C000131194

STREET ATLAS
Tyne & Wear
Northumberland

First published in 1996 as
'Tyne and Wear' by

George Philip Ltd, a division of
Octopus Publishing Group Ltd
2–4 Heron Quays, London E14 4JP

First colour edition 2001
First impression 2001

ISBN 0-540-07807-7

© George Philip Ltd 2001

 Ordnance Survey®

This product includes mapping data licensed
from Ordnance Survey® with the permission of
the Controller of Her Majesty's Stationery Office.
© Crown copyright 2001. All rights reserved.
Licence number 100011710

Printed and bound in Spain
by Cayfosa-Quebecor

Contents

II   **Key to map symbols**

III   **Key to Navigator® map symbols**

IV   **Key to map pages**

VI   **Route planning**

X   **Administrative and Postcode Boundaries**

1   **Street maps** at 3 ½ inches to 1 mile

98   **Street maps of Newcastle upon Tyne and Sunderland city centres** at 7 inches to 1 mile

104   **Navigator® mapping of Northumberland** at ⅞ inches to 1 mile

136   **Town maps** of Alnwick, Amble, Berwick-upon-Tweed and Rothbury

138   **Index** of towns and villages

140   **Index** of streets, hospitals, industrial estates, railway stations, schools, shopping centres and universities and places of interest

Digital Data

The exceptionally high-quality mapping found in this atlas is available as digital data in TIFF format, which is easily convertible to other bit mapped (raster) image formats.

The index is also available in digital form as a standard database table. It contains all the details found in the printed index together with the National Grid reference for the map square in which each entry is named and feature codes for places of interest in eight categories such as education and health.

For further information and to discuss your requirements, please contact Philip's on 020 7531 8440 or george.philip@philips-maps.co.uk

Motorway with junction number	
Primary route – dual/single carriageway	
A road – dual/single carriageway	
B road – dual/single carriageway	
Minor road – dual/single carriageway	
Other minor road – dual/single carriageway	
Road under construction	
Pedestrianised area	
DY7 **Postcode boundaries**	
County and unitary authority boundaries	
Railway	
Railway under construction	
Tramway, miniature railway	
Rural track, private road or narrow road in urban area	
Gate or obstruction to traffic (restrictions may not apply at all times or to all vehicles)	
Path, bridleway, byway open to all traffic, road used as a public path	

The representation in this atlas of a road, track or is no evidence of the existence of a of a right of way

98 **Adjoining page indicators**
(The colour of the arrow indicates the scale of the adjoining page - see scales below)
84

102 **The map area within the pink band is shown at a larger scale on the page indicated by the red block and arrow**

		Railway station
	Walsall	
		Tyne and Wear Metro station
		Private railway station
		Bus, coach station
		Ambulance station
		Coastguard station
		Fire station
		Police station
		Accident and Emergency entrance to hospital
		Hospital
		Place of worship
		Information Centre (open all year)
		Parking
		Park and Ride
		Post Office
		Camping site
		Caravan site
		Golf course
		Picnic site
		Important buildings, schools, colleges, universities and hospitals
	Prim Sch	
	River Medway	**Water name**
		River, stream
		Lock, weir
		Water
		Tidal water
		Woods
		Houses
	Church	**Non-Roman antiquity**
	ROMAN FORT	**Roman antiquity**

Abbr	Full	Abbr	Full
Acad	**Academy**	Mkt	**Market**
Allot Gdns	**Allotments**	Meml	**Memorial**
Cemy	**Cemetery**	Mon	**Monument**
C Ctr	**Civic Centre**	Mus	**Museum**
CH	**Club House**	Obsy	**Observatory**
Coll	**College**	Pal	**Royal Palace**
Crem	**Crematorium**	PH	**Public House**
Ent	**Enterprise**	Recn Gd	**Recreation Ground**
Ex H	**Exhibition Hall**	Resr	**Reservoir**
Ind Est	**Industrial Estate**	Ret Pk	**Retail Park**
IRB Sta	**Inshore Rescue Boat Station**	Sch	**School**
		Sh Ctr	**Shopping Centre**
Inst	**Institute**	TH	**Town Hall/House**
Ct	**Law Court**	Trad Est	**Trading Estate**
L Ctr	**Leisure Centre**	Univ	**University**
LC	**Level Crossing**	Wks	**Works**
Liby	**Library**	YH	**Youth Hostel**

■ The small numbers around the edges of the maps identify the 1 kilometre National Grid lines ■ The dark grey border on the inside edge of some pages indicates that the mapping does not continue onto the adjacent page

The scale of the maps is 5.52 cm to 1 km
3¹/₂ inches to 1 mile • 1: 18103

0 — ¹/₄ — ¹/₂ — ³/₄ — 1 mile
0 — 250 m — 500 m — 750 m — 1 kilometre

The scale of the maps on pages numbered in red is 11.04 cm to 1 km • 7 inches to 1 mile • 1: 9051.4

0 — 220 yards — 440 yards — 660 yards — ¹/₂ mile
0 — 125 m — 250 m — 375 m — ¹/₂ kilometre

Key to Navigator® map symbols on pages 104–135

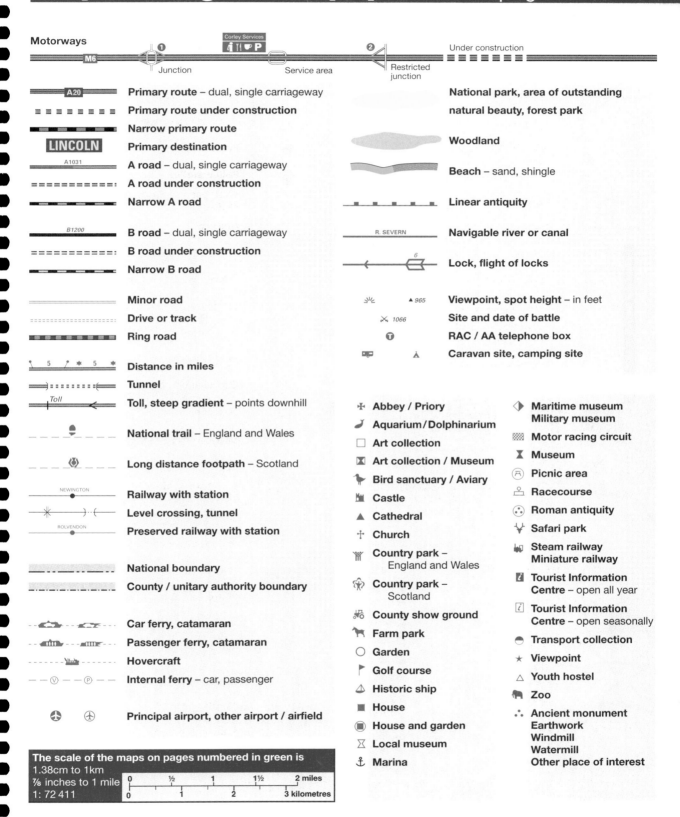

Motorways

① Junction
Corley Services — Service area
② Restricted junction
Under construction

A20	**Primary route** – dual, single carriageway
	Primary route under construction
	Narrow primary route
LINCOLN	**Primary destination**
A1031	**A road** – dual, single carriageway
	A road under construction
	Narrow A road
B1200	**B road** – dual, single carriageway
	B road under construction
	Narrow B road
	Minor road
	Drive or track
	Ring road
5 5	**Distance in miles**
	Tunnel
Toll	**Toll, steep gradient** – points downhill
	National trail – England and Wales
	Long distance footpath – Scotland
NEWINGTON	**Railway with station**
	Level crossing, tunnel
ROLVENDON	**Preserved railway with station**
	National boundary
	County / unitary authority boundary
	Car ferry, catamaran
	Passenger ferry, catamaran
	Hovercraft
—Ⓥ——Ⓟ—	**Internal ferry** – car, passenger
✈ ✈	**Principal airport, other airport / airfield**

National park, area of outstanding natural beauty, forest park

Woodland

Beach – sand, shingle

Linear antiquity

R. SEVERN — **Navigable river or canal**

← 6 **Lock, flight of locks**

⚜ ▲ 965 **Viewpoint, spot height** – in feet

✕ 1066 **Site and date of battle**

🕾 **RAC / AA telephone box**

🚐 Å **Caravan site, camping site**

✠ **Abbey / Priory**
🐬 **Aquarium / Dolphinarium**
☐ **Art collection**
✠ **Art collection / Museum**
🐦 **Bird sanctuary / Aviary**
🏰 **Castle**
▲ **Cathedral**
✝ **Church**
🎪 **Country park** – England and Wales
🎎 **Country park** – Scotland
🐎 **County show ground**
🐴 **Farm park**
○ **Garden**
⚑ **Golf course**
⛵ **Historic ship**
■ **House**
⊞ **House and garden**
⊠ **Local museum**
⚓ **Marina**

◇ **Maritime museum / Military museum**
▨ **Motor racing circuit**
✕ **Museum**
Ⓐ **Picnic area**
♘ **Racecourse**
⊙ **Roman antiquity**
♈ **Safari park**
🚂 **Steam railway / Miniature railway**
🄸 **Tourist Information Centre** – open all year
🄸 **Tourist Information Centre** – open seasonally
⊖ **Transport collection**
★ **Viewpoint**
△ **Youth hostel**
🐘 **Zoo**
∴ **Ancient monument / Earthwork / Windmill / Watermill / Other place of interest**

The scale of the maps on pages numbered in green is
1.38cm to 1km
⅞ inches to 1 mile
1: 72 411

0	½	1	1½	2 miles
0	1	2		3 kilometres

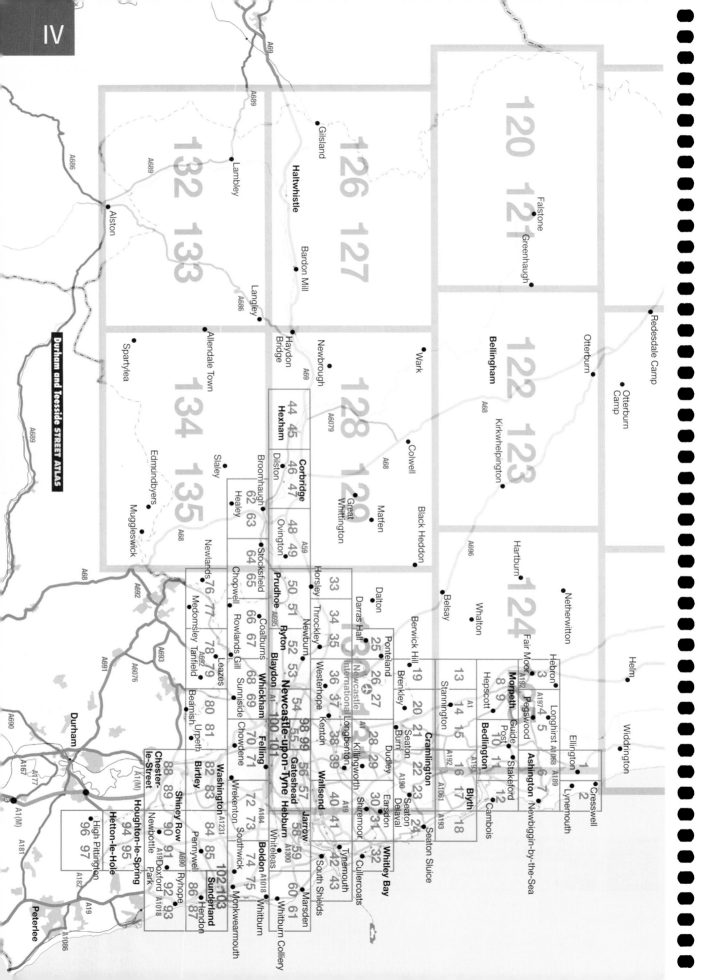

Durham and Teesside STREET ATLAS

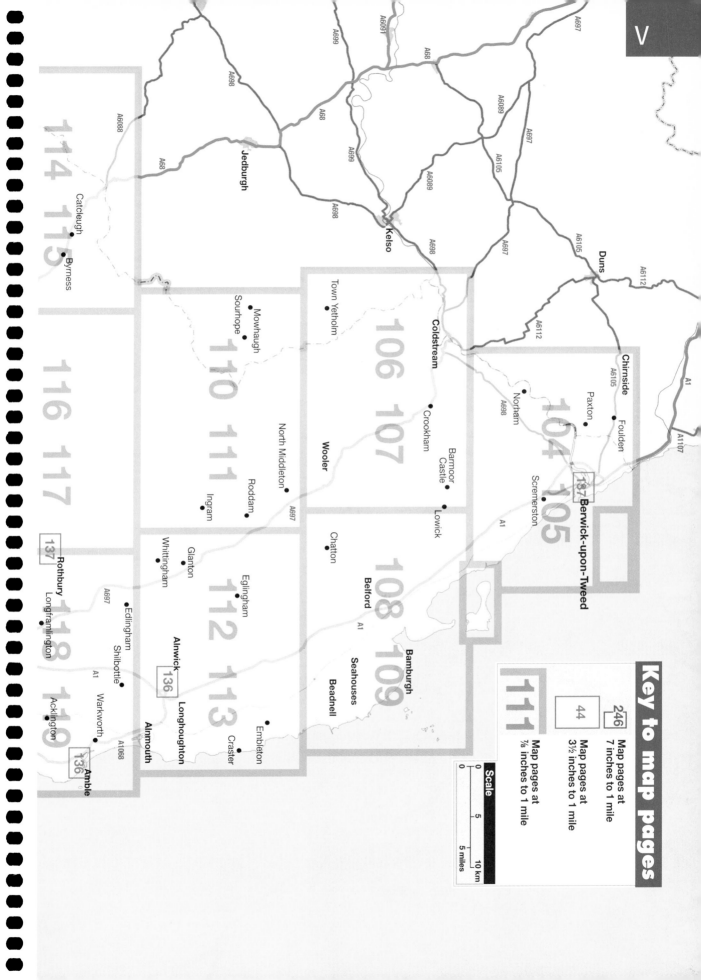

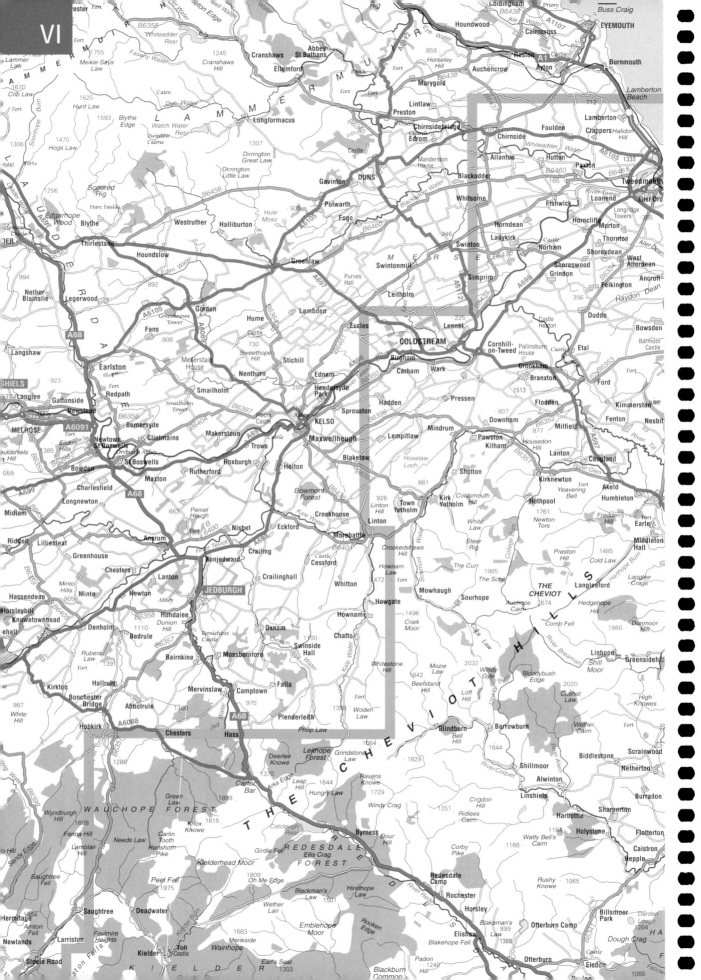

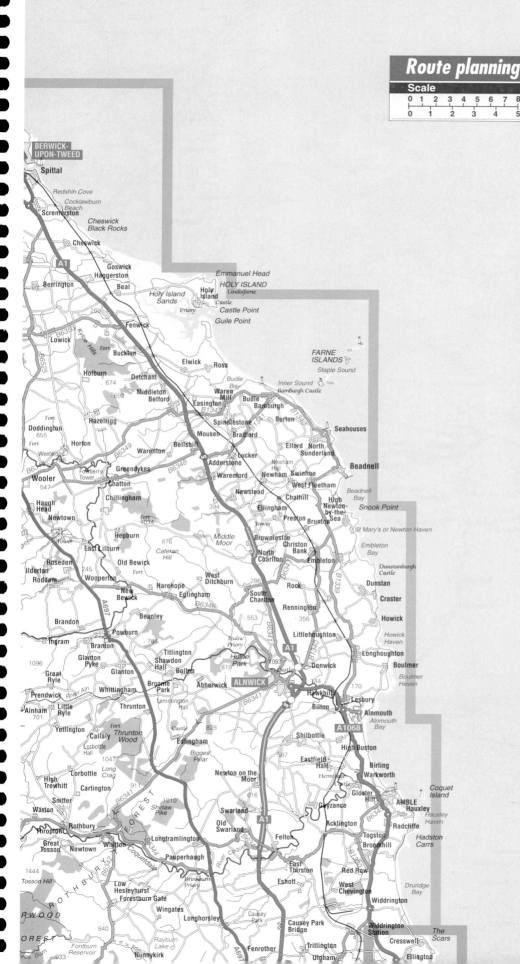

Route planning

Scale

0 1 2 3 4 5 6 7 8 km

0 1 2 3 4 5 miles

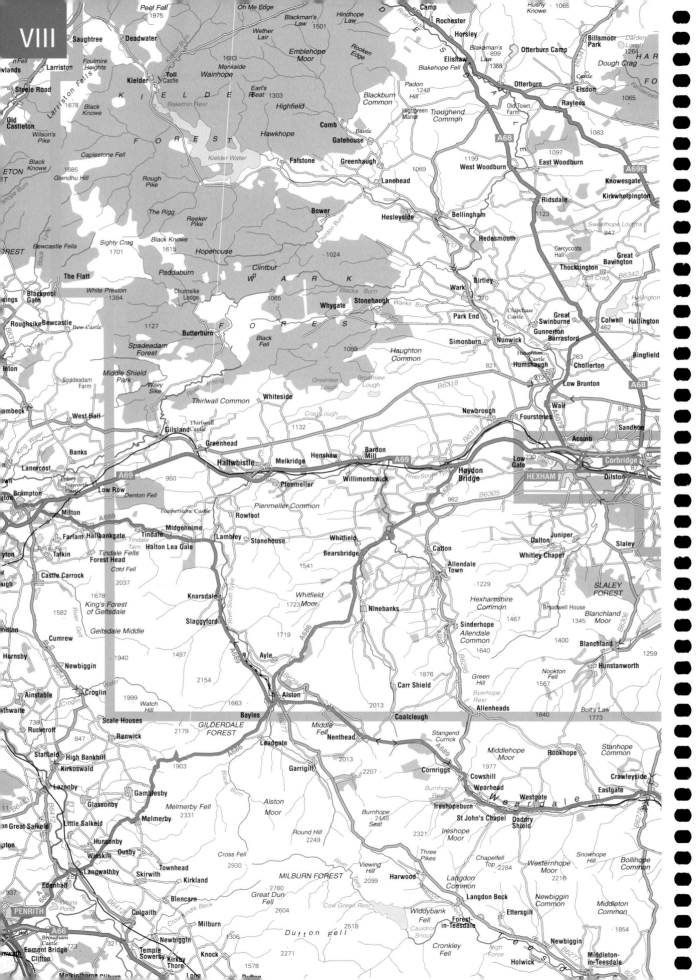

Route planning

Scale

0 1 2 3 4 5 6 7 8 km
0 1 2 3 4 5 miles

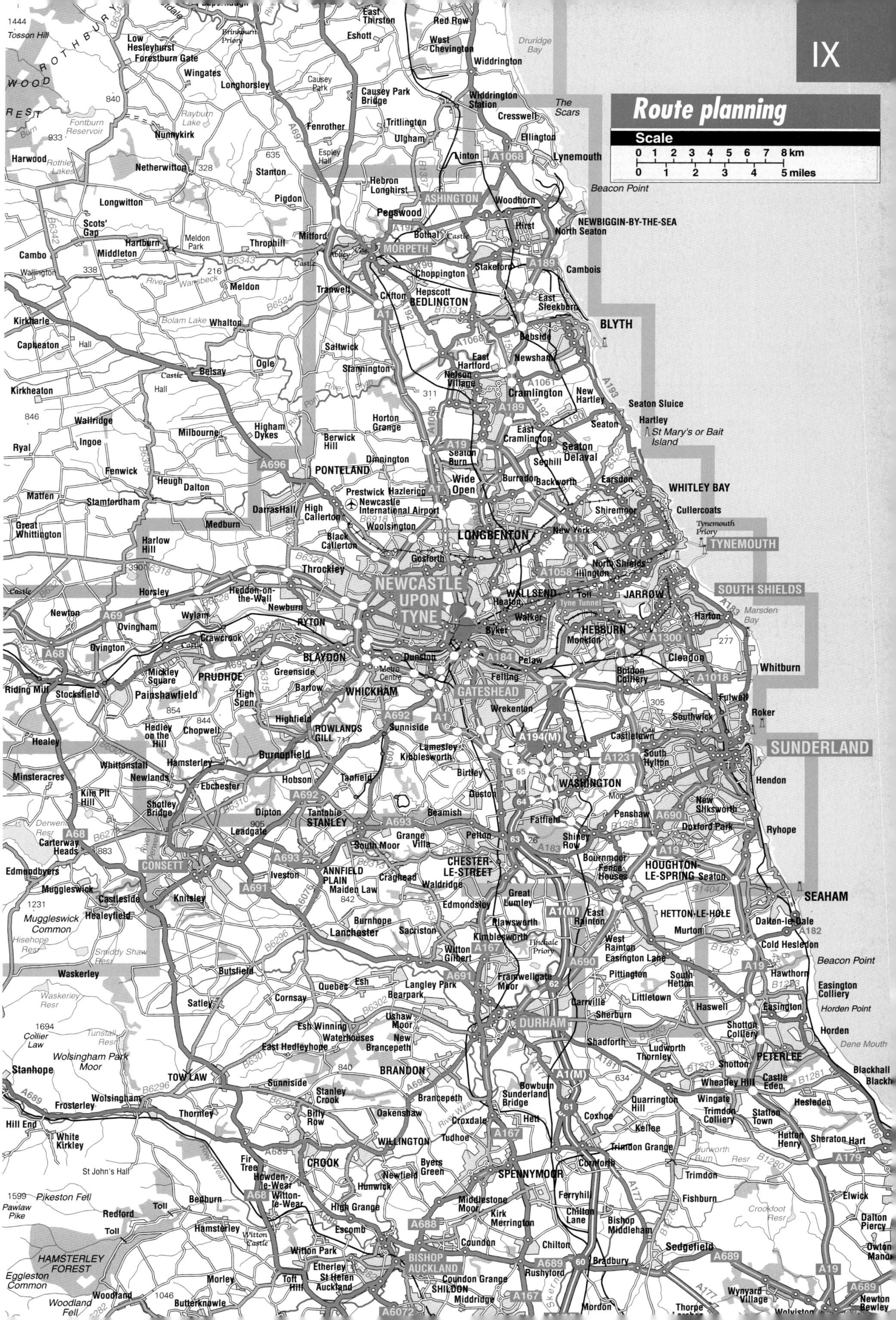

ROTHBURY WOOD FOREST

Tosson Hill 1444
Low Hesleyhurst
Forestburn Gate
Wingates
Longhorsley
Brinkburn Priory
Eshott
East Thriston
Red Row
West Chevington
Widdrington
Druridge Bay
The Scars

Harwood
Nunnykirk
Netherwitton
Rothley Lakes
Rayburn Lake
Fontburn Reservoir
Causey Park
Causey Park Bridge
Tritlington
Ulgham
Widdrington Station
Cresswell
Ellington
Lynemouth
Beacon Point

Cambo
Hartburn
Middleton
Throphill
Stanton
Pigdon
Hebron
Longhirst
Pegswood
ASHINGTON
Woodhorn
North Seaton
NEWBIGGIN-BY-THE-SEA

Scots' Gap
Wallington
Longwitton
Meldon Park
Meldon
Mitford
MORPETH
Bothal
Castle
Hirst
Choppington
Stakeford
Cambois

Kirkharle
Capheaton
Belsay
Ogle
Saltwick
Stannington
Clifton
Hepscott
BEDLINGTON
East Sleekburn
Bebside
Newsham
BLYTH

Kirkheaton
Wallridge
Ingoe
Higham Dykes
Berwick Hill
Dinnington
Horton Grange
East Hartford
Nelson Village
Cramlington
New Hartley
Seaton Sluice
Hartley
St Mary's or Bait Island

Matfen
Fenwick
Heugh
Dalton
Stamfordham
PONTELAND
Prestwick
Hazlerigg
Seaton Burn
East Cramlington
Seghill
Seaton Delaval
Earsdon
WHITLEY BAY
Cullercoats

Great Whittington
Harlow Hill
Medburn
Darras Hall
High Callerton
Newcastle International Airport
Woolsington
Black Callerton
Wide Open
Burradon
Backworth
Shiremoor
New York
Tynemouth Priory
TYNEMOUTH

Horsley
Newton
Ovingham
Wylam
Heddon-on-the-Wall
Newburn
Throckley
Gosforth
LONGBENTON
North Shields
Billington
SOUTH SHIELDS

Ovington
Riding Mill
Stocksfield
Painshawfield
RYTON
BLAYDON
Greenside
Newburn
Dunston
NEWCASTLE UPON TYNE
Heaton
Byker
Walker
WALLSEND
JARROW
Harton
Marsden Bay

PRUDHOE
Mickley Square
Crawcrook
High Spen
Highfield
WHICKHAM
Metro Centre
GATESHEAD
Felling
Pelaw
HEBBURN
Monkton
Cleadon
Whitburn

Healey
Hedley on the Hill
Chopwell
ROWLANDS GILL
Sunniside
Wrekenton
Bill Quay
Boldon Colliery
Fulwell
Roker

Minsteracres
Whittonstall
Newlands
Hamsterley
Burnopfield
Lamesley
Kibblesworth
Birtley
A194(M)
Castletown
South Hylton
Southwick
SUNDERLAND
Hendon

Kiln Pit Hill
Shotley Bridge
Ebchester
Dipton
Tantobie
Hobson
Tanfield
Beamish
Ouston
WASHINGTON
Usworth
New Silksworth
Doxford Park
Ryhope

Carterway Heads
Edmundbyers
Muggleswick
Castleside
Healeyfield
Knitsley
Iveston
STANLEY
South Moor
Grange Villa
Pelton
Fatfield
Penshaw
Shiney Row
Bournmoor
Fence Houses
HOUGHTON-LE-SPRING
Seaton
SEAHAM

CONSETT
Leadgate
ANNFIELD PLAIN
Maiden Law
Craghead
Waldridge
CHESTER-LE-STREET
Great Lumley
Bournmoor
HETTON-LE-HOLE
Murton
Dalton-le-Dale
Cold Hesledon
Beacon Point

Muggleswick Common
Burnhope
Lanchester
Sacriston
Edmondsley
Plawsworth
A1(M)
East Rainton
West Rainton
Easington Lane
Pittington
South Hetton
Hawthorn
Easington Colliery
Horden Point

Waskerley
Butsfield
Satley
Quebec
Esh
Langley Park
Bearpark
Witton Gilbert
Kimblesworth
Finchale Priory
Framwellgate Moor
Carrville
Sherburn
Haswell
Shotton Colliery
Easington
Horden
Dene Mouth

Collier Law
Wolsingham Park Moor
Cornsay
Esh Winning
Waterhouses
New Brancepeth
Ushaw Moor
DURHAM
Shadforth
Ludworth
Thornley
Shotton
PETERLEE
Castle Eden
Blackhall
Blackh

Stanhope
TOW LAW
Sunniside
Stanley Crook
Billy Row
Oakenshaw
BRANDON
Bowburn
Sunderland Bridge
Coxhoe
Quarrington Hill
Kelloe
Wheatley Hill
Wingate
Trimdon Colliery
Hesleden

Hill End
Frosterley
Wolsingham
Thornley
CROOK
Howden-le-Wear
Witton-le-Wear
High Grange
Fir Tree
Newfield
Byers Green
WILLINGTON
Tudhoe
Hett
Coxhoe
Cornforth
Trimdon Grange
Station Town
Hutton Henry
Sheraton
Hart

Pikeston Fell
Pawlaw Pike
Redford
Bedburn
Hamsterley
Witton Park
Escomb
Coundon
SPENNYMOOR
Ferryhill
Chilton Lane
Trimdon
Fishburn
Elwick
Dalton Piercy
Owton
Manor
Newton Bewley

HAMSTERLEY FOREST
Eggleston Common
Woodland Fell
Woodland
Butterknowle
Morley
Toft Hill
St Helen Auckland
BISHOP AUCKLAND
Coundon Grange
SHILDON
Middridge
Chilton
Bishop Middleham
Sedgefield
Bradbury
Rushyford
Mordon
Thorpe
Wynyard Village
Wolviston

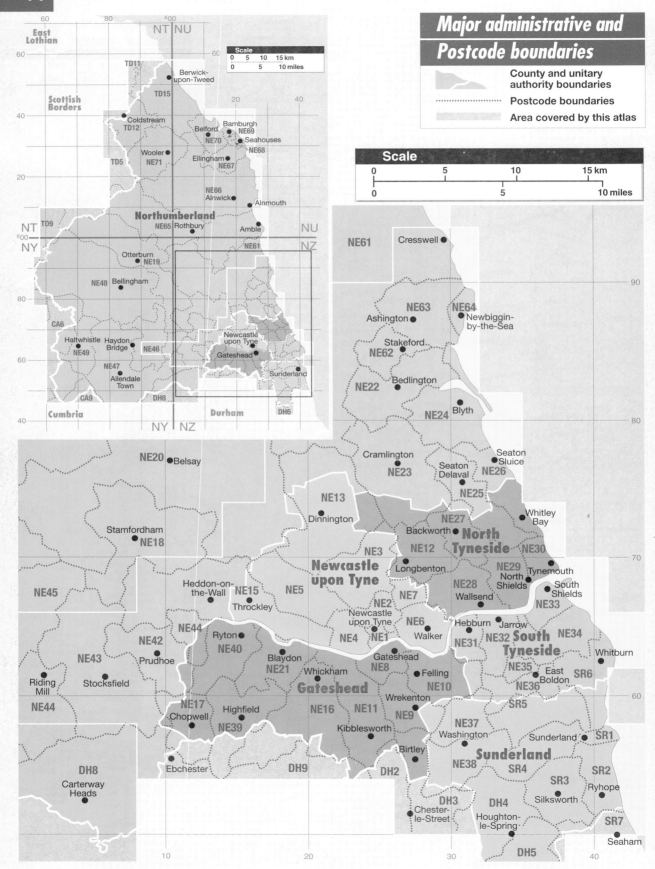

Major administrative and Postcode boundaries

- County and unitary authority boundaries
- Postcode boundaries
- Area covered by this atlas

Scale
0 5 10 15 km
0 5 10 miles

Scale
0 5 10 15 km
0 5 10 miles

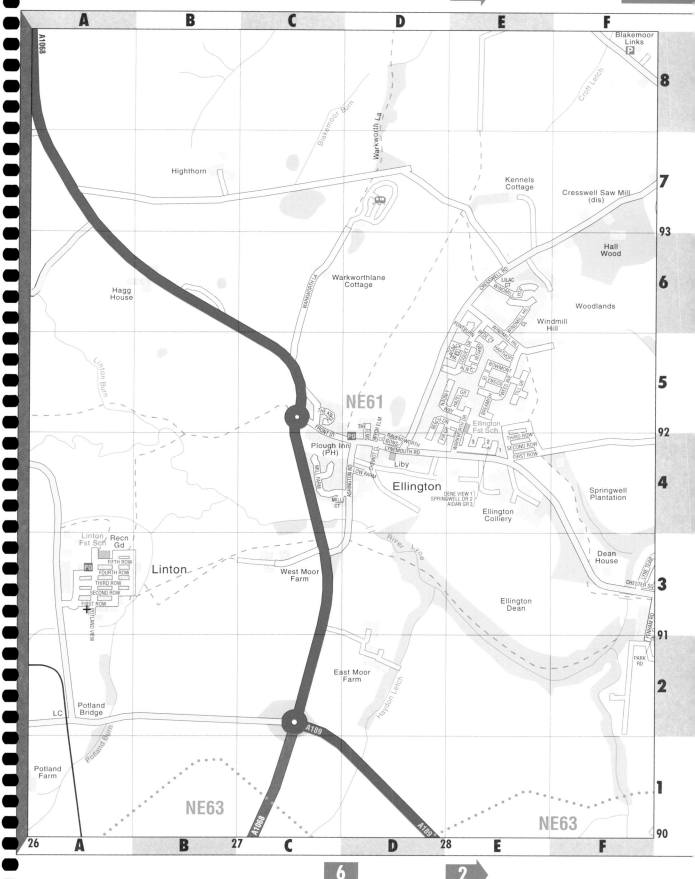

2

Blakemoor Links
P

Croft Letch

8

A1068

Blakemoor Burn

Warkworth La

Highthorn

Kennels
Cottage

Cresswell Saw Mill
(dis)

7

93

Hall
Wood

6

WARKWORTH LA

Hagg
House

Warkworthlane
Cottage

CRESSWELL RD

LILAC
CT

WINDMILL
CT

Woodlands

Windmill
Hill

Linton Burn

FONTBURN

RED CT

WINDMILL HILL

HARTHOPE

WINDMILL HILL
CL

5

THE KIL

FRONT ST

NE61

BECK CL
CODDET DR
ALN CT

IRTHM

BOWMONT

GLENSIDE

WEDD AVE

BREAMISH

TILL GR

92

PO

Ellington
Fst. Sch

THIRD ROW

SECOND ROW

THE
ELMS

WYCH ELM

HAZEL

GR

WARKWORTH DR

3

2

FIRST ROW

Plough Inn
(PH)

RAVENSWORTH
GDNS

CHEWITT CL

LYNEMOUTH RD

Liby

Ellington

DENE VIEW 1
SPRINGWELL DR 2
AIDAN GR 3

Springwell
Plantation

92

4

MILL FARM

ASHINGTON RD

Low FARM

Ellington
Colliery

MILL
CT

River Lyne

Dean
House

LYNE TERR

Linton
Fst Sch

Recn
Gd

FIFTH ROW

West Moor
Farm

CHESTER SQ

3

PO

FOURTH ROW

THIRD ROW

Linton

Ellington
Dean

FENHAM RD

SECOND ROW

FIRST ROW

POTLAND VIEW

91

East Moor
Farm

Haydon Letch

PARK
RD

2

LC

Potland
Bridge

Potland Burn

A189

Potland
Farm

NE63

A1068

A189

1

90

26

A

B

27

C

D

28

E

F

8

SOUTH SIDE

St BARTHOLOMEWS CL

+ St Bartholomews

7

Cresswell

Sea Lodge

93

P

Caravan Site

6

P

Snab Point

5

NE61

92

CRESSWELL HOME FARM COTTS

4

Cresswell Home Farm

Chugdon Wood

Bewick Drift

JUBILEE COTTS

CHESTER SQ

CORONATION COTTS

River Lyne

ROLAND RD

RIVER VIEW

DUNLIN CT

3

EDEN TERR

Lynemouth Fst Sch

DALTON AVE

Liby +

INGLEBY TERR

ALBION TERR

CHURCH SQ

GUILDFORD SQ

HENLEY SQ

JERSEY SQ

OAKLAND TERR

+

PO

KINGSLEY RD

SEA VIEW

91

QUEEN ST

Lynemouth

MATLOCK SQ 1

NEVILLE SQ 2

BRIDGE RD

MARKET SQ

Sewage Works

Lyne Hill

2

PARK RD

Cemy

Works

PORT RD

1

Works

Power Station

Lyne Sands

90

NE63

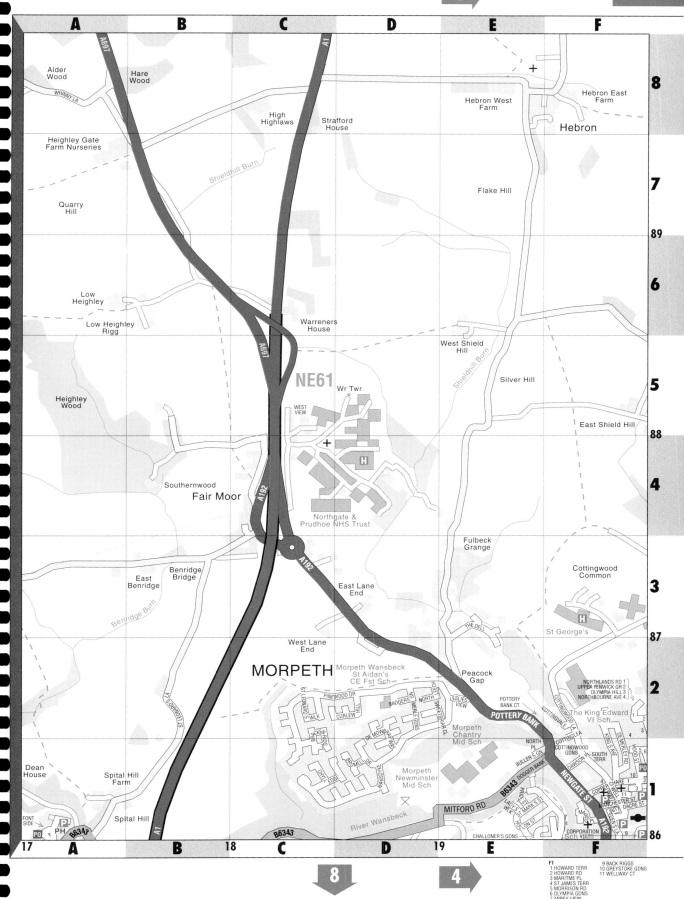

A **B** **C** **D** **E** **F**

Alder Wood

Hare Wood

High Highlaws

Strafford House

Hebron West Farm

Hebron East Farm

Hebron

8

WHINNY LA

Heighley Gate Farm Nurseries

Shieldhill Burn

Flake Hill

7

Quarry Hill

89

Low Heighley

6

Low Heighley Rigg

Warreners House

West Shield Hill

Shieldhill Burn

Heighley Wood

A697

NE61

Wr Twr

WEST VIEW

Silver Hill

5

East Shield Hill

88

A192

Southernwood

Fair Moor

H

Northgate & Prudhoe NHS Trust

Fulbeck Grange

4

East Benridge

Benridge Bridge

A192

East Lane End

Cottingwood Common

3

Benridge Burn

THE DELL

St George's

H

87

West Lane End

MORPETH

Morpeth Wansbeck St Aidan's CE Fst Sch

Peacock Gap

POTTERY BANK CT

Pottery Bank

Cottingvale

Cottingwood La

NORTHLANDS RD 1
UPPER FENWICK GR 2
OLYMPIA HILL 3
NORTHBOURNE AVE 4

The King Edward VI Sch

2

ST LEONARD'S

PINEWOOD DR

BADGERS

NORTH MERLE GDNS

SWEETBRIAR CL

LESLIE'S VIEW

Morpeth Chantry Mid Sch

NORTH PL

Cottingwood Gdns

Cottinglea

De Merley Rd

King's Ave

SOUTH TERR

Dean House

ST LEONARDS LA

CURLEW

CHAILEY

DE MONT

RAVENSWAY

BRAMWELL DR

CHILL EDGE

PANSYKE

Morpeth Newminster Mid Sch

BULLER S DN

Cottingwood

DAWSON PL

NEWGATE ST

A192

1

Spital Hill Farm

A1

B6343

DOGGER BANK

MITFORD RD

River Wansbeck

CHALLONER'S GDNS

86

Font Side

PO

P

PH

B6343

Spital Hill

B6343

17 **A** **B** **18** **C** **D** **19** **E** **F**

F1
1 HOWARD TERR
2 HOWARD RD
3 MARITIME PL
4 ST JAMES TERR
5 MORRISON RD
6 OLYMPIA GDNS
7 ABBEY VIEW
8 ABBEY TERR
9 BACK RIGGS
10 GREYSTOKE GDNS
11 WELLWAY CT

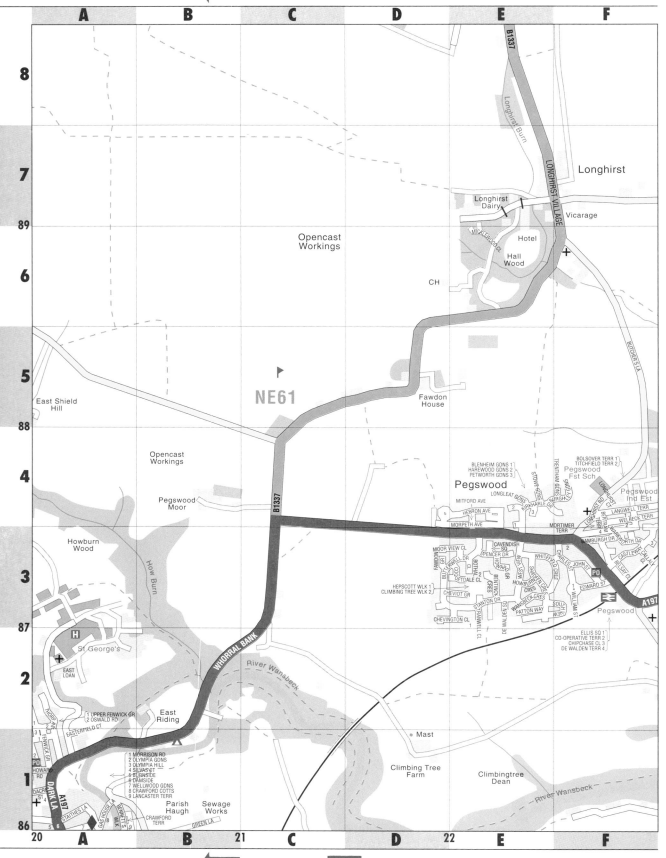

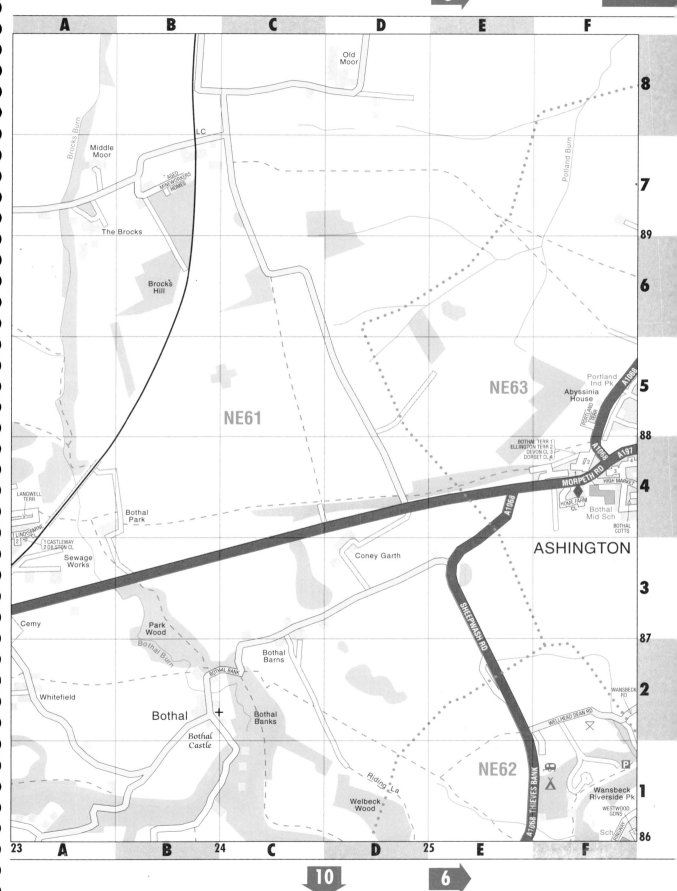

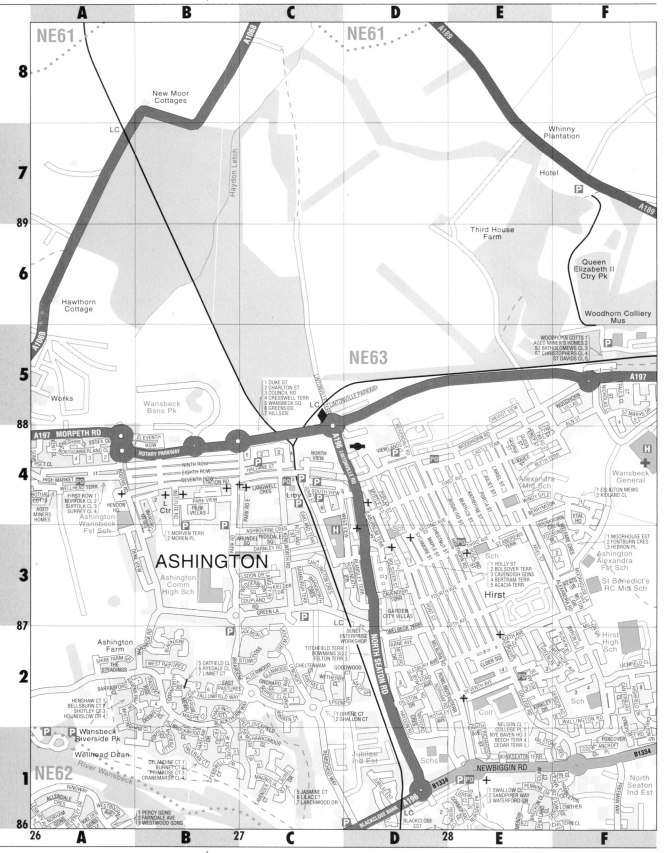

ASHINGTON

Hirst

NE61
NE63
NE62

1 LINSHIELS GDNS
2 LINDISFARNE HO
3 SIMONBURN LA
4 SALLY DAVISON CT
5 CALLERTON CL
6 HESLEYSIDE
7 ALWINTON SQ
8 WINCHESTER CL
9 SALISBURY CL

A **B** **C** **D** **E** **F**

8

7

89

6

Works

Woodhorn Grange

Woodhorn Burn

Lynefield House

Woodhorn Mill (dis)

Church Farm

St Mary's Church (Mus)

Woodhorn

Queen Elizabeth II Ctry Pk

A189

A197

Beacon Point

Newbiggin Moor

Woodhorn Demesne

WOODHORN CRES

5

SMALLHOLDINGS

CHURCH VIEW

MAY AVE 1
IVY AVE 2
HOLLY AVE 3

WOODHORN RD

Moorside Fst Sch

A797

1 KING ST
2 QUEENS PL
3 WAVERLEY BLDGS
4 RUSTIC TERR
5 CARLTON HO
6 ROBINSON SQ
7 HENDERSON'S BLDGS
8 SEA VIEW LA

CH

88

ST MARY'S DR

Woodbridge

Wansbeck General

H

NE63

NE64

Newbiggin Mid Sch

IRB Sta

Newbiggin Point

4

SUMMERHOUSE LA

Newbiggin Bay

FRONT ST

B1334

GIBSON ST

Libyl

1 CORONATION ST
2 LOCARNO PL
3 VICTORIA TERR
4 JUBILEE TERR
5 THIRLMERE TERR
6 BAY VIEW W
7 OCEAN VIEW

Windsor Fst Sch

NEWBIGGIN-BY-THE-SEA

3

NORTH SEATON RD

Spital Burn

Coniston Ave

Spital House Farm

Sewage Works

Welbeck Com Fst Sch

North Seaton

The Hollows

The Demesne

South Ridge

B1334

A189

87

Spital Point

2

1

86

MORPETH

Mitford

Mitford Castle

Castle Plantation

Mitford Steads

Mill Farm

Highford Bridge

Abbey Mills Farm

Borough Wood

Newminster Abbey

High House

Nature Reserve

West High House

Abbeyfields Fst Sch

St Christopher's Ho

High Church

Morpeth Cottage

Morpeth Common

Silver Hill

High Common House

Grindle Hill

Loansdean Hill Farm

Loansdean

Works

Factory

NE61

Rock Cottages

Tranwell

Tranwell Farm

The Gubeon

Commongate Plantation

Catch Burn

Crag Plantation

CH

Gubeon Plantations

Gubeon Wood

Woodside Cottage

Prospect Cottage

Glororum

Airfield (disused)

Wellhill Plantation

Cockhill Moor

Bet's La

Mast

Wr Twr

Well Hill

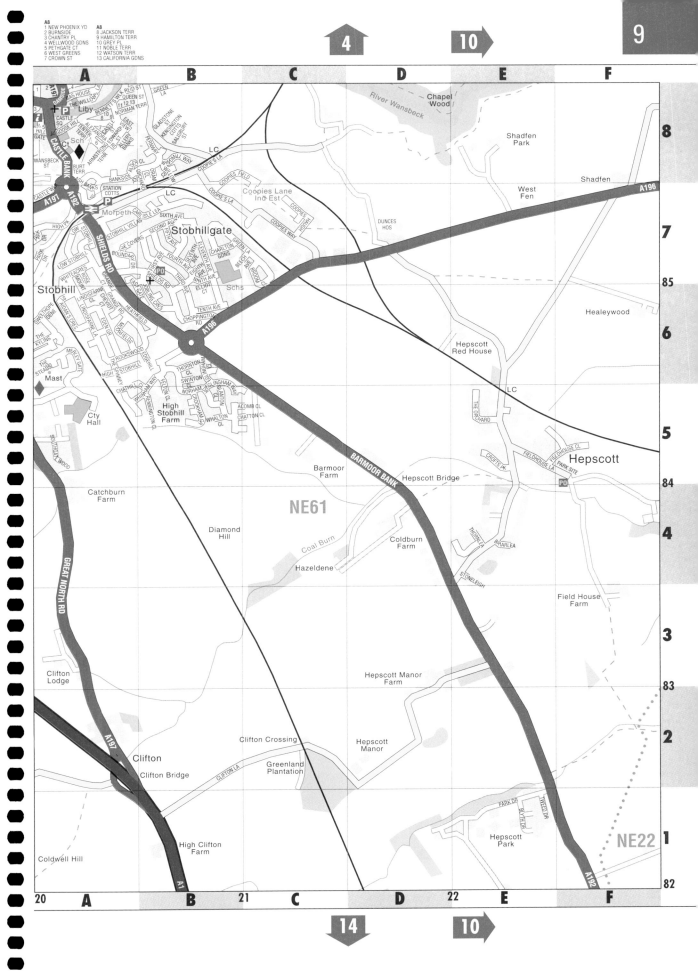

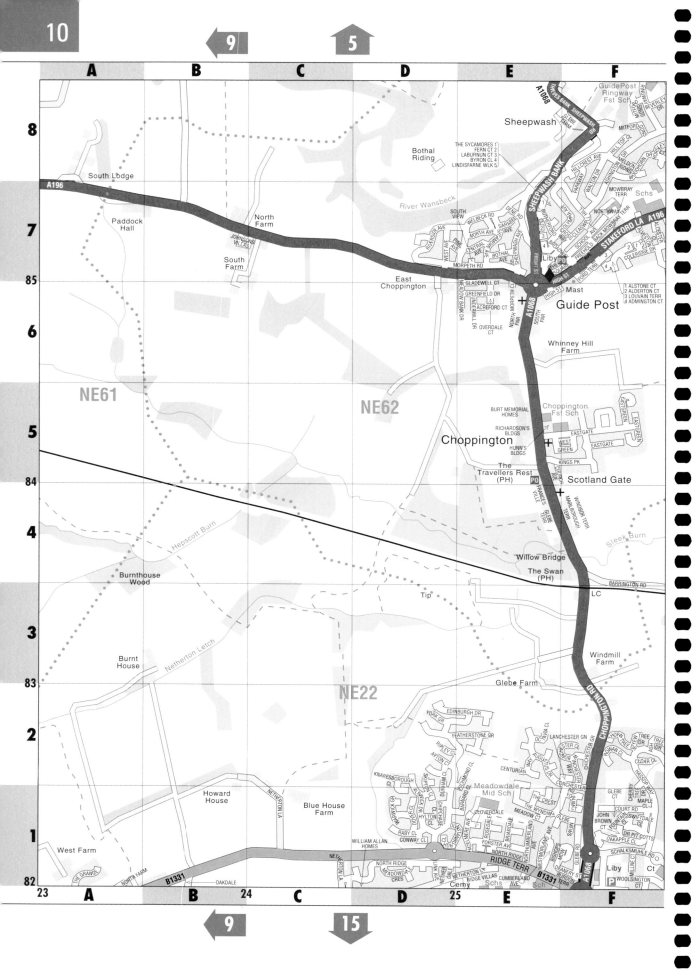

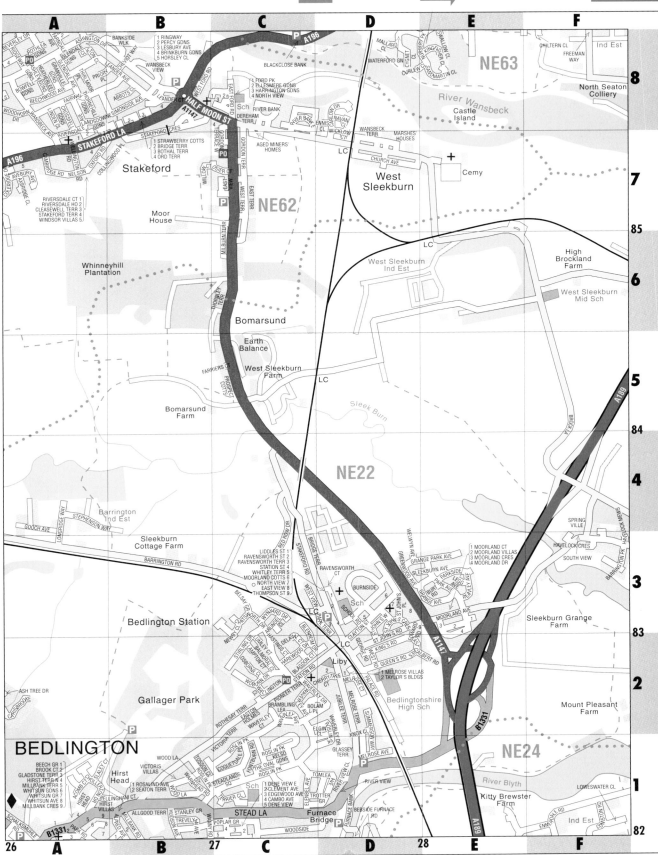

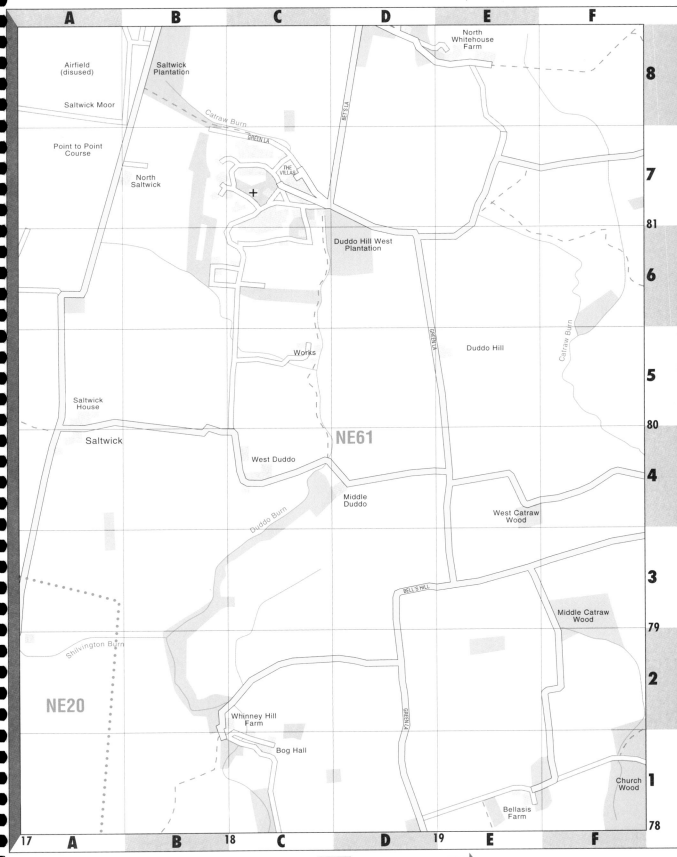

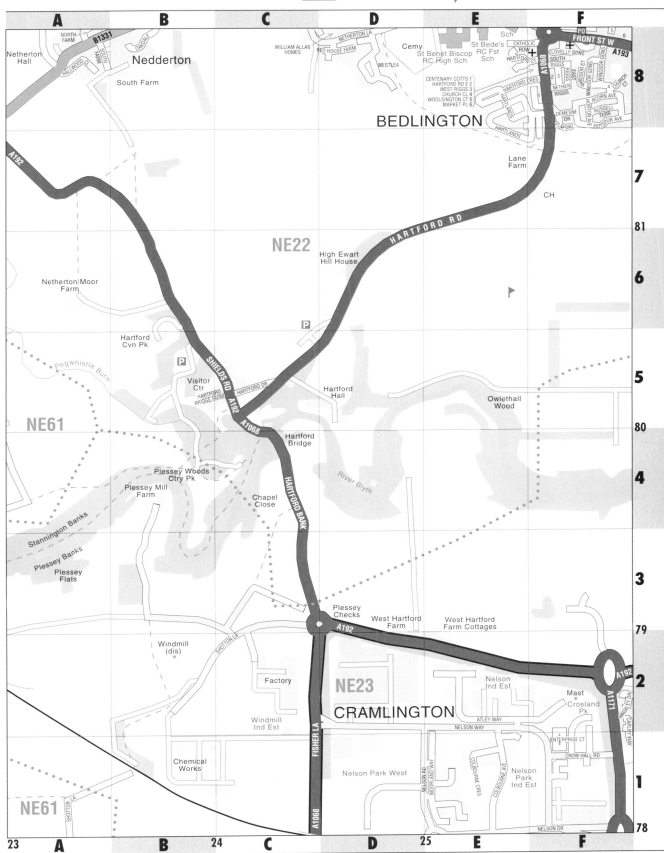

A **B** **C** **D** **E** **F**

NORTH FARM

Netherton Hall

B1331

SOUTH FARM

HALLWOOD CT

OAKDALE

Nedderton

South Farm

NETHERTON LA

WILLIAM ALLAN HOMES

RED HOUSE FARM

WESTLEA

Cemy

St Benet Biscop RC High Sch

St Bede's RC Fst Sch

Sch

CATHOLIC ROW

HARTFORD CT

PO

FRONT ST W

A193

CLOVELLY GDNS

SOUTH RIGGS

NETHER RIGGS

A1068

EAST RIGGS

WINDSOR GDNS

HORTON AVE

SNODON GDNS

WINDSOR GDNS

ACORN AVE

RUSSELL TERR

HOTSPUR AVE

CHURCH CT

8

CENTENARY COTTS 1
HARTFORD RD E 2
WEST RIGGS 3
CHURCH CL 4
WOOLSINGTON CT 5
MARKET PL 6

HARTFORD CRES

HARTLANDS

DEMESNE DR

ELM DR

HARTLANDS

BEDLINGTON

A192

Lane Farm

CH

NE22

High Ewart Hill House

HARTFORD RD

81

7

Netherton Moor Farm

6

Hartford Cvn Pk

P

Pegwhistle Burn

P

Visitor Ctr

SHIELDS RD

HARTFORD BRIDGE FARM

HARTFORD DR

A192

Hartford Hall

Owlethall Wood

5

NE61

A1068

Hartford Bridge

HARTFORD BANK

River Blyth

80

4

Plessey Woods Ctry Pk

Plessey Mill Farm

Chapel Close

Stannington Banks

Plessey Banks

Plessey Flats

3

Plessey Checks

A192

West Hartford Farm

West Hartford Farm Cottages

79

Windmill (dis)

SHOTTON LA

Factory

NE23

CRAMLINGTON

Nelson Ind Est

Mast

Crosland Pk

A192

A1171

MAUD ST

GARDEN EST

CARLBY WAY

2

ATLEY WAY

ENTERPRISE CT

Windmill Ind Est

FISHER LA

NELSON WAY

NELSON RD

MOORLAND WAY

COLBOURNE CRES

COLBOURNE AVE

Nelson Park Ind Est

CROW HALL RD

Chemical Works

Nelson Park West

A1068

NELSON DR

NE61

SHOTTON LA

1

78

23 **A** **B** 24 **C** **D** 25 **E** **F**

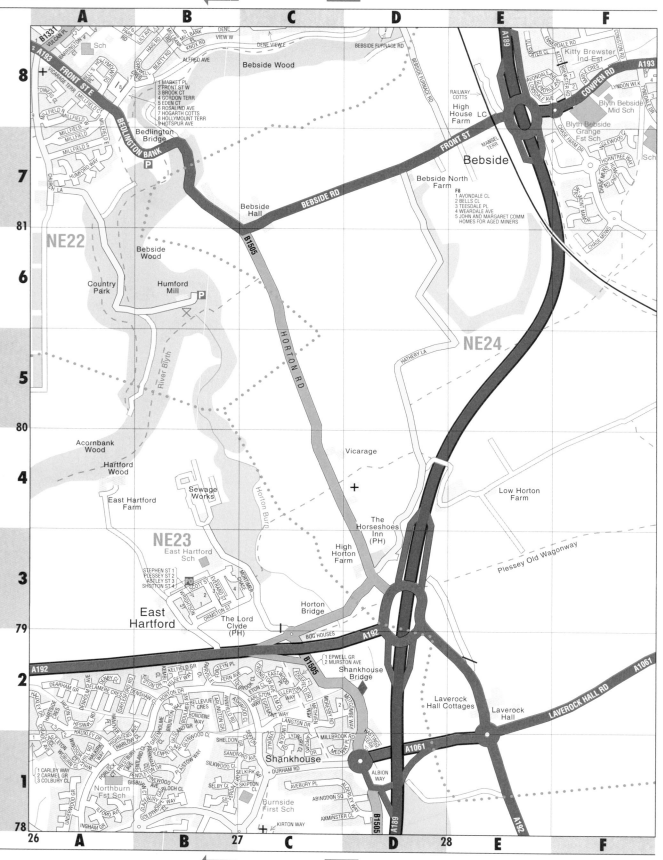

12

D8
1 PORTLAND ST
2 BALFOUR ST
3 THE GABLES
4 WEST SALISBURY ST
5 ARCOT TERR

18

F8
1 WAPPING
2 SUSSEX ST
3 BREWERY ST
4 POST OFFICE ST
5 FREEHOLD ST
6 SEXTANT HO

7 QUAYSIDE CT
8 TATE ST
9 FIELDFARE HO
10 WELLINGTON STREET E

17

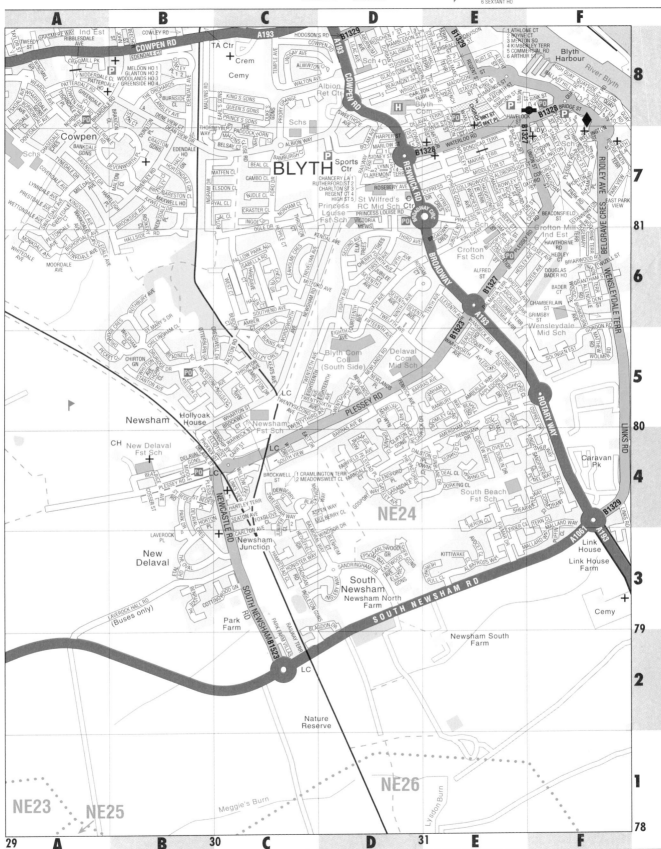

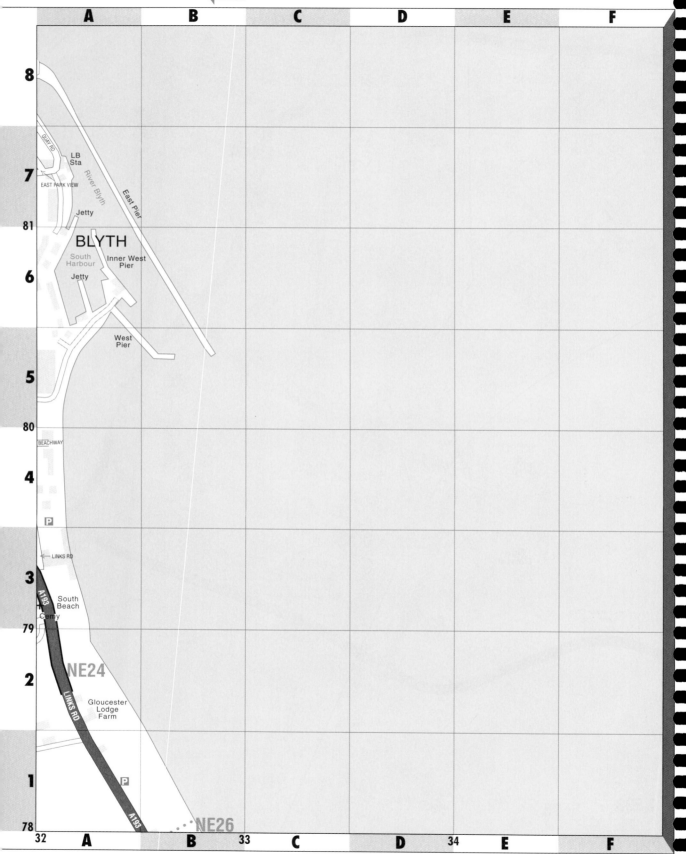

17

17 24

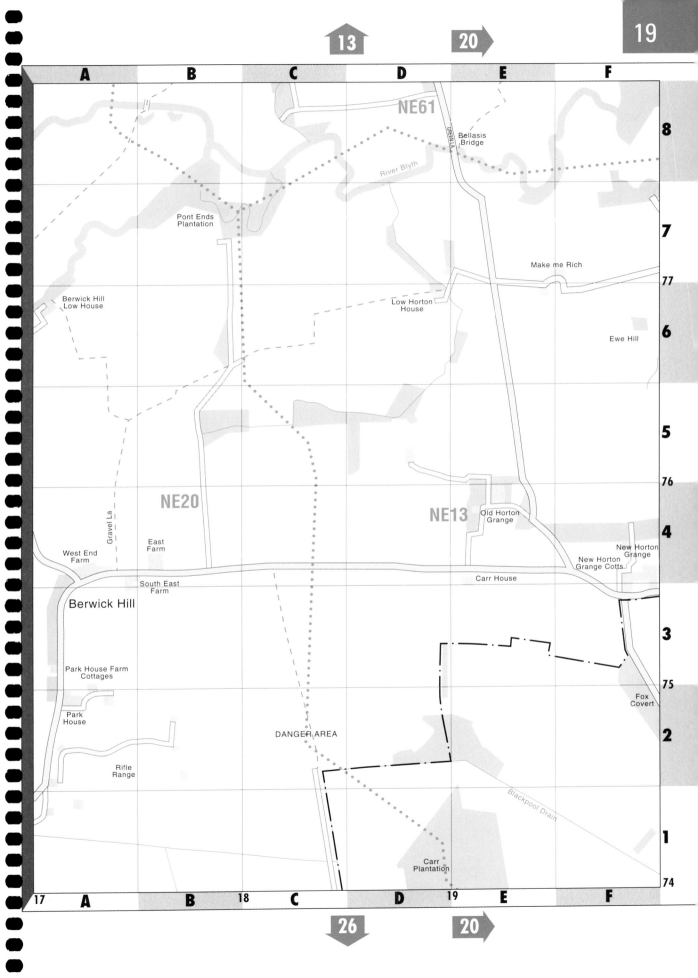

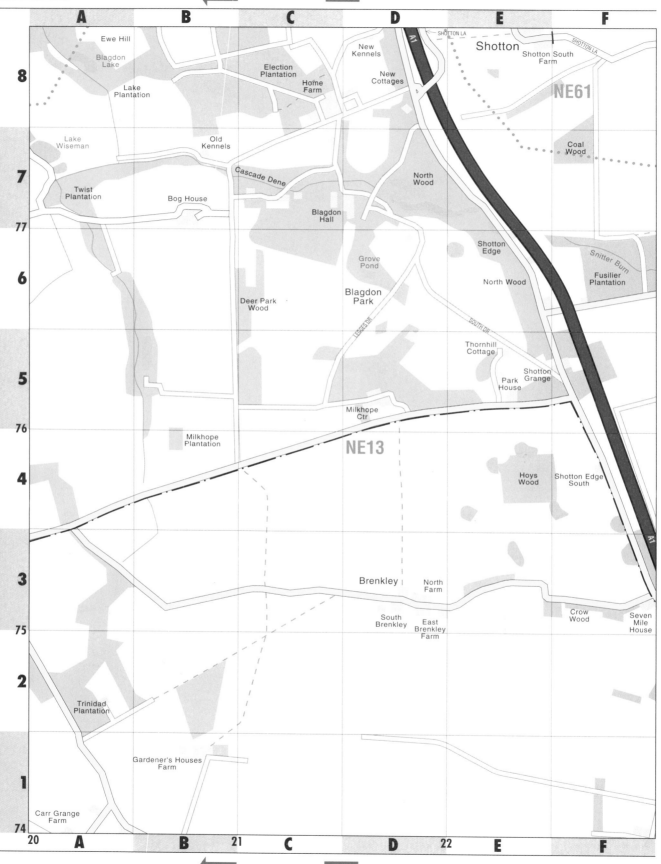

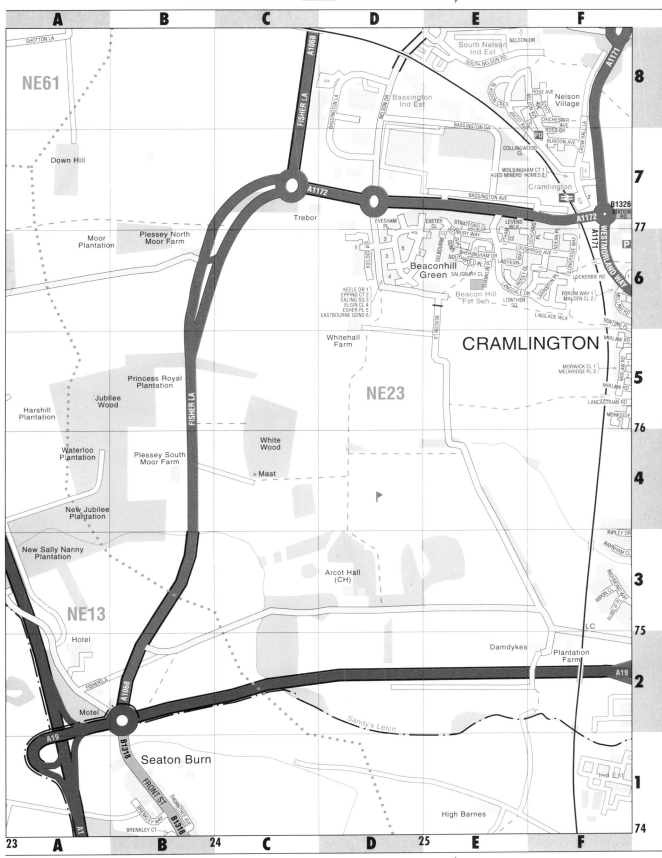

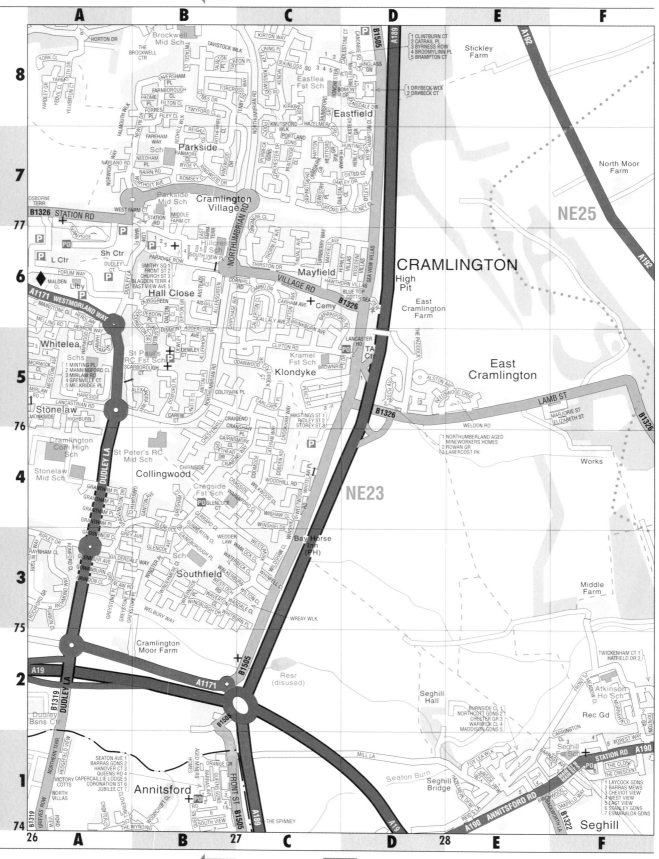

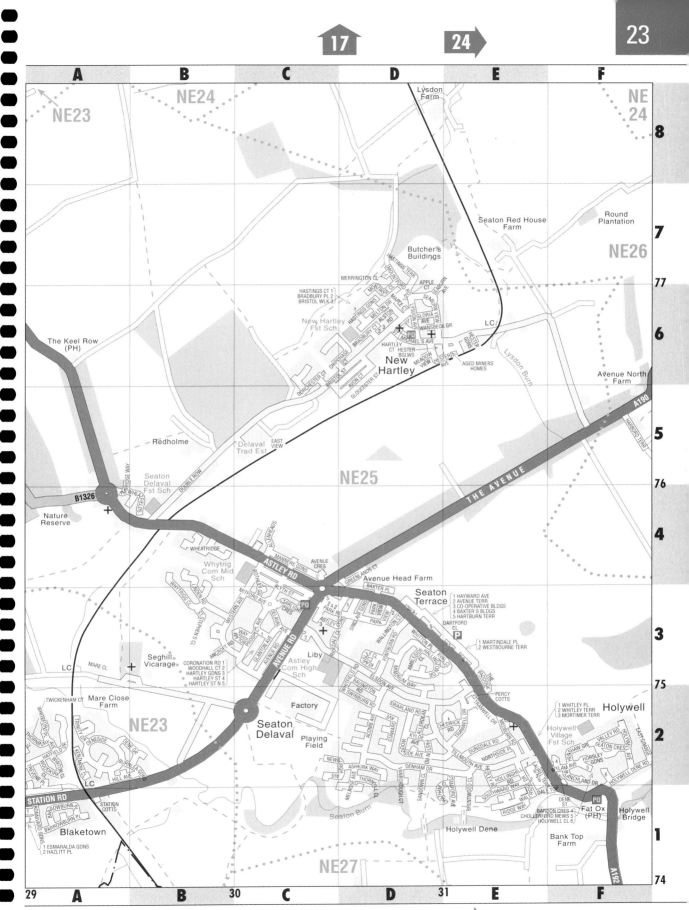

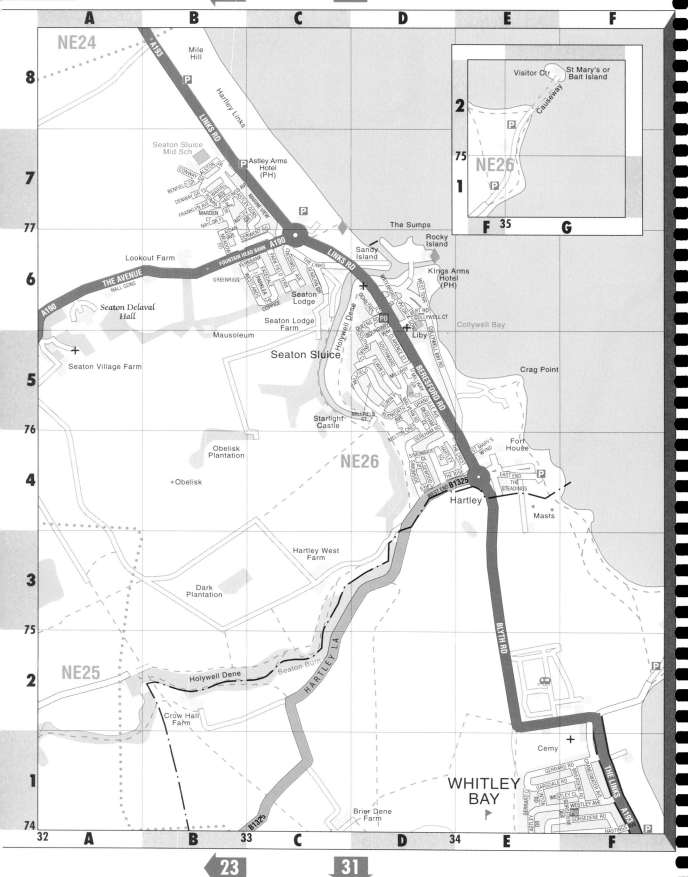

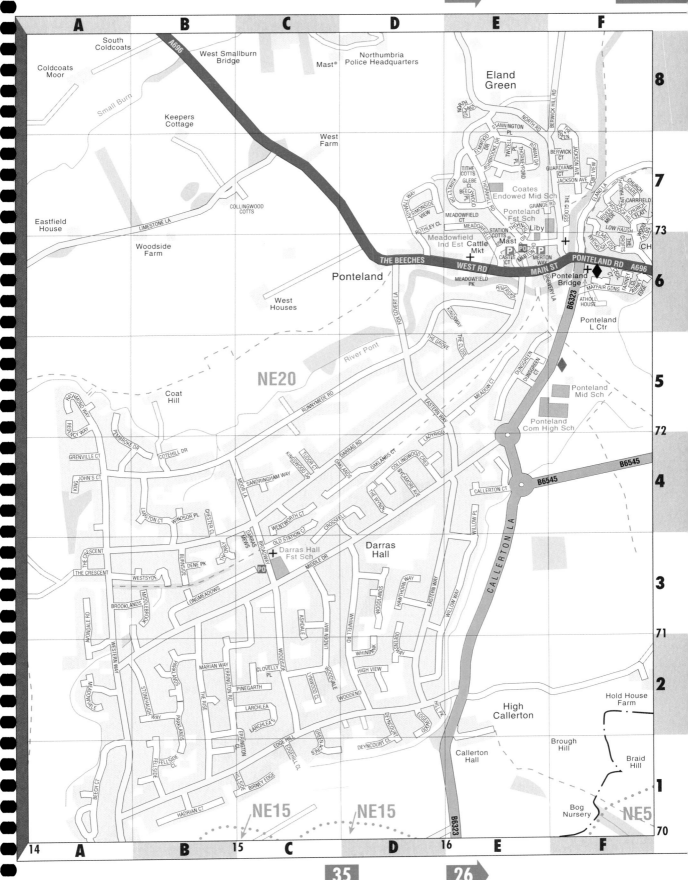

A **B** **C** **D** **E** **F**

8
7
73
6
5
72
4
71
3
71
2
1
70

South Coldcoats
Coldcoats Moor
Keepers Cottage
West Smallburn Bridge
Mast
Northumbria Police Headquarters
Eland Green
Small Burn
A696
West Farm
Eastfield House
Collingwood Cotts
Limestone La
Woodside Farm
West Houses
Ponteland
The Beeches
WEST RD
MAIN ST
PONTELAND RD A696
Ponteland Bridge
Coates Endowed Mid Sch
Ponteland Fst Sch
Meadowfield Ind Est
Cattle Mkt
Meadowfield PK
Ponteland L Ctr
River Pont
NE20
Coat Hill
Runnymede Rd
Eastern Way
Ponteland Mid Sch
Ponteland Com High Sch
B6323
B6545
B6545
Darras Rd
Oaklands
Collingwood Cres
Sycamore Ave
Callerton Ct
Sandringham Way
Kingswood Dr
Tudor Ct
The Wynd
Darras Hall Fst Sch
Darras Hall
Middle Dr
Broadway
Crossfell
Willow Pl
CALLERTON LA
The Crescent
Westsyde
Middlebrook
Longmeadows
Brooklands
Avondale Rd
Western Way
Parklands
Marian Way
Errington Rd
The Rise
Clovelly Pl
Woodside
Lynwood Ct
Woodend
Hawthorn Way
Whinfell Rd
Whinbank
High View
Queensway
Eastern Way
Willow Way
High Callerton
Hold House Farm
Brough Hill
Braid Hill
Callerton Hall
Hadrian Ct
Fellside
Birney Edge
Edge Hill
Fossmill Cl
Green La
Deyncourt
Eugene Cl
B6323
Bog Nursery
NE15
NE15
NE5
NE15
70

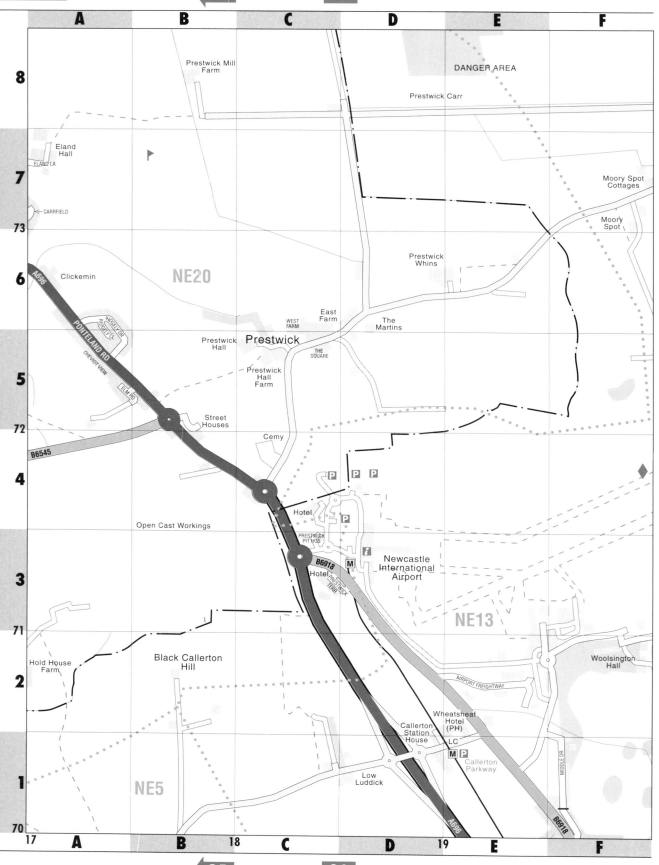

8

Prestwick Mill
Farm

DANGER AREA

Prestwick Carr

Eland
Hall
ELAND LA

7

CARRFIELD

73

Clickemin

NE20

Moory Spot
Cottages

Moory
Spot

6

A696

PONTELAND RD

RIDGEVA DR
RIDGELY CL

CHEVIOT VIEW

ELM RD

Prestwick Whins

East
Farm

WEST
FARM

Prestwick
Hall

Prestwick

The
Martins

5

Prestwick Hall
Farm

THE
SQUARE

Street
Houses

72

Cemy

4

B6545

Open Cast Workings

P

P P

Hotel

P

PRESTWICK
PIT HOS

i

Newcastle
International
Airport

3

B6918

M

Hotel

PRESTWICK
TERR

NE13

71

Hold House
Farm

Black Callerton
Hill

Woolsington
Hall

2

AIRPORT FREIGHTWAY

Wheatsheaf
Hotel
(PH)

Callerton
Station
House

LC

M P

MIDDLE DR

Callerton
Parkway

1

NE5

Low
Luddick

A696

B6918

70

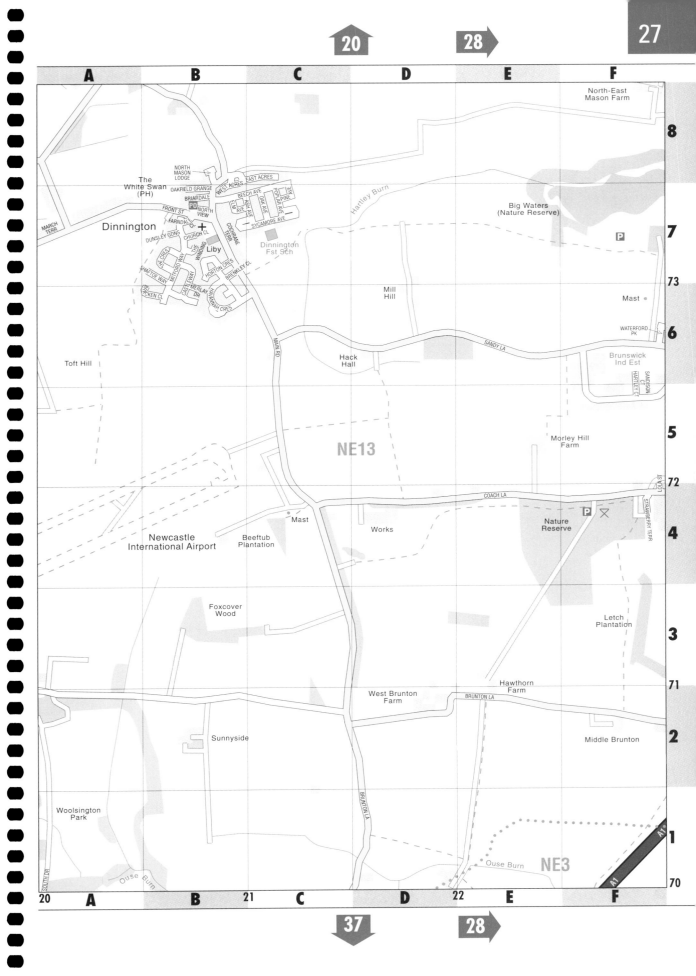

20
28

North-East
Mason Farm

The
White Swan
(PH)

NORTH
MASON
LODGE

OAKFIELD GRANGE

WEST ACRES
EAST ACRES

BEECH AVE
ELM
ASH AVE
OAK AVE
PINE
POPLAR AVE
3YM

BRIARDALE
PO
NORTH
VIEW

Dinnington

FRONT ST
FARNDALE

DUNSLEY GDNS

COCHRANE TERR

CHURCH CL

Liby

THE WINDING

HORTON CRES

BRENKLEY CL

Dinnington
Fst Sch

Big Waters
(Nature Reserve)

Hartley Burn

P

SHAFTOE WAY
ICE CRES
MITFORD WAY
CASTLEWAY
MERLAY DR
HYANNIH CRES
BRACKEN CL

Mill
Hill

Mast

Toft Hill

MAIN RD

Hack
Hall

SANDY LA

WATERFORD
PK

Brunswick
Ind Est

SANDISON
CT
HARTLEY CT

NE13

Morley Hill
Farm

COACH LA

HOLT IS

72

Mast

Newcastle
International Airport

Beeftub
Plantation

Works

Nature
Reserve

P

STRAWBERRY TERR

Foxcover
Wood

Letch
Plantation

Hawthorn
Farm

West Brunton
Farm

BRUNTON LA

Middle Brunton

Sunnyside

BRUNTON LA

Woolsington
Park

SOUTH DRI

Ouse Burn

Ouse Burn

NE3

A1

A1

↑ 22   30 →
↓ 39   30 →

A | **B** | **C** | **D** | **E** | **F**

8

NE23

West Field

7

Holywell Grange Farm

73

East Holywell

Fenwick's Close Farm

6

West Holywell

NE25

Cemy

Brierdene Burn

West Farm

B1322

Middle Farm

ECCLES CT

ST JOHN'S CT

CHURCH MEWS

THOMAS TAYLDR COTTS

MELROSE AVE

CHURCH RD

LC

Wks

5

BACKWORTH LA

B1317

Backworth Park Prim Sch

Recn Gd

ASHBURN GDNS
TELFORD CL
ST CLARE PL
STRETTON WAY
SIMONSIDE DR
SWARLAND CT

HARLEBURY

CASTLE SQ

RUSHBURY CT

CLARA AVE 1
LOWER CRONE ST 2
UPPER CRONE ST 3
BRIDGE TERR 4
EARSDON VIEW 5

72

A19

KILLINGWORTH LA

KILLINGWORTH AVE

CH

ECCLES CL

NE27

Moor Edge Farm

Shiremoor Mid Sch

PH

Recn Gd
BYWELL GR

HECTOR ST
SOUTH ST
WARK AVE
GRANGE AVE

MORLEY PL 6
HUGH AVE 7
CHARLES AVE 8
JAMES AVE 9

4

Backworth

Holystone Farm

Moor View

HARTSIDE CRES

HARLOW RD
HALTON RD

ANN ST 1
HARROW ST 2

MOOR EDGE RD

Shiremoor

M

ETAL CL
ETAL GDNS

BELFORD AVE
BAMBURGH CRES
CRASTER AVE

PARK LA
PARK CRES

1 GARFIELD CL
2 HARWOOD DR

ST MARKS CT 1
CO-OPERATIVE TERR 2

Shiremoor

MATFEN AVE
PARK RD

SIMONSIDE WAY

HAYDON GDNS 1
HAVELOCK RD 2

STATION RD

EMERSON PL

BOYNE GDNS

BRANDON AVE

FELTON CL
WITTON RD
FAIRE RD
BEAL RD

HORSLEY
ALSTON

3

B1317

East House Farm

NEW YORK ROAD

Shiremoor Prim Sch

BRENKLEY AVE

BRUNTON CL
CARRINGTON AVE
KIRKLEY
WARKWORTH
AVE

PARK LA
ANGERTON AVE
HARBOTTLE AVE

71

NE12

Killingworth Moor

Holystone Farm

A186

Holystone Prim Sch

B1322

NEW YORK RD

ST JOHNS VIEW

Hypermarket

BRUNSWICK RD

BRUNSWICK SQ

PARK LA

2

PH

HOLYSTONE DR

WINDSOR PL

A191

HOLYFIELDS

SOUTH VIEW
HOLLY AVE

MURRAYFIELDS

WEST ST
PH

TURNER ST

PO

BENTON RD

The Allotment

THE SILVERLINK N

Algernon Ind Est

A191

1 PALMERSVILLE
2 CO-OPERATIVE TERR
3 CLARABAD TERR
4 BANNISTER DR
5 THORNTON TERR
6 ELIZABETH CT
7 KELVIN PL
8 KELVIN PL
9 ROSEBERRY GRANGE

Palmersville

Holystone

ST CUTHBERT'S RD

WESLEY WAY

DEVONSHIRE PL

ST BEDES WAY

ST CUTHBERTS WAY

WHITLEY RD
ST PUTHBERTS
AIDAN CL

HOWARD CT
HOLYSTONE GRANGE

HOLYSTONE WAY

Silverlink Park

Mon

1

LAUREL AVE

B1505

LAUREL END

Palmersville

WESLEY DR

Benton Square Ind Est

WESLEY DR

ST AIDAN'S SQ

AIDAN CL

CARLISLE CL

BACKWORTH TERR 1
HOLYWELL TERR 2
RYTON TERR 3

CARLISLE CL

12 West Allotment

70

FEETHAM CT

GREAT LIME RD

M

B1505

Benton Square

ST AIDAN'S SQ

A191

A19

29 | **A** | **B** | 30 | **C** | **D** | 31 | **E** | **F**

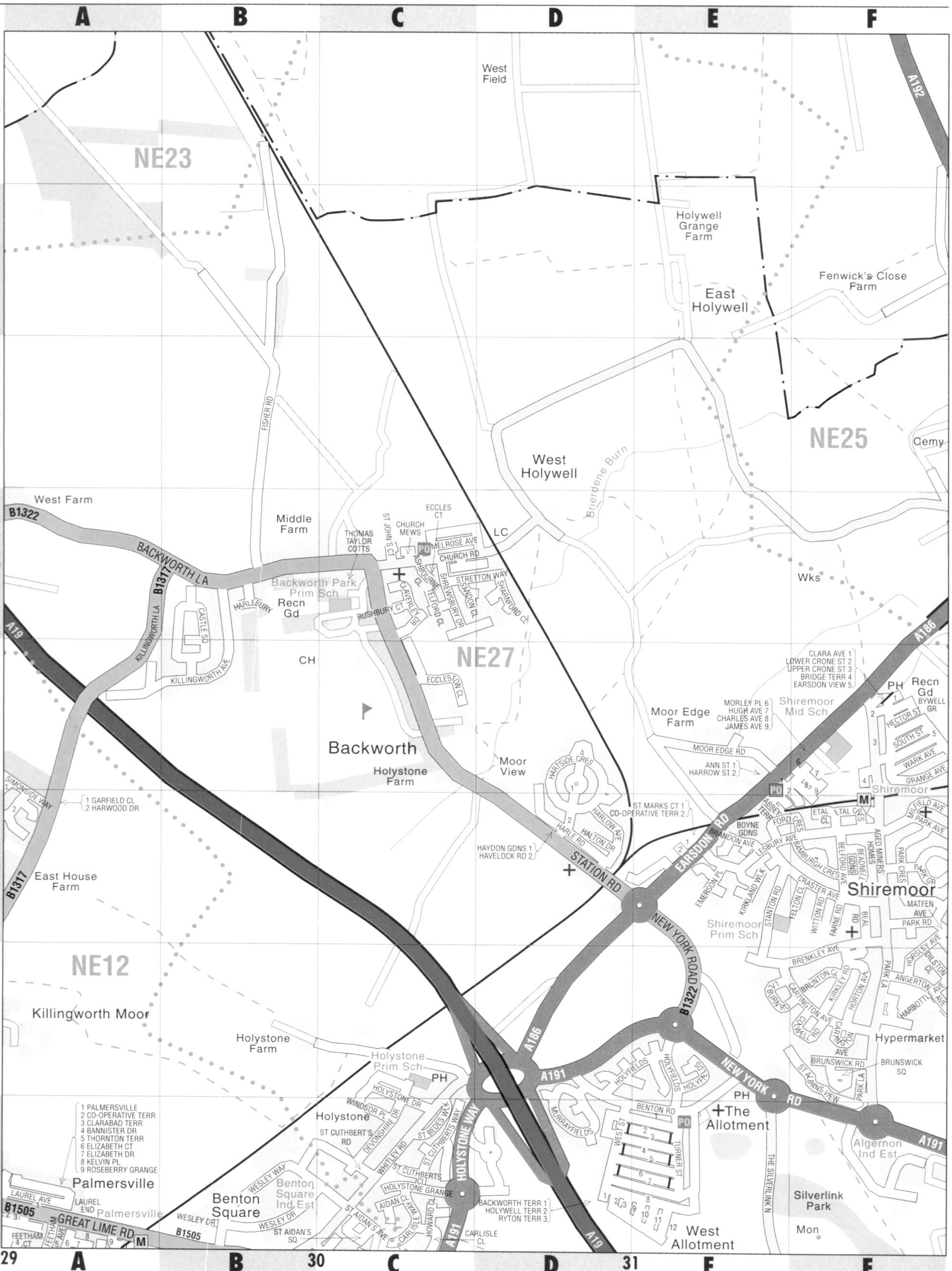

E1
1 NORTH TERR
2 ECCLES TERR
3 CARLISLE TERR
4 BUDDLE TERR
5 MAUD TERR
6 LAMB TERR
7 GRIFFITH TERR
8 TAYLOR TERR
9 EARSDON TERR

10 CRAMLINGTON TERR
11 CO-OPERATIVE TERR
12 PRESTON TERR

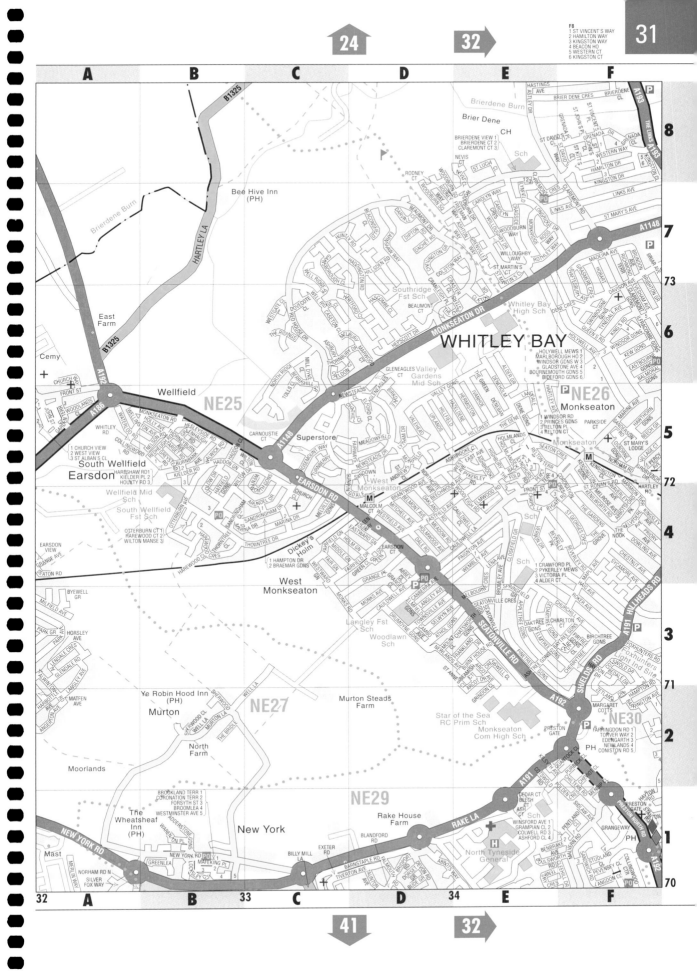

A B C D E F

8
7
73
6
5
72
4
3
71
2
1
70

Whitley Links

ST MARK'S AVE MONKSEATON DR
A1148 A193 THE LINKS
Northern Promenade
DAVISON AVE LINKS CT
GLENDALE AVE
SHFIELD GR
BOURNEMOUTH GDNS
CROMER GDNS
NE26
1 EASTBOURNE GDNS
2 ILFRACOMBE GDNS
3 MARINE CT W
4 MARINE CT E
CLIFTONVILLE GDNS
VENTNOR GDNS
CLOVELLY GDNS
BIDEFORD GDNS
WATTS RD
PROMENADE
Central Lower Promenade
ELMWOOD GR PARK TERR
A193 PARK RD
A193
Schs
Liby

WHITLEY BAY

1 ESPLANADE AVE
2 LINDEN TERR
3 TREWIT RD
4 VICTORIA MEWS
5 MAFEKING ST

B4
1 ALBANY GDNS
2 CLARENCE CRES
3 ALEXANDRA TERR
4 ALBERT TERR
5 WATERFORD CRES
6 DEVONSHIRE TERR
7 GLADSTONE TERR
8 STANLEY CRES

PARK VIEW CT
BEACH GR
DUCHESS ME
COUNTESS ME
COQUET AVE
HOLLY AVE
HOLLY MEWS
BEACH AVE
BRIAR CT
PERCY AVE
DUKE ST
ALNWICK AVE
WARWORTH AVE
NORHAM RD
QUEEN'S DR
GROSVENOR DR

EAST PAR
BROOK ST
CHARTS RD
OCEAN VIEW
EAST PAR
NORTH PAR
SOUTH PAR
ROXBURGH HO
YORK RD
NRTHMBRLND SQ
ROXBURGH TERR
LABURNUM AVE
CLIFTON TERR
VICTORIA TERR
STATION RD
JESMOND TERR

PARK AVE
PARK PAR
CAMBRIDGE AVE
MARINE GDNS
PO

KITTYWAKE HO 1
ESPLANADE
WHITLEY RD
PERCY RD
VICTORIA AVE
HELENA AVE
PROMENADE

1 GORDON TERR
2 ROCKCLIFFE

Southern Promenade

1 ROCKCLIFFE GDNS
2 GUARDIAN CT
3 COLLINGWOOD TERR
4 ROMNEY CL
5 WESTMINSTER CL

EXCHANGE BLDGS
PERCY PL
ALGERNON PL
EDWARDS RD
OXFORD ST
GORDON SQ
DR LAVAL RD
ROCKCLIFFE ST
GRAFTON RD
WINDSOR AVE
WINDSOR CRES
WINDSOR AVE

Brown's Bay

THE CRESCENT
P M
Whitley Bay
PRIORY AVE
Sports Ctr
CRESCENT VALE
Sch
RD A191
A193 MARDEN RD S
HILLHEADS
A191
KINGSLEY
HILLHEADS CT
LOVAINE AVE
HOTSPUR AVE
PERCY RD
ST PAUL'S GDNS
STUDLEY GDNS
DILSTON AVE
CHOLLERFORD AVE
FELTON AVE
ETAL AVE
PLESSEY CRES
RELSAY AVE
AMBLE AVE
MARDEN CRES
NATERS ST
ALMA PL
PRINCES RD
BRINTON TERR
LISH AVE
CHEVIOT CT
ESKDALE
SOUTHCLIFF
NORMA CRES
CEIFF ROW
PROMONTORY TERR
Mast
Brown's Point

NE25

BRAESIDE CL 1
SHADFEN PARK RD 2
SHAFTESBURY CRES
BROADWAY
MARDEN FARM DR
CRANBOURNE GR
HAMBLEDON AVE
HIGHCROSS AVE
BERESFORD GDNS
SANDFIELD RD
MANDALE AVE
ELLERMORE
KESWICK AVE
FAIRFIELD DR
LONGSTONE AVE
FOXTON AVE
HATHERTON AVE
NEWTON AVE
SHORESTONE AVE
BIRKSIDE RD

M
Liby
DOVE CT
BANK TOP
IRB Sta
1 VICTORIA CT
2 DOVE ROW
3 BEVERLEY VILLAS
4 BEDE CT
Cullercoats Bay
Tynemouth North Point
Cullercoats
Cullercoats Prim Sch
BEVERLEY TERR
BEVERLEY GDNS

FARRINGDON RD
Sch
KIRKSTONE AVE
TILBURY GR
CARDIGAN GR
HAMPTON RD
TORVER WAY
LORTON AVE
THIRLMERE AVE
PENRITH AVE
ENNERDALE RD
KIRKLINTON RD
SOLWAY AVE
DERWENT RD
THURSBY AVE
DEEPDALE RD
GRANGE RD
SILLOTH DR
KENDAL AVE
SEDGE
FAIRFIELD DR
SANDHURST AVE
SEACROFT AVE
SUNILA AVE
WARSBECK AVE
SEACOMBE AVE
Mast LA
LINKS RD
P

1 EDENGARTH
2 NEWLANDS
3 CONISTON RD
4 BLENCATHRA

SHAP RD
PO
KINGSTON
EDEN PL
HARTINGTON RD
BUTTERMERE RD
HARTLEY
Marden
STAN RD
AWORTH
HARAM AVE
STANTON RD
STANTON GR
MOLESDON
ANGERTON AVE
MONKHOUSE AVE
Monkhouse Prim Sch
HARTBURN RD
CAMBO
PRESTON WOOD
BEVCH WAY
EDLINGTON RD
EGLINGTON RD
BOLAM GR
WALLINGTON AVE
NEASDON CRES
INGHOE
BEACH RD
MONKSTONE GRANGE
MONKSTONE CRES
Marden High Sch
GREEN CL
NORTHLANDS
HENLEY RD
BEACH CROFT AVE
EALING DR
WHITTINGHAM CL
WHITTINGHAM RD
GLENEARN CL
NE30
1 EGLINGHAM AVE
2 RENNINGTON AVE
3 AYDON CL
4 SEACREST APARTMENTS
THE BROADWAY
AMBER AVE
MEDBURN AVE
LINKS AVE

Tynemouth Sealife Ctr
GRAND PAR
KENNERSDENE
LOUGHBOROUGH AVE
REGENT ST
SAXON DR
KENNETONE DR
REGENT RD
BEACH RD
ALDENHAM GDNS
PARKSIDE
1 THE DRIVE
2 PARKSIDE CRES

SOUTHLANDS Sch
BEACH RD
A1058
MONKS WAY
MILL VIEW
MARSHALL
A1058
SOUTHLANDS
A193

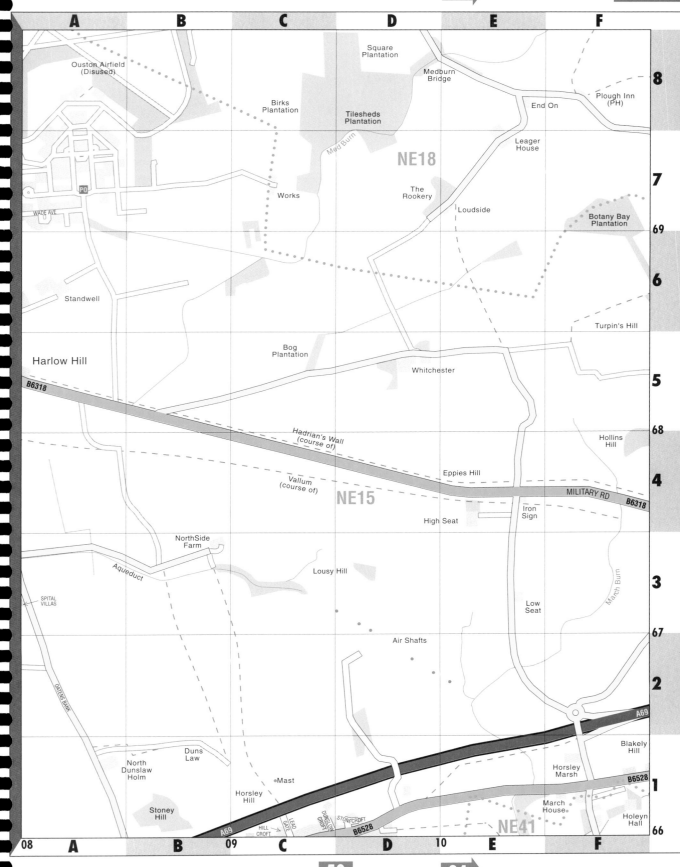

A B C D E F

8

Ouston Airfield
(Disused)

Square
Plantation

Medburn
Bridge

End On

Plough Inn
(PH)

Birks
Plantation

Tilesheds
Plantation

Mod Burn

NE18

7

Leager
House

Works

The
Rookery

Loudside

Botany Bay
Plantation

69

WADE AVE

PO

Standwell

6

Turpin's Hill

Harlow Hill

Bog
Plantation

Whitchester

5

B6318

Hadrian's Wall
(course of)

Hollins
Hill

68

Vallum
(course of)

Eppies Hill

MILITARY RD   B6318

NE15

High Seat

Iron
Sign

4

NorthSide
Farm

Lousy Hill

Low
Seat

March Burn

3

Aqueduct

SPITAL
VILLAS

Air Shafts

67

OATENS BANK

A69

Blakely
Hill

2

North
Dunslaw
Holm

Duns
Law

Horsley
Marsh

B6528

Horsley
Hill

Mast

HILL
CROFT

LEAD
GATE

DUNSLOW
CROFT

STONECRDFT

March
House

NE41

1

Stoney
Hill

A69

B6528

Holeyn
Hall

66

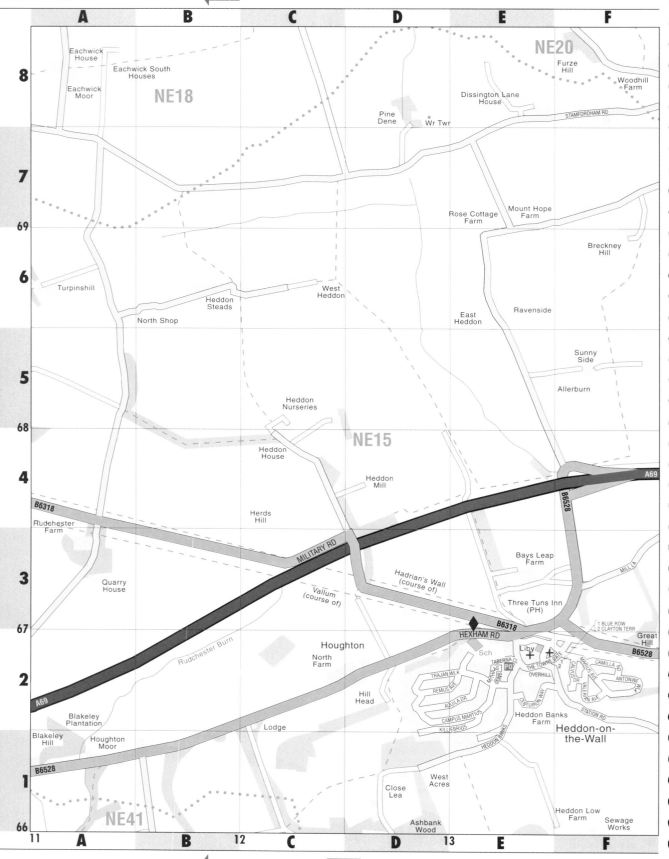

A B C D E F

8

7

69

6

68

5

4

3

67

2

1

66

11 A B 12 C D 13 E F

NE20

Eachwick House
Eachwick South Houses
NE18
Eachwick Moor

Furze Hill
Woodhill Farm
STAMFORDHAM RD

Dissington Lane House
Pine Dene
Wr Twr

Rose Cottage Farm
Mount Hope Farm

Breckney Hill

Turpinshill

Heddon Steads
West Heddon
North Shop

East Heddon
Ravenside

Sunny Side
Allerburn

Heddon Nurseries
NE15

Heddon House
Heddon Mill

B6318
Rudchester Farm

Herds Hill

MILITARY RD

Hadrian's Wall (course of)
Vallum (course of)

Bays Leap Farm

MILL LA

Quarry House

Three Tuns Inn (PH)

67
B6318
HEXHAM RD

1 BLUE ROW
2 CLAYTON TERR
Great Hill
B6528

Rudchester Burn

Houghton
North Farm

Sch
PO
The Towne Gate
Overhill

Liby

TRAJAN WLK
REMUS AVE
AQUILA DR
CAMPUS MARTIUS
KILLIEBRIGS
MITHRAS CL
TABERNA CL
CENTURION WAY

MARIUS AVE
CALVUS DR
VALERIAN AVE
CAMILLA RD
ANTONINE
STATION RD

A69

Blakeley Plantation
Hill Head

Heddon Banks Farm
Heddon-on-the-Wall

Blakeley Hill
Houghton Moor
Lodge

HEDDON BANKS

B6528

NE41

Close Lea
West Acres

Heddon Low Farm
Sewage Works

Ashbank Wood

Woodhill Farm
NE20
Birney Hall
Fell House
NE20
B6323
CALLERTON LA

8

Windmill (disused)
Birney Hill Farm
Callerton Common
Callerton Grange
Broom Hall

7

Heddon Law
Heddon Laws Farm
Throckley Marsh
Callerton Lane End
STAMFORDHAM RD
B6324
Callerton Lane End Cotts
NE5

69

Crescent Farm
Lough House
B6324

6

West Woodside
Throckley Common
Heddon Birks
BIRKS RD
PONTELAND RD
Dewley Burn
Dewley Hill

NE15

5

68

Holmside
Birds Hill
Burnside Farm
Dewley Farm
B6323

4

Dewley Park House

BLACKROW LA
MILL LA
Black Row Farm
DROVE RD
A6085
Throckley North Farm
Westway Ind Est
Walbottle Campus Tech Coll

3

A69

D2
1 OAK ST
2 HADRIAN HO
3 VICTORIA TERR
4 FIELD TERR
5 RADCLIFFE COTTS
6 RAVENBURN WLK
7 HILDA TERR
8 ORCHARD TERR
9 THE CRESCENT
Works
GRADYS YD
LILY ST
LIME ST
PINE ST 1
POPLAR ST 2
LAUREL ST
SYCAMORE ST
WESLEY WAY
High Dewley Burn
FINCHALE GDNS
WESTWAY
AMBLESIDE GDNS
BRAMPTON GDNS
TANCREDGDNS
INGLETON DR
Talbot House Specl Sch

67

1 FRENCHMAN'S ROW
2 AGED MINE WORKERS HOMES
Hadrian's wall (course of)
AINDERBY RD
Throckley Mid Sch
STEPHENSON TERR
HAWTHORN ST 1
GEORGE ST 2

Vallum (course of)
HEXHAM RD
Bank Top
OLLERTON DR
SHERINGHAM GDNS
HORNCLIFFE PL
HILL HO RD
THE MOUNT
TENTER GARTH
CLIPSTONE CL
STUART GDNS
P
HADRIAN
VALLUM RD
CALLERTON RD
1 CALLERTON RD
2 ST MARY'S PL
3 ELMFIELD RD
4 EVERSLEIGH PL
5 APPIAN PL
Vallum (course of)
Walbottle
HAWTHORN TERR
B6528

2

WOODLANDS CT
WOODLANDS
VALESIDE
COQUET GR
WALSWAY
THE BRIARY
Throckley Fst Sch
DERESIDE
BROOM HILL RD
PO
MOUNT PLEASANT
WOODSIDE AVE
Walbottle Dene
DENE HEAD COTTS
RICHMOND TERR
WHITEHALL RD
GROVE WLK
THE PADDOCK
PO
THE GREEN

Heddon Hall
STATION RD
REETH WAY
WELLFIELD CL
COACH RD
HEYN RD
TILLMOUTH PARK RD
HAWKWELL
BYE BY-WAY
GATE
THE WILLOWS
MOUNT CT
HEWLEY CRES
THE CAUSEWAY
NEWBURN RD
BRIAR LA
MAYFIELD AVE
MAYFIELD GDNS
New Burn
Small Burn
RICHMOND TERR
BANKHEAD RD
WALBOTTLE RD
DENE TERR

1

Throckley House
WINDSHIELDS WLK 1
LYDNEY CL 2
COLLIER CL 3
BOLAM CT 4
ISABELLA WLK 5
LEAZES PARKWAY
THE LEAZES
TYNE WLK
HALLOW DR
Throckley
Tyne Riverside Country Park
Hallow Hill
RICHARD
BROWELL RD
FOSSE LAWN
PARKSIDE
Rye Hill
A6085

66

A B C D E F

8 Black Callerton

Woolsington
NE13

Woolsington Bridge

THE PADDOCK
THE OVAL
HOLLYWELL GR

7 Ouse Burn

Black La

Harvey Dene

A696

69 ARMSTRONG ST

SHORT ROW
Callerton
Burn Close
Butterlaw

MORTON CRES
SEVERS TERR

Low Newbiggin Farm

6 B6324

Lough Bridge

Whorlton Hall

LOWBIGGIN
HAREYDENE

BEDEBURN FOOT
WEST THORP
PRIORY WAY

5 NE5

STAMFORDHAM RD

Simonside Fst Sch

BEDEBURN RD
EAST THORP
WESTGARTH
NEWBIGGIN LA

P

68 Fell House Farm

Great Whinstone Dike

1 CALLERTON VIEW
2 CLAVERDON ST
3 NEDDERTON CL
4 WHORLTON TERR

The Jingling Gate (PH)

WHORLTON GRANGE COTTS
CH

E3
1 WHORLTON PL
2 AGED MINERS HOMES
3 MARSHAM RD
4 COUNDEN RD
5 KENSINGTON VILLAS

SHIRLAW CL 1
BARDON CL 2

St Mark's RC Prim Sch

4 Westerhope Community Recn Ctr

REDBURN RD

WIMBOURNE GN 1
BUXTON GN 2
CHATSWORTH GDNS 3
PILTON WLK 4
BOYD TERR 5
BELMONT COTTS 6

TREVELYAN DR

3 North Walbottle

CORONATION RD

1 DULVERSTON CL
2 DUMAS WLK
3 DICKENS WLK

Sch

Westerhope

Westerhope Ind Unit

BUXTON GDNS
MATLOCK GDNS

B6324

67 A69

NE15

1 MILSTED CT
2 MELTHAM CT
3 COTTER RIGGS WLK

Parkway Sch

LANGDON RD
ROACHBURN RD

WEST AVE

THOMAS ST
JAMES ST
BRUCE
GREELY RD

Linhope Fst Sch

2 Chapel House Mid Sch

Sch

Byron

West Denton High Sch

DENTON PARK HO

CONCORD
LINKS WLK
HAWKSLEY

Hadrian's Wall (course of)

BRACKWELL GDNS
BLACKSIDE GDNS
BROOKFIELD GDNS

CHAPEL HOUSE DR

West Denton

P Denton Park Shopping Ctr
Lby P P
WEST DENTON WAY
LOW LEAM CT

1 Vallum (course of)
Walbottle Hall

BURT TERR
BEVERLEY TERR

1 COQUET BLDGS
2 WEST SPENCER TERR
3 STEPHENSON TERR
4 SPENCER TERR
5 SIMPSON TERR
6 BOYD TERR
7 BLUCHER TERR

THE CHESTERS

NORTHCOTE AVE
WESTLANDS

HARELAW GR

RIDSDALE AVE

DEIGHTON WLK 1
NORTHUMBRIA WLK 2
DUNSTAN WLK 3

Percy Arms (PH)

WELBOTTLE HALL GDNS

B6528 A69
THE ROMAN WAY
WESTERN AVE
MIDDLE GATE

66

C1
1 ANGRAM WLK
2 ASKRIGG WLK
3 AUDLAND WLK
4 AUSTWICK WLK
C2
1 HANOVER WLK
2 HANOVER CL
3 ELGAR AVE
4 THE SHOPPING CTR

E1
1 BIRKSHAW WLK
2 BICKERTON WLK
3 KNARSDALE PL
4 HIGHWELL LA

F2
1 FRANKHAM ST
2 BARENTS CL
3 FAIRSPRING
4 FENTON WLK
5 FORESTBORN CT
6 FOURSTONES
7 FORDMOSS WLK

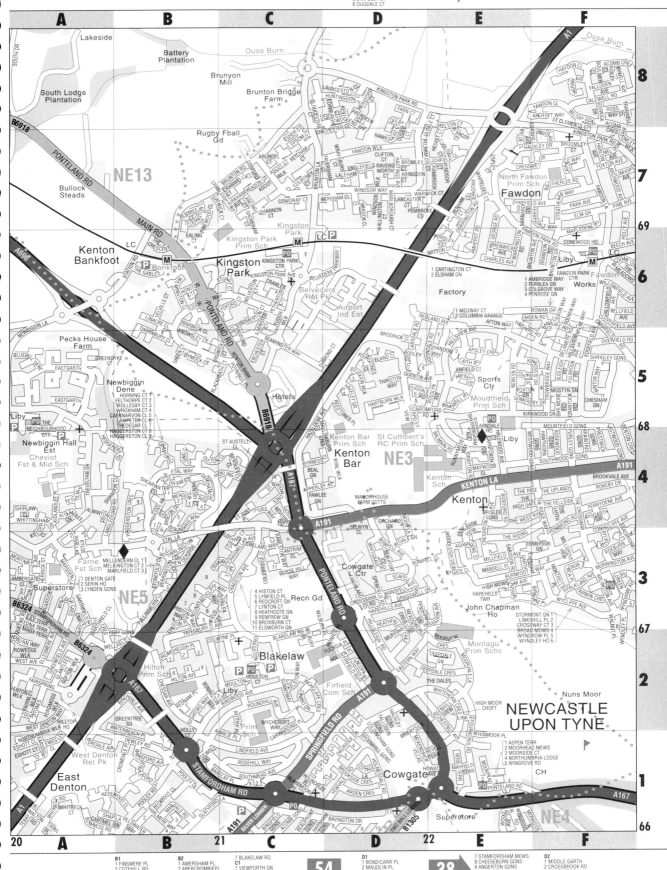

27
38

D5
1 GUNNERSTON GR
2 DUNNYKIRK AVE
3 LAVEROCK PL
4 HAZELEY WAY
5 STAPELEY CT
6 DUGDALE CT

7 CASTLE CL
8 BELLINGHAM CT

54
38

B1
1 FINSMERE PL
2 COTEHILL RD
3 BUTTERMERE CL
4 LOWESWATER RD

B2
1 AMERSHAM PL
2 ABERCROMBIE PL
3 CHANDRA PL PL
4 WALTHAM PL
5 MELVIN PL
6 CURZON PL

7 BLAKELAW RD
C1
1 VIEWFORTH GN
2 OAKWOOD PL
3 HADSTONE PL
4 TOGSTONE PL
5 DEEPBROOK RD

D1
1 BONDICARR PL
2 MAUDLIN PL
3 MORWICK PL
4 DOXFORD GDNS
5 EMBLETON GDNS
6 CHEVINGTON GDNS

7 STAMFORDHAM MEWS
8 CHEESEBURN GDNS
9 ANGERTON GDNS
10 OVINGTON GR
11 WESTERHOPE GDNS

D2
1 MIDDLE GARTH
2 CROSSBROOK RD
3 RADCLIFFE PL
4 BIRLING PL
5 RENNINGTON PL

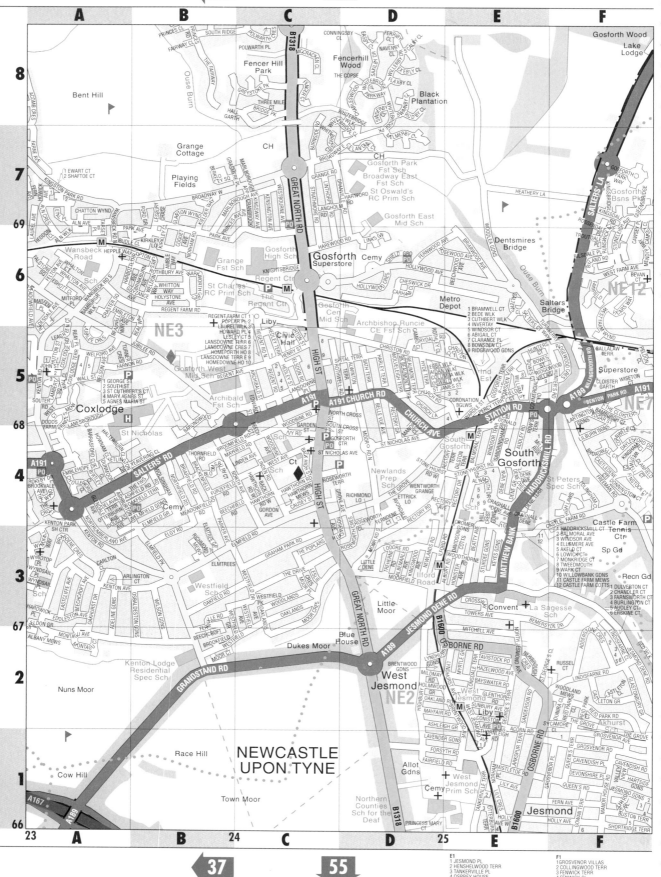

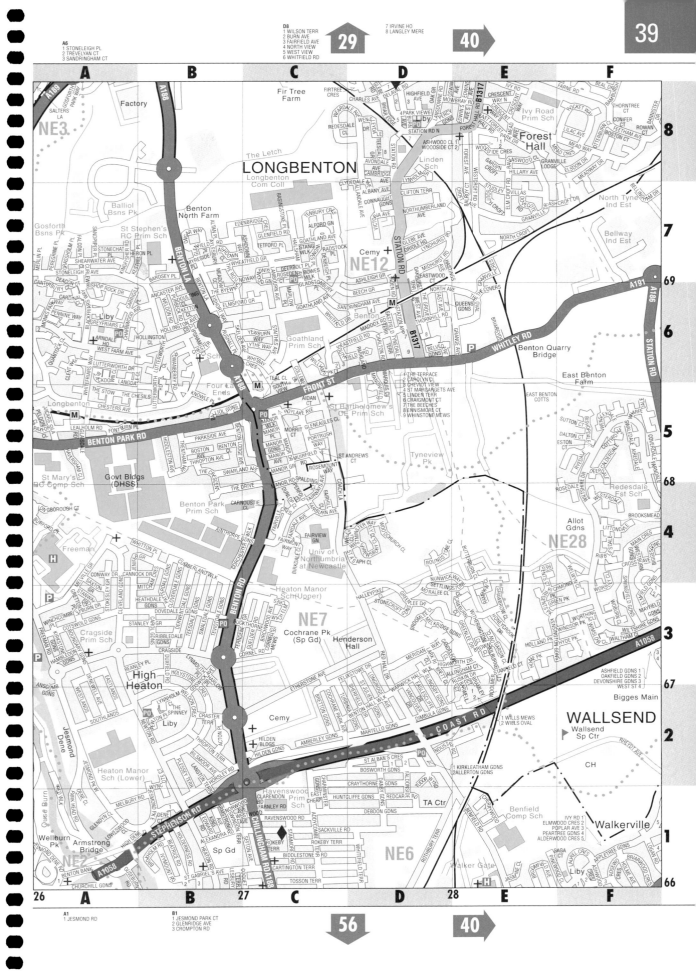

WALLSEND

NE27 · NE12 · NE29 · NE28 · NE6

Rising Sun Ctry Pk · Rising Sun Farm · Scaffold Hill Farm · Battle Hill · Willington · Willington Square · Holy Cross · Rosehill · Point Pleasant · Hadrian Road

North Tyne Ind Est · Hypermarket · Nature Reserve · Visitor Ctr · Hadrian Park Fst Sch · Hadrian Park Mid Sch · North Tyneside Coll · Willington Comm High Sch · Duke of Northumberland · Playing Fields · Willington Farm

St Bernadette's RC Prim Sch · High Farm Mid Sch · Parkside Specl Sch · Wallsend Jubilee Fst Sch · Sir GB Hunter Memorial Park · St Columba's RC Prim Sch · Arts Ctr · Wallsend Burn · Burn Closes · Cemy · War Meml

Station Rd · Coast Rd · High St E · High St W · Shields Rd · Hadrian Rd · Wagon Way · Church Bank · Rosehill · Tynemouth Rd · Buddle St

River Tyne · Willington Gut · Point Pleasant Ind Est · Brittania Ho · Carville Station Cotts · Mus · Ind Est

Index lists (bottom)

B1
1 SAKER PL
2 THE FORUM
3 SANDERLINGS
4 ELSDON TERR
5 EDEN CT
6 TIBERIUS CL
7 MAUDE GDNS
8 CAIRNSMORE CL

B2
1 BURN AVE
2 WINDSOR ST
3 JUBILEE ST
4 COBDEN ST
5 BLENKINSOP ST
6 HARRINGTON ST
7 DOUGLAS ST
8 HOPPER ST
9 TOWN SQ

F4
1 STANWIX
2 VINDOLANDA
3 CORSTOPITUM
4 CARVORAN
5 CHESTERS
6 HOUSTEADS
7 DOVECREST CT
8 SANDRINGHAM MEWS
9 GARDEN PK

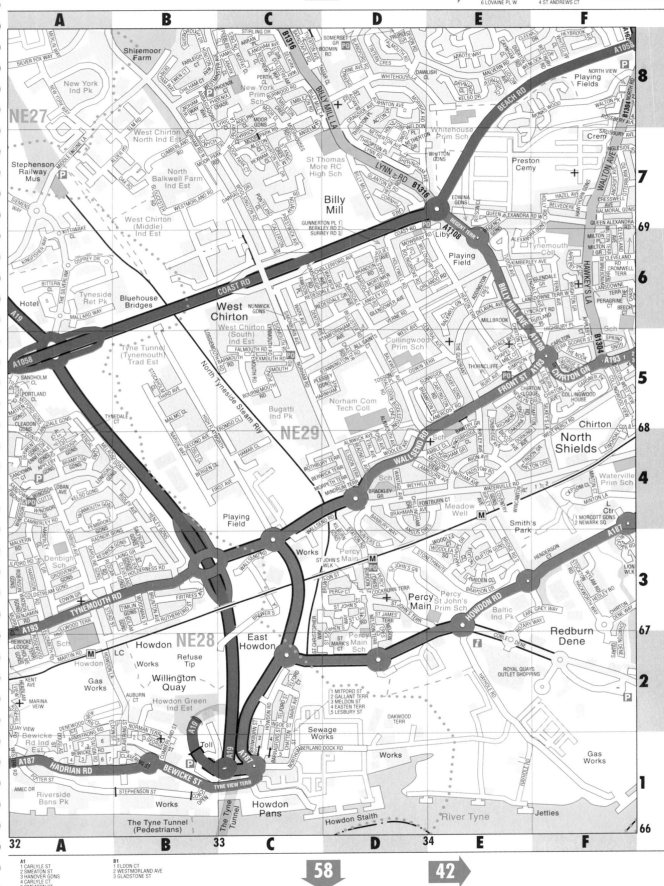

A5
1 SOUTH PRESTON GR
2 SOUTH PRESTON TERR
3 ALBION HOUSE
4 WIDDRINGTON TERR
5 HOPPER ST
6 HYLTON TERR

7 YORK TERR
8 LOVAINE AVE
9 WATERVILLE TERR
10 RAILWAY ST
11 WELLINGTON ST
12 WELLINGTON ST W
13 RUDYERD ST

A5
14 WILLIAM ST W
15 CHIRTON WEST VIEW
16 WATERVILLE PL
17 HYLTON ST
18 PRUDHOE TERR
19 PRUDHOE ST BACK

20 SPENCER ST
21 THEATRE PL

A6
1 GROSVENOR MEWS
2 ETAL CT
3 THE CHASE
4 THE ORCHARD
5 SPRINGFIELD
6 ASHFIELD GR

7 EDITH MOFFAT HOUSE
8 ALBION TERR
9 NORTHUMBERLAND PL
10 UPPER CAMDEN ST
11 NORFOLK MEWS

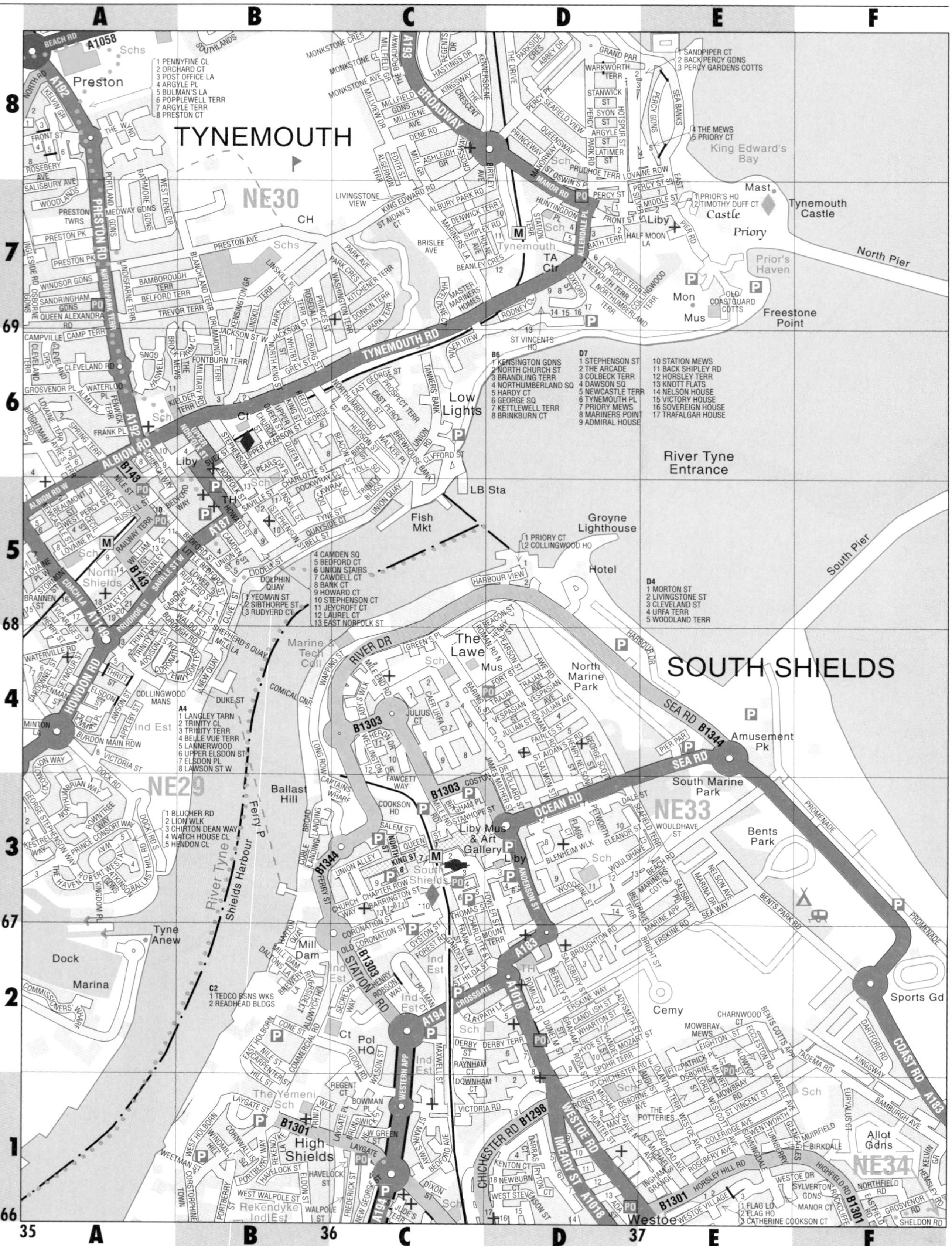

Grid columns: A B C D E F

Rows: 8 7 69 6 5 68 4 3 67 2 1 66

41
32
41
59

Map labels:
TYNEMOUTH
NE30
Preston
Preston Pk
NE29
North Shields
Low Lights
River Tyne Entrance
SOUTH SHIELDS
NE33
The Lawe
North Marine Park
South Marine Park
Bents Park
NE34
High Shields
Westoe
Tyne Anew
Dock Marina
King Edward's Bay
Tynemouth Castle
Priory
North Pier
South Pier
Freestone Point
Prior's Haven
Groyne Lighthouse
Sports Gd
Allot Gdns

B6
1 KENSINGTON GDNS
2 NORTH CHURCH ST
3 BRANDLING TERR
4 NORTHUMBERLAND SQ
5 HARDY CT
6 GEORGE SQ
7 KETTLEWELL TERR
8 BRINKBURN CT

D7
1 STEPHENSON ST
2 THE ARCADE
3 COLBECK TERR
4 DAWSON SQ
5 NEWCASTLE TERR
6 TYNEMOUTH PL
7 PRIORY MEWS
8 MARINERS POINT
9 ADMIRAL HOUSE

10 STATION MEWS
11 BACK SHIPLEY RD
12 HORSLEY TERR
13 KNOTT FLATS
14 NELSON HOUSE
15 VICTORY HOUSE
16 SOVEREIGN HOUSE
17 TRAFALGAR HOUSE

D4
1 MORTON CT
2 LIVINGSTONE ST
3 CLEVELAND ST
4 URFA TERR
5 WOODLAND TERR

4 CAMDEN SQ
5 BEDFORD CT
6 UNION STAIRS
7 CAWDELL CT
8 BANK CT
9 HOWARD CT
10 STEPHENSON CT
11 JEYCROFT CT
12 LAUREL CT
13 EAST NORFOLK ST

1 PRIORY CT
2 COLLINGWOOD HO

A4
1 LANGLEY TARN
2 TRINITY CL
3 TRINITY TERR
4 BELLE VUE TERR
5 LANNERWOOD
6 UPPER ELSDON ST
7 ELSDON PL
8 LAWSON ST W

1 BLUCHER ST
2 LION WLK
3 CHIRTON DEAN WAY
4 WATCH HOUSE CL
5 HENDON CL

C2
1 TEDCO BSNS WKS
2 READHEAD BLDGS

1 FLAG LO
2 FLAG HO
3 CATHERINE COOKSON CT

C3
1 STATION APP
2 SMITHY ST
3 KEPPEL ST
4 ALBEMARLE ST
5 BURROW ST
6 WILLIAM ST
7 RUSSELL ST
8 WATERLOO VALE
9 EAST ST

10 WATERLOO SQ
11 NELSON ST
12 WALLIS ST
13 CORNWALLIS ST

C4
1 AGRICOLA CT
2 FORT SQ
3 CAESAR'S WLK
4 CLAUDIUS CT
5 HEDLEY CT
6 MORTON WLK
7 HEDLEY CL
8 LIVINGSTONE PL
9 CLEVELAND CT

10 ALBION CT
11 CLASPER CT
12 PETREL CL

D1
1 NEWMARKET WLK
2 HALSTEAD PL
3 JOHN CLAY ST
4 CLAYSIDE HOUSE
5 WEST STAINTON ST
6 WEST MOFFETT ST
7 WEST STEVENSON ST
8 MADEIRA TERR
9 IMEARY GR

10 EAST STAINTON ST
11 EAST MOFFETT ST
12 EAST STEVENSON ST
13 EAST GEORGE POTTS ST
14 WAWN ST
15 DELAVAL CT
16 MILTON ST
17 WEST GEORGE POTTS ST
18 SHAKESPEARE ST

D2
1 SOUTH WOODBINE ST
2 SELBOURNE ST
3 LYNDHURST ST
4 BOLINGBROKE ST
5 PERCY ST
6 BRENTWOOD CT
7 ELIZABETH ST
8 ROBINSON ST
9 BURLEIGH ST

10 BEETHOVEN ST
11 TENNYSON ST

D3
1 SHORTRIDGE ST
2 WOODBINE ST
3 CATHERINE ST
4 SAVILLE ST
5 SAVILLE LODGE
6 KESTREL LODGE FLATS

7 WINCHESTER ST
8 CHATSWORTH CT
9 WALLINGTON GR
10 LONGLEAT GDNS
11 HATFIELD SQ
12 EASTBOURNE GR
13 BRODRICK ST
14 SYDENHAM TERR

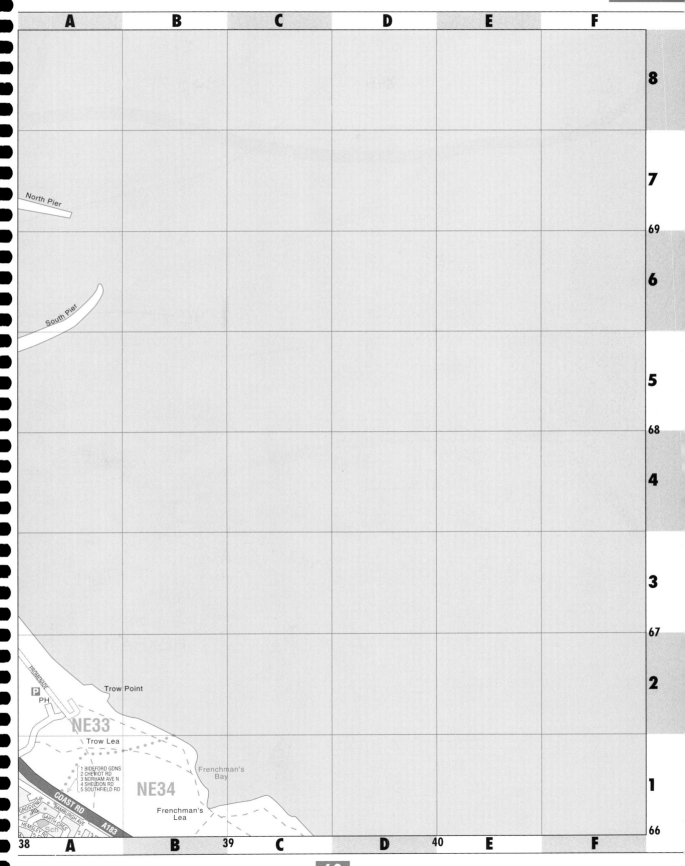

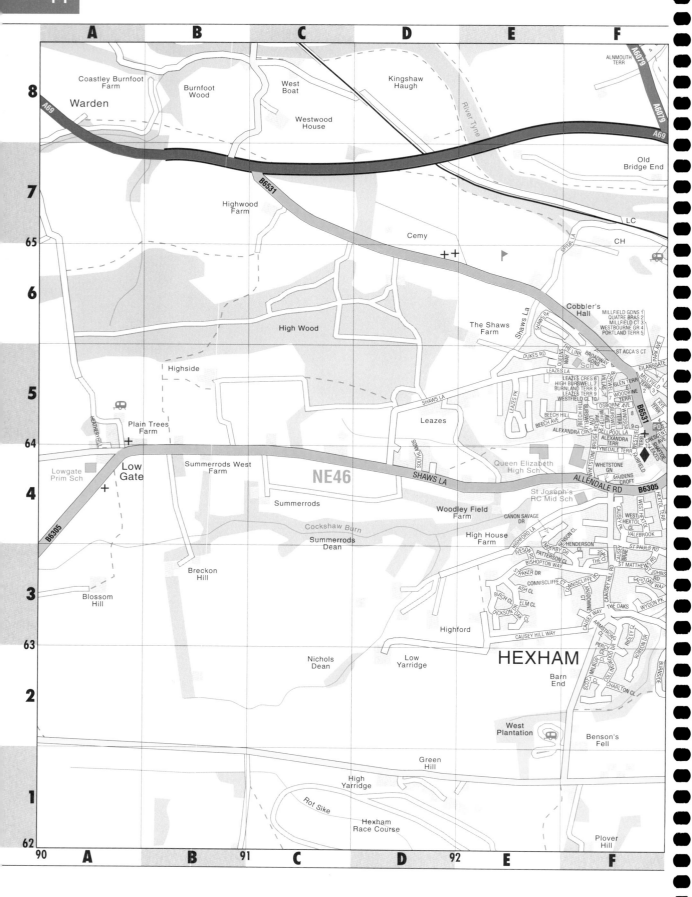

Riding Farm

Acomb

Target House

East Oakwood Farm

Oakwood

Anick

West Oakwood

The Rat (PH)

Anick Grange

Bank Foot

The Hermitage

Tyne Green

The Oaklands

Bridge End

Harwood Meadows

Tyne Green Country Park

Bridge End Ind Est

Auction Mart

Factory

NE46

Sewage Wks

Haugh Lane Ind Est

Tyne Mills Ind Est

Anickgrange Haugh

1 CHURCH ROW
2 MARKET PL
3 PUDDING MEWS
4 ST MARY'S WYND
5 ST MARY'S CHARE
6 MEAL MKT

Tyne Mills

Hexham

Broomhaugh Island

River Tyne

Wentworth L Ctr

Abbey
The Liby
Seal

1 PEARSON'S TERR
2 MILLFIELD TERR
3 WESTBOURNE GR
4 FENWICK GR
5 KINGSGATE
6 DUNWOODIE TERR
7 COCKSHAW CT
8 GIBSON PL
9 COCKSHAW TERR

DEAN ST

PETH HEAD

CORBRIDGE RD

DENE AVE DENE PK

Hexham General

Hexham Priory Sch

EAST WOODLANDS

Craneshaugh

MONKS MEADOWS

Hexham Mid Sch

Hexham East Fst Sch

Bogle Hole

1 MONK'S TERR
2 WOODLANDS
3 WOODSIDE
4 CHURCHLANDS
5 ELDON RD
6 GLANTON RD

Cock Wood

EASTGATE

Delegate Hall

GALLOWS BANK

Halfmile Wood

Hexham Hackwood Park Sch

Gallowsbank Wood

Golden Hill

Duke's House

Wydon Burn

Coalpits Flat

Dukeshouse Wood

High Shield

Outdoor Ctr

Milking Hill

Sunnyside Plantation

Mount Pleasant

Loughbrow

Ochrelands Farm

Ochrelands Ho

Black House

CAUSEY HILL RD

Sunnyside

Devil's Water

A4
1 PRIESTLANDS AVE
2 CROFT TERR
3 ST OSWALD'S RD
4 HENCOTES CT
5 GIBSON HO
6 ST WILFRID'S CT
7 ETHEL TERR
8 HENCOTES MEWS
9 SELE CT

10 HIGH ST CUTHBERT'S AVE

B4
1 NEWMAN'S WAY
2 JUBILEE BLDGS
3 DIAMOND SQ

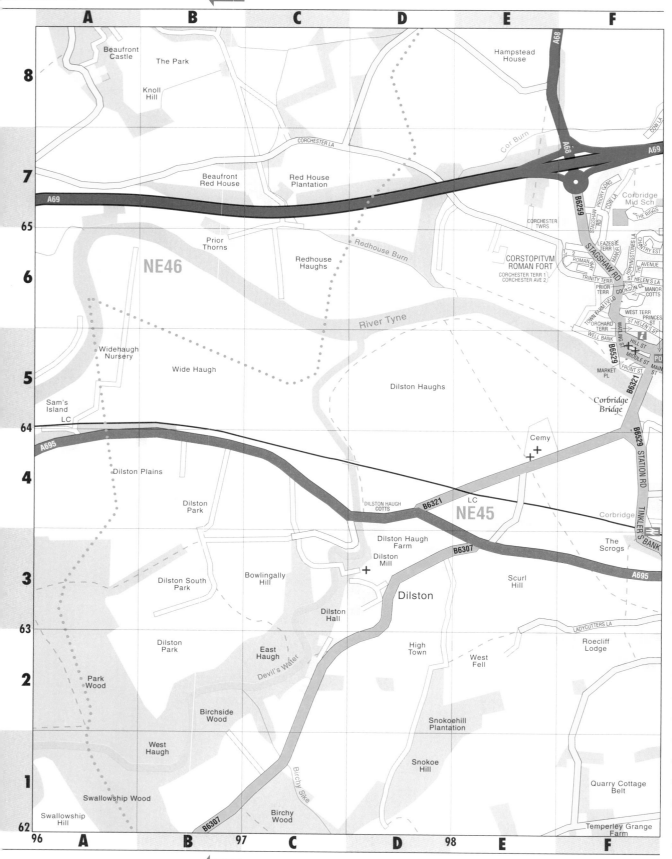

47

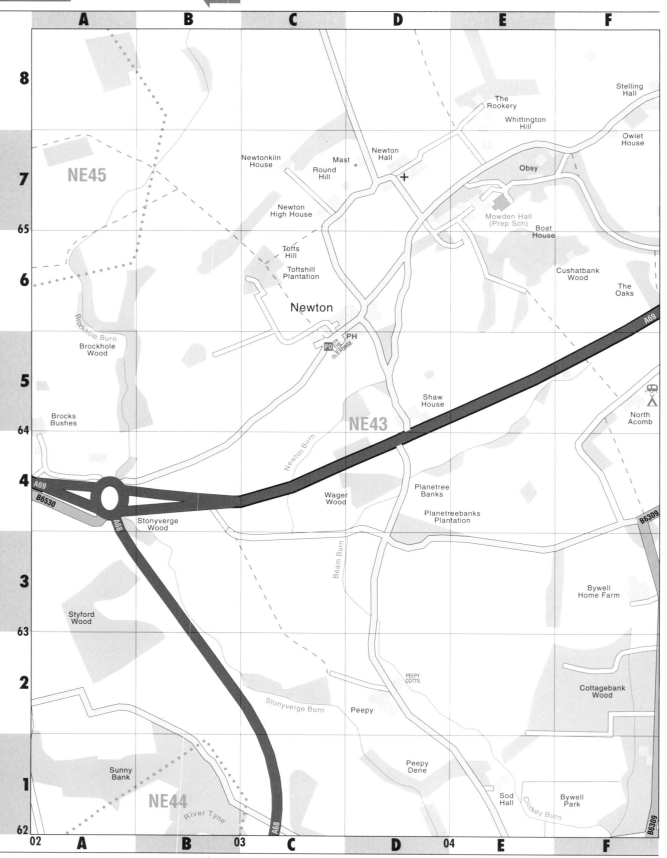

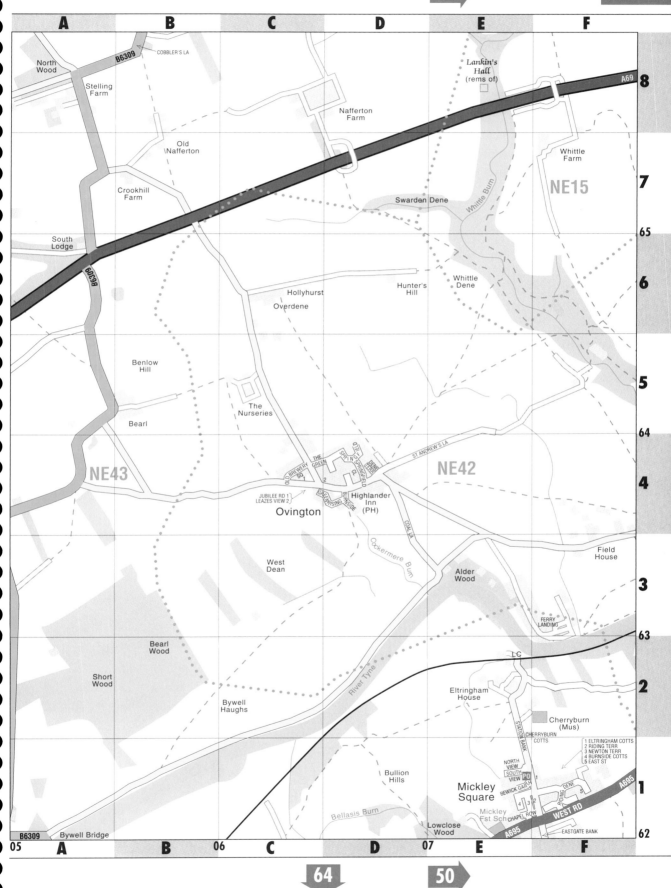

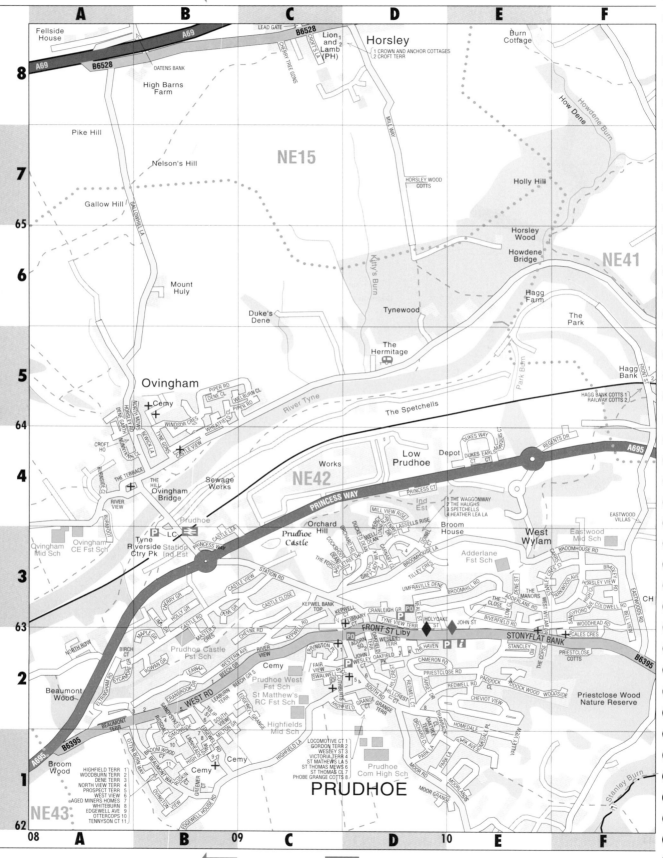

A   B   C   D   E   F

Fellside House

A69   B6528

8

OATENS BANK

High Barns Farm

Pike Hill

Nelson's Hill

7

Gallow Hill

65

Mount Huly

6

LEAD GATE   B6528

Lion and Lamb (PH)

Horsley
1 CROWN AND ANCHOR COTTAGES
2 CROFT TERR

CROFT TERR

CHERRY TREE GDNS

NE15

MILL WAY

HORSLEY WOOD COTTS

Burn Cottage

How Dene   Howdene Burn

Holly Hill

Horsley Wood

Howdene Bridge

NE41

Duke's Dene

Kitty's Burn

Tynewood

Hagg Farm

The Park

The Hermitage

5

Ovingham

PIPER RD

DENE CL   WELBURN CL

WINDSOR CRES   PIPER RD

WHEATLEY CL

Cemy

NORTH MEWS   HORSLEY RD   DENE GARTH   MUNDAY PK CL   BEWICK LA   TYNE GDNS   CASTLE VIEW

River Tyne

The Spetchells

Park Burn

HAGG BANK COTTS 1
RAILWAY COTTS 2

Hagg Bank

FRONT ST

64

CROFT HO

BURNSIDE CL   RUNSIDE CL   THE TERRACE   RIVER VIEW   THE HILL

Ovingham Bridge

Sewage Works

Works

Low Prudhoe

Depot   DUKES WAY   DUKES EARLS CT   REGENTS DR

A695

4

NE42

Prudhoe

BURNEDGE

Ovingham Mid Sch   Ovingham CE Fst Sch

Tyne Riverside Ctry Pk   P   LC   Station   Ind Est

CASTLE LEA

PRINCESS WAY

PRINCESS WAY   PRINCESS CT

Ind Est

1 THE WAGGONWAY
2 THE HAUGHS
3 SPETCHELLS
4 HEATHER LEA LA

Broom House

EASTWOOD VILLAS

West Wylam

Eastwood Mid Sch

CH

3

Prudhoe Castle

Orchard Hill

COCKSHOT   ORCHARD HILL   DUKE'S DENE   WELL DEAN   MILL VIEW RISE   LASSELLS RISE

THE FORD   PLUMTREE CT   GREY CT   KW LA   CARNEGIE   TILLEY CRES   BROOMHOUSE LA

Adderlane Fst Sch

ADDERLANE RD   THE MANORS   DENE ST   HORSLEY VIEW   PARKWOOD AVE   BRADLEY CT   EASTWOODS RD

UMFRAVILLE DENE   BROOMHILL RD   THE CLOSE   LOW WEST WYLAM   SANDYFORD   WOODHEAD RD   COLDWELL RD   BELL VIEW

63

NORTH ROW   BIRCH CT   MAPLE GR   CHERRY GR   HOLLY GR   LIME GR   CASTLE RD   DENE GR   CASTLE CLOSE   CHEYNE RD   KEPWELL   KEPWELL RD   KEPWELL BANK TOP   LIBRARY   KEPWELL CT   CRANLEIGH CT   P   PO   TYNE VIEW TERR   HOLYOAKE ST   JOHN ST   BIVERFIELD RD   CALES CRES

SYCAMORE GR   ROWAN GR   MASTER'S CRES   FRONT ST Liby   STONYFLAT BANK   B6395

Prudhoe Castle Fst Sch   ERRINGTON   WESLEY TERR   THE HAVEN   P   i   STANCLEY   THE COPSE   PRIESTCLOSE COTTS

FETTERINGHAM RD   RIVER VIEW   WESTERN AVE   BEECH GR   LEAFIELD   ADORN SQ   JOHN WESLEY CT   OAKFIELD CT   CAMERON RD   PRIESTCLOSE RD   REDWELL CT   PADDOCK CL   PADDOCK WOOD   WOODSIDE

2

Beaumont Wood

SANDY SYKES   CRANBROOK GR   LEABURN   STEP UP   SOUTH VIEW   MILTON GR   GREENER CT   EDGEWELL GRANGE   SWALWELL   FAIR VIEW   ST CUTHBERTS   HIGHFIELD   GRANGE CT   GRANGE TERR   SOUTH RD   HILLCREST CT   TARSET DR   CHEVIOT VIEW   HOMEDALE   VALLEY VIEW   MOORLANDS

West Rd   WEST RD

Cemy   Prudhoe West Fst Sch   St Matthew's RC Fst Sch

Cemy

Highfields Mid Sch

Priestclose Wood Nature Reserve

1

Broom Wood

B6395   A695

COTTERBURN WAY   BROOM WOOD CT   BEAUMONT WAY   RUSKIN   OVINGTON VIEW   EDGEWELL HOUSE RD   HIGHFIELD LA

LOCOMOTIVE CT 1
GORDON TERR 2
WESLEY ST 3
VICTORIA TERR 4
ST MATHEWS LA 5
ST THOMAS MEWS 6
ST THOMAS CT 7
PHOBE GRANGE COTTS 8

Prudhoe Com High Sch

MOOR RD   MOOR GRANGE   ORCHARD CT   ORCHARD LA   PARK LA   OAK TREE   DRAYDALE   HOMEDALE PL   PARK AVE   HOMEDALE RD

Stanley Burn

Cemy   Cemy

HIGHFIELD TERR 1
WOODBURN TERR 2
DENE TERR 3
NORTH VIEW TERR 4
PROSPECT TERR 5
WEST VIEW 6
AGED MINERS HOMES 7
WHITEBURN 8
EDGEWELL AVE 9
OTTERCOPS 10
TENNYSON CT 11

NE43

PRUDHOE

62

08   A   B   09   C   D   10   E   F

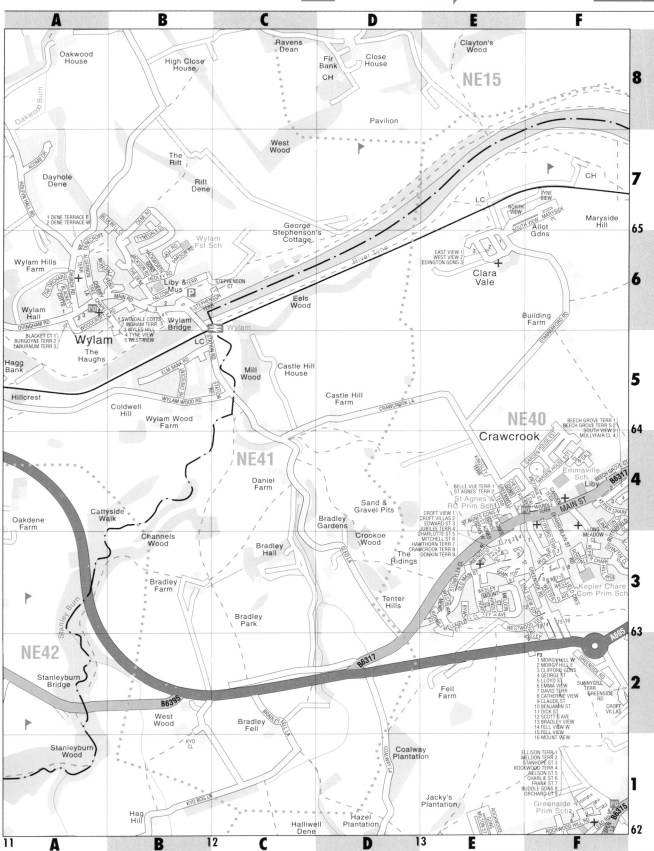

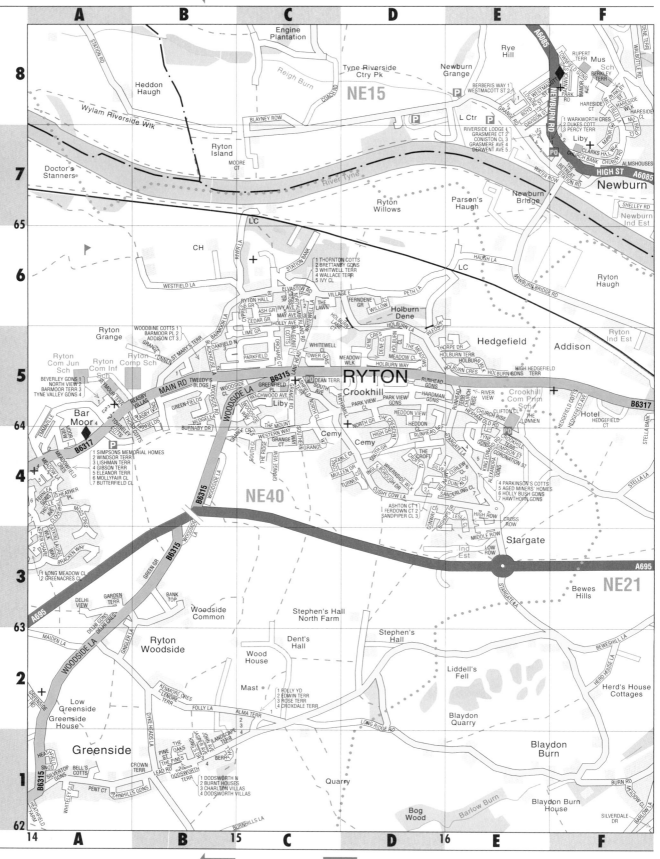

36 54

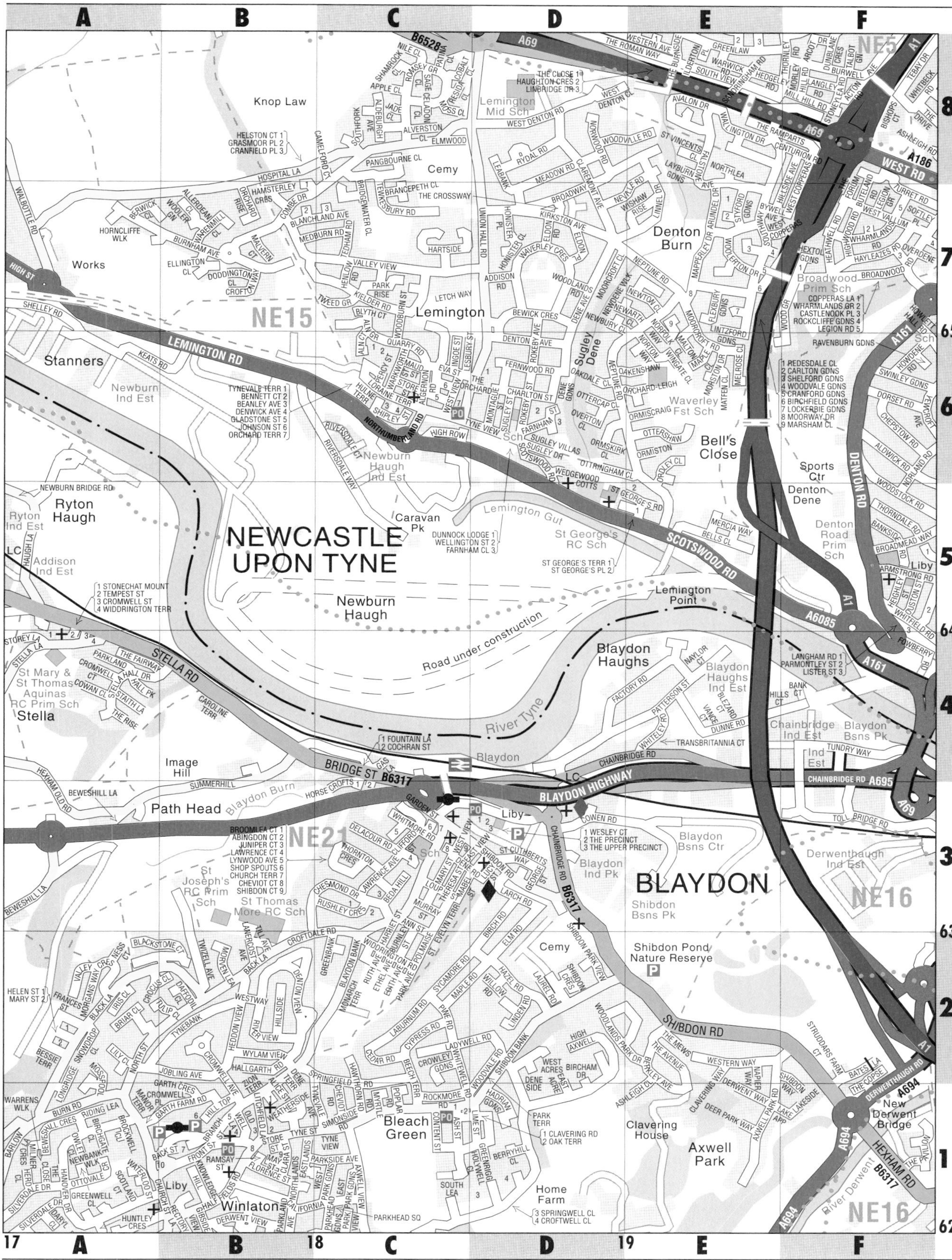

NEWCASTLE UPON TYNE

NE15

NE21

NE16

Major places and labels:

- Knop Law
- Works
- Stanners
- Ryton Haugh
- Ryton Ind Est
- Addison Ind Est
- Newburn Ind Est
- Newburn Haugh Ind Est
- Newburn Haugh
- Caravan Pk
- Lemington
- Lemington Point
- Lemington Gut
- Sugley Dene
- Denton Burn
- Denton Dene
- Bell's Close
- Waverley Fst Sch
- Sports Ctr
- Broadwood Prim Sch
- Scotswood Rd
- Blaydon Haughs
- Blaydon Haughs Ind Est
- Chainbridge Ind Est
- Blaydon Bsns Pk
- River Tyne
- Road under construction
- Stella
- St Mary & St Thomas Aquinas RC Prim Sch
- Image Hill
- Summerhill
- Path Head
- Blaydon Burn
- Horse Crofts
- St Joseph's RC Prim Sch
- St Thomas More RC Sch
- Bridge St
- Blaydon
- Blaydon Highway
- Blaydon Ind Pk
- Blaydon Bsns Ctr
- BLAYDON
- Shibdon Bsns Pk
- Shibdon Pond Nature Reserve
- Cemy
- Derwenthaugh Ind Est
- Chainbridge Rd
- Bleach Green
- Winlaton
- Home Farm
- Clavering House
- Axwell Park
- Shibdon Rd
- New Derwent Bridge
- Hexham Rd
- River Derwent
- **NE16**

Roads: B6528, A69, A186, WEST RD, A1, A161, A6085, A695, A694, B6317, Lemington Rd, Stella Rd, Denton Rd

B1
1 LITCHFIELD ST
2 LITCHFIELD CRES
3 LITCHFIELD TERR
4 OLDWELL AVE
5 MOUNT PLEASANT
6 ROOKSLEIGH
7 THE GARTH
8 COMMERCIAL ST
9 GARDEN TERR
10 NORTH LODGE APARTMENTS

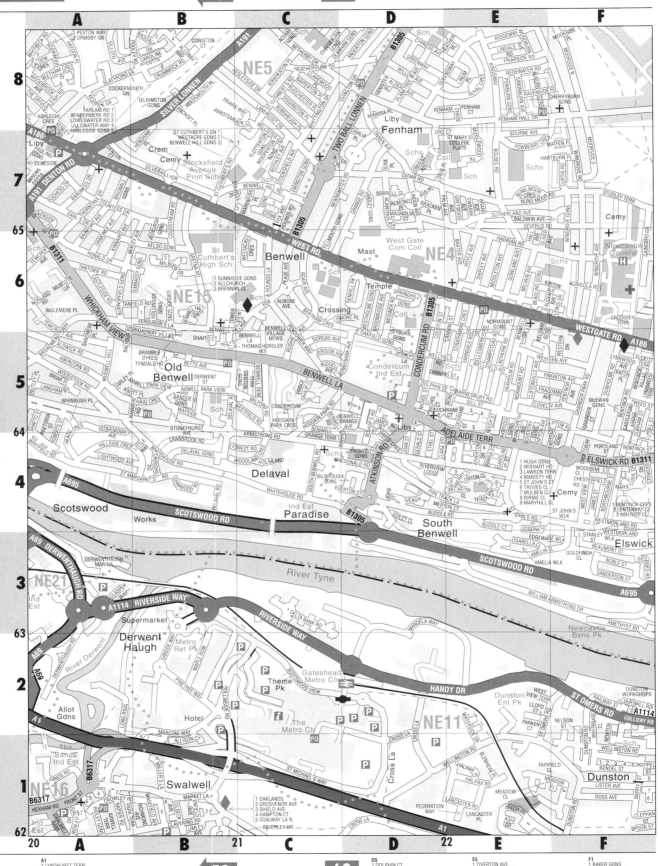

A1
1 LYNDHURST TERR
2 CROWLEY
3 SPENCERS BANK
4 HOOD ST
5 BREWERY LA
6 BREWERY BANK
7 JUBILEE TERR

D5
1 DOLPHIN CT
2 BOND ST
3 NICHOL ST
4 ST JAMES LODGE
5 ATKINSON TERR
6 ST JAMES' GDNS
7 DAVID ADAMS HO
8 BENWELL GRANGE CL
9 BENWELL GRANGE

E5
1 TIVERTON AVE
2 NORMOUNT AVE
3 ADELAIDE HO
4 CLENNEL HO
5 THE ADELAIDE CTR

F1
1 BAKER GDNS
2 FOWLER GDNS
3 KELVIN GDNS
4 TYNDAL GDNS
5 PARSONS GDNS
6 JOHNSON ST
7 RUSKIN AVE
8 KINGSLEY PL

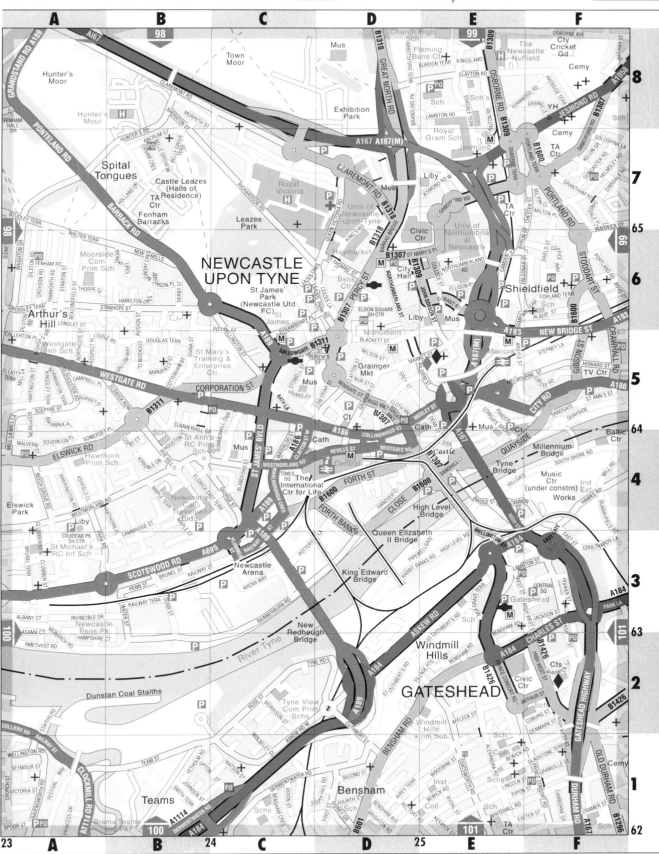

For full street detail of the
highlighted area see pages
98, 99, 100 and 101.

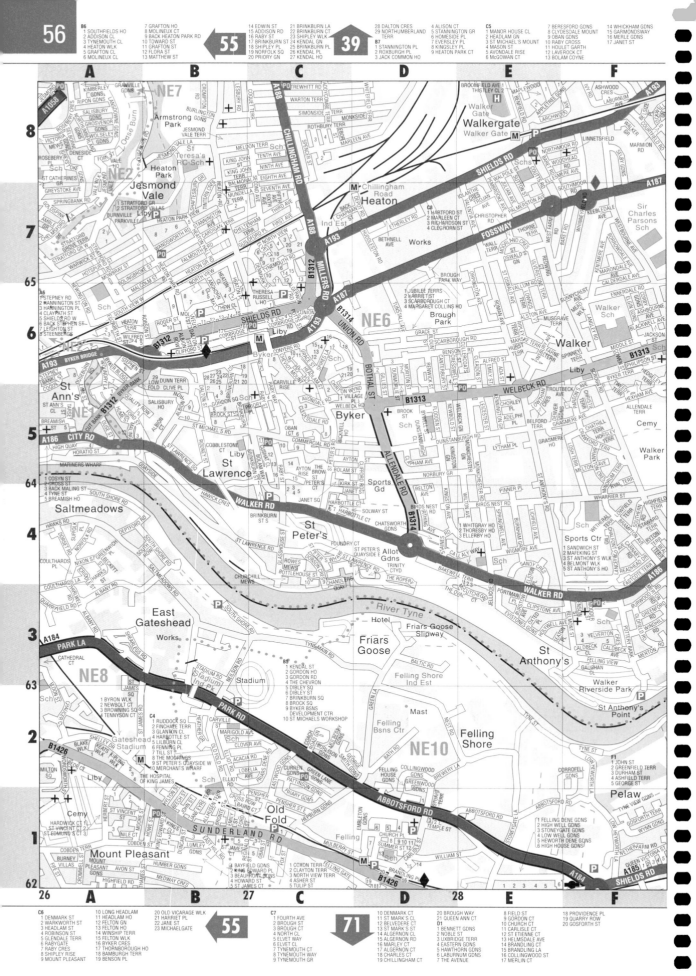

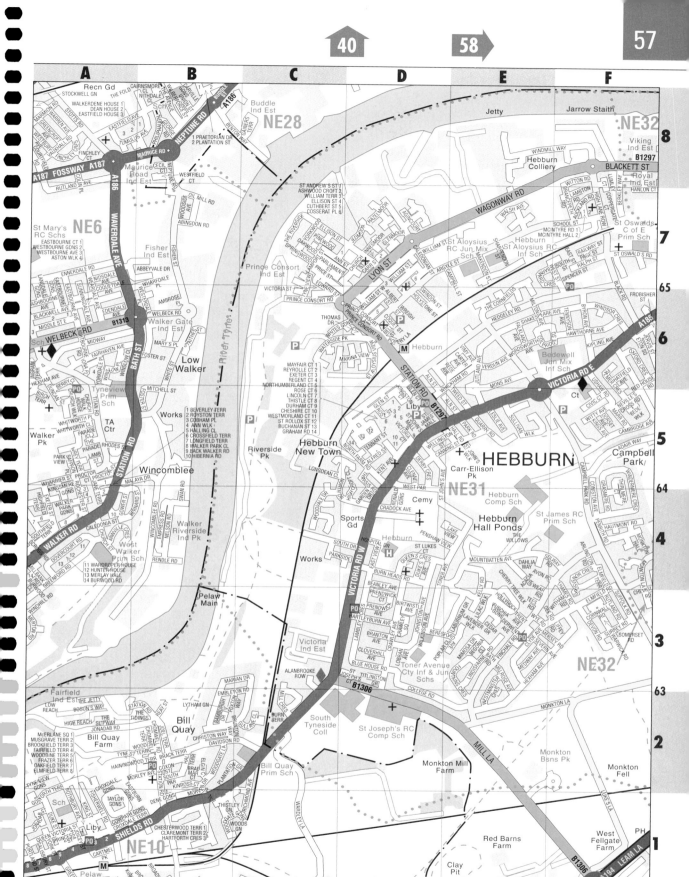

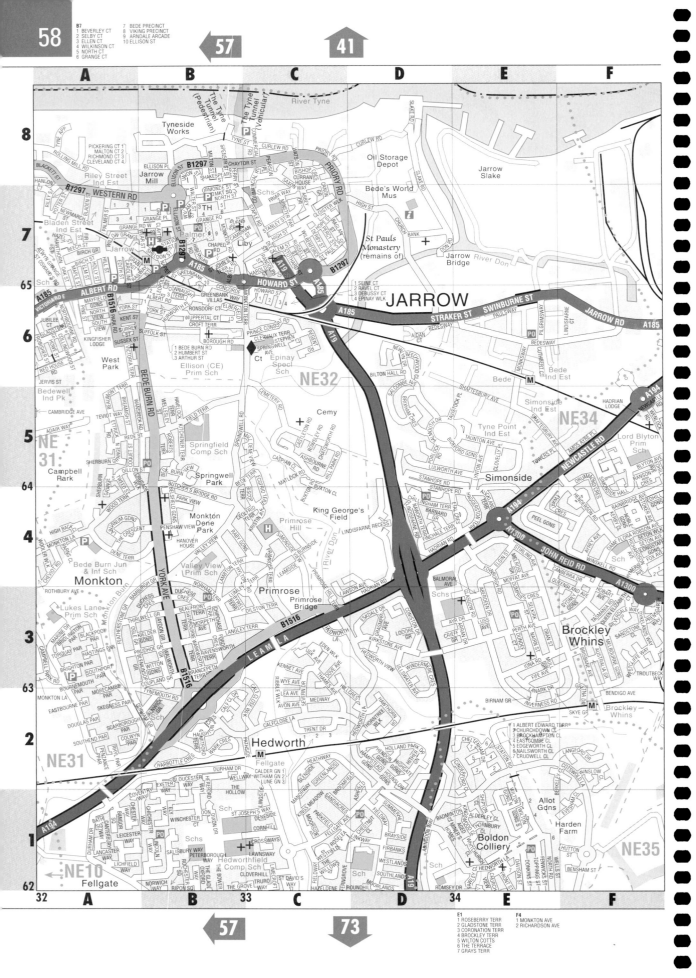

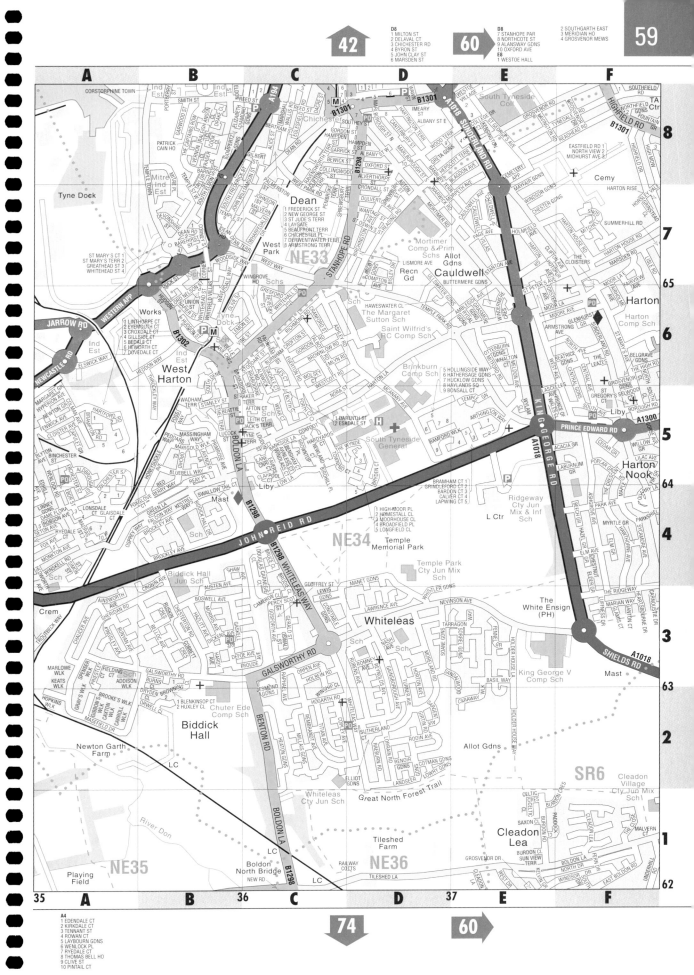

42

60

D8
7 STANHOPE PAR
8 NORTHCOTE ST
9 ALANSWAY GDNS
10 OXFORD AVE

E8
1 WESTOE HALL

2 SOUTHGARTH EAST
3 MERIDIAN HO
4 GROSVENOR MEWS

59

D8
1 MILTON ST
2 DELAVAL CT
3 CHICHESTER RD
4 BYRON ST
5 JOHN CLAY ST
6 MARSDEN ST

A4
1 EDENDALE CT
2 KIRKDALE CT
3 TENNANT ST
4 ROWAN CT
5 LAYBOURN GDNS
6 WENLOCK PL
7 RYEDALE CT
8 THOMAS BELL HO
9 CLIVE ST
10 PINTAIL CT

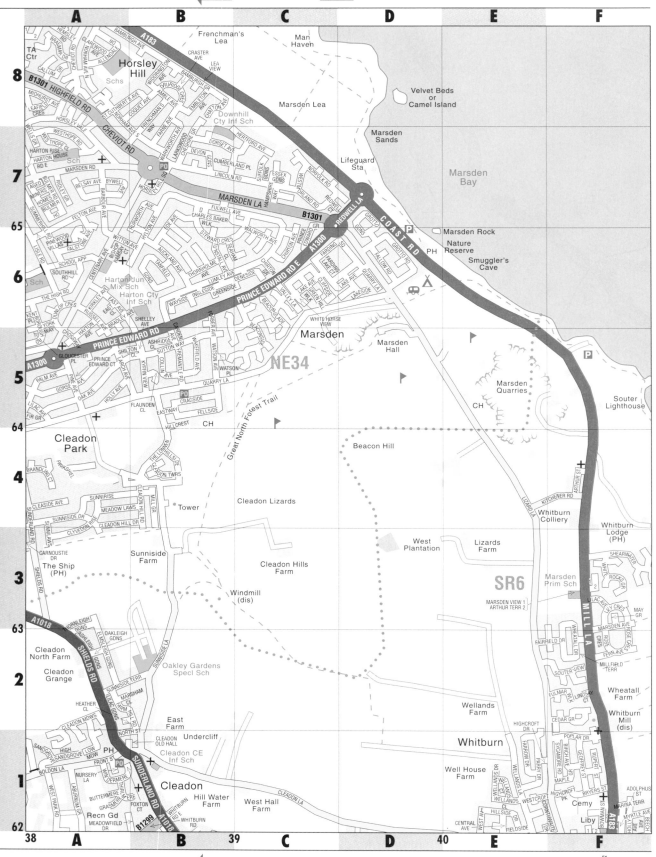

A   B   C   D   E   F

Frenchman's Lea

Man Haven

TA Ctr

Horsley Hill

Schs

Velvet Beds or Camel Island

Marsden Lea

Marsden Sands

Marsden Bay

Lifeguard Sta

Downhill Cty Inf Sch

MARSDEN LA

B1301

Marsden Rock

Nature Reserve

PH

Smuggler's Cave

COAST RD

REDWELL LA

Marsden

Marsden Hall

Marsden Quarries

CH

NE34

Souter Lighthouse

PRINCE EDWARD RD

Cleadon Park

White Horse View

Beacon Hill

Great North Forest Trail

MILL LA

Cleadon Lizards

Tower

Whitburn Colliery

Whitburn Lodge (PH)

Sunniside Farm

West Plantation

Lizards Farm

Cleadon Hills Farm

SR6

Marsden Prim Sch

The Ship (PH)

Windmill (dis)

MARSDEN VIEW 1
ARTHUR TERR 2

A1018

Cleadon North Farm

Oakleigh Gdns

Oakley Gardens Specl Sch

Cleadon Grange

Wellands Farm

Wheatall Farm

East Farm

Undercliff

Cleadon Old Hall

Cleadon CE Inf Sch

Whitburn Mill (dis)

PH

PO

Cleadon

Hill Water Farm

West Hall Farm

CLEADON LA

Whitburn

Well House Farm

SUNDERLAND RD

B1299

A1018

Recn Gd

Whitburn Rd

Cemy

Liby

A183

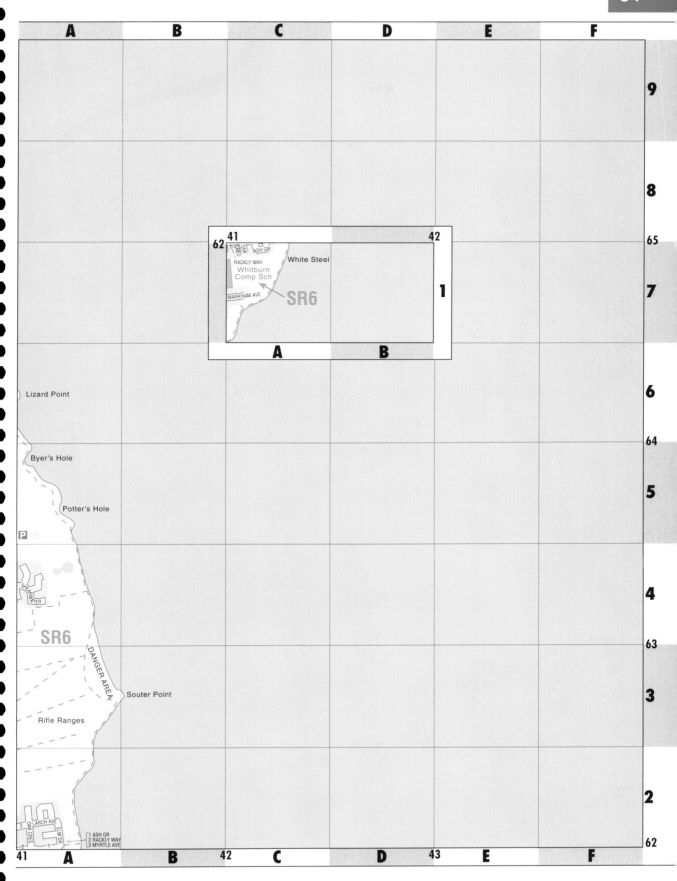

A B C D E F

9

8

65

41 42
62

OAK CRES
ASH GR
RACKLY WAY White Steel
Whitburn
Comp Sch
MARKHAM AVE SR6
1
7

A B

Lizard Point 6

64

Byer's Hole

5
Potter's Hole

P

64

SEABREAKWATER

SR6 4

DANGER AREA 63

Souter Point 3

Rifle Ranges

2

LARCH AVE
OAK CRES
ELM DR
3 1 ASH GR
2 RACKLY WAY
3 MYRTLE AVE
2
62

41 A B 42 C D 43 E F

47

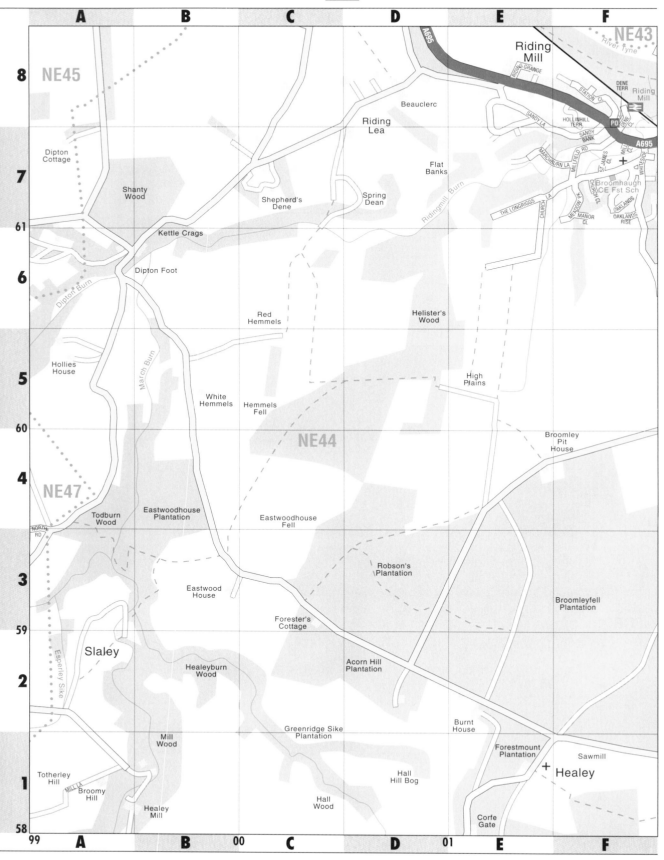

NE43

NE45

NE47

NE44

Riding Mill

River Tyne

A695

RIDING GRANGE

DENE TERR

Riding Mill

STATION CL

HOLLINHILL TERR

SANDY LA

SANDY BANK

A695

Dipton Cottage

Beauclerc

Riding Lea

Flat Banks

Ridingmill Burn

MARCYBURN LA

MILLFIELD RD

MILL TERR

CHURCH CL

ST JAMES CL

WHITESIDE

Broomhaugh CE Fst Sch

Shanty Wood

Shepherd's Dene

Spring Dean

THE LONGRIGGS

CHURCH LA

MEADOW PK

MANOR CL

OAKLANDS

OAKLANDS RISE

Kettle Crags

Dipton Burn

Dipton Foot

Red Hemmels

Helister's Wood

March Burn

Hollies House

White Hemmels

Hemmels Fell

High Plains

Broomley Pit House

Eastwoodhouse Plantation

Eastwoodhouse Fell

Robson's Plantation

Broomleyfell Plantation

NORTH RD

Todburn Wood

Eastwood House

Forester's Cottage

Acorn Hill Plantation

Slaley

Esperley Sike

Healeyburn Wood

Greenridge Sike Plantation

Burnt House

Forestmount Plantation

Sawmill

Healey

Mill Wood

Hall Hill Bog

Totherley Hill

MILL LA

Broomy Hill

Healey Mill

Hall Wood

Corfe Gate

99   00   01

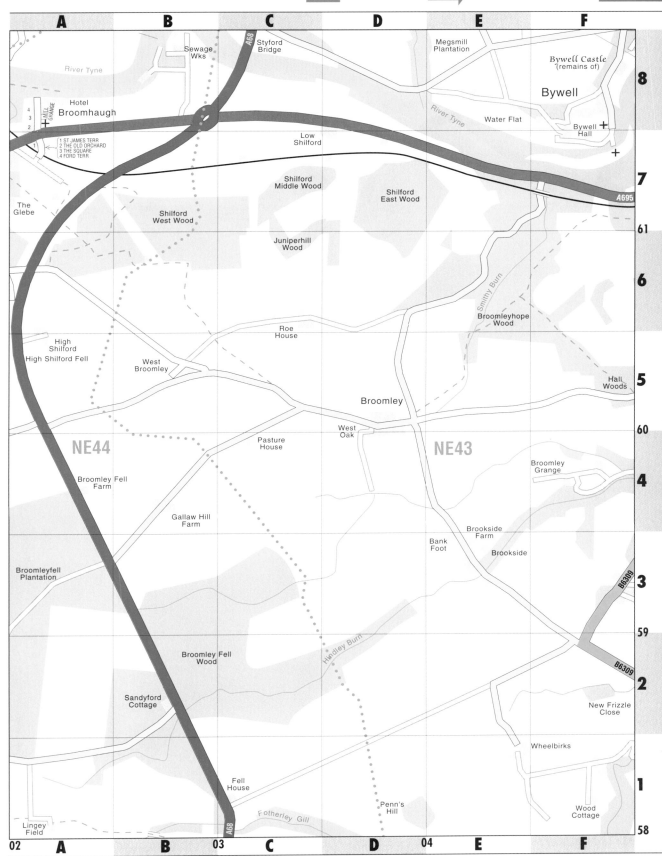

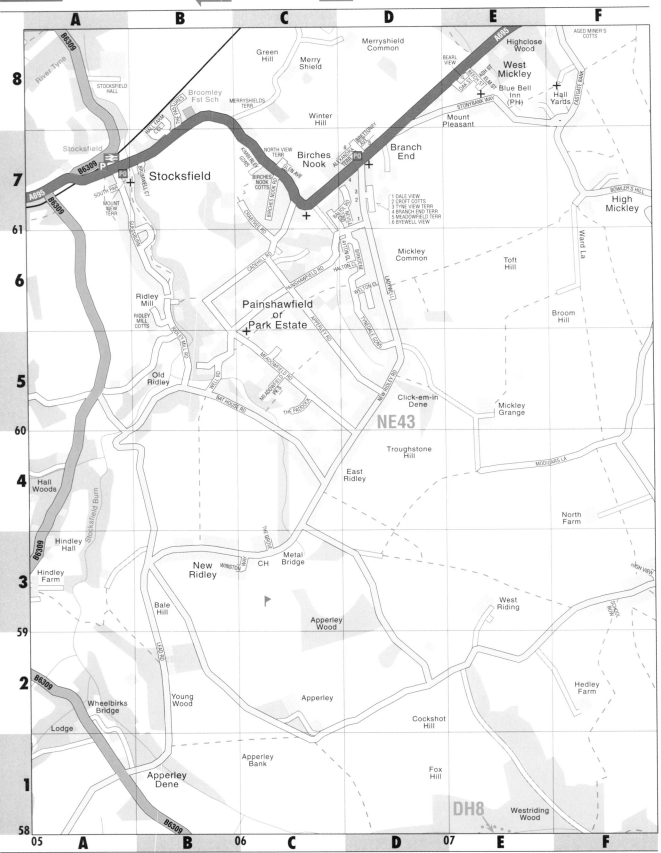

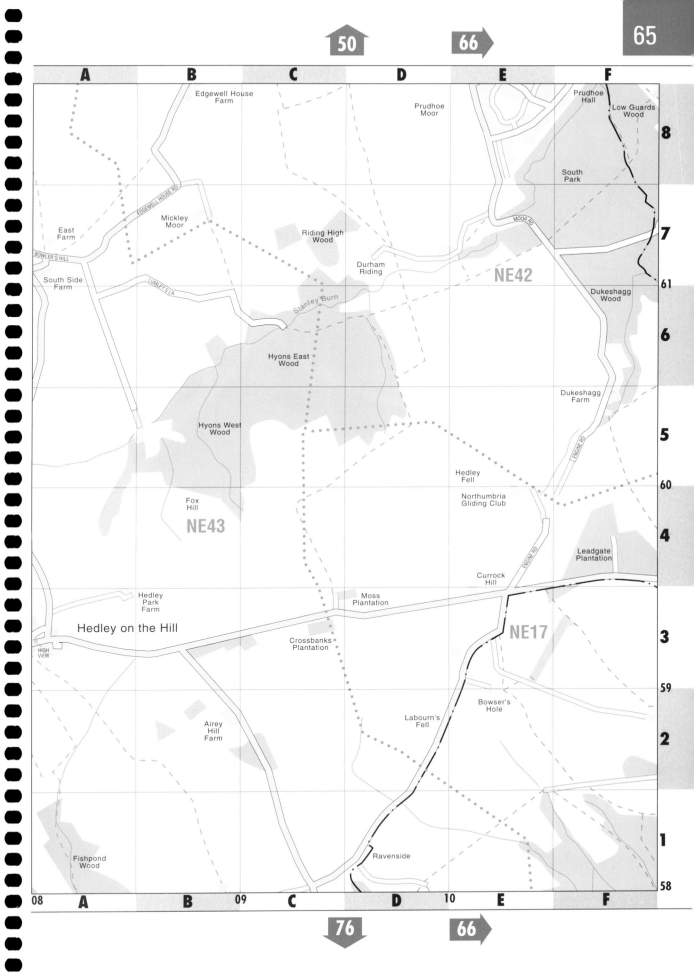

A B C D E F

8

Edgewell House Farm

Prudhoe Moor

Prudhoe Hall

Low Guards Wood

South Park

7

East Farm

Mickley Moor

EDGEWELL HOUSE RD

Riding High Wood

Durham Riding

MOOR RD

NE42

61

BOWLER'S HILL

South Side Farm

LUMLEY'S LA

Stanley Burn

Dukeshagg Wood

6

Hyons East Wood

Dukeshagg Farm

5

Hyons West Wood

ENGINE RD

Hedley Fell

60

Fox Hill

NE43

Northumbria Gliding Club

4

Leadgate Plantation

Currock Hill

ENGINE RD

Hedley Park Farm

Moss Plantation

NE17

3

Hedley on the Hill

HIGH VIEW

Crossbanks Plantation

59

Airey Hill Farm

Labourn's Fell

Bowser's Hole

2

1

Fishpond Wood

Ravenside

58

08 A B 09 C D 10 E F

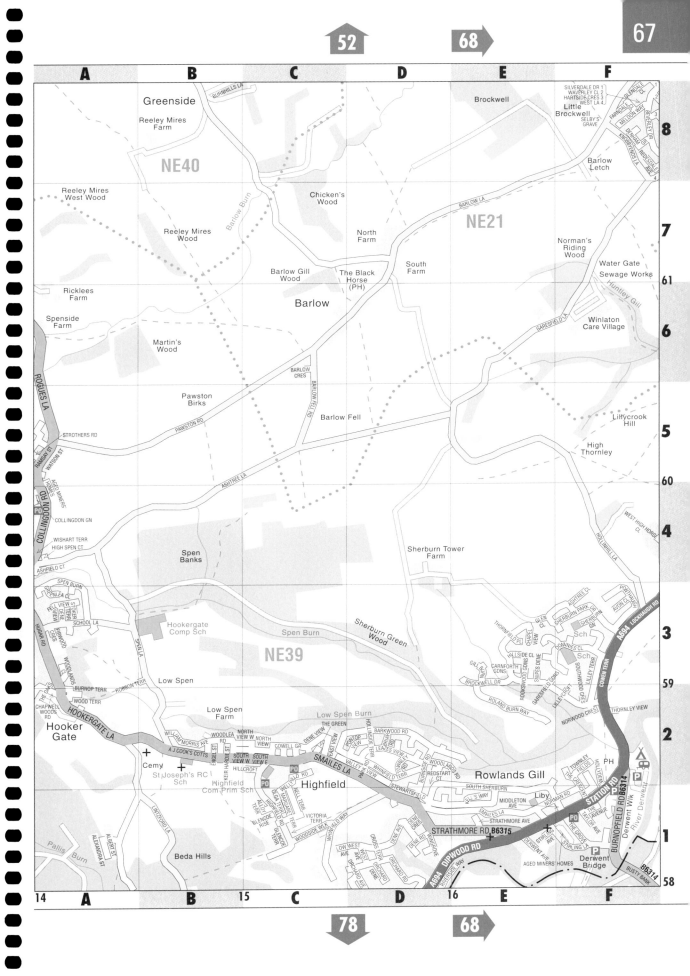

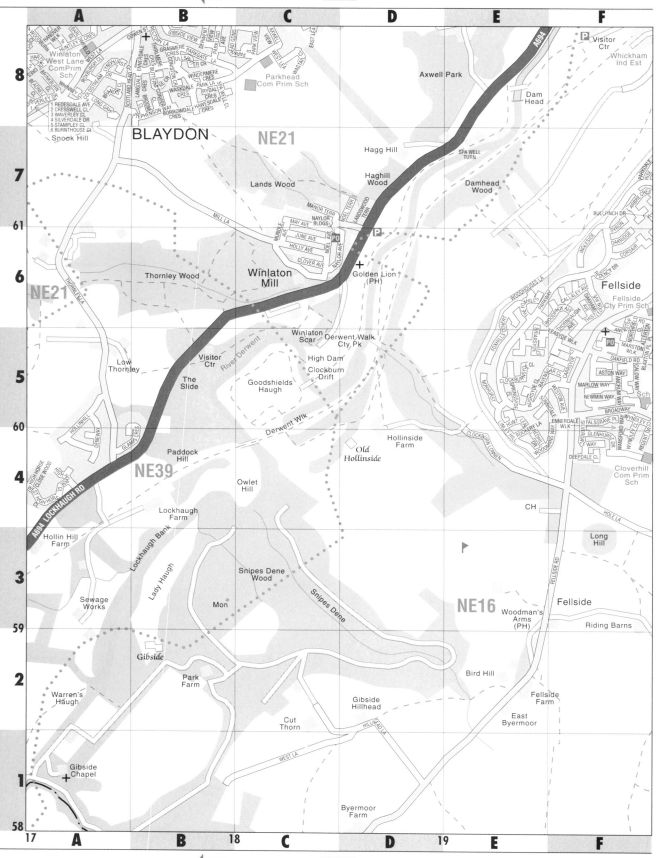

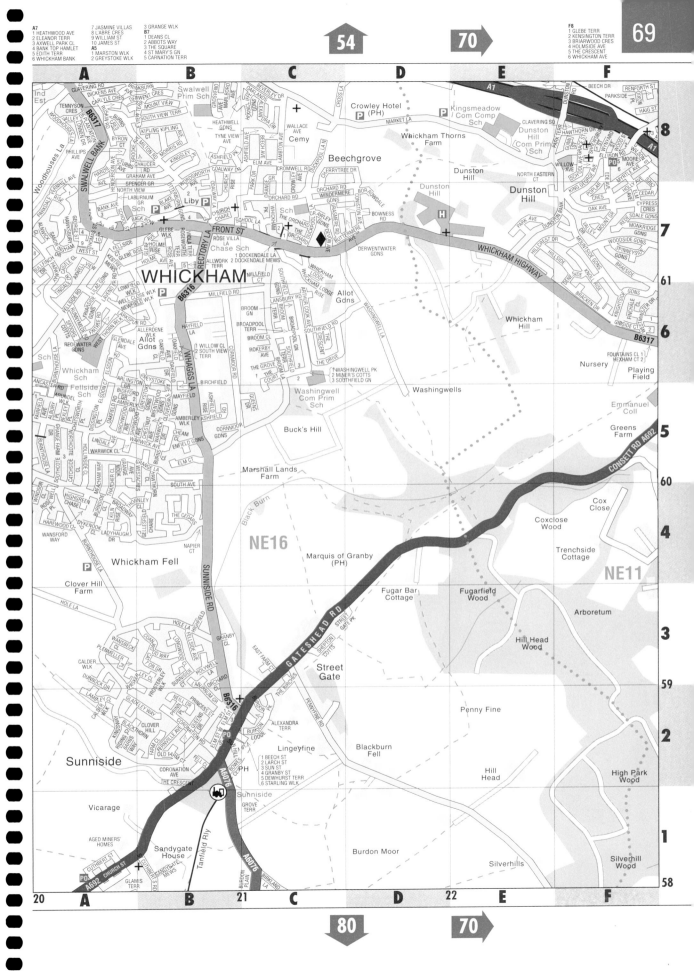

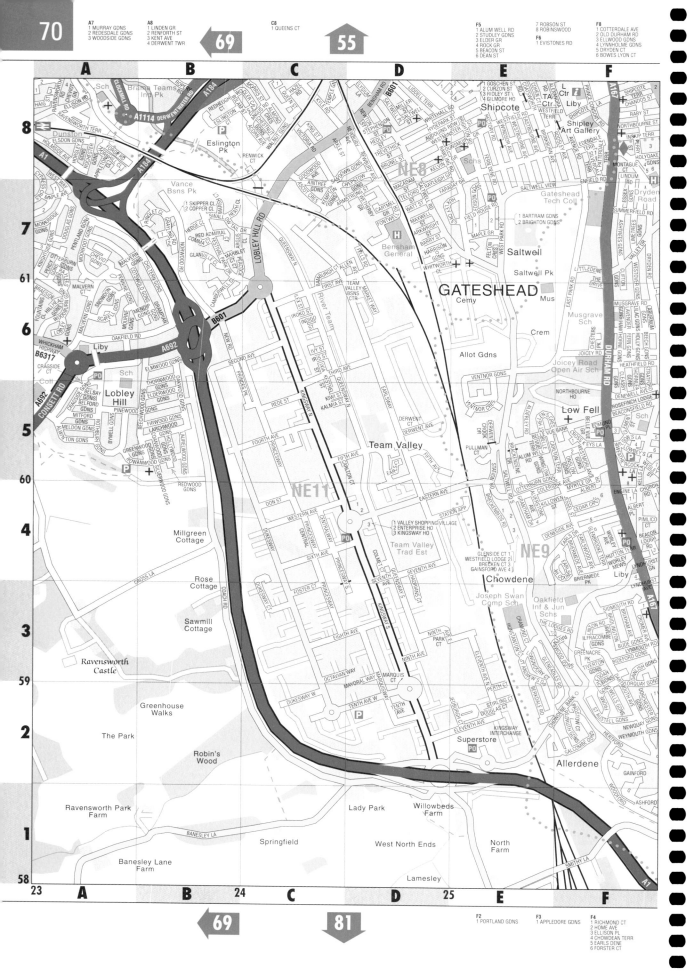

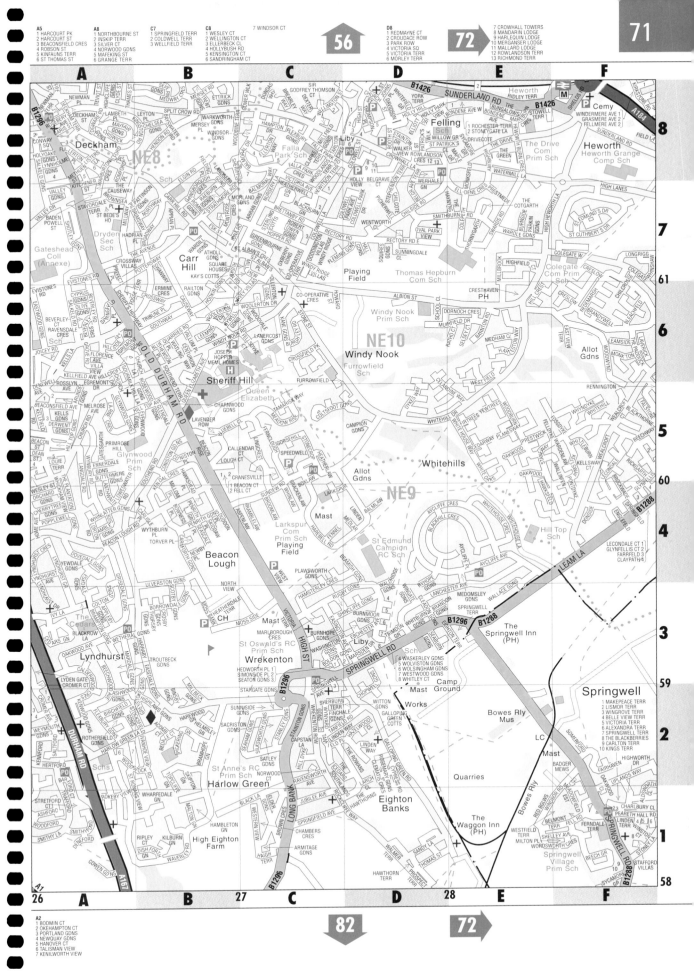

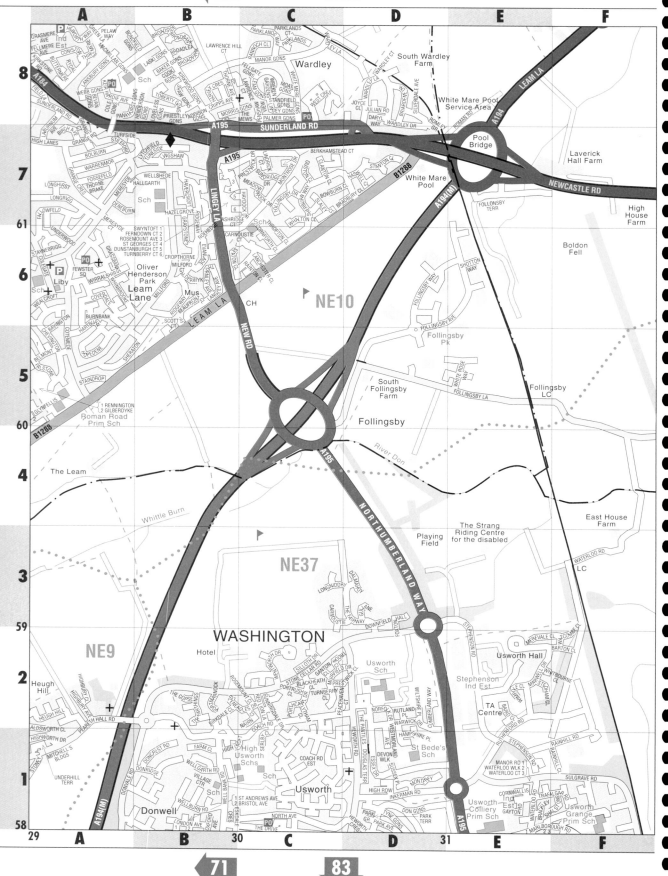

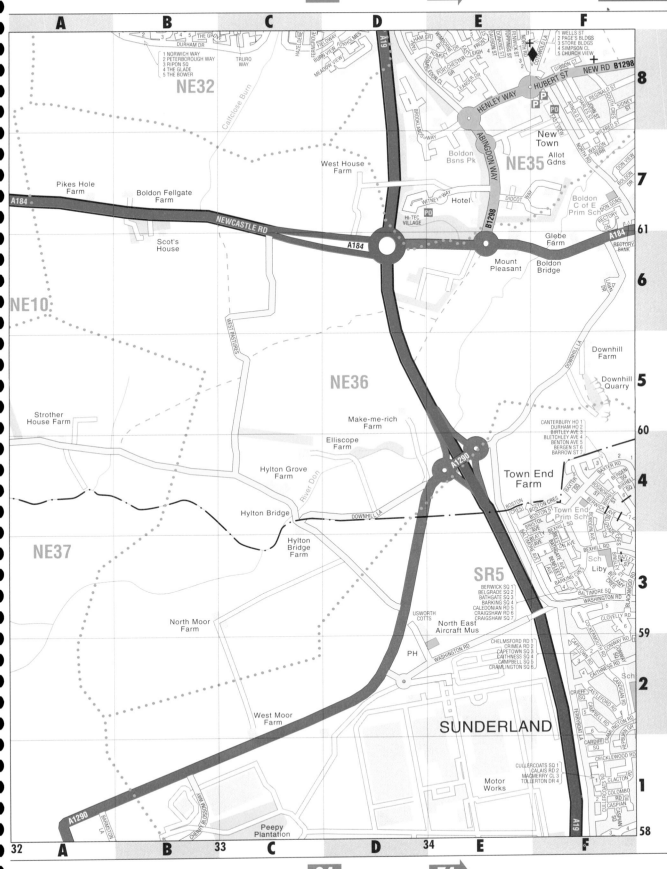

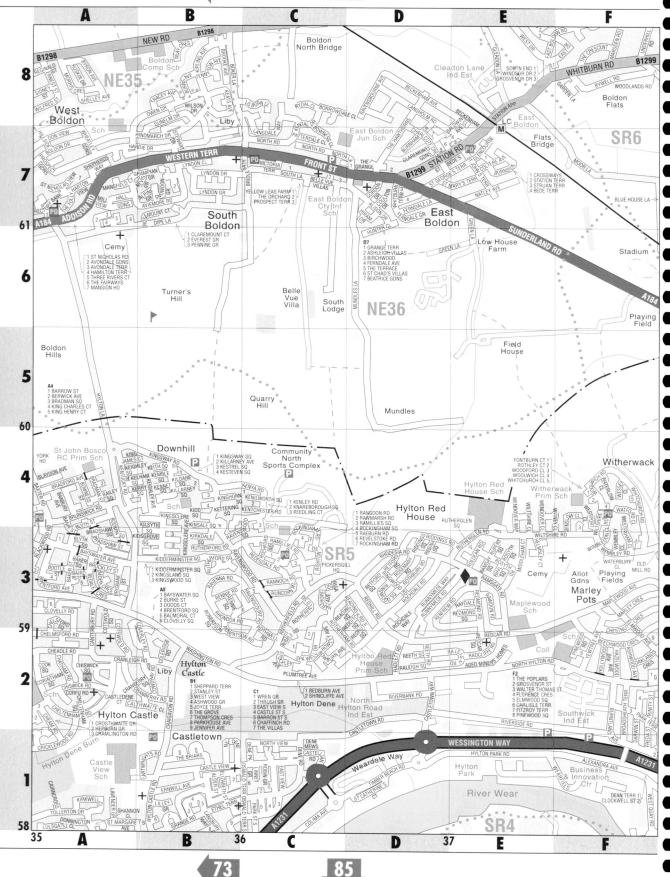

NE35

West Boldon

New Rd
B1298
B1298
Boldon Comp Sch

Boldon North Bridge

Cleadon Lane Ind Est

WHITBURN RD
B1299

SOUTH END 1
WINDSOR DR 2
GROSVENOR DR 3

Boldon Flats

SR6

East Boldon

Flats Bridge

WESTERN TERR

FRONT ST
B1299
STATION RD

Liby

South Boldon

Yellow Leas Farm 1
THE ORCHARD 2
PROSPECT TERR 3

VICTORIA TERR
BELLE VUE VILLAS

East Boldon Cty/Inf Sch

East Boldon Jun Sch

1 GRANGE TERR
2 ASHLEIGH VILLAS
3 BIRCHWOOD
4 FERNDALE AVE
5 THE TERRACE
6 ST CHAD'S VILLAS
7 BEATRICE GDNS

1 CROSSWAYS
2 STATION TERR
3 STRUAN TERR
4 BEDE TERR

SUNDERLAND RD

Low House Farm

Stadium

A184

ADDISON RD

A184

Cemy

1 ST NICHOLAS RD
2 AVONDALE GDNS
3 AVONDALE TERR
4 HAMILTON TERR
5 THREE RIVERS CT
6 THE FAIRWAYS
7 MANSION HO

1 CLAREMOUNT CT
2 EVEREST GR
3 PENNINE GR

Turner's Hill

Belle Vue Villa

South Lodge

NE36

Playing Field

Boldon Hills

Quarry Hill

Mundles

Field House

A4
1 BARROW ST
2 BERWICK AVE
3 BRADMAN ST
4 KING CHARLES CT
5 KING HENRY CT

St John Bosco RC Prim Sch

Downhill

1 KINGSWAY SQ
2 KILLARNEY AVE
3 KESTREL SQ
4 KESTEVEN SQ

Community North Sports Complex

FONTBURN CT 1
ROTHLEY CT 2
WOODFORD CL 3
WOOLWICH CL 4
WHITCHURCH CL 5

Witherwack

Witherwack Prim Sch

Hylton Red House Sch

Hylton Red House

1 RANGOON RD
2 RAWMARSH RD
3 RAMILLIES SQ
4 ROCKINGHAM SQ
5 RAEBURN RD
6 REVELSTOKE RD
7 ROCKINGHAM RD

1 KENLEY RD
2 KNAREBOROUGH SQ
3 REEDLING CT

SR5

Cemy

Allot Gdns

Marley Pots

Maplewood Sch

Playing Fields

A5
1 BAYSWATER SQ
2 BURKE ST
3 DODDS CT
4 BRENTFORD SQ
5 BALMORAL CT
6 CLOVELLY SQ

1 KIDDERMINSTER SQ
2 KINGSLAND SQ
3 KINGSWOOD SQ

Coll

F2
1 THE POPLARS
2 GROSVENOR ST
3 WALTER THOMAS ST
4 FLORENCE CRES
5 ELMWOOD SQ
6 CARLISLE TERR
7 FITZROY TERR
8 PINEWOOD SQ

Hylton Castle

Liby

Hylton Castle

B1
1 SHEPPARD TERR
2 STANLEY SQ
3 WEST VIEW
4 ASHWOOD GR
5 JOYCE TERR
6 THE GROVE
7 THOMPSON CRES
8 PARKHOUSE AVE
9 JENNIFER AVE

C1
1 WREN GR
2 THRUSH GR
3 EAST VIEW S
4 CASTLE ST S
5 BARRON ST S
6 CHAFFINCH RD
7 THE VILLAS

1 BEDBURN AVE
2 SHINCLIFFE AVE

Hylton Dene

North Hylton Road Ind Est

Riverbank Rd

Southwick Ind Est

Castle View Sch

1 CROSTHWAITE GR
2 HEPBURN GR
3 DRAMLINGTON RD

Castletown

DENE MEWS

NORTH VIEW

Riverside Rd

WESSINGTON WAY

HYLTON PARK RD

Hylton Park

Business Innovation Ctr

A1231

A1231

Weardale Way

River Wear

DEAN TERR 1
CLOCKWELL ST 2

SR4

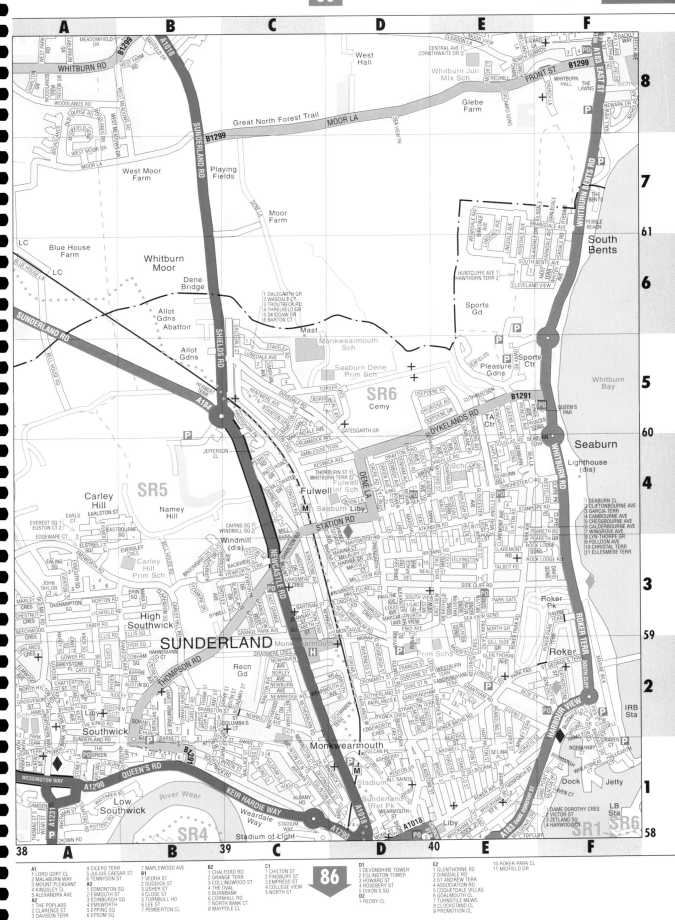

A1
1 LORD GORT CL
2 MALABURN WAY
3 MOUNT PLEASANT
4 KINGSLEY CL
5 ALEXANDRA AVE

A2
1 THE POPLARS
2 CLARENCE ST
3 DAVISON TERR

4 CICERO TERR
5 JULIUS CAESAR ST
6 TENNYSON ST

A3
1 EDMONTON SQ
2 EXMOUTH ST
3 EDINBURGH SQ
4 EMSWORTH
5 EPPING SQ
6 EPSOM SQ

7 MAPLEWOOD AVE

B1
1 VEDRA ST
2 SUDDICK ST
3 USHER ST
4 CLOSE ST
5 TURNBULL HO
6 LEE ST
7 PEMBERTON CL

B2
1 CHALFORD RD
2 GRANGE TERR
3 COLLINGWOOD SQ
4 THE OVAL
5 BURNBANK
6 CORNHILL RD
7 NORTH BANK CT
8 MAYPOLE CL

C1
1 CHILTON ST
2 FINSBURY ST
3 EMPRESS ST
4 COLLEGE VIEW
5 NORTH ST

D1
1 DEVONSHIRE TOWER
2 EGLINGTON TOWER
3 HOWARD ST
4 ROSEBERY ST
5 DIXON S SQ

D2
1 REDBY CL

E2
1 GLENTHORNE RD
2 DINSDALE RD
3 ST ANDREW TERR
4 ASSOCIATION RD
5 COQUETDALE VILLAS
6 GOALMOUTH CL
7 TURNSTILE MEWS
8 CLOCKSTAND CL
9 PROMOTION CL

10 ROKER PARK CL
11 MIDFIELD DR

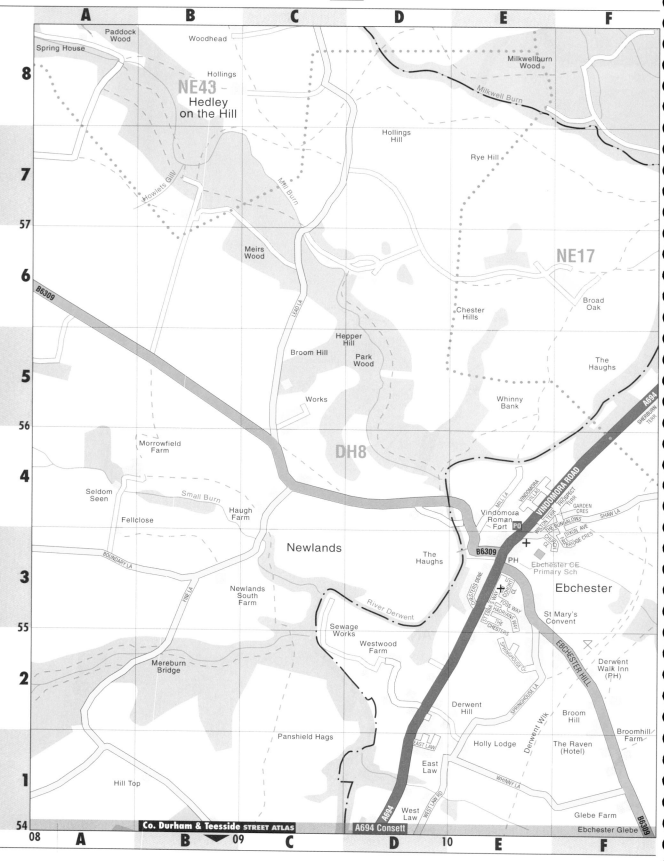

A B C D E F

8

Spring House
Paddock Wood
Woodhead
Hollings
NE43
Hedley on the Hill

7

Howlets Gill
Mill Burn
Hollings Hill
Rye Hill

57

Meirs Wood

NE17

6

B6309
Broad Oak
Chester Hills

Lead La
Hepper Hill
Broom Hill
Park Wood
The Haughs

5

Works
Whinny Bank

56

DH8

Morrowfield Farm

4

Seldom Seen
Small Burn
Haugh Farm
Vindomora Roman Fort
Vindomora Villas
MILL LA
VINDOMORA ROAD
PROSPECT TERR
WILTON TERR
GARDEN CRES
SHAW LA
THE BUNGALOWS
DIXON AVE
BRIDGE CRES
CHURCH CL

Fellclose

Newlands
The Haughs
B6309
PH
Ebchester CE Primary Sch

3

Boundary La
Fine La
Newlands South Farm
River Derwent
Chesters Dene
St Ebba's Wk
Foss Way
Hadrian's Way
The Chesters
St Mary's Convent
Ebchester

55

Sewage Works
Westwood Farm
Springhouse Cl
Ebchester Hill
Derwent Walk Inn (PH)

2

Mereburn Bridge
Springhouse La
Derwent Hill
Derwent Wlk
Broom Hill
Broomhill Farm

Panshield Hags
East Law
Holly Lodge
The Raven (Hotel)
Whinny La

1

Hill Top
East Law
West Law Rd
A694
Glebe Farm
B6309

54

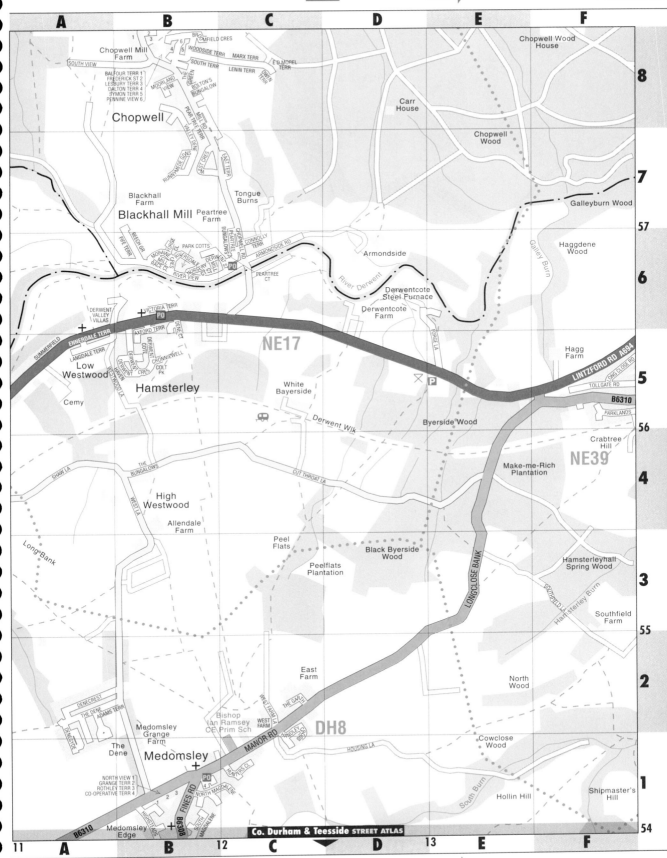

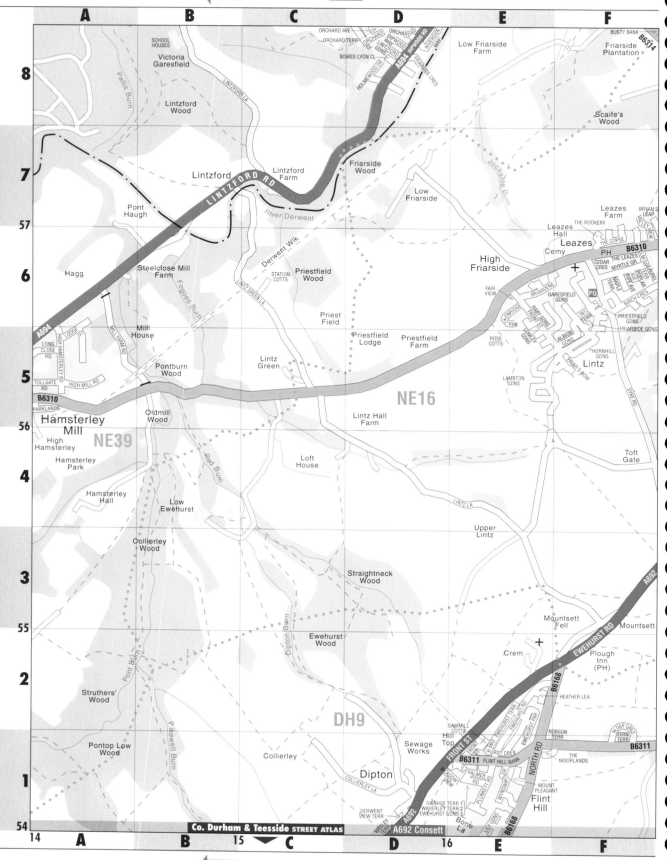

A | B | C | D | E | F

8 West Wood · Blackamoor Hill · Mast · A692 · Busty Bank · Leapmill Burn · Strathmore Cres · LOBLEYHILL RD · High Marley Hill · Longfield House Farm · SCHOOLHOUSE LA · Ravensworth Cres · Bowes Cres · Gibside Cres · Byermoor RC Prim Sch · Byermoor

7 Bryan's Leap · Sandypath La · New Rd · The Oaks · Sheep Hill · PH · ST CUTHBERT S RD · The Larches · Westwood Cl · Busty Bank · Hill Crest · Derwent Terr · Oakfields · Chapel Ave · Raglan Pl · Grove Terr · Oak Terr · The Close

57 Leazes Villas · Willow View · West View · Dene View · Park Terr · Derwent View · Wood St · Eden Ave · B6314 · Front St · Watson Terr · B6310 · Gibside Terr · Co-operative Terr · Lilby · Crookbank Farm · Wheatley's Gill

6 Birch Cres · Aged Miners Homes · Cricket Terr · Lilac Cres · Park View · Fell Terr · Crookfield Farm · 1 Broom Terr · 2 Heather Terr · Low Barcus Close · Fortune Hill · Burnopfield Prim Sch · Burnopfield · Fieldfare Terr · Beech Terr · Briar Terr · Hazel Gr · Holly Terr · The Sycamores · Crookgate Bank · NE16

5 Black Hill · Bowesville · Fieldfare Ct · Plover Terr · Lapwing Ct · Barcusclose La · Bobgins Burn · Beckley · Ind Est · Causey Gill · Great North Forest Trail

56 Tanfield Grange Farm

4 The Meadows · Mulberry Gr · Cragleas · Cavendish Pl · Front St · Hobson · CH · PH · Townhead · Pickering Nook · Tanfield Moor · The Hardings · St Margaret's Dr · Hawthorne Terr · Maud Terr · Old Front St · Old Rectory Cl · Tudor Dr · Folly Hill · Tanfield Hall · Sewage Works · Tanfield Rly · Oxpasture Hill · 1 Robinson Terr · 2 Moyle Terr · 3 Cawthorne Terr · 4 Prospect Terr · 5 Wigham Terr · 6 Edward St

3 She Rd · B6173 · Clough Dene · PH · Tanfield · Cemy · Tanfield Lane Farm · DH9

55 Clough Dene · Tantobie · Woodside Gr · Hwy Pl · Palm Terr · Ever Ready Ind Est · East Tanfield · Houghwell Burn

2 Clough Cotts · Cherry Cotts · Elm Terr · Blanche Terr · Unity Terr · B6311 · South View · Beda Cotts · Jubilee Terr · Chapel St · Tanfield Leith Farm · Tanfield Lea Ind Est

1 Corvan Terr · Butts Terr · White-le-Head Gdns · PH · Worley Terr · Front St · Larch Terr · West Rd · White-le-Head · Wester Leith · Margerley La · Margaret Terr · King Edward St · Tanfield Lea Jun & Inf Sch · Parkside · Parkside Cotts · North Leigh · New Front St · South Leigh · B6173 · Tanfield Lea · Tanfield Lea South Ind Est · Stanelaw Way · Station Field · St Andrews Rd · James St · Oaks Rd · Oaks St

1 Ash Terr · 2 Liberty Terr · 3 Oak Terr · 4 Bailey St · 5 Mitchell St · 6 Federation Terr · 7 Owen Terr · 8 Neale St · 9 Clarence St · 10 Martha St · 11 Havelock Terr

54

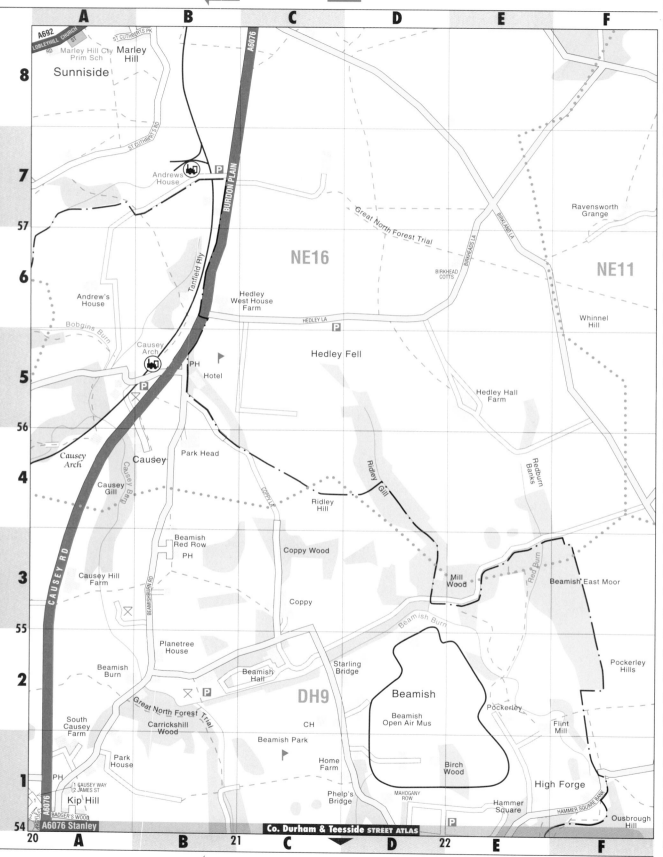

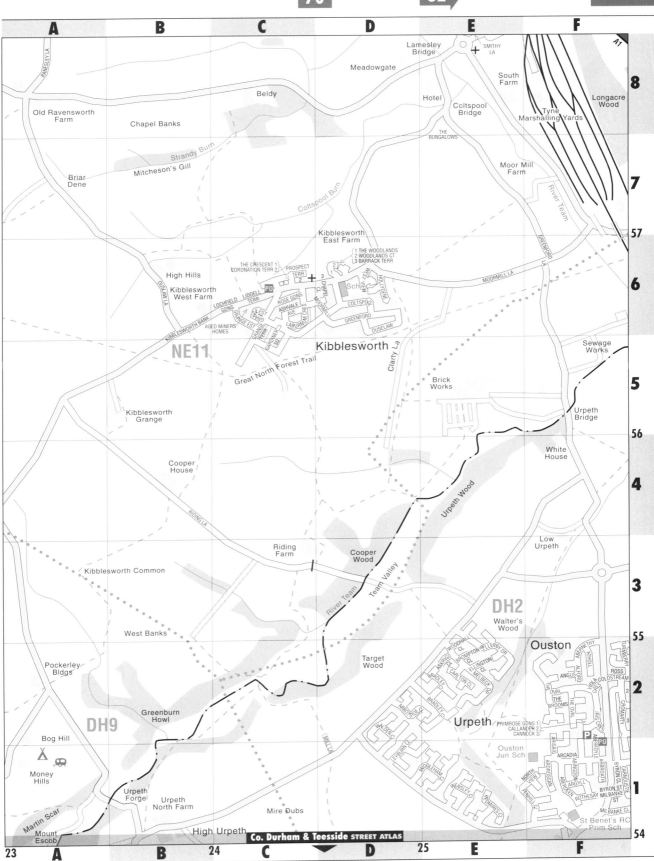

A1

Lamesley Bridge

SMITHY LA

Meadowgate

Beldy

South Farm

Hotel

Coltspool Bridge

Longacre Wood

Tyne Marshalling Yards

8

Old Ravensworth Farm

Chapel Banks

THE BUNGALOWS

Moor Mill Farm

7

Strandy Burn

Briar Dene

Mitcheson's Gill

Coltspool Burn

River Team

Greenford LA

57

Kibblesworth East Farm

High Hills

1 THE WOODLANDS
2 WOODLANDS CT
3 BARRACK TERR

MOORMILL LA

6

Kibblesworth West Farm

THE CRESCENT 1
CORONATION TERR 2

PROSPECT TERR
2

Sch

ASH VIEW

HOLYERNE

MOORMILL LA

OUSLAW LA

KIBBLESWORTH BANK

LOCHFIELD GDNS

LIDDELL TERR

ROSE GDNS

CHAPEL

COLTSPO

GREENFORD

NE11

LE EST

GRANGE EST

ASHVALE AVE

ABURN CRES

OUSELAW

AGED MINERS HOMES

GARDNER

Kibblesworth

Clarty La

Sewage Works

5

Kibblesworth Grange

Great North Forest Trail

Brick Works

Urpeth Bridge

56

Cooper House

White House

4

RIDING LA

Urpeth Wood

Low Urpeth

West Banks

Kibblesworth Common

Riding Farm

Cooper Wood

Team Valley

River Team

DH2

Walter's Wood

55

Ouston

3

Pockerley Bldgs

Target Wood

WOODHALL CL

BROMPTON CL

ELLERBY DR

ASRIGG CL

ELLINGTON CL

MELBECK CL

CARLTON CL

BRADLEY CL

THE OVAL

THE BROOMS

ABERNETHY

NHOLL

ALFORD

ANGUS

COLDSTREAM

ROSS

CROMARTY

TURNERBY

Urpeth

PRIMROSE GDNS 1
CALLANDER 2
CANNOCK 3

2

DH9

Greenburn Howl

WELBECK CL

EYBURN CL

MIDDLEHAM

WENSLEY

PONTFRES CT

Ouston Jun Sch

ARCADIA

ARISAIG

ARGYLL

ABERDEEN

ABINGDON

AYR CRES

IRIS CRES

BYRON ST

CARNOUSTIE

ABERFELDY

ARBROATH

Bog Hill

Money Hills

NORTH VIEW

PENILL CL

AGRISSAN

ROTHESAY

MILBANKE ST

1

Martin Scar

Urpeth Forge

Urpeth North Farm

Mire Dubs

St Benet's RC Prim Sch

Mount Escob

High Urpeth

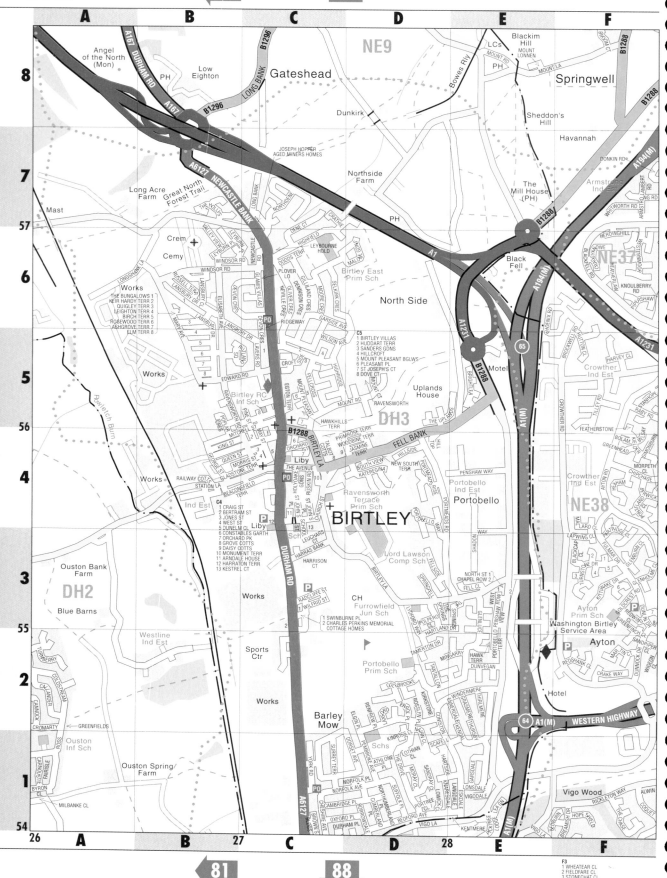

Angel of the North (Mon)

Low Eighton

NE9

Gateshead

Dunkirk

Blackim Hill

MOUNT LONNEN

Springwell

Sheddon's Hill

Havannah

Joseph Hopper Aged Miners Homes

Northside Farm

The Mill House (PH)

Armstrong Ind Est

NE37

Long Acre Farm

Great North Forest Trail

Herdinghill

Knoulberry Rd

Crem

Cemy

Mast

Works

THE BUNGALOWS 1
KEIR HARDY TERR 2
QUIGLEY TERR 3
LEIGHTON TERR 4
BIRCH TERR 5
ROSEWOOD TERR 6
ASHGROVE TERR 7
ELM TERR 8

Birtley East Prim Sch

North Side

Black Fell

Crowther Ind Est

Harvey Cl

Works

C5
1 BIRTLEY VILLAS
2 HUDDART TERR
3 SANDERS GDNS
4 HILLCROFT
5 MOUNT PLEASANT BGLWS
6 PLEASANT PL
7 ST JOSEPH'S CT
8 DOVE CT

Uplands House

Ravensworth

DH3

Motel

Featherstone

65

Works

Birtley RC Inf Sch

Liby

Primrose Terr
Woodbine Terr
Jasmine Terr

South View

FELL BANK

Hillside

New South Terr

Penshaw Way

Portobello Ind Est

Crowther Ind Est

NE38

Works

Railway Cot

Station La

Ind Est

C4
1 CRAIG ST
2 BERTRAM ST
3 JONES ST
4 WEST ST
5 DUNELM CL
6 CONSTABLES GARTH
7 ORCHARD PK
8 GROVE COTTS
9 DAISY COTTS
10 MONUMENT TERR
11 ARNDALE HOUSE
12 HARRATON TERR
13 KESTREL CT

Liby

Ravensworth Terrace Prim Sch

Portobello

BIRTLEY

Lord Lawson Comp Sch

DH2

Ouston Bank Farm

Blue Barns

Furrowfield Jun Sch

NORTH ST 1
CHAPEL ROW 2

Ayton Prim Sch

Washington Birtley Service Area

Works

1 SWINBURNE PL
2 CHARLES PERKINS MEMORIAL COTTAGE HOMES

Ayton

Westline Ind Est

Sports Ctr

Portobello Prim Sch

Hotel

Works

Barley Mow

Schs

Ouston Inf Sch

64

A1(M)

WESTERN HIGHWAY

Ouston Spring Farm

Vigo Wood

Milbanke Cl

NORFOLK PL
NORFOLK AVE

F3
1 WHEATEAR CL
2 FIELDFARE CL
3 STONECHAT CL
4 CORMORANT CL
5 PLOVER CL
6 WHITETHROAT CL
7 TEAL CL
8 WREN CL

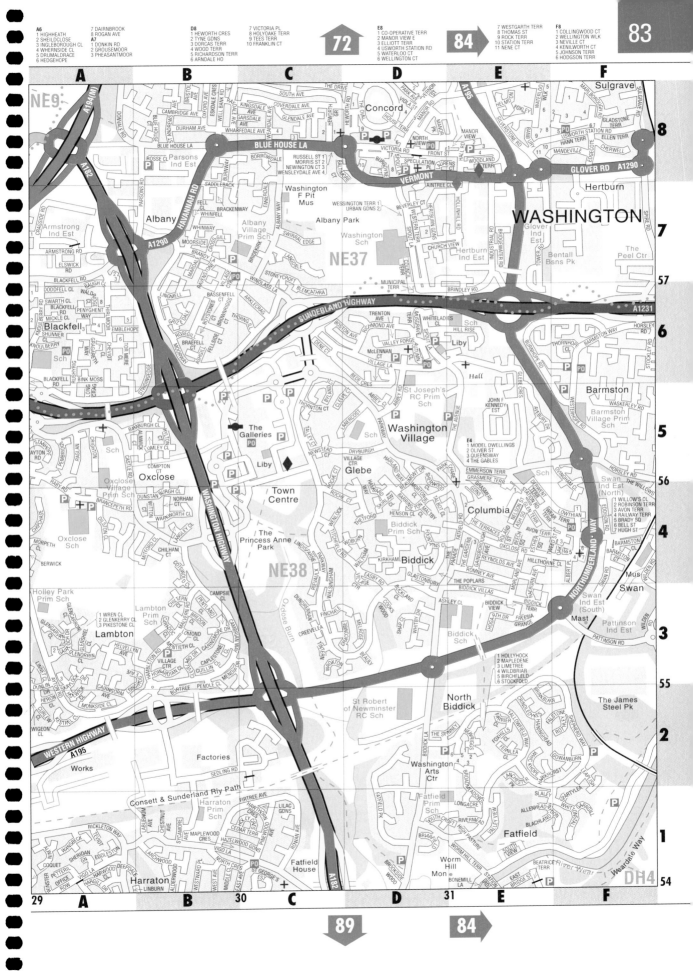

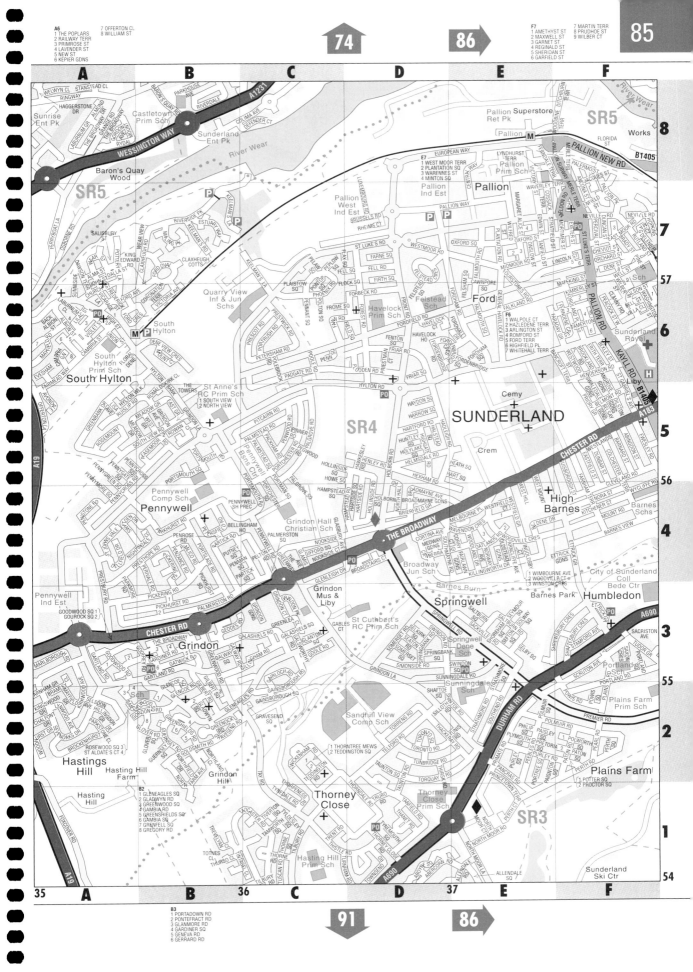

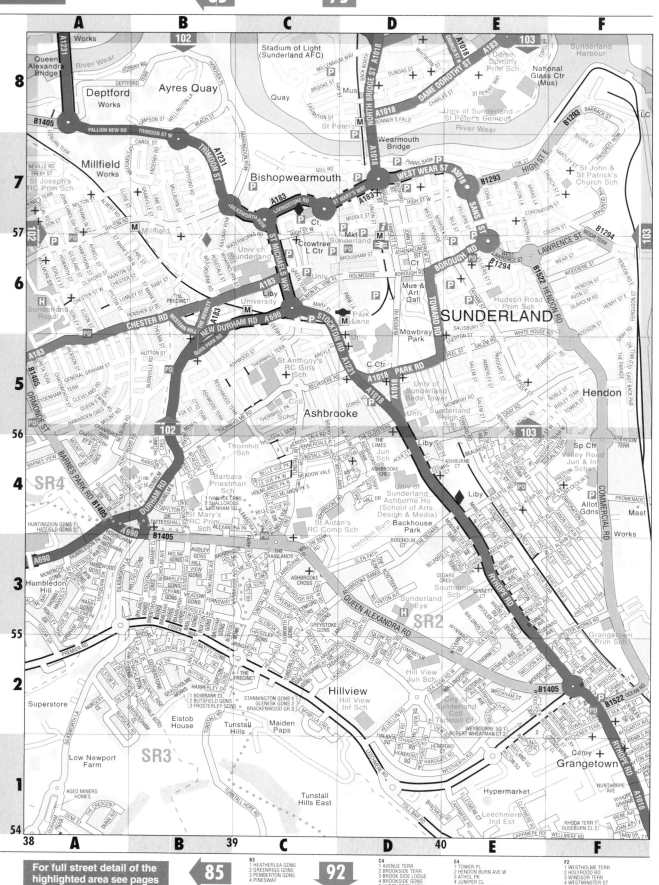

For full street detail of the highlighted area see pages 102 and 103.

85

92

B3
1 HEATHERLEA GDNS
2 GREENRIGG TERR
3 PEMBERTON GDNS
4 PINESWAY

C4
1 AVENUE TERR
2 BROOKSIDE TERR
3 BROOK SIDE LODGE
4 BROOKSIDE GDNS
5 HUMBLEDON VIEW
6 ASHBROOKE MOUNT

E4
1 TOWER PL
2 HENDON BURN AVE W
3 ATHOL PK
4 JUNIPER CL
5 VILLETTE BROOK ST
6 HENDON VALLEY CT
7 ERNEST ST
8 ROWLANDSEN TERR
9 TAYLOR GDNS

F2
1 WESTHOLME TERR
2 HOLYROOD RD
3 WINDSOR TERR
4 WESTMINSTER ST
5 RYHOPE ST
6 OCEAN RD N
7 OCEAN RD S
8 STOCKTON TERR
9 HEMMING ST
10 CARNEGIE ST

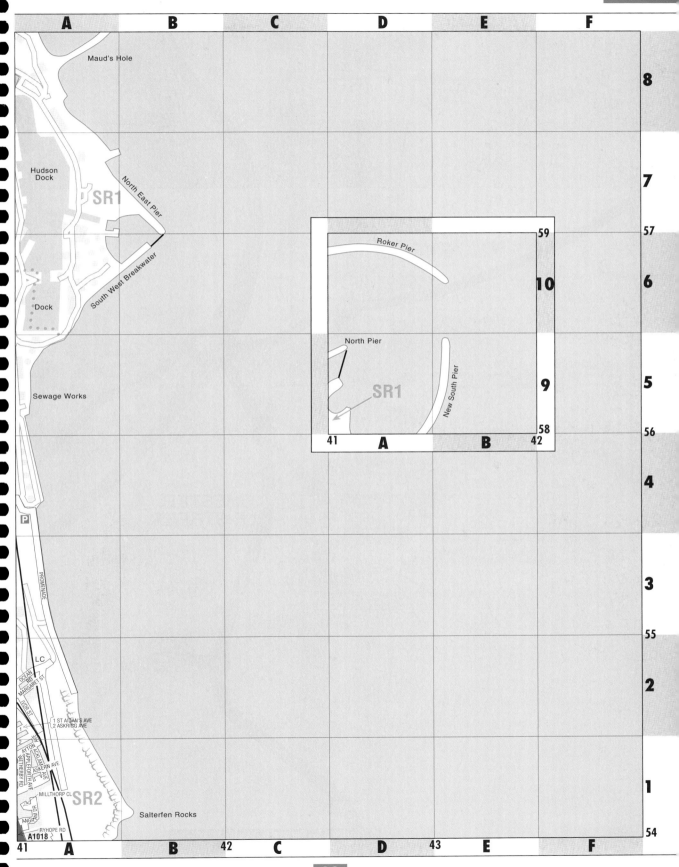

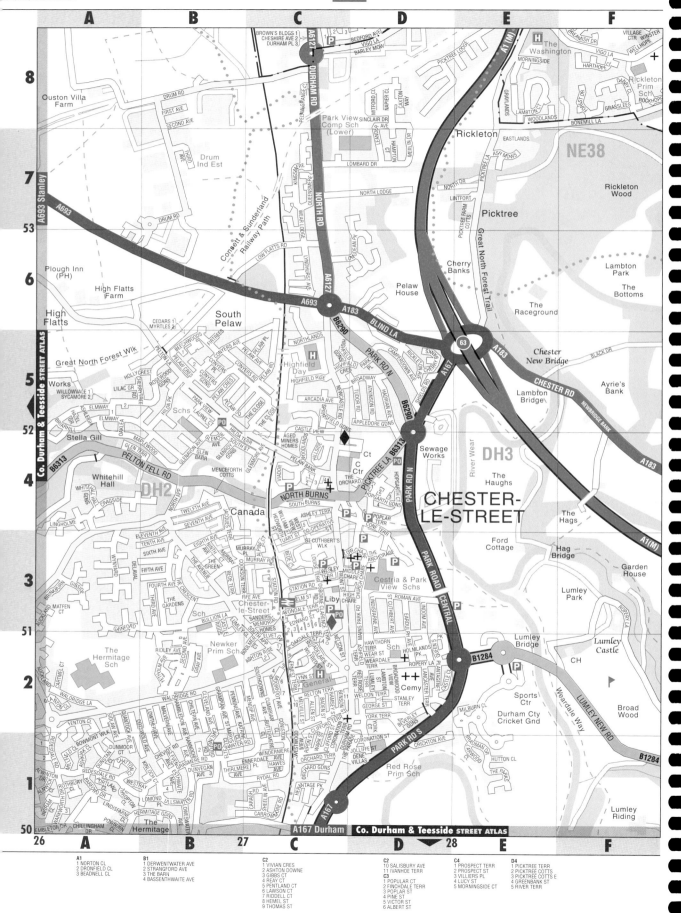

A1
1 NORTON CL
2 DRONFIELD CL
3 BEADNELL CL

B1
1 DERWENTWATER AVE
2 STRANGFORD AVE
3 THE BARN
4 BASSENTHWAITE AVE

C2
1 VIVIAN CRES
2 ASHTON DOWNE
3 GIBBS CT
4 REAY CT
5 PENTLAND CT
6 LAWSON CT
7 RIDDELL CT
8 HEMEL ST
9 THOMAS ST

C2
10 SALISBURY AVE
11 IVANHOE TERR
C3
1 POPULAR CT
2 FINCHDALE TERR
3 POPLAR ST
4 PINE ST
5 VICTOR ST
6 ALBERT ST

C4
1 PROSPECT TERR
2 PROSPECT ST
3 VILLIERS PL
4 LUCY ST
5 MORNINGSIDE CT

D4
1 PICKTREE TERR
2 PICKTREE COTTS
3 PICKTREE COTTS E
4 GREENBANK ST
5 RIVER TERR

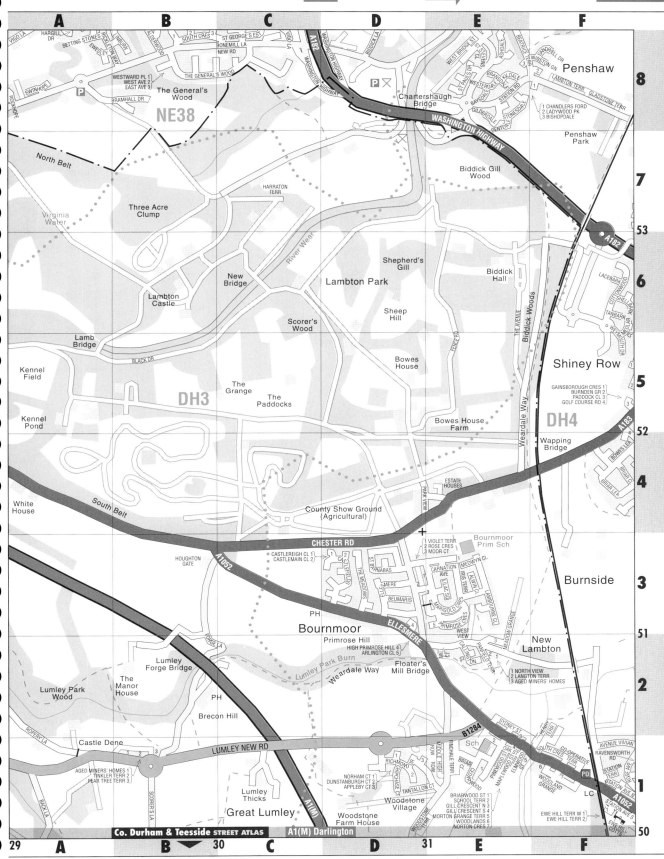

Penshaw

The General's Wood

NE38

North Belt

Virginia Water

Three Acre Clump

HARRATON TERR

River Wear

Biddick Gill Wood

Penshaw Park

Shepherd's Gill

Lambton Park

Biddick Hall

New Bridge

Lambton Castle

Scorer's Wood

Sheep Hill

BLACK DR

Lamb Bridge

Biddick Woods

The Avenue

Shiney Row

Kennel Field

DH3

The Grange

The Paddocks

Bowes House

Weardale Way

GAINSBOROUGH CRES 1
BURNDEN GR 2
PADDOCK CL 3
GOLF COURSE RD 4

DH4

Kennel Pond

Bowes House Farm

Wapping Bridge

White House

South Belt

ESTATE HOUSES

PARK VIEW

County Show Ground (Agricultural)

CHESTER RD

A1052

HOUGHTON GATE

CASTLEREIGH CL 1
CASTLEMAIN CL 2

1 VIOLET TERR
2 ROSE CRES
3 MOOR CT

Bournmoor Prim Sch

Burnside

CT

ST BARNABAS

The Meadows

CARNATION AVE

MEDWYN CL

IRIS TERR

LAMBOURNE CL

MARIGOLD CRES

PRIMROSE CRES

WEST VIEW

MEADOW GRANGE

New Lambton

PH

Bournmoor

ELLESMERE

Primrose Hill

HIGH PRIMROSE HILL 4
ARLINGTON CL 5

Floater's Mill Bridge

MILL

CALLING DN

PANFIELD TERR

1 NORTH VIEW
2 LANGTON TERR
3 AGED MINERS' HOMES

FORGE LA

Lumley Forge Bridge

The Manor House

PH

Brecon Hill

Lumley Park Wood

Lumley Park Burn

Weardale Way

SYDNEY ST

MIDDLE HIGH ROW

FINCHALE ROW

B1284

Sch

CO-OPERATIVE TERR

AVENUE VIVIAN

RAVENSWORTH RD

ROPERY LA

Castle Dene

LUMLEY NEW RD

RICHMOND

CHIRCHASE DR

JR

TANTALLON CT

SOUTH CRES

WOODLAND GRANGE

STATION AVE N

STATION AVE

AGED MINERS' HOMES 1
TINKLER TERR 2
PEAR TREE TERR 3

SCORER'S LA

A1(M)

Lumley Thicks

Great Lumley

Woodstone Farm House

NORHAM CT 1
DUNSTANBURGH CT 2
APPLEBY CT 3

Woodstone Village

BACK LA

BRIARWOOD ST 1
SCHOOL TERR 2
GILL CRESCENT N 3
GILL CRESCENT S 4
MORTON GRANGE TERR 5
WOODLANDS 6
NORTON CRES 7

EWE HILL TERR W 1
EWE HILL TERR 2

A1052

STATION AVE M

EWE HILL COTTS

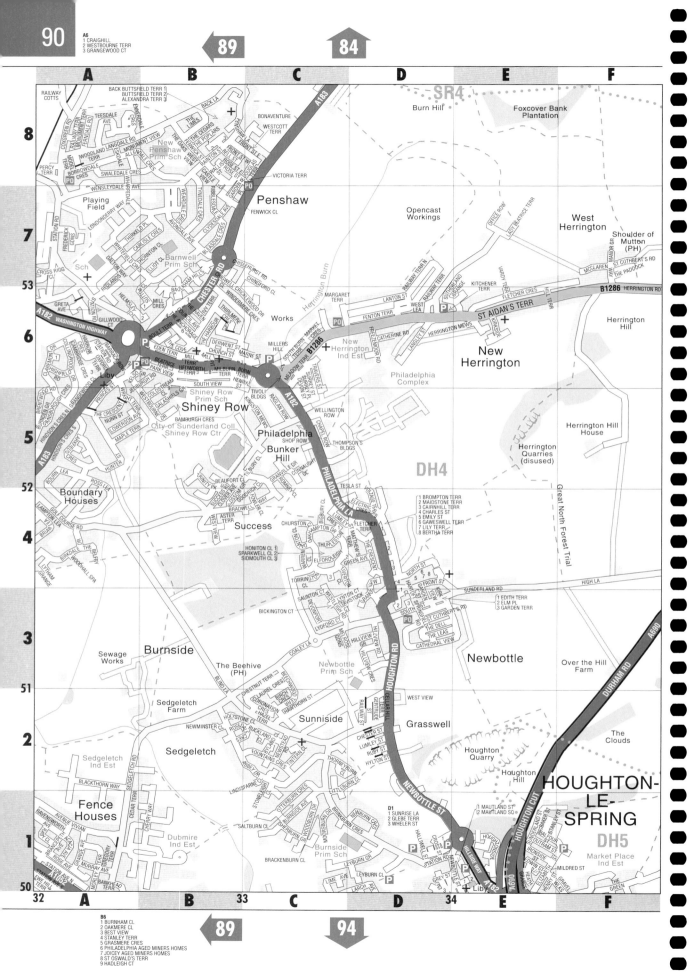

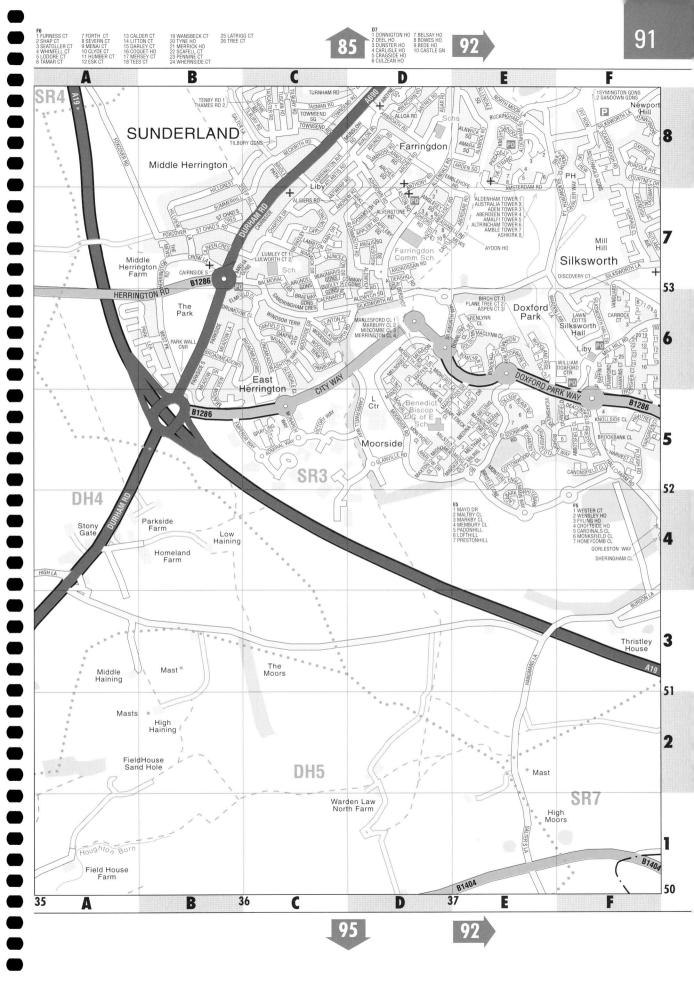

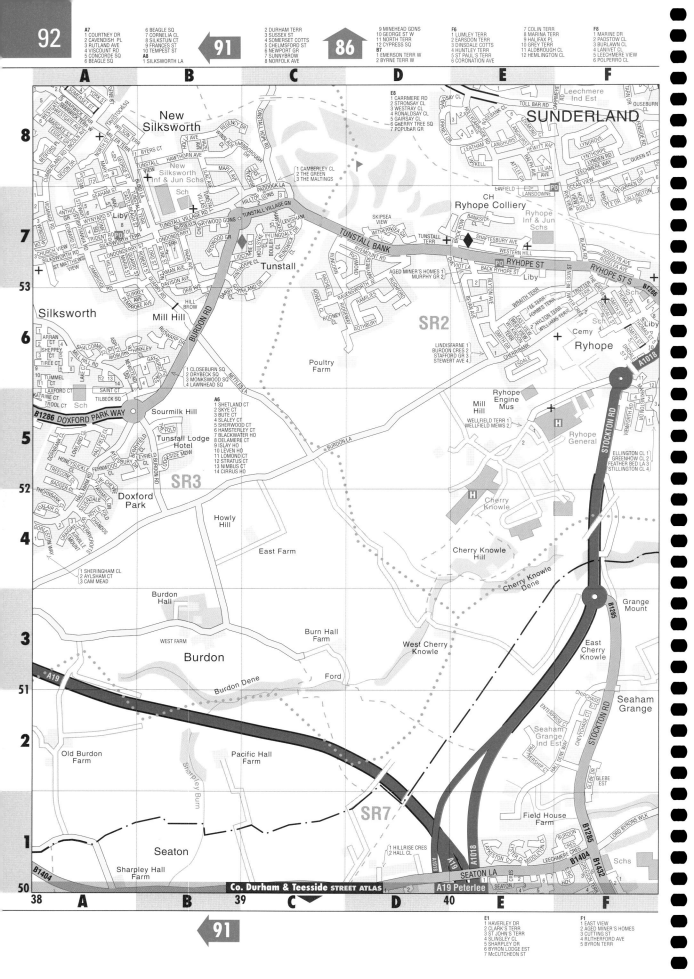

A7
1 COURTNEY DR
2 CAVENDISH PL
3 RUTLAND AVE
4 VISCOUNT RD
5 CONCORDE SQ
6 BEAGLE SQ

6 BEAGLE SQ
7 CORNELIA CL
8 SILKSTUN CT
9 FRANCES ST
10 TEMPEST ST
A8
1 SILKSWORTH LA

2 DURHAM TERR
3 SUSSEX ST
4 SOMERSET COTTS
5 CHELMSFORD ST
6 NEWPORT GR
7 SUNNYBROW
8 NORFOLK AVE

9 MINEHEAD GDNS
10 GEORGE ST W
11 NORTH TERR
12 CYPRESS SQ
B7
1 EMERSON TERR W
2 BYRNE TERR W

F6
1 LUMLEY TERR
2 EARSDON TERR
3 DINSDALE COTTS
4 HUNTLEY TERR
5 ST PAUL'S TERR
6 CORONATION AVE

7 COLIN TERR
8 MARINA TERR
9 HALIFAX PL
10 GREY TERR
11 ALDBROUGH CL
12 HEMLINGTON CL

F8
1 MARINE DR
2 PADSTOW CL
3 BURLAWN CL
4 LANIVET CL
5 LEECHMERE VIEW
6 POLPERRO CL

E8
1 CARRMERE RD
2 STRONSAY CL
3 WESTRAY CL
4 RONALDSAY CL
5 GAIRSAY CL
6 CHERRY TREE SQ
7 POPULAR GR

E1
1 HAVERLEY DR
2 CLARK'S TERR
3 ST JOHN'S TERR
4 SLINGLEY CL
5 SHARPLEY DR
6 BYRON LODGE EST
7 McCUTCHEON ST

F1
1 EAST VIEW
2 AGED MINER'S HOMES
3 CUTTING ST
4 RUTHERFORD AVE
5 BYRON TERR

Ryhope Nook

1 TOLL BAR RD
2 MARINE DR
3 LEECHMERE WAY
4 QUEEN ST
5 LADOCK CL
6 POLPERRO CL

Maiden's Flat

CLIFF VIEW

THE VILLAGE

A6
1 FLORALIA AVE
2 GREY TERR
3 GORDON TERR
4 KILBURN CL
5 ERNEST TERR
6 RICHARDSON TERR
7 FAWCETT TERR
8 THOMPSON TERR
9 CRANSTON PL
10 ROBSON PL
11 ARTHUR ST
12 MOIR TERR
13 CHARLES ST
14 JOHN ST

Halliwell Banks

SR2

Pincushion

Ryhope Dene House (Convent)

Ryhope Dene

SR7

Hall Farm

Seaham Hall

LC

LORD BYRONS WLK

Seaham Dene

NEW DR

1 BURNWAY
2 NEWLANDS RD W
3 NEWARK CRES
4 NAVENBY CL

SEAHAM

1 SUTHERLAND ST
2 EMBANKMENT RD

PROMENADE

B1287 NORTH RD

THE CASTLEREAGH HOMES

Northlea

Seaham Sch

Co. Durham & Teesside STREET ATLAS

41   A   B   42   C   D   43   E   F

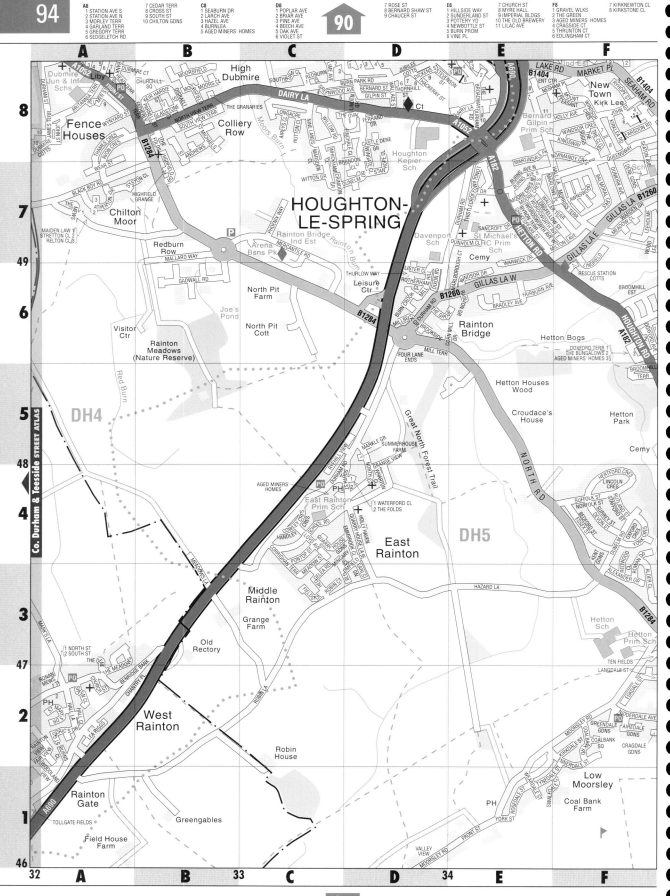

A8
1 STATION AVE S
2 STATION AVE N
3 MORLEY TERR
4 GARLAND TERR
5 GREGORY TERR
6 SEDGELETCH RD

7 CEDAR TERR
8 CROSS ST
9 SOUTH ST
10 CHILTON GDNS

C8
1 SEABURN DR
2 LARCH AVE
3 HAZEL AVE
4 BURNLEA
5 AGED MINERS' HOMES

D8
1 POPLAR AVE
2 BRIAR AVE
3 PINE AVE
4 BEECH AVE
5 OAK AVE
6 VIOLET ST

7 ROSE ST
8 BERNARD SHAW ST
9 CHAUCER ST

E8
1 HILLSIDE WAY
2 SUNDERLAND ST
3 POTTERY YD
4 NEWBOTTLE ST
5 BURN PROM
6 VINE PL

7 CHURCH ST
8 MYRE HALL
9 IMPERIAL BLDGS
10 THE OLD BREWERY
11 LILAC AVE

F8
1 GRAVEL WLKS
2 THE GREEN
3 AGED MINERS' HOMES
4 CRAGSIDE CT
5 THRUNTON CT
6 EDLINGHAM CT

7 KIRKNEWTON CL
8 KIRKSTONE CL

90
96

Co. Durham & Teesside STREET ATLAS

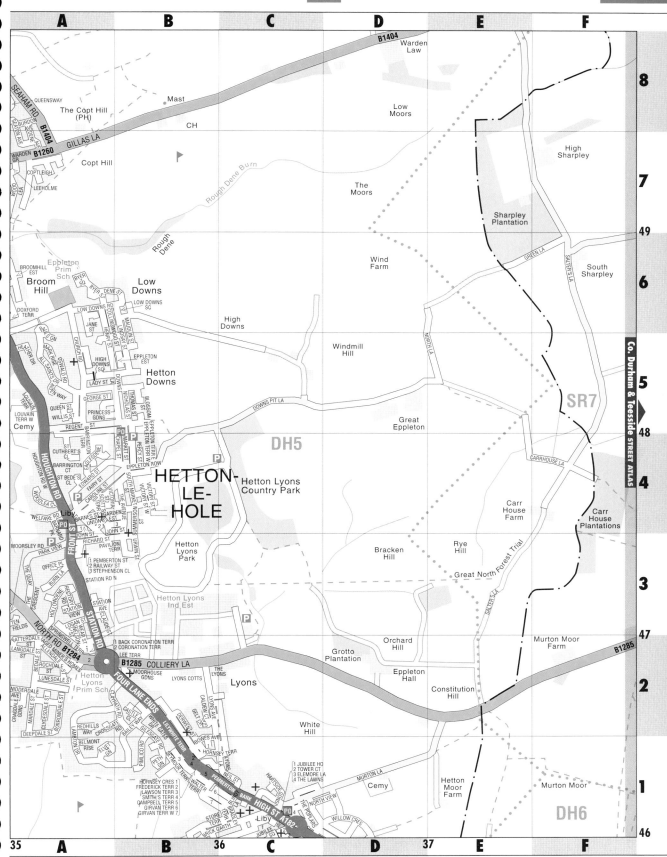

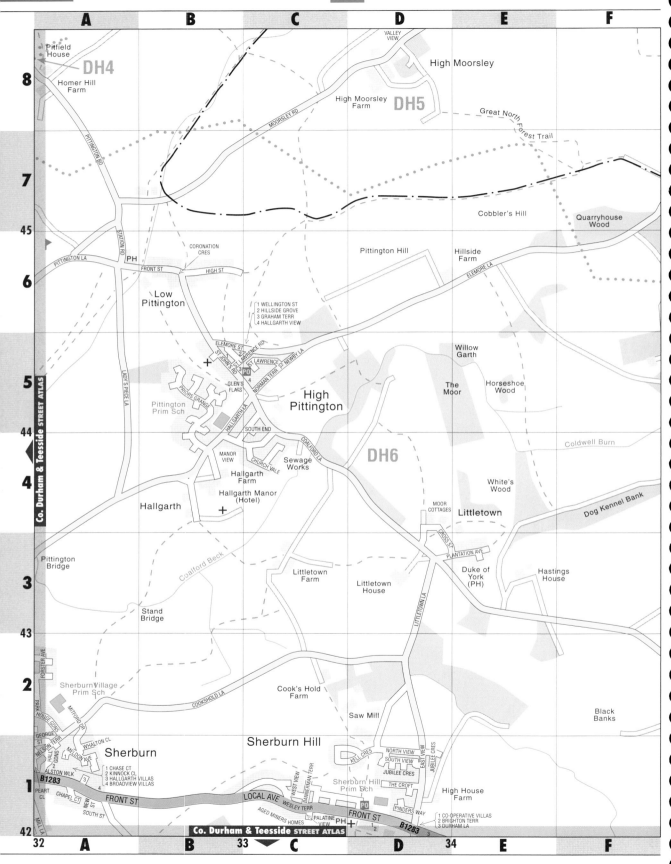

A   B   C   D   E   F

Pitfield House

DH4

Homer Hill Farm

PITTINGTON RD

MOORSLEY RD

VALLEY VIEW

High Moorsley

High Moorsley Farm

DH5

Great North Forest Trail

Cobbler's Hill

Quarryhouse Wood

8

7

45

6

STATION RD

Pittington La

PH

FRONT ST

CORONATION CRES

HIGH ST

Low Pittington

Pittington Hill

Hillside Farm

ELEMORE LA

LADY'S PIECE LA

1 WELLINGTON ST
2 HILLSIDE GROVE
3 GRAHAM TERR
4 HALLGARTH VIEW

ELEMORE ST

ST LAWRENCE RD

NEWBY LA

LAWRENCE

PO

NORMAN TERR

Willow Garth

GLEN'S FLATS

High Pittington

The Moor

Horseshoe Wood

5

44

PRIORS GRANGE

Pittington Prim Sch

HALLGARTH LA

SOUTH END

MANOR VIEW

CHURCH VALE

Sewage Works

COALFORD LA

DH6

Coldwell Burn

Hallgarth Farm

Hallgarth

Hallgarth Manor (Hotel)

White's Wood

MOOR COTTAGES

Littletown

Dog Kennel Bank

4

Pittington Bridge

Coalford Beck

CROSS ST

PLANTATION AVE

Duke of York (PH)

Hastings House

3

Stand Bridge

Littletown Farm

Littletown House

LITTLETOWN LA

43

FORSTER AVE

Sherburn Village Prim Sch

COOKSHOLD LA

Cook's Hold Farm

Saw Mill

Black Banks

2

PARK HOUSE GDNS

MITFORD DR

Cook's Hold Farm

GEORGE ST

NELSON TERR

HALL TERR

MELDON AVE

WHALTON CL

MELDON GDNS

Sherburn

1 CHASE CT
2 KINNOCK CL
3 HALLGARTH VILLAS
4 BROADVIEW VILLAS

Sherburn Hill

KELL CRES

NORTH VIEW

SOUTH VIEW

EAST VIEW

JUBILEE CRES

THE CROFT

High House Farm

1

ALSTON WLK

B1283

PEART CL

CHAPEL CT

NEW ST

FRONT ST

SOUTH ST

WEST VIEW

BANNERMAN TERR

WESLEY TERR

LOCAL AVE

AGED MINERS HOMES

PALATINE VIEW

PH

FRONT ST

Sherburn Hill Prim Sch

PO

PINDERS WAY

B1283

1 CO-OPERATIVE VILLAS
2 BRIGHTON TERR
3 DURHAM LA

42

32   A   B   33   C   D   34   E   F

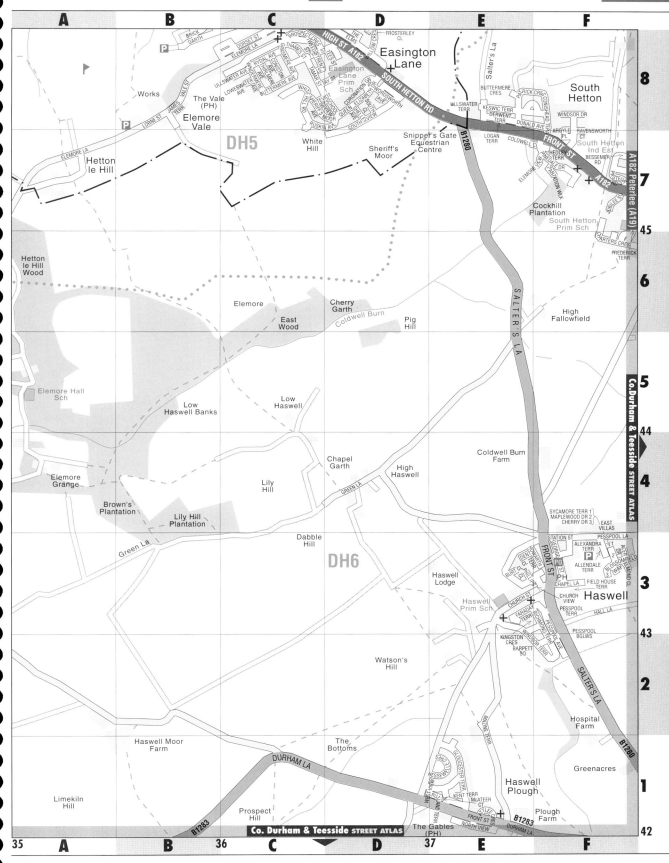

A182 Peterlee (A19)

Co.Durham & Teesside STREET ATLAS

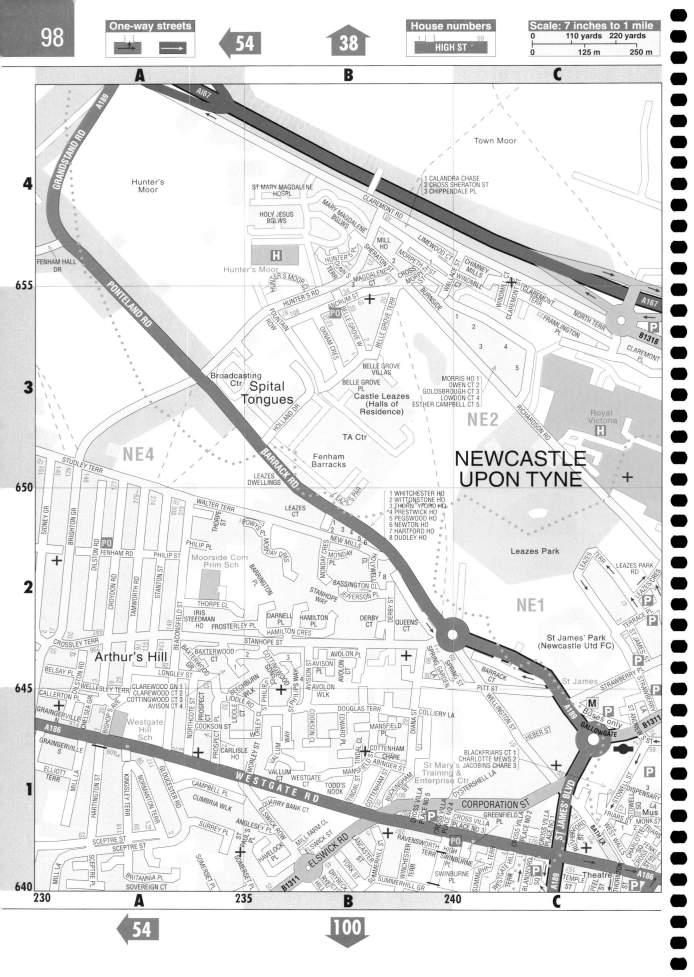

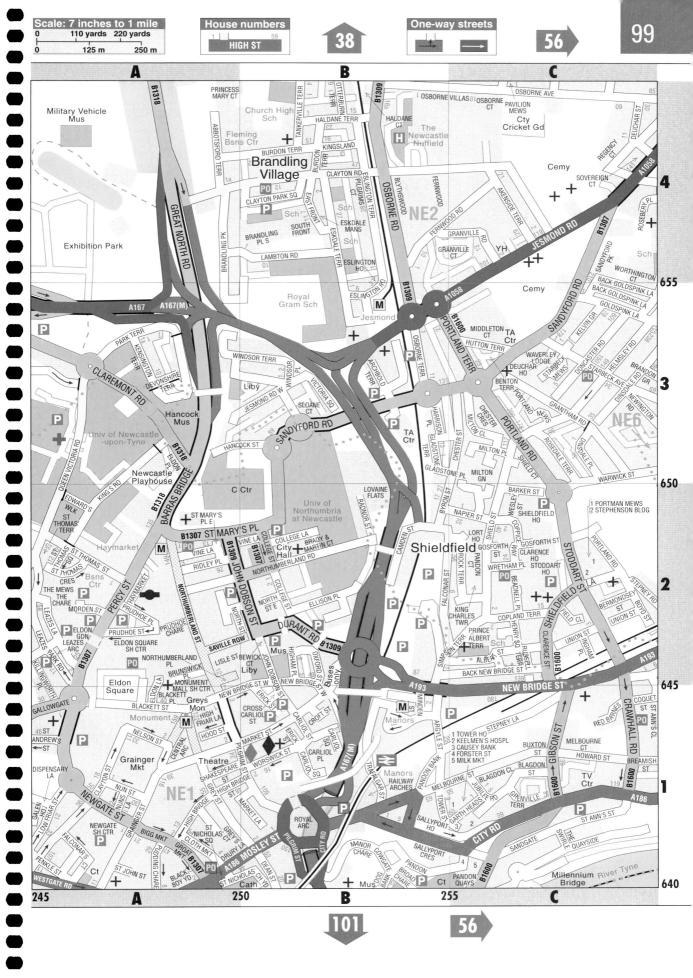

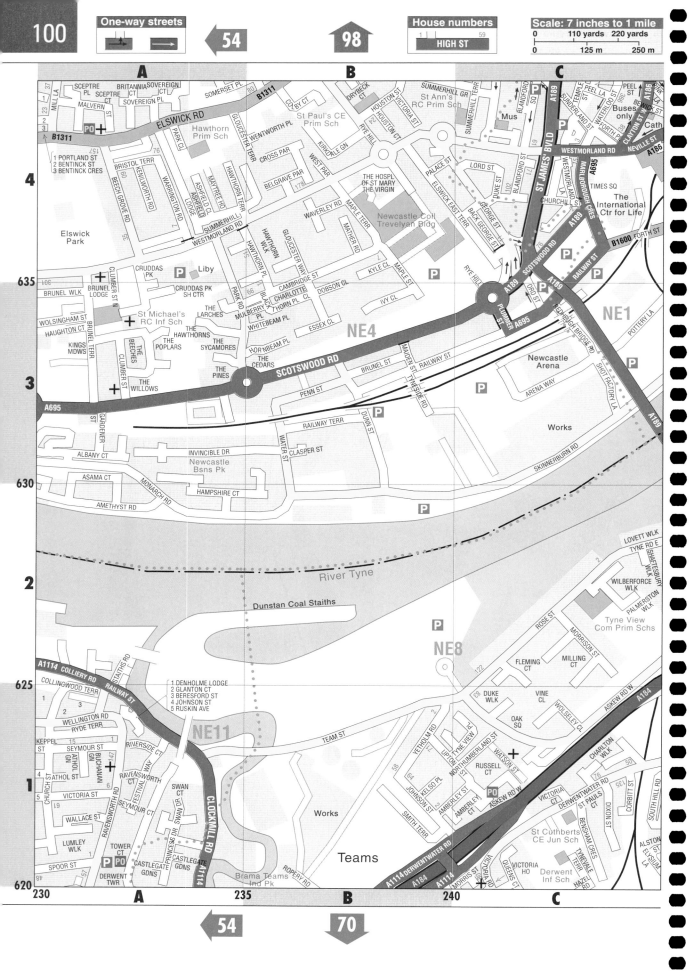

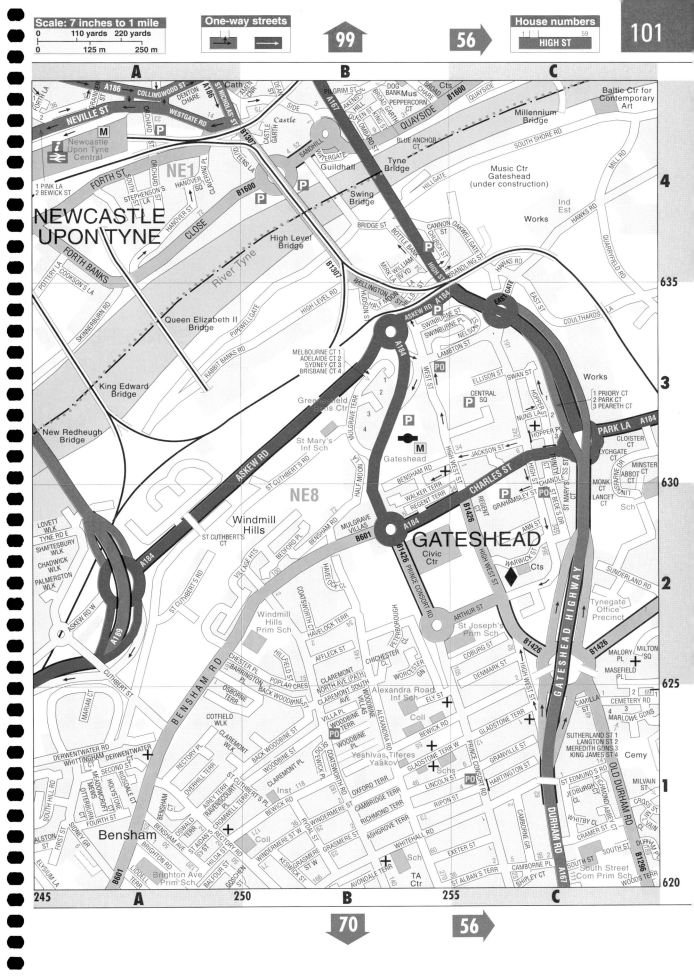

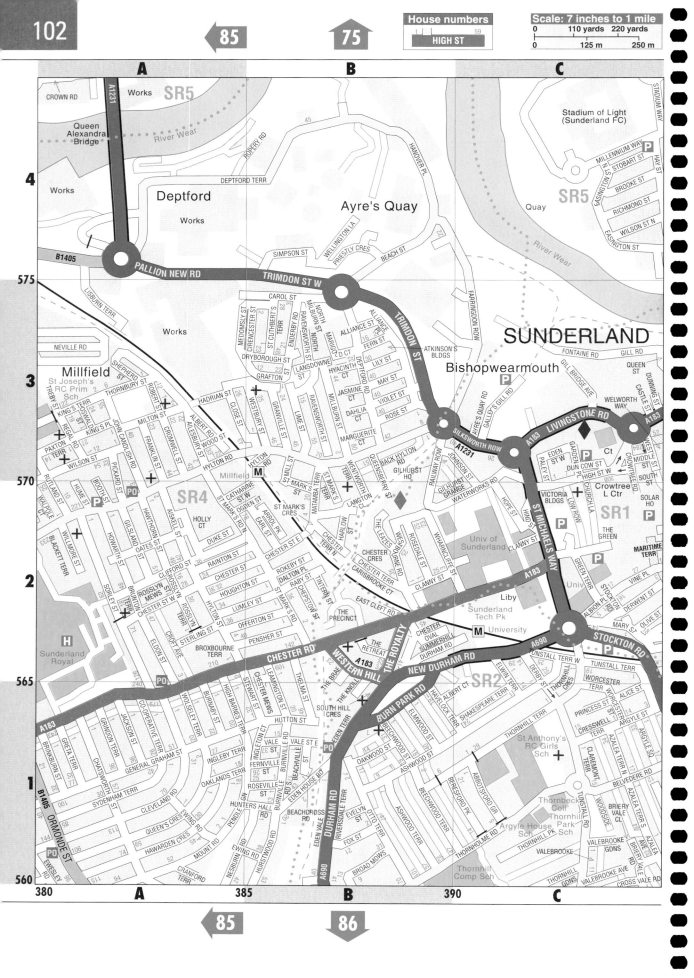

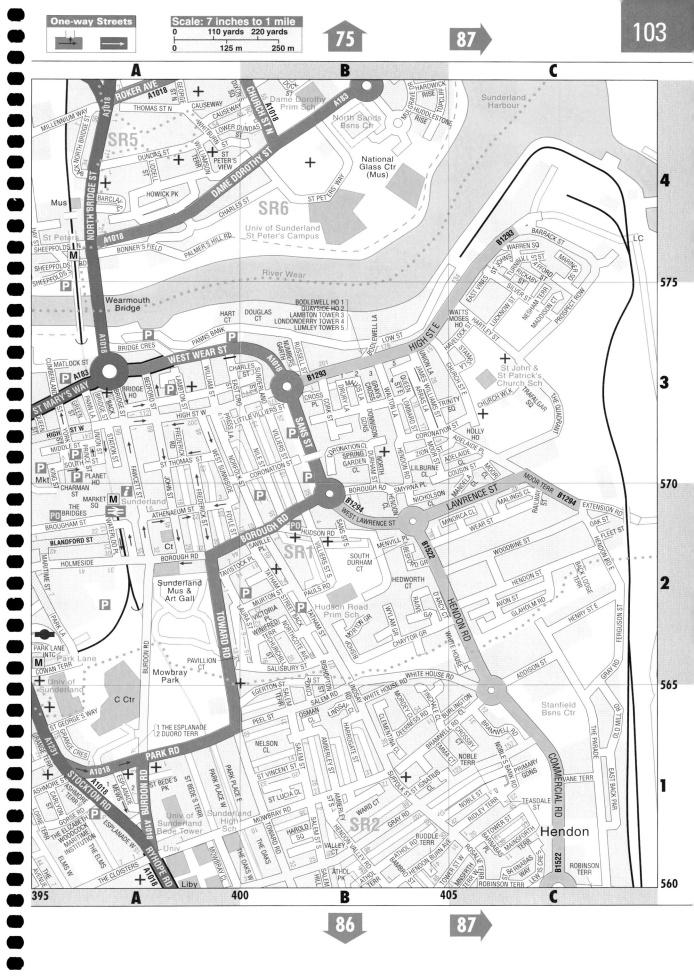

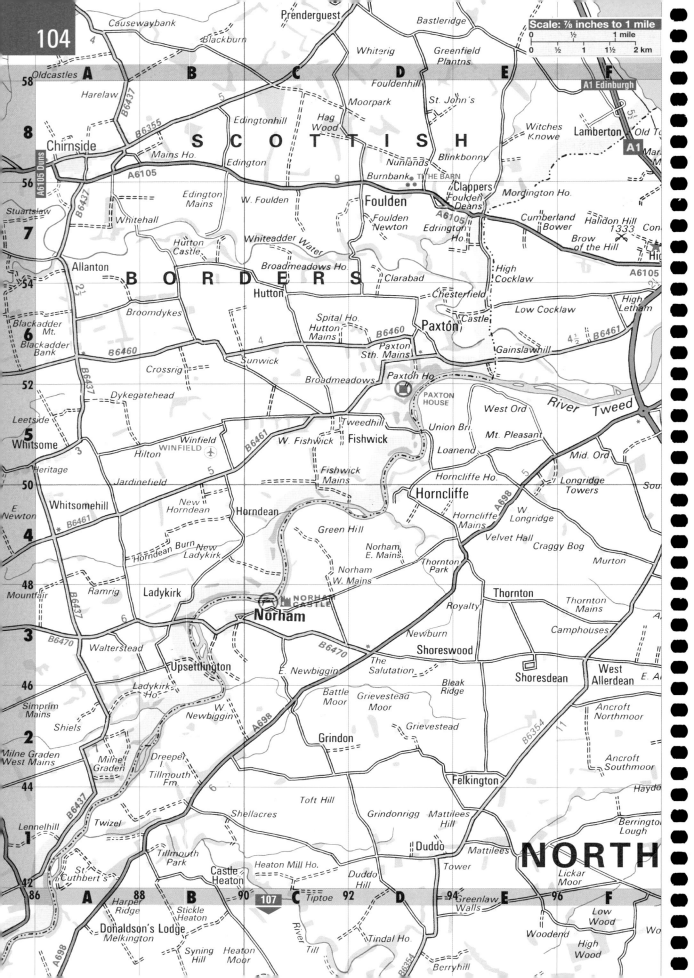

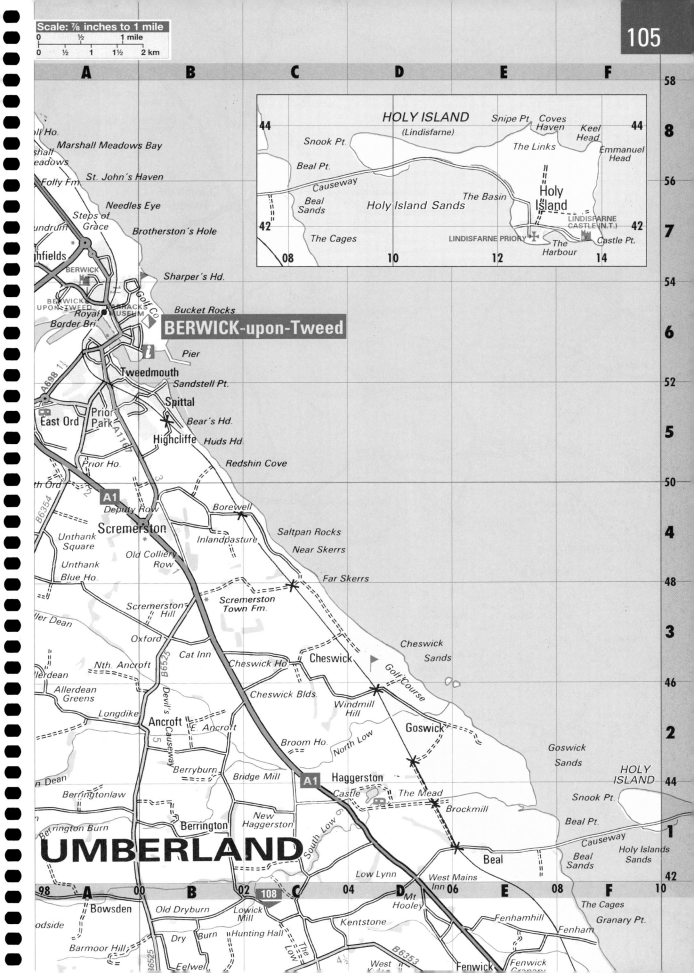

Scale: ⅞ inches to 1 mile

0 ½ 1 mile
0 ½ 1 1½ 2 km

A B C D E F

58
8
56
7
54
6
52
5
50
4
48
3
46
2
44
1
42

HOLY ISLAND inset

HOLY ISLAND
(Lindisfarne)

44 — Snook Pt. — Snipe Pt. — Coves Haven — Keel Head — 44
Beal Pt. — The Links — Emmanuel Head
Causeway
Beal Sands — Holy Island Sands — The Basin — Holy Island
42 — The Cages — LINDISFARNE PRIORY — The Harbour — LINDISFARNE CASTLE (N.T.) — Castle Pt. — 42

08 — 10 — 12 — 14

Main map

oll Ho.
Marshall Meadows Bay
shall eadows
St. John's Haven
Folly Fm.
Needles Eye
Steps of Grace
undrum
Brotherston's Hole
ghfields
BERWICK
Sharper's Hd.
BERWICK-UPON-TWEED
Bucket Rocks
Royal MUSEUM
BARRACKS
Border Bri.
BERWICK-upon-Tweed
Pier
Tweedmouth
Sandstell Pt.
Spittal
East Ord
Prior Park
Bear's Hd.
Highcliffe — Huds Hd.
Prior Ho.
Redshin Cove
th Ord
A1
Deputy Row
Borewell
Scremerston
Unthank Square
Inlandpasture
Saltpan Rocks
Near Skerrs
Old Colliery Row
Unthank Blue Ho.
Far Skerrs
ler Dean
Scremerston Hill
Scremerston Town Fm.
Oxford
Cheswick Sands
Cat Inn
Nth. Ancroft
Cheswick Ho.
Cheswick
lerdean
Cheswick Blds.
Golf Course
Allerdean Greens
Windmill Hill
Longdike
Ancroft
E. Ancroft
Goswick
Berryburn
Broom Ho.
North Low
Goswick Sands
Bridge Mill
A1
Haggerston
HOLY ISLAND
n Dean
Berringtonlaw
Castle
The Mead
Brockmill
Snook Pt.
New Haggerston
Beal Pt.
Berrington
Causeway
Berrington Burn
South Low
Beal
Beal Sands
Holy Islands Sands
UMBERLAND
Low Lynn
West Mains Inn
42

98 A 00 B 02 108 C 04 D Mt. Hooley E 06 08 F 10

Bowsden
Old Dryburn
Lowick Mill
The Cages
odside
Kentstone
Fenhamhill
Granary Pt.
Dry Burn
Hunting Hall
Fenham
Barmoor Hill
Eelwell
West
B6353
Fenwick
Fenwick Granary

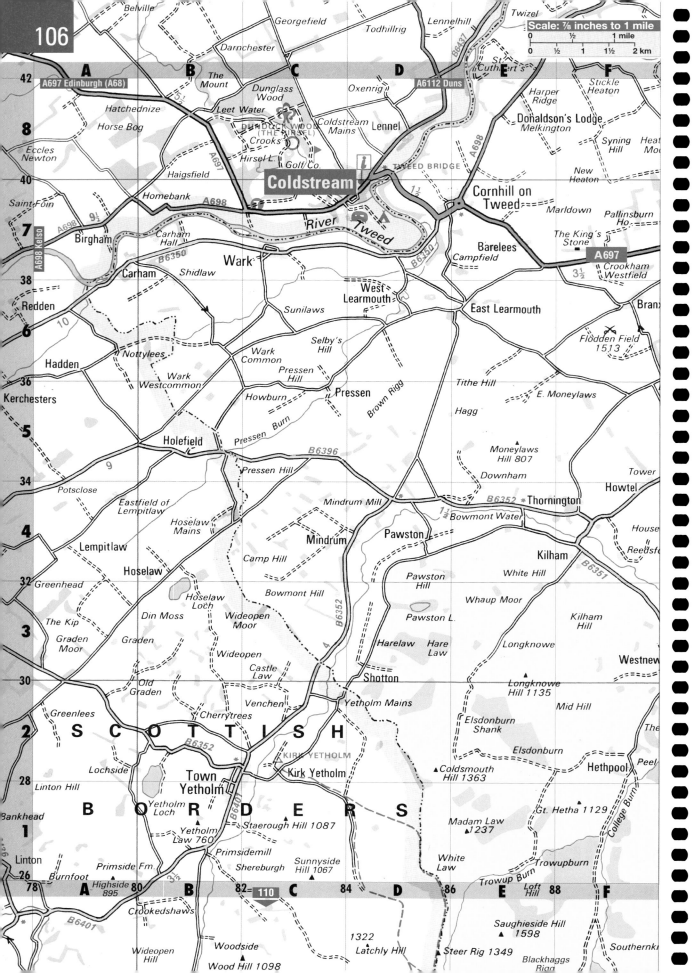

Scale: ⅞ inches to 1 mile

0   ½   1 mile
0   ½   1   1½   2 km

Belville
Georgefield
Todhillrig
Lennelhill
Twizel

Darnchester
Oxenrig
St. Cuthbert's

A697 Edinburgh (A68)
The Mount
Dunglass Wood
A6112 Duns
Stickle Heaton

Hatchednize
Leet Water
Harper Ridge
Donaldson's Lodge

Horse Bog
DUNDOCK WOOD (THE HIRSEL)
Coldstream Mains
Lennel
Melkington
Syning Hill
Heat Moo

Eccles Newton
Crooks
Hirsel L.
New Heaton

Haigsfield
Golf Co.
Coldstream
TWEED BRIDGE
Cornhill on Tweed
Marldown
Pallinsburn Ho.

Saint-Foin
Homebank
A698
Barelees
The King's Stone
A697

A698 Kelso
Birgham
Carham Hall
River Tweed
Campfield
Crookham Westfield

B6350
Wark
Shidlaw
West Learmouth
East Learmouth
Branx

Carham
Redden
Sunilaws
Flodden Field 1513

Hadden
Nottylees
Wark Common
Selby's Hill
Pressen Hill
Tithe Hill
E. Moneylaws

Kerchesters
Wark Westcommon
Howburn
Pressen
Brown Rigg
Hagg

Holefield
Pressen Burn
B6396
Moneylaws Hill 807
Tower

Potsclose
Pressen Hill
Downham
Howtel

Eastfield of Lempitlaw
Mindrum Mill
B6352
Thornington

Hoselaw Mains
Bowmont Water
House Reedsf

Lempitlaw
Mindrum
Pawston
Kilham

Hoselaw
Camp Hill
Pawston Hill
White Hill
B6351

Greenhead
Hoselaw Loch
Bowmont Hill
Whaup Moor
Kilham Hill

The Kip
Din Moss
Graden
Wideopen Moor
Pawston L.

Graden Moor
Wideopen
Harelaw
Hare Law
Longknowe
Westnew

Old Graden
Castle Law
Shotton
Longknowe Hill 1135
Mid Hill

Greenlees
Venchen
Cherrytrees
Yetholm Mains
Elsdonburn Shank
The

S C O T T I S H
B6352
Elsdonburn
Hethpool
Peel

Lochside
KIRK YETHOLM
Coldsmouth Hill 1363

Town Yetholm
Kirk Yetholm
Gt. Hetha 1129

B O R D E R S
Yetholm Loch
B6401
Madam Law 1237
College Burn

Bankhead
Linton Hill
Yetholm Law 760
Staerough Hill 1087
White Law
Trowupburn

Linton
Primside Fm.
Primsidemill
Shereburgh
Sunnyside Hill 1067
Trowup Burn
Loft Hill

Burnfoot
A Highside 895
B
110
C
D
E
88
F

Crookedshaws
B6401
Saughieside Hill 1598

Woodside
1322
Latchly Hill
Steer Rig 1349
Blackhaggs Rigg
Southernk

Wideopen Hill
Wood Hill 1098

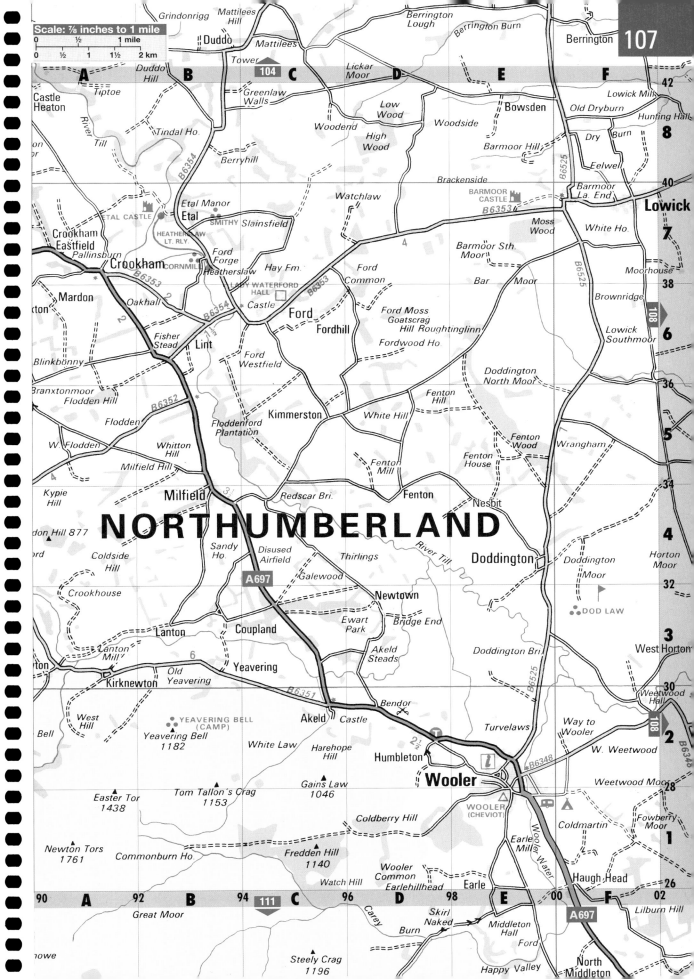

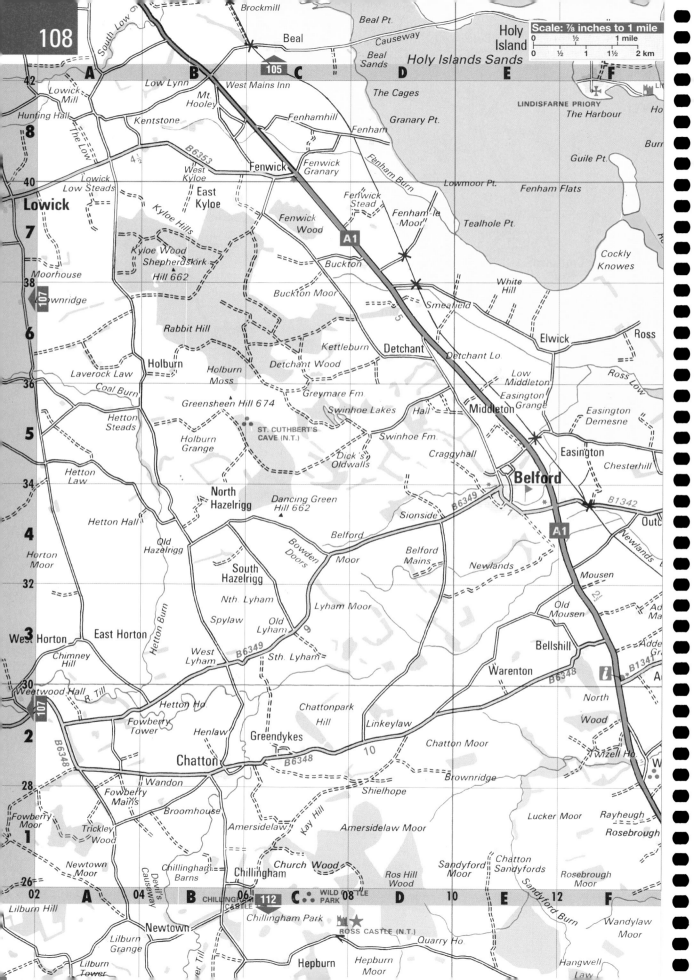

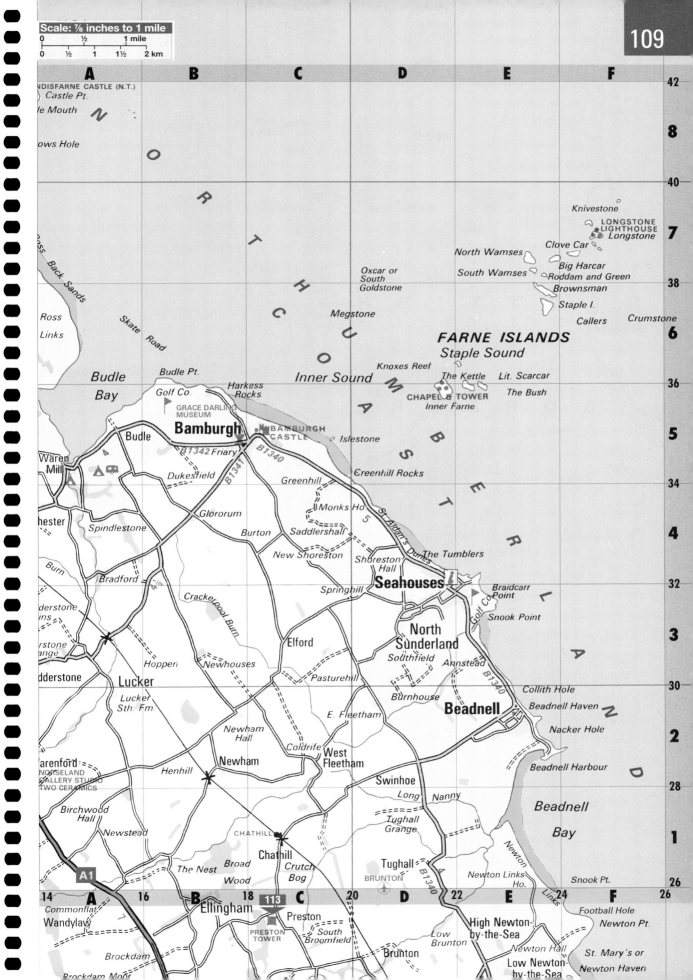

Scale: ⅞ inches to 1 mile

0 ½ 1 mile
0 ½ 1 1½ 2 km

A B C D E F

42

8

40

LINDISFARNE CASTLE (N.T.)
) Castle Pt.
e Mouth

ows Hole

N O R T H C U M B E R L A N D

Knivestone

LONGSTONE
LIGHTHOUSE
Longstone

Clove Car

North Wamses

Big Harcar
Roddam and Green
Brownsman

South Wamses

Staple I.

Callers   Crumstone

Oxcar or
South
Goldstone

Megstone

FARNE ISLANDS
Staple Sound

ss Back Sands

Ross
Links

Skate Road

Inner Sound

Knoxes Reef

The Kettle   Lit. Scarcar

The Bush

CHAPEL & TOWER
Inner Farne

Budle
Bay

Budle Pt.

Harkess
Rocks

Golf Co.

GRACE DARLING
MUSEUM

BAMBURGH
CASTLE

Islestone

Bamburgh

Budle

B1342 Friary
B1340

Dukesfield

B1341

Greenhill

Greenhill Rocks

Waren
Mill

Spindlestone

Glororum

Monks Ho
St. Aidan's Dunes

Saddlershall

The Tumblers

hester

Dukesfield

Burton

New Shoreston

Shoreston
Hall

Burn

Bradford

Crackerpool Burn

Springhill

Seahouses

Braidcarr
Point

Snook Point

derstone
ins

Elford

North
Sunderland

Golf Co.

rstone
ange

Hoppen

Newhouses

Pasturehill

Southfield

Annstead

B1340

Collith Hole

dderstone

Lucker

Burnhouse

Beadnell

Beadnell Haven

Nacker Hole

Lucker
Sth. Fm.

E. Fleetham

arenford
NORSELAND
GALLERY STUDIO
TWO CERAMICS

Newham
Hall

Henhill

Newham

Coldrife

West
Fleetham

Swinhoe

Beadnell Harbour

Birchwood
Hall

Newstead

Long   Nanny

Tughall
Grange

Beadnell

Bay

CHATHILL

Chathill

Tughall

Newton
Links

A1

The Nest

Broad
Wood

Crutch
Bog

BRUNTON

Newton Links
Ho.

Snook Pt.

14   A   16   B   18   113   C   20   D   22   E   24   F   26

Commonflat

Football Hole

Newton Pt.

Wandylaw

Ellingham

Preston

High Newton-
by-the-Sea

PRESTON
TOWER

South
Broomfield

Low
Brunton

Newton Hall

St. Mary's or
Newton Haven

Brockdam

Brunton

Newton-
by-the-Sea

Low Newton-
by-the-Sea

7

38

6

36

5

34

4

32

3

30

2

28

1

26

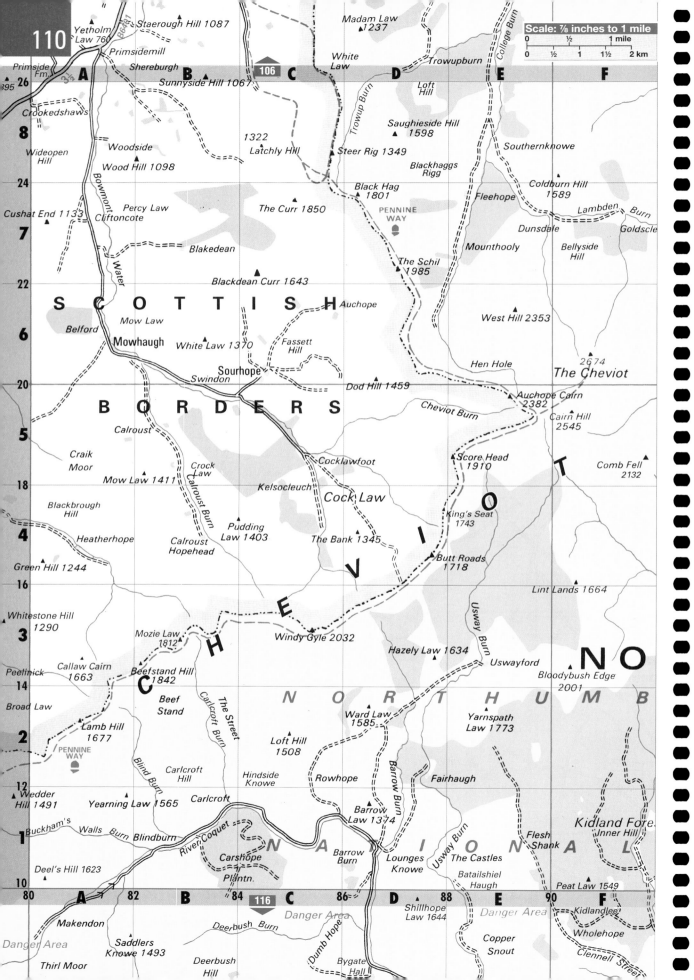

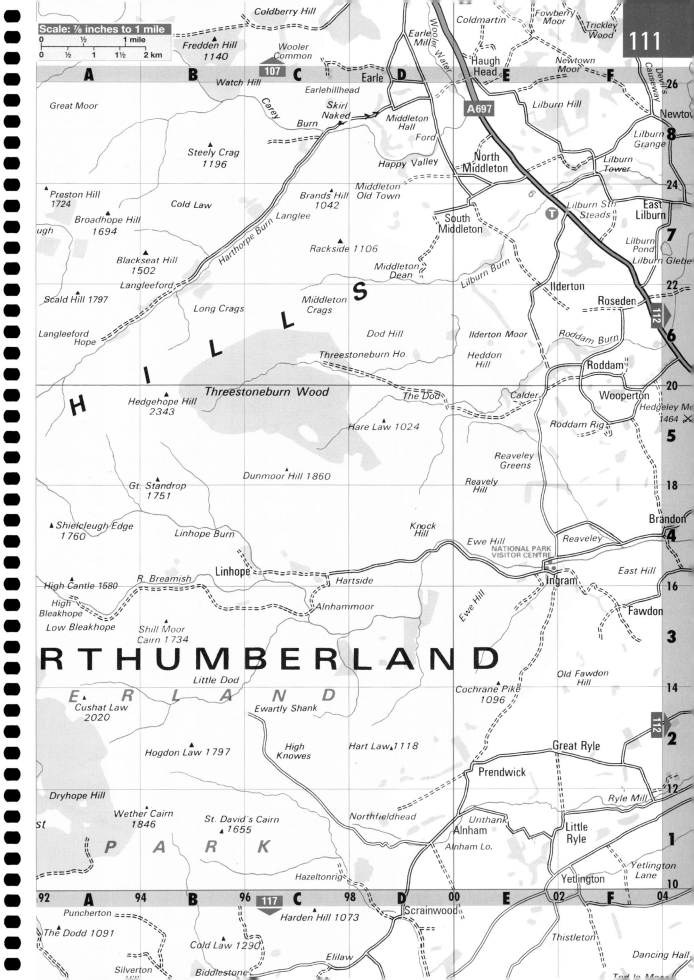

Scale: ⅞ inches to 1 mile

0 ½ 1 mile
0 ½ 1 1½ 2 km

A B 107 C D E F

Coldberry Hill

Coldmartin Fowberry Moor Trickley Wood

Fredden Hill 1140

Earle Mill Newtown Moor

Wooler Common

Haugh Head

Devil's Causeway

26

Watch Hill Earle Earlehillhead

Great Moor

A697 Lilburn Hill Newtow

Carey Burn

Skirl Naked

Middleton Hall Ford

North Middleton

Lilburn Grange 8

Steely Crag 1196

Happy Valley

Lilburn Tower 24

Preston Hill 1724

Cold Law

Brands Hill 1042

Middleton Old Town

Lilburn Sth Steads East Lilburn

T

Langlee

Broadhope Hill 1694

Langlee South Middleton

Lilburn Pond 7

Harthorpe Burn

Blackseat Hill 1502

Rackside 1106 Middleton Dean

Lilburn Burn Lilburn Glebe

Langleeford

Middleton Dean

Ilderton 22

Scald Hill 1797

Long Crags

S

Middleton Crags

Lilburn Burn Roseden 112

Langleeford Hope

Dod Hill Ilderton Moor Roddam Burn 6

H I L L

Threestoneburn Ho.

Heddon Hill Roddam

Threestoneburn Wood

The Dod Calder Wooperton 20

H Hedgehope Hill 2343

Hare Law 1024 Roddam Rig Hedgeley M 1464

Dunmoor Hill 1860

Reaveley Greens 5

Gt. Standrop 1751

Reavely Hill 18

Shielcleugh Edge 1760

Linhope Burn

Knock Hill Reaveley

Ewe Hill NATIONAL PARK VISITOR CENTRE Brandon 4

High Cantle 1580

R. Breamish Linhope Hartside

East Hill

High Bleakhope

Alnhammoor

Ewe Hill Ingram 16

Low Bleakhope

Shill Moor Cairn 1734

Fawdon 3

R T H U M B E R L A N D

Little Dod

Old Fawdon Hill 14

E R L A N D

Cushat Law 2020

Ewartly Shank

Cochrane Pike 1096 112 2

Hogdon Law 1797

High Knowes

Hart Law 1118 Great Ryle

Dryhope Hill

Prendwick

Ryle Mill 12

Wether Cairn 1846

St. David's Cairn 1655

Northfieldhead

Unthank Little Ryle 1

st

Alnham Alnham Lo.

Yetlington Lane

P A R K

Hazeltonrig

Yetlington 10

92 A 94 B 96 117 C 98 D 00 E 02 F 04

Puncherton

Scrainwood

The Dodd 1091

Harden Hill 1073

Thistleton

Cold Law 1290

Silverton Biddlestone Elilaw

Dancing Hall

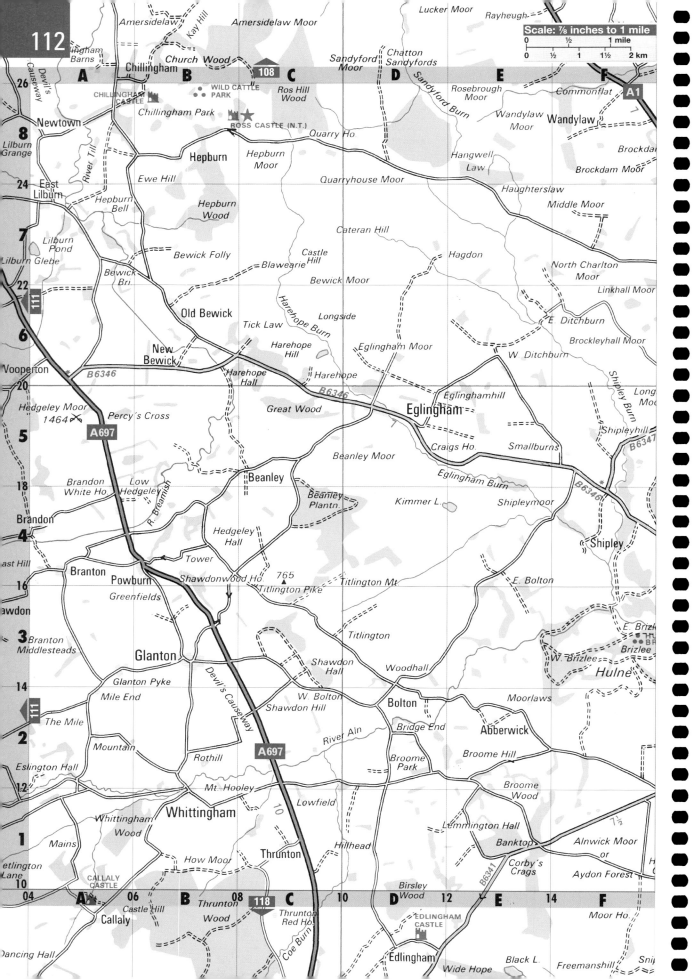

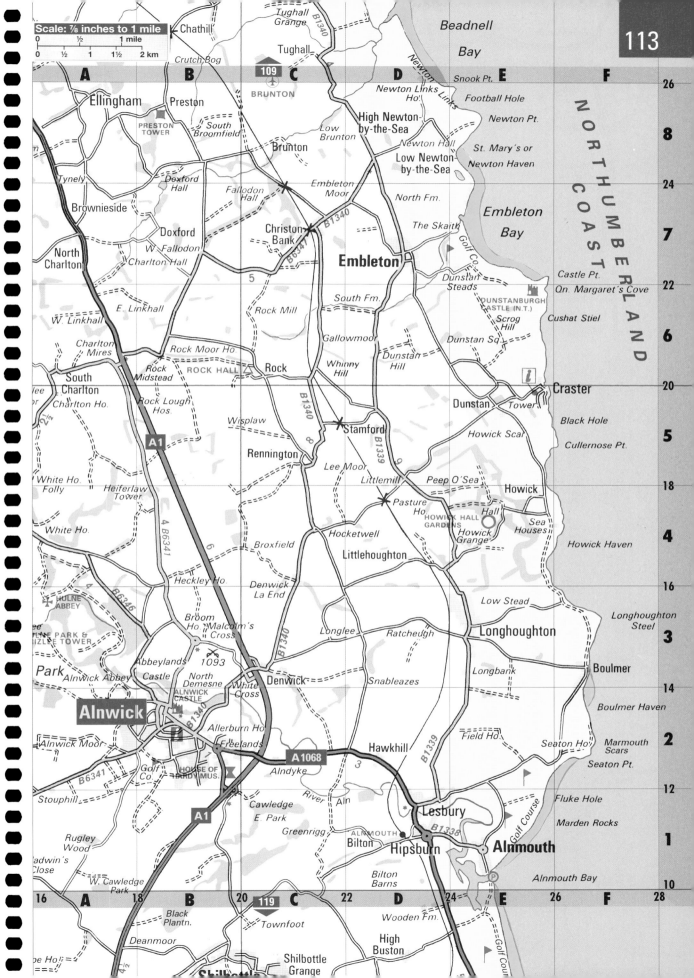

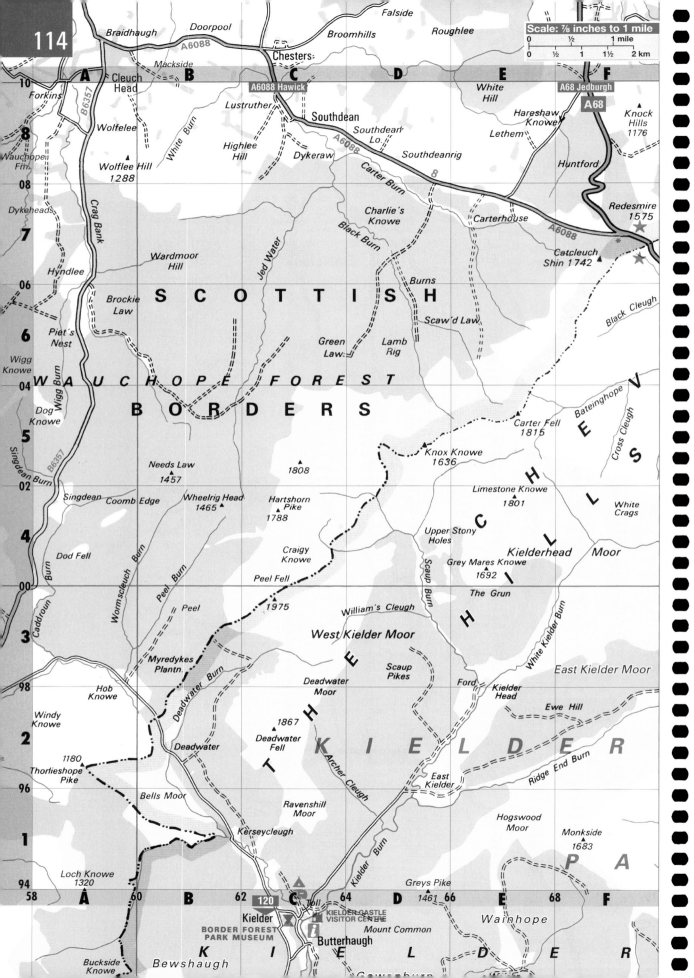

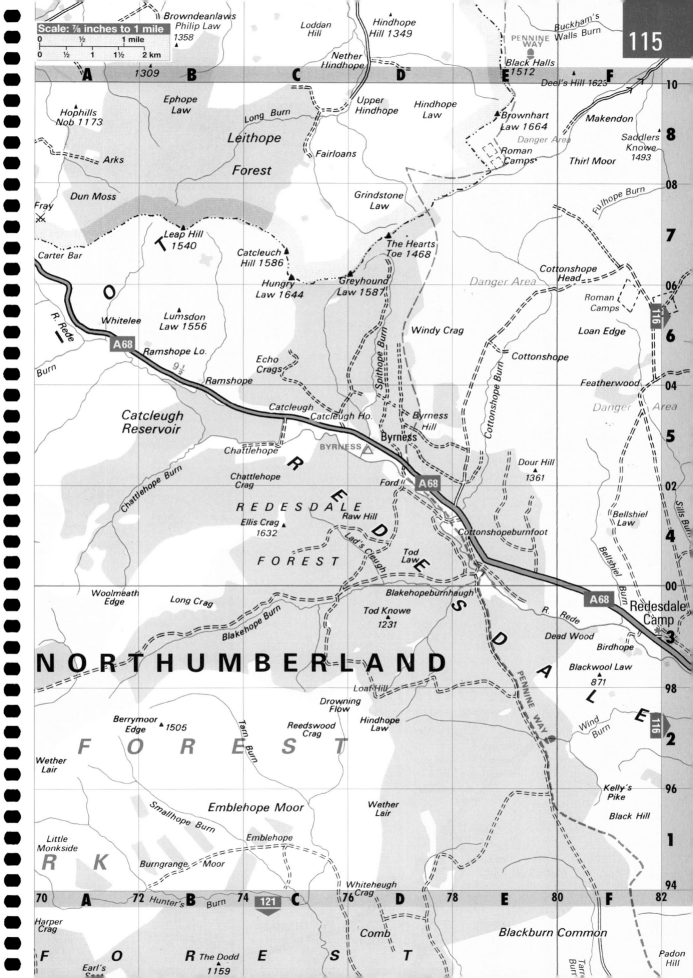

Scale: ⅞ inches to 1 mile
0   ½   1 mile
0   ½   1   1½   2 km

A **B** **C** **D** **E** **F**

Browndeanlaws
Philip Law
1358

Loddan
Hill

Hindhope
Hill 1349

Buckham's
Walls Burn

PENNINE
WAY

Black Halls
1512

Deel's Hill 1623

10

Ephope
Law

Nether
Hindhope

Upper
Hindhope

Hindhope
Law

Brownhart
Law 1664

Makendon

8

Hophills
Nob 1173

Long Burn

Fairloans

Danger Area

Roman
Camps

Saddlers
Knowe
1493

Arks

Leithope

Forest

Grindstone
Law

Thirl Moor

08

Dun Moss

Fulhope Burn

7

Fray

Leap Hill
1540

Catcleuch
Hill 1586

The Hearts
Toe 1468

Cottonshope
Head

Danger Area

Roman
Camps

06

Carter Bar

Hungry
Law 1644

Greyhound
Law 1587

Loan Edge

116

6

Whitelee

Lumsdon
Law 1556

Windy Crag

Cottonshope

R. Rede

A68

Ramshope Lo.

9½

Echo
Crags

Spithope Burn

Cottonshope Burn

Featherwood

04

Burn

Ramshope

Catcleugh

Catcleugh Ho.

Byrness
Hill

Danger   Area

5

Catcleugh
Reservoir

Chattlehope

BYRNESS

Byrness

Dour Hill
1361

Bellshiel
Law

02

Chattlehope
Crag

Ford

A68

Sills Burn

Chattlehope Burn

REDESDALE

Ellis Crag
1632

Raw Hill

Cottonshopeburnfoot

00

Woolmeath
Edge

Long Crag

Lad's Cleugh

FOREST

Tod
Law

Blakehopeburnhaugh

R. Rede

A68

Redesdale
Camp

3

NORTHUMBERLAND

Blakehope Burn

Tod Knowe
1231

Dead Wood

Birdhope

Loaf Hill

PENNINE WAY

Blackwool Law
871

98

Berrymoor
Edge 1505

Drowning
Flow

Reedswood
Crag

Hindhope
Law

Wind
Burn

116

2

Wether
Lair

Tarn Burn

FOREST

Kelly's
Pike

96

Little
Monkside

Emblehope Moor

Wether
Lair

Black Hill

1

R K

Smallhope Burn

Emblehope

94

Burngrange   Moor

Whiteheugh
Crag

70 **A** **72** **B** **74** 121 **C** **76** **D** **78** **E** **80** **F** **82**

Harper
Crag

Hunter's   Burn

Comb

Blackburn Common

Tarn Burn

Padon
Hill

F   O   R   E   S   T

Earl's
Seat

R The Dodd
1159

E   S   T

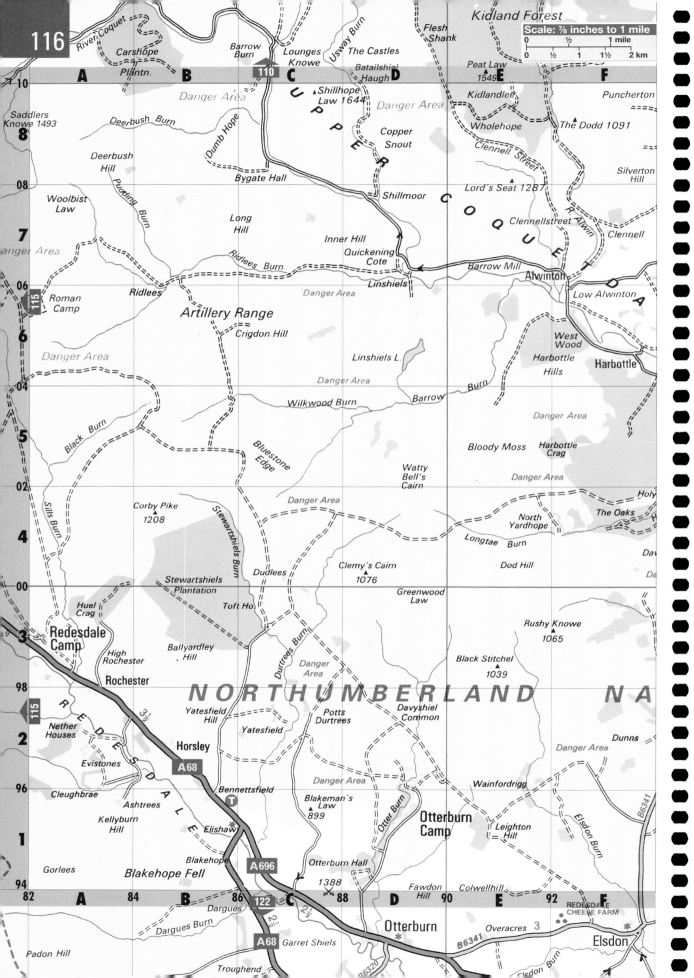

Kidland Forest

Scale: 7/8 inches to 1 mile

| 0 | ½ | 1 mile |
| 0 | ½ | 1 | 1½ | 2 km |

River Coquet

Carshope Plantn.

Barrow Burn

Lounges Knowe

Usway Burn

The Castles

Flesh Shank

A   B   110   C   D   E   F
10

Danger Area

Shillhope Law 1644

Danger Area

Peat Law 1549

Kidlandlee

Puncherton

Saddlers Knowe 1493

Deerbush Burn

Dumb Hope

Batailshiel Haugh

Wholehope

The Dodd 1091

8

Deerbush Hill

Copper Snout

Clennell Street

Silverton Hill

08

Bygate Hall

Shillmoor

Lord's Seat 1287

Woolbist Law

Pudding Burn

Long Hill

Inner Hill

Clennellstreet

Clennell

7

Ridlees Burn

Quickening Cote

Barrow Mill

anger Area

Danger Area

Alwinton

06

115   Roman Camp

Ridlees

Linshiels

Low Alwinton

Danger Area

Artillery Range

West Wood

6

Crigdon Hill

Linshiels L.

Harbottle Hills

Harbottle

04

Danger Area

Wilkwood Burn

Barrow   Burn

Danger Area

5

Black Burn

Bluestone Edge

Watty Bell's Cairn

Bloody Moss

Harbottle Crag

02

Danger Area

Danger Area

Corby Pike 1208

Stewartshiels Burn

Danger Area

North Yardhope

The Oaks

Holy

4

Dudlees

Clemy's Cairn 1076

Longtae   Burn

Dod Hill

Da

00

Stewartshiels Plantation

Toft Ho.

Durtrees Burn

Greenwood Law

Da

Huel Crag

Rushy Knowe 1065

3

Redesdale Camp

High Rochester

Ballyardley Hill

Danger Area

Black Stitchel 1039

Rochester

NORTHUMBERLAND   NA

98

115   Nether Houses

Yatesfield Hill

Yatesfield

Potts Durtrees

Davyshiel Common

2

Horsley

A68

Bennettsfield

Danger Area

Dunns

Evistones

Wainfordrigg

Danger Area

96

Cleughbrae

Ashtrees

Blakeman's Law 899

B6341

Kellyburn Hill

Elishaw

Otter Burn

Otterburn Camp

Leighton Hill

Elsdon Burn

1

Gorlees

Blakehope

A696

Otterburn Hall 1388

Fawdon Hill

Colwellhill

94

A   84   B   86   122   C   88   D   90   E   92   F

82

A68   Garret Shiels

Dargues

Dargues Burn

Otterburn

Overacres   3

REDESDALE CHEESE FARM

Elsdon

Padon Hill

Troughend

B6341

Elsdon Burn

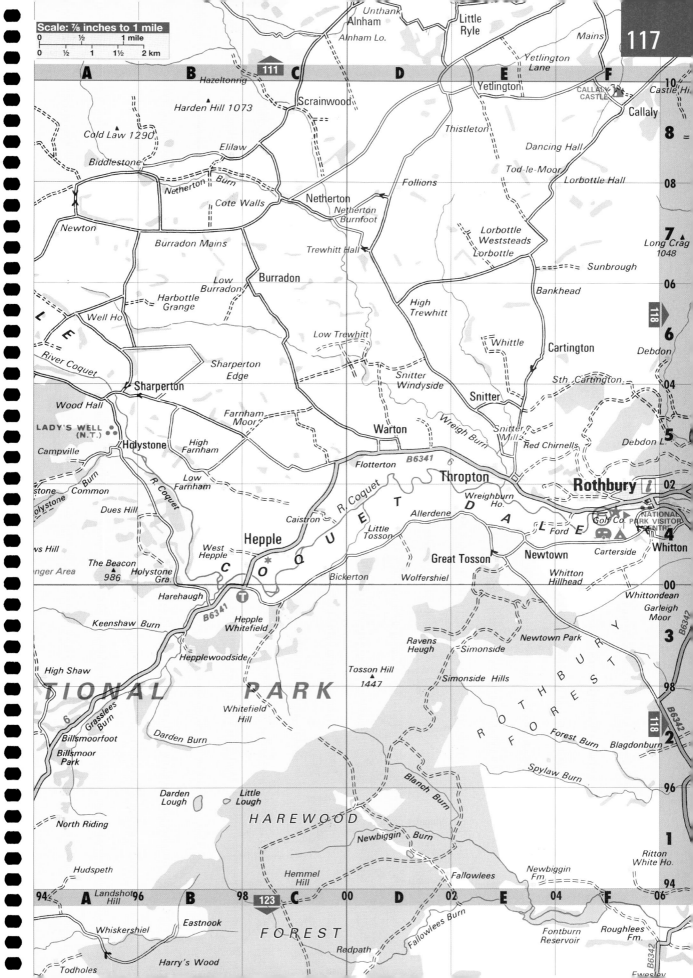

Scale: 7/8 inches to 1 mile
0   ½   1 mile
0   ½   1   1½   2 km

A   B   111   C   D   E   F

Unthank
Alnham
Little Ryle
Alnham Lo.
Mains
Yetlington Lane
10
Hazeltonrig
Scrainwood
Yetlington
CALLALY CASTLE
Castle Hi.
Callaly
Harden Hill 1073
8
Cold Law 1290
Thistleton
Dancing Hall
Elilaw
Follions
Tod-le-Moor
Lorbottle Hall
08
Biddlestone
Netherton Burn
Netherton
Burradon Mains
Cote Walls
Netherton Burnfoot
Lorbottle Weststeads
7
Long Crag 1048
Newton
Trewhitt Hall
Lorbottle
Sunbrough
Well Ho.
Low Burradon
Burradon
High Trewhitt
Bankhead
06
Harbottle Grange
Whittle
Cartington
L E
Low Trewhitt
Debdon
6
River Coquet
Sharperton Edge
Sth. Cartington
Sharperton
Snitter Windyside
Snitter
Wood Hall
Farnham Moor
Warton
Wreigh Burn
Snitter Mill
Red Chirnells
Debdon L.
5
LADY'S WELL (N.T.)
Holystone
High Farnham
B6341   6
Flotterton
Throopton
Rothbury
i
02
Campville
Low Farnham
Wreighburn Ho.
Golf Co.
NATIONAL PARK VISITOR CENTRE
...stone Common
R. Coquet
Caistron
Little Tosson
Allerdene
D
Ford
Whitton
4
...lystone
Dues Hill
C   O   Q   U   E   T
Great Tosson
Newtown
Carterside
...vs Hill
West Hepple
Hepple
Bickerton
Wolfershiel
Whitton Hillhead
00
The Beacon 986
Holystone Gra.
Newtown Park
...nger Area
Harehaugh
Whittondean
Garleigh Moor
Keenshaw Burn
B6341
Hepple Whitefield
Ravens Heugh
Simonside
R O T H B U R Y   F O R E S T
3
High Shaw
Hepplewoodside
Simonside Hills
98
T I O N A L   P A R K
Whitefield Hill
Tosson Hill 1447
Forest Burn
Grasslees Burn
Darden Burn
Blagdonburn
2
Billsmoorfoot
Spylaw Burn
Billsmoor Park
Darden Lough
Little Lough
Blanch Burn
96
North Riding
H A R E W O O D
Newbiggin Burn
Newbiggin Fm.
1
Hudspeth
Ritton White Ho.
94   A   Landshot Hill   96   B   98   123   C   00   D   02   E   04   F   06
Whiskershiel
Eastnook
F O R E S T
Fallowlees Burn
Fontburn Reservoir
Roughlees Fm.
Todholes
Harry's Wood
Redpath

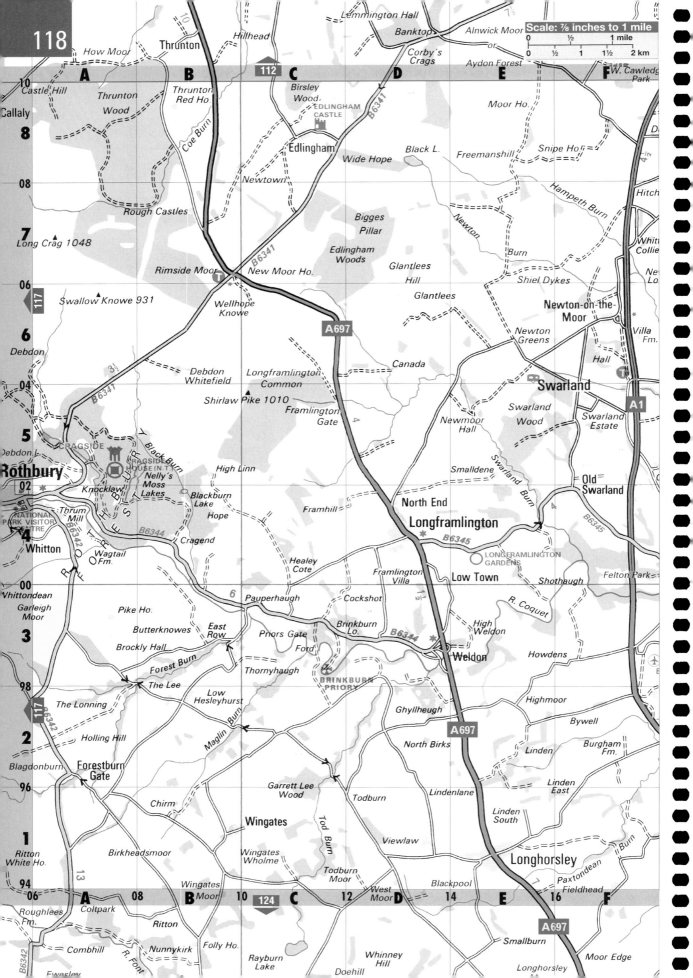

Scale: ⅞ inches to 1 mile
0   ½   1 mile
or
0   ½   1   1½   2 km

Lemmington Hall
Hillhead
Thrunton
How Moor
Banktops
Alnwick Moor
Corby's Crags
Aydon Forest
W. Cawledge Park

Castle Hill
Callaly
Thrunton Wood
Thrunton Red Ho.
Birsley Wood
EDLINGHAM CASTLE
Moor Ho.

Edlingham
Black L.
Freemanshill
Snipe Ho.
Hitch

Newtown
Wide Hope
Hampeth Burn
Whitt Collie

Rough Castles
Bigges Pillar
Newton
Burn
Ne Lo

Long Crag 1048
Edlingham Woods
Glantlees Hill
Shiel Dykes

Rimside Moor
New Moor Ho.
Glantlees
Newton-on-the-Moor
Villa Fm.

Swallow Knowe 931
Wellhope Knowe
Newton Greens
Hall

Debdon
Debdon Whitefield
Longframlington Common
Canada
Newmoor Hall
Swarland
Swarland Wood
Swarland Estate

Shirlaw Pike 1010
Framlington Gate
Smalldene
Old Swarland

CRAGSIDE
Debdon L.
CRAGSIDE HOUSE (N.T.)
Nelly's Moss Lakes
High Linn
Framhill
North End
Longframlington
Swarland Burn

Rothbury
Knocklaw
Blackburn Lake Hope
LONGFRAMLINGTON GARDENS
Low Town
Felton Park

NATIONAL PARK VISITOR CENTRE
Thrum Mill
Cragend
Healey Cote
Framlington Villa
High Weldon
R. Coquet

Whitton
Wagtail Fm.
Pauperhaugh
Cockshot
Shothaugh

Vhittondean
Garleigh Moor
Pike Ho.
East Row
Priors Gate
Brinkburn Lo.
Weldon
Howdens

Butterknowes
Ford
BRINKBURN PRIORY
Highmoor

Brockly Hall
Forest Burn
The Lee
Thornyhaugh
Ghyllheugh
Bywell

The Lonning
Low Hesleyhurst
North Birks
Linden
Burgham Fm.

Holling Hill
Maglin Burn
Lindenlane
Linden East

Blagdonburn
Forestburn Gate
Garrett Lee Wood
Todburn
Linden South

Chirm
Wingates
Tod Burn
Viewlaw
Longhorsley

Ritton White Ho.
Birkheadsmoor
Wingates Wholme
Todburn Moor
Blackpool
Paxtondean Fieldhead

Roughlees Fm.
Coltpark
Ritton
Wingates Moor
West Moor
Smallburn

Combhill
Nunnykirk
Folly Ho.
Rayburn Lake
Whinney Hill
Longhorsley
Moor Edge

Ewasley
Doehill

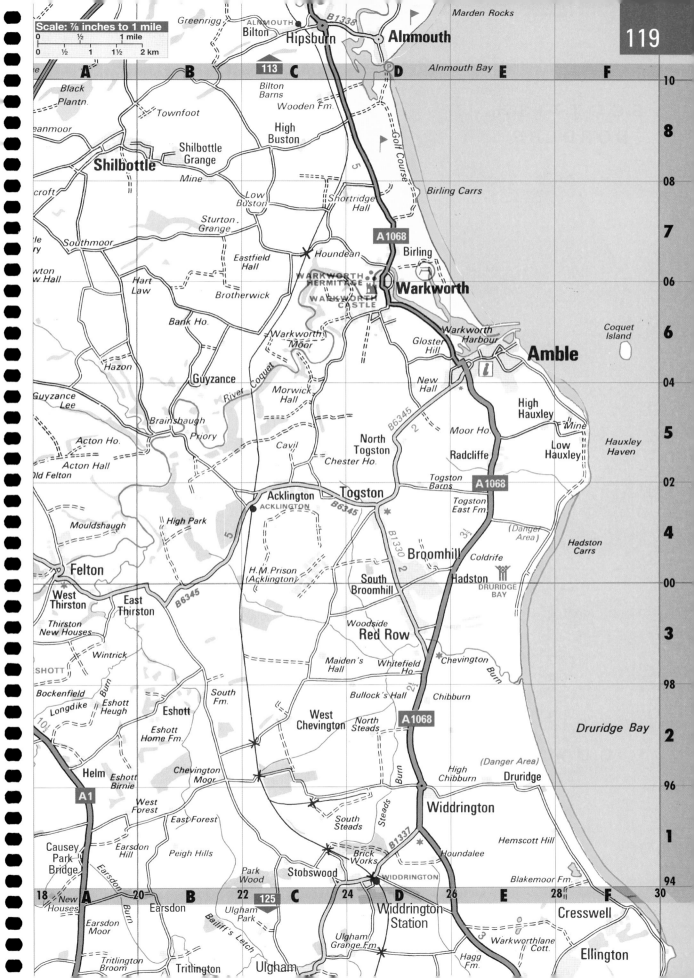

Scale: 7/8 inches to 1 mile

0   ½   1 mile
0   ½   1   1½   2 km

113

125

A   B   C   D   E   F

Marden Rocks

Greenrigg   B1338

ALNMOUTH   Bilton

Hipsburn   Alnmouth

Alnmouth Bay

10

Black Plantn.

Bilton Barns

Wooden Fm.

8

eanmoor   Townfoot

High Buston

Shilbottle Grange

Golf Course

08

Shilbottle   Mine

Low Buston

Shortridge Hall

Birling Carrs

croft

Sturton Grange   Eastfield Hall

A1068

7

tle ry   Southmoor

Hart Law   Brotherwick   Houndean   Birling

06

wton w Hall   Bank Ho.   WARKWORTH HERMITAGE   Warkworth

WARKWORTH CASTLE

Warkworth Harbour   Amble

6

Hazon   Warkworth Moor   Gloster Hill   Coquet Island

04

Guyzance Lee   Guyzance   Morwick Hall   New Hall   High Hauxley   Mine

River Coquet

Brainshaugh Priory   Cavil   North Togston   Moor Ho.   Low Hauxley   Hauxley Haven

5

Acton Ho.   Chester Ho.   Radcliffe

Acton Hall

Old Felton   Acklington   ACKLINGTON   Togston Barns   A1068

02

Mouldshaugh   High Park   B6345   Togston   Togston East Fm.   (Danger Area)   Hadston Carrs

4

H.M.Prison (Acklington)   B1330   Broomhill   Coldrife

Felton   South Broomhill   Hadston   DRURIDGE BAY

West Thirston   East Thirston   B6345   Woodside   00

Thirston New Houses   Red Row

3

Wintrick   Maiden's Hall   Whitefield Ho.   Chevington   Chevington Burn   98

SHOTT   Bockenfield   Longdike   Eshott Heugh   South Fm.   Bullock's Hall   Chibburn

Eshott   West Chevington   North Steads   A1068   2

Helm   Eshott Home Fm.   Chibburn   High Chibburn   (Danger Area)   Druridge   Druridge Bay

Eshott Birnie   96

A1   West Forest   Chevington Moor   Steads Burn   Widdrington

East Forest   South Steads   B1337   Hemscott Hill   1

Causey Park Bridge   Earsdon Hill   Peigh Hills   Brick Works   Houndalee   Blakemoor Fm.   94

New Houses   Earsdon   Park Wood   Stobswood   WIDDRINGTON   Cresswell

Earsdon Moor   Ulgham Park   Widdrington Station

Tritlington Broom   Ulgham Grange Fm.   Hagg Fm.   Ellington

Bailiff's Letch   Ulgham   Warkworthlane Cott.

18   20   22   24   26   28   30

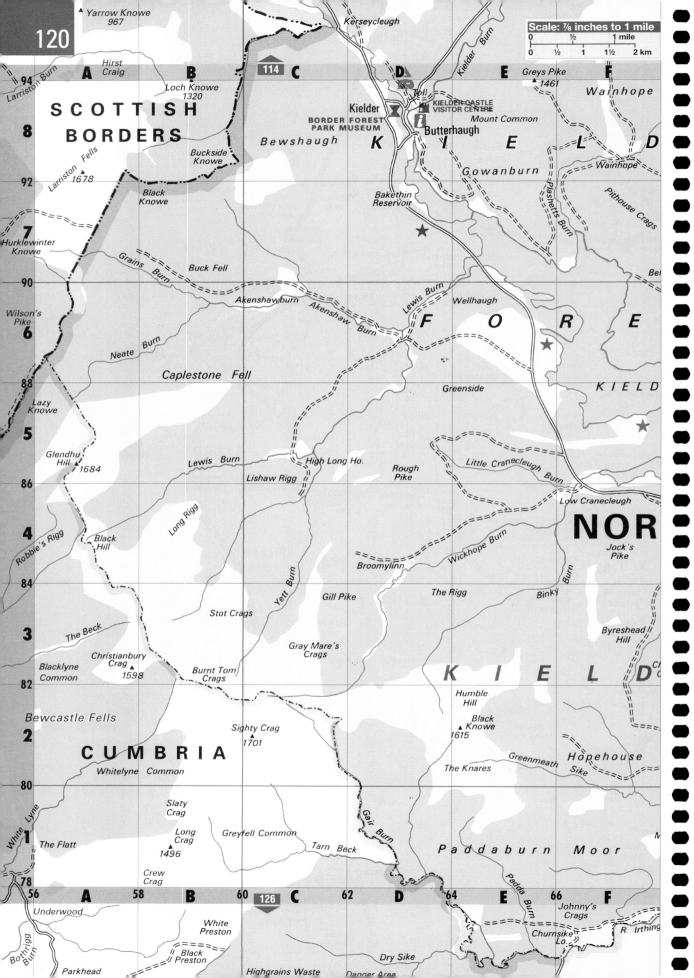

Scale: 7/8 inches to 1 mile

SCOTTISH BORDERS

CUMBRIA

Yarrow Knowe 967
Kerseycleugh
Hirst Craig
Loch Knowe 1320
Buckside Knowe
Black Knowe
Larriston Fells 1678
Hurklewinter Knowe
Wilson's Pike
Lazy Knowe
Glendhu Hill 1684
Robbie's Rigg
Black Hill
The Beck
Blacklyne Common
Christianbury Crag 1598
Burnt Tom Crags
Bewcastle Fells
Sighty Crag 1701
Whitelyne Common
Slaty Crag
Long Crag 1496
Crew Crag
Greyfell Common
The Flatt
White Lyne
Bothrigg Burn
Parkhead
Underwood
White Preston
Black Preston
Highgrains Waste
Danger Area
Dry Sike
Tarn Beck
Gail Burn
Padda Burn
Paddaburn Moor
Johnny's Crags
Churnsike Lo.
R. Irthing

Larriston Burn
Grains Burn
Buck Fell
Akenshawburn
Akenshaw Burn
Neate Burn
Caplestone Fell
Lewis Burn
High Long Ho.
Lishaw Rigg
Long Rigg
Yett Burn
Stot Crags
Gray Mare's Crags
Gill Pike
Broomylinn
Wickhope Burn
Rough Pike
Greenside
Lewis Burn
Wellhaugh
Low Cranecleugh
Little Cranecleugh Burn
Binky Burn
The Rigg
Jock's Pike
Byreshead Hill
Humble Hill
Black Knowe 1615
The Knares
Greenmeath Sike
Hopehouse

KIELDER FOREST

Kielder
BORDER FOREST PARK MUSEUM
Bewshaugh
KIELDER CASTLE VISITOR CENTRE
Toll
Butterhaugh
Mount Common
Gowanburn
Bakethin Reservoir
Kielder Burn
Greys Pike 1461
Wainhope
Wainhope
Pithouse Crags
Plasherts Burn

NOR

114
126

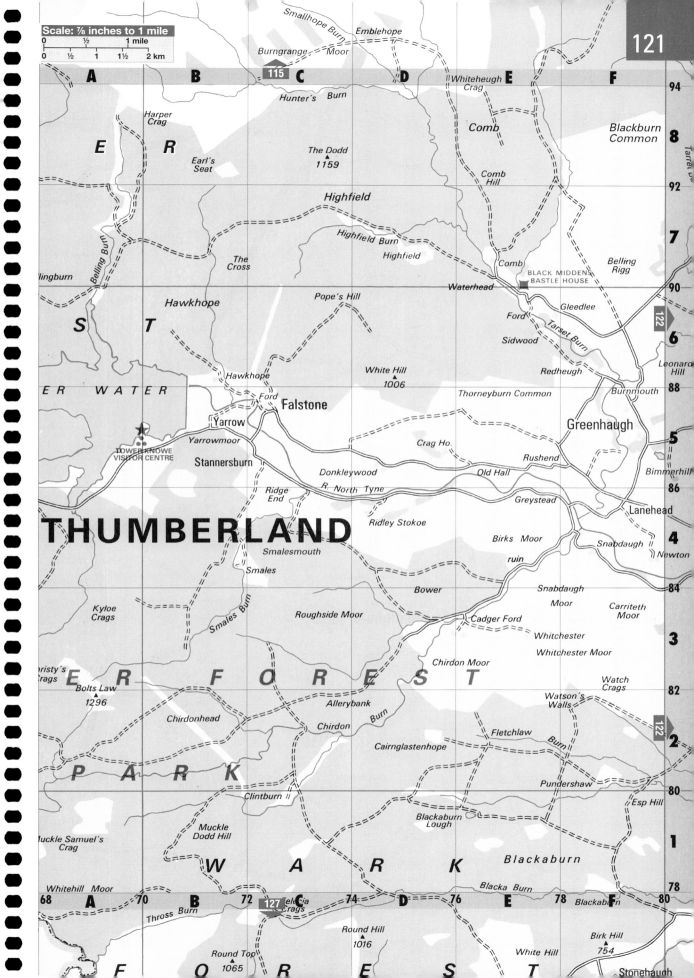

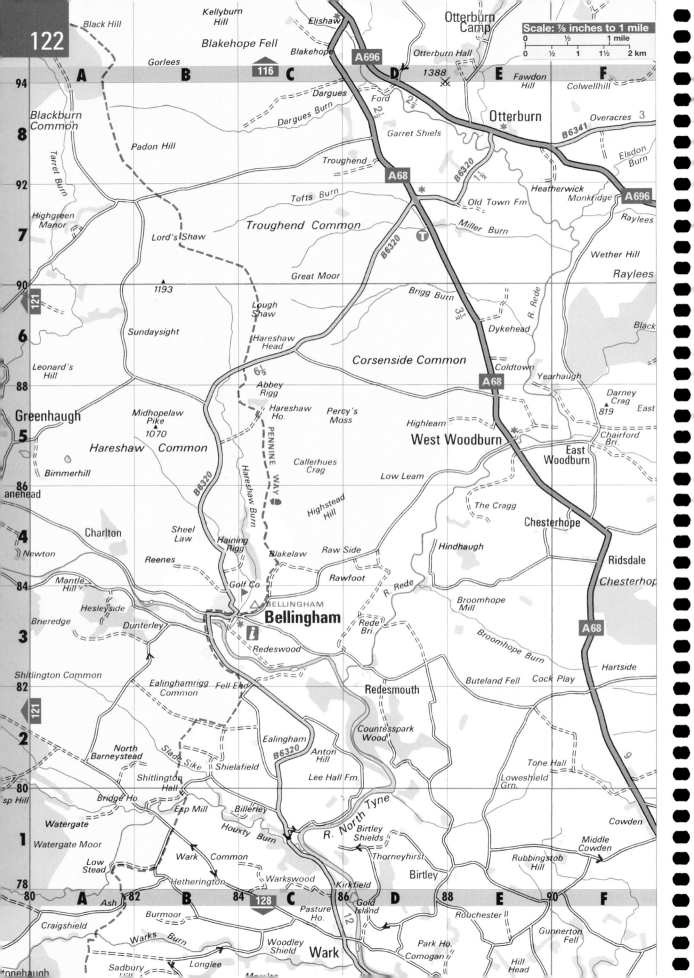

Scale: ⅞ inches to 1 mile

Black Hill
Gorlees
Kellyburn Hill
Blakehope Fell
Blakehope
Elishaw
Otterburn Camp
Otterburn Hall
1388
Fawdon Hill
Colwellhill

Blackburn Common
Dargues
Dargues Burn
Ford
Garret Shiels
Otterburn
Overacres
Elsdon Burn

Padon Hill
Troughend
Tofts Burn
Heatherwick
Monkridge
Raylees

Highgreen Manor
Lord's Shaw
Troughend Common
Old Town Fm.
Miller Burn
Wether Hill
Raylees

1193
Great Moor
Brigg Burn
Dykehead
R. Rede
Black

Lough Shaw
Sundaysight
Hareshaw Head
Corsenside Common
Coldtown
Yearhaugh

Leonard's Hill
6½
Abbey Rigg
Hareshaw Ho.
Percy's Moss
Highleam
Darney Crag 819
East

Greenhaugh
Midhopelaw Pike 1070
West Woodburn
Chairford Bri.

Hareshaw Common
Hareshaw Burn
Callerhues Crag
Low Leam
East Woodburn

Bimmerhill
PENNINE WAY
Highstead Hill
The Cragg
Chesterhope

anehead
Charlton
Sheel Law
Haining Rigg
Raw Side
Hindhaugh
Ridsdale

Newton
Reenes
Blakelaw
Rawfoot
Chesterhope

Mantle Hill
Golf Co.
R. Rede
Broomhope Mill
A68

Hesleyside
Bellingham
Rede Bri.
Broomhope Burn
Hartside

Brieredge
Dunterley
Redeswood
Buteland Fell
Cock Play

Shitlington Common
Ealinghamrigg Common
Fell End
Redesmouth
Countesspark Wood

North Barneystead
Ealingham
Anton Hill
Tone Hall
Loweshield Grn.

Slade Sike
Shielafield
Lee Hall Fm.
Cowden

Shitlington Hall
Bridge Ho.
Esp Mill
Billerley
Houxty Burn
R. North Tyne
Birtley Shields
Middle Cowden

Watergate
Watergate Moor
Wark Common
Thorneyhirst
Birtley
Rubbingstob Hill

Low Stead
Hetherington
Warkswood
Kirkfield
Gold Island

Craigshield
Burmoor
Pasture Ho.
Roucester
Gunnerton Fell

Warks Burn
Woodley Shield
Wark
Park Ho. Comogan
Hill Head

Sadbury
Longlee

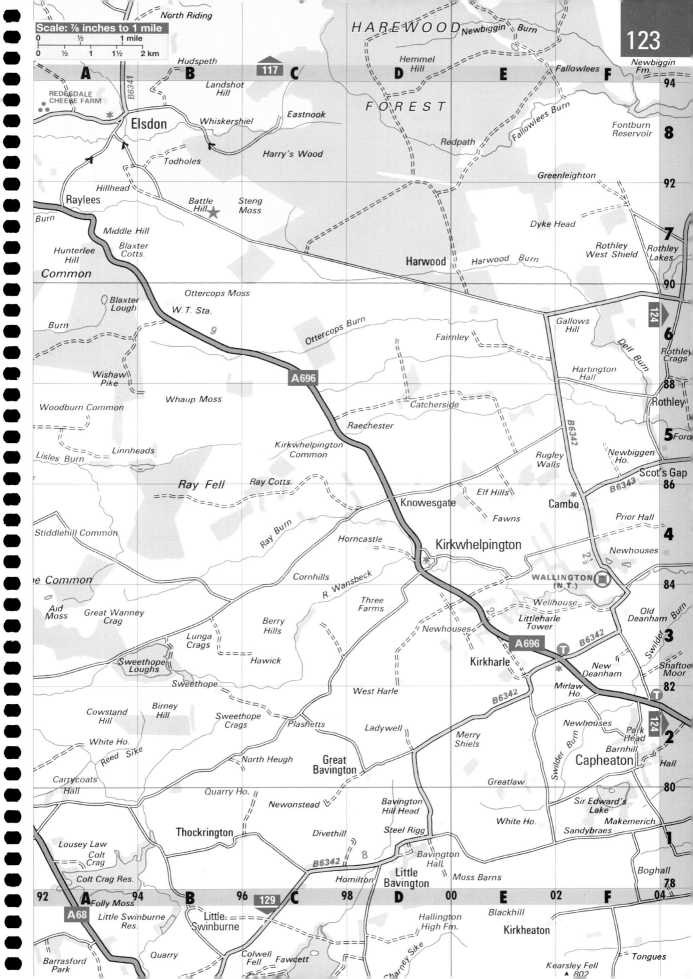

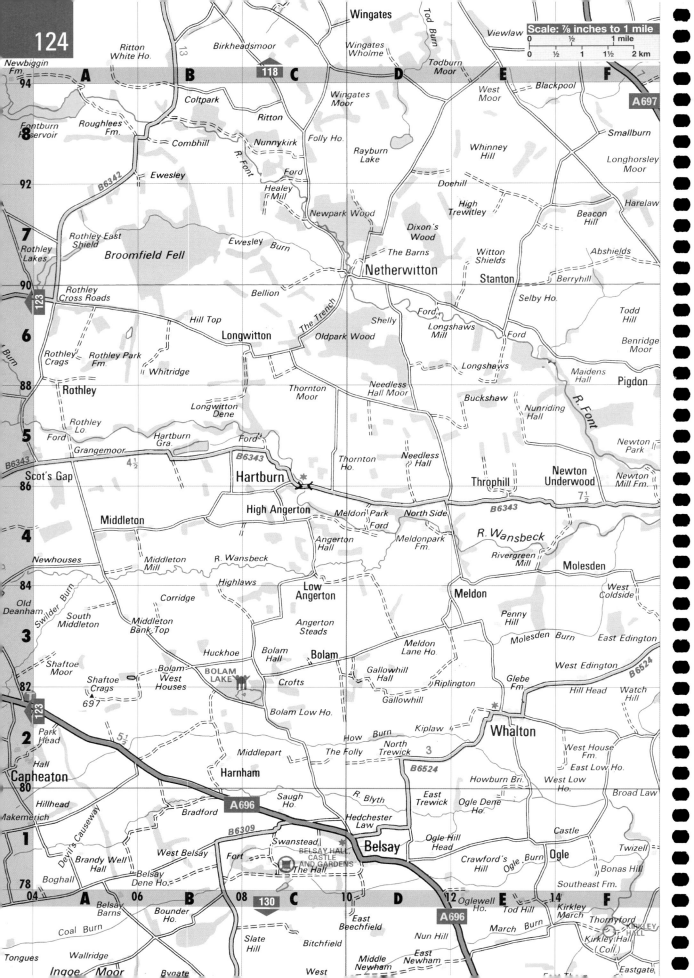

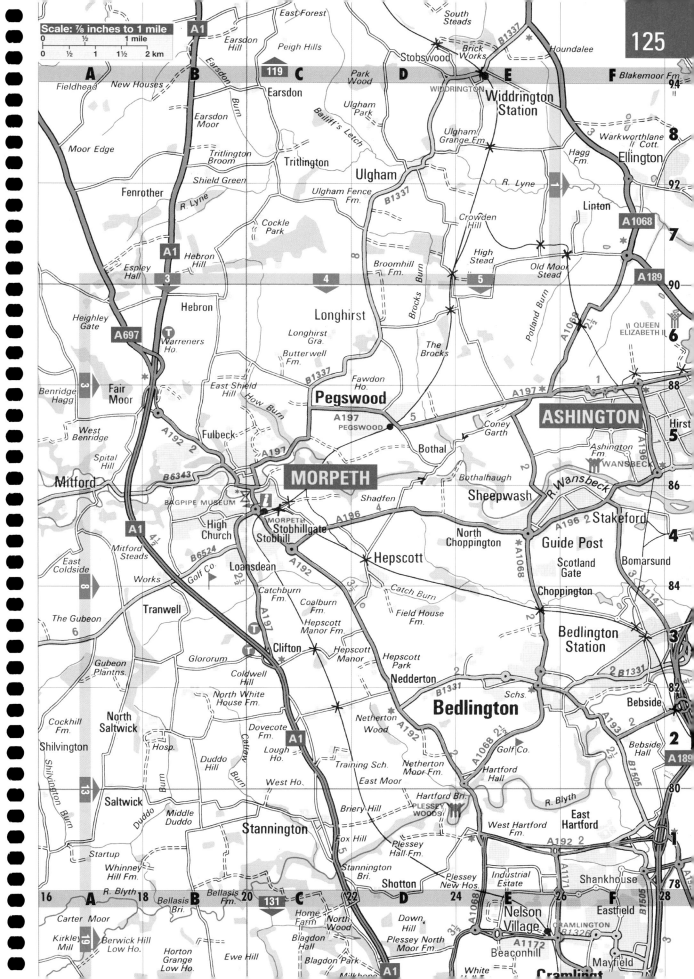

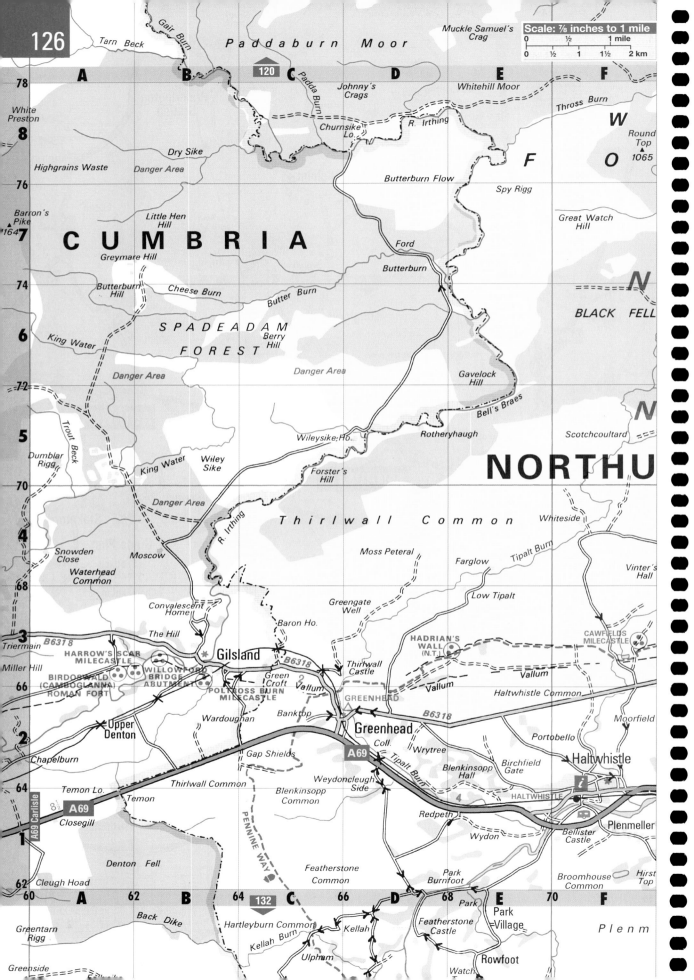

Tarn Beck
Gair Burn
Paddaburn Moor
Muckle Samuel's Crag

A   B   120   C   Padda Burn   D   E   F

78

Johnny's Crags
Whitehill Moor
Thross Burn

White Preston

8

Churnsike Lo.
R. Irthing
W O F O

76

Dry Sike
Danger Area
Butterburn Flow
Spy Rigg

Highgrains Waste

Round Top 1065

Barron's Pike 1164

7

Little Hen Hill
CUMBRIA
Ford
Butterburn
Great Watch Hill

74

Greymare Hill
Cheese Burn
Butter Burn
Butterburn

BLACK FELL

Butterburn Hill

6

SPADEADAM
Berry Hill

King Water
FOREST
N

72

Danger Area
Danger Area
Gavelock Hill

Trout Beck
Bell's Braes
N

5

Wileysike Ho.
Rotheryhaugh
Scotchcoultard

Dumblar Rigg
King Water
Wiley Sike
NORTHU

70

Forster's Hill

Danger Area
Thirlwall   Common
Whiteside

4

R. Irthing
Moss Peteral
Farglow
Tipalt Burn
Vinter's Hall

Snowden Close
Moscow
Greengate Well
Low Tipalt

68

Waterhead Common
Convalescent Home
Baron Ho.

3

Triermain
B6318
The Hill
HADRIAN'S WALL (N.T.)
CAWFIELDS MILECASTLE

Miller Hill
HARROW'S SCAR MILECASTLE
Gilsland
B6318
Thirlwall Castle
Vallum
Vallum

66

BIRDOSWALD (CAMBOGLANNA) ROMAN FORT
WILLOWFORD BRIDGE ABUTMENT
Green Croft
GREENHEAD
Haltwhistle Common

POLTROSS BURN MILECASTLE
Vallum

Upper Denton
Wardoughan
Banktop
Greenhead
B6318
Moorfield

2

Chapelburn
Gap Shields
Coll.
Wrytree
Blenkinsopp Hall
Birchfield Gate
Portobello
Haltwhistle

64

Temon Lo.
Thirlwall Common
Weydoncleugh Side
HALTWHISTLE

A69 Carlisle
8½ A69
Temon
Blenkinsopp Common
Tipalt Burn
Redpeth
Bellister Castle
Plenmeller

1

Closegill
PENNINE WAY
Wydon

Denton Fell
Featherstone Common
Park Burnfoot
Broomhouse Common
Hirst Top

62

Cleugh Hoad
A   62   B   64   132   C   66   D   68   Park   E   70   F

Greentarn Rigg
Back Dike
Hartleyburn Common
Kellah Burn
Kellah
Featherstone Castle
Park Village
Plenm

Greenside
Ulpham
Watch
Rowfoot

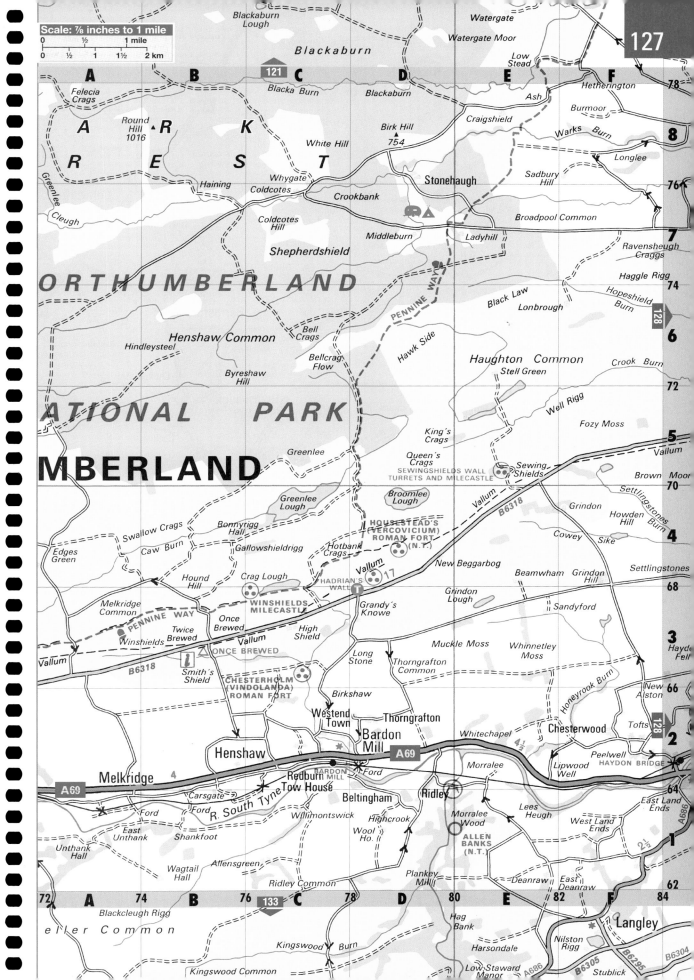

Scale: ⅞ inches to 1 mile

0   ½   1 mile
0   ½   1   1½   2 km

A   B   121   C   D   E   F   78

8
7
6
5
4
3
2
1

Felecia Crags

Round Hill 1016   R

Blacka Burn   Blackaburn   Ash   Hetherington

Birk Hill 754   Craigshield   Burmoor

A   R   K   E   S   T

Warks   Burn   Longlee

White Hill   Stonehaugh   Sadbury Hill

Haining   Whygate   Crookbank   Broadpool Common
Coldcotes

Greenlee Cleugh   Coldcotes Hill   Middleburn   Ladyhill   Ravensheugh Craggs

Shepherdshield   Haggle Rigg

ORTHUMBERLAND   Black Law   Hopeshield Burn
Lonbrough   128

Henshaw Common   Bell Crags   Hawk Side   Haughton Common   Crook Burn
Hindleysteel   Stell Green

Byreshaw Hill   Bellcrag Flow   Well Rigg

ATIONAL   PARK   King's Crags   Fozy Moss

MBERLAND   Greenlee   Queen's Crags   Sewing Shields   Brown Moor
SEWINGSHIELDS WALL TURRETS AND MILECASTLE   Vallum

Swallow Crags   Greenlee Lough   Broomlee Lough   Grindon   Settlingstones Burn
Bonnyrigg Hall   HOUSESTEAD'S (VERCOVICIUM) ROMAN FORT (N.T.)   B6318   Howden Hill

Caw Burn   Gallowshieldrigg   Hotbank Crags   Cowey   Sike

Edges Green   New Beggarbog   Beamwham   Grindon Hill   Settlingstones

Hound Hill   Crag Lough   Vallum   17
Melkridge Common   HADRIAN'S WALL   Grindon Lough   Sandyford
WINSHIELDS MILECASTLE   Grandy's Knowe   Muckle Moss   Whinnetley Moss   Hayde Fell

PENNINE WAY   Once Brewed   High Shield   Long Stone   Thorngrafton Common   Honeyrook Burn   New Alston
Winshields   Twice Brewed   Vallum   ONCE BREWED   Birkshaw   Chesterwood   Tofts   128
Vallum   B6318   Smith's Shield   CHESTERHOLM (VINDOLANDA) ROMAN FORT   Westend Town   Thorngrafton   Whitechapel   Lipwood Well   Peelwell   HAYDON BRIDGE
Henshaw   Bardon Mill   A69   Morralee   HAYDON BRIDGE
Melkridge   A69   Redburn   Tow House   Beltingham   Ridley   Lees Heugh   East Land Ends
Carsgate   R. South Tyne   Ford   Morralee Wood   West Land Ends
Ford   Ford   Willimontswick   Highcrook   ALLEN BANKS (N.T.)
East Unthank   Shankfoot   Wool Ho.
Unthank Hall   Wagtail Hall   Allensgreen   Ridley Common   Plankey Mill   Deanraw   East Deanraw

72   A   74   B   76   133   C   78   D   80   E   82   F   84   62

eller   Common   Blackcleugh Rigg   Hag Bank   Langley
Kingswood   Burn   Harsondale   Nilston Rigg   B6295   B6304
Kingswood Common   Low Staward Manor   A686   B6305   Stublick

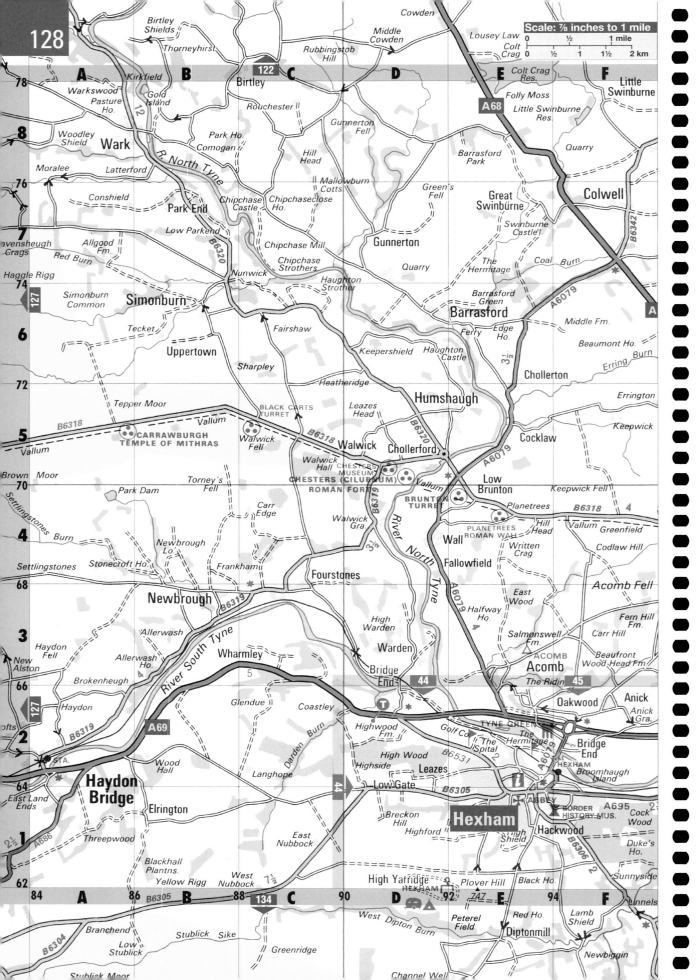

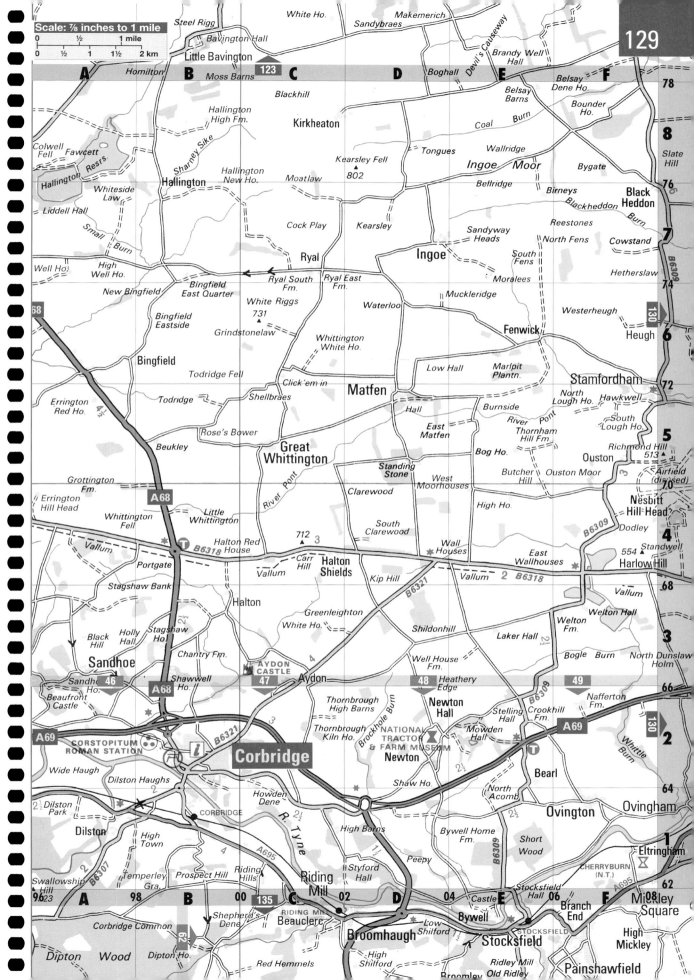

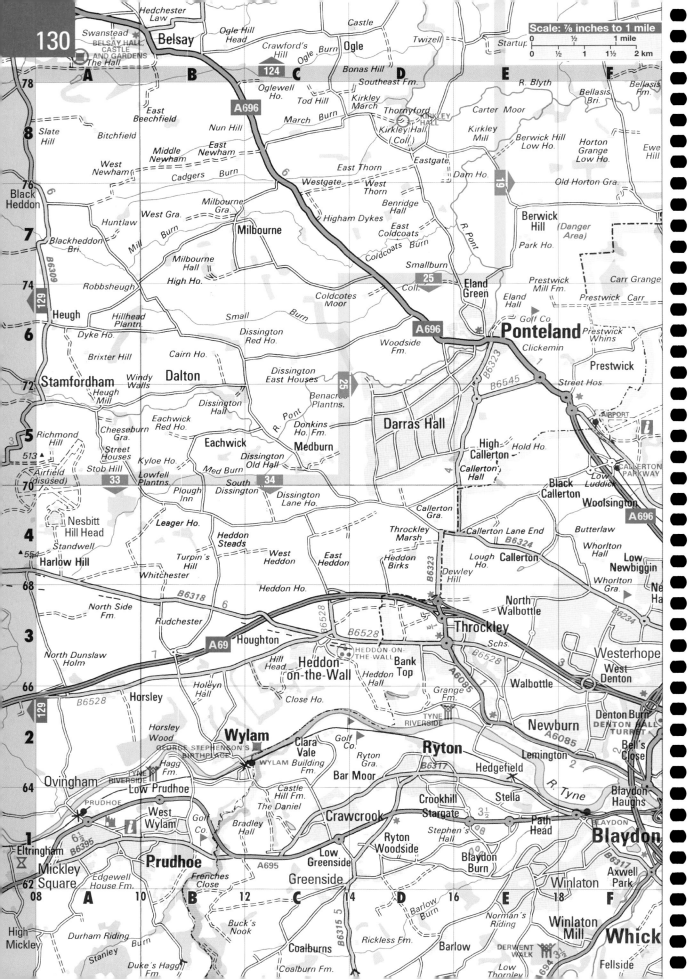

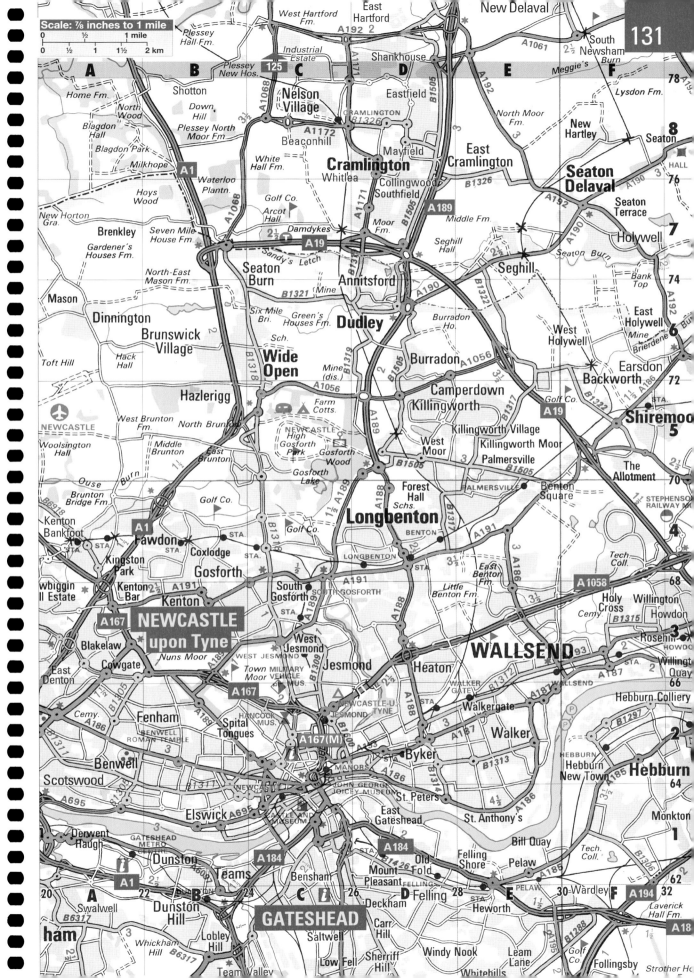

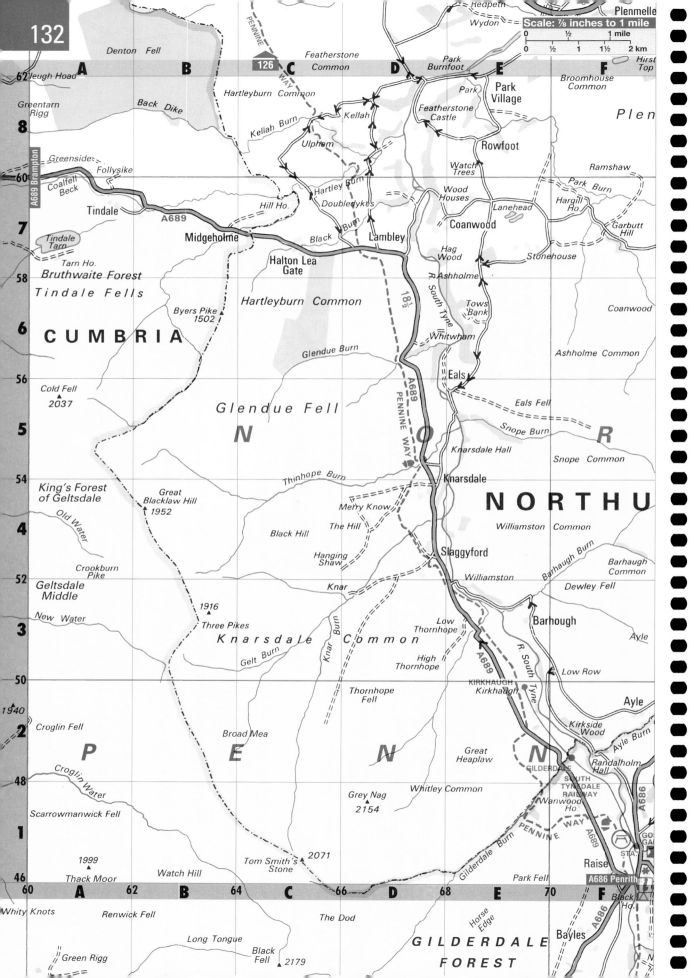

Scale: ⅞ inches to 1 mile

A **B** 126 **C** **D** **E** **F**

62 Jeugh Hoad

Denton Fell

Heapeth
Wydon
Plenmelle

Featherstone
Common

Park
Burnfoot

Broomhouse
Common

Hirst
Top

8

Greentarn
Rigg

Back Dike

Hartleyburn Common

Kellah

Park

Park Village

P l e n

Kellah Burn

Featherstone
Castle

Rowfoot

Ramshaw

60

Greenside
Follysike

Coalfell
Beck

Hartley Burn

Watch
Trees

Park
Burn

Hargill
Ho.

7

Tindale

A689

Hill Ho.

Doubledykes

Wood
Houses

Lanehead

Garbutt
Hill

Midgeholme

Black Burn

Lambley

Coanwood

58

Tarn Ho.

Halton Lea
Gate

Hag
Wood

Stonehouse

Bruthwaite Forest

R. Ashholme

Coanwood

T i n d a l e   F e l l s

Hartleyburn   Common

Tows
Bank

Ashholme Common

6

C U M B R I A

Byers Pike
1502

18½

Whitwham

56

Glendue Burn

Eals

Cold Fell
2037

G l e n d u e   F e l l

Eals Fell

5

N

O

Snope Burn

R

Knarsdale Hall

Snope   Common

54

King's Forest
of Geltsdale

Thinhope Burn

Knarsdale

N O R T H U

Great
Blacklaw Hill
1952

Merry Know

Williamston Common

4

Old Water

Black Hill

The Hill

Slaggyford

Barhaugh Burn

Barhaugh
Common

52

Geltsdale
Middle

Hanging
Shaw

Williamston

Dewley Fell

New Water

Crookburn
Pike

Knar

Barhough

Ayle

3

1916

Knar Burn

Low
Thornhope

Low Row

Three Pikes

K n a r s d a l e   C o m m o n

Gelt Burn

High
Thornhope

A689

R. South Tyne

50

Croglin Fell

Broad Mea

Thornhope
Fell

KIRKHAUGH
Kirkhaugh

Ayle

1940

P

E

N

N

Kirkside
Wood

Ayle Burn

2

Croglin Water

Great
Heaplaw

GILDERDALE

Randalholm
Hall

48

Scarrowmanwick Fell

Whitley Common

Grey Nag
2154

SOUTH
TYNEDALE
RAILWAY

Wanwood
Ho.

PENNINE   WAY

1

1999

2071

Tom Smith's
Stone

STA.

Raise

A686 Penrith

46

Thack Moor

Watch Hill

Park Fell

Gilderdale Burn

Black
Ho.

60 **A** **62** **B** **64** **C** 66 **D** **68** **E** **70** **F**

Whity Knots

Renwick Fell

The Dod

Horse
Edge

Bayles

Green Rigg

Long Tongue

Black
Fell   2179

G I L D E R D A L E
F O R E S T

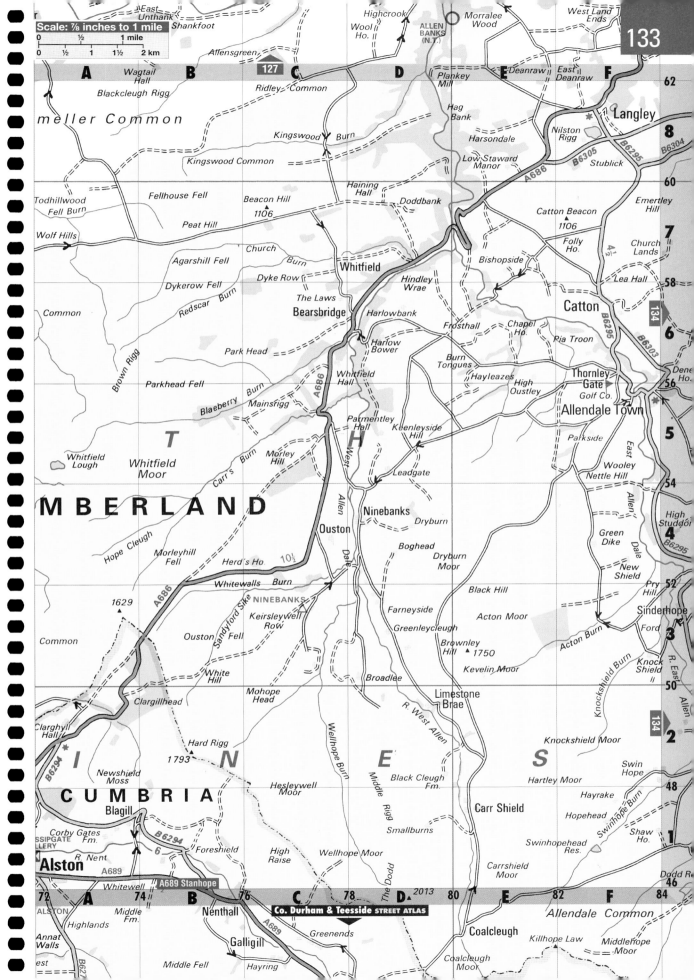

Scale: ⅞ inches to 1 mile
0   ½   1 mile
0   ½   1   1½   2 km

East Unthank
Shankfoot
Highcrook
Wool Ho.
Morralee Wood
West Land Ends

ALLEN BANKS (N.T.)

A Wagtail Hall **B** Allensgreen **127** **C** **D** Plankey Mill **E** Deanraw East Deanraw **F** 62

Blackcleugh Rigg
Ridley Common
Hag Bank
Langley
Nilston Rigg
B6305
B6304
8

meller Common
Kingswood Burn
Harsondale
Low Staward Manor
A686
Stublick
B6295

Kingswood Common
Haining Hall
Doddbank
Catton Beacon 1106
Folly Ho.
Emertley Hill
60

Todhillwood Fell Burn
Fellhouse Fell
Beacon Hill 1106
Peat Hill
Church Burn
Whitfield
Hindley Wrae
Bishopside
4½
Church Lands
7

Wolf Hills
Agarshill Fell
Dyke Row
The Laws
Lea Hall
58

Dykerow Fell
Redscar Burn
Bearsbridge
Harlowbank
Frosthall
Chapel Ho.
Pia Troon
Catton
B6303
6

Common
Brown Rigg
Park Head
Harlow Bower
Burn Tongues
Hayleazes
High Oustley
Thornley Gate
Golf Co.
Dene Ho.
56

Parkhead Fell
Whitfield Hall
A686
Parmentley Hall
Keenleyside Hill
Allendale Town
Parkside
East Allen Dale
5

Whitfield Lough
Whitfield Moor
Blaeberry Burn
Mainsrigg
Morley Hill
Leadgate
West Allen Dale
Wooley
Nettle Hill
54

Carr's Burn
Ouston
Ninebanks
Dryburn
Green Dike
High Studdon
B6295
4

M B E R L A N D
Hope Cleugh
Morleyhill Fell
Herd's Ho. 10½
Whitewalls Burn
Boghead
Dryburn Moor
New Shield
Pry Hill
52

1629
Sandyford Sike
NINEBANKS
Keirsleywell Row
Farneyside
Black Hill
Acton Moor
Acton Burn
Sinderhope
Ford
3

Common
A686
Ouston Fell
Greenleycleugh
Brownley Hill 1750
Kevelin Moor
Knockshield Burn
Knock Shield
R. East Allen

Clarghyll Hall
Clargillhead
White Hill
Broadlee
Limestone Brae
R. West Allen
Knockshield Moor
134
2

Hard Rigg 1793
Mohope Head
Wellhope Burn
Swin Hope
48

I N E S
Newshield Moss
Hesleywell Moor
Middle Rigg
Black Cleugh Fm.
Hartley Moor
Hayrake
Hopehead
Swinhope Burn
Shaw Ho.
1

C U M B R I A
Blagill
B6294
Foreshield
High Raise
Wellhope Moor
Smallburns
Carr Shield
Swinhopehead Res.
Carrshield Moor

Corby Gates Fm.
SSIPGATE LLERY
R. Nent
B6294
6

Alston
A689
Whitewell
A689 Stanhope
Co. Durham & Teesside STREET ATLAS
Coalcleugh
Killhope Law
Middlehope Moor

ALSTON Middle Fm. Highlands
Nenthall
Greenends
2013
Allendale Common

Galligill
Middle Fell
Hayring
The Dodd
Coalcleugh Moor
Dodd Rd.
46

72 **A** **74** **B** **76** **C** **78** **D** **80** **E** **82** **F** **84**

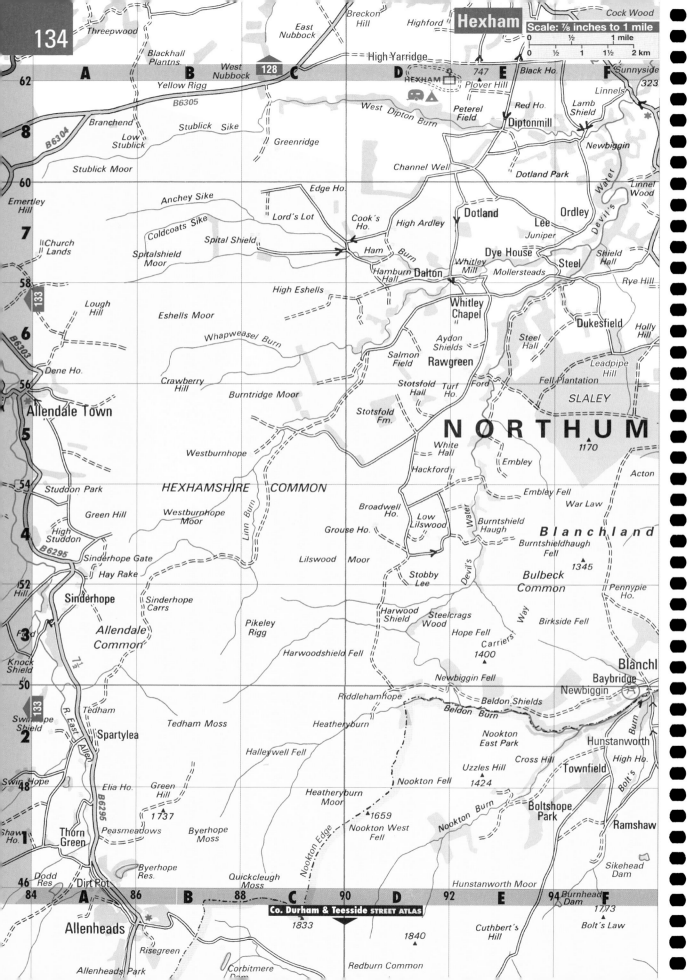

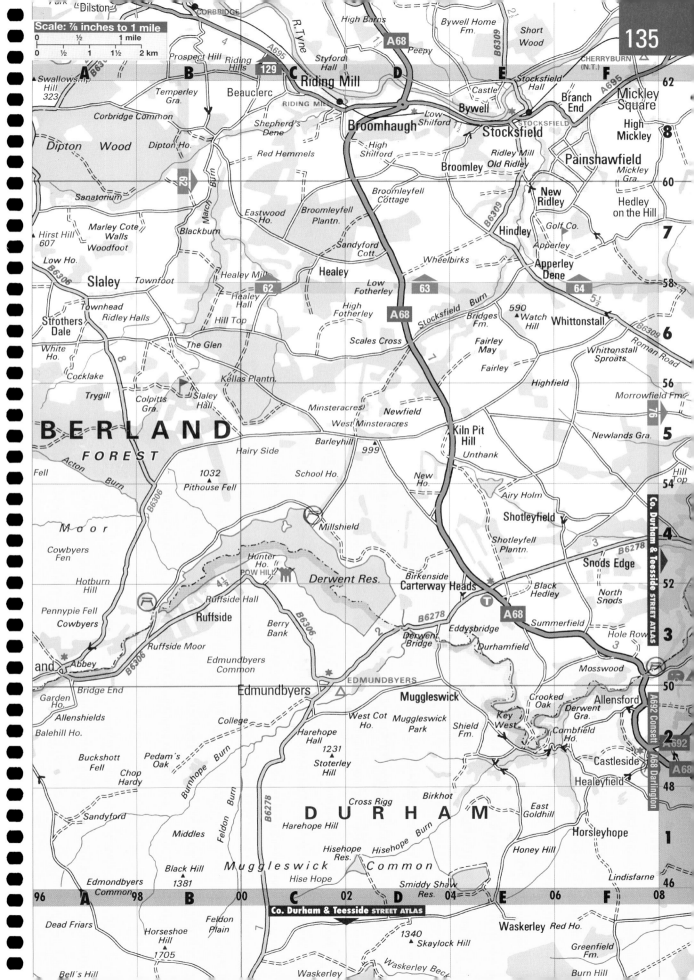

Scale: ⅞ inches to 1 mile

½ 1 mile
½ 1 1½ 2 km

A **B** 129 **C** **D** **E** **F**

CORRIDGE
Dilston
Park
High Barns
Bywell Home Fm.
Short Wood
CHERRYBURN (N.T.)

R. Tyne
A695
A68
Peepy
B6309

Swallowship Hill 323
Prospect Hill
Riding Hills
Styford Hall
Riding Mill
Castle
Stocksfield Hall
Branch End
Mickley Square
62

Temperley Gra.
Beauclerc
Bywell
Stocksfield
High Mickley
8

Corbridge Common
Shepherd's Dene
Broomhaugh
Low Shilford
STOCKSFIELD
Painshawfield

Dipton Wood
Dipton Ho.
Red Hemmels
High Shilford
Broomley
Ridley Mill
Old Ridley
Mickley Gra.

62
Sanatorium
Broomleyfell Plantn.
Broomleyfell Cottage
New Ridley
Hedley on the Hill
60

Marley Cote Walls
Blackburn
Eastwood Ho.
Hindley
Golf Co.
Apperley
7

Hirst Hill 607
Woodfoot
Sandyford Cott.
Wheelbirks
Apperley Dene

Low Ho.
B6306
Healey Mill
Healey
Low Fotherley
63
Stocksfield Burn
64
5½
58

Slaley
Townfoot
Healey Hall
High Fotherley
A68
Bridges Fm.
590
Watch Hill
Whittonstall
Roman Road
6

Strothers Dale
Townhead
Ridley Halls
Hill Top
Scales Cross
Fairley May
Whittonstall Sproats

White Ho.
The Glen
Fairley
56

Cocklake
Kellas Plantn.
Highfield
Morrowfield Fm.

Trygill
Colpitts Gra.
Slaley Hall
Minsteracres
Newfield
Newlands Gra.
76
5

B E R L A N D
West Minsteracres
Kiln Pit Hill

F O R E S T
Hairy Side
Barleyhill
999
Unthank
Hill Top
54

Fell
Acton Burn
1032
Pithouse Fell
School Ho.
New Ho.
Airy Holm

Moor
Millshield
Shotleyfield
Snods Edge
B6278
4

Cowbyers Fen
Hunter Ho.
POW HILL
Shotleyfell Plantn.
3
52

Hotburn Hill
Derwent Res.
Birkenside
Carterway Heads
Black Hedley
North Snods

Pennypie Fell
Cowbyers
Ruffside Hall
A68
Summerfield
Hole Row
3

Ruffside
Berry Bank
B6306
Derwent Bridge
B6278
Eddysbridge
Durhamfield
Mosswood

and
Abbey
Ruffside Moor
2
Edmundbyers Common
EDMUNDBYERS
Crooked Oak
Derwent Gra.
Allensford
50

Bridge End
College
Muggleswick
Key West
Combfield Ho.
Castleside
A692 Consett

Garden Ho.
Allenshields
Harehope Hall
West Cot Ho.
Muggleswick Park
Shield Fm.
Healeyfield
2
A68 Darlington
48

Balehill Ho.
Pedam's Oak
1231
Stoterley Hill
East Goldhill
Horsleyhope
A692

Buckshott Fell
Chop Hardy
Bunhope Burn
Cross Rigg
Birkhot
Honey Hill
1

Sandyford
Middles
Feldon Burn
B6278
Harehope Hill
Hisehope Burn
Lindisfarne

Edmondbyers Common
Black Hill 1381
M u g g l e s w i c k
Hisehope Res.
C o m m o n
Smiddy Shaw Res.
46

96 **A** 98 **B** 00 **C** 02 **D** 04 **E** 06 **F** 08

Dead Friars
Horseshoe Hill 1705
Feldon Plain
Hise Hope
Waskerley
Red Ho.

Bell's Hill
Waskerley
1340
Skaylock Hill
Waskerley Beck
Greenfield Fm.
Burn Hill

Co. Durham & Teesside STREET ATLAS

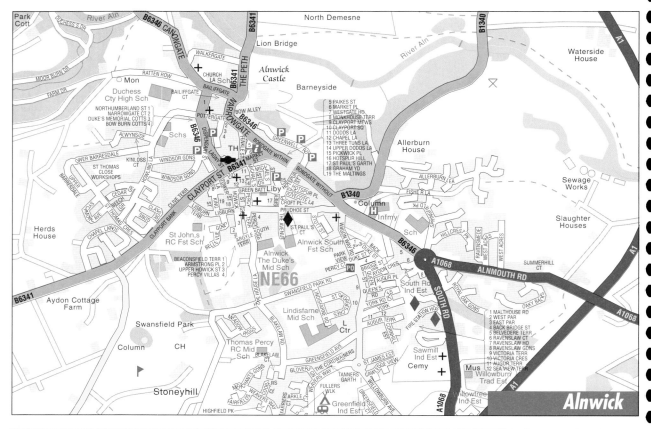

Alnwick

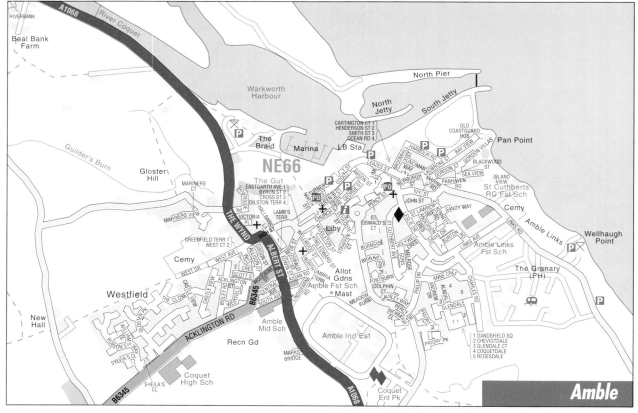

Amble

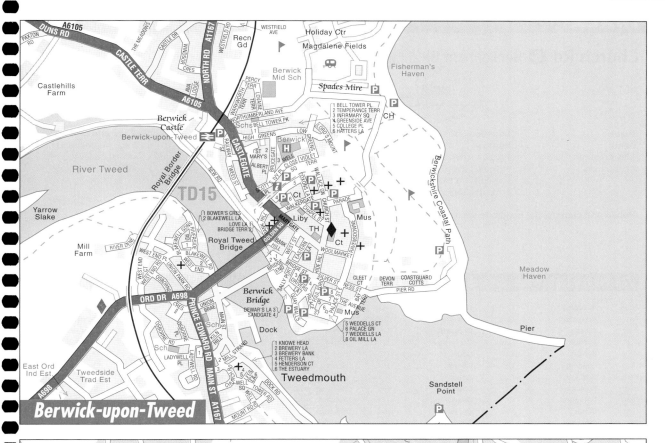

Berwick-upon-Tweed

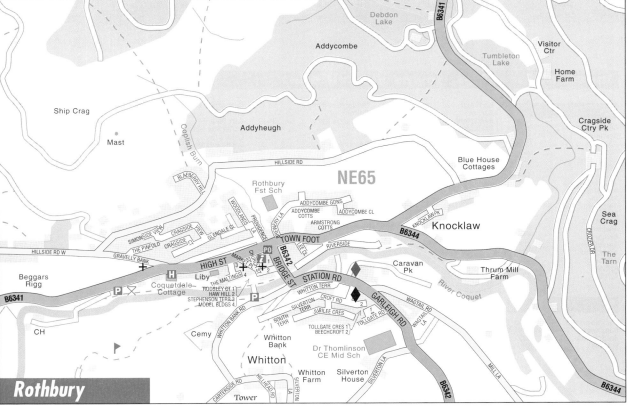

Rothbury

Index

Church Rd **6** Beckenham BR2..........**53** C6

Place name	Location number	Locality, town or village	Postcode district	Page and grid square
May be abbreviated on the map	Present when a number indicates the place's position in a crowded area of mapping	Shown when more than one place has the same name	District for the indexed place	Page number and grid reference for the standard mapping

Public and commercial buildings are highlighted in magenta   **Places of interest** are highlighted in blue with a star★

Abbreviations used in the index

Acad	**Academy**	Comm	**Common**	Gd	**Ground**	L	**Leisure**	Prom	**Prom**
App	**Approach**	Cott	**Cottage**	Gdn	**Garden**	La	**Lane**	Rd	**Road**
Arc	**Arcade**	Cres	**Crescent**	Gn	**Green**	Liby	**Library**	Recn	**Recreation**
Ave	**Avenue**	Cswy	**Causeway**	Gr	**Grove**	Mdw	**Meadow**	Ret	**Retail**
Bglw	**Bungalow**	Ct	**Court**	H	**Hall**	Meml	**Memorial**	Sh	**Shopping**
Bldg	**Building**	Ctr	**Centre**	Ho	**House**	Mkt	**Market**	Sq	**Square**
Bsns, Bus	**Business**	Ctry	**Country**	Hospl	**Hospital**	Mus	**Museum**	St	**Street**
Bvd	**Boulevard**	Cty	**County**	HQ	**Headquarters**	Orch	**Orchard**	Sta	**Station**
Cath	**Cathedral**	Dr	**Drive**	Hts	**Heights**	Pal	**Palace**	Terr	**Terrace**
Cir	**Circus**	Dro	**Drove**	Ind	**Industrial**	Par	**Parade**	TH	**Town Hall**
Cl	**Close**	Ed	**Education**	Inst	**Institute**	Pas	**Passage**	Univ	**University**
Cnr	**Corner**	Emb	**Embankment**	Int	**International**	Pk	**Park**	Wk, Wlk	**Walk**
Coll	**College**	Est	**Estate**	Intc	**Interchange**	Pl	**Place**	Wr	**Water**
Com	**Community**	Ex	**Exhibition**	Junc	**Junction**	Prec	**Precinct**	Yd	**Yard**

Index of localities, towns and villages

A

Abberwick 112 E2
Acklington 119 C4
Acomb 45 A8
Acomb 128 E3
Adderstone 108 F3
Akeld 107 C2
Allanton 104 A7
Allendale Town 133 F5
Allensford 135 F2
Alnham 111 D1
Alnmouth 113 E1
Alnwick 113 B2
Alston 132 F1
Alwinton 116 F7
Amble 119 E6
Ancroft 105 B2
Annitsford 22 B1
Ashington 6 B3
Aydon 129 C3
Ayle 132 F2

B

Backworth 30 C4
Bamburgh 109 B5
Bardon Mill 127 C2
Barelees 106 E7

Barhough 132 E3
Barlow 67 C6
Barrasford 128 D6
Baybridge 134 F3
Beadnell 109 E2
Beal 105 E1
Beamish 80 D2
Beanley 112 C5
Bearsbridge 133 D6
Bebside 16 E7
Bedlington 11 A1
Belford 108 E4
Bellingham 122 B3
Bellshill 108 F3
Belsay 124 D1
Beltingham 127 D1
Berrington 105 B1
Berwick-upon-Tweed ..105 A6
Biddick Hall 59 B2
Bilton 113 D1
Bingfield 129 A6
Birgham 106 A7
Birling 119 D7
Birtley 82 D4
Birtley 122 D1
Black Heddon 129 F7
Blackhall Mill 77 B7
Blagill 133 A1
Blanchland 135 A3
Blaydon 53 E3
Blyth 17 C7
Bolam 124 C3

Boldon Colliery 58 E1
Bolton 112 D2
Boltshope Park 134 F1
Bothal 5 B2
Boulmer 113 F3
Bournmoor 89 D3
Bowsden 107 E8
Brandon 112 A4
Branton 112 A4
Branxton 106 F6
Brockley Whins 58 F3
Broomhill 119 D4
Brownieside 113 A7
Brunswick Village ...28 A6
Brunton 113 C8
Budle 109 A5
Burdon 92 B3
Burnopfield 79 A6
Burnside 90 B3
Burradon 117 C7
Butterhaugh 120 D8
Byermoor 79 D7
Byrness 115 D5
Bywell 63 F8

C

Callaly 117 F8
Cambo 123 F4
Cambois 12 C5

Capheaton 123 F2
Carham 106 A7
Carr Shield 133 E1
Carterway Heads 135 E3
Cartington 117 E6
Castle Heaton 107 A8
Castleside 135 F2
Catton 133 F6
Causey Park Bridge ..119 A1
Charlton 122 A4
Chathill 109 C1
Chatton 108 B2
Chester le Street ...88 D4
Chesterhope 122 F4
Chesterwood 127 F2
Cheswick 105 C3
Chillingham 108 B1
Chirnside 104 A8
Chollerford 128 D5
Chollerton 128 E6
Choppington 10 E5
Chopwell 66 B1
Christon Bank 113 C7
Cleadon 60 B1
Coanwood 132 E7
Cocklaw 128 E5
Coldstream 106 D7
Colwell 128 F7
Corbridge 47 B5
Cornhill-on-Tweed ...106 E7
Coupland 107 B3

Cramlington 21 F5
Craster 113 E5
Crawcrook 51 E4
Cresswell 2 A7
Crookham 107 A7
Crookham Eastfield ..107 A7

D

Dalton 130 B5
Dalton 134 D7
Denwick 113 C3
Detchant 108 D6
Dinnington 27 B7
Dipton 78 D1
Diptonmill 134 E8
Doddington 107 E4
Donaldson's Lodge ...106 E8
Dotland 134 E7
Doxford 113 B7
Druridge 119 E2
Duddo 104 D1
Dudley 29 A7
Dukesfield 134 F6
Dunstan 113 E5
Dunston 54 F1
Dye House 134 E7

E

Eachwick	130	B5
Eals	132	E6
Earle	107	E1
Earsdon	31	A5
Earsdon	125	C8
Easington	108	F5
Easington Lane	97	D8
East Boldon	74	D7
East Cramlington	22	E5
East Hartford	16	B3
East Horton	108	A3
East Kyloe	108	B7
East Learmouth	106	E6
East Lilburn	112	A7
East Ord	105	A5
East Rainton	94	D4
East Sleekburn	12	A3
East Thirston	119	A3
East Woodburn	122	F5
Ebchester	76	F3
Edlingham	118	C8
Edmundbyers	135	C2
Eglingham	112	D5
Elford	109	C3
Ellingham	113	A8
Ellington	1	D4
Elrington	128	B1
Elsdon	123	A8
Elwick	108	E6
Embleton	113	D7
Eshott	119	B2
Etal	107	B7

F

Fallowfield	128	E4
Falstone	121	C5
Fawdon	111	F3
Felkington	104	E2
Felton	119	A4
Fence Houses	94	A8
Fenrother	125	A8
Fenton	107	D4
Fenwick	108	C8
Fenwick	129	E6
Fishwick	104	C3
Ford	107	C6
Fordhill	107	C6
Forestburn Gate	118	A2
Foulden	104	D7
Fourstones	128	C3

G

Gateshead	55	E2
Gateshead	101	C2
Gilsland	126	B3
Glanton	112	B3
Goswick	105	D2
Great Bavington	123	D2
Great Lumley	89	C4
Great Ryle	111	F2
Great Swinburne	128	E7
Great Tosson	117	E4
Great Whittington	129	C5
Greendykes	108	C2
Greenhaugh	121	F5
Greenhead	126	C2
Greenside	52	A1
Grindon	104	C2
Guide Post	10	F6
Gunnerton	128	D7
Guyzance	119	B6

H

Hadden	106	A6
Hadston	119	E5
Haggerston	105	C1
Hallington	129	B7
Halton	129	B3
Halton Lea Gate	132	C7
Halton Shields	129	C4
Haltwhistle	126	F2
Hamsterley	77	B5
Hamsterley Mill	78	A3
Harbottle	116	F6
Harlow Hill	33	A5
Harnham	124	B2
Hartburn	124	C5
Harwood	123	E7
Haswell	97	F3
Haugh Head	107	F1

Hauxley	119	F5
Hawkhill	113	D2
Haydon Bridge	128	A2
Hazlerigg	28	A4
Healeyfield	135	F2
Hebburn	57	E5
Heddon-on-the-Wall	34	F2
Hedley on the Hill	65	A3
Hedworth	58	C2
Helm	119	A2
Henshaw	127	C2
Hepburn	112	B8
Hepple	117	C4
Hepscott	9	F5
Hethpool	106	F2
Hetton le Hole	95	B4
Heugh	130	A6
Hexham	44	E2
High Angerton	124	C4
High Buston	119	C8
High Hauxley	119	E5
High Newton-by-the-Sea	113	D8
High Pittington	96	C5
High Spen	66	F4
Highcliffe	105	B5
Highfields	105	A7
Hipsburn	113	D1
Holburn	108	B6
Holefield	106	B5
Holy Island	105	F1
Holystone	117	A5
Holywell	23	F2
Horncliffe	104	D4
Horndean	104	B4
Horsley	50	D8
Horsley	116	B2
Horsleyhope	135	F1
Hoselaw	106	B4
Houghton-le-Spring	94	D7
Howick	113	E4
Howtel	106	F4
Humbleton	107	D2
Humshaugh	128	D5
Hunstanworth	134	F4
Hutton	104	C6

I

Ilderton	111	E6
Ingoe	129	D7
Ingram	111	E4

J

Jarrow	58	D6

K

Kibblesworth	81	D5
Kielder	120	D8
Kilham	106	F4
Killingworth	29	D3
Kiln Pit Hill	135	E5
Kimmerston	107	C5
Kirk Yetholm	106	C2
Kirkharle	123	E3
Kirkheaton	129	C8
Kirknewton	107	A3
Kirkwhelpington	123	D4
Knarsdale	132	D4
Knowesgate	123	D4

L

Ladykirk	104	B3
Lamberton	104	F8
Lambley	132	D7
Lanehead	121	F4
Langley	133	F8
Lanton	107	B3
Lee	134	F7
Lempitlaw	106	A4
Lennel	106	D8
Lesbury	113	D1
Limestone Brae	133	D2
Linhope	111	C4
Lint	107	B6
Linton	1	B3
Little Bavington	123	D1
Little Ryle	111	E1
Little Swinburne	128	F8
Littlehoughton	113	D4
Longbenton	39	C8

Longframlington	118	D4
Longhorsley	118	E1
Longhoughton	113	E3
Longhurst	4	F7
Longwitton	124	B6
Low Angerton	124	C4
Low Brunton	128	E4
Low Newton-by-the-Sea	113	D8
Low Town	118	D4
Lowick	107	F7
Lucker	109	A3
Lynmouth	2	B2

M

Mardon	107	A6
Matfen	129	D5
Medburn	130	C5
Medomsley	77	B1
Meldon	124	D3
Melkridge	127	A1
Mickley Square	49	E1
Middleton	108	E5
Middleton	124	B4
Midgeholme	132	B7
Milbourne	130	B7
Milfield	107	B4
Mindrum	106	D4
Mitford	3	A8
Molesden	124	F4
Moorside	135	F2
Morpeth	8	F8
Mowhaugh	110	A6
Muggleswick	135	E2

N

Nedderton	15	B8
Nesbit	107	E4
Netherton	117	C7
Netherwitton	124	C7
New Bewick	112	B6
New Hartley	23	D6
New Herrington	90	E6
New Silksworth	92	B8
Newbiggin	134	F2
Newbiggin-by-the-Sea	7	E3
Newbottle	90	E3
Newbrough	128	B3
Newburn	52	F7
Newcastle-upon-Tyne	55	C6
Newcastle-upon-Tyne	98	C3
Newham	109	B2
Newlands	76	C3
Newton	48	C6
Newton	117	E4
Newton Underwood	124	F5
Newton-on-the-Moor	118	F6
Newtown	107	D3
Newtown	112	A8
Ninebanks	133	D4
Norham	104	C3
North Charlton	113	A7
North Hazelrigg	108	B4
North Middleton	111	E8
North Shields	41	F4
North Sunderland	109	D3
North Togston	119	D5

O

Oakwood	45	E8
Ogle	124	E1
Old Bewick	112	B6
Ordley	134	F7
Otterburn	122	E8
Otterburn Camp	116	D1
Ouston	81	F2
Ouston	129	F5
Ouston	133	C4
Outchester	108	F4
Ovingham	50	B5
Ovington	49	C4

P

Park End	128	B7
Park Village	132	E8
Pawston	106	D4
Paxton	104	D6
Pegswood	4	E4
Penshaw	90	C7
Pigdon	124	F6

Plenmeller	126	F1
Ponteland	25	D6
Powburn	112	B4
Prendwick	111	E2
Pressen	106	C5
Preston	113	B8
Prior Park	105	A5
Prudhoe	50	D1

R

Radcliffe	119	E5
Raise	132	F1
Ramshaw	134	F1
Rawgreen	134	E6
Raylees	123	A7
Red Row	119	D3
Redburn	127	C2
Redesdale Camp	116	A3
Redesmouth	122	D3
Rennington	113	C5
Riding Mill	62	E8
Ridley	127	D1
Ridsdale	122	F4
Rochester	116	A3
Rock	113	C6
Roddam	111	F6
Roseden	111	F6
Ross	108	F6
Rothbury	117	F4
Rothley	124	A6
Rowfoot	132	E8
Rowlands Gill	67	E2
Ruffside	135	B3
Ryal	129	C7
Ryhope	92	F6
Ryton	52	D5

S

Sandhoe	129	A3
Scot's Gap	124	A5
Scrainwood	117	C8
Scremerston	105	B4
Seaham	93	C1
Seahouses	109	D3
Seaton	92	B1
Seaton Burn	21	B1
Seaton Delaval	23	C2
Seaton Sluice	24	C5
Seghill	22	F1
Sharperton	117	A5
Sherburn	96	A1
Sherburn Hill	96	C1
Shilbottle	119	A8
Shilbottle Grange	119	B8
Shilvington	124	F2
Shiney Row	90	B5
Shipley	112	F4
Shiremoor	30	F3
Shoresdean	104	E3
Shoreswood	104	D3
Shotleyfield	135	F4
Shotton	20	E8
Shotton	106	D3
Silksworth	91	F7
Simonburn	128	B6
Sinderhope	134	A4
Slaggyford	132	D4
Slaley	62	A2
Slaley	135	A6
Snitter	117	E5
Snods Edge	135	F4
Sourhope	110	C6
South Broomhill	119	D3
South Charlton	113	A6
South Hazelrigg	108	B4
South Hetton	97	F8
South Middleton	111	D7
South Shields	42	E4
Southdean	114	C8
Spartylea	134	A2
Spittal	105	B5
Springwell	71	F2
Stakeford	11	B7
Stamford	113	D5
Stamfordham	130	A5
Stannersburn	121	C5
Stannington	14	D3
Stanton	124	E7
Steel	134	F7
Stobswood	119	C1
Stocksfield	64	B7
Stonehaugh	127	D8
Strothers Dale	135	A6
Sunderland	86	E6
Sunderland	102	C3
Sunniside	69	A2

Swarland	118	F5
Swinhoe	109	D2

T

Tanfield	79	D3
Tanfield Lea	79	D1
Tantobie	79	B2
Thockrington	123	B1
Thorn Green	134	A1
Thorngrafton	127	D2
Thornington	106	F4
Thornley Gate	133	F6
Thornton	104	E3
Throckley	35	D1
Throphill	124	E4
Thropton	117	E5
Thrunton	112	C1
Tindale	132	A7
Togston	119	D4
Tow House	127	C2
Town Yetholm	106	B1
Townfield	134	F2
Tritlington	125	C8
Tughall	109	D1
Tweedmouth	105	A6
Tynemouth	42	B8

U

Ulgham	125	D8
Upper Denton	126	A2
Uppertown	128	B6
Upsettlington	104	B3
Urpeth	81	E2

W

Walbottle	35	F2
Wall	128	D4
Wall Houses	129	D4
Wallsend	40	D2
Walwick	128	D5
Wandylaw	112	F8
Warden	128	D3
Warenford	108	F2
Warenton	108	E3
Wark	106	C7
Wark	128	A8
Warkworth	119	D6
Warren Mill	109	A5
Warton	117	D5
Washington	83	F7
Weldon	118	D3
West Allerdean	104	F3
West Boldon	74	A8
West Chevington	119	C2
West Fleetham	109	C2
West Horton	108	A3
West Learmouth	106	D6
West Rainton	94	B2
West Sleekburn	11	D7
West Thirston	119	A3
West Woodburn	122	E5
Westend Town	127	C2
Westnewton	107	A3
Whalton	124	E2
Wharmley	128	B3
Whickham	69	B7
Whitburn	60	E1
Whiteleas	59	D3
Whitfield	133	C7
Whitley Bay	31	E6
Whitley Chapel	134	E6
Whitsome	104	A5
Whitsomehill	104	A4
Whittingham	112	B1
Whitton	117	F4
Whittonstall	135	F6
Widdrington	119	D1
Widdrington Station	125	E8
Wide Open	28	C3
Wingates	118	B1
Winlaton Mill	68	C6
Wooler	107	E2
Woolsington	36	E8
Wooperton	111	F6
Wylam	51	A5

Y

Yarrow	121	B5
Yeavering	107	B3
Yetlington	117	E8

A

A J Cook's Cotts NE39 ...67 B2
Abbay St SR5 ...75 A1
Abbey Cl Whitley Bay NE25 31 D4
Washington NE38 ...83 D5
Abbey Ct NE8 ...101 C1
Abbey Dr Burnside DH4 ...90 C2
Tynemouth NE30 ...42 D8
Jarrow NE32 ...58 C7
Newcastle-upon-Tyne NE5 ..36 B4
Abbey Gate NE61 ...8 D7
Abbey Mdws NE61 ...8 D7
Abbey Rd NE38 ...83 D5
Abbey Terr
Shiremoor NE27 ...30 E3
8 Morpeth NE61 ...3 F1
Abbey View Hexham NE46 .45 C4
7 Morpeth NE61 ...3 F1
Abbeyfields Fst Sch NE61 .8 E8
Abbeyvale Dr NE6 ...57 B7
Abbot Ct NE8 ...101 C3
Abbot's Way NE61 ...8 E8
Abbots Cl NE62 ...11 B8
Abbots Way
2 Whickham NE16 ...69 B7
Tynemouth NE29 ...41 E8
Abbotsfield Cl SR3 ...91 F5
Abbotsford Gr SR2 ...102 C1
Abbotsford Pk NE25 ...31 F4
Abbotsford Rd NE10 ...56 D1
Abbotsford Terr NE2 ...99 A4
Abbotside Cl DH2 ...81 D2
Abbotside Pl NE5 ...36 D2
Abbotsmeade Cl NE5 ...54 C8
Abbs St SR5 ...75 D1
Abercorn Pl NE28 ...40 E6
Abercorn Rd
Newcastle-upon-Tyne NE15 .54 A5
Sunderland SR3 ...91 D8
Abercrombie Pl 2 NE5 ...37 B2
Aberdare Rd SR3 ...91 E7
Aberdeen DH2 ...81 F1
Aberdeen Ct NE3 ...37 D8
Aberdeen Dr NE32 ...58 E3
Aberdeen Tower SR3 ...91 E8
Aberfoyle DH2 ...81 F1
Abernethy DH2 ...81 F2
Abersford Cl NE5 ...36 B3
Abigail Ct NE3 ...38 E5
Abingdon DH2 ...81 F1
Abingdon Ct
Blaydon NE21 ...53 C3
Newcastle-upon-Tyne NE3 .37 D7
Abingdon Rd NE6 ...57 B7
Abingdon Sq NE23 ...16 C1
Abingdon St SR4 ...85 F5
Abingdon Way NE35 ...73 E7
Abinger St NE4 ...98 B1
Aboyne Sq SR3 ...85 D1
Acacia Ave DH4 ...90 A1
Acacia Gr Hebburn NE31 ..57 E4
South Shields NE34 ...59 F5
Acacia Rd NE10 ...56 B2
Acacia Terr NE63 ...6 D3
Acanthus Ave NE4 ...54 D7
Acer Ct SR2 ...86 D4
Acer Dr DH6 ...97 F3
Acklam Ave SR2 ...87 A1
Acomb Ave
Seaton Delaval NE25 ...23 D2
Wallsend NE28 ...40 D7
Acomb Cl NE61 ...9 C5
Acomb Cres NE3 ...38 A8
Acomb Ct
Killingworth NE12 ...29 D3
Bedlington NE22 ...11 A1
Gateshead NE9 ...71 B2
Sunderland SR2 ...86 F1
Acomb Dr NE41 ...51 A7
Acomb Gdns NE5 ...37 C1
Acorn Ave Bedlington NE22 15 F8
Gateshead NE8 ...70 C8
Acorn Rd NE2 ...38 E2
Acorn Sq NE42 ...50 D2
Acreford Ct NE62 ...10 E6
Acton Dr NE29 ...41 D8
Acton Pl NE7 ...39 B2
Acton Rd NE5 ...53 F8
Ada St South Shields NE33 .42 D1
Newcastle-upon-Tyne NE6 .56 E6
Adair Ave NE15 ...54 C6
Adair Way NE31 ...58 A5
Adams Terr DH8 ...77 A2
Adderlane Fst Sch NE42 .50 E3
Adderlane Rd NE42 ...50 E3
Adderstone Ave NE23 ...22 B5
Adderstone Cres NE2 ...38 F2
Adderstone Gdns NE29 ...31 B1
Addington Cres NE29 ...41 E6
Addington Dr Blyth NE24 .17 E5
Wallsend NE28 ...40 D7
Addison Cl 2 NE6 ...56 B6
Addison Ct
7 Wallsend NE28 ...41 A1
Ryton NE40 ...52 B5
Addison Gdns NE10 ...72 B8
Addison Ind Est NE21 ...53 A5
Addison Rd
Newcastle-upon-Tyne, Lemington NE15 ...53 D7
West Boldon NE36 ...74 A7
Addison Rd *continued*
15 Newcastle-upon-Tyne NE6 ...56 B6
Addison St
North Shields NE29 ...42 A4
Sunderland SR2 ...103 C2
Addison Wlk NE34 ...59 A3
Addycombe Terr NE6 ...39 C1
Adelaide Cl SR1 ...103 C3
Adelaide Ct NE8 ...101 B3
Adelaide Ctr The 5 NE4 .54 E5
Adelaide Ho 3 NE4 ...54 E5
Adelaide Pl SR1 ...103 C3
Adelaide St DH3 ...88 C2
Adelaide Terr NE4 ...54 E4
Adeline Gdns NE3 ...38 A3
Adelphi Cl NE29 ...41 C8
Adelphi Pl NE6 ...56 E5
Aden Tower SR3 ...91 E8
Admington Ct NE62 ...10 F7
Admiral Way SR3 ...91 C5
Admirals House 9 NE30 .42 D7
Adolphus St SR6 ...60 F1
Affleck St NE8 ...101 B2
Afton Ct NE34 ...59 C5
Afton Way NE3 ...37 E6
Agar Rd SR3 ...91 D8
Aged Miners' Cotts NE43 .64 F8
Aged Miners' Homes
Chester le Street DH2 ...88 C4
Great Lumley DH3 ...89 B1
Bournmoor DH4 ...89 E2
5 Houghton-le-Spring DH4 94 C8
East Rainton DH5 ...94 C4
Hetton le Hole DH5 ...95 A2
Hetton le Hole DH5 ...94 F6
3 Houghton-le-Spring, New Town DH5 ...94 F8
Sherburn Hill DH6 ...96 C1
Kibblesworth NE11 ...81 C6
Brunswick Village NE13 ...28 A6
Burnopfield NE16 ...79 A6
Sunniside NE16 ...69 A1
Annitsford NE23 ...22 B1
Cramlington NE23 ...21 F7
Dudley NE23 ...29 A6
Cambois NE24 ...12 D4
New Hartley NE25 ...23 E6
Shiremoor NE27 ...30 F3
South Shields NE34 ...60 A7
Boldon Colliery NE35 ...58 D1
High Spen NE39 ...67 A4
Rowlands Gill NE39 ...67 F1
Ryton NE40 ...52 E4
Prudhoe NE42 ...50 B1
2 Newcastle-upon-Tyne NE5 ...36 E3
Stakeford NE62 ...11 C8
Ashington NE63 ...6 A4
Ashington NE63 ...6 F5
Newbiggin-by-the-Sea NE64 .7 D3
Ryhope SR2 ...92 E7
New Silksworth SR3 ...86 A1
Sunderland SR5 ...74 E2
2 Seaham SR7 ...92 F1
Aged Mineworkers Homes
Throckley NE15 ...35 B2
Longhurst NE61 ...5 B7
Agincourt
Killingworth NE12 ...29 D4
Hebburn NE31 ...57 D7
Agnes Maria St NE3 ...38 A5
Agricola Ct 1 NE33 ...42 C4
Agricola Gdns NE28 ...40 D7
Agricola Rd NE4 ...54 F6
Aidan Ave NE26 ...24 B6
Aidan Cl
Brunswick Village NE13 ...28 A6
Wallsend NE27 ...30 C1
Aidan Ct Jarrow NE32 ...58 D6
Longbenton NE7 ...39 C5
Aidan Gr NE61 ...1 E4
Aidan Wlk NE3 ...38 E5
Aiden Way DH5 ...95 A5
Ailesbury St SR4 ...102 A3
Ainderby Rd NE15 ...35 B2
Ainsdale Gdns NE5 ...36 C2
Ainslie Pl NE5 ...37 C2
Ainsworth Ave NE34 ...59 A3
Ainthorpe Cl SR3 ...92 B7
Ainthorpe Gdns NE7 ...39 C4
Aintree Cl
Washington NE37 ...83 D7
Ashington NE63 ...6 C2
Aintree Gdns NE8 ...70 C7
Aintree Rd SR3 ...91 D8
Airedale NE28 ...39 F5
Airedale Gdns DH5 ...94 F2
Airey Terr
Newcastle-upon-Tyne NE6 ..57 A5
Gateshead NE8 ...101 A1
Aireys Cl DH4 ...94 C8
Airport Freightway NE13 .26 E2
Airport Ind Est NE3 ...37 D6
Airville Mount SR3 ...92 A4
Aisgill Cl NE23 ...22 B6
Aisgill Dr NE5 ...36 C1
Aiskell St SR4 ...102 A2
Akeld Cl NE23 ...22 B5
Akeld Ct NE3 ...38 E4
Akeman Way NE34 ...59 B5
Akenside Hill NE1 ...101 B4
Akenside Terr NE2 ...99 C4
Akhurst Sch NE2 ...38 F2
Alamein Ave DH5 ...94 F8
Alanbrooke Row NE31 ...57 C3
Alansway Gdns 9 NE33 .59 D8
Albany Ave NE12 ...39 D7
Albany Ct NE4 ...100 A3
Albany Gdns 1 NE26 ...32 B4
Albany Ho SR5 ...75 C1
Albany Mews NE3 ...38 A2
Albany Rd NE8 ...56 A3
Albany St E NE33 ...59 D8
Albany St W NE33 ...59 D8
Albany Village Prim Sch NE37 ...83 C7
Albany Way NE37 ...83 C7
Albatross Way NE24 ...17 E3
Albemarle Ave NE2 ...38 D3
Albemarle St 4 NE33 ...42 C3
Albert Ave NE28 ...40 B2
Albert Ct SR2 ...102 B1
Albert Dr NE9 ...70 F4
Albert Edward Terr NE35 .58 E2
Albert Pl Washington NE38 83 F4
Gateshead NE9 ...70 F4
Albert Rd Bedlington NE22 .11 E2
Seaton Sluice NE26 ...24 D6
Jarrow NE32 ...58 A6
Sunderland SR4 ...102 A3
Albert St
6 Chester le Street DH3 ...88 C3
Newcastle-upon-Tyne NE2 ...99 C2
Blyth NE24 ...17 E8
Hebburn NE31 ...57 D6
Rowlands Gill NE39 ...67 A1
Albert Terr
Longbenton NE12 ...29 C1
4 Whitley Bay NE26 ...32 B4
Albion Ct
10 South Shields NE33 ...42 C4
Newcastle-upon-Tyne NE6 ...56 B5
Albion Gdns NE16 ...78 F5
Albion House 3 NE29 ...42 A5
Albion Pl SR1 ...102 C2
Albion Rd NE29,NE30 ...42 A6
Albion Rd W NE29 ...42 A5
Albion Ret Ctr NE24 ...17 D8
Albion Row
Newcastle-upon-Tyne NE6 ..56 B6
Newcastle-upon-Tyne, St Lawrence NE6 ...56 B5
Albion St Gateshead NE10 .71 D6
Sunderland SR4 ...85 A6
Albion Terr
8 North Shields NE29 ...42 A6
Hexham NE46 ...45 A5
Lynmouth NE61 ...2 A3
Albion Way
Cramlington NE23 ...16 D1
Blyth NE24 ...17 C7
Albury Park Rd NE30 ...42 C7
Albury Pl NE16 ...69 A5
Albury Rd NE2 ...38 D3
Albyn Gdns SR3 ...86 A3
Alcester Cl NE62 ...10 F7
Alconbury Cl NE24 ...17 E5
Alcroft Cl NE5 ...36 B3
Aldborough St NE24 ...17 E7
Aldbrough Cl 11 SR2 ...92 F6
Aldbrough St NE34 ...59 A5
Aldeburgh Ave NE15 ...53 C8
Aldenham Gdns NE30 ...32 C1
Aldenham Rd SR3 ...91 E8
Aldenham Tower SR3 ...91 E8
Alder Ave NE4 ...54 D8
Alder Cl Hetton le Hole DH5 94 F3
Morpeth NE61 ...9 A8
Alder Cres DH9 ...78 F2
Alder Ct NE25 ...31 E4
Alder Gr NE25 ...31 E6
Alder Rd Wallsend NE28 ...40 E6
Shiremoor NE29 ...41 B7
Alder St SR5 ...74 B1
Alder Way NE12 ...29 C4
Alderley Cl NE35 ...58 E1
Alderley Dr NE12 ...29 F4
Alderley Rd NE9 ...70 E5
Alderley Way NE23 ...16 D1
Alderney Gdns NE5 ...36 C2
Aldershot Rd SR3 ...91 D7
Aldershot Sq SR3 ...91 D7
Aldertone Ct NE62 ...10 F7
Alderwood
Washington NE38 ...89 B8
Ashington NE63 ...6 C2
Alderwood Cres NE6 ...39 F1
Alderwyk NE10 ...72 B6
Aldwick Rd NE15 ...54 A5
Aldwych Dr NE29 ...41 B7
Aldwych Ho NE33 ...42 B2
Aldwych Rd SR3 ...91 D7
Aldwych Sq SR3 ...91 D6
Aldwych St NE33 ...42 E2
Alemouth Rd NE46 ...45 B5
Alexander Dr DH5 ...94 F3
Alexander Terr
Hazlerigg NE13 ...28 A5
Sunderland SR6 ...75 D3
Alexandra Ave SR5 ...74 F1
Alexandra Cres NE46 ...44 F5
Alexandra Dr NE16 ...69 C8
Alexandra Gdns
North Shields NE29 ...41 E6
Ryton NE40 ...52 E4
Alexandra Pk SR2 ...86 C4
Alexandra Rd
Newcastle-upon-Tyne NE6 ..39 B1
Morpeth NE61 ...9 A8
Ashington NE63 ...6 F3
Gateshead NE8 ...101 B1
Alexandra St
Wallsend NE28 ...40 C2
Rowlands Gill NE39 ...67 A1
Alexandra Terr
Penshaw DH4 ...90 B8
Haswell DH6 ...97 F3
Sunniside NE16 ...69 C2
3 Whitley Bay NE26 ...32 B4
Stocksfield NE43 ...64 D7
Hexham NE46 ...44 F5
Newcastle-upon-Tyne NE5 ..36 F3
Springwell NE9 ...71 F1
Alexandra Way NE23 ...22 B5
Alford DH2 ...81 F2
Alford Gn NE12 ...39 C7
Alfred Ave NE22 ...11 B1
Alfred St Blyth NE24 ...17 E6
Hebburn NE31 ...57 D5
Newcastle-upon-Tyne NE6 ..56 E6
Algernon NE12 ...29 D5
Algernon Cl 14 NE6 ...56 C7
Algernon Ct 17 NE6 ...56 C7
Algernon Ind Est NE27 ...30 F1
Algernon Pl NE26 ...32 B4
Algernon Rd
Newcastle-upon-Tyne, Lemington NE15 ...53 C6
15 Newcastle-upon-Tyne, Heaton NE6 ...56 C7
Algernon Terr
Tynemouth NE30 ...42 C8
Wylam NE41 ...51 A6
Algiers Rd SR3 ...91 C7
Alice St Blaydon NE21 ...53 B1
South Shields NE33 ...59 C8
Sunderland SR2 ...102 C1
Alice Well Villas SR4 ...84 B3
Aline St SR3 ...92 B7
Alison Ct 4 NE6 ...56 B7
Alison Dr NE36 ...74 D7
All Saints CE Inf Sch NE34 ...59 C5
All Saints CE Jun Mix Sch NE34 ...59 B4
All Saints Ct NE29 ...41 D6
All Saints Dr DH5 ...95 A5
All Saints Ho SR6 ...75 D1
Allan Rd NE64 ...7 D5
Allandale Ave NE12 ...39 D7
Allanville NE12 ...29 C5
Allchurch NE15 ...54 B6
Allchurch Dr NE63 ...7 A3
Allen Ave NE11 ...70 D7
Allen Banks (N.T.)* NE47 ...127 E1
Allen Dr NE46 ...45 B4
Allen St DH3 ...88 C2
Allendale Ave NE28 ...40 B4
Allendale Cres
Penshaw DH4 ...90 B8
Shiremoor NE27 ...31 A3
Stakeford NE62 ...6 A1
Allendale Dr NE34 ...60 A8
Allendale Pl NE30 ...42 D7
Allendale Rd Blyth NE24 ..17 F6
Hexham NE46 ...44 F4
Newcastle-upon-Tyne NE6 .56 D5
Sunderland SR3 ...91 D8
Allendale Sq SR3 ...91 E8
Allendale St DH5 ...95 A2
Allendale Terr
Haswell DH6 ...97 F3
Newcastle-upon-Tyne NE6 ..56 F5
Allenhead NE38 ...83 E1
Allenheads
Seaton Delaval NE25 ...23 C4
Newcastle-upon-Tyne NE5 ..36 E1
Allensgreen NE23 ...22 B6
Allerdean Cl
Newcastle-upon-Tyne NE15 .53 B7
Seaton Delaval NE25 ...23 D2
Allerdene Wlk NE16 ...69 B6
Allerhope NE23 ...22 B5
Allerton Gdns NE6 ...39 D2
Allerton Pl NE16 ...68 F5
Allerwash NE5 ...36 E1
Allery Banks NE61 ...9 A8
Allgood Terr NE22 ...11 B1
Allhusen Terr NE8 ...56 B1
Alliance Pl SR4 ...102 B3
Alliance St SR4 ...102 B3
Allingham Ct NE7 ...39 E3
Allison Ct NE11 ...54 B1
Alloa Rd SR3 ...91 D8
Allonby Way NE5 ...54 B8
Alloy Terr NE39 ...67 C1
Allwork Terr NE16 ...69 B7
Alma Pl Whitley Bay NE26 .32 C4
North Shields NE29 ...42 A6
Alma St SR4 ...85 A7
Alma Terr NE40 ...52 C2
Almond Cl DH6 ...97 F3
Almond Cres NE8 ...70 C8
Almond Dr SR5 ...85 A8
Almond Pl NE4 ...54 D7
Almshouses NE15 ...52 F7
Aln Ave NE3 ...38 A7
Aln Cres NE3 ...38 A7
Aln Ct
Newcastle-upon-Tyne NE15 .53 C6
Ellington NE61 ...1 E5
Aln Gr NE15 ...53 C7
Aln St Hebburn NE31 ...57 D6
Ashington NE63 ...6 F5
Aln Wlk NE3 ...38 A6
Alnham Ct NE3 ...37 E7
Alnham Gr NE5 ...36 C2
Alnmouth Ave NE29 ...41 D4
Alnmouth Dr NE3 ...38 E4
Alnmouth Terr NE46 ...44 F8
Alnwick Ave
Whitley Bay NE26 ...32 A5
North Shields NE29 ...41 D4
Alnwick Castle* NE66 ..113 B2
Alnwick Cl
Chester le Street DH2 ...88 A1
Whickham NE16 ...69 A7
Alnwick Ct NE38 ...83 B5
Alnwick Dr NE22 ...10 D1
Alnwick Gr NE32 ...58 B2
Alnwick Rd
South Shields NE34 ...59 C6
Sunderland SR3 ...91 E8
Alnwick Sq SR3 ...91 E8
Alnwick St Newburn NE15 .52 F8
Wallsend NE28 ...40 C2
Alnwick Terr NE13 ...28 C7
Alpine Ct DH2 ...88 C3
Alpine Gr NE36 ...74 B7
Alpine Way SR3 ...86 A3
Alresford NE12 ...29 D4
Alston Ave
East Cramlington NE23 ...22 D5
Newcastle-upon-Tyne NE6 ..56 E6
Alston Cl Wallsend NE28 ..41 A4
Tynemouth NE29 ...41 C7
Alston Cres SR6 ...75 C4
Alston Gdns NE15 ...35 D3
Alston Gr NE26 ...24 B7
Alston Rd
New Hartley NE25 ...23 D6
Washington NE38 ...84 B6
Alston St NE8 ...101 A1
Alston Wlk DH6 ...96 A1
Alstone Ct NE62 ...10 F7
Altan Pl NE12 ...39 B7
Altrincham Tower SR3 ...91 E8
Alum Well Rd
Gateshead NE9 ...70 E5
1 Gateshead, Low Fell NE9 70 F5
Alverston Cl NE15 ...53 C8
Alverstone Ave NE9 ...70 E4
Alverstone Rd SR3 ...91 D7
Alverthorpe St NE33 ...59 D8
Alveston Cl NE62 ...10 F7
Alwin NE38 ...83 A1
Alwin Cl DH4 ...89 E3
Alwinton Ave NE29 ...41 D8
Alwinton Cl Blyth NE24 ...17 C8
Newcastle-upon-Tyne NE5 .37 A4
Alwinton Dr DH2 ...88 A1
Alwinton Gdns NE11 ...70 A5
Alwinton Rd NE27 ...31 A3
Alwinton Sq 7 NE63 ...6 F2
Alwinton Terr NE3 ...38 D5
Amalfi Tower SR3 ...91 E8
Amara Sq SR3 ...91 E8
Ambassadors Way NE29 .41 B8
Amber Ct NE24 ...17 C6
Ambergate Cl NE5 ...37 A3
Amberley Chase NE12 ...29 E4
Amberley Cl NE28 ...41 A3
Amberley Ct NE8 ...100 C1
Amberley Gdns NE7 ...39 C2
Amberley Prim Sch NE12 29 E4
Amberley St
Gateshead NE8 ...100 C1
Sunderland SR2 ...103 B1
Amberley St S SR2 ...103 B1
Amberley Way NE24 ...17 E5
Amberley Wlk NE16 ...69 B5
Amberly Gr NE16 ...69 A5
Amble Ave
Whitley Bay NE25 ...32 B4
South Shields NE34 ...60 B8
Amble Cl Blyth NE24 ...17 C5
North Shields NE29 ...41 E4
Amble Gr NE2 ...56 A7
Amble Pl NE12 ...29 F1
Amble Tower SR3 ...91 E8
Amble Way NE3 ...38 B6
Ambleside NE15 ...35 E3
Ambleside Ave NE34 ...59 E6
Ambleside Cl NE25 ...23 D3
Ambleside Gdns
Newcastle-upon-Tyne NE5 ..54 B8
Gateshead NE9 ...71 A4
Ambleside Terr SR6 ...75 C4
Ambridge Way
Seaton Delaval NE25 ...23 A4
Newcastle-upon-Tyne NE3 ..37 F5
Ambrose Pl NE6 ...57 B6
Ambrose Rd SR3 ...91 D8
Amec Dr NE28 ...41 A1
Amec Way NE28 ...40 E1
Amelia Cl NE4 ...54 E3
Amelia Gdns SR3 ...91 C7
Amelia Wlk NE4 ...54 E3
Amen Cnr NE1 ...101 B4
Amersham Pl 1 NE5 ...37 B2
Amersham Rd NE24 ...17 E4
Amesbury Cl NE5 ...36 B3
Amethyst Rd NE4 ...100 A2
Amethyst St 1 SR4 ...85 F7
Amherst Rd NE3 ...37 E6
Amos Ayre Pl NE34 ...58 F5
Amsterdam Rd SR3 ...91 E8
Amy St SR5 ...75 B2
Ancaster Ave NE12 ...39 B6
Ancaster Rd NE16 ...68 F6
Anchorage The
Chester le Street DH3 ...88 D3
Penshaw DH4 ...90 B6
Ancona St SR4 ...85 F7
Ancroft Ave NE29 ...41 F7
Ancroft Pl
Newcastle-upon-Tyne NE5 ..54 B8
Ashington NE63 ...6 F1

Ancroft Rd NE25 23 B3
Ancroft Way NE3 37 F8
Ancrum St NE2 98 B3
Ancrum Way NE16 68 F5
Anderson St NE33 42 D3
Andover Pl NE28 40 E6
Andrew Rd SR3 91 D7
Andrews House Sta★
NE16 80 B7
Anfield Ct NE3 37 E5
Anfield Rd NE3 37 E5
Angel of the North (mon)★
NE9 82 A8
Angerton Ave
Shiremoor NE27 30 F2
Tynemouth NE30 32 A1
Angerton Gdns NE5 54 D8
Angerton Terr NE23 28 F8
Angle Terr NE28 40 F2
Anglesey Gdns NE5 36 C2
Anglesey Pl NE4 98 B1
Anglesey Rd SR3 91 D7
Anglesey Sq SR3 91 D7
Angram Dr SR2 87 A1
Angram Wlk 1 NE5 36 C1
Angrove Gdns SR4 85 F5
Angus DH2 81 F2
Angus Cl NE12 29 C3
Angus Cres NE29 41 D3
Angus House NE4 54 E4
Angus Rd NE8 70 C8
Angus Sq SR3 91 D7
Ann St Blaydon NE21 53 C3
Shiremoor NE27 30 E4
Hebburn NE31 57 C7
Gateshead NE8 101 C2
Ann Wlk NE6 57 A4
Ann's Row NE24 12 E1
Anne Dr NE12 40 A8
Annfield Rd NE23 16 B2
Annie St SR6 75 E4
Annitsford Dr NE23 29 B8
Annitsford Rd NE23 22 E1
Annville Cres NE6 57 A4
Anscomb Gdns NE7 39 A3
Anson Cl NE33 59 B8
Anson Pl NE5 36 F3
Anson St NE8 56 B1
Anstead Cl NE23 22 B6
Anthony Rd SR3 91 D8
Anton Pl NE23 22 B5
Antonine Wlk NE15 34 F2
Antrim Cl NE5 37 C3
Antwerp Rd SR3 91 C7
Apperley NE5 36 E1
Apperley Ave NE3 37 C4
Apperley Rd NE43 64 C6
Appian Pl Throckley NE15 35 E2
Gateshead NE9 71 B7
Apple Cl NE15 53 C8
Apple Ct NE25 23 D6
Appleby Ct
Bournmoor DH4 89 D1
North Shields NE29 41 F5
Appleby Gdns
Wallsend NE28 41 A4
Gateshead NE9 71 A3
Appleby Pk NE29 41 F6
Appleby Rd SR3 91 D7
Appleby Sq SR3 91 D7
Appleby St NE29 42 A4
Appledore Cl NE40 66 E8
Appledore Gdns
Chester le Street DH3 88 D5
1 Gateshead NE9 70 F3
Appledore Rd NE24 17 E5
Appleforth Ave SR2 87 A1
Appleton Cl NE11 70 A8
Appletree Dr NE42 50 D3
Appletree Gardens Fst Sch
NE25 31 E4
Appletree Gdns
Whitley Bay NE25 31 E3
Newcastle-upon-Tyne NE6 39 F1
Appletree La NE45 47 A5
Appletree Rise NE45 47 A5
Applewood NE12 29 F3
Appley Terr SR6 75 E2
Apsley Cres NE3 37 E5
Aqua Terr NE64 7 D4
Aquila Dr NE15 34 E2
Arbroath DH2 81 F1
Arbroath Rd SR3 91 D8
Arcade The 2 NE30 42 D7
Arcadia DH2 81 F1
Arcadia Ave DH3 88 C5
Arcadia Terr NE24 17 E6
Archbishop Runcie CE Fst
Sch NE3 38 D5
Archbold Terr NE2 99 B3
Archer Rd SR3 91 D8
Archer Sq SR3 91 D8
Archer St NE28 40 E3
Archer Villas NE28 40 D3
Archibald Fst Sch NE3 38 C5
Archibald St NE3 38 C5
Arcot Ave
Cramlington NE23 21 E8
Whitley Bay NE25 31 E3
Arcot Dr Whitley Bay NE25 31 E3
Newcastle-upon-Tyne NE5 53 F8
Arcot Terr 5 NE24 17 D8
Arden Ave NE3 28 B1
Arden Cl NE28 40 D7
Arden Cres NE5 37 D1
Arden Sq SR3 91 E8
Ardrossan DH2 81 F1
Ardrossan Rd SR3 91 D7
Arena Bsns Pk DH4 94 C7
Arena Way NE4 100 C3
Argus Cl NE11 70 B7
Argyle Ct DH9 80 A1
Argyle House Sch SR2 102 C1
Argyle Pl South Hetton DH6 97 F7
Tynemouth NE29 42 A8
Argyle Sq SR2 102 C1
Argyle St
Newcastle-upon-Tyne NE1 99 B1
Blyth NE24 12 E1
Tynemouth NE30 42 D8
Hebburn NE31 57 D7
Sunderland SR2 102 C1
Argyle Terr
Tynemouth NE29 42 A8
Hexham NE46 45 B4
Newbiggin-by-the-Sea NE64 7 D4
Argyll DH2 81 F1
Ariel St NE63 6 E3
Arisaig DH2 81 F1
Arkle Rd SR3 91 D7
Arkle St Hazlerigg NE13 28 A4
Gateshead NE8 70 C8
Arklecrag NE37 83 C6
Arkleside Pl NE5 36 D1
Arkwright St NE8 70 D7
Arlington Ave NE3 37 F3
Arlington Cl DH4 89 E3
Arlington Ct NE3 38 A3
Arlington Gr
Whickham NE16 69 A6
Cramlington NE23 16 B2
Arlington Rd NE31 57 F4
Arlington St 3 SR4 85 F6
Armitage Gdns NE9 71 C1
Armondside Rd NE17 77 C6
Armstrong Ave
South Shields NE34 59 E6
Newcastle-upon-Tyne NE6 39 B1
Armstrong Cl NE46 44 F3
Armstrong Dr NE12 29 B2
Armstrong Ind Est NE37 83 A7
Armstrong Rd
Newcastle-upon-Tyne NE15,
NE4 54 B5
Wallsend NE28 41 A1
Washington NE37 83 A7
Armstrong St
Woolsington NE5 36 B7
Gateshead NE8 70 D7
Armstrong Terr
South Shields NE33 59 C8
Morpeth NE61 9 A8
Arn Dr SR2 92 F8
Arncliffe Ave SR4 85 E4
Arncliffe Gdns NE5 36 C2
Arndale Arc 9 NE32 58 B7
Arndale Ho
Newcastle-upon-Tyne NE3 37 E5
6 Washington NE37 83 D8
Arndale House
11 Birtley DH3 82 C4
Longbenton NE12 39 A6
Arnold Rd SR3 91 D8
Arnold St NE35 73 F8
Arnside Wlk NE5 36 C2
Arran Ct SR3 92 A6
Arran Dr NE32 58 E3
Arran Gdns NE10 71 C7
Arran Pl NE29 41 C8
Arras La SR1 103 B3
Arrol Pk SR4 102 B2
Arrow Cl NE12 29 B2
Arthington Way NE34 59 E5
Arthur Ave SR2 93 A6
Arthur Cook Ave NE16 69 C6
Arthur St Blyth NE24 17 E8
Jarrow NE32 58 B6
Gateshead NE8 101 C2
11 Ryhope SR2 93 A6
Whitburn SR6 60 F4
Arthur Terr SR6 60 F3
Arundel Cl
Brunswick Village NE13 28 A5
Bedlington NE22 11 C3
Arundel Ct NE3 37 C7
Arundel Dr
Newcastle-upon-Tyne NE15 53 E7
Whitley Bay NE25 31 C4
Arundel Gdns
Gateshead NE9 71 A5
Sunderland SR3 91 C7
Arundel Rd SR3 91 D8
Arundel Sq NE63 6 C3
Arundel Wlk NE16 69 A5
Asama Ct NE4 100 A3
Ascham House Sch NE3 38 C4
Ascot Cl NE28 40 D6
Ascot Cres NE8 70 C7
Ascot Ct
Newcastle-upon-Tyne NE3 37 C7
Sunderland SR3 91 D7
Ascot Gdns NE34 59 D7
Ascot Wlk NE3 37 C7
Ascott Gr NE63 6 D2
Ash Ave NE13 27 C7
Ash Banks NE61 9 A7
Ash Cl NE46 44 E3
Ash Ct NE29 31 E1
Ash Gr Dunston NE11 54 E1
Wallsend NE28 40 D1
Ryton NE40 52 C6
Morpeth NE61 8 E7
Whitburn SR6 61 A2
Ash Mdws NE38 88 E7
Ash Sq NE38 83 E4
Ash St Blaydon NE21 53 C1
Ash St *continued*
Mickley Square NE43 64 E8
Ash Terr DH9 79 B2
Ash Tree Dr NE22 10 F2
Ashberry Gr SR6 75 D1
Ashbourne Ave NE6 56 F6
Ashbourne Cl NE27 30 C5
Ashbourne Cres NE63 6 C3
Ashbourne Rd NE32 58 C5
Ashbrooke NE25 31 E5
Ashbrooke Cl NE25 31 E5
Ashbrooke Cres SR2 86 D4
Ashbrooke Cross SR2 86 C3
Ashbrooke Dr NE20 25 E7
Ashbrooke Gdns NE28 40 E3
Ashbrooke Mount 6
SR2 86 C4
Ashbrooke Range SR2 86 D3
Ashbrooke Rd SR2 86 C4
Ashbrooke St NE3 37 E3
Ashbrooke Terr SR2 86 D4
Ashburn Rd NE28 40 E6
Ashburne Ct SR2 86 D4
Ashburton Rd NE3 38 A4
Ashbury NE25 31 C6
Ashby St SR2 86 F3
Ashcroft Dr NE12 39 E7
Ashdale Penshaw DH4 89 E8
Ponteland NE20 25 C3
Ashdale Cres NE5 36 D1
Ashdown Cl NE12 39 B7
Ashdown Rd SR3 91 D7
Ashdown Way NE12 39 B7
Asher St NE10 56 C1
Ashfield NE32 58 D2
Ashfield Ave NE16 69 C8
Ashfield Cl NE4 100 A4
Ashfield Ct NE39 67 A4
Ashfield Gdns NE28 40 A3
Ashfield Gr
Whitley Bay NE26 32 A7
6 North Shields NE29 42 A6
Ashfield Lodge NE4 100 A4
Ashfield Pk NE16 69 B8
Ashfield Rd
Whickham NE16 69 B5
Newcastle-upon-Tyne NE3 38 A4
Ashfield Rise NE16 69 B5
Ashfield Terr
Chester le Street DH3 88 D2
4 Gateshead NE10 56 F1
Ryton NE40 52 C5
Ashford NE9 71 A1
Ashford Cl Blyth NE24 17 E5
Tynemouth NE29 31 F1
Ashford Gr NE5 36 B4
Ashford Rd SR3 91 D7
Ashgill NE37 83 B6
Ashgrove Ave NE34 59 F4
Ashgrove Terr Birtley DH3 82 B5
Gateshead NE8 101 B1
Ashill Ct SR2 86 D4
Ashington Alexandra Fst Sch
NE63 6 F3
Ashington Alexandra Mid Sch
NE63 6 E4
Ashington Central Fst Sch
NE63 6 D3
Ashington Comm High Sch
NE63 6 B3
Ashington Dr NE62 11 A8
Ashington Hawthorn Fst Sch
NE63 6 D1
Ashington Hirst Park Mid Sch
NE63 6 E3
Ashington Hospl NE63 6 C3
Ashington Rd NE61 1 D4
Ashington Seaton Hirst Com
Mid Sch NE63 7 A2
Ashington Wansbeck Fst Sch
NE63 6 A4
Ashkirk Annitsford NE23 29 A8
Sunderland SR3 91 E8
Ashkirk Cl DH2 88 A1
Ashkirk Way NE25 23 D2
Ashleigh DH2 88 A5
Ashleigh Cl NE21 53 E1
Ashleigh Cres NE5 54 A8
Ashleigh Gdns SR6 60 A2
Ashleigh Gr
Longbenton NE12 39 D7
Newcastle-upon-Tyne NE2 38 D2
Tynemouth NE30 42 C8
Sunderland SR6 75 E4
Ashleigh Rd NE5 54 A8
Ashleigh Sch NE30 42 B5
Ashleigh Special Sch
NE30 42 A6
Ashleigh Villas 2 NE36 74 D7
Ashley Cl Killingworth NE12 29 F4
Washington NE38 83 D3
Ashley Gdns NE62 11 A8
Ashley Rd NE34 59 C6
Ashley Road Cty Prim Sch
NE34 59 C6
Ashley Terr DH3 88 C4
Ashmead Cl NE12 29 E4
Ashmore St SR2 103 A1
Ashmore Terr SR2 103 A1
Asholme NE5 36 E1
Ashridge Cl NE34 60 B5
Ashridge Ct NE10 72 C7
Ashton Cl NE5 36 B4
Ashton Ct NE40 52 D4
Ashton Downe 2 DH2 88 C2
Ashton Rise DH2 88 C2
Ashton Way
Whitley Bay NE26 31 E7
Ashton Way *continued*
Sunderland SR3 91 C6
Ashtree Cl
Rowlands Gill NE39 67 F3
Newcastle-upon-Tyne NE4 54 F4
Ashtree Gdns NE25 31 E3
Ashtree La NE21,NE39 67 B5
Ashtrees Gdns NE9 70 F7
Ashvale Ave NE11 81 C6
Ashwell Rd SR3 91 D7
Ashwood Ave SR5 74 F2
Ashwood Cl
Longbenton NE12 39 E8
Cramlington NE23 16 C2
Ashwood Cres NE6 39 F1
Ashwood Croft NE31 57 D7
Ashwood Gdns NE9 71 A2
Ashwood Gr
Wide Open NE13 28 B5
4 Sunderland SR5 74 B1
Ashwood Rd NE46 45 C4
Ashwood St SR2 102 B1
Ashwood Terr SR2 102 B1
Askern Ave SR2 87 A1
Askew Rd NE8 101 B3
Askew Rd W NE8 100 C1
Askrigg Ave
Wallsend NE28 40 D7
Sunderland SR2 86 F1
Askrigg Cl DH2 81 E2
Askrigg Wlk 2 NE5 36 C1
Aspen Ct SR3 91 E6
Aspen Terr NE5 37 E1
Aspen Way NE24 17 D4
Aspenlaw NE9 71 C4
Aspley Cl SR3 92 A6
Association Rd 4 SR6 75 E2
Aster Pl NE4 54 C7
Aster Terr DH4 90 B4
Astley Com High Sch
NE25 23 C3
Astley Ct NE12 29 D3
Astley Dr NE26 31 E8
Astley Gdns
Seaton Delaval NE25 23 C3
Seaton Sluice NE26 24 B7
Astley Gr NE26 24 B7
Astley Rd NE25 23 C4
Astley St NE23 16 B3
Aston Sq SR3 91 D7
Aston St NE33 59 D7
Aston Way NE16 68 F5
Aston Wlk NE6 57 A6
Athelhampton NE38 84 A5
Athelstan Rigg SR2 93 A7
Athenaeum St SR1 103 A2
Atherton Dr
Fence Houses DH4 94 A7
Newcastle-upon-Tyne NE4 54 E4
Atherton House NE4 54 E4
Athlone Ct NE24 17 E8
Athlone Pl DH3 82 D1
Athol Gdns
Whitley Bay NE25 31 D3
Ryhope SR2 93 A6
Athol Gn NE11 100 A1
Athol Gr SR3 92 A7
Athol House NE20 25 F6
Athol Pk 3 SR2 86 E4
Athol Rd SR2 103 B1
Athol St NE11 100 A1
Athol Terr SR2 103 B1
Atholl DH2 81 F2
Atholl Gdns NE9 71 B7
Atkin St NE12 29 B5
Atkinson Gdns NE29 42 A3
Atkinson Ho Sch NE23 22 F2
Atkinson Rd
Chester le Street DH3 88 D5
Newcastle-upon-Tyne NE4 54 D4
Sunderland SR6 75 E4
Atkinson Road Prim Sch
NE4 54 D4
Atkinson St NE28 40 B1
Atkinson Terr
Wallsend NE28 40 B1
5 Newcastle-upon-Tyne
NE4 54 D5
Atkinson's Bldgs SR4 102 B3
Atlantis Rd SR3 91 C8
Atley Way NE23 15 E2
Attlee Cl NE23 29 B5
Attlee Cres DH6 97 E1
Attlee Gr SR2 92 E8
Attlee Terr NE64 7 F5
Attwood Gr SR5 75 B2
Aubone Ave NE15 54 C6
Auburn Cl NE28 41 A2
Auburn Ct NE28 41 B2
Auburn Gdns NE4 54 E8
Auburn Pl NE61 8 E8
Auckland DH2 88 A3
Auckland Ave NE34 60 B6
Auckland Rd NE31 57 F7
Auckland Terr NE32 58 E4
Auden Gr NE4 54 E6
Audland Wlk 3 NE5 36 C1
Audley Ct NE2 38 F2
Audley Gdns SR3 86 B3
Audley Rd NE3 38 E4
Audouins Row NE8 70 E8
August Pl NE33 42 D1
Augusta Ct NE28 40 E6
Augusta Sq SR3 91 D7
Augustus Dr NE22 10 E2
Austen Ave NE34 59 B4
Austin Sq SR5 75 B2
Austral Pl NE13 28 A5
Australia Gr NE34 58 F3
Australia Tower SR3 91 E8
Austwick Wlk 4 NE5 36 C1
Autumn Cl NE38 83 D6
Avalon Dr NE15 53 E8
Avalon Rd SR3 91 D8
Avebury Ave NE62 11 A7
Avebury Dr NE38 83 E5
Avebury Pl NE23 16 C1
Avenue Cres NE25 23 C4
Avenue Rd
Seaton Delaval NE25 23 C3
Gateshead NE8 70 F8
Avenue Terr
Seaton Delaval NE25 23 D3
1 Sunderland SR2 86 C4
Avenue The
Chester le Street DH2 88 B3
Birtley DH3 82 C4
Bournmoor DH3 89 E6
Hetton le Hole DH5 95 B4
7 Gateshead, Felling NE10 56 D1
Blaydon NE21 53 E2
Seaton Delaval NE25,NE26 23 E5
Seaton Sluice NE26 24 A6
Whitley Bay NE26 32 A5
Wallsend NE28 40 B1
Washington NE38 83 E5
Rowlands Gill NE39 67 F1
Corbridge NE45 46 F6
Morpeth NE61 8 F6
Gateshead, Carr Hill NE9 71 B7
Sunderland SR2 103 A1
Avenue Vivian
Fence Houses DH4 90 A1
Great Lumley DH4 89 F1
Aviemore Rd NE36 74 B7
Avis Ave NE64 7 C3
Avison Ct NE4 98 B2
Avison Pl NE4 98 B2
Avison St NE4 98 B2
Avocet Cl NE24 17 E3
Avolon Ct NE4 98 B2
Avolon Pl NE4 98 B2
Avolon Wlk NE4 98 B2
Avon Ave
North Shields NE29 41 E4
Hedworth NE32 58 C2
Avon Cl Wallsend NE28 40 D6
Rowlands Gill NE39 67 F3
Avon Cres DH4 94 A8
Avon Ct NE25 23 D6
Avon Rd NE31 57 F4
Avon St Gateshead NE8 56 A1
Sunderland SR2 103 C2
Avon Terr
Washington NE38 83 E4
Washington NE38 83 F4
Avondale SR4 85 A5
Avondale Ave
Penshaw DH4 90 B7
Longbenton NE12 39 D8
Blyth NE24 16 E8
Avondale Cl 1 NE24 16 F8
Avondale Ct NE3 38 D4
Avondale Gdns
West Boldon NE36 74 A7
Ashington NE63 7 A2
Avondale Ho NE6 56 C5
Avondale Rd
Ponteland NE20 25 A2
Newcastle-upon-Tyne NE6 56 C5
Avondale Rise 5 NE6 56 C5
Avondale Terr
Chester le Street DH3 88 C3
West Boldon NE36 74 A7
Gateshead NE8 101 B1
Avonlea Way NE5 37 C3
Avonmouth Rd SR3 91 D7
Avonmouth Sq SR3 91 D7
Awnless Ct NE34 59 C5
Axbridge Cl NE62 11 A7
Axbridge Gdns NE4 54 E5
Axford Terr NE17 77 B6
Axminster Cl NE23 16 D1
Axwell Dr NE24 17 B7
Axwell Park Cl 3 NE16 69 A7
Axwell Park Rd NE21 53 E1
Axwell Park View NE15 54 B5
Axwell Terr NE16 54 A1
Axwell View
Whickham NE16 69 A7
Blaydon NE21 53 C1
Aycliffe Ave NE9 71 E4
Aycliffe Cres NE9 71 D4
Aycliffe Pl NE9 71 E4
Aydon Ave NE45 47 A6
Aydon Castle★ NE45 129 C3
Aydon Cl NE30 32 C1
Aydon Cres NE45 47 B6
Aydon Dr NE45 47 A6
Aydon Gdns NE45 47 A6
Aydon Gr Jarrow NE32 58 B3
Corbridge NE45 47 A6
Aydon Ho SR3 91 E7
Aydon Rd NE45 47 C7
Aydon Rd Est NE45 47 A6
Aydon Wlk NE5 36 E1
Aylesbury Dr SR3 92 A5
Aylesbury Pl NE12 39 B7
Aylesford Sq NE24 17 E5
Aylsham Cl NE5 36 B4
Aylsham Ct SR3 92 A4
Aylyth Pl NE3 37 F3
Ayr Dr NE32 58 E3

Ayre's Quay Rd SR1 102 C3
Ayre's Terr NE29 42 A6
Ayrey Ave NE34 58 F4
Aysgarth Ave
Wallsend NE28 40 D7
Sunderland SR2 86 F2
Aysgarth Gn NE3 37 F4
Ayton Ave SR2 87 A1
Ayton Cl Stocksfield NE43 64 D6
Newcastle-upon-Tyne NE5 36 E3
Ayton Ct NE22 10 D2
Ayton Prim Sch NE38 82 F3
Ayton Rd NE38 82 F4
Ayton Rise NE6 56 C5
Ayton St NE6 56 D5
Azalea Ave SR2 102 C1
Azalea Terr N SR2 102 C1
Azalea Terr S SR2 102 C1

B

Back Albion St SR4 85 A6
Back Beaumont Terr
NE3 38 D5
Back Bridge St SR1 103 A3
Back Buttsfield Terr DH4 90 B8
Back Chapman St NE6 56 C7
Back Coronation Terr
DH5 95 A2
Back Croft Rd NE24 17 E7
Back George St NE4 100 C4
Back Goldspink La NE2 99 C3
Back Hawthorn Rd W
NE3 38 C4
Back Heaton Park Rd 9
NE6 56 B6
Back High St NE3 38 C4
Back Hylton Rd SR4 102 B3
Back La Great Lumley DH3 89 A1
Penshaw DH4 90 B8
Blaydon NE21 53 B2
Whitley Bay NE25 31 E5
Back Lodge Terr SR1 103 C2
Back Maling St NE6 56 A5
Back Mitford St NE4 100 B3
Back Mowbray Terr NE62 10 F7
Back New Bridge St NE1,
NE2 99 C2
Back North Bridge St
SR5 103 A4
Back Percy Gdns NE30 42 D8
Back Riggs 9 NE61 3 F1
Back Row Whickham NE16 69 B7
Hexham NE46 45 B5
Back Ryhope St SR2 102 E7
Back Shipley Rd 11 NE30 42 D7
Back St NE21 53 B1
Back Stephen St 6 NE6 56 A6
Back Walker Rd NE6 57 A4
Back Woodbine St NE8 101 B1
Backview Ct SR5 75 C3
Backworth La NE23,NE27 29 F7
Backworth Park Prim Sch
NE27 30 C5
Backworth Terr NE27 30 D1
Baden Cres SR5 74 A3
Baden Powell St NE9 71 A7
Baden St DH3 88 C2
Bader Ct NE24 17 F6
Badger Cl SR3 92 A5
Badger Mews NE9 71 F2
Badger's Wood DH9 80 A1
Badgers Gn NE61 3 D2
Badminton Cl NE35 58 E1
Baffin Ct SR3 91 F6
Baildon Cl NE28 40 C4
Bailey Green Prim Sch
NE12 29 C4
Bailey Sq SR5 74 A4
Bailey St DH9 79 B2
Bailey Way DH5 95 B2
Bainbridge Ave
South Shields NE34 58 F4
Sunderland SR3 86 B3
Bainbridge Holme Cl
SR3 86 B3
Bainbridge Holme Rd
SR3 86 C3
Bainford Ave NE15 54 A7
Baird Ave NE28 41 C2
Baird Cl NE37 72 E2
Baird Ct NE8 56 B1
Baird St SR5 74 A3
Baker Gdns
Gateshead NE10 72 B8
1 Dunston NE11 54 F1
Baker Sq SR5 74 A3
Baker St
Houghton-le-Spring DH5 90 E1
Sunderland SR5 74 A3
Bakewell Terr NE6 56 D4
Baldersdale Gdns SR2 86 B2
Baldwin Ave
East Boldon NE36 74 E8
Newcastle-upon-Tyne NE4 54 F7
Balfour Rd NE15 54 A6
Balfour St
Houghton-le-Spring DH5 90 E1
2 Blyth NE24 17 D8
Gateshead NE8 101 A1
Balfour Terr NE17 66 B1
Balgonie Cotts NE40 52 C5
Baliol Rd NE43 64 D7
Balkwell Ave NE29 41 D5
Balkwell Gn NE29 41 E6
Ballast Hill NE24 17 F8
Ballast Hill Rd NE29 42 A3
Balliol Ave NE12 29 C1
Balliol Bsns Pk NE12 39 A7
Balliol Gdns NE7 39 B5
Balliol Prim Sch NE12 39 B6
Balmain Rd NE5 37 E4
Balmlaw NE9 71 D4
Balmoral Ave
Newcastle-upon-Tyne NE3 38 E4
Brockley Whins NE32 58 E3
Balmoral Cl NE22 11 C2
Balmoral Cres DH5 94 F7
Balmoral Ct 5 SR5 74 A3
Balmoral Dr NE10 71 C8
Balmoral Gdns
Whitley Bay NE26 31 F6
Tynemouth NE29 41 F7
Balmoral St NE28 40 B2
Balmoral Terr
Newcastle-upon-Tyne,
South Gosforth NE3 38 E4
Newcastle-upon-Tyne, Heaton
NE6 56 B8
Sunderland, Grangetown
SR2 86 F2
Sunderland, East Herrington
SR3 91 C7
Balmoral Way
Gateshead NE10 71 C8
Blyth NE24 17 C3
Balroy Ct NE12 39 E7
Baltic Ctr for Contemporary
Art NE8 101 C4
Baltic Ind Pk NE28 41 E3
Baltic Rd NE10 56 D3
Baltimore Ave SR5 73 E3
Baltimore Ct NE37 83 C8
Baltimore Sq SR5 73 F3
Bamborough Ct NE23 29 A8
Bamborough Terr NE30 42 A7
Bambro' St SR2 103 B1
Bamburgh Ave NE33,
NE34 43 A1
Bamburgh Castle*
NE69 109 C5
Bamburgh Cl Blyth NE24 17 C7
Washington NE38 83 B5
Bamburgh Cres
Shiney Row DH4 90 B5
Shiremoor NE27 30 F3
Bamburgh Ct
Newcastle-upon-Tyne NE7 38 F5
Gateshead NE8 70 C7
Bamburgh Dr
Gateshead NE10 57 B2
Wallsend NE28 40 F2
Pegswood NE61 4 F3
Bamburgh Gdns SR3 86 B3
Bamburgh Gr
Jarrow NE32 58 B4
South Shields NE34 60 B8
Bamburgh Ho NE5 36 E3
Bamburgh Rd
Longbenton NE12 29 F1
Newcastle-upon-Tyne NE5 36 E3
Bamburgh Sch NE34 60 A8
Bamburgh Terr
18 Newcastle-upon-Tyne
NE6 56 C6
Ashington NE63 6 C3
Bamburgh Wlk NE3 38 A6
Bamford Terr NE12 29 F1
Bamford Wlk NE34 59 D5
Bampton Ave SR6 75 C5
Banbury NE37 83 E8
Banbury Ave SR5 74 A4
Banbury Gdns NE28 40 D5
Banbury Rd NE3 37 F6
Banbury Terr NE33,NE34 59 D8
Banbury Way Blyth NE24 17 E5
North Shields NE29 41 D4
Bancroft Terr SR4 85 F6
Banesley La NE11 70 B1
Banff St SR5 74 A4
Bangor Sq NE32 58 A1
Bank Ave NE16 69 A7
Bank Ct Blaydon NE21 53 F4
North Shields NE30 42 B5
Bank Head NE46 45 B5
Bank Top Tynemouth NE30 32 C3
Crawcrook NE40 51 E3
Greenside NE40 52 B3
Bank Top Hamlet 4
NE16 69 A7
Bankdale Gdns NE24 17 A7
Bankfoot Sta NE3 37 B6
Bankhead Rd NE15 35 F1
Bankhead Terr DH4 94 A8
Bankside NE61 9 A8
Bankside La NE34 59 C5
Bankside Rd NE15 53 F5
Bankside Wlk NE62 11 B8
Bankwell La NE8 101 B4
Bannerman Terr DH6 96 C1
Bannister Dr NE12 40 A8
Bannockburn NE12 29 C4
Barbara Priestman Sch
SR2 86 B4
Barbara St SR2 86 F2
Barbary Dr SR6 75 F2
Barbondale Lonnen NE5 36 C2
Barbour Ave NE34 60 A7
Barclay Pl NE5 37 B1
Barclay St SR6 103 A4
Barcusclose La DH9,NE16 79 D5
Bardolph Rd NE29 41 D6
Bardon Cl NE5 36 F4
Bardon Cres NE25 23 F2
Bardon Ct NE34 59 E5
Bardsey Pl NE12 39 B7
Barehirst St NE33 59 B7
Barents Cl 2 NE5 36 F2
Baret Rd
Newcastle-upon-Tyne, Walker
NE6 56 F7
Newcastle-upon-Tyne, Walkergate
NE6 56 E8
Barford Ct NE9 71 A2
Barford Dr DH2 88 A1
Baring St NE33 42 D4
Barker St NE2 99 C2
Barking Cres SR5 73 F3
Barking Sq SR5 73 F3
Barkwood Rd NE39 67 D2
Barley Mow DH3 88 D8
Barley Mow Prim Schs
DH3 82 D1
Barlow Cres NE21 67 C6
Barlow Fell Rd NE21 67 C5
Barlow La NE21 67 E7
Barlowfield Cl NE21 68 A8
Barmoor Bank NE61 9 D5
Barmoor Castle* TD15 107 E7
Barmoor La NE40 52 B5
Barmoor Pl NE40 52 B5
Barmoor Terr NE40 52 A5
Barmouth Cl NE28 40 D5
Barmouth Rd NE29 41 C5
Barmston Cl NE38 83 F4
Barmston Ct NE38 83 F4
Barmston La NE38 84 C6
Barmston Rd NE38 84 A4
Barmston Village Prim Sch
NE38 83 F5
Barmston Way NE38 83 F6
Barn The 3 DH2 88 B1
Barnabas Pl SR2 103 C1
Barnard Cl NE22 10 E1
Barnard Cres NE31 57 E7
Barnard Gn NE3 37 E7
Barnard Gr NE32 58 D4
Barnard Pk DH5 95 A4
Barnard St Blyth NE24 17 E7
Sunderland SR4 85 F5
Barnes Jun & Inf Schs
SR4 85 F4
Barnes Park Rd SR4 86 A4
Barnes St DH5 95 A4
Barnes View SR4 85 F4
Barnes' Rd NE33 59 B8
Barnesbury Rd NE4 54 E5
Barnett Ct SR5 75 B2
Barningham NE38 84 A5
Barningham Cl SR3 86 B2
Barns Cl NE32 58 A4
Barnstaple Cl NE28 40 C5
Barnstaple Rd NE29 31 D1
Barnston NE63 7 B3
Barnton Rd NE10 71 E6
Barnwell Prim Sch DH4 90 B7
Barnwood Cl NE28 40 C5
Baron's Quay Rd SR5 85 B8
Baroness Dr NE15 54 A7
Baronswood NE3 38 B5
Barpett Sq DH6 97 F3
Barr Cl NE28 40 E5
Barrack Ct NE4 98 C2
Barrack Rd NE2,NE4 98 B3
Barrack Row DH4 90 A6
Barrack St SR1 103 C4
Barrack Terr NE11 81 D6
Barracks Museum*
TD15 105 B6
Barras Ave
Annitsford NE23 22 B1
Blyth NE24 17 E5
Barras Ave W NE24 17 D5
Barras Bridge NE1 99 A2
Barras Dr SR3 86 B3
Barras Gdns NE23 22 B1
Barras Mews NE23 22 F1
Barrasford Cl
Newcastle-upon-Tyne NE3 38 A4
Ashington NE63 6 A2
Barrasford Dr NE13 28 C5
Barrasford Rd NE23 22 C6
Barrasford St NE28 41 C1
Barrass Ave NE23 22 F1
Barrie Sq SR5 75 B2
Barrington Ave NE30 31 F2
Barrington Ct
Hetton le Hole DH5 95 A4
Bedlington NE22 16 A8
Barrington Dr NE38 83 D4
Barrington Ind Est NE22 11 B4
Barrington Pk NE22 11 F3
Barrington Pl
Newcastle-upon-Tyne NE4 98 B2
Gateshead NE8 101 A2
Barrington Rd NE22 11 B3
Barrington St NE33 42 C3
Barrington Terr DH5 95 A5
Barron St S 5 SR5 74 C1
Barrow St SR5 73 F4
Barrowburn Pl NE23 23 A1
Barry St Dunston NE11 54 F1
Gateshead NE8 70 D7
Barton Cl Wallsend NE28 40 D5
Tynemouth NE30 32 B1
Washington NE37 72 F2
Barton Ct SR6 75 C5
Bartram Gdns NE8 70 E7
Bartram St SR5 75 C3
Barwell Cl NE28 40 D5
Barwell Ct NE7 39 E3
Basil Way NE34 59 E3
Basildon Gdns NE28 40 C5
Basingstoke Pl NE12 39 C7
Baslow Gdns SR3 86 B3
Bassenfell Ct NE37 83 B6
Bassenthwaite Ave 4
DH2 88 B1
Bassington Ave NE23 21 E7
Bassington Cl NE4 98 B2
Bassington Dr NE23 21 E8
Bassington Ind Est NE23 21 D8
Bassington La NE23 21 D8
Bat House Rd NE43 64 B5
Bates La NE21 53 F2
Bath Cl NE28 40 E5
Bath La
Newcastle-upon-Tyne NE1,
NE4 98 C1
Blyth NE24 17 F7
Bath Rd Gateshead NE10 56 D2
Hebburn NE31 57 E3
Bath Sq NE32 58 A1
Bath St NE6 57 B6
Bath Terr Blyth NE24 17 F7
Newcastle-upon-Tyne NE3 38 D5
Tynemouth NE30 42 D7
Bathgate Ave SR5 73 F3
Bathgate Cl NE28 40 E5
Bathgate Sq SR5 73 F3
Batley St SR5 73 F3
Battle Hill NE46 45 B4
Battle Hill Dr NE28 40 D5
Battle Hill Fst Sch NE28 40 D5
Baugh Cl NE37 83 A7
Baulkham Hills DH4 90 B7
Bavington NE10 72 A5
Bavington Dr NE5 37 D1
Bavington Gdns NE30 32 B1
Bavington Rd NE25 23 D2
Bawtry Gr NE29 41 E5
Baxter Ave NE4 54 E6
Baxter Pl NE25 23 D3
Baxter Rd SR5 73 F4
Baxter Sq SR5 73 F4
Baxter's Bldgs NE25 23 D3
Baxterwood Ct NE4 98 A2
Baxterwood Gr NE4 98 A2
Bay View W NE64 7 E4
Baybridge Rd NE5 36 E3
Bayfield Gdns NE8 56 B1
Baysdale DH4 89 E8
Bayswater Ave SR5 74 A3
Bayswater Rd
Newcastle-upon-Tyne NE2 38 E2
Gateshead NE8 71 B8
Bayswater Sq 1 SR5 74 A3
Baytree Gdns NE25 31 F3
Baywood Gr NE28 40 C5
Beach Ave NE26 32 A5
Beach Croft Ave NE30 32 B1
Beach Rd Tynemouth NE29 42 A8
South Shields NE33 42 E3
Beach St SR4 102 B4
Beach Terr NE64 7 D3
Beach Way NE30 32 A1
Beachcross Rd SR4 102 B1
Beaches The NE4 100 A3
Beachville St SR4 102 B1
Beachway NE24 18 A4
Beacon Ct
Brunswick Village NE13 28 A6
Gateshead NE9 71 B5
Beacon Dr
Brunswick Village NE13 28 A5
Sunderland SR6 75 F1
Beacon Glade NE34 60 C6
Beacon Ho 4 NE26 31 F8
Beacon La NE23 21 E6
Beacon Lough Rd NE9 71 A4
Beacon Rise NE9 71 B5
Beacon St
North Shields NE30 42 C6
South Shields NE33 42 D5
Gateshead NE9 71 A5
Beaconsfield Ave NE9 71 A5
Beaconsfield Cl NE25 31 D7
Beaconsfield Cres 3
NE9 71 A5
Beaconsfield Rd NE9 70 F5
Beaconsfield St
Blyth NE24 17 F7
Newcastle-upon-Tyne NE4 98 A2
Beaconsfield Terr
Birtley DH3 82 B4
Chopwell NE17 66 B1
Beaconside NE34 60 C5
Beadling Gdns NE4 54 E6
Beadnell Ave NE29 41 D4
Beadnell Cl
3 Chester le Street DH2 88 A1
Blaydon NE21 68 A8
Beadnell Ct NE28 40 E5
Beadnell Gdns NE27 30 F3
Beadnell Pl NE2 99 C2
Beadnell Rd NE24 17 B5
Beadnell Way NE3 38 A6
Beagle Sq 6 SR3 92 A7
Beal Cl NE24 17 C7
Beal Dr NE12 29 F1
Beal Gdns NE28 40 F5
Beal Gn NE5 37 C4
Beal Rd NE27 30 F3
Beal Terr NE6 56 F4
Beal Way NE3 38 B6
Beaminster Way NE3 37 C5
Beamish Cl NE28 40 C5
Beamish Ct NE25 31 E3
Beamish Gdns NE9 71 D4
Beamish Open Air Mus*
DH9 80 D2
Beamishburn Rd DH9,
NE16 80 B3
Beamsley Terr NE63 6 D3
Beanley Ave
Newcastle-upon-Tyne NE15 53 C6
Hebburn NE31 57 D4
Beanley Cres NE30 42 D7
Beanley Pl NE7 39 A3
Bearl View NE43 64 E8
Beatrice Ave NE24 17 B4
Beatrice Gdns
South Shields NE34 59 F6
7 East Boldon NE36 74 D7
Beatrice Rd NE6 39 B1
Beatrice St Ashington NE63 6 E4
Sunderland SR6 75 E2
Beatrice Terr
Penshaw DH4 89 E8
Shiney Row DH4 90 B6
Beattie St NE34 59 B5
Beatty Ave
Newcastle-upon-Tyne NE2 38 E3
Sunderland SR5 73 F3
Beatty Rd NE22 16 B8
Beaufort Cl
Shiney Row DH4 90 B5
Newcastle-upon-Tyne NE5 37 D3
Beaufort Gdns NE28 40 C5
Beaufront Ave NE46 45 D4
Beaufront Cl NE10 72 B6
Beaufront Gdns NE5 37 C1
Beaufront Terr
Jarrow NE32 58 B3
South Shields NE33 59 C8
Beauly NE38 83 D3
Beaumaris Gdns SR3 91 C7
Beaumaris Way NE5 37 B4
Beaumont Ct NE25 31 D6
Beaumont Dr
Whitley Bay NE25 31 D7
Washington NE38 83 D5
Beaumont Manor NE24 16 F7
Beaumont St Blyth NE24 17 D8
North Shields NE29 42 A5
Newcastle-upon-Tyne NE4 54 F3
Hexham NE46 45 B5
Sunderland SR2 86 E4
Sunderland, Southwick SR5 75 A2
Beaumont Terr
Brunswick Village NE13 28 A6
Newcastle-upon-Tyne, Gosforth
NE3 38 D5
Jarrow NE32 58 A5
Prudhoe NE42 50 A2
Newcastle-upon-Tyne,
Westerhope NE5 36 F3
Beaumont Way NE42 50 B1
Bebdon Ct NE24 17 C6
Bebside Furnace Rd
NE22,NE24 16 D8
Bebside Rd NE24 16 C7
Beckenham Ave NE36 74 D8
Beckenham Cl NE36 74 E8
Beckenham Gdns NE28 40 C4
Beckett St NE8 56 A4
Beckfoot Cl NE5 37 B1
Beckford NE38 84 A4
Beckford Cl NE28 40 C5
Beckside Gdns NE5 36 B1
Beckwith Rd SR3 91 C8
Beda Cotts DH9 79 A2
Beda Hill NE21 53 C3
Bedale Cl NE28 40 C5
Bedale Cres SR5 74 A3
Bedale Ct
South Shields NE34 59 A5
Gateshead NE9 71 B2
Bedale Dr NE25 31 F3
Bedale Gn NE5 37 D3
Bedale St DH5 95 A2
Bedburn NE38 82 F1
Bedburn Ave SR5 74 C2
Bede Burn Jun & Inf Sch
NE32 58 A4
Bede Burn Rd NE32 58 B5
Bede Burn View NE32 58 B5
Bede Cl NE12 40 C8
Bede Com Prim Sch
NE10 56 B2
Bede Cres Wallsend NE28 40 E3
Washington NE38 83 D6
Bede Ct
Chester le Street DH3 88 C3
Tynemouth NE30 32 C3
Gateshead NE8 56 A2
Bede Ho 9 SR3 91 D7
Bede Ind Est NE32 58 E6
Bede Precinct 7 NE32 58 B7
Bede St SR5 75 E2
Bede Sta NE32 58 E6
Bede Terr
Chester le Street DH2 88 B3
Jarrow NE32 58 C5
East Boldon NE36 74 E7
Bede Wlk
Newcastle-upon-Tyne NE3 38 E5
Hebburn NE31 57 F5
Bede's World (Mus)*
NE32 58 D7
Bedeburn Foot NE5 36 F5
Bedeburn Rd NE5 36 F5
Bedesway NE32 58 E6
Bedewell Ind Pk NE31 58 A5
Bedewell Jun Mix & Inf Sch
NE31 57 F6

Bedford Ave Birtley DH3 ..82 D1
Chester le Street DH3 .....88 D8
Wallsend NE28 .....40 A3
South Shields NE33 ....42 C1
Bedford Ct NE30 ....42 B5
Bedford Pl
Newcastle-upon-Tyne NE5 ..36 C1
Gateshead NE8 ....101 B2
New Silksworth SR3 ....92 A8
Bedford St
Hetton le Hole DH5 ....94 F4
North Shields NE29,NE30 ..42 B5
Sunderland SR1 ....103 A3
Bedford Way NE29 ....42 B5
Bedlington Bank NE22, NE24 ....16 A7
Bedlington West End Fst Sch NE22 ....10 E1
Bedlingtonshire High Sch NE22 ....11 D2
Beech Ave
4 Houghton-le-Spring DH4 94 D8
Dinnington NE13 ....27 B7
Whickham NE16 ....69 C8
Cramlington NE23 ....22 D5
Newcastle-upon-Tyne NE3 ..37 F6
Hexham NE46 ....44 E5
Morpeth NE61 ....9 C7
Whitburn SR6 ....60 F1
Beech Cl NE3 ....28 C1
Beech Ct Ponteland NE20 .25 A1
North Shields NE29 ....41 F6
Tynemouth NE29 ....31 E1
Newcastle-upon-Tyne NE3 ..38 C4
Beech Dr Dunston NE11 ...54 E1
Corbridge NE45 ....47 B6
Ellington NE61 ....1 D5
Beech Gdns NE9 ....70 F6
Beech Gr Longbenton NE12 39 D6
Blackhall Mill NE17 ....77 B6
Bedlington NE22 ....11 A1
Whitley Bay NE26 ....31 F5
Wallsend NE28 ....40 B2
South Shields NE34 ....59 F4
Prudhoe NE42 ....50 B2
Springwell NE9 ....71 F1
Beech Gr S NE42 ....50 B2
Beech Grove Ct NE40 ...51 F4
Beech Grove Rd NE4 ...100 A4
Beech Grove Terr NE40 .51 F4
Beech Grove Terr S NE40 51 F4
Beech Hill NE46 ....44 E5
Beech Sq NE38 ....83 E4
Beech St Sunniside NE16 ..69 B2
Jarrow NE32 ....58 A7
Newcastle-upon-Tyne NE4 ..54 E5
Mickley Square NE43 ....64 E8
Gateshead NE8 ....56 B1
Beech Terr
Burnopfield NE16 ....79 C6
Blaydon NE21 ....53 C2
Ashington NE63 ....6 E2
Beech Way NE12 ....29 C4
Beechburn Wlk NE4 ....98 A1
Beechcroft NE3 ....38 B2
Beechcroft Ave NE3 ....38 A3
Beecher St NE24 ....17 B8
Beeches The
Longbenton NE12 ....39 D6
Ponteland NE20 ....25 D6
Stannington NE61 ....14 C4
Beechfield Gdns NE28 ...40 A3
Beechfield Rd NE3 ....38 B4
Beechlea NE61 ....14 C3
Beecholm Ct SR2 ....86 D3
Beechway Gateshead NE10 71 F5
Ashington NE63 ....7 A3
Beechwood Ave
Whitley Bay NE25 ....31 D4
Newcastle-upon-Tyne NE3 ..38 E6
Ryton NE40 ....52 C5
Stakeford NE62 ....11 A8
Gateshead NE9 ....71 A3
Beechwood Cl NE32 ....58 D6
Beechwood Cres SR5 ....74 F2
Beechwood Gdns NE11 ...70 B5
Beechwood Pl NE20 ....25 F2
Beechwood St SR2 ......102 B1
Beechwood Terr
Burnside DH4 ....90 C2
Sunderland SR2 ....102 B1
Beechwoods DH2 ....88 B5
Beeston Ave SR5 ....73 F3
Beetham Cres NE5 ....54 A8
Beethoven St 10 NE33 ...42 D2
Begonia Cl NE31 ....57 E3
Beldene Dr SR4 ....85 E4
Belford Ave NE27 ....30 F3
Belford Cl Wallsend NE28 .40 D5
Sunderland SR2 ....86 D3
Belford Gdns NE11 ....70 A5
Belford Rd SR2 ....86 E3
Belford Terr
Tynemouth NE30 ....42 A7
Newcastle-upon-Tyne NE6 ..56 E5
Sunderland SR2 ....86 E3
Belfry The DH4 ....90 A4
Belgrade Cres SR5 ....73 F4
Belgrade Sq SR5 ....73 F3
Belgrave Cres NE24 ....17 F6
Belgrave Ct NE10 ....71 D8
Belgrave Gdns
South Shields NE34 ....59 F6
Ashington NE63 ....7 A2
Belgrave Par NE4 ....100 B4
Belgrave Terr
Gateshead NE10 ....71 D7
South Shields NE33 ....42 D3
Bell Gr NE12 ....29 B4
Bell House Rd
Sunderland SR5 ....75 A5
Sunderland, High Southwick SR5 ....75 B3
Bell Rd NE41 ....51 B6
Bell St Penshaw DH4 ....90 B8
North Shields NE30 ....42 B5
Hebburn NE31 ....57 D6
Washington NE38 ....83 F4
Sunderland SR4 ....85 F6
Bell View NE42 ....50 F3
Bell's Cotts NE40 ....52 A1
Bell's Ct NE1 ....99 B1
Bell's Hill NE61 ....13 D3
Bell's Pl NE22 ....16 A8
Bellamy Cres SR5 ....73 F3
Bellburn Ct NE23 ....22 D8
Belle Gr W NE2 ....98 B3
Belle Grove Pl NE2 ....98 B3
Belle Grove Terr NE2 ...98 B3
Belle Grove Villas NE2 ...98 B3
Belle View Terr NE9 ....71 F1
Belle Vue NE39 ....66 F5
Belle Vue Ave NE3 ....38 D5
Belle Vue Bank NE9 ....70 E5
Belle Vue Cres
South Shields NE33 ....59 B6
Sunderland SR2 ....86 C4
Belle Vue Dr SR2 ....86 C4
Belle Vue Gr NE9 ....70 F5
Belle Vue Pk SR2 ....86 C4
Belle Vue Pk W SR2 ....86 C4
Belle Vue Rd SR2 ....86 C4
Belle Vue St NE30 ....32 C3
Belle Vue Terr
4 North Shields NE29 ...42 A4
Crawcrook NE40 ....51 F4
Gateshead NE9 ....70 E5
Belle Vue Villas NE36 ...74 C7
Bellerby Dr DH2 ....81 E2
Bellevue Cres NE23 ....16 B2
Bellfield Ave NE3 ....37 F6
Bellgreen Ave NE3 ....28 D1
Bellingham Cl NE28 ....40 D4
Bellingham Ct
Bedlington NE22 ....11 A1
8 Newcastle-upon-Tyne NE3 ....37 D5
Bellingham Dr NE12 ....40 A8
Bellingham Ho SR4 ....85 B4
Bellister Gr NE5 ....54 C7
Bellister Rd NE29 ....41 D6
Belloc Ave NE34 ....59 B3
Bells Cl
Newcastle-upon-Tyne NE15 .53 E5
2 Blyth NE24 ....16 F8
Bellsburn Ct NE63 ....6 B2
Bellshill Cl NE28 ....40 E6
Bellway Ind Est NE12 ....39 F7
Belmont NE10 ....72 A5
Belmont Ave NE25 ....31 D4
Belmont Cl NE28 ....40 E5
Belmont Cotts NE5 ....36 F3
Belmont Rd SR4 ....85 F5
Belmont Rise DH5 ....95 A1
Belmont St NE6 ....56 F3
Belmont Terr NE9 ....71 E1
Belmont Wlk NE6 ....56 F3
Belmount Ave NE3 ....28 D1
Belper Cl NE28 ....40 C5
Belsay NE38 ....82 F4
Belsay Ave Hazlerigg NE13 28 A4
Whitley Bay NE25 ....32 B4
South Shields NE34 ....60 A7
Belsay Cl Wallsend NE28 ..40 C5
Pegswood NE61 ....4 F3
Belsay Ct NE24 ....17 C7
Belsay Gdns
Dunston NE11 ....70 A5
Newcastle-upon-Tyne NE3 ..37 F8
Sunderland SR4 ....85 F5
Belsay Gr NE22 ....11 C3
Belsay Hall Castle and Gardens* NE20 ....124 C1
Belsay Ho 7 SR3 ....91 D7
Belsay Pl NE4 ....98 A2
Belsfield Gdns NE32 ....58 B4
Belsize Pl NE6 ....56 F8
Beltingham NE5 ....36 E1
Belvedere NE29 ....41 F7
Belvedere Ave NE25 ....31 F4
Belvedere Ct 12 NE6 ....56 C7
Belvedere Gdns NE12 ....39 D6
Belvedere Parkway NE3 ...37 D6
Belvedere Rd SR2 ....102 C1
Belvedere Ret Pk NE3 ....37 C6
Bemersyde Dr NE2 ....38 E3
Benbrake Ave NE29 ....31 E1
Bendigo Ave NE34 ....58 F3
Benedict Biscop C of E Prim Sch SR3 ....91 D5
Benedict Rd SR6 ....75 F2
Benfield Comp Sch NE6 .39 E1
Benfield Gr NE26 ....24 B7
Benfield Rd NE6 ....39 E1
Benfleet Ave SR5 ....73 F3
Benjamin Rd NE28 ....41 A3
Benjamin St 10 NE40 ....51 F3
Bennett Ct
Newcastle-upon-Tyne NE15 .53 C6
Sunderland SR2 ....86 E3
Bennett Gdns 1 NE10 ....56 D1
Bennett's Wlk NE61 ....9 A8
Benridge Bank DH4 ....94 A2
Benridge Pk NE24 ....17 B3
Bensham Ave NE8 ....101 A1
Bensham Cres NE8 ....100 C1
Bensham Ct
South Shields NE34 ....59 C5
Gateshead NE8 ....101 A1
Bensham General Hospl NE8 ....70 D7
Bensham Rd
Gateshead NE8 ....101 B3
Gateshead, Bensham NE8 .101 A1
Gateshead, Windmill Hills NE8 ....101 B2
Bensham St NE35 ....58 F1
Benson Cl NE46 ....44 E4
Benson Pl 19 NE6 ....56 C6
Benson Rd NE6 ....56 D6
Benson St DH3 ....88 C2
Bentall Bsns Pk NE37 ...83 F7
Bentinck Cres
Newcastle-upon-Tyne NE4 ..54 F4
Pegswood NE61 ....4 E3
Bentinck Rd NE4 ....54 F5
Bentinck St NE4 ....54 F4
Bentinck Villas NE4 ....54 F5
Benton Ave SR5 ....73 F4
Benton Bank NE2 ....39 A1
Benton Cl NE7 ....39 B5
Benton Hall Wlk NE7 ...39 D2
Benton La NE12 ....39 B7
Benton Lodge Ave NE7 ..39 B5
Benton Park Prim Sch NE7 ....39 B4
Benton Park Rd NE7 ....39 A5
Benton Rd Shiremoor NE27 30 E1
Biddick Hall NE34 ....59 C2
Newcastle-upon-Tyne NE7 ..39 B3
Benton Square Ind Est NE12 ....30 B1
Benton Sta NE12 ....39 D6
Benton Terr NE2 ....99 C3
Benton Way
Wallsend NE28 ....40 B1
Wallsend NE28 ....57 B8
Bents Cotts App NE33 ...42 E2
Bents Park Rd NE33 ....42 E3
Bents The SR6 ....75 F7
Benwell Dene Terr NE15 .54 C5
Benwell Gr NE4 ....54 E5
Benwell Grange 9 NE15 .54 D5
Benwell Grange Ave NE15 ....54 D5
Benwell Grange Cl 8 NE15 ....54 D5
Benwell Grange Rd NE15 54 C5
Benwell Grange Terr NE15 ....54 C5
Benwell Hall Dr NE15 ...54 B6
Benwell Hill Gdns NE5 ..54 C7
Benwell Hill Rd NE5 ....54 C7
Benwell La
Newcastle-upon-Tyne NE15 .54 C5
Newcastle-upon-Tyne, Old Benwell NE15 ....54 B5
Benwell Village NE15 ...54 B6
Benwell Village Mews NE15 ....54 C6
Berberis Way NE15 ....52 E8
Beresford Ave NE31 ....57 E3
Beresford Gdns 7 NE6 ....56 C5
Beresford Pk SR2 ....102 C1
Beresford Rd
Seaton Sluice NE26 ....24 D5
Tynemouth NE30 ....32 A3
Beresford St NE11 ....100 A1
Bergen Cl NE29 ....41 B4
Bergen Sq SR5 ....73 F4
Bergen St SR5 ....73 F4
Berkdale Rd NE9 ....70 E2
Berkeley Cl
Killingworth NE12 ....29 E4
Boldon Colliery NE35 ....58 E2
Sunderland SR3 ....91 C7
Berkeley Sq NE3 ....38 B7
Berkely St NE33 ....42 D2
Berkhamstead Ct NE10 ..72 C7
Berkley Ave NE21 ....53 E2
Berkley Cl NE28 ....40 C5
Berkley Rd NE29 ....41 D6
Berkley St NE15 ....52 F8
Berkley Terr NE15 ....52 F8
Berkley Way NE31 ....57 F8
Berkshire Cl NE5 ....36 F2
Bermondsey St NE2 ....99 C2
Bernard Gilpin Prim Sch DH5 ....94 E8
Bernard Shaw St 8 DH4 94 D8
Bernard St
Houghton-le-Spring DH4 ...94 D8
Newcastle-upon-Tyne NE6 ..57 B4
Berrington Dr NE5 ....37 B3
Berrishill Gr NE25 ....31 C6
Berry Cl Wallsend NE28 ..40 C5
Newcastle-upon-Tyne NE6 ..57 A6
Berry Hill NE40 ....52 B1
Berryfield Cl SR3 ....92 A5
Berryhill Cl NE21 ....53 D1
Berrymoor NE63 ....6 E4
Bertha Terr DH4 ....90 D4
Bertram Cres NE15 ....54 C6
Bertram St 2 Birtley DH3 .82 C4
South Shields NE33 ....59 C8
Bertram Terr
Pegswood NE61 ....4 F4
Ashington NE63 ....6 D3
Berwell Roman Temple* NE15 ....54 D6
Berwell Vallum Crossing* NE15 ....54 D6
Berwick NE38 ....82 F4
Berwick Castle* TD15 ..105 A6
Berwick Cl NE15 ....53 A7
Berwick Ct NE20 ....25 F7
Berwick Dr NE28 ....40 D5
Berwick Hill Rd NE20 ....25 F8
Berwick Sq SR5 ....73 F3
Berwick Terr NE29 ....41 D4
Besford Gr SR1 ....103 B2
Bessemer Rd DH6 ....97 F7
Bessie Terr NE21 ....53 A2
Best View 3 DH4 ....90 B6
Bet's La NE61 ....13 D8
Bethnell Ave NE6 ....56 D7
Betts Ave NE15 ....54 B5
Beumaris DH4 ....89 D3
Bevan Ave SR2 ....92 E6
Bevan Ct NE12 ....38 F6
Bevan Gdns NE10 ....72 A8
Beverley Cl NE3 ....28 B2
Beverley Cres NE9 ....71 A6
Beverley Ct
1 Jarrow NE32 ....58 B7
Washington NE37 ....83 D7
Gateshead NE9 ....71 A6
Beverley Dr
Whickham NE16,NE21 ....69 C8
Blaydon NE21 ....67 F8
Stakeford NE62 ....6 A1
Beverley Gdns
Chester le Street DH3 ....88 D2
Tynemouth NE30 ....32 C2
Ryton NE40 ....52 A5
Beverley Pk NE25 ....31 E4
Beverley Pl NE28 ....40 F3
Beverley Rd
Whitley Bay NE25 ....31 F4
Gateshead NE9 ....71 A6
Sunderland SR2 ....86 F2
Beverley Terr
Walbottle NE15 ....36 A2
Tynemouth NE30 ....32 C3
Newcastle-upon-Tyne NE6 ..57 A5
Beverley Villas NE30 ...32 C3
Beweshill Cres NE21 ....53 A1
Beweshill La NE21 ....53 A3
Bewick Cres NE15 ....53 D7
Bewick Ct NE1 ....99 B2
Bewick Garth NE43 ....49 E1
Bewick La NE42 ....50 B4
Bewick Pk NE28 ....40 F5
Bewick Rd NE8 ....101 B1
Bewick St
Newcastle-upon-Tyne NE1 101 A4
South Shields NE33 ....59 C8
Bewicke Lodge NE28 ...41 A2
Bewicke Rd NE28 ....41 A1
Bewicke Rd Ind Est NE28 41 A1
Bewicke St NE28 ....41 B1
Bewley Gdns NE28 ....40 D5
Bexhill Prim Sch SR5 ...73 F3
Bexhill Rd SR5 ....73 F3
Bexhill Sq Blyth NE24 ....17 E5
Sunderland SR5 ....73 F4
Bexley Ave NE15 ....54 B6
Bexley Pl NE16 ....69 A5
Bexley St SR4 ....85 F6
Bickerton Wlk 2 NE5 ....36 E1
Bickington Ct DH4 ....90 C3
Bicknell Ho NE6 ....56 C5
Biddick Hall Cty Inf Sch NE34 ....59 A3
Biddick Hall Cty Jun Sch NE34 ....59 B4
Biddick Hall Dr NE34 ....59 B4
Biddick La NE38 ....83 D2
Biddick Prim Sch NE38 .83 D4
Biddick Sch NE38 ....83 E3
Biddick Terr NE38 ....83 E3
Biddick View NE38 ....83 E3
Biddick Villas NE38 ....83 E3
Biddlestone Cres NE29 ..41 D5
Biddlestone Rd NE6 ....39 C1
Bideford Gdns
Whitley Bay NE26 ....32 A6
Jarrow NE32 ....58 E5
South Shields NE34 ....43 A1
Gateshead NE9 ....70 F3
Bideford Gr NE16 ....69 A5
Bideford Rd NE3 ....37 E4
Bideford St SR2 ....86 F2
Big Waters Nature Reserve* NE13 ....28 A7
Bigbury Cl DH4 ....90 C4
Bigg Mkt NE1 ....99 A1
Bigges Gdns NE28 ....39 F4
Bilbrough Gdns NE4 ....54 D4
Bill Quay Prim Sch NE10 57 C2
Billy Mill Ave NE29 ....41 E6
Billy Mill La NE29 ....41 D8
Bilsdale SR6 ....75 F7
Bilsdale Pl NE12 ....38 F6
Bilsmoor Ave NE7 ....39 B2
Bilton Hall Rd NE32 ....58 D6
Binchester St NE34 ....59 A5
Bingfield Gdns NE5 ....37 C1
Bingley Cl NE28 ....40 E5
Bingley St SR5 ....73 F3
Bink Moss NE37 ....83 A6
Binsby Gdns NE9 ....71 B2
Binswood Ave NE5 ....37 C2
Birch Ave Gateshead NE10 72 A7
Whitburn SR6 ....60 F1
Birch Cl NE46 ....44 E3
Birch Cres Burnside DH4 ..90 C2
Burnopfield NE16 ....79 A6
Birch Ct Prudhoe NE42 ...50 A2
Silksworth SR3 ....91 E6
Birch Gr Wallsend NE28 ..40 C5
Jarrow NE32 ....58 A7
Birch Rd NE21 ....53 D3
Birch St NE32 ....58 A7
Birch Terr NE6 ....57 A5
Bircham Dr NE21 ....53 D1
Birches Nook Cotts NE43 64 C7
Birches Nook Rd NE43 ..64 C7
Birches The NE16 ....69 C3
Birchfield NE16 ....69 B5
Birchfield Gdns
Newcastle-upon-Tyne NE15 .53 E7
Gateshead NE9 ....71 A2
Birchfield Rd SR2 ....86 B4
Birchfleld NE38 ....83 E2
Birchgate Cl NE21 ....53 A1
Birchington Ave NE33 ...59 D7
Birchtree Gdns NE25 ....31 F3
Birchvale Ave NE5 ....37 B2
Birchwood 3 NE36 ....74 D7
Birchwood Ave
Wide Open NE13 ....28 C5
Whickham NE16 ....69 A5
Newcastle-upon-Tyne NE7 ..39 C3
Birchwood Cl NE23 ....22 F1
Bird St NE30 ....42 C6
Birdhill Pl NE34 ....59 C5
Birdoswald (Camboglanna) Roman Fort* CA6 ....126 A3
Birds Nest Rd
Newcastle-upon-Tyne NE6 .56 D4
Newcastle-upon-Tyne NE6 .56 E4
Birkdale Whitley Bay NE25 .31 D5
South Shields NE33 ....42 E1
Birkdale Ave SR6 ....75 E7
Birkdale Cl Wallsend NE28 40 C4
Washington NE37 ....72 B2
Newcastle-upon-Tyne NE7 ..39 C4
Birkdale Dr DH4 ....90 A4
Birkdene NE43 ....64 D6
Birkhead Cotts NE11 ....80 E6
Birkheads La NE11 ....80 E6
Birkland La DH9,NE11, NE16 ....80 E7
Birks Rd NE15 ....35 B5
Birkshaw Wlk 1 NE5 ....36 E1
Birling Pl 4 NE5 ....37 D2
Birnam Gr NE32 ....58 E2
Birney Edge NE20 ....25 C1
Birnham Pl NE3 ....37 F3
Birnie Cl NE4 ....54 E4
Birrell Sq SR5 ....73 F4
Birrell St SR5 ....73 F4
Birtley Ave
Tynemouth NE30 ....42 D8
Sunderland SR5 ....73 F4
Birtley Cl NE3 ....38 A4
Birtley East Cty Prim Sch DH3 ....82 C6
Birtley Golf Course DH3 .82 D2
Birtley La DH3 ....82 D3
Birtley RC Inf Sch DH3 ..82 C5
Birtley RC Jun Sch DH3 .82 C4
Birtley Villas 1 DH3 ....82 C5
Birtwistle Ave NE31 ....57 D3
Biscop Terr NE32 ....58 C4
Bishop Cres NE32 ....58 C8
Bishop Harland C of E Prim Sch SR5 ....74 C3
Bishop Ian Ramsey CE Prim Sch DH8 ....77 C1
Bishop Morton Gr SR1 .103 B2
Bishop Ramsay Ct NE34 .60 A6
Bishop Rock Dr NE12 ...39 A6
Bishop's Ave NE4 ....98 A1
Bishop's Rd NE15 ....54 D5
Bishopdale Penshaw DH4 .89 E8
Wallsend NE28 ....39 F5
Bishopdale Ave NE24 ....17 A6
Bishopdale House NE4 ..54 E4
Bishops Cl NE28 ....40 E2
Bishops Ct NE5 ....53 F8
Bishops Dr NE40 ....52 D4
Bishops Mdw NE22 ....10 F1
Bishops Way SR3 ....91 E5
Bishopton St Blyth NE24 ..17 E6
Sunderland SR2 ....103 B1
Bishopton Way NE46 ....44 E3
Bisley Dr NE34 ....59 D7
Bittern Cl NE28 ....41 A6
Biverfield Rd NE42 ....50 E3
Black Boy Rd DH4 ....94 A7
Black Boy Yd NE1 ....99 A1
Black Carts Turret* NE47 ....128 C5
Black Dr DH3 ....89 B5
Black La Blaydon NE21 ...53 A2
Gateshead NE9 ....71 C1
Black Middens Bastle House* NE48 ....121 E7
Black Rd Hebburn NE31 ...57 F6
Ryhope SR2 ....92 F7
Blackberries The NE9 ....71 F1
Blackburn Gn NE10 ....71 C7
Blackcap Cl NE38 ....82 F3
Blackclose Bank NE63 ....6 D1
Blackclose Est NE63 ....6 D1
Blackdene NE63 ....6 B2
Blackdown Cl NE12 ....39 A6
Blackett Cotts NE41 ....51 A6
Blackett Pl NE1 ....99 A1
Blackett St
Newcastle-upon-Tyne NE1 ..99 A1
Hebburn NE31,NE32 ....57 F8
Blackett Terr SR4 ....102 A2
Blackfell Prim Sch NE37 .83 A6
Blackfell Rd NE37 ....82 F6

Blackfriars Ct NE1 98 C1
Blackfriars Mus★ NE1 98 C1
Blackfriars Way NE12 39 A6
Blackheath Cl NE37 72 C2
Blackheath Ct NE3 37 B5
Blackhill Ave NE28 40 F6
Blackhill Cres NE9 71 D4
Blackhouse La NE40 52 B5
Blackpool Par NE31 58 A3
Blackrow La
Heddon-on-the-Wall NE15 35 A4
Gateshead NE9 71 A3
Blackstone Ct NE21 53 A2
Blackthorn Cl NE16 69 A2
Blackthorn Dr NE28 40 C5
Blackthorn Pl NE4 100 B3
Blackthorn Way
Fence Houses DH4 90 A2
Blyth NE24 17 C4
Ashington NE63 6 B2
Blackthorne NE10 71 F5
Blackwater Ho 7 SR3 92 A6
Blackwell Ave NE6 57 A6
Blackwood Rd SR5 74 A3
Bladen St NE32 58 A7
Bladen Street Ind Est NE32 58 A7
Blagdon Ave NE34 59 E8
Blagdon Cl
Newcastle-upon-Tyne NE1 99 C1
Morpeth NE61 8 E8
Blagdon Cres NE23 21 E8
Blagdon Ct NE22 11 C2
Blagdon Dr NE24 17 C3
Blagdon St NE1 99 C1
Blagdon Terr
Seaton Burn NE13 28 B8
Cramlington NE23 22 B6
Blake Ave NE16 69 B7
Blake Wlk NE8 56 A2
Blakelaw Rd
7 Newcastle-upon-Tyne NE5 37 B2
Newcastle-upon-Tyne NE5 37 C2
Blakemoor Pl NE5 37 C1
Blanche Terr DH9 79 B2
Blanchland NE38 83 E1
Blanchland Ave
Wide Open NE13 28 B6
Newcastle-upon-Tyne NE15 53 C7
Blanchland Cl NE28 40 D5
Blanchland Dr
Seaton Delaval NE25 23 F2
Sunderland SR5 75 C3
Blanchland Terr NE30 42 B7
Blandford Rd NE29 41 D8
Blandford Sq NE1 100 C4
Blandford St
Newcastle-upon-Tyne NE1 100 C4
Sunderland SR1 103 A2
Blandford Way NE28 40 D5
Blaxton Pl NE16 68 F5
Blaydon Ave SR5 74 A4
Blaydon Bank NE21 53 C2
Blaydon Bsns Ctr NE21 53 E3
Blaydon Bsns Pk NE21 53 F4
Blaydon Haughs Ind Est NE21 53 E4
Blaydon Highway NE21 53 D3
Blaydon Ind Pk NE21 53 D3
Blaydon West Prim Sch NE21 53 C3
Blaykeston Cl SR7 92 E1
Blayney Row NE15 52 C8
Bleachfeld NE10 71 F6
Bleasdale Cres DH4 90 B7
Blencathra
Tynemouth NE30 32 A2
Washington NE37 83 C6
Blenheim NE12 29 D4
Blenheim Ct NE24 17 D3
Blenheim Dr NE22 11 C2
Blenheim Gdns NE61 4 E4
Blenheim Pl NE11 54 E1
Blenkinsop Ct NE34 59 B3
Blenkinsop Gr NE32 58 B3
Blenkinsop St 5 NE28 40 B2
Bletchley Ave SR5 73 F4
Blezard Ct NE21 53 E4
Blind La
Chester le Street DH3 88 D6
Burnside DH4 90 B3
New Silksworth SR3 92 B7
Blindy La DH5 95 C1
Bloomfield Ct SR6 75 F2
Bloomfield Dr DH5 94 D3
Bloomsbury Ct NE3 38 B4
Blossom Gr DH4 90 B4
Blossomfield Way DH6 97 F3
Blount St NE6 56 D6
Blucher Rd
Killingworth NE12 29 C2
North Shields NE29 41 F3
Blucher Terr NE15 35 B1
Blue Anchor Ct NE8 101 B4
Blue House Ct NE37 83 B8
Blue House La
Washington NE37 83 C8
Cleadon SR5,SR6 75 A6
Blue House Rd NE31 57 D3
Blue Quarries Rd NE9 71 B6
Blue Row NE15 34 F2
Blue Top Cotts NE23 22 D6
Bluebell Cl Wylam NE41 51 B7
Gateshead NE9 71 B5
Bluebell Dene NE5 37 A5
Bluebell Way NE34 59 B5
Blueburn Dr NE12 29 F3
Blumer St DH4 94 A8
Blyth Bebside Mid Sch NE24 16 F8
Blyth Cl NE23 28 F8
Blyth Com Coll (North Side) NE24 17 A7
Blyth Com Coll (South Side) NE24 17 D5
Blyth Community Hospl NE24 17 D8
Blyth Ct
Newcastle-upon-Tyne NE15 53 C7
South Shields NE34 59 C5
Blyth Dr NE61 9 E1
Blyth Horton Grange Fst Sch NE24 16 F8
Blyth Rd NE26 24 E2
Blyth Sq SR5 74 A3
Blyth St Chopwell NE17 66 C1
Seaton Delaval NE25 23 C3
Sunderland SR5 74 A4
Blyth Terr NE63 6 E4
Blythswood NE2 99 B4
Blyton Ave
South Shields NE34 58 F5
Ryhope SR2 92 E6
Bodlewell Ho SR1 103 B3
Bodlewell La SR1 103 B3
Bodley Cl NE3 37 D5
Bodmin Cl NE28 40 E5
Bodmin Ct 1 NE9 71 A2
Bodmin Rd NE29 41 C8
Bodmin Sq SR5 74 A4
Bodmin Way NE3 37 F6
Bog Houses NE23 16 C2
Bognor St SR5 73 F4
Bohemia Terr NE24 17 E6
Boker La NE35 74 B8
Bolam NE38 82 F4
Bolam Ave Blyth NE24 17 D7
Tynemouth NE30 32 A1
Bolam Coyne 13 NE6 56 C5
Bolam Ct NE15 35 D1
Bolam Dr NE63 6 E2
Bolam Gdns NE28 41 B3
Bolam Gr NE30 32 A1
Bolam Lake★ NE20 124 B3
Bolam Pl NE22 11 C2
Bolam Rd NE12 29 C3
Bolam St
Newcastle-upon-Tyne NE6 56 C5
Gateshead NE8 70 B8
Bolam Street Prim Sch NE6 56 C5
Bolam Way
Seaton Delaval NE25 23 C3
Newcastle-upon-Tyne NE6 56 C5
Boland Rd NE61 2 A3
Bolbec Rd NE4 54 E7
Bolburn NE10 72 A7
Boldon Bsns Pk NE35 73 E7
Boldon C of E Prim Sch NE36 73 F7
Boldon Cl NE28 40 D5
Boldon Comp Sch NE35 74 B8
Boldon Dr NE36 74 A7
Boldon Gdns NE9 71 C3
Boldon La
South Shields NE34 59 B5
East Boldon NE35,NE36 59 C1
Cleadon SR6 59 F1
Bolingbroke Rd NE29 41 D6
Bolingbroke St
4 South Shields NE33 42 D2
Newcastle-upon-Tyne NE6 56 A7
Bollihope Dr SR3 86 B2
Bolsover St NE63 6 D3
Bolsover Terr
Pegswood NE61 4 F4
Ashington NE63 6 D3
Bolton's Bglw NE17 77 B8
Bomont Dr NE23 22 D8
Bonaventure DH4 90 C8
Bonchester Cl NE22 10 F2
Bonchester Ct NE28 40 E5
Bonchester Pl NE23 22 D8
Bond Cl SR5 75 C1
Bond Ct NE4 54 E5
Bond St 2 NE4 54 D5
Bondene Ave NE10 71 E8
Bondene Ave W NE10 71 E8
Bondene Way NE23 16 B2
Bondfield Cl NE28 40 F3
Bondfield Gdns NE10 72 A8
Bondgate Cl NE46 45 B4
Bondgate Ct NE46 45 B4
Bondicar Terr NE24 17 E7
Bondicarr Pl 1 NE5 37 D1
Bonemill La
Chester le Street NE38 88 F8
Washington NE38 89 C8
Bonington Way NE5 37 B2
Bonner's Field SR6 103 A4
Bonnivard Gdns NE23 23 A1
Bonsall Ct NE34 59 D5
Booth St Gateshead NE10 71 D8
Sunderland SR4 102 A2
Booths Rd NE63 6 A4
Bootle St SR5 74 A3
Bordeaux Cl SR3 91 E6
Border Forest Park Museum★ NE48 120 D8
Border History & Tourist Ctr NE46 45 B5
Border Rd NE28 40 B1
Boreham Cl NE28 40 D5
Borodin Ave SR5 73 F4
Borough Rd
North Shields NE29 42 A5
Jarrow NE32 58 B6
South Shields NE34 60 A5
Sunderland SR1 103 B2
Borrowdale Birtley DH3 82 D1
Whickham NE16 69 D7
Washington NE37 83 C8
Borrowdale Ave
Blyth NE24 17 A8
Newcastle-upon-Tyne NE6 56 F7
Sunderland SR6 75 D5
Borrowdale Cl NE36 74 C8
Borrowdale Cres
Penshaw DH4 90 A8
Blaydon NE21 68 B8
Borrowdale Gdns NE9 71 B3
Borrowdale St DH5 95 A2
Boscombe Dr NE28 40 C4
Boston Ave
Washington NE38 83 D6
Newcastle-upon-Tyne NE7 39 B5
Boston Cl NE28 40 D5
Boston Cres SR5 73 E4
Boston Ct NE12 39 F8
Boston St SR5 73 F4
Bosun's Way NE10 57 A2
Boswell Ave NE34 59 B3
Bosworth NE12 29 D4
Bosworth Gdns NE6 39 D2
Bothal Ave NE62 10 E7
Bothal Bank NE61 5 C2
Bothal Cl Blyth NE24 17 C7
Pegswood NE61 4 E3
Bothal Cotts NE63 5 F4
Bothal Mid Sch NE63 5 F4
Bothal St NE6 56 D6
Bothal Terr
Stakeford NE62 11 B8
Ashington NE63 5 F4
Bottle Bank NE8 101 B4
Bottlehouse St NE6 56 C4
Boulby Cl SR3 92 C7
Boulmer Ave NE23 16 B2
Boulmer Cl NE3 37 F8
Boulmer Ct DH2 88 C2
Boulmer Gdns NE13 28 B6
Boulsworth Rd NE29 31 E1
Boult Terr DH4 90 B6
Boundary Dr NE61 9 A7
Boundary Gdns NE7 39 A3
Boundary La DH8 76 A3
Boundary St SR5 75 C2
Boundary Way NE26 24 D6
Bourn Lea DH4 90 A5
Bourne Ave NE4 54 E7
Bournemouth Ct NE28 40 E5
Bournemouth Gdns
Whitley Bay NE26 32 A6
Newcastle-upon-Tyne NE5 36 F3
Bournemouth Par NE31 58 A3
Bournemouth Rd NE29 41 C5
Bournmoor Prim Sch DH4 89 E3
Bourtree Cl NE28 40 C4
Bowbank Cl SR3 86 B2
Bowburn Ave SR5 74 C2
Bowburn Cl NE10 72 C7
Bower St SR6 75 D4
Bower The NE32 73 B8
Bowes Ave DH5 95 B1
Bowes Cl NE16 69 B2
Bowes Cres NE16 79 D8
Bowes Ct NE3 38 E5
Bowes Ho 8 SR3 91 D7
Bowes Lea DH4 89 F4
Bowes Lyon Cl NE39 78 D8
Bowes Lyon Ct 6 NE9 70 F8
Bowes Rly★ NE9 82 E8
Bowes Rly Mus★ NE9 71 E2
Bowes St Blyth NE24 17 E8
Newcastle-upon-Tyne NE3 38 E5
Bowes Wlk NE12 39 C7
Bowesville NE16 79 B5
Bowfell Ave NE5 37 D3
Bowfell Cl NE5 37 D3
Bowfell Gdns NE62 11 A8
Bowfield Ave NE3 28 C1
Bowler's Hill NE43 64 F7
Bowlynn Cl SR3 91 E6
Bowman Dr NE23 29 B8
Bowman Pl NE33 42 C1
Bowman Sq NE63 6 D2
Bowman St SR6 60 F1
Bowmont NE61 1 E5
Bowmont Wlk DH2 88 A1
Bowness Ave NE28 40 E6
Bowness Cl NE36 74 C7
Bowness Pl NE9 71 B4
Bowness Rd
Whickham NE16 69 D7
Newcastle-upon-Tyne NE5 37 A1
Bowness St SR5 74 A4
Bowness Terr NE28 40 E5
Bowsden Ct NE3 38 E5
Bowsden Terr NE3 38 E5
Bowtrees SR2 86 D3
Boxlaw NE9 71 C5
Boyd Cres NE28 40 C2
Boyd Rd NE28 40 D2
Boyd St Newburn NE15 52 E8
Newcastle-upon-Tyne NE2 99 C2
Boyd Terr
Newcastle-upon-Tyne NE15 36 B1
Newcastle-upon-Tyne, Westerhope NE5 36 F3
Boyne Ct NE24 17 E8
Boyne Gdns NE27 30 E3
Boystones Ct NE37 83 B6
Brabourne St NE34 59 C6
Brack Terr NE10 57 B2
Bracken Ave NE28 40 C5
Bracken Cl NE13 27 B6
Bracken Dr NE11 69 F6
Bracken Pl NE4 54 D7
Bracken Ridge NE61 3 C1
Bracken Way NE40 52 A3
Brackenburn Cl DH4 90 C1
Brackendene Dr NE9 70 E5
Brackenfield Rd NE3 38 B4
Brackenlaw NE9 71 C3
Brackenridge NE16 78 E6
Brackenside NE3 28 C1
Brackenway NE37 83 B7
Brackenwood Gr SR2 86 C2
Brackley NE37 72 E1
Brackley Gr NE29 41 D4
Bracknell Cl SR3 92 C8
Bracknell Gdns NE5 36 C1
Bradbury Cl NE10 72 D7
Bradbury Ct NE25 23 D6
Bradbury Pl NE25 23 D6
Bradford Ave
Wallsend NE28 40 D5
Sunderland SR5 74 A4
Bradley Ave
Houghton-le-Spring DH5 94 E6
South Shields NE34 60 A6
Bradley Cl DH2 81 E2
Bradley Fell La NE41 51 C2
Bradley Fell Rd NE40, NE42 66 C8
Bradley Rd NE42 50 F3
Bradley Terr DH5 95 C1
Bradley View 13 NE40 51 F3
Bradman Dr DH3 88 E1
Bradman Sq 3 SR5 74 A4
Bradman St SR5 74 A4
Bradshaw Sq SR5 74 A3
Bradshaw St SR5 74 A3
Bradwell Rd NE3 37 E5
Bradwell Way DH4 90 C4
Brady & Martin Ct NE1 99 B2
Brady Sq NE38 83 F4
Brady St SR4 85 F7
Brae The SR2 102 B2
Braebridge Pl NE3 37 F3
Braefell Ct NE37 83 B6
Braemar Ct NE10 57 B2
Braemar Dr NE34 60 A8
Braemar Gdns
Whitley Bay NE25 31 C4
Sunderland SR3 86 B3
Sunderland SR3 91 C6
Braeside Dunston NE11 69 F7
Sunderland SR2 86 B4
Braeside Cl NE30 32 A3
Brahman Ave NE29 41 D4
Braintree Gdns NE3 37 F4
Brama Teams Ind Est NE8 70 B8
Bramble Dykes NE15 54 B6
Bramblelaw NE9 71 C4
Brambling Lea NE22 11 C2
Bramhall Dr NE38 89 B8
Bramham Ct NE34 59 E5
Bramhope Gn NE9 71 B2
Bramley Cl SR4 85 A3
Bramley Ct NE7 39 E3
Brampton Ave NE6 56 F4
Brampton Ct NE23 22 C8
Brampton Gdns
Throckley NE15 35 E2
Wallsend NE28 41 A4
Gateshead NE9 71 A3
Brampton Pl NE29 41 E5
Brampton Rd NE34 59 A5
Bramwell Ct NE3 38 E5
Bramwell Rd SR2 103 B1
Brancepeth Ave
Fence Houses DH4 90 A1
Newcastle-upon-Tyne NE4 54 E5
Brancepeth Cl NE15 53 C7
Brancepeth Rd
Hebburn NE31 57 F7
Washington NE38 83 A4
Brancepeth Terr NE32 58 B3
Branch End Terr NE43 64 D7
Branch St NE21 53 B1
Brand Ave NE4 54 E7
Brandling Ct
14 Gateshead NE10 56 D1
South Shields NE34 60 A4
Brandling Dr NE3 28 D1
Brandling La 15 NE10 56 D1
Brandling Mews NE3 28 D1
Brandling Pk NE2 99 A4
Brandling Pl NE10 56 D1
Brandling Pl S NE2 99 B4
Brandling Prim Sch NE10 56 D1
Brandling St
Gateshead NE8 101 C4
Sunderland SR6 75 E2
Brandling St S SR6 75 E1
Brandling Terr 3 NE30 42 B6
Brandon Ave NE27 30 E3
Brandon Cl
Houghton-le-Spring DH4 94 D7
Blaydon NE21 68 A8
Blyth NE24 17 B8
Brandon Gdns NE9 71 D3
Brandon Gr NE2 99 C3
Brandon Rd
North Shields NE29 41 D6
Newcastle-upon-Tyne NE3 37 F6
Brandy La NE37 83 B7
Brandywell NE10 71 F6
Brannen St NE29 42 A5
Bransdale DH4 89 E8
Bransdale Ave SR6 75 F7
Branston St SR5 75 B2
Branton Ave NE31 57 D3
Brantwood Ave NE25 31 D4
Branxton Cres NE6 56 F5
Bray Cl NE28 40 D5
Braydon Dr NE29 41 E3
Brayside NE32 58 D1
Breamish NE61 1 E5
Breamish Dr NE38 88 F8
Breamish Ho NE1 56 A5
Breamish St
Newcastle-upon-Tyne NE1 56 A5
Jarrow NE32 58 A5
Brearley Way NE10 71 C8
Brecken Ct NE9 70 E4
Breckenbeds Rd NE9 70 E4
Breckon Cl NE63 6 E1
Brecon Cl NE5 37 B4
Bredon Cl NE38 83 B3
Brendale Ave NE5 36 E3
Brenkley Ave NE27 30 F2
Brenkley Cl NE13 27 B7
Brenkley Ct NE13 28 B8
Brenkley Way NE13 21 B1
Brenlynn Cl SR3 91 E6
Brennan Cl
Newcastle-upon-Tyne NE15 54 B6
Ashington NE63 7 A3
Brentford Ave SR5 74 A3
Brentford Sq 4 SR5 74 A3
Brentwood Ave
Newcastle-upon-Tyne NE2 38 E2
Newbiggin-by-the-Sea NE64 7 D5
Brentwood Cl NE25 23 E2
Brentwood Gdns
Whickham NE16 69 B5
Newcastle-upon-Tyne NE2 38 D2
Sunderland SR3 86 B3
Brentwood Gr NE28 40 D1
Brentwood Pl 6 NE33 42 D2
Brentwood Rd DH4 90 A5
Brett Cl NE7 39 D3
Brettanby Gdns NE40 52 C6
Brettanby Rd NE10 71 C7
Bretton Gdns NE7 39 C2
Brettonby Ave NE43 64 D7
Brewer Terr SR2 93 A6
Brewer's La NE28,NE29 41 C3
Brewery Bank 6 NE16 54 A1
Brewery La
Gateshead NE10 56 D2
5 Whickham NE16 54 A1
Ponteland NE20 25 E6
South Shields NE33 42 B2
Brewery St 3 NE24 17 F8
Brewhouse Bank NE30 42 C6
Briar Ave
2 Houghton-le-Spring DH4 94 D8
Whitley Bay NE26 32 A6
Briar Cl Great Lumley DH4 89 E1
Shiney Row DH4 89 F4
Blaydon NE21 53 A2
Wallsend NE28 40 C5
Briar Ct NE26 32 A5
Briar Edge NE12 39 D8
Briar Field NE38 83 D1
Briar La NE15 35 E1
Briar Pl NE15 54 A5
Briar Rd NE39 67 D2
Briar Terr NE16 79 C6
Briar Wlk NE15 54 A5
Briardale Dinnington NE13 27 B7
Bedlington NE22 10 E1
Briardale Rd NE24 17 A8
Briardene
Burnopfield NE16 78 E6
Ashington NE63 6 B2
Briardene Cl SR3 91 C6
Briardene Cres NE3 38 A3
Briardene Dr NE10 72 D8
Briarfield Rd NE3 38 B4
Briarhill DH2 88 A5
Briarlea NE61 9 E4
Briars The SR5 74 B1
Briarside NE5 37 A3
Briarsyde NE12 39 E6
Briarsyde Cl NE16 68 E5
Briarwood NE23 29 B8
Briarwood Ave NE3 38 E6
Briarwood Cres
3 Dunston NE11 69 F8
Newcastle-upon-Tyne NE6 39 F1
Briarwood Rd NE24 17 F6
Briarwood St DH4 89 E1
Briary The NE15 35 C2
Brick Garth DH5 95 C1
Brick Row SR2 92 E7
Bridekirk NE37 83 C7
Bridge Cotts NE23 29 B8
Bridge Cres SR1 103 A3
Bridge End Ind Est NE46 45 C6
Bridge House SR1 103 A3
Bridge Pk NE3 38 C8
Bridge Rd NE61 2 A2
Bridge Rd S NE29 41 E3
Bridge St
Seaton Burn NE13 28 B8
Blaydon NE21 53 C4
Blyth NE24 17 F7
Blyth NE24 17 F8

Bridge St *continued*
Morpeth NE61 .8 F8
Newbiggin-by-the-Sea NE64 .7 E4
Gateshead NE8 .101 B4
Sunderland SR1 .103 A3
Bridge Terr
Bedlington NE22 .11 C3
Shiremoor NE27 .30 F4
Stakeford NE62 .11 B8
Bridges The SR1 .103 A2
Bridgewater Cl
Newcastle-upon-Tyne NE15 .53 C7
Wallsend NE28 .40 C4
Bridgewater Rd NE37 .83 E7
Bridle Path
East Boldon NE36 .74 C7
Sunderland SR3 .91 C8
Bridle The NE27 .31 B2
Bridlington Ave NE9 .70 F3
Bridlington Cl NE28 .40 D5
Bridlington Par NE31 .58 A3
Bridport Rd NE29 .31 D1
Brier Dene Cres NE26 .31 F8
Brierdene Cl NE26 .31 F8
Brierdene Ct NE26 .31 E8
Brierdene Rd NE26 .24 F1
Brierdene View NE26 .31 E8
Brierfield Gr SR4 .85 D4
Brierley Cl NE24 .17 B7
Brierley Rd NE24 .17 B7
Briermede Ave NE9 .70 F4
Briermede Pk NE9 .70 F4
Briery Hill La NE61 .14 C3
Briery Vale Cl SR2 .102 C1
Briery Vale Rd SR2 .86 C4
Brieryside NE5 .37 D2
Brigham Ave NE3 .37 E3
Brigham Pl NE33 .42 C3
Bright St
South Shields NE33 .42 E2
Sunderland SR6 .75 E1
Brightlea DH3 .82 E5
Brightman Rd NE29 .42 A6
Brighton Ave Prim Sch
NE8 .101 A1
Brighton Cl NE28 .40 E5
Brighton Gdns NE8 .70 E7
Brighton Gr
Whitley Bay NE26 .31 F6
North Shields NE29 .41 F6
Newcastle-upon-Tyne NE4 .98 A2
Brighton Par NE31 .58 A3
Brighton Rd NE8 .70 E8
Brighton Terr DH6 .96 D1
Brignall Gdns NE15 .54 A7
Brignall Rise SR3 .86 B2
Brigside Cotts NE13 .28 C8
Brindley Rd NE37 .83 E6
Brinkburn
Chester le Street DH2 .88 A3
Washington NE38 .83 E2
Brinkburn Ave
Whickham NE16 .69 B8
Cramlington NE23 .22 C6
Blyth NE24 .17 F6
Newcastle-upon-Tyne NE3 .38 B6
Gateshead NE8 .70 E8
Brinkburn Cl
Blaydon NE21 .68 A8
Newcastle-upon-Tyne NE6 .56 B6
Brinkburn Comp Sch
NE34 .59 D6
Brinkburn Cres
Burnside DH4 .90 C1
Ashington NE63 .6 E4
Brinkburn Ct
8 North Shields NE30 .42 B6
22 Newcastle-upon-Tyne
NE6 .56 B6
Brinkburn Gdns NE62 .11 A8
Brinkburn La 21 NE6 .56 B6
Brinkburn Pl 25 NE6 .56 B6
Brinkburn Priory*
NE65 .118 C3
Brinkburn Sq 7 NE6 .56 B5
Brinkburn St
North Shields NE28 .41 C1
South Shields NE34 .59 B6
17 Newcastle-upon-Tyne
NE6 .56 B6
Newcastle-upon-Tyne, St
Lawrence NE6 .56 B5
Sunderland SR4 .102 A1
Brinkburn St S NE6 .56 C4
Brisbane Ave NE34 .58 F3
Brisbane Ct NE8 .101 B3
Brisbane St SR5 .74 A3
Brislee Ave NE30 .42 C7
Brislee Gdns NE3 .37 E4
Bristlecone SR3 .91 E5
Bristol Ave
Washington NE37 .83 B8
Sunderland SR5 .73 F4
Bristol Dr NE28 .40 D5
Bristol St NE25 .23 D6
Bristol Terr NE4 .100 A4
Bristol Wlk NE25 .23 D6
Britannia Ct NE4 .100 A4
Britannia Pl NE4 .98 A1
Britannia Rd SR3 .92 A7
Britannia Terr DH4 .94 A8
Brittania Ho NE28 .40 F1
Brixham Ave NE9 .70 F3
Brixham Cres NE32 .58 D5
Brixham Gdns SR3 .86 B3
Broad Chare NE1 .101 B4
Broad Garth NE1 .101 B4
Broad Landing NE33 .42 B3
Broad Meadows
Newcastle-upon-Tyne NE3 .37 F3
Sunderland SR2 .102 B1
Broad Oak Terr NE17 .66 B1
Broadbank NE10 .72 B8
Broadfield Pl NE34 .59 D5
Broadgates NE46 .45 B4
Broadlands SR6 .75 A7
Broadlea NE10 .72 B8
Broadmayne Ave SR4 .85 D4
Broadmayne Gdns SR4 .85 D4
Broadmead Way NE15 .54 A5
Broadmeadows
Washington NE38 .83 E2
Sunderland SR3 .91 B6
Broadoak NE10 .57 B1
Broadpark NE10 .72 B8
Broadpool Gn NE16 .69 C6
Broadpool Terr NE16 .69 C6
Broadsheath Terr SR5 .74 F2
Broadside NE10 .72 B8
Broadstairs Ct SR4 .85 D4
Broadstone Gr NE5 .36 C1
Broadstone Way NE28 .40 C4
Broadview Villas DH6 .96 A1
Broadwater NE10 .57 B1
Broadway
Chester le Street DH3 .88 D5
Newcastle-upon-Tyne NE15 .53 D7
Whickham NE16 .69 A4
Ponteland NE20 .25 C3
Blyth NE24 .17 E6
Guide Post NE62 .10 F7
Gateshead NE9 .71 B7
Broadway Circ NE24 .17 E7
Broadway Cl NE30 .32 B3
Broadway Cres NE24 .17 E6
Broadway E NE3 .38 C7
Broadway East Fst Sch
NE3 .38 D7
Broadway Gdns NE46 .44 F5
Broadway Jun Sch SR4 .85 D4
Broadway The
Houghton-le-Spring DH4 .94 E8
Tynemouth NE30 .32 B2
Sunderland, Grindon SR4 .85 B3
Sunderland, Springwell SR4 85 D4
Sunderland, Castletown
SR5 .85 A8
Broadway Villas NE15 .54 B6
Broadway W NE3 .38 B7
Broadwell Ct NE3,NE7 .38 F4
Broadwood Prim Sch
NE15 .53 F7
Broadwood Rd NE15 .53 F7
Broadwood View DH3 .88 D2
Brock Farm Ct NE30 .42 B6
Brock La NE22,NE62 .11 F5
Brock Sq 8 NE6 .56 B5
Brock St NE6 .56 B5
Brockenhurst Dr SR4 .85 A2
Brockhampton Cl NE35 .58 E2
Brockley Ave NE34 .59 B4
Brockley St SR5 .74 A3
Brockley Terr 4 NE35 .58 E1
Brockley Whins Sta NE32 58 F2
Brockwade NE10 .71 F4
Brockwell Cl NE21 .53 A1
Brockwell Ct NE24 .17 C5
Brockwell Ctr The NE23 .22 B8
Brockwell Dr NE39 .67 E3
Brockwell Mid Sch NE23 .22 B8
Brockwell Rd NE38 .82 F5
Brockwell St NE24 .17 C4
Brockwood Cl NE63 .6 B1
Brodie Cl NE34 .59 C4
Brodrick Cl NE3 .37 D5
Brodrick St 13 NE33 .42 D3
Brokenheugh NE5 .36 F1
Bromarsh Ct SR6 .75 F1
Bromford Rd NE3 .37 D5
Bromley Ave NE25 .31 E4
Bromley Ct NE3 .37 D7
Bromley Gdns Blyth NE24 .17 E5
Wallsend NE28 .40 D5
Brompton Cl DH2 .81 E2
Brompton Terr DH4 .90 D4
Bromsgrove Cl NE28 .40 E5
Bronte St NE8 .56 B1
Brook Ct Bedlington NE22 .11 A1
Bedlington NE22 .16 A8
Brook Side Lodge 3
SR2 .86 C4
Brook St Whitley Bay NE26 32 B6
Newcastle-upon-Tyne NE6 .56 D5
Brookbank Cl SR3 .91 F5
Brooke Ave
Whickham NE16 .69 A8
West Boldon NE35 .74 B8
Brooke St SR5 .102 C4
Brooke's Wlk NE34 .59 A2
Brookfield NE3 .38 B2
Brookfield Cres NE5 .36 C1
Brookfield Terr NE10 .57 B2
Brookland Dr NE12 .29 E3
Brookland Rd SR4 .85 F6
Brookland Terr NE29 .31 B1
Brooklands NE20 .25 A3
Brooklands Way NE35 .73 D8
Brookside
Houghton-le-Spring DH5 .94 D6
Annitsford NE23 .29 A7
Brookside Ave
Brunswick Village NE13 .28 A6
Blyth NE24 .17 B7
Brookside Cres NE5 .37 D1
Brookside Gdns 4 SR2 .86 C4
Brookside Terr 2 SR2 .86 C4
Brookside Wood NE38 .83 D1
Brooksmead NE28 .40 A4
Brookvale Ave NE3 .38 A4
Broom Cl Whickham NE16 .69 C6
Blaydon NE21 .68 B8
Morpeth NE61 .9 C7
Broom Ct NE9 .82 F8
Broom Gn NE16 .69 C6
Broom La NE16 .69 C6
Broom Terr
Burnopfield NE16 .79 C6
Whickham NE16 .69 C6
Broom Wood Ct NE42 .50 B1
Broome Cl NE3 .37 F6
Broomfield NE32 .58 C2
Broomfield Ave
Wallsend NE28 .40 C5
Newcastle-upon-Tyne NE6 .39 E1
Broomfield Cres NE17 .77 B8
Broomfield Rd NE3 .38 B4
Broomhaugh CE Fst Sch
NE44 .62 F7
Broomhaugh Cl NE46 .45 C4
Broomhill Est DH5 .94 F6
Broomhill Gdns NE5 .37 D1
Broomhill Rd NE42 .50 E3
Broomhill Terr DH5 .94 F5
Broomhouse La NE42 .50 D3
Broomhouse Rd NE42 .50 F3
Broomlaw NE9 .71 C4
Broomlea NE29 .31 B1
Broomlea Ct NE21 .53 C3
Broomlee NE63 .6 E2
Broomlee Cl NE7 .39 D3
Broomlee Rd NE12 .29 D3
Broomley Ct NE3 .37 F7
Broomley Fst Sch NE43 .64 B8
Broomley Wlk NE3 .37 F7
Broomridge Ave NE15 .54 D6
Brooms The DH2 .81 F2
Broomshields Ave SR5 .75 B3
Broomshields Cl SR5 .75 B3
Broomy Hill Rd NE15 .35 D2
Broomylinn Pl NE23 .22 C8
Brotherlee Rd NE3 .37 F7
Brough Ct 3 NE6 .56 C7
Brough Gdns NE28 .41 A4
Brough Park Way NE6 .56 D7
Brough St 2 NE6 .56 C7
Brough Way 20 NE6 .56 C7
Brougham St SR1 .103 A2
Broughton Rd NE33 .42 D2
Brow The NE6 .56 C5
Brown Cres NE9 .71 C1
Brown's Bldgs DH3 .82 C1
Browne Rd SR6 .75 E3
Browning Cl NE34 .59 B3
Browning Sq NE8 .56 A2
Brownlow Cl NE7 .39 E3
Brownlow Rd NE34 .59 C6
Brownrigg Dr NE23 .22 C5
Brownriggs Ct NE37 .83 B6
Brownsea Pl NE9 .71 A7
Browntop Pl NE34 .59 C5
Broxbourne Terr SR4 .102 A2
Broxburn Cl NE28 .40 E5
Broxburn Ct NE5 .37 C3
Broxholm Rd NE6 .39 B1
Bruce Cl Whiteleas NE34 .59 C4
Newcastle-upon-Tyne NE5 .36 F2
Bruce Gdns NE5 .54 C7
Brumell Dr NE61 .3 D1
Brumwell Ct NE43 .64 B7
Brundon Ave NE26 .31 F7
Brunel Dr SR6 .75 F2
Brunel Lodge NE4 .100 A3
Brunel St
Newcastle-upon-Tyne NE4 100 B3
Gateshead NE8 .70 D8
Brunel Terr NE4 .100 A3
Brunel Wlk NE4 .100 A3
Brunswick Gr NE13 .28 A6
Brunswick Ind Est NE13 .27 F6
Brunswick Park Ind Est
NE13 .28 A6
Brunswick Pl NE1 .99 A2
Brunswick Rd
Shiremoor NE27 .30 F2
Sunderland SR5 .74 A4
Brunswick Sq NE27 .30 F2
Brunswick St NE33 .42 C1
Brunton Ave
Wallsend NE28 .41 B3
Newcastle-upon-Tyne NE3 .37 F6
Brunton Cl NE27 .30 F2
Brunton Gr NE3 .37 F6
Brunton La Hazlerigg NE13 27 E2
Newcastle-upon-Tyne,
Kingston Park NE3 .37 C7
Newcastle-upon-Tyne,
Brunton Park NE3,NE13 .28 B2
Brunton Rd NE3 .37 C7
Brunton St NE29 .41 D3
Brunton Terr SR4 .102 A2
Brunton Turret* NE46 .128 E4
Brunton Way
Gateshead NE10 .57 B2
Cramlington NE23 .16 B2
Brussels Rd
Wallsend NE28 .40 B1
Sunderland SR4 .85 D7
Bryan's Leap NE16 .79 A7
Bryden Ct NE34 .59 D5
Bryers St SR6 .60 F1
Buchanan Gn NE11 .100 A1
Buchanan St NE31 .57 D5
Buck's Nook La NE40 .66 C7
Buckingham SR3 .91 E8
Buckingham Cl 1 SR6 .75 F8
Buckingham St NE4 .98 B1
Buckland Cl Burnside DH4 90 C2
Washington NE38 .83 D3
Buckthorne Gr NE7 .39 C3
Buddle Ct NE4 .54 E4
Buddle Rd NE4 .54 D4
Buddle St NE28 .40 C1
Buddle Terr
4 Shiremoor NE27 .30 E1
Sunderland SR2 .103 B1
Bude Ct NE28 .40 C4
Bude Gdns NE9 .70 F3
Bude Gr NE29 .31 D1
Budle Cl Blyth NE24 .17 C7
Newcastle-upon-Tyne NE3 .38 A6
Budleigh Rd NE3 .37 F5
Budworth Ave NE26 .24 D5
Bugatti Ind Pk NE29 .41 C5
Buller's Gn NE61 .3 E1
Bullfinch Dr NE16 .69 A7
Bullion La DH2 .88 B3
Bullion La Sch DH2 .88 B3
Bulman's La NE29 .42 A8
Bulmer Ho NE34 .60 A7
Bulmer Rd NE34 .60 A7
Bungalows The
Birtley DH3 .82 B6
Hetton le Hole DH5 .94 F6
Ebchester DH8 .76 F4
Gateshead NE10 .71 E8
Kibblesworth NE11 .81 E8
Medomsley NE17 .77 B4
Wallsend NE28 .40 F3
Bunyan Ave NE34 .59 A3
Burdale Ave NE5 .37 A1
Burdon Ave
Houghton-le-Spring DH5 .95 A8
Cramlington NE23 .21 F7
Burdon Cl SR6 .59 E1
Burdon Cres Ryhope SR2 .92 E6
Cleadon SR6 .59 E1
Seaham SR7 .92 F1
Burdon La SR2,SR3 .92 C5
Burdon Lodge NE16 .69 C2
Burdon Main Row NE29 .42 A4
Burdon Pk NE16 .69 C2
Burdon Plain NE16 .80 B7
Burdon Rd
Sunderland SR1, SR2 .103 A1
Burdon SR3 .92 B5
New Silksworth SR3 .92 B6
Cleadon SR6 .59 E1
Burdon St NE29 .41 D3
Burdon Terr
Newcastle-upon-Tyne NE2 .99 B4
Bedlington NE22 .10 F1
Burford Ct NE7 .39 A4
Burford Gdns SR3 .86 B3
Burghley Gdns NE61 .4 E4
Burghley Rd NE10 .71 C6
Burgoyne Ct NE37 .83 D8
Burke St 2 SR5 .74 A3
Burlawn Cl 3 SR2 .92 F8
Burleigh St 9 NE33 .42 D2
Burlington Cl SR2 .103 C1
Burlington Ct
Newcastle-upon-Tyne NE2 .38 F2
Wallsend NE28 .40 E7
Burlington Gdns NE6 .56 B8
Burlison Gdns NE10 .56 C2
Burn Ave
2 Longbenton NE12 .39 D8
1 Wallsend NE28 .40 B2
Burn Closes Cres NE28 .40 E3
Burn Crook DH5 .94 D6
Burn Heads Rd NE31 .57 D4
Burn La Hetton le Hole DH5 95 A3
Hexham NE46 .45 A6
Burn Park Rd
Houghton-le-Spring DH4 .94 D8
Sunderland SR2 .102 B1
Burn Prom 5 DH4 .94 E8
Burn Rd NE21 .53 A1
Burn Terr Shiney Row DH4 .90 B6
Wallsend NE28 .40 F2
Hebburn NE31 .57 C2
Burn View Annitsford NE23 29 B8
Hedworth NE32 .73 D8
Burnaby Dr NE40 .52 B4
Burnaby St SR4 .102 A1
Burnbank Gateshead NE10 72 A6
Seaton Burn NE13 .28 B8
5 Sunderland SR5 .75 B2
Burnbank Ave NE25 .31 B5
Burnbridge NE13 .28 B8
Burnden Gr DH4 .90 A5
Burnet Cl NE28 .40 C5
Burnet Ct NE63 .6 B1
Burney Villas NE8 .56 A1
Burnfoot NE42 .50 A4
Burnfoot Terr NE26 .32 C4
Burnfoot Way NE3 .37 E3
Burnhall Dr SR7 .93 A1
Burnham Ave NE15 .53 B7
Burnham Cl
1 Penshaw DH4 .90 B6
Blyth NE24 .17 E5
Burnham Gr
East Boldon NE36 .74 D7
Newcastle-upon-Tyne NE6 .56 E4
Burnham St NE34 .59 C6
Burnhills Gdns NE40 .52 A1
Burnhills La NE40 .67 B8
Burnhope Dr SR5 .75 B3
Burnhope Gdns NE9 .71 D3
Burnhope Rd NE38 .83 E6
Burnland Terr NE46 .44 F5
Burnlea 4 DH4 .94 C8
Burnlea Gdns NE23 .23 B2
Burnley St NE21 .53 C2
Burnmoor Gdns NE9 .71 D3
Burnop Terr NE39 .67 A2
Burnopfield Gdns NE15 .54 A6
Burnopfield Prim Sch
NE16 .79 A6
Burnopfield Rd NE39 .67 F1
Burns Ave N DH5 .94 E7
Burns Ave Blyth NE24 .17 C5
West Boldon NE35 .74 B8
Burns Ave S DH5 .94 E7
Burns Cl West Rainton DH4 94 A2
Whickham NE16 .69 B5
Biddick Hall NE34 .59 B3
Burns Cres NE16 .69 A8
Burns St NE32 .58 B7
Burnside Gateshead NE10 .71 E7
Newcastle-upon-Tyne NE2 .98 B3
Ponteland NE20 .25 B3
Bedlington NE22 .11 D3
Jarrow NE32 .58 C4
East Boldon NE36 .74 E7
Ovington NE42 .49 D4
Hexham NE46 .44 F2
Morpeth NE61 .4 A1
Ashington NE63 .7 A3
Burnside Ave
Burnside DH4 .90 C1
Annitsford NE23 .29 B8
Burnside Cl
Whickham NE16 .69 A4
Seghill NE23 .22 E1
Blyth NE24 .17 B8
Ovingham NE42 .50 A4
Burnside Comm High Sch
NE28 .40 D2
Burnside Cotts
Annitsford NE23 .29 C8
Mickley Square NE43 .49 E1
Burnside Fst Sch NE23 .16 C1
Burnside Prim Sch DH4 .90 D1
Burnside Rd
Newcastle-upon-Tyne NE3 .38 C7
Tynemouth NE30 .32 B3
Rowlands Gill NE39 .67 D2
Burnside The NE5 .36 E1
Burnside View NE23 .22 E1
Burnstones NE5 .36 E1
Burnt House Rd NE25 .31 E3
Burnt Houses NE40 .52 B1
Burnthouse Cl NE21 .68 A8
Burnthouse La
Whickham NE16 .69 A5
Whickham NE16 .69 A6
Whickham, Whickham Fell
NE16 .69 A4
Burntland Ave SR5 .74 F2
Burnville NE6 .56 A7
Burnville Rd SR4 .102 B1
Burnville Rd S SR4 .102 B1
Burnway Washington NE37 83 B8
Seaham SR7 .93 A1
Burradon Farm Cotts
NE23 .29 D7
Burradon Prim Sch NE23 .29 C5
Burradon Rd NE23 .29 C7
Burrow St 5 NE33 .42 C3
Burscough Cres SR6 .75 D2
Burstow Ave NE6 .56 E3
Burswell Ave NE46 .44 F5
Burswell Villas NE46 .44 F5
Burt Ave NE29 .41 E5
Burt Cl DH6 .97 E3
Burt Cres NE23 .29 B8
Burt Memorial Homes
NE62 .10 E5
Burt Rd NE22 .11 E3
Burt St NE24 .17 E8
Burt Terr Walbottle NE15 .36 A2
Morpeth NE61 .9 A8
Burtree NE38 .83 B3
Burwell Ave NE5 .53 F8
Burwood Cl NE6 .57 A4
Burwood Rd
Tynemouth NE29 .41 C8
Newcastle-upon-Tyne NE6 .56 F3
Business & Innovation Ctr
SR5 .74 F1
Buston Terr NE2 .38 F1
Busty Bank
Burnopfield NE16 .79 B7
Burnopfield NE16,NE39 .79 A8
Butcher's Bridge Rd
NE32 .58 B4
Butcher's La NE61 .4 F5
Bute Ct 3 SR3 .92 A6
Bute Dr NE39 .66 F4
Bute Rd N NE39 .66 F4
Bute Rd S NE39 .66 F3
Bute St DH9 .79 A2
Buteland Rd NE15 .53 F7
Buteland Terr NE64 .7 D4
Butsfield Gdns SR3 .86 B2
Butterburn Cl NE7 .39 E4
Butterfield Cl NE40 .51 F4
Buttermere
Gateshead NE10 .72 A8
Cleadon SR6 .60 A1
Buttermere Ave
Easington Lane DH5 .97 C8
Whickham NE16 .69 D7
Buttermere Cl
Chester le Street DH2 .88 C2

Buttermere Cl *continued*
Killingworth NE12 .29 C3
3 Newcastle-upon-Tyne NE5 .37 B1
Buttermere Cres
South Hetton DH6 .97 E8
Blaydon NE21 .68 B8
Buttermere Gdns
South Shields NE34 .59 E6
Gateshead NE9 .71 A5
Buttermere Rd NE30 .32 A2
Buttermere St SR2 .86 E2
Buttermere Way NE24 .12 B1
Butterwell Dr NE61 .4 E3
Buttsfield Terr DH4 .90 B8
Buxton Cl Wallsend NE28 .40 D5
Jarrow NE32 .58 C5
Buxton Gdns
Newcastle-upon-Tyne NE5 .36 F3
Sunderland SR3 .86 B3
Buxton Gn NE5 .36 F3
Buxton Rd NE32 .58 C5
Buxton St NE1 .99 C1
By-Way The NE15 .35 D1
Byer Sq DH5 .95 A6
Byer St DH5 .95 A6
Byermoor RC Prim Sch NE16 .79 D7
Byers Ct SR3 .92 B8
Byeways The NE12 .39 B6
Byewell Gr NE27 .31 A3
Byewell View NE43 .64 D7
Bygate Cl NE3 .37 E3
Bygate Rd NE25 .31 E4
Byker Bank NE6 .56 A5
Byker Bldgs NE6 .56 A6
Byker Bridge NE1,NE6 .56 A6
Byker Bsns Development Ctr 9 NE6 .56 B5
Byker Cres 16 NE6 .56 C6
Byker Metro Sta NE6 .56 C6
Byker Prim Sch NE6 .56 B5
Byker Terr NE6 .56 F6
Byland Cl DH4 .90 C2
Byland Ct NE38 .83 C5
Byland Rd NE12 .38 F6
Bylands Gdns SR3 .86 B3
Byony Toft SR2 .93 A7
Byrne Terr W 2 SR3 .92 B7
Byrness NE5 .36 E1
Byrness Cl NE3 .37 C4
Byrness Ct NE28 .40 E5
Byrness Row NE23 .22 C8
Byron Ave Blyth NE24 .17 C6
6 Wallsend NE28 .41 A1
Hebburn NE31 .57 F6
West Boldon NE35 .74 A8
Byron Cl NE62 .10 E7
Byron Ct Whickham NE16 .69 A8
Newcastle-upon-Tyne NE5 .36 C2
Byron Lodge Est 6 SR7 .92 E1
Byron Pl NE63 .6 F2
Byron Rd SR5 .75 A2
Byron St Ouston DH2 .81 F1
Newcastle-upon-Tyne NE2 .99 B2
4 South Shields NE33 .59 D8
Sunderland SR5 .75 C1
Byron Terr
Houghton-le-Spring DH5 .94 E7
5 Seaham SR7 .92 F1
Byron Wlk NE8 .56 A2
Bywell Ave
Newcastle-upon-Tyne, Denton Burn NE15 .53 E7
Newcastle-upon-Tyne, Fawdon NE3 .37 F8
South Shields NE34 .60 A7
Hexham NE46 .45 D4
Sunderland SR5 .75 C3
Bywell Cl NE40 .51 E3
Bywell Gdns
Dunston NE11 .70 A5
Gateshead NE9 .71 B6
Bywell Rd Ashington NE63 .6 D2
Cleadon SR6 .74 F8
Bywell St NE6 .56 D5
Bywell Terr NE32 .58 B3

C

Cadehill Rd NE43 .64 C6
Cadlestone Ct NE23 .22 D8
Caedmon Prim Sch NE8 101 B1
Caer Urfa Cl NE33 .42 C4
Caernarvon Cl NE5 .37 B4
Caernarvon Dr SR3 .91 C6
Caesar's Wlk 3 NE33 .42 C4
Cairncross SR5 .74 A1
Cairnglass Gn NE23 .22 D8
Cairngorm Ave NE38 .83 A2
Cairnhill Terr DH4 .90 D4
Cairns Rd SR5 .75 C4
Cairns Sq SR5 .75 C4
Cairns Way NE3 .37 F7
Cairnside SR3 .91 C7
Cairnside S SR3 .91 B7
Cairnsmore Cl
Cramlington NE23 .22 B4
Newcastle-upon-Tyne NE6 .57 B8
Cairnsmore Dr NE38 .83 B3
Cairo St SR2 .86 F3
Caithness Rd SR5 .73 F2
Caithness Sq SR5 .73 F2
Calais Rd SR5 .73 F1
Calandra Chase NE2 .98 B4
Caldbeck Ave NE6 .56 F3
Caldbeck Cl NE6 .56 F3
Calder Ct 13 SR3 .91 F6
Calder Gn NE32 .58 C2
Calder Wlk
Sunniside NE16 .69 A2
Sunniside NE16 .69 A3
Calderbourne Ave SR6 .75 E4
Calderdale NE28 .39 F5
Calderdale Ave NE6 .56 F7
Calderwood Cres NE9 .71 A3
Caldew Cres NE5 .54 A8
Caldew Ct DH5 .95 B2
Caldwell Rd NE3 .37 F8
Caledonia St NE6 .57 A4
Caledonian Rd SR5 .73 F3
Caledonian St NE31 .57 D7
Calf Cl Dr NE32 .58 B2
Calf Close Wlk NE32 .58 C2
Calfclose La NE32 .58 C2
California NE21 .53 B1
California Gdns 13 NE61 .9 A8
Callaley Ave NE16 .68 F6
Callaly Ave NE23 .22 C6
Callaly Castle* NE66 .117 F8
Callaly Cl NE61 .4 F3
Callaly Way NE6 .56 D4
Callander DH2 .82 A2
Callendar Ct NE9 .71 C5
Callerdale Rd NE24 .17 A7
Callerton NE12 .29 D5
Callerton Ave NE29 .41 C6
Callerton Cl
Cramlington NE23 .22 C6
5 Ashington NE63 .6 F2
Callerton Ct NE20 .25 E4
Callerton La NE5,NE15, NE20 .25 E3
Callerton Lane End Cotts NE5 .35 E7
Callerton Parkway Sta NE13 .26 E1
Callerton Pl NE4 .98 A1
Callerton Rd NE15 .35 E2
Callerton View NE5 .36 B4
Callington Cl DH4 .89 E2
Callington Dr SR2 .92 F7
Callum Dr NE34 .60 A8
Calow Way NE16 .68 F5
Calthwaite Cl SR5 .74 B2
Calver Ct NE34 .59 E5
Calvus Dr NE15 .34 F2
Cam Mead SR3 .92 A4
Camberley Cl SR3 .92 C8
Camberley Rd NE28 .41 A4
Camberwell Cl NE11 .70 B6
Camberwell Way SR3 .91 D5
Cambo Ave
Bedlington NE22 .11 C1
Whitley Bay NE25 .31 D3
Cambo Cl Blyth NE24 .17 C7
Wallsend NE28 .40 D6
Newcastle-upon-Tyne NE3 .38 D5
Cambo Dr NE23 .22 C6
Cambo Gn NE5 .37 C2
Cambo Pl NE30 .32 A1
Cambois Fst Sch NE24 .12 C4
Camborne Gr NE8 .101 C1
Camborne Pl NE8 .101 C1
Cambourne Ave SR6 .75 E4
Cambria Gn SR4 .85 A6
Cambria St SR4 .85 A6
Cambrian St NE32 .58 B7
Cambrian Way NE38 .83 B3
Cambridge Ave
Longbenton NE12 .39 D8
Whitley Bay NE26 .32 A5
Wallsend NE28 .40 A3
Hebburn NE31 .57 F5
Washington NE37 .83 B8
Cambridge Cres DH4 .90 A6
Cambridge Pl DH3 .82 C1
Cambridge Rd
Stakeford NE62 .11 A7
New Silksworth SR3 .92 A7
Cambridge St NE4 .100 B4
Cambridge Terr NE8 .101 B1
Camden Sq NE30 .42 B5
Camden St
Newcastle-upon-Tyne NE1, NE2 .99 B2
North Shields NE30 .42 B5
Sunderland SR5 .75 A1
Camelford Ct NE15 .53 C8
Cameron Cl NE34 .59 C3
Cameron Rd NE42 .50 D2
Camerton Pl NE28 .40 E7
Camilla Rd NE15 .34 F2
Camilla St NE8 .101 C1
Camp Terr NE29 .42 A6
Campbell Park Rd NE31 .57 F5
Campbell Pl NE4 .98 A1
Campbell Rd SR5 .73 F2
Campbell Sq SR5 .73 F2
Campbell St NE31 .57 E7
Campbell Terr DH5 .95 B1
Camperdown NE5 .36 F1
Camperdown Ave
Chester le Street DH3 .88 D5
Killingworth NE12 .29 B4
Camperdown Ind Est NE12 .29 B5
Campion Gdns NE10 .71 D5
Campion Way NE63 .6 C2
Campsie Cl NE38 .83 B3
Campsie Cres NE30 .32 A1
Campus Martius NE15 .34 E2
Campville NE29 .42 A6
Camsey Cl NE12 .38 F7
Camsey Pl NE12 .38 F7
Canberra Ave NE25 .31 D3
Canberra Dr NE34 .58 F4
Canberra Rd SR4 .85 D4
Candelford Cl NE7 .39 D3
Candlish St NE33 .42 D2
Canning St Hebburn NE31 .57 E5
Newcastle-upon-Tyne NE4 .54 E5
Canning Street Prim Sch NE4 .54 D5
Cannock NE12 .29 D4
Cannock Dr NE7 .39 A4
Cannon St NE8 .101 B4
Canon Cockin St SR2 .86 F4
Canon Gr NE32 .58 C7
Canon Savage Dr NE46 .44 E4
Canonbie Sq NE23 .22 D8
Canonsfield Cl
Newcastle-upon-Tyne NE15 .36 B3
Silksworth SR3 .91 F5
Canterbury Ave NE28 .40 D6
Canterbury Cl
Longbenton NE12 .39 A7
Ashington NE63 .6 F2
Canterbury Ho SR5 .73 F4
Canterbury Rd SR5 .74 A3
Canterbury St
South Shields NE33 .59 D8
Newcastle-upon-Tyne NE6 .56 D6
Canterbury Way
Wide Open NE13 .28 B5
Hedworth NE32 .58 A1
Capercaillie Lodge NE23 .22 B1
Capetown Rd SR5 .73 F2
Capetown Sq SR5 .73 F2
Caplestone Cl NE38 .83 B3
Capstan La NE9 .71 C2
Captains Row The NE33 .59 B8
Captains Wharf NE33 .42 C3
Capulet Gr NE34 .59 A5
Capulet Terr SR2 .86 E4
Caradoc Cl NE38 .83 B3
Caragh Rd DH2 .88 C1
Caraway Wlk NE34 .59 E2
Carden Ave NE34 .60 B5
Cardiff Sq SR5 .73 F1
Cardigan Gr NE30 .32 A3
Cardigan Rd SR5 .73 F2
Cardigan Terr NE6 .56 B7
Cardinal Cl
Longbenton NE12 .39 A6
Newcastle-upon-Tyne NE15 .36 B3
Cardinals Cl 5 SR3 .91 F5
Cardonnel St NE29 .42 A4
Cardwell St SR6 .75 E1
Careen Cres SR3 .91 B7
Carew Ct NE23 .22 B5
Carham Ave NE23 .22 C6
Carham Cl
Newcastle-upon-Tyne NE3 .38 D6
Corbridge NE45 .47 B5
Caris St NE8,NE9 .71 A8
Carisbrooke NE22 .11 A2
Carisbrooke Ct SR1 .102 B2
Carlcroft Pl NE23 .22 C5
Carley Hill Prim Sch SR5 75 B3
Carley Hill Rd SR5 .75 B3
Carley Rd SR5 .75 B2
Carlingford Rd DH2 .88 B1
Carliol Pl NE1 .99 B1
Carliol Sq NE1 .99 B1
Carliol St NE1 .99 B1
Carlisle Cl NE27 .30 C1
Carlisle Cres DH4 .90 B7
Carlisle Ct 11 NE10 .56 D1
Carlisle Ho
Newcastle-upon-Tyne NE4 .98 A1
4 Sunderland SR3 .91 D7
Carlisle Lea NE61 .9 A7
Carlisle Pl NE9 .71 B4
Carlisle St NE10 .56 D1
Carlisle Terr
3 Shiremoor NE27 .30 E1
6 Sunderland SR5 .74 F2
Carlisle Way NE27 .30 C1
Carlow Dr NE62 .11 D8
Carlton Ave NE24 .17 C3
Carlton Cl Urpeth DH2 .81 E2
Newcastle-upon-Tyne NE3 .38 A3
Carlton Cres SR3 .91 C7
Carlton Ct NE11 .70 C5
Carlton Gdns NE15 .53 E7
Carlton Gr NE63 .6 F1
Carlton Ho NE64 .7 E5
Carlton Rd NE12 .39 D6
Carlton St NE24 .17 F7
Carlton Terr Blyth NE24 .17 D8
North Shields NE29 .41 F5
Gateshead NE9 .70 F5
Springwell NE9 .71 F1
Carlyle Cres NE16 .69 A8
Carlyle Ct 4 NE28 .41 A1
Carlyle St 1 NE28 .41 A1
Carlyon St SR2 .103 A1
Carmel Gr NE23 .16 A1
Carnaby Cl NE42 .50 D3
Carnaby Rd NE6 .56 F4
Carnation Ave DH4 .89 E3
Carnation Terr 5 NE16 .69 B7
Carnegie Cl NE34 .59 C4
Carnegie St 10 SR2 .86 F2
Carnforth Cl NE28 .40 E7
Carnforth Gdns
Rowlands Gill NE39 .67 E3
Gateshead NE9 .71 B4
Carnforth Gn NE3 .37 E4
Carnoustie Ouston DH2 .82 A1
Washington NE37 .72 C3
Carnoustie Cl NE7 .39 C4
Carnoustie Ct
Gateshead NE10 .72 B6
Whitley Bay NE25 .31 C5
Carnoustie Dr NE34 .59 F3
Carol Gdns NE7 .39 B3
Carol St SR4 .102 B3
Caroline Cotts NE5 .54 B8
Caroline Gdns NE28 .41 A3
Caroline St
Hetton le Hole DH5 .95 A4
Jarrow NE32 .58 A7
Newcastle-upon-Tyne NE4 .54 E4
Caroline Terr NE21 .53 B4
Carolyn Cl NE12 .39 C6
Carolyn Cres NE26 .31 E7
Carolyn Way NE26 .31 E7
Carpenter St NE33 .42 B2
Carr Hill Rd N10,NE9 .71 B7
Carr Hill Sch NE9 .71 B7
Carr St Blyth NE24 .17 C4
Hebburn NE31 .57 D7
Carrawburgh Temple of Mithras* NE47 .128 A5
Carrfield NE20 .25 F7
Carrfield Rd NE3 .37 F5
Carrhouse La SR7 .95 F4
Carrick Dr NE24 .17 D4
Carrigill Pl NE12 .39 A6
Carrington Cl NE23 .22 F1
Carrmere Rd SR2 .86 E1
Carrock Ct SR3 .91 F6
Carroll Wlk NE34 .59 A2
Carrowmore Rd DH2 .88 C1
Carrs Cl NE42 .50 F3
Carrsfield NE45 .47 A5
Carrsyde Cl NE16 .68 F5
Carsdale Rd NE3 .37 D5
Cartington Ave NE27 .30 F2
Cartington Ct NE3 .37 E7
Cartington Rd NE29 .41 E5
Cartington Terr NE6 .39 C1
Cartmel Ct DH2 .88 A2
Cartmel Gn NE5 .37 A1
Cartmel Gr NE8 .70 D7
Cartmel Pk NE10 .57 A1
Cartwright Rd SR5 .74 B1
Carville Fst Sch NE28 .57 B8
Carville Gdns NE28 .57 B8
Carville Rd NE28 .40 B1
Carville Rise NE6 .56 C6
Carville St NE10 .56 B2
Carville Station Cotts NE28 .40 C1
Carvoran 4 NE28 .40 F4
Carwarding Pl NE5 .37 C2
Caseton Cl NE25 .31 C6
Caspian Cl NE32 .58 C5
Caspian Rd SR5 .73 F1
Caspian Sq SR5 .73 F1
Castellian Rd SR5 .74 C1
Casterton Gr NE5 .36 B3
Castle Bank NE61 .9 A8
Castle Cl
Chester le Street DH3 .88 D2
Hetton le Hole DH5 .95 B2
Whickham NE16 .69 A7
7 Newcastle-upon-Tyne NE3 .37 D5
Prudhoe NE42 .50 C3
Morpeth NE61 .8 F8
Castle Ct NE20 .25 E6
Castle Dene Gr DH4 .94 D8
Castle Farm Cotts NE7 .38 E3
Castle Farm Mews NE2 .38 E3
Castle Farm Rd NE2,NE7 .38 F4
Castle Farm Tennis Ctr NE7 .38 F4
Castle Garth NE1 .101 B4
Castle Gn 10 SR3 .91 D7
Castle Lea NE42 .50 B3
Castle Leazes (Halls of Residence) NE2 .98 B3
Castle Mdws NE61 .8 E7
Castle Mews SR3 .91 D7
Castle Rd
Washington NE38 .83 A5
Prudhoe NE42 .50 B3
Castle Riggs DH2 .88 B3
Castle Sq Backworth NE27 .30 B5
Morpeth NE61 .9 A8
Castle St Hazlerigg NE13 .28 A4
Morpeth NE61 .9 A8
Sunderland SR1 .102 C3
Castle St S 4 SR5 .74 C1
Castle Terr NE63 .6 E4
Castle View
Chester le Street DH3 .88 C5
Penshaw DH4 .90 B8
Ovingham NE42 .50 B4
Prudhoe NE42 .50 C3
Sunderland SR5 .74 B1
Castle View Sch SR5 .74 A1
Castle Wlk NE61 .9 A7
Castledale Ave NE24 .17 A6
Castledene Ct
Newcastle-upon-Tyne NE3 .38 F4
Sunderland SR5 .74 A2
Castlefields DH4 .89 D3
Castleford Rd SR5 .73 F2
Castlegate Gdns NE8 .100 A1
Castlemain Cl DH4 .89 D3
Castlenook Pl NE15 .53 F7
Castlereagh Homes The SR7 .93 D1
Castlereagh St SR3 .92 A7
Castlereigh Cl DH4 .89 D3
Castles Gn NE12 .29 E3
Castleside Rd NE15 .54 A6
Castleton Cl
Newcastle-upon-Tyne NE2 .38 F2
Cramlington NE23 .16 A1
Castleton Gr NE2 .38 F2
Castleton Lodge NE4 .54 F5
Castleton Rd NE32 .58 C5
Castletown Prim Sch SR5 .85 B8
Castletown Rd SR5 .74 D2
Castletown Way SR5 .74 D2
Castleway Dinnington NE13 27 B7
Pegswood NE61 .4 F3
Castlewood Cl NE5 .36 D2
Catchside Cl NE16 .69 A5
Cateran Way NE23 .22 C4
Catharine St W SR4 .102 A2
Cathedral Ct NE8 .56 A3
Cathedral View DH4 .90 D3
Catherine Cookson Ct NE33 .42 E1
Catherine Rd DH4 .90 D6
Catherine St 3 NE33 .42 D3
Catherine View 8 NE40 .51 F3
Catholic Row NE22 .15 E8
Catkin Wlk NE40 .52 A3
Cato Sq SR5 .75 A2
Cato St SR5 .75 A2
Catrail Pl NE23 .22 C8
Cattle Market NE46 .45 B4
Catton Gr NE16 .69 B3
Catton Pl NE28 .40 E6
Cauldwell Ave
Whitley Bay NE25 .31 D3
South Shields NE34 .59 E7
Cauldwell Cl NE25 .31 E4
Cauldwell La NE25 .31 E4
Cauldwell Pl NE34 .59 E7
Cauldwell Villas NE34 .59 E7
Causeway Gateshead NE9 .71 B6
Sunderland SR6 .103 A4
Causeway The
Throckley NE15 .35 D1
Gateshead NE9 .71 A8
Causey Arch* DH9 .80 A4
Causey Arch Sta* NE16 .80 B5
Causey Bank NE1 .99 B1
Causey Brae NE46 .44 F3
Causey Hill Rd
Hexham NE46 .44 F3
Hexham NE46 .45 B1
Causey Hill Way NE46 .44 E3
Causey Pk NE46 .44 F4
Causey Rd DH9,NE16 .80 A3
Causey St NE3 .38 C4
Causey Way Tanfield DH9 .80 A1
Hexham NE46 .44 F3
Cavalier Way SR3 .91 F7
Cavendish Gdns NE63 .6 D3
Cavendish Pl
Burnopfield NE16 .79 A4
Newcastle-upon-Tyne NE2 .38 F1
New Silksworth SR3 .91 F7
Cavendish Rd NE2 .38 F1
Cavendish Sq NE61 .4 E3
Cavendish Terr NE63 .6 D3
Caversham Rd NE5 .36 B3
Cawburn Cl NE7 .39 E3
Cawdell Ct NE30 .42 B5
Cawfields Milecastle* NE49 .126 F3
Cawnpore Sq SR4 .85 E7
Cawthorne Terr NE16 .79 A4
Caxton Way DH3 .88 D8
Caxton Wlk NE34 .59 A2
Caynham Cl NE29 .41 E8
Cayton Gr NE5 .36 B2
Cecil Ct Ponteland NE20 .25 F6
Wallsend NE28 .57 B8
Cecil St NE29 .42 A5
Cecil Terr NE46 .45 B5
Cedar Cl Bedlington NE22 .10 F2
Whitley Bay NE25 .31 F3
Cedar Cres Dunston NE11 .69 F7
Burnopfield NE16 .78 F6
Gateshead NE9 .70 F4
Cedar Ct NE29 .31 E1
Cedar Gr Wallsend NE28 .40 D2
Hebburn NE31 .57 E3
South Shields NE34 .59 F5
Ryton NE40 .52 C6
Whitburn SR6 .60 F2
Cedar Rd Blaydon NE21 .53 C2
Newcastle-upon-Tyne NE4 .54 D7
Cedar Terr
Fence Houses DH4 .90 A1
Washington NE38 .83 C1
Ashington NE63 .6 E2
Cedar Way NE12 .29 E1
Cedars DH2 .88 B5
Cedars Cres SR2 .86 E3
Cedars Ct SR2 .86 D4
Cedars Gn NE9 .71 A3
Cedars Pk SR2 .86 E3
Cedars Specl Sch The NE9 .71 A3
Cedars The Penshaw DH4 .90 B8
Whickham NE16 .69 B4
Newcastle-upon-Tyne NE4 100 B3
Gateshead NE9 .71 C2
Sunderland SR2 .86 D4
Cedartree Gdns NE25 .31 E3
Cedarway NE10 .71 E5
Cedarwood DH4 .89 E1
Cedarwood Ave NE6 .40 A1
Cedarwood Gr SR2 .86 D2

Cedric Cres SR2 . . . . .86 B4
Celadon Cl NE15 . . . . .53 C8
Celandine Cl NE3 . . . . .38 D7
Celandine Ct NE63 . . . . .6 B1
Celandine Way NE10 . . . .71 E5
Cellar Hill Terr DH4 . . . . .90 D2
Celtic Cl SR6 . . . . .59 E1
Celtic Cres SR6 . . . . .59 E1
Cemetery App NE34 . . . . .59 E8
Cemetery Rd Jarrow NE32 58 C5
  Gateshead NE8 . . . . .101 C1
Centenary Ave NE34 . . . . .60 A6
Centenary Cotts NE22 . . .15 F8
Centenary Ct NE4 . . . . . . .54 F4
Central Arc NE1 . . . . .99 A1
Central Ave
  North Shields NE29 . . . . .41 E5
  South Shields NE34 . . . . .59 F6
  Guide Post NE62 . . . . .10 E7
  Whitburn SR6 . . . . .60 E1
Central Gdns NE34 . . . . . .59 F6
Central Newcastle High Sch
  NE2 . . . . .99 B4
Central Newcastle High Sch
  The NE3 . . . . .38 C4
Central Sq NE8 . . . . .101 C3
Central Way SR4 . . . . . . .85 E8
Centralway NE11 . . . . .70 C4
Centurion Rd NE15 . . . . . .53 F8
Centurion Way
  Heddon-on-the-Wall NE15 . .34 E2
  Gateshead NE9 . . . . .71 B6
Ceolfrid Terr NE32 . . . . . .58 C4
Cestria Cty Prim Sch
  DH3 . . . . .88 D3
Chacombe NE38 . . . . .83 D3
Chadderton Dr NE5 . . . . . .36 B3
Chadwick St NE28 . . . . . . .40 B1
Chadwick Wlk NE8 . . . . .101 A2
Chaffinch Ct NE63 . . . . .6 B2
Chaffinch Rd 6 SR5 . . . . .74 C1
Chaffinch Way NE12 . . . . .29 C4
Chainbridge Ind Est
  NE21 . . . . .53 F4
Chainbridge Rd
  Blaydon NE21 . . . . .53 D3
  Blaydon, Derwenthaugh
  NE21 . . . . .53 F4
Chainbridge Road Ind Est
  NE21 . . . . .53 F4
Chalfont Gr SR4 . . . . .85 A2
Chalfont Rd NE6 . . . . .56 F4
Chalford Rd 1 SR5 . . . . . .75 B2
Challoner's Gdns NE61 . . . .3 E1
Chamberlain St
  Blyth NE24 . . . . .17 F6
  Crawcrook NE40 . . . . .51 F4
Chambers Cres NE9 . . . . .71 C1
Chancery La NE24 . . . . . . .17 D7
Chandler Ct NE2 . . . . .38 F2
Chandlers Ford DH4 . . . . .89 F8
Chandlers Quay NE6 . . . . .56 C4
Chandless St NE8 . . . . . .101 A2
Chandos SR3 . . . . .92 A4
Chandos St NE8 . . . . .70 F8
Chandra Pl 3 NE5 . . . . . .37 B2
Chantry Cl SR3 . . . . .91 E5
Chantry Dr NE13 . . . . .28 B6
Chantry Est NE45 . . . . . . .46 F6
Chantry Pl
  West Rainton DH4 . . . . .94 A2
  3 Morpeth NE61 . . . . .9 A8
Chapel & Tower★ 109 D5
Chapel Ave NE16 . . . . .79 B6
Chapel Cl
  Kibblesworth NE11 . . . . . . .81 D6
  Newcastle-upon-Tyne NE3 . .28 D1
Chapel Ct Sherburn DH6 . .96 A1
  Seaton Burn NE13 . . . . . . .28 B8
Chapel House Dr NE5 . . . .36 C1
Chapel House Gr NE5 . . . .36 C1
Chapel House Mid Sch
  NE5 . . . . .36 B2
Chapel House Rd NE5 . . . .36 C1
Chapel La Haswell DH6 . . .97 F3
  Whitley Bay NE25 . . . . .31 E4
  Wylam NE41 . . . . .51 A6
Chapel Park Mid Sch
  NE5 . . . . .36 C3
Chapel Pl NE13 . . . . .28 B8
Chapel Rd NE32 . . . . .58 B7
Chapel Row Birtley DH3 . .82 E3
  Penshaw DH4 . . . . .90 C5
  Mickley Square NE43 . . . . .49 E1
Chapel St
  Hetton le Hole DH5 . . . . . .95 B4
  Tantobie DH9 . . . . .79 B8
  North Shields NE29 . . . . . .41 E5
Chapel View
  Brunswick Village NE13 . . .28 A6
  Rowlands Gill NE39 . . . . . .67 E3
Chapelville NE13 . . . . .28 B8
Chapman St SR6 . . . . .75 E4
Chapter Row NE33 . . . . . .42 C3
Chapwell Woods Rd
  NE39 . . . . .67 A3
Chare The NE1 . . . . .99 A2
Chareway NE46 . . . . .45 A6
Chareway La NE46 . . . . . . .45 A6
Charlbury Cl NE12 . . . . . . .71 F1
Charlcote Cres NE36 . . . . .74 D7
Charles Ave
  Longbenton NE12 . . . . .39 D8
  Whitley Bay NE26 . . . . .32 B5
  Shiremoor NE27 . . . . .30 F4
  Newcastle-upon-Tyne NE3 . .37 E6
Charles Baker Wlk NE34 . .60 B7

Charles Ct 18 NE6 . . . . . .56 C7
Charles Dr NE23 . . . . .29 B8
Charles Perkins Memorial
  Cottage Homes DH3 . . . .82 C3
Charles St Newbottle DH4 .90 D4
  Hazlerigg NE13 . . . . .28 A4
  West Boldon NE35 . . . . . . .73 F8
  Pegswood NE61 . . . . .4 F3
  Gateshead NE8 . . . . .101 C2
  Sunderland SR1 . . . . .103 B3
  18 Ryhope SR2 . . . . .93 A6
  Sunderland, Monkwearmouth
  SR6 . . . . .103 A4
Charleswood NE3 . . . . . . .38 C8
Charlie St NE40 . . . . .51 F1
Charlotte Cl NE4 . . . . . . .100 B3
Charlotte Mews NE1 . . . . .98 C1
Charlotte Sq NE1 . . . . . . .98 C1
Charlotte St
  Wallsend NE28 . . . . .40 C2
  North Shields NE30 . . . . . .42 B6
  South Shields NE33 . . . . . .42 C2
  Crawcrook NE40 . . . . .51 E3
Charlton Cl NE46 . . . . .44 F2
Charlton Ct NE25 . . . . .31 E3
Charlton Gdns NE61 . . . . . .9 B7
Charlton Gr SR6 . . . . .75 A8
Charlton Rd SR5 . . . . .75 C3
Charlton St
  Newcastle-upon-Tyne NE15 .53 D6
  Blyth NE24 . . . . .17 D7
  Ashington NE63 . . . . .6 C4
Charlton Villas NE40 . . . . .52 B1
Charlton Wlk NE8 . . . . . .100 C1
Charman St SR1 . . . . .103 A3
Charminster Gdns NE6 . . .39 C1
Charnwood Ave NE12 . . . .39 A6
Charnwood Ct NE33 . . . . .42 E4
Charnwood Gdns NE9 . . . .71 B5
Charter Dr SR3 . . . . .91 C7
Charters Cres DH6 . . . . . .97 F7
Chase Ct DH6 . . . . .96 A1
Chase Farm Dr NE24 . . . .16 F7
Chase Mdws NE24 . . . . . .16 F6
Chase Mews NE24 . . . . . .16 F7
Chase Sch NE16 . . . . .69 B7
Chase The
  Killingworth NE12 . . . . .29 A2
  North Shields NE29 . . . . . .41 F6
  Washington NE38 . . . . .82 F1
  Hexham NE46 . . . . .44 F2
Chasedale Cres NE24 . . . .17 A7
Chatham Cl NE25 . . . . .23 D1
Chatham Rd SR5 . . . . .74 A2
Chathill Cl
  Whitley Bay NE25 . . . . .31 D5
  Morpeth NE61 . . . . .9 B6
Chathill Terr NE6 . . . . .56 F5
Chatsworth Cres NE4 . . . .86 A4
Chatsworth Ct 8 NE33 . . .42 D3
Chatsworth Dr NE22 . . . . .11 C3
Chatsworth Gdns
  Whitley Bay NE25 . . . . .31 E3
  Newcastle-upon-Tyne,
  Westerhope NE5 . . . . .36 F3
  Newcastle-upon-Tyne, Walker
  NE6 . . . . .56 D4
Chatsworth Pl NE16 . . . . .69 A5
Chatsworth Rd NE32 . . . . .58 C5
Chatsworth St SR4 . . . . .102 A1
Chatsworth St S SR4 . . . .86 A1
Chatterton St SR5 . . . . . .75 A2
Chatton Ave
  Cramlington NE23 . . . . . . .22 C6
  South Shields NE34 . . . . . .60 B8
Chatton Cl
  Chester le Street DH2 . . . . .88 A1
  Morpeth NE61 . . . . .9 C5
Chatton St NE28 . . . . .41 C1
Chatton Wynd NE3 . . . . . .38 A7
Chaucer Ave NE34 . . . . . .59 A3
Chaucer Cl NE8 . . . . .56 A2
Chaucer Rd NE16 . . . . . . .69 B8
Chaucer St 9 DH4 . . . . . .94 D8
Chaytor Gr SR1 . . . . .103 B3
Chaytor St NE32 . . . . .58 B8
Cheadle Ave
  Cramlington NE23 . . . . . . .16 A1
  Wallsend NE28 . . . . .40 E6
Cheadle Rd SR5 . . . . .74 A2
Cheam Cl NE16 . . . . .69 B5
Cheam Rd SR5 . . . . .74 A2
Cheddar Gdns NE9 . . . . . .70 F3
Cheldon Ct NE25 . . . . .31 C6
Chelford Ct NE28 . . . . .40 E7
Chelmsford Gr NE2 . . . . . .56 A7
Chelmsford Rd SR5 . . . . . .74 A2
Chelmsford Sq SR5 . . . . . .74 A3
Chelmsford St 5 SR3 . . . .92 A8
Chelsea Gdns NE8 . . . . . .71 B8
Chelsea Gr NE4 . . . . .98 A1
Cheltenham Ct NE63 . . . . . .6 C2
Cheltenham Dr NE35 . . . . .58 E2
Cheltenham Rd SR5 . . . . .74 A2
Cheltenham Sq SR5 . . . . .74 A2
Cheltenham Terr NE6 . . . .56 B7
Chelton Cl NE13 . . . . .28 B4
Chepstow Gdns NE8 . . . . .70 D7
Chepstow Rd NE15 . . . . . .53 F6
Chepstow St SR4 . . . . . .102 B2
Cherribank SR2 . . . . .92 E6
Cherry Banks DH3 . . . . . .88 D5
Cherry Blossom Way
  NE37 . . . . .73 B1
Cherry Cotts DH9 . . . . . . .79 B2
Cherry Dr DH6 . . . . .97 F3
Cherry Gr
  Killingworth NE12 . . . . .29 C4

Cherry Gr continued
  Prudhoe NE42 . . . . .50 B3
Cherry Knowle Hospl
  SR2 . . . . .92 E4
Cherry Tree Dr NE22 . . . . .10 F1
Cherry Tree Gdns NE15 . . .50 C8
Cherry Tree La NE41 . . . . .51 A6
Cherry Tree Sq 6 SR2 . . . .92 E8
Cherry Tree Wlk NE31 . . . .57 E4
Cherry Trees NE24 . . . . . .17 D6
Cherry Way
  Fence Houses DH4 . . . . . . .90 B1
  Killingworth NE12 . . . . .29 C4
Cherryburn Cotts NE43 . . .49 E2
Cherryburn Gdns NE4 . . . .54 E8
Cherrytree Cl NE12 . . . . . .29 F2
Cherrytree Ct NE21 . . . . . .11 D2
Cherrytree Dr NE16 . . . . . .69 C8
Cherrytree Gdns
  Whitley Bay NE25 . . . . .31 F3
  Gateshead NE8 . . . . .71 A4
Cherrytree Rd DH2 . . . . . .88 A5
Cherrywood NE6 . . . . .39 E1
Cherrywood Gdns SR3 . . .92 B7
Cherwell NE37 . . . . .83 F8
Cherwell Sq NE12 . . . . . . .29 C1
Chesham Gdns NE5 . . . . . .36 B2
Chesham Gn NE3 . . . . .37 F5
Cheshire Ave DH3 . . . . . . .82 C1
Cheshire Cl NE63 . . . . .6 A4
Cheshire Ct NE31 . . . . . . .57 D5
Cheshire Gdns NE28 . . . . .40 A3
Cheshire Gr NE34 . . . . . . .60 B7
Chesils The NE12 . . . . .39 A5
Chesmond Dr NE21 . . . . . .53 C3
Chessar Ave NE5 . . . . .37 B2
Chester Ave NE28 . . . . . . .40 F3
Chester Cl NE20 . . . . .25 B4
Chester Cres
  Newcastle-upon-Tyne NE2 . .99 C3
  Sunderland SR1 . . . . .102 B2
Chester Ct NE12 . . . . .39 B6
Chester Gdns NE34 . . . . . .59 E7
Chester Gr Seghill NE23 . . .22 E1
  Blyth NE24 . . . . .17 C6
Chester Mews SR4 . . . . .102 B2
Chester Oval SR2 . . . . . .102 B2
Chester Pl NE8 . . . . .101 B2
Chester Rd
  Chester le Street DH3 . . . . .88 F5
  Bournmoor DH3,DH4 . . . . .89 D3
  Penshaw DH4 . . . . .90 B7
  Shiney Row DH4 . . . . .90 B7
  Sunderland, High Barnes
  SR1 SR2,SR4 . . . . .85 F5
  Sunderland SR1,SR4 . . . . .102 B2
  Sunderland, Grindon SR4 . . .85 B3
Chester Sq NE61 . . . . .2 A3
Chester St Newbottle DH4 .90 D2
  Newcastle-upon-Tyne NE2 . .99 C3
  Sunderland SR4 . . . . .102 A2
Chester St E SR4 . . . . . . .102 A2
Chester St W SR4 . . . . . .102 A2
Chester Terr SR1 . . . . . . .102 B2
Chester Terr N SR4 . . . . .102 A2
Chester Way NE32 . . . . . . .58 A1
Chester-le-Street CE Jun
  Sch DH2 . . . . .88 B5
Chester-le-Street General
  Hospl DH3 . . . . .88 C2
Chester-le-Street Sta
  DH3 . . . . .88 C3
Chesterfield Rd NE4 . . . . .54 F4
Chesterhill NE23 . . . . .22 B5
Chesterholm (Vindolanda)
  Roman Fort★ NE47 . . . .127 C3
Chesters 5 NE28 . . . . .40 F4
Chesters (Cilurnum) Roman
  Fort★ NE46 . . . . .128 C5
Chesters Ave NE12 . . . . . .39 A5
Chesters Dene DH8 . . . . . .76 E3
Chesters Gdns NE40 . . . . .51 E4
Chesters Museum★
  NE46 . . . . .128 D5
Chesters Pk NE9 . . . . .70 F6
Chesters The
  Ebchester DH8 . . . . .76 E3
  Whitley Bay NE25 . . . . .31 E4
  Newcastle-upon-Tyne NE5 . .36 C1
Chesterton Rd NE34 . . . . .59 B3
Chesterwood Dr NE28 . . . .40 A2
Chesterwood Terr NE10 . . .57 B1
Chestnut Ave
  Whickham NE16 . . . . .69 B5
  Blyth NE24 . . . . .12 D1
  Whitley Bay NE25 . . . . .31 F4
  Washington NE38 . . . . .83 B1
  Newcastle-upon-Tyne NE5 . .37 E2
Chestnut Cl
  Killingworth NE12 . . . . .29 B4
  Hedworth NE32 . . . . .58 D1
Chestnut Cres SR5 . . . . . .74 F3
Chestnut Gdns NE8 . . . . . .70 C8
Chestnut Gr NE34 . . . . . . .59 F4
Chestnut St
  Wallsend NE28 . . . . .40 C1
  Ashington NE63 . . . . .6 D3
Chestnut Terr DH4 . . . . . . .90 C3
Cheswick Dr NE3 . . . . .38 D6
Chevin Cl NE28,NE6 . . . . .40 B1
Chevington NE10 . . . . .72 A5
Chevington Cl NE61 . . . . . .4 E3
Chevington Gdns 6 NE5 . .36 F3
Chevington Gr NE25 . . . . .31 D7
Cheviot Cl
  Tynemouth NE29 . . . . .31 F2
  Washington NE37 . . . . .83 A6
  Ellington NE61 . . . . .1 D4

Cheviot Ct Blaydon NE21 . .53 C3
  Whitley Bay NE26 . . . . .32 C4
  Morpeth NE61 . . . . .9 A6
Cheviot Cty Jun Mix Sch
  NE34 . . . . .60 A8
Cheviot Fst Sch NE5 . . . . .37 A4
Cheviot Gdns NE11 . . . . . .70 A7
Cheviot Gn NE11 . . . . .70 A8
Cheviot Gr NE61 . . . . .4 E3
Cheviot Grange NE23 . . . .29 C6
Cheviot La SR2 . . . . .92 E7
Cheviot Mount NE6 . . . . . .56 C6
Cheviot Rd
  Chester le Street DH2 . . . . .88 B1
  Blaydon NE21 . . . . .53 C1
  Hebburn NE32 . . . . .58 A4
  South Shields NE34 . . . . . .60 A7
  South Shields NE34 . . . . . .60 A8
Cheviot St SR43 . . . . .85 F7
Cheviot View
  Longbenton NE12 . . . . .39 C6
  Brunswick Village NE13 . . .28 A6
  Ponteland NE20 . . . . .26 A5
  Seghill NE23 . . . . .22 F1
  Whitley Bay NE26 . . . . .32 B5
  Prudhoe NE42 . . . . .50 E2
  Ashington NE63 . . . . .6 E5
Cheviot Way
  Hexham NE46 . . . . .45 A4
  Stakeford NE62 . . . . .11 B8
Chevron The 4 NE6 . . . . .56 B5
Chevychase Ct SR7 . . . . . .92 F2
Chevyside Mid Sch NE5 . . .37 A4
Cheyne Rd NE42 . . . . .50 C2
Cheyne The SR3 . . . . .92 A5
Chichester Ave NE23 . . . . .21 F8
Chichester Cl
  Newcastle-upon-Tyne NE3 . .37 D8
  Ashington NE63 . . . . .7 A2
  Gateshead NE8 . . . . .101 B2
Chichester Gr NE22 . . . . . .10 F2
Chichester Pl NE33 . . . . . .59 C8
Chichester Rd
  South Shields NE33 . . . . . .42 D1
  Sunderland SR6 . . . . .75 E4
Chichester Rd E NE33 . . . .42 D1
Chichester Sta NE33 . . . . .59 C8
Chichester Way NE32 . . . .58 B1
Chick's La 4 SR6 . . . . .75 F8
Chicken Rd NE28 . . . . .40 A4
Chigwell Cl DH4 . . . . .90 B7
Chilcote NE10 . . . . .71 D7
Chilcrosse NE10 . . . . .71 F6
Chilham Ct
  Tynemouth NE29 . . . . .41 B8
  Washington NE38 . . . . .83 B4
Chillingham Castle★
  NE66 . . . . .112 B8
Chillingham Cl NE24 . . . . .17 B5
Chillingham Cres NE63 . . . .6 C3
Chillingham Ct 19 NE6 . . .56 C7
Chillingham Dr
  Chester le Street DH2 . . . . .88 A1
  North Shields NE29 . . . . . .41 D4
Chillingham Ind Est NE6 . .56 C7
Chillingham Rd NE6 . . . . . .56 C8
Chillingham Road Prim Sch
  NE6 . . . . .56 C8
Chillingham Road Sta
  NE6 . . . . .56 D7
Chillingham Terr NE32 . . . .58 D4
Chilside Rd NE10 . . . . .71 D7
Chiltern Ave DH2 . . . . .88 B2
Chiltern Cl
  Washington NE38 . . . . .83 B3
  Ashington NE63 . . . . .6 F1
Chiltern Dr NE12 . . . . .29 B1
Chiltern Gdns NE11 . . . . . .70 A7
Chiltern Rd NE29 . . . . .31 F2
Chilton Gdns 10 DH4 . . . .94 A8
Chilton St 1 SR5 . . . . .75 C1
Chimney Mills NE2 . . . . . .98 C4
China St SR2 . . . . .86 C3
Chingford Cl DH4 . . . . .90 C7
Chip The NE61 . . . . .8 F5
Chipchase NE38 . . . . .82 F4
Chipchase Ave NE23 . . . . .22 B6
Chipchase Cl
  Bedlington NE22 . . . . .10 D1
  Pegswood NE61 . . . . .4 F3
Chipchase Cres NE5 . . . . .36 E3
Chipchase Ct
  Bournmoor DH4 . . . . .89 D1
  New Hartley NE25 . . . . . . .23 D6
  Seaham SR7 . . . . .92 F2
Chipchase Terr NE32 . . . . .58 B3
Chippendale Pl NE2 . . . . .98 B4
Chirdon Cres NE46 . . . . . .45 C4
Chirnside NE23 . . . . .22 B4
Chirton Ave
  North Shields NE29 . . . . . .41 F5
  South Shields NE34 . . . . . .60 C6
Chirton Dean Way NE29 . .42 A3
Chirton Dene Quays
  NE28 . . . . .41 F2
Chirton Gn Blyth NE24 . . . .17 B5
  North Shields NE29 . . . . . .41 F5
Chirton Gr NE34 . . . . .60 C6
Chirton Hill Dr NE29 . . . . .41 C7
Chirton La NE29 . . . . .41 E5
Chirton Lodge NE29 . . . . .41 E5
Chirton West View NE29 . .41 F5
Chirton Wynd NE6 . . . . . . .56 C5
Chislehurst Rd DH4 . . . . . .90 B7
Chiswick Gdns NE8 . . . . . .71 A8

Chiswick Rd
  Seaton Delaval NE25 . . . . .23 E2
  Sunderland SR5 . . . . .74 A2
Chiswick Sq SR5 . . . . .74 A2
Chollerford Ave
  Whitley Bay NE25 . . . . .32 B4
  North Shields NE29 . . . . . .41 D6
Chollerford Cl NE3 . . . . . . .38 A4
Chollerford Mews NE25 . .23 F2
Chollerton Dr
  Longbenton NE12 . . . . .40 A8
  Bedlington NE22 . . . . .11 A1
Choppington Fst Sch
  . . . . .10 E5
Choppington Rd
  Bedlington NE22,NE62 . . . .10 F2
  Morpeth NE61 . . . . .9 B6
Chopwell Gdns NE9 . . . . . .71 A2
Chopwell Prim Sch NE17 .66 B1
Chopwell Rd NE17 . . . . . . .77 C6
Chopwell Wood Wlks★
  NE39 . . . . .66 F2
Chorley Pl NE6 . . . . .56 E5
Chowdean Terr 4 NE9 . . . .70 F4
Chowdene Bank NE11,
  NE9 . . . . .70 F2
Christ Church CE Prim Sch
  Newcastle-upon-Tyne NE2 . .99 C2
  North Shields NE30 . . . . . .42 A6
Christal Terr SR6 . . . . .75 D3
Christie Terr NE6 . . . . .56 F5
Christon Cl NE3 . . . . .38 E5
Christon Rd NE3 . . . . .38 D5
Christon Way NE10 . . . . . .57 B2
Christopher Rd NE6 . . . . . .56 E7
Chudleigh Gdns NE5 . . . . .36 B2
Church Ave
  Newcastle-upon-Tyne NE3 . .38 D5
  Choppington NE62 . . . . . . .10 E5
  West Sleekburn NE62 . . . . .11 D7
Church Bank
  Newburn NE15 . . . . .52 F7
  Wallsend NE28 . . . . .40 D2
  Jarrow NE32 . . . . .58 D7
  Sunderland SR5 . . . . .75 A1
Church Chare
  Chester le Street DH3 . . . . .88 C3
  Whickham NE16 . . . . .69 B7
  Ponteland NE20 . . . . .25 F7
Church Cl Ebchester DH8 . .76 E3
  Dinnington NE13 . . . . .27 B7
  Bedlington NE22 . . . . .15 F8
  Whitley Bay NE25 . . . . .31 C4
  Riding Mill NE44 . . . . .62 F7
Church Ct
  10 Gateshead NE10 . . . . . .56 D1
  Bedlington NE22 . . . . .15 F8
Church Dr NE9 . . . . .71 A6
Church Flatt NE20 . . . . . . .25 F7
Church High Sch NE2 . . . .99 B4
Church La
  Bedlington NE22 . . . . .16 A7
  Newcastle-upon-Tyne NE3 . .38 D5
  Riding Mill NE44 . . . . .62 E7
  Gateshead NE9 . . . . .71 B6
  Sunderland SR1 . . . . .102 C2
  Whitburn SR6 . . . . .75 F8
Church Mews NE27 . . . . . .30 C5
Church Pl NE10 . . . . .56 D1
Church Rd
  Hetton le Hole DH5 . . . . . .95 A5
  Newburn NE15 . . . . .52 F7
  Backworth NE27 . . . . .30 C5
  Newcastle-upon-Tyne NE3 . .38 D5
  Wylam NE41 . . . . .51 A6
  Stannington NE61 . . . . .14 C3
  Gateshead NE9 . . . . .71 A5
Church Rise
  Whickham NE16 . . . . .69 B7
  Ryton NE40 . . . . .52 E5
Church Row NE46 . . . . . . .45 B5
Church Sq NE61 . . . . .2 B3
Church St Birtley DH3 . . . .82 C4
  Penshaw DH4 . . . . .90 B6
  West Rainton DH4 . . . . .94 A2
  7 Houghton-le-Spring DH4,
  DH5 . . . . .94 E8
  Haswell DH6 . . . . .97 E3
  Gateshead, Felling NE10 . . .71 D8
  Dunston NE11 . . . . .100 A4
  Sunnyside NE16 . . . . .69 A1
  Blaydon NE21 . . . . .53 B1
  Cramlington NE23 . . . . . . .22 B6
  Blyth NE24 . . . . .17 E8
  North Shields NE30 . . . . . .42 B6
  Hebburn NE31 . . . . .57 D7
  Newcastle-upon-Tyne NE6 . .57 A4
  Gateshead NE8 . . . . .101 B4
  Sunderland, South Hylton
  SR4 . . . . .85 A6
  Sunderland, Southwick SR5 .75 F8
Church St E SR1 . . . . . . .103 C3
Church St N SR6 . . . . . . .103 B4
Church Terr NE21 . . . . . . .53 C3
Church Vale DH6 . . . . .97 F3
Church View Haswell DH6 .97 F3
  Earsdon NE25 . . . . .31 A5
  Wallsend NE28 . . . . .40 D2
  Boldon Colliery NE35 . . . . .58 E1
  Washington NE37 . . . . .83 D7
  Newbiggin-by-the-Sea NE64 . .7 C5
  New Silksworth SR3 . . . . . .92 B7
Church Way Earsdon NE25 31 A6
  North Shields NE29,NE30 . .42 A6
  South Shields NE33 . . . . . .42 C3

Church Wlk
Newcastle-upon-Tyne NE6 57 A5
Morpeth NE61 8 E7
Sunderland SR1 103 C3
Churchburn Dr NE61 8 F6
Churchdown Cl NE35 58 E2
Churcher Gdns NE28 40 A4
Churchill Ave
Whitley Bay NE25 31 F3
Sunderland SR5 75 A2
Churchill Gdns NE2 39 A1
Churchill Mews NE6 56 C4
Churchill Sq DH4 94 B8
Churchill St
Newcastle-upon-Tyne NE1 100 C4
Wallsend NE28 40 F4
Sunderland SR1 103 B2
Churchlands NE46 45 D4
Churchwalk House NE6 57 A5
Churston Cl DH4 90 C4
Chuter Ede Comp Sch
NE34 59 B2
Chyll Edge NE61 3 C1
Cicero Terr 4 SR5 75 A2
Cinderford Cl NE35 58 E2
Circle Pl NE46 45 A5
Cirencester St SR4 102 B3
Cirrus Ho 14 SR3 92 A6
Citadel E NE12 29 D3
Citadel W NE12 29 D3
City Hall NE1 99 B2
City of Sunderland Coll
SR5 74 E2
City of Sunderland Coll Bede
Ctr SR3 85 F3
City of Sunderland Coll
Shiney Row Ctr DH4 90 B5
City of Sunderland Coll
Tunstall Ctr SR2 86 E2
City Rd NE1 99 C1
City Way SR3 91 C6
Civic Ct NE31 57 F5
Clacton Rd SR5 73 F1
Clanfield Ct NE7 38 F4
Clanny Ho SR4 85 F6
Clanny St Sunderland SR1 102 B2
Sunderland SR1 102 C2
Clanton Cl NE10 72 C7
Clapham Ave NE6 56 D5
Clara Ave NE27 30 F4
Clara St Blaydon NE21 53 B1
Newcastle-upon-Tyne NE4 54 D4
Clarabad Terr NE12 30 A1
Clarance Pl NE3 38 E5
Claremont Ave
Newcastle-upon-Tyne NE15 53 D7
Sunderland SR6 75 E3
Claremont Cres NE26 31 E7
Claremont Ct NE26 31 E8
Claremont Dr DH4 90 A6
Claremont Gdns
Whitley Bay NE26 31 F6
East Boldon NE36 74 D7
Claremont North Avenue
Path NE8 101 B2
Claremont Pl
Newcastle-upon-Tyne NE2 98 C3
Gateshead NE8 101 B1
Claremont Rd
Newcastle-upon-Tyne NE2 98 B4
Whitley Bay NE26 31 F7
Sunderland SR6 75 E3
Claremont South Ave
NE8 101 B1
Claremont St NE2 98 C3
Claremont Terr
Gateshead NE10 57 B1
Newcastle-upon-Tyne NE2 98 C3
Blyth NE24 17 D7
Sunderland SR2 102 C1
Claremont Wlk NE8 101 A1
Claremount Ct NE36 74 B7
Clarence Cres 2 NE26 32 B4
Clarence Ho NE2 99 C2
Clarence St Tantobie DH9 79 B2
Newcastle-upon-Tyne NE1,
NE2 99 C2
Seaton Sluice NE26 24 D5
2 Sunderland SR5 75 A2
Clarence Terr DH3 88 C3
Clarendon Rd NE6 39 C1
Clarendon Sq SR5 75 B3
Clarewood Ave NE34 60 A8
Clarewood Ct NE4 98 B2
Clarewood Gn NE4 98 A2
Clarewood Pl NE5 54 C8
Clark's Terr 2 SR7 92 E1
Clarke Terr NE10 71 C8
Clarke's Terr NE23 29 A6
Clarks Field NE61 8 E8
Clarks Hill Wlk NE15 52 F7
Clasper Ct 11 NE33 42 C4
Clasper St NE4 100 B3
Clasper Way NE16 54 A3
Claude St
Hetton le Hole DH5 95 A3
9 Crawcrook NE40 51 F3
Claudius Ct 4 NE33 42 C4
Claverdon St NE5 36 B4
Clavering Pl NE1 101 A4
Clavering Rd
Whickham NE16 54 B1
Blaydon NE21 53 C1
Clavering Sq NE11 69 F8
Clavering St NE28 41 B1
Clavering Way NE21 53 E2
Claverley Dr NE27 30 C5
Claxheugh Cotts SR4 85 B7
Claxheugh Rd SR4 85 B7
Claymere Rd SR2 86 E1
Claypath NE10 71 F4
Claypath La NE33 42 D2
Claypath Rd DH5 95 B2
Claypath St 4 NE6 56 A6
Claypool Ct NE34 59 C5
Clayside House 4 NE33 42 D1
Clayton Park Sq NE2 99 B4
Clayton Rd NE2 99 B4
Clayton St
Newcastle-upon-Tyne NE1 99 A1
Bedlington NE22 11 D3
Dudley NE23 28 F8
Jarrow NE32 58 B7
Clayton St W NE1 100 C4
Clayton Terr
Heddon-on-the-Wall NE15 34 F2
Gateshead NE8 56 C1
Clayton Terrace Rd
High Spen NE13,NE39 66 D4
Chopwell NE17 66 C2
Clayworth Rd NE3 28 B1
Cleadon CE Inf Sch SR6 60 B1
Cleadon Gdns
Wallsend NE28 41 A5
Gateshead NE9 71 D3
Cleadon Hill Dr NE34 60 A4
Cleadon Hill Rd NE34 60 B4
Cleadon La SR6 60 C1
Cleadon Lane Ind Est
NE36 74 E8
Cleadon Lea SR6 59 F1
Cleadon Mdws SR6 60 A2
Cleadon Old Hall SR6 60 A1
Cleadon St NE6 56 E6
Cleadon Twrs NE34 60 B4
Cleadon Village Cty Jun Mix
Sch SR6 59 F1
Cleasby Gdns NE9 70 F6
Cleasewell Terr NE62 11 A7
Cleaside Ave NE34 60 A4
Cleaswell Hill NE62 10 F7
Cleaswell Hill Special Sch
NE62 10 F7
Cleehill Dr NE29 31 F1
Cleeve Ct NE38 83 C5
Cleghorn St 4 NE6 56 C8
Clematis Cres NE9 71 D2
Clement Ave NE22 11 C1
Clement St NE9 70 F5
Clementina Cl SR2 103 B1
Clennel Ave NE31 57 D5
Clennel Ho 4 NE4 54 E5
Clent Way NE12 39 A6
Clephan St NE11 54 F1
Clervaux Terr NE32 58 C6
Cleveland Ave
Chester le Street DH2 88 B2
North Shields NE29 41 F6
Newbiggin-by-the-Sea NE64 7 D4
Cleveland Cres NE29 42 A6
Cleveland Ct Jarrow NE32 58 A7
9 South Shields NE33 42 C4
Cleveland Dr NE38 83 B3
Cleveland Gdns
Wallsend NE28 41 B3
Newcastle-upon-Tyne NE7 39 A3
Cleveland Rd
North Shields NE29 42 A6
Sunderland SR4 85 F5
Cleveland St 3 NE33 42 D4
Cleveland Terr
North Shields NE29 42 A6
Newbiggin-by-the-Sea NE64 7 D4
Cleveland View SR6 75 E6
Cliff Rd SR2 93 A6
Cliff Row NE26 32 C4
Cliff Terr SR2 93 A6
Cliff View SR2 93 A6
Cliffe Ct SR6 75 F4
Cliffe Pk SR6 75 F4
Clifford Gdns 3 NE40 51 F3
Clifford Rd NE6 56 D5
Clifford St
Chester le Street DH3 88 C1
Blaydon NE21 53 C3
North Shields NE30 42 C6
Newcastle-upon-Tyne NE6 56 B6
Sunderland SR4 102 A2
Clifford Terr
Chester le Street DH3 88 C2
Crawcrook NE40 51 F3
Cliffside NE34 60 C6
Clifton Ave Wallsend NE28 40 B2
South Shields NE34 59 E7
Clifton Cl Ryton NE40 52 E4
Stakeford NE62 11 A8
Clifton Ct NE3 37 D7
Clifton Gdns Blyth NE24 17 D4
North Shields NE29 41 E3
Gateshead NE9 70 F7
Clifton Gr NE25 31 E6
Clifton La NE61 9 B2
Clifton Rd
Cramlington NE23 22 C5
Newcastle-upon-Tyne NE4 54 F5
Sunderland SR6 75 E4
Clifton Terr
Longbenton NE12 39 D7
Whitley Bay NE26 32 B5
South Shields NE33 59 C8
Clifton Wlk NE5 36 B2
Cliftonbourne Ave SR6 75 E4
Cliftonville Ave NE4 54 E5
Cliftonville Gdns NE26 32 A6
Climbing Tree Wlk NE61 4 E3
Clintburn Ct NE23 22 C8
Clinton Pl Hazlerigg NE3 28 B2
Sunderland SR3 91 C6
Clipsham Cl NE12 39 B6
Clipstone Ave NE6 56 E3
Clipstone Cl NE15 35 C2
Clive Pl NE6 56 B5
Clive St North Shields NE29 42 B5
9 South Shields NE34 59 A4
Clockburn Lonnen NE16 68 E4
Clockburnsyde Cl NE16 68 E5
Clockmill Rd NE11,NE8 100 A1
Clockstand Cl 8 SR6 75 E2
Clockwell St SR5 74 F1
Cloggs The NE20 25 F7
Cloister Ave NE34 59 A5
Cloister Ct NE8 101 C3
Cloister Garth NE7 38 F5
Cloister Wlk NE32 58 C7
Cloisters The
South Shields NE34 59 F7
Newcastle-upon-Tyne NE7 38 F5
Sunderland SR2 103 A1
Close NE1 101 A4
Close E The DH2 88 C5
Close St
Sunderland, Millfield SR4 102 A3
4 Sunderland, Southwick
SR5 75 B1
Close The
Chester le Street DH2 88 C5
Houghton-le-Spring DH5 94 F8
Burnopfield NE16 79 C7
Ponteland NE20 25 E5
Blaydon NE21 53 A1
Seghill NE23 22 F1
Blyth NE24 12 E1
Prudhoe NE42 50 E3
Newcastle-upon-Tyne NE5 53 E8
Stannington NE61 14 C3
Cleadon SR6 59 F1
Closeburn Sq SR3 92 B6
Closefield Gr NE25 31 E4
Cloth Mkt NE1 99 A1
Clough Dene
Tantobie DH9 79 B2
Tantobie, Pickering Nook
NE16 79 A3
Clough La NE1 99 A1
Clousden Dr NE12 29 E1
Clousden Grange NE12 29 E1
Clovelly Ave NE4 54 E5
Clovelly Gdns
Bedlington NE22 15 F8
Whitley Bay NE26 32 A6
Clovelly Pl Ponteland NE20 25 C2
Jarrow NE32 58 E5
Clovelly Sq 6 SR5 74 A3
Clover Ave
Shiney Row DH4 90 B4
Gateshead NE10 56 B2
Winlaton Mill NE21 68 C6
Clover Hill NE16 69 B2
Cloverdale NE22 10 E1
Cloverdale Gdns
Whickham NE16 69 B5
Newcastle-upon-Tyne NE7 39 B3
Cloverfield Ave NE3 37 F6
Cloverhill NE32 58 C1
Cloverhill Ave NE31 57 D3
Cloverhill Cl NE23 22 A1
Cloverhill Com Prim Sch
NE16 68 F4
Cloverhill Dr NE40 52 A4
Clumber St NE4 100 A3
Clumber St N NE4 100 A3
Clyde Ave NE31 57 E3
Clyde Ct 10 SR3 91 F6
Clyde St Chopwell NE17 66 C1
Gateshead NE8 71 A8
Clydedale Ave NE12 39 D8
Clydesdale Ave DH4 90 B7
Clydesdale Mount 8
NE6 56 C5
Clydesdale Rd NE6 56 C5
Clydesdale St DH5 95 A2
Clyvedon Rise NE34 60 A3
Co-operative Bldgs
NE25 23 D3
Co-operative Cres NE10 71 C7
Co-operative St DH3 88 C4
Co-operative Terr
Great Lumley DH4 89 F1
Medomsley DH8 77 B1
Gateshead NE10 71 C7
Longbenton NE12 30 A1
Brunswick Village NE13 28 A6
Burnopfield NE16 79 B6
Backworth NE27 30 E3
11 Shiremoor NE27 30 E1
1 Washington NE37 83 E8
High Spen NE39 66 F5
Pegswood NE61 4 F3
Sunderland SR4 102 A1
Co-operative Villas DH6 96 D1
Coach La
Brunswick Village NE13 27 E4
Hazlerigg NE13 28 B4
Dinnington NE13,NE3 27 E4
North Shields NE29 42 A5
Newcastle-upon-Tyne NE7 39 C4
Coach Open NE28 41 B1
Coach Rd
Kibblesworth NE11 70 B3
Throckley NE15 35 C1
Wallsend NE28 40 C1
Coach Rd *continued*
Washington NE37 72 C2
Coach Rd Est NE37 72 C1
Coach Road Gn NE10 56 C2
Coal La NE42 49 D4
Coalbank Rd DH5 94 F2
Coalbank Sq DH5 94 F2
Coaley La DH4 90 C3
Coalford La DH6 96 C4
Coalway Dr NE16 69 B8
Coalway La
Whickham NE16 69 B7
Greenside NE40, NE41 51 D1
Coalway La N NE16 54 B1
Coanwood Dr NE23 22 C5
Coanwood Gdns NE11 70 B5
Coanwood Rd NE15 54 B4
Coanwood Way NE16 69 B3
Coast Rd
Shiremoor NE28,NE29 41 C6
Wallsend NE28,NE29 40 C4
Tynemouth NE29 41 C6
South Shields NE34,SR6 60 D6
Newcastle-upon-Tyne NE7 39 E2
Coates Endowed Mid Sch
NE20 25 E7
Coatsworth Ct NE8 101 B2
Coatsworth Rd NE8 101 B1
Cobalt Cl NE15 53 C8
Cobbett Cres NE34 59 B3
Cobbler's La NE43 49 B8
Cobblestone Ct NE6 56 B5
Cobden Rd NE23 22 C4
Cobden St
4 Wallsend NE28 40 B2
Gateshead NE8 56 A1
Cobden Terr NE8 56 A1
Cobham Pl NE6 57 A4
Cobham Sq SR5 75 B2
Coble Dene NE29 41 E2
Coble Landing NE33 42 B3
Coburg St Blyth NE24 17 F7
North Shields NE30 42 B6
Gateshead NE8 101 C2
Coburn Cl NE23 29 C5
Cochran St NE21 53 C4
Cochrane Ct NE4 54 E5
Cochrane Park Ave NE7 39 C2
Cochrane St NE4 54 E5
Cochrane Terr NE13 27 B7
Cockburn Terr NE29 41 D3
Cockermouth Gn NE5 54 A8
Cockermouth Rd SR5 73 F2
Cockshaw NE46 45 A5
Cockshaw Ct NE46 45 A5
Cockshaw Terr NE46 45 A5
Cockshoot Dean NE42 50 D3
Cohen Ct NE8 70 E8
Cohort Cl DH8 76 E3
Colbeck Ave NE16 54 B1
Colbeck Terr 3 NE30 42 D7
Colbourne Ave NE23 15 E1
Colbourne Cres NE23 15 E1
Colbury Cl NE23 16 A2
Colby Ct NE4 100 B4
Colchester St NE34 59 A5
Colchester Terr SR4 85 F5
Coldbeck Ct NE23 22 C5
Coldingham Gdns NE5 37 D2
Coldside Gdns NE5 36 B3
Coldstream DH2 82 A2
Coldstream Ave SR5 75 B2
Coldstream Cl DH4 90 B5
Coldstream Dr NE21 68 A8
Coldstream Gdns NE28 41 A3
Coldstream Rd NE15 54 B7
Coldstream Way NE29 41 C8
Coldwell Cl DH6 97 F7
Coldwell La NE10 71 C7
Coldwell Park Ave NE10 71 D7
Coldwell Park Dr NE10 71 D7
Coldwell Rd NE42 50 F3
Coldwell St NE10 71 D8
Coldwell Terr 2 NE10 71 C7
Cole Gdns NE10 72 A8
Colebridge Cl NE5 37 C3
Colebrooke DH3 82 D2
Colegate NE10 71 F7
Colegate Com Prim Sch
NE10 71 F7
Colegate W NE10 71 F7
Colepeth NE10 71 E7
Coleridge Ave
South Shields NE33 42 E1
Gateshead NE9 70 E4
Coleridge Rd SR5 74 B2
Coleridge Sq NE31 57 E6
Coley Gn NE5 36 B4
Coley Hill Cl NE5 36 C4
Coley Terr SR6 75 E3
Colgrove Pl NE3 37 E5
Colgrove Way NE3 37 F5
Colima Ave SR5 85 C8
Colin Pl NE6 57 A8
Colin Terr 7 SR2 92 F6
College Burn Rd SR3 91 E5
College Dr NE33 59 E8
College La
Newcastle-upon-Tyne NE1 99 B2
Longbenton NE7 39 C6
College Pl NE63 6 E2
College Rd Hebburn NE31 57 D2
Ashington NE63 6 E2
College St NE1 99 B2
College View 4 SR5 75 C1
Collier Cl NE15 35 D1
Collierley La DH9 78 D1
Colliery La
Hetton le Hole DH5 95 B2
Newcastle-upon-Tyne NE4 98 B1
Colliery Rd NE11 54 F2
Collin Ave NE34 60 B5
Collingdon Gn NE39 67 A4
Collingdon Rd NE39 67 A4
Collingwood Ave NE28 40 B4
Collingwood Cl NE23 21 F8
Collingwood Cotts NE20 25 B7
Collingwood Cres NE20 25 D4
Collingwood Ct 1 NE37 83 F8
Collingwood Ctr NE29 31 F1
Collingwood Dr
Shiney Row DH4 90 A6
Hexham NE46 44 F2
Collingwood Gdns NE10 56 D2
Collingwood Ho
North Shields NE29 41 F5
South Shields NE33 42 D5
Collingwood Mansions
NE29 42 B4
Collingwood Pl NE62 11 A7
Collingwood Prim Sch
NE29 41 D5
Collingwood Rd
Earsdon NE25 31 A5
Newbiggin-by-the-Sea NE64 7 D5
Collingwood St
Hetton le Hole DH5 95 A6
Newcastle-upon-Tyne NE1 101 A4
16 Gateshead NE10 56 D1
Hebburn NE31 58 A6
South Shields NE33 59 C8
3 Sunderland SR5 75 B2
Collingwood Terr
Dunston NE11 100 A1
1 Newcastle-upon-Tyne
NE2 38 F1
Blyth NE24 17 E7
Whitley Bay NE26 32 C4
Tynemouth NE30 42 D7
Collingwood View NE29 41 F5
Collywell Bay Rd NE26 24 D5
Collywell Ct NE26 24 D6
Colman Ave NE34 59 A5
Colmet Ct NE11 70 D4
Colnbrook Cl NE3 37 D7
Colomba Wlk NE3 38 E5
Colombo Rd SR5 73 F1
Colston St NE4 54 D6
Colston Way NE25 31 D7
Colt Pk NE17 77 B5
Coltere Ave NE36 74 E7
Colton Gdns NE9 71 A3
Coltpark NE5 36 F1
Coltpark Pl NE23 22 B5
Coltsfoot Gdns NE10 71 C5
Coltspool NE11 81 D6
Columba St SR5 75 B2
Columbia Grange NE3 37 E5
Columbia Terr NE24 17 E6
Colwell Pl NE5 54 B7
Colwell Rd
Shiremoor NE27 30 F2
Tynemouth NE29 31 F1
Ashington NE63 6 F1
Colwyn Par NE31 58 A2
Colwyne Pl NE5 37 B2
Combe Dr NE15 53 B7
Comet Row NE12 29 C2
Comet Sq SR3 92 A7
Comical Cnr NE33 42 B4
Comma Ct NE11 70 B7
Commercial Rd
Blyth NE24 17 E8
Newcastle-upon-Tyne,
South Gosforth NE3 38 E5
Jarrow NE32 58 C8
South Shields NE33 42 B1
Newcastle-upon-Tyne, Byker
NE6 56 C5
Sunderland SR2 86 F4
Commercial St 8 NE21 53 B1
Commissioners' Wharf
NE29 42 A2
Compton Ave NE34 59 D7
Compton Ct NE38 83 B5
Compton Rd NE29 41 F5
Concord Ho NE5 36 F2
Concorde Sq 5 SR3 92 A7
Concorde Way NE32 58 B6
Condercum Ct NE15 54 C5
Condercum Ind Est NE4 54 D5
Condercum Rd NE4 54 D5
Cone St NE33 42 B2
Cone Terr DH3 88 D4
Conewood House NE3 37 F6
Conhope La NE15,NE4 54 D5
Conifer Cl NE21 68 B8
Conifer Ct NE12 39 F8
Coniscliffe Ave NE3 37 F4
Conishead Terr DH6 97 F8
Coniston Birtley DH3 82 D2
Gateshead NE10 72 A8
Coniston Ave
Easington Lane DH5 97 C8
Whickham NE16 69 D7
Newcastle-upon-Tyne NE2 38 E2
Hebburn NE31 57 F4
Newbiggin-by-the-Sea NE64 7 C3
Sunderland SR5 75 C4
Coniston Cl
Chester le Street DH2 88 C2
Killingworth NE12 29 C3
Newburn NE15 52 E7
Coniston Cres NE21 68 B8
Coniston Ct NE5 54 B8

Coniston Dr NE32 ....58 D3
Coniston Gdns NE9 .....71 B5
Coniston Pl NE9 ....71 B5
Coniston Rd Blyth NE24 ..12 A1
Wallsend NE28 ....44 A1
Tynemouth NE30 ....32 A2
Connaught Cl DH4 ......90 C5
Connaught Gdns NE12 ..39 D7
Connaught Terr NE32 ...58 B6
Conningsby Cl NE3 .....38 D8
Conniscliffe Ct NE46 ...44 F3
Conniscliffe Rd NE46 ...44 F3
Connolly Terr NE17 .....77 C6
Consett Rd NE11 ....70 A5
Constable Cl NE40 ......52 C4
Constable Gdns NE34 ....59 C3
Constables Garth 6 DH3 82 C4
Content St NE21 ....53 C1
Convent Rd NE4 ....54 D7
Conway Cl
Bedlington NE22 ....10 D1
Ryton NE40 ....52 D4
Conway Dr NE7 ....39 A4
Conway Gdns
Wallsend NE28 ....40 A4
Sunderland SR3 ....91 C7
Conway Gr NE26 ....24 B7
Conway Rd SR5 ....73 F2
Conway Sq Gateshead NE9 71 A8
Sunderland SR5 ....73 F2
Conyers Ave DH2 ....88 B5
Conyers Gdns DH2 ....88 B5
Conyers Pl DH2 ....88 B5
Conyers Rd
Chester le Street DH2 .....88 C5
Newcastle-upon-Tyne NE6 ..56 C6
Cook Cl NE33 ....59 B8
Cook Gdns NE10 ....72 B8
Cook Sq SR5 ....74 A2
Cooks Wood NE38 ....83 D3
Cookshold La
Sherburn DH6 ....96 B2
Sherburn Hill DH6 ....96 B2
Cookson Cl
Newcastle-upon-Tyne NE4 ..98 B1
Corbridge NE45 ....46 F6
Cookson House NE33 ....42 C3
Cookson St NE4 ....98 A1
Cookson Terr DH2 ....88 B3
Cookson's La NE1 ....101 A4
Coomassie Rd NE24 ......17 E7
Coomside NE23 ....22 C4
Cooper St SR6 ....75 E1
Coopies Field NE61 ......9 B8
Coopies Haugh NE61 ......9 C7
Coopies La NE61 ....9 B7
Coopies Lane Ind Est
NE61 ....9 C7
Coopies Way NE61 ....9 C7
Copland Terr NE2 ....99 C2
Copley Ave NE34 ....59 C2
Copley Dr SR3 ....86 B2
Copper Chare NE61 ....3 F1
Copper Cl NE11 ....70 B7
Copperas La NE15 ....53 F7
Coppergate Ct NE31 .....57 F7
Coppice The NE26 ....24 C6
Coppice Way NE2 ....99 C2
Coppy La DH9 ....80 C4
Copse The Prudhoe NE42 ..50 E2
Burnopfield NE16 ....78 F6
Blaydon NE21 ....53 F2
Newcastle-upon-Tyne NE3 ..38 D8
Washington NE37 ....72 B2
Coptleigh DH5 ....95 A7
Coquet NE38 ....82 F1
Coquet Ave Blyth NE24 ..17 E5
Whitley Bay NE26 ....32 A5
Newcastle-upon-Tyne NE3 ..38 B6
South Shields NE34 ....60 B8
Coquet Bldgs NE15 ......36 B1
Coquet Dr NE61 ....1 E5
Coquet Gr NE15 ....35 C2
Coquet Ho 16 SR3 ....91 F6
Coquet Park Fst Sch
NE26 ....32 A6
Coquet St
Newcastle-upon-Tyne NE1 ..56 A6
Chopwell NE17 ....66 C1
Hebburn NE31 ....57 D6
Jarrow NE32 ....58 A5
Ashington NE63 ....6 E4
Coquet Terr Dudley NE23 ..28 F8
Newcastle-upon-Tyne NE6 ..56 B8
Coquetdale Ave NE6 .....57 A6
Coquetdale Cl NE61 ......4 E3
Coquetdale Pl NE22 .....11 C1
Coquetdale Villas 5 SR6 .75 E2
Corbiere Cl SR3 ....91 E6
Corbitt St NE8 ....100 C1
Corbridge Ave NE13 .....28 B6
Corbridge CE Fst Sch
NE45 ....47 A6
Corbridge Cl NE28 ......40 E6
Corbridge Mid Sch NE45 .46 F7
Corbridge Rd
Hexham NE46 ....45 D4
Newcastle-upon-Tyne NE6 ..56 C6
Corbridge St NE6 ....56 B6
Corby Gate SR2 ....86 D4
Corby Gdns NE6 ....56 F6
Corby Hall Dr SR2 ......86 D4
Corchester La NE46,NE45 .46 C7
Corchester Rd NE22 .....10 F2
Corchester Twrs NE45 ...46 E7
Corchester Wlk NE7 .....39 C4
Corfu Rd SR5 ....74 A2
Corinthian Sq SR5 ......74 A2
Cork St SR1 ....103 B3
Cormorant Cl Blyth NE24 .17 F4
4 Washington NE38 ....82 F3
Ashington NE63 ....6 E1
Corn Mill Dr DH5 ....94 D6
Cornbank Cl SR3 ....92 A5
Corndean NE38 ....84 A4
Cornel Mews NE7 ....39 C3
Cornel Rd NE7 ....39 C3
Cornelia Cl 7 SR3 ......92 A7
Corney St NE33 ....59 B7
Cornfields The NE31 ....57 E6
Cornforth Cl
Gateshead NE10 ....72 C6
Ashington NE63 ....6 B2
Cornhill Hedworth NE32 ..58 C1
Newcastle-upon-Tyne NE5 ..36 F1
Cornhill Ave NE3 ....37 F7
Cornhill Cres NE29 .....41 D7
Cornhill Rd
Cramlington NE23 ....22 C6
6 Sunderland SR5 ....75 B2
Cornmill* TD12 ....107 B7
Cornmoor Gdns NE16 ....69 B5
Cornmoor Rd NE16 ....69 B6
Cornthwaite Dr SR6 .....75 E8
Cornwall Rd NE31 ....57 F3
Cornwallis Sq NE33 .....42 B1
Cornwallis St 13 NE33 ..42 C3
Cornwell Cres NE22 .....16 B8
Cornwell Ct NE7 ....38 F4
Coronation Ave
Sunniside NE16 ....69 B2
6 Ryhope SR2 ....92 F6
Coronation Bglws NE3 ...38 D5
Coronation Cl SR1 .....103 B3
Coronation Cotts NE61 ...2 A3
Coronation Cres
Burnside DH4 ....90 C2
Whitley Bay NE25 ....31 F4
Coronation Gn DH5 ......97 D8
Coronation Rd
Sunniside NE16 ....69 B2
Seaton Delaval NE25 ......23 C3
Newcastle-upon-Tyne NE5 ..36 B3
Coronation St
Chester le Street DH3 .....88 D1
Annitsford NE23 ....22 B1
Blyth NE24 ....17 E6
Wallsend NE28 ....40 C2
North Shields NE29 ....42 A4
South Shields NE33 ....42 C2
Ryton NE40 ....52 E4
Newbiggin-by-the-Sea NE64 ..7 E5
Sunderland SR1 ....103 B3
Coronation Terr
Chester le Street DH3 .....88 C2
Hetton le Hole DH5 ....95 A2
Kibblesworth NE11 ....81 C6
Tynemouth NE29 ....31 B1
3 Boldon Colliery NE35 ...58 E1
Ashington NE63 ....6 E1
Sunderland SR4 ....85 B6
Corporation Rd SR2 .....86 F4
Corporation St NE4 .....98 C1
Corporation Yd NE61 .....3 F1
Corpus Christie RC Prim Sch
NE8 ....70 E8
Corrighan Terr DH5 .....94 C4
Corrofell Gdns NE10 ....56 F1
Corry Ct SR4 ....85 E4
Corsair NE16 ....68 F6
Corsenside NE5 ....36 F1
Corstopitum 3 NE28 .....40 F4
Corstopitvm Roman Fort*
NE45 ....46 E6
Corstorphine Town NE33 .42 B1
Cortina Ave SR4 ....85 D4
Corvan Terr DH9 ....79 A2
Cosford Ct NE3 ....37 C7
Cossack Terr SR4 ....85 E7
Cosser St NE24 ....17 B4
Cosserat Pl NE31 ....57 D7
Coston Dr NE33 ....42 C3
Cosyn St NE6 ....56 A5
Cotehill Dr NE20 ....25 B4
Cotehill Rd 2 NE5 ......37 B1
Cotemede NE10 ....72 A5
Cotfield Wlk NE8 ......101 A1
Cotgarth The NE10 ......71 E7
Cotherstone Ct SR3 .....86 B2
Cotman Gdns NE34 ....59 D2
Cotswold Ave
Chester le Street DH2 .....88 B1
Longbenton NE12 ....29 B1
Cotswold Cl NE38 ....83 B4
Cotswold Dr
Whitley Bay NE25 ....31 F3
Ashington NE63 ....6 F1
Cotswold Gdns
Dunston NE11 ....70 A7
Newcastle-upon-Tyne NE7 ..39 A3
Cotswold La NE35 ....58 F2
Cotswold Rd
Tynemouth NE29 ....31 E2
Sunderland SR5 ....74 A2
Cotswold Sq SR5 ....74 A3
Cottage La NE5 ....37 D1
Cottenham Chare NE4 ....98 B1
Cottenham St NE4 ....98 B1
Cotter Riggs Pl NE5 ....36 B2
Cotter Riggs Wlk NE5 ...36 B2
Cotterdale NE28 ....39 F5
Cotterdale Ave 1 NE8 ...70 F8
Cottersdale Gdns NE5 ...36 B3
Cottinglea NE61 ....3 F2
Cottingvale NE61 ....3 F2
Cottingwood Ct NE4 .....98 B2
Cottingwood Gdns
Newcastle-upon-Tyne NE4 ..98 B2
Morpeth NE61 ....3 F1
Cottingwood Gn NE24 ....17 C3
Cottingwood La NE61 .....3 F2
Cottonwood
Shiney Row DH4 ....89 F6
Silksworth SR3 ....91 E5
Coulson Park Fst Sch
NE63 ....6 F2
Coulthards La NE8 .....101 C3
Coulthards Pl NE8 ......56 A4
Coulton Dr NE36 ....74 D7
Council Ave DH4 ....90 B6
Council Rd NE63 ....6 C4
Council Terr NE37 ......83 D7
Counden Rd 4 NE5 ....36 E3
Countess Ave NE26 ......32 A5
Countess Dr NE15 ....54 A7
Coupland Gr NE32 ....58 B3
Coupland Rd NE63 ....6 C3
Court Rd NE22 ....10 F1
Court The NE16 ....69 C6
Courtfield Rd NE6 ......56 F8
Courtney Ct NE3 ....37 C7
Courtney Dr SR3 ....91 F8
Cousin St SR1 ....103 C3
Coutts Rd NE6 ....56 E8
Cove The DH4 ....90 B6
Coventry Gdns
North Shields NE29 ....41 E4
Newcastle-upon-Tyne NE4 ..54 E4
Coventry Way NE32 ......58 B1
Coverdale Gateshead NE10 72 A6
Wallsend NE28 ....39 F5
Coverdale Ave Blyth NE24 17 A7
Washington NE37 ....83 C8
Coverley Rd SR5 ....74 B2
Covers The
Longbenton NE12 ....39 E6
Wallsend NE28 ....40 B3
Morpeth NE61 ....9 A7
Cow La NE45 ....46 F7
Cowan Cl NE21 ....53 A4
Cowan Terr SR2 ....103 A2
Cowans Ave NE12 ....29 C4
Cowdray Ct NE3 ....37 C7
Cowdray Rd SR5 ....74 B2
Cowell Gr NE39 ....67 C2
Cowen Gdns NE9 ....71 A1
Cowen Rd NE21 ....53 D3
Cowen St Blaydon NE21 ..68 B8
Newcastle-upon-Tyne NE6 ..56 F6
Cowen Terr NE39 ....67 F3
Cowgarth NE46 ....45 A5
Cowgate NE1 ....99 B1
Cowgate L Ctr NE5 ....37 D3
Cowgate Prim Sch NE4 ...54 D8
Cowley Cres DH5 ....94 C4
Cowley Pl NE24 ....17 B8
Cowley Rd NE24 ....12 B1
Cowpath Gdns NE10 ......57 B2
Cowpen Rd NE24 ....17 C8
Cox Chare NE1 ....99 C1
Coxfoot Cl NE34 ....59 C5
Coxgreen Rd DH4 ....84 B2
Coxlodge Rd NE3 ....38 A5
Coxlodge Terr NE3 ......38 A5
Coxon St Gateshead NE10 .57 B2
Sunderland SR2 ....103 B1
Coxon Terr NE8 ....56 C1
Crabtree Rd NE43 ....64 C7
Cradock Ave NE31 ....57 D4
Craggyknowe NE37 ....82 F6
Craghall Dene NE2 ......38 E4
Craghall Dene Ave NE2 ..38 E4
Cragleas NE16 ....79 A4
Cragside
Chester le Street DH2 .....88 A4
Brunswick Village NE13 ...28 B6
Cramlington NE23 ....22 C4
Whitley Bay NE26 ....31 E7
South Shields NE34 ....60 B5
Corbridge NE45 ....47 B7
Cragside* NE65 ....118 A5
Newcastle-upon-Tyne NE7 ..39 B3
Cragside Ave NE29 ......41 D8
Cragside Ct
4 Houghton-le-Spring DH5 .94 F8
Dunston NE11 ....70 A6
Cragside Cty Prim Sch
NE7 ....39 A3
Cragside Fst Sch NE23 ..22 B4
Cragside Gdns
Dunston NE11 ....70 A5
Killingworth NE12 ....29 F4
Wallsend NE28 ....40 F3
Cragside Ho 5 SR3 ......91 D7
Cragside House (N.T.)*
NE65 ....118 A5
Cragside Rd NE37 ....83 A7
Cragston Ave NE5 ....37 C3
Cragston Cl NE5 ....37 C2
Cragton Gdns NE24 ......17 B7
Craig Cres NE23 ....29 A8
Craig St 1 DH3 ....82 C4
Craigavon Rd SR5 ....74 B2
Craigend NE23 ....22 B5
Craighill 1 DH4 ....90 A6
Craiglands The SR3 .....86 C3
Craigmill Pk NE24 ......17 A8
Craigmillar Ave NE5 ....37 C3
Craigmillar Cl NE5 .....37 C3
Craigmont Ct NE12 ......39 D6
Craigshaw Rd SR5 ....73 F3
Craigshaw Sq SR5 ....73 F3
Craigwell Dr SR3 ....92 A4
Craik Ave NE34 ....59 B5
Crake Way NE38 ....82 F2
Cramer St NE8 ....101 C1
Cramilngton Terr 10
NE27 ....30 E1
Cramlington Beacon Hill Fst
Sch NE23 ....21 E6
Cramlington Com High Sch
NE23 ....22 A4
Cramlington Rd SR5 .....73 F2
Cramlington Sq SR5 .....73 F2
Cramlington Sta NE23 ...21 F7
Cramlington Terr NE24 ..17 C4
Cramond Ct NE9 ....70 E3
Cramond Way NE23 ....22 B4
Cranberry Rd SR5 ....74 B2
Cranberry Sq SR5 ....74 A2
Cranborne SR3 ....91 C6
Cranbourne Gr NE30 .....32 B3
Cranbrook Ave NE3 ......38 C7
Cranbrook Ct NE3 ....37 E7
Cranbrook Dr NE42 ......50 B2
Cranbrook Rd NE15 ......54 B4
Cranemarsh Cl NE63 ......6 C1
Craneshaugh Cl NE46 ....45 E4
Cranesville NE9 ....71 C5
Caneswater Ave NE26 ....24 F1
Cranfield Pl NE15 ......53 C7
Cranford Gdns NE15 .....53 E7
Cranford St NE34 ....59 C6
Cranford Terr SR4 .....102 A1
Cranham Cl NE12 ....29 F4
Cranlea NE3 ....37 C6
Cranleigh Ave NE3 ......37 C7
Cranleigh Gr NE42 ......50 D3
Cranleigh Pl NE25 ......31 D6
Cranleigh Rd SR5 ....74 A2
Cranshaw Pl NE23 ....22 C5
Cranston Pl 9 SR2 ......93 A6
Crantock Rd NE3 ....37 F5
Cranwell Ct NE3 ....37 C7
Cranwell Dr NE13 ....28 B6
Craster Ave
Longbenton NE12 ....29 F1
Shiremoor NE27 ....30 F3
South Shields NE34 ....60 B8
Craster Cl Blyth NE24 ..17 C7
Whitley Bay NE25 ....31 D7
Craster Gdns NE28 ......40 F3
Craster Rd NE29 ....41 D5
Craster Sq NE3 ....38 A6
Craster Terr NE7 ....39 B2
Crathie DH3 ....82 C7
Craven Ct SR6 ....75 F1
Crawcrook La NE40, NE41 51 D5
Crawcrook Terr NE40 ....51 E3
Crawford Cotts NE61 .....4 A1
Crawford Ct SR3 ....91 F6
Crawford Pl NE25 ....31 E4
Crawford St NE24 ....12 D1
Crawford Terr
Newcastle-upon-Tyne NE6 ..56 F5
Morpeth NE61 ....4 A1
Crawhall Cres NE61 ......8 E7
Crawhall Cty Fst Sch
NE23 ....22 A5
Crawhall Rd NE1 ....99 C1
Crawley Ave NE31 ....57 D3
Crawley Gdns NE16 ......69 C7
Crawley Rd NE28 ....40 B1
Crawley Sq NE31 ....57 D3
Craythorne Gdns NE6 ....39 D2
Creeve lea NE38 ....83 C3
Creighton Ave NE3 ......37 E4
Creland Way NE5 ....37 C3
Crescent Ave NE46 ......44 F5
Crescent The
Chester le Street DH2 .....88 B3
Newbottle DH4 ....90 D4
Shiney Row DH4 ....90 A5
Hetton le Hole DH5 ....95 A3
5 Dunston NE11 ....69 F8
Kibblesworth NE11 ....81 C6
Newcastle-upon-Tyne,
Kenton Bankfoot NE13 ....37 B6
9 Throckley NE15 ....35 D2
Sunniside NE16 ....69 B2
Whickham NE16 ....69 C6
Ponteland NE20 ....25 A3
Seghill NE23 ....22 F1
Whitley Bay NE26 ....32 B4
Wallsend NE28 ....40 B3
Tynemouth NE30 ....42 C8
Jarrow NE32 ....58 A4
South Shields NE34 ....59 F5
High Spen NE39 ....66 F3
Rowlands Gill NE39 ....67 F2
Ryton NE40 ....52 D5
Wylam NE41 ....51 B5
Morpeth NE61 ....8 F6
Newcastle-upon-Tyne NE7 ..39 B5
New Silksworth SR3 ......86 A1
Cleadon SR6 ....74 F8
Crescent Vale NE26 .....32 A4
Crescent Way NE12 ......39 E8
Crescent Way N NE12 ....39 E8
Crescent Way S NE12 ....39 E8
Creslow NE10 ....71 F6
Cressbourne Ave SR6 ....75 E4
Cresswell Ave
Longbenton NE12 ....29 F1
Seaton Sluice NE26 ......24 C6
Tynemouth NE29 ....41 F7
Cresswell Cl Blaydon NE21 68 A8
Whitley Bay NE25 ....31 E3
Cresswell Dr Blyth NE24 .17 C5
Newcastle-upon-Tyne NE3 ..37 E7
Cresswell Home Farm Cotts
NE61 ....2 B4
Cresswell Rd
Wallsend NE28 ....40 A1
Ellington NE61 ....1 E6
Cresswell St NE6 ....56 D6
Cresswell Terr
Ashington NE63 ....6 C4
Sunderland SR2 ....102 C1
Crest The Dinnington NE13 .27 B7
Bedlington NE22 ....10 E1
Seaton Sluice NE26 ......24 E4
Cresthaven NE10 ....71 E6
Crichton Ave DH3 ....88 D1
Cricket Terr NE16 ......79 A6
Cricklewood Dr DH4 .....90 B6
Cricklewood Rd SR5 .....74 A1
Criddle St NE8 ....56 A4
Crieff Gr NE32 ....58 D3
Crieff Sq SR5 ....73 F2
Crigdon Hill NE5 ....36 F1
Crighton NE38 ....83 A5
Crimdon Gr DH4 ....94 C7
Crimea Rd SR5 ....73 F2
Crindledykes NE38 ......83 E2
Cripps Ave NE10 ....72 B8
Crocus Cl NE21 ....53 A2
Croft Ave Longbenton NE12 39 E7
Wallsend NE28 ....40 C2
Sunderland SR4 ....102 A2
Croft Cl NE40 ....52 D4
Croft Cotts NE43 ....64 D7
Croft Ho NE42 ....50 A4
Croft House Sch NE46 ...44 F5
Croft Rd NE24 ....17 E7
Croft St NE1 ....99 B1
Croft Terr Horsley NE15 ..50 C8
Jarrow NE32 ....58 B6
2 Hexham NE46 ....45 A4
Croft The
Sherburn Hill DH6 ....96 D1
Killingworth NE12 ....29 E4
Newcastle-upon-Tyne NE3 ..38 A4
Ryton NE40 ....52 D4
Croft View NE40 ....51 E3
Croft Villas 2 NE40 .....51 E3
Croft's La NE15 ....50 C8
Croftdale Rd NE21 ......53 B2
Crofter Cl NE23 ....22 A1
Crofthead Dr NE23 ......22 B4
Crofton Fst Sch NE24 ....17 E6
Crofton Mill Ind Est NE24 17 F7
Crofton St Blyth NE24 ...17 E7
South Shields NE34 ....59 C6
Crofton Way NE15 ....53 B7
Crofts Ave NE45 ....47 B5
Crofts Cl NE45 ....47 B5
Crofts Pk NE61 ....9 E5
Crofts The NE20 ....25 F6
Crofts Way NE45 ....47 A6
Croftside DH3 ....82 C5
Croftside Ave 2 SR6 ....75 F8
Croftside Ho 3 SR3 .....91 F5
Croftsway NE4 ....54 F4
Croftwell Cl NE21 ......53 D1
Cromarty St SR6 ....75 D2
Cromdale Pl NE5 ....37 B1
Cromer Ave NE9 ....70 F3
Cromer Ct NE9 ....71 A3
Cromer Gdns
Newcastle-upon-Tyne NE2 ..38 E3
Whitley Bay NE26 ....32 A6
Crompton Rd NE6 ....56 B8
Cromwell Ave NE21 ......53 B2
Cromwell Ct NE21 ....53 A4
Cromwell Pl NE21 ....53 A1
Cromwell Rd
Gateshead NE10 ....57 B2
Whickham NE16 ....69 C8
Cromwell St Ryton NE21 ..53 A4
Gateshead NE8 ....56 A1
Sunderland SR4 ....102 A3
Cromwell Terr
North Shields NE29 ....41 F6
Gateshead NE8 ....101 A1
Crondall St NE33 ....59 D7
Cronin Ave NE34 ....59 B4
Cronniewell NE17 ....77 B5
Crookham Gr NE61 ....9 B5
Crookham Way NE23 ......22 C4
Crookhill Com Prim Sch
NE40 ....52 E5
Crookhill Terr NE40 ....52 E4
Cropthorne NE10 ....72 B6
Crosby Gdns NE9 ....71 B3
Crosland Pk NE23 ....15 F2
Cross Ave NE28 ....39 F4
Cross Camden La NE29,
NE30 ....42 B5
Cross Carliol St NE1 ...99 B1
Cross Dr NE40 ....52 C6
Cross Keys La NE9 ......70 F5
Cross La Dunston NE11 ...54 D2
Kibblesworth NE11 ....70 B4
Cross Morpeth St NE2 ...98 B4
Cross Par NE4 ....100 B4
Cross Pl SR1 ....103 B3
Cross Rigg Cl DH4 ......90 A7
Cross Row Ryton NE40 ...52 E4
Gateshead NE8 ....56 B1
Cross Sheraton St NE2 ..98 B4
Cross St
8 Fence Houses DH4 ......94 A8
Houghton-le-Spring DH4 ...90 D1
High Pittington DH6 .....96 D3
Newcastle-upon-Tyne NE1 ..98 C1

Cross St *continued*
Newcastle-upon-Tyne, St Ann's NE6 .56 A5
Gateshead NE8 .101 C1
Cross Terr NE39 .67 D1
Cross Vale Rd SR2 .86 C4
Cross Villa Place No 1 NE4 .98 C1
Cross Villa Place No 2 NE4 .98 C1
Cross Villa Place No 3 NE4 .98 C1
Cross Villa Place No 4 NE4 .98 B1
Cross Villa Place No 5 NE4 .98 B1
Cross Way The NE61 .8 F6
Crossbank Rd NE5 .37 D3
Crossbrook Rd 2 NE5 .37 D2
Crossby Ct SR2 .103 C1
Crossfell NE20 .25 C4
Crossfell Gdns NE62 .11 A8
Crossfield Pk NE10 .71 C6
Crossfield Terr NE6 .57 A4
Crossgate NE33 .42 C2
Crossgate Rd DH5 .95 A2
Crossgill NE37 .83 B7
Crosshill Rd NE15 .54 B4
Crosslaw NE5 .36 F1
Crosslea Ave SR3 .86 B3
Crossley Terr
Longbenton NE12 .29 F1
Newcastle-upon-Tyne NE4 .98 A2
Crossway
Newcastle-upon-Tyne NE2 .38 E3
Tynemouth NE30 .42 C8
South Shields NE34 .60 A5
Guide Post NE62 .10 F7
Gateshead NE9 .71 B6
Crossway Ct NE5 .37 F3
Crossway The
Newcastle-upon-Tyne, Lemington NE15 .53 D7
Newcastle-upon-Tyne, Kenton NE3 .37 F4
Crossway Villas NE9 .71 A6
Crossways Hedworth NE32 58 C1
East Boldon NE36 .74 E7
New Silksworth SR3 .91 F7
Crossways The NE13 .28 A4
Crosthwaite Gr SR5 .74 A1
Croudace Row 2 NE10 .71 D8
Crow Bank NE28 .40 C2
Crow Hall La NE23 .21 F7
Crow Hall Rd NE23 .15 F1
Crow La SR3 .91 B7
Crowhall La NE10 .71 D8
Crowhall Towers 7 NE10 .71 D8
Crowley 2 NE16 .54 A1
Crowley Ave NE16 .69 C8
Crowley Gdns NE21 .53 C2
Crowley Rd NE16 .54 A1
Crown And Anchor Cotts NE15 .50 C8
Crown Rd SR5 .75 A1
Crown St Blyth NE24 .17 F7
7 Morpeth NE61 .9 A8
Crown Terr NE40 .52 B1
Crowther Ind Est
Birtley NE37 .82 F4
Washington NE38 .82 F5
Crowther Rd NE38 .82 F5
Crowtree L Ctr SR1 .102 C2
Crowtree Rd SR1 .102 C3
Croxdale Ct NE34 .59 A5
Croxdale Gdns NE10 .57 B2
Croxdale Terr
Gateshead NE10 .57 B2
Greenside NE40 .52 C1
Croydon Rd NE4 .98 A2
Crozier St SR5 .75 C1
Cruddas Pk NE4 .100 A4
Cruddas Pk Sh Ctr NE4 .100 A4
Crudwell Cl NE35 .58 E2
Crummock Ave SR6 .75 C4
Crummock Rd NE5 .54 B8
Crumstone Ct NE12 .29 E4
Crusade Wlk NE32 .58 A5
Cty Cricket Gd NE2 .99 C4
Cuba St SR2 .86 E4
Cuillin Cl NE38 .83 B3
Culford Pl NE28 .40 E6
Cullercoats Prim Sch NE30 .32 C3
Cullercoats Rd SR5 .73 F1
Cullercoats Sq SR5 .73 F1
Cullercoats St NE6 .56 E6
Cullercoats Sta NE30 .32 C3
Culloden Wlk NE12 .29 D4
Culzean Ho 6 SR3 .91 D7
Cumberland Ave
Bedlington NE22 .10 E1
Newbiggin-by-the-Sea NE64 .7 D4
Cumberland Pl
Birtley DH3 .82 D1
South Shields NE34 .60 B7
Cumberland Rd
Shiremoor NE29 .41 B7
New Silksworth SR3 .92 A8
Cumberland St
Wallsend NE28 .40 C2
Wallsend, Willington Quay NE28 .41 B1
Sunderland SR1 .103 A3
Cumberland Way NE37 .72 D2
Cumberland Wlk NE7 .39 B4
Cumbria Wlk NE4 .98 A1
Cumbrian Ave
Chester le Street DH2 .88 C2
Sunderland SR6 .75 C5
Cummings St NE24 .17 E8
Curlew Cl
Longbenton NE12 .39 A7
Washington NE38 .83 A2
Ryton NE40 .52 E4
Ashington NE63 .11 E8
Curlew Hill NE61 .3 D2
Curlew Rd Jarrow NE32 .58 C8
Jarrow NE32 .58 D8
Curlew Way NE24 .17 E4
Curly Kews NE61 .8 E8
Curran House NE32 .58 C8
Curren Gdns NE10 .56 C2
Curtis Rd NE4 .54 F7
Curzon Pl 6 NE5 .37 B2
Curzon Rd W NE28 .40 B1
Curzon St NE8 .70 E8
Cushat Cl NE6 .56 C5
Cushy Cow La NE40 .52 D4
Cut Bank NE1 .56 A5
Cut Throat La NE17,NE39 .77 C4
Cuthbert Ct NE32 .58 E6
Cuthbert St
Sunniside NE16 .69 A1
Hebburn NE31 .57 D7
Gateshead NE8 .101 A2
Cuthbert Wlk NE3 .38 E5
Cuthbertson Cl SR6 .75 E5
Cutting St 3 SR7 .92 F1
Cygnet Cl
Newcastle-upon-Tyne NE5 .36 D4
Ashington NE63 .11 D8
Cyncopa Way NE5 .37 D2
Cypress Ave NE4 .54 D8
Cypress Cres
Dunston NE11 .70 A7
Blyth NE24 .17 E7
Cypress Dr NE24 .17 E7
Cypress Gdns
Killingworth NE12 .29 C4
Blyth NE24 .17 E7
Cypress Gr NE40 .52 C6
Cypress Rd Blaydon NE21 .53 C2
Gateshead NE9 .71 D2
Cypress Sq 11 SR3 .92 A8
Cyprus Gdns NE9 .71 A6

D

D'arcy Ct SR1 .103 B2
Dachet Rd NE25 .31 D7
Dacre Rd SR6 .75 D4
Dacre St
South Shields NE33 .59 C8
Morpeth NE61 .3 F1
Daffodil Cl NE21 .53 B2
Dahlia Ct SR4 .102 B3
Dahlia Pl NE4 .54 D7
Dahlia Way NE31 .57 E4
Dainton Cl DH4 .90 C4
Dairnbrook 7 NE37 .83 A6
Dairy La DH4 .94 C8
Daisy Cotts 9 DH3 .82 C4
Dale Rd NE25 .31 D4
Dale St Cambois NE24 .12 E1
South Shields NE33 .42 D3
Crawcrook NE40 .51 F4
Dale Terr SR6 .75 E3
Dale Top NE25 .23 F1
Dale View NE43 .64 D7
Dale View Gdns NE40 .51 F3
Dalegarth Gr SR6 .75 C5
Dales The NE5 .37 E2
Dalla St SR4 .85 A7
Dalmahoy NE37 .72 D3
Dalmatia Terr NE24 .17 E6
Dalston Pl NE24 .17 E4
Dalton Ave NE61 .2 A3
Dalton Cl NE23 .22 B6
Dalton Cres 28 NE6 .56 B6
Dalton Ct NE28 .39 F5
Dalton Pl
Newcastle-upon-Tyne NE5 .36 C3
Sunderland SR4 .102 B2
Dalton St
Newcastle-upon-Tyne NE6 .56 B5
Newcastle-upon-Tyne NE6 .56 B6
Dalton Terr NE17 .77 B8
Dalton Way DH4 .90 A7
Daltons La NE33 .42 B2
Dame Allan's Boys Sch NE4 .54 E7
Dame Allan's Girls Sch NE4 .54 E7
Dame Dorothy Cres SR6 .75 E1
Dame Dorothy Prim Sch SR6 .103 B4
Dame Dorothy St SR6 .103 A4
Dame Flora Robson Ave NE34 .58 F4
Damside NE61 .9 A8
Danby Cl Washington NE38 88 F8
New Silksworth SR3 .92 B6
Danby Gdns NE6 .39 D1
Danville Rd SR6 .75 E4
Darden Cl NE12 .29 F4
Darden Lough NE5 .36 F1
Darenth St NE34 .59 C6
Darien Ave SR6 .75 D4
Dark La NE61 .4 A1
Darley Ct 15 SR3 .91 F6
Darley Pl NE15 .54 A5
Darnell Pl NE4 .98 B2
Darnley Rd NE63 .6 C3
Darras Ct NE33 .42 D1
Darras Dr NE29 .41 C7
Darras Hall Fst Sch NE20 25 C3
Darras Mews NE20 .25 C4
Darras Rd NE20 .25 D4
Darrell St NE13 .28 A6
Dartford Cl NE25 .23 E3
Dartford Rd
South Shields NE33 .42 F2
Sunderland SR6 .75 D4
Dartmouth Ave NE9 .70 F2
Darvall Cl NE25 .31 D7
Darwin Cres NE3 .37 F3
Darwin St SR5 .74 F2
Daryl Cl NE21 .53 A1
Daryl Way NE10 .72 D8
Davenport Dr NE3 .28 B1
Davenport Sch DH5 .94 D7
David Adams Ho 7 NE15 54 D5
David Gdns SR6 .75 F3
David St NE28 .40 B2
David Terr 7 NE40 .51 F3
Davidson Cotts NE2 .38 E3
Davidson Rd NE10 .57 B2
Davidson St NE10 .71 D8
Davison Ave
Whitley Bay NE26 .31 F6
New Silksworth SR3 .92 B7
Davison St Newburn NE15 .52 E8
Blyth NE24 .17 E8
Boldon Colliery NE35 .58 E1
Davison Terr 3 SR5 .75 A2
Davy Bank NE28 .40 D1
Dawlish Cl NE29 .41 D8
Dawlish Gdns NE9 .70 F3
Dawlish Pl NE5 .36 C3
Dawson Pl NE61 .3 F1
Dawson Sq 4 NE30 .42 D7
Dawson Terr SR4 .85 A7
Daylesford Dr NE3,NE7 .38 F4
Daylesford Rd NE23 .16 A2
Dayshield NE5 .36 F1
De Merley Rd NE61 .3 F1
De Mowbray Way NE61 .3 D2
De Walden Sq NE61 .4 E3
De Walden Terr NE61 .4 F3
Deacon Cl NE15 .36 B2
Deacon Ct NE12 .39 A7
Deaconsfield Cl SR3 .91 F5
Deadridge La NE45 .47 B7
Deal Cl NE24 .17 E4
Dean House NE6 .57 A8
Dean Rd
South Shields NE33 .59 B7
South Shields, Dean NE33 .59 C8
Dean St
Newcastle-upon-Tyne NE1 .99 B1
Hexham NE46 .45 C5
Gateshead NE9 .71 A5
Dean Terr
South Shields NE33 .59 B7
Ryton NE40 .52 C5
Sunderland SR5 .75 A1
Dean View Dr NE24 .17 B8
Deanery St NE22 .10 F1
Deanham Gdns NE5 .54 D8
Deans Ave NE64 .7 C5
Deans Cl 1 NE16 .69 B7
Deansfield Cl SR3 .91 F5
Deansfield Gr NE15 .36 B3
Dearham Gr NE23 .16 A2
Debdon Gdns NE6 .39 D1
Debdon Pl NE23 .22 B6
Debdon Rd NE63 .6 F2
Debussy Ct NE32 .58 C6
Deckham St NE8 .71 A8
Deckham Terr NE8,NE9 .71 A8
Dee Rd NE31 .57 F3
Dee St NE32 .58 C7
Deel Ho 2 SR3 .91 D7
Deepbrook Rd 5 NE5 .37 C1
Deepdale Wallsend NE28 .39 F5
Washington NE38 .83 A1
Deepdale Cl NE16 .68 F4
Deepdale Cres NE5 .37 E2
Deepdale Gdns NE12 .29 C3
Deepdale Gn NE5 .37 E2
Deepdale Rd NE30 .32 B2
Deepdale St DH5 .95 A2
Deepdene Gr SR6 .75 E5
Deepdene Rd SR6 .75 D5
Deer Bush NE5 .36 F1
Deer Park Way NE21 .53 E1
Deerbolt Pl NE12 .39 C7
Deerfell Cl NE63 .6 B2
Deerness Rd SR2 .103 B1
Dees Ave NE28 .40 B3
Defender Ct SR5 .85 C8
Defoe Ave NE34 .59 C3
Deighton Wlk NE5 .36 F1
Delacour Rd NE21 .53 C3
Delamere Cres NE23 .16 A2
Delamere Ct 8 SR3 .92 A6
Delamere Rd NE3 .37 F5
Delaval DH2 .88 A3
Delaval Ave
Seaton Delaval NE25 .23 C3
North Shields NE29 .41 E6
Delaval Com Mid Sch NE24 .17 D5
Delaval Com Prim Sch NE15 .54 B5
Delaval Cres NE24 .17 B4
Delaval Ct
Killingworth NE12 .29 E1
Delaval Ct *continued*
Bedlington NE22 .11 C2
15 South Shields NE33 .42 D1
Delaval Gdns
Newcastle-upon-Tyne NE15 .54 B4
Blyth NE24 .17 B4
Delaval Rd
Newcastle-upon-Tyne, Delaval NE15 .54 B4
Newcastle-upon-Tyne, Old Benwell NE15 .54 B5
Whitley Bay NE26 .32 C4
Delaval St NE24 .17 B4
Delaval Terr Blyth NE24 .17 E8
Newcastle-upon-Tyne NE3 .38 A4
Delaval Trad Est NE25 .23 C5
Delhi Cres NE40 .52 A3
Delhi Gdns NE40 .52 A3
Delhi View NE40 .52 A3
Dell The Newbottle DH4 .90 D3
Morpeth NE61 .3 E3
Dellfield Dr SR4 .85 A4
Demesne Dr NE22 .15 F8
Demesne The NE63 .7 B2
Dempsey Rd NE13 .28 B4
Denbeigh Pl NE12 .39 C7
Denbigh Ave
Wallsend NE28 .41 A3
Sunderland SR6 .75 D4
Denbigh Community Prim Sch NE28 .41 A3
Denby Cl NE23 .16 A2
Dene Ave
Houghton-le-Spring DH5 .95 A7
Killingworth NE12 .29 A2
Brunswick Village NE13 .28 A6
Newcastle-upon-Tyne, Denton Burn NE15 .53 D7
Newcastle-upon-Tyne, South Gosforth NE3 .38 E4
Rowlands Gill NE39 .67 D1
Hexham NE46 .45 C4
Dene Bank View NE3 .37 E3
Dene Cl Ryton NE40 .52 D5
Ovingham NE42 .50 B5
Riding Mill NE44 .62 F8
Newcastle-upon-Tyne NE7 .39 A1
Dene Cres
Whitley Bay NE26 .31 F6
Wallsend NE28 .40 D2
Newcastle-upon-Tyne NE3 .38 E4
Rowlands Gill NE39 .67 D1
Ryton NE40 .52 D5
Dene Ct Birtley DH3 .82 C7
Hamsterley NE17 .77 B6
Washington NE38 .83 C6
Newcastle-upon-Tyne NE7 .39 B1
Dene Garth NE42 .50 A5
Dene Gdns
Houghton-le-Spring DH5 .94 F7
Gateshead NE10 .57 B1
Newcastle-upon-Tyne NE15 .53 D6
Whitley Bay NE25 .31 E5
Dene Gr Seghill NE23 .23 B2
Newcastle-upon-Tyne NE3 .38 E4
Prudhoe NE42 .50 B3
Dene Head Cotts NE15 .35 E2
Dene La Cleadon SR6 .75 C7
Sunderland SR6 .75 D4
Dene Mews SR5 .74 C1
Dene Pk Ponteland NE20 .25 B3
Hexham NE46 .45 C4
Sunderland SR5 .74 C1
Dene Rd Blaydon NE21 .53 D3
Tynemouth NE30 .42 C8
Rowlands Gill NE39 .67 D1
Wylam NE41 .51 B7
Guide Post NE62 .10 E7
Sunderland SR5 .74 C1
Dene Side NE21 .53 D2
Dene St Hetton le Hole DH5 95 B6
Holywell NE25 .23 F2
Prudhoe NE42 .50 E3
New Silksworth SR3 .86 A1
Sunderland SR4 .85 F7
Dene Terr Newburn NE15 .52 F8
Blaydon NE21 .53 B2
Newcastle-upon-Tyne NE3 .38 E4
Jarrow NE32 .58 A4
Ovington NE42 .49 D4
Riding Mill NE44 .62 F8
Dene Terrace E NE41 .51 A7
Dene Terrace W NE41 .51 A7
Dene The
West Rainton DH4 .94 A2
Medomsley DH8 .77 A2
Whitley Bay NE25 .31 E5
Wylam NE41 .51 B6
Dene View
Burnopfield NE16 .79 A6
Bedlington NE22 .11 C1
Newcastle-upon-Tyne NE3 .38 E4
High Spen NE39 .67 A3
Rowlands Gill NE39 .67 C2
Ellington NE61 .1 E4
Ashington NE63 .6 B3
Dene View Cres SR4 .85 B6
Dene View Ct NE24 .17 B7
Dene View Dr NE24 .17 B8
Dene View E NE22 .11 C1
Dene View W NE22 .16 B8
Dene Villas DH3 .88 D1
Denebank NE25 .31 E5
Deneburn NE10 .72 A7
Denecrest DH8 .77 A2
Denecroft NE41 .51 A6
Deneford NE9 .71 A1
Deneholm
Whitley Bay NE25 .31 E5
Wallsend NE28 .40 D3
Denelands NE46 .45 C5
Deneside Dunston NE11 .69 F7
Newcastle-upon-Tyne, Denton Burn NE15 .54 A7
Seghill NE23 .23 A2
Hedworth NE32 .58 C1
South Shields NE34 .60 C6
Newcastle-upon-Tyne, Newbiggin Hall Est NE5 .36 F4
Deneside Ave NE9 .70 F4
Deneside Cl NE15 .35 D2
Deneside Ct NE2 .56 A8
Denesyde DH8 .77 A2
Deneway NE39 .68 A4
Denewell Ave
Newcastle-upon-Tyne NE7 .39 A3
Gateshead NE9 .70 F5
Denewood NE12 .29 E2
Denewood Ct NE28 .41 A2
Denham Ave SR6 .75 D4
Denham Dr NE25 .23 D2
Denham Gr NE21 .67 F8
Denham Wlk NE5 .36 C3
Denhill Pk NE15 .54 D6
Denholm Ave NE23 .16 A2
Denholme Lodge NE11 .100 A1
Denmark Ct 10 NE6 .56 C7
Denmark St
1 Newcastle-upon-Tyne NE6 .56 C6
Gateshead NE8 .101 C2
Dennison Cres DH3 .82 C6
Denshaw Cl NE23 .16 B2
Dent Cl DH6 .97 E3
Dent St Blyth NE24 .17 F6
Sunderland SR6 .75 D4
Dentdale DH4 .89 E8
Denton Ave
Newcastle-upon-Tyne NE15 .53 D6
North Shields NE29 .41 C6
Denton Chare NE1 .101 A4
Denton Ct NE5 .54 A7
Denton Gate NE5 .37 A3
Denton Gdns NE15 .54 C5
Denton Gr NE5 .37 A3
Denton Park Ho NE5 .36 E2
Denton Park Mid Sch NE5 .36 F2
Denton Park Sh Ctr NE5 .36 E2
Denton Rd NE15 .53 F6
Denton Road Prim Sch NE15 .53 F5
Denton View NE21 .53 B2
Denver Gdns NE6 .56 E5
Denway Gr NE26 .24 B7
Denwick Ave NE15 .53 C6
Denwick Terr NE30 .42 C7
Depot Rd NE6 .56 D7
Deptford Rd
Gateshead NE8 .56 A4
Sunderland SR4 .102 B3
Deptford Terr SR4 .102 A4
Derby Cres NE31 .57 D5
Derby Ct NE4 .98 B2
Derby Gdns NE28 .40 A3
Derby St Jarrow NE32 .58 C7
South Shields NE33 .42 C2
Newcastle-upon-Tyne NE4 .98 B2
Sunderland SR2 .102 C2
Derby Terr NE33 .42 D2
Dereham Cl NE26 .24 D5
Dereham Ct NE5 .37 B4
Dereham Rd NE26 .24 D5
Dereham Terr NE62 .11 C8
Dereham Way NE29 .41 B8
Derry Ave SR6 .75 E4
Derwent Ave
Gateshead NE11 .70 D5
Newburn NE15 .52 E7
Hebburn NE31 .57 E3
Rowlands Gill NE39 .67 E1
Derwent Cote NE17 .77 B5
Derwent Cres
Whickham NE16 .69 B8
Hamsterley NE17 .77 B5
Derwent Crook Dr NE9 .70 E5
Derwent Ct NE11 .70 D5
Derwent Gdns
Wallsend NE28 .41 A4
Gateshead NE9 .71 A5
Derwent Haven NE17 .77 B5
Derwent Inf Sch NE8 .100 C1
Derwent Rd
Seaton Sluice NE26 .24 C6
Tynemouth NE30 .32 B2
Hexham NE46 .45 C4
Derwent St Penshaw DH4 .90 B6
Hetton le Hole DH5 .95 B2
Newcastle-upon-Tyne NE15 .54 B5
Blackhall Mill NE17 .77 C6
Chopwell NE17 .66 B1
Sunderland SR1 .102 C2
Derwent Terr
South Hetton DH6 .97 E8
Burnopfield NE16 .79 B7
Washington NE38 .83 E4
Derwent Tower NE11 .100 A1
Derwent Valley Villas NE17 .77 A6
Derwent View
Burnopfield NE16 .79 B6
Chopwell NE17 .66 C2
Blaydon NE21 .53 B1
Derwent View Terr DH9 .78 D1

Derwent Walk Cty Pk★
NE16,NE21,NE39 68 C5
Derwent Way
Killingworth NE12 29 C3
Blaydon NE21 53 E1
Derwentcote Steel Furnace★
NE17 77 E6
Derwentdale Gdns NE7 39 B3
Derwenthaugh Ind Est
NE16 53 F3
Derwenthaugh Marina
NE21 54 A3
Derwenthaugh Rd NE21 54 A3
Derwentwater Ave 1
DH2 88 B1
Derwentwater Ct NE8 101 A1
Derwentwater Gdns
NE16 69 D7
Derwentwater Rd
Newbiggin-by-the-Sea NE64 7 C3
Gateshead NE8 100 C1
Derwentwater Terr NE33 59 C8
Deuchar Ho NE2 99 C3
Deuchar St NE2 99 C4
Devon Ave NE16 69 C7
Devon Cl NE63 5 F4
Devon Cres DH3 82 B6
Devon Dr SR3 92 A8
Devon Gdns
South Shields NE34 60 B7
Gateshead NE9 70 F7
Devon Rd Tynemouth NE29 31 D1
Hebburn NE31 57 F3
Devon St Penshaw DH4 90 C6
Hetton le Hole DH5 94 F4
Devon Wlk NE37 72 D1
Devonport DH4 90 C3
Devonshire Dr NE27 30 C1
Devonshire Gdns NE28 40 A3
Devonshire Pl NE2 38 F1
Devonshire St
South Shields NE33 59 B7
Sunderland SR5 75 C1
Devonshire Terr
Newcastle-upon-Tyne NE2 99 A3
6 Whitley Bay NE26 32 B4
Devonshire Tower 1
SR5 75 D1
Devonworth Pl NE24 17 A7
Dewberry Cl NE24 17 C4
Dewhurst Terr NE16 69 B2
Dewley NE23 22 B5
Dewley Ct NE23 22 B5
Dewley Pl NE5 36 E4
Dewley Rd NE5 37 B1
Dewsgreen NE23 22 B6
Dexter Way NE10 71 C8
Deyncourt NE20 25 D2
Deyncourt Cl NE20 25 D1
Diamond Ct NE3 37 D5
Diamond Hall Jun & Inf Sch
SR4 85 F7
Diamond Sq 3 NE46 45 B4
Diamond St NE28 40 B2
Diana St NE4 98 B1
Dibley Sq 5 NE6 56 B5
Dibley St 6 NE6 56 B5
Dick St 11 NE40 51 F3
Dickens Ave
Whickham NE16 69 A8
Biddick Hall NE34 59 B3
Dickens St
Houghton-le-Spring DH4 94 D8
Sunderland SR5 75 A1
Dickens Wlk NE5 36 C3
Dickson Dr NE46 44 E3
Didcot Ave NE29 41 E4
Didcot Way NE36 73 E7
Dillon St NE32 58 A5
Dilston Ave
Whitley Bay NE25 32 B4
Hexham NE46 45 D4
Dilston Cl Shiremoor NE27 30 F2
Washington NE38 83 A4
Pegswood NE61 5 A3
Dilston Dr
Newcastle-upon-Tyne NE5 36 E3
Ashington NE63 6 D2
Dilston Gdns SR4 85 F5
Dilston Haugh Cotts
NE45 46 D4
Dilston Rd NE4 98 A2
Dilston Terr
Newcastle-upon-Tyne NE3 38 E4
Jarrow NE32 58 C3
Dimbula Gdns NE7 39 D2
Dinmont Pl NE23 22 B5
Dinnington Fst Sch NE13 27 C7
Dinsdale Ave NE28 40 C4
Dinsdale Cotts 3 SR2 92 F6
Dinsdale Pl NE2 99 C3
Dinsdale Rd
Newcastle-upon-Tyne NE2 99 C3
2 Sunderland SR6 75 E2
Dinsdale St SR2 92 F6
Dinsdale St S SR2 92 F6
Dipe La NE36 74 B7
Dipton Ave NE4 54 E4
Dipton Cl NE46 45 E4
Dipton Gdns SR3 86 B2
Dipton Gr NE23 22 B6
Dipton Rd NE25 31 D7
Dipwood Rd NE39 67 E1
Dipwood Way NE39 78 D8
Discovery Ct SR3 91 F7
Dishforth Gn NE9 71 B1
Dispensary La NE1 99 A1
Disraeli St
Fence Houses DH4 94 B8
Blyth NE24 17 D8
Blyth NE24 17 E8
Disraeli Terr NE17 66 B1
Dissington Pl
Whickham NE16 69 A5
Newcastle-upon-Tyne NE5 54 C8
Ditchburn Terr SR4 85 F8
Dixon Ave DH8 76 F4
Dixon Pl NE11 69 F8
Dixon Rd DH5 94 D6
Dixon St
South Shields NE33 42 C1
Gateshead NE8 100 C1
Dixon's Sq SR6 103 A4
Dobson Cl NE4 100 B3
Dobson Cres NE6 56 C4
Dock Rd NE29 42 A4
Dock Rd S NE29 42 A3
Dock St South Shields NE33 59 B7
Sunderland SR6 75 E1
Dockendale La NE16 69 C7
Dockendale Mews NE16 69 C7
Dockwray Cl NE30 42 C6
Dockwray Sq NE30 42 B5
Dod Law★ NE71 107 F3
Doddfell Cl NE37 83 A6
Doddington Cl NE15 53 B7
Doddington Dr NE23 22 B6
Doddington Villas NE10 71 C7
Dodds Ct 3 SR5 74 A3
Dodds Farm NE3 38 A5
Dodds Terr DH3 82 C6
Dodsworth N NE40 52 B1
Dodsworth Terr NE40 52 B1
Dodsworth Villas NE40 52 B1
Dog Bank NE1 101 B4
Dogger Bank NE61 3 E1
Dolphin Ct 1 NE4 54 D5
Dolphin Quay NE29 42 B5
Dolphin St NE4 54 D5
Dolphin Villas NE13 28 B4
Dominies Cl NE39 67 F3
Don Dixon Dr NE32 58 B1
Don Gdns
West Boldon NE36 73 F7
Washington NE37 72 D1
Don Rd NE32 58 D7
Don St NE11 70 C4
Don View NE36 74 A7
Donald Ave DH6 97 F8
Donald St NE3 38 E5
Doncaster Rd NE2 99 C3
Doncrest Rd NE37 72 B1
Donkin Rd NE37 82 F7
Donkin Terr
North Shields NE30 42 C7
Crawcrook NE40 51 E3
Donkins St NE35 58 E1
Donnington Ho 1 SR3 91 D7
Donnington Cl SR5 74 A1
Donnington Ct NE3,NE7 38 F4
Donnison Gdns SR1 103 B3
Donridge NE37 72 B1
Donside NE10 71 F4
Donvale Rd NE37 72 A1
Donwell Cty Jun Sch
NE37 72 C1
Dorcas Ave NE15 54 C5
Dorcas Terr 3 NE37 83 D8
Dorchester Cl NE5 36 B3
Dorchester Ct NE25 23 C6
Dorchester Gdns NE9 70 F2
Dorking Ave NE29 41 E4
Dorking Cl NE24 17 E4
Dorking Rd SR6 75 E4
Dornoch Cres NE10 71 E6
Dorrington Rd NE3 37 E7
Dorset Ave Birtley DH3 82 D1
Wallsend NE28 40 A3
Hebburn NE31 57 F5
South Shields NE34 60 B7
Sunderland SR6 75 E4
Dorset Cl NE63 5 F4
Dorset Gr NE29 31 D1
Dorset Rd
Newcastle-upon-Tyne NE15 53 F6
Gateshead NE8 56 A4
Dorset St DH5 97 C8
Dotland Cl NE46 45 E4
Double Row NE25 23 B5
Douglas Ave NE3 38 A4
Douglas Bader Ho NE24 17 F6
Douglas Cl NE34 59 C4
Douglas Ct
Gateshead NE11 70 E2
Sunderland SR1 103 B3
Douglas Gdns NE11 70 A7
Douglas Par NE31 58 A2
Douglas Rd SR6 75 E4
Douglas St
7 Wallsend NE28 40 B2
Wallsend, Willington Quay
NE28 41 A1
Douglas Terr
Penshaw DH4 90 C8
Washington NE37 72 D1
Newcastle-upon-Tyne NE4 98 B1
Doulting Cl NE12 39 B6
Dove Ave NE32 58 C3
Dove Cl NE12 29 C4
Dove Ct 8 Birtley DH3 82 C5
Tynemouth NE30 32 C3
Dove Row NE30 32 C3
Dovecote Cl NE25 31 C6
Dovecote Rd NE12 39 E7
Dovecrest Ct 7 NE28 40 F4
Dovedale Ave NE24 17 A8
Dovedale Ct NE34 59 A5
Dovedale Gdns
Newcastle-upon-Tyne NE7 39 B3
Gateshead NE9 71 A4
Dovedale Rd SR6 75 C5
Dover Cl Bedlington NE22 10 D1
Newcastle-upon-Tyne NE5 36 C3
Dovercourt Rd NE6 57 A4
Dowling Ave NE25 31 F4
Downe Cl NE24 17 E4
Downend Rd NE5 36 E3
Downfield NE37 72 D3
Downham NE5 36 F1
Downham Ct NE33 42 C1
Downhill Cty Inf Sch
NE34 60 B7
Downhill La
Hedworth NE36 73 D4
West Boldon NE37 73 F5
Downhill Prim Sch SR5 74 B4
Downing Dr NE61 8 E7
Downs La DH5 95 B5
Downs Pit La DH5 95 C5
Downswood NE12 29 F3
Doxford Ave DH5 94 F6
Doxford Gdns 4 NE5 37 D1
Doxford Park Way SR3 91 E6
Doxford Pl NE23 22 B5
Doxford Terr DH5 94 F6
Dr Henry Russell Ct
NE15 54 A5
Dr Pit Cotts NE22 10 F1
Drake Cl NE33 59 B8
Drawback Cl NE42 50 D2
Drayton Rd
Newcastle-upon-Tyne NE3 37 E4
Sunderland SR6 75 D4
Drey The NE20 25 B3
Drive Com Prim Sch The
NE10 71 E8
Drive The Birtley DH3 82 D1
Gateshead, Felling NE10 71 E8
Whickham NE16 69 C6
Wallsend NE28 40 B2
Newcastle-upon-Tyne, Gosforth
NE3 38 C3
Tynemouth NE30 42 D8
Washington NE37 72 C1
Newcastle-upon-Tyne, East
Denton NE5 54 A8
Newcastle-upon-Tyne NE7 39 B4
Gateshead, Saltwell NE9 70 F6
Drivecote NE10 71 E8
Dronfield Cl 2 DH2 88 A1
Drove Rd NE15 35 B3
Drum Ind Est DH2 88 B7
Drum Rd DH2,DH3 88 B8
Drumaldrace 5 NE37 83 A6
Drummond Cres NE34 58 F5
Drummond Rd NE3 37 F4
Drummond Terr NE30 42 B6
Drumoyne Cl SR3 91 B6
Drumoyne Gdns NE25 31 D3
Drumsheugh Pl NE5 37 B2
Druridge Ave SR6 75 E5
Druridge Bay★ NE61 119 E4
Druridge Cres Blyth NE24 17 B5
South Shields NE34 60 B8
Druridge Dr Blyth NE24 17 B5
Newcastle-upon-Tyne NE5 37 D2
Drury La
Newcastle-upon-Tyne NE1 99 A1
Tynemouth NE29 41 C7
Sunderland SR1 103 B3
Drybeck Ct
Cramlington NE23 22 D8
Newcastle-upon-Tyne NE4 98 B1
Drybeck Sq SR3 92 B6
Drybeck Wlk NE23 22 D8
Dryborough St SR4 102 B3
Dryburgh NE38 83 D5
Dryburgh Cl NE29 41 E8
Dryden Cl NE34 59 B2
Dryden Ct 5 NE9 70 F8
Dryden Rd NE9 70 F7
Dryden Road Hospl NE9 70 F8
Dryden Sec Sch NE9 71 A7
Dryden St SR5 75 A2
Drysdale Cres NE13 28 A6
Drysdale Ct NE13 28 B6
Dubmire Cotts DH4 94 A8
Dubmire Ct DH4 94 A8
Dubmire Ind Est DH4 90 B1
Dubmire Jun & Inf Schs
DH4 94 A8
Duchess Cres NE32 58 B3
Duchess Cres E NE32 58 B3
Duchess Dr NE15 54 A7
Duchess St NE26 32 A5
Duckets Dean NE42 50 D3
Duckpool La NE16 69 C7
Duckpool La N NE16 69 C8
Duddon Pl NE9 71 B4
Dudley Ave SR6 75 D4
Dudley Bsns Ctr NE23 22 A2
Dudley Ct NE23 22 A6
Dudley Dr NE23 29 A8
Dudley Gdns SR3 91 C7
Dudley House NE4 98 B2
Dudley La
Seaton Burn NE13,NE23 28 D8
Cramlington NE23 22 A4
Dudley Lane Cotts NE13 28 C8
Dugdale Ct 6 NE3 37 D5
Dugdale Rd NE3 37 D5
Duke of Northumberland Ct
NE28 40 E5
Duke St
Newcastle-upon-Tyne NE1 100 C4
Gateshead NE10 57 A1
Whitley Bay NE26 32 A5
North Shields NE29 42 B4
Ashington NE63 6 C4
Sunderland SR4 102 A2
Duke St N SR6 75 D2
Duke Wlk NE8 100 C1
Duke's Ave NE31 57 D4
Duke's Gdns NE24 17 C8
Dukes Cott NE15 52 F7
Dukes Ct NE42 50 E4
Dukes Dr NE3 28 B1
Dukes Mdw NE13 36 E8
Dukes Rd NE46 44 E5
Dukes Way NE42 50 E4
Dukesfield NE23 22 B6
Dukesway NE11 70 C4
Dukesway Ct NE11 70 C3
Dukesway W NE11 70 C2
Dulverton Cl NE5 36 C3
Dulverton Ave NE33 59 D7
Dulverton Ct NE2 38 F2
Dumas Wlk NE5 36 C3
Dumfries Cres NE32 58 E3
Dun Cow St SR1 102 C3
Dunbar Cl NE5 36 C3
Dunbar St SR4 85 F5
Dunblane Cres NE5 36 F1
Dunblane Dr NE24 17 E4
Dunblane Rd SR6 75 E4
Dunbreck Gr SR4 86 A4
Duncan Gdns NE61 8 F7
Duncan St
Newcastle-upon-Tyne NE6 57 A5
Gateshead NE8 56 B1
Sunderland SR4 85 F7
Dunces Hos NE61 9 D7
Dundas St SR6 103 A4
Dundas Way NE10 71 C8
Dundee Cl NE5 36 C3
Dundee Ct NE32 58 E3
Dundock Wood (The
Hirsel)★ TD12 106 C8
Dundrennan NE38 83 C3
Dunelm SR2 86 B4
Dunelm Cl 5 DH3 82 C4
Dunelm Dr
Houghton-le-Spring DH4 94 D7
West Boldon NE36 74 B8
Dunelm Rd DH5 94 F4
Dunelm S SR4 86 B4
Dunelm St NE33 42 D2
Dunford Gdns NE5 36 D4
Dunholm Cl DH5 94 E7
Dunholme Rd NE4 54 F5
Dunira Cl NE2 38 F2
Dunkeld Cl NE24 17 E4
Dunkirk Ave DH5 94 F7
Dunlin Cl NE40 52 E4
Dunlin Ct NE61 2 A3
Dunlin Dr Blyth NE24 17 E4
Washington NE38 82 F3
Dunlop Cl NE7 39 C4
Dunlop Cres NE34 60 A6
Dunmoor Cl NE3 38 A4
Dunmoor Ct DH2 88 A1
Dunmore Ave SR6 75 E4
Dunmorlie St NE6 56 D6
Dunn Ave SR3 86 A1
Dunn St NE4 100 B3
Dunn St Prim Sch NE32 58 C7
Dunn Terr NE6 56 B6
Dunn's Terr NE2 98 B4
Dunne Rd NE21 53 E4
Dunning St SR1 102 C3
Dunnlynn Cl SR3 91 E6
Dunnock Dr
Sunniside NE16 69 A3
Washington NE38 82 F2
Dunnock Lodge NE15 53 D6
Dunnykirk Ave 2 NE3 37 D5
Dunsdale Dr NE23 22 D8
Dunsdale Rd NE25 23 E2
Dunsgreen NE20 25 E5
Dunsgreen Ct NE20 25 E5
Dunsley Gdns NE13 27 B7
Dunslow Croft NE15 33 C1
Dunsmuir Gr NE8 70 D8
Dunstable Pl NE5 36 B3
Dunstan Cl DH2 88 A1
Dunstan Wlk NE5 36 F1
Dunstanburgh Castle (N.T.)★
NE66 113 E6
Dunstanburgh Cl
Bedlington NE22 10 D1
Washington NE38 83 B4
Newcastle-upon-Tyne NE6 56 D5
Dunstanburgh Ct
Bournmoor DH4 89 D1
Gateshead NE10 72 B7
Dunstanburgh Rd NE6 56 D5
Dunster Ho 3 SR3 91 D7
Dunston Bank NE11 69 F7
Dunston Ent Pk NE11 54 E2
Dunston Hill Com Prim Sch
NE11 69 F8
Dunston Hill Hospl NE11 69 D7
Dunston Pl NE24 17 B8
Dunston Rd NE11 54 F1
Dunston Riverside Prim Sch
NE11 54 F1
Dunston Sta NE11 70 A8
Dunston Workshops
NE11 54 F2
Dunvegan DH3 82 E2
Dunvegan Ave DH2 88 B1
Dunwoodie Terr NE46 45 A5
Duoro Terr SR2 103 A1
Durant Rd NE1 99 B2
Durban St NE24 17 D8
Durham Ave NE37 83 B8
Durham Cl NE22 10 D2
Durham Ct NE31 57 D5
Durham Cty Cricket Gd
DH3 88 E2
Durham Dr NE32 58 B2
Durham Gr NE32 58 B2
Durham Ho SR5 73 F4
Durham La Haswell DH6 97 C1
Sherburn Hill DH6 96 D1
Durham Pl Birtley DH3 82 D1
Gateshead NE8 101 C1
Durham Rd Birtley DH3 82 C3
Chester le Street DH3 88 C1
Chester le Street, Barley Mow
DH3 88 C8
East Rainton DH5 94 C4
Houghton-le-Spring DH5 90 F3
Houghton-le-Spring DH5 94 E7
Cramlington NE23 16 C1
Gateshead NE8,NE9 70 F6
Gateshead NE9 82 B8
Sunderland SR3 85 E2
Durham St
Fence Houses DH4 94 A8
3 Gateshead NE10 56 F1
Wallsend NE28 40 C2
Newcastle-upon-Tyne NE4 54 F5
Durham St W NE28 40 C2
Durham Terr SR3 86 A1
Duxfield Rd NE7 39 B3
Dwyer Cres SR2 92 F6
Dyer Sq SR5 75 B2
Dyke Heads La NE40 52 B1
Dykefield Ave NE3 37 E7
Dykelands Rd SR6 75 E5
Dykelands Way NE34 58 F3
Dykenook Cl NE16 69 A4
Dykes Way NE10 71 D5
Dymock Ct NE3 37 B5

E

E D Morel Terr NE17 77 C8
Eaglescliffe Dr NE7 39 D2
Eaglesdene DH5 95 A4
Ealing Ct NE3 37 B6
Ealing Dr NE30 32 C1
Ealing Sq
Cramlington NE23 21 D6
Sunderland SR5 75 A3
Eardulph Ave DH3 88 D3
Earl Grey Way NE29 41 F3
Earl St SR4 102 B2
Earl's Dr NE15 54 A7
Earl's Gdns NE24 17 C8
Earlington Ct NE12 29 E1
Earls Ct Gateshead DH98 70 D5
Prudhoe NE42 50 E4
Sunderland SR5 75 A4
Earls Dene 5 NE9 70 F4
Earls Dr NE9 70 F4
Earls Gn DH5 94 D3
Earlston St SR5 75 A4
Earlston Way NE23 16 C2
Earlsway DH98,NE11,NE82 70 D5
Earlswood Ave NE9 70 F4
Earlswood Gr NE24 17 D3
Earlswood Pk NE9 70 F4
Earnshaw Way NE25 31 D7
Earsdon Cl NE5 37 A1
Earsdon Ct NE25 31 D4
Earsdon Rd
Houghton-le-Spring DH5 94 F8
Earsdon NE25 31 C4
Whitley Bay NE25 31 C4
Shiremoor NE27 30 E4
Newcastle-upon-Tyne NE3 37 E3
Earsdon Terr
9 Shiremoor NE27 30 E1
2 Ryhope SR2 92 F6
Earsdon View NE27 30 F4
Earth Balance★ NE22 11 C5
Easby Cl NE3 38 D8
Easby Rd NE38 83 D4
Easdale Ave NE3 28 C1
Easedale NE26 24 C6
Easedale Gdns NE9 71 B3
Easington Ave
Cramlington NE23 16 C2
Gateshead NE9 71 C3
Easington Lane Prim Sch
DH5 97 D8
Easington St SR5 102 C4
Easington St N SR5 102 C4
East Acre NE21 53 D1
East Acres NE13 27 C8
East Ave Longbenton NE12 39 D6
Whitley Bay NE25 31 E5
South Shields NE34 60 A6
Washington NE38 83 B1
East Back Par SR2 103 C1
East Bailey NE12 29 F3
East Benton Cotts NE12 39 E5
East Boldon Inf Sch
NE36 74 D7
East Boldon Jun Sch
NE36 74 D7
East Boldon Rd SR6 59 F1
East Boldon Sta NE36 74 E8

East Bridge St DH4 83 E1
East Cl NE34 60 A6
East Cleft Rd SR2 102 B2
East Cres NE22 11 D2
East Cross St SR1 103 A3
East Dr Blyth NE24 17 C4
Cleadon SR6 74 F8
East End NE26 24 E4
East Farm Ct NE16 69 C3
East Farm Terr NE23 22 B6
East Fields SR6 75 F8
East Ford Rd NE62 11 C8
East Forest Hall Rd NE12 39 E8
East Front NE2 99 B4
East Gate Morpeth NE61 9 A6
Gateshead NE8 101 C3
East George Potts St 13 NE33 42 D1
East George St NE30 42 C6
East Gr SR4 85 B5
East Grange
Holywell NE25 23 F2
Sunderland SR5 75 C3
East Hartford Sch NE23 16 B3
East Herrington Prim Sch SR3 91 C7
East Hill Rd NE8 56 B1
East Holborn NE33 42 B2
East Law DH8 76 D1
East Lea Blaydon NE21 68 C8
Newbiggin-by-the-Sea NE64 7 E5
East Loan NE61 4 A2
East Moffett St 11 NE33 42 D1
East Moor Rd SR4 85 F7
East Oakwood NE46 45 E8
East Par NE26 32 B5
East Park Gdns NE21 53 C1
East Park Rd NE9 70 F6
East Park View NE24 18 A7
East Pastures NE63 6 B2
East Percy St NE30 42 C6
East Rainton Prim Sch DH5 94 C4
East Riggs NE22 15 F8
East Sea View NE64 7 F5
East St Chopwell NE17 66 D1
Tynemouth NE30 42 E7
Hebburn NE31 57 F7
9 South Shields NE33 42 C3
High Spen NE39 66 F4
Mickley Square NE43 49 F1
Gateshead NE8 101 C3
Whitburn SR6 75 E8
East Stainton St 10 NE33 42 D1
East Stevenson St 12 NE33 42 D1
East Tanfield Sta DH9 79 E2
East Terr Chopwell NE17 77 C7
Stakeford NE62 11 C7
East Thorp NE5 36 F5
East View
Sherburn Hill DH6 96 D1
Wide Open NE13 28 B7
Burnopfield NE16 79 A6
Blaydon NE21 53 D3
Bedlington NE22 11 D3
Seghill NE23 22 F1
New Hartley NE25 23 C5
Hebburn NE31 57 D4
West Boldon NE35 73 F8
Rowlands Gill NE39 67 C2
Crawcrook NE40 51 E6
Morpeth NE61 9 A8
Stakeford NE62 11 C7
Ryhope SR2 92 E6
Sunderland, Castletown SR5 74 C1
Sunderland, Roker SR6 75 E3
1 Seaham SR7 92 F1
East View Ave NE23 22 B6
East View S 3 SR5 74 C1
East View Terr
Gateshead NE10 71 F6
Whickham NE16 69 B8
Dudley NE23 29 A8
East Villas DH6 97 F4
East Vines SR1 103 C3
East Woodlands NE46 45 D4
Eastbourne Ave
Newcastle-upon-Tyne NE6 57 A6
Gateshead NE8 70 E8
Eastbourne Ct NE6 57 A6
Eastbourne Gdns
Cramlington NE23 21 D6
Whitley Bay NE26 32 A6
Newcastle-upon-Tyne NE6 57 A6
Eastbourne Gr 12 NE33 42 D3
Eastbourne Par NE31 58 E2
Eastbourne Sq SR5 75 A4
Eastburn Gdns NE10 57 B2
Eastcheap NE6 39 C1
Eastcliffe Ave NE3 38 A3
Eastcombe Cl NE35 58 E2
Eastcote Terr NE6 56 F4
Easten Terr NE28 41 C1
Easterfield Ct NE61 4 A1
Eastern Ave NE11,NE9 70 D4
Eastern Gdns 4 NE10 56 D1
Eastern Way
Ponteland NE20 25 D3
Newcastle-upon-Tyne NE5 37 D2
Eastfield Ave
Whitley Bay NE25 31 D4
Newcastle-upon-Tyne NE28, NE6 57 A8
Eastfield House NE6 57 A8
Eastfield Rd
Longbenton NE12 39 D6
South Shields NE34 59 F8
Eastfield St SR4 85 F5
Eastfield Terr NE12 39 D6
Eastfields NE46 45 D4
Eastgarth NE5 37 A5
Eastgate Hexham NE46 45 B4
Choppington NE62 10 F5
Eastgate Bank NE43 64 F8
Eastgate Gdns NE4 54 E4
Eastgreen NE62 10 F5
Eastlands Blaydon NE21 53 B1
Chester le Street NE38 88 E7
Newcastle-upon-Tyne NE7 39 A3
Eastlea Fst Sch NE23 22 C8
Eastleigh Cl NE35 73 E8
Easton Holmes NE22 11 C2
Eastward Gn NE25 31 D4
Eastway NE34 60 B5
Eastwood Ave NE24 17 D3
Eastwood Cl NE23 29 C5
Eastwood Ct NE12 39 D7
Eastwood Gdns
Gateshead, Old Fold NE10 56 C2
Newcastle-upon-Tyne NE3 37 F4
Gateshead, Low Fell NE9 71 A6
Eastwood Grange Ct NE46 45 E4
Eastwood Grange Rd NE46 45 E4
Eastwood Mid Sch NE42 50 F3
Eastwood Pl NE23 16 C2
Eastwood Villas NE42 50 F4
Eastwoods Rd NE42 50 F3
Eaton Pl NE4 54 F5
Eavers Ct NE34 59 C5
Ebba Wlk NE3 38 D5
Ebchester Ave NE9 71 D3
Ebchester CE Primary Sch DH8 76 E3
Ebchester Ct NE3 37 C5
Ebchester Hill DH8 76 F2
Ebchester St NE34 59 A5
Ebdon La SR6 75 D4
Ebor St South Shields NE34 59 A4
Newcastle-upon-Tyne NE6 56 C8
Eccles Ct NE27 30 C5
Eccles Terr 2 NE27 30 E1
Eccleston Cl NE27 30 C4
Eccleston Rd NE33 42 E2
Ecgfrid Terr NE32 58 C4
Eddison Rd NE38 83 F4
Eddleston NE38 83 A1
Eddleston Ave NE3 38 A3
Eddrington Gr NE5 36 C2
Ede Ave Dunston NE11 69 F8
South Shields NE34 60 B7
Eden Ave NE16 79 A6
Eden Cl NE5 36 C2
Eden Ct Bedlington NE22 16 A8
5 Wallsend NE28 40 B1
Eden Dale NE40 51 F4
Eden Gr NE61 9 A6
Eden House Rd SR2,SR4 102 B1
Eden Pl NE30 32 A1
Eden St NE28 40 B1
Eden St W SR1 102 C3
Eden Terr Penshaw DH4 90 B6
Lynmouth NE61 2 A3
Sunderland SR2 102 B1
Eden Vale SR2 102 B1
Eden Wlk NE32 58 C3
Edenbridge Cres NE12 39 B7
Edendale Ave Blyth NE24 17 B8
Newcastle-upon-Tyne NE6 57 A6
Edendale Ct Blyth NE24 17 B8
1 South Shields NE34 59 A4
Edendale Ho NE24 17 B7
Edendale Terr NE8 70 F8
Edengarth NE30 32 A2
Edgar St NE3,NE7 38 F5
Edge Hill NE20 25 C1
Edge Mount NE12 29 E4
Edgecote NE37 83 F8
Edgefield Ave NE3 37 F5
Edgefield Dr NE23 16 C2
Edgehill NE61 9 B6
Edgehill Cl NE20 25 C1
Edgeware Ct SR5 75 A3
Edgeware Wlk NE4 54 E3
Edgewell Ave NE42 50 B1
Edgewell Grange NE42 50 C2
Edgewell House Rd NE42, NE43 65 B8
Edgewell Rd NE42 50 B1
Edgewood Ponteland NE20 25 D2
Hexham NE46 45 D4
Edgewood Ave NE22 11 C1
Edgeworth Cl NE35 58 E2
Edgeworth Cres SR6 75 D2
Edgmond Ct SR2 92 E8
Edgware Rd NE8 71 A8
Edhill Ave NE34 59 A4
Edhill Gdns NE34 58 F4
Edinburgh Ct NE3 37 D8
Edinburgh Dr NE22 10 E2
Edinburgh Rd NE32 58 E4
Edinburgh Sq 3 SR5 75 A3
Edington Gdns NE40 51 E6
Edington Gr NE30 32 A1
Edington Rd NE30 32 A1
Edison Gdns NE8 70 E7
Edith Ave NE21 53 C2
Edith Moffat House 7 NE29 42 A6
Edith St Tynemouth NE30 42 C8
Edith St *continued*
Jarrow NE32 58 A7
Sunderland SR2 86 E4
Sunderland, Southwick SR5 75 C2
Edith Terr Newbottle DH4 90 D3
5 Whickham NE16 69 A7
Edlingham Castle* NE66 118 C8
Edlingham Cl NE3,NE7 38 F4
Edlingham Ct 6 DH5 94 F8
Edmonton Sq 1 SR5 75 A3
Edmund Pl NE9 70 F5
Edna Terr NE5 37 A3
Edward Burdis St SR5 75 B2
Edward Pl NE4 98 B1
Edward Rd Birtley DH3 82 B5
Bedlington NE22 11 D3
Wallsend NE28 40 F3
Edward St
Chester le Street DH3 88 C3
Hetton le Hole DH5 95 A4
Burnopfield NE16 79 A4
Blyth NE24 17 D7
Newcastle-upon-Tyne NE3 38 C5
Hebburn NE31 57 C6
Crawcrook NE40 51 E3
Morpeth NE61 9 A8
Pegswood NE61 4 F3
New Silksworth SR3 92 A7
Edward's Wlk NE1 99 A2
Edwards Rd NE26 32 C4
Edwin Gr NE28 41 A3
Edwin St
Houghton-le-Spring DH5 90 E1
Brunswick Village NE13 28 A6
14 Newcastle-upon-Tyne NE6 56 B6
Sunderland SR4 85 E7
Edwin Terr NE40 52 C2
Edwin's Ave S NE12 39 E8
Edwina Gdns NE29 41 E7
Edwins Ave NE12 39 E8
Egerton Rd NE34 59 C6
Egerton St
Newcastle-upon-Tyne NE4 54 D4
Sunderland SR2 103 B1
Eggleston Dr SR3 86 A2
Egham Rd NE5 36 C2
Eglesfield Rd NE33 59 C8
Eglingham Ave NE30 32 C1
Eglingham Cl NE61 9 B6
Eglingham Way NE61 9 B6
Eglinton Tower 2 SR5 75 D1
Eglinton St SR5 75 C1
Eglinton St N SR5 75 C1
Egremont Dr NE9 71 A6
Egremont Gdns NE9 71 A6
Egremont Pl NE26 32 B4
Egremont Way NE23 16 C2
Egton Terr DH3 82 C5
Eider Cl NE24 17 E3
Eighteenth Ave NE24 17 D5
Eighth Ave
Chester le Street DH2 88 B3
Gateshead NE11 70 D3
Blyth NE24 17 D6
Newcastle-upon-Tyne NE6 56 C8
Morpeth NE61 9 B7
Ashington NE63 6 E2
Eighth Row NE63 6 B4
Eighton Terr NE9 71 E3
Eilansgate NE46 45 A5
Eilansgate Terr NE46 45 A5
Eilanville NE46 45 A5
Eishort Way NE12 39 B6
Eland Cl NE3 37 D5
Eland Edge NE20 25 F6
Eland La NE20 25 F7
Elberfeld Ct NE32 58 B6
Elder Gdns NE9 71 C1
Elder Gr
South Shields NE34 59 F3
3 Gateshead NE9 70 F5
Elder Sq NE63 6 E2
Elderwood Gdns NE11 70 B5
Eldon Ct 1 NE28 41 B1
Eldon Gdn NE1 99 A2
Eldon La NE1 99 A1
Eldon Pl
Newcastle-upon-Tyne NE1 99 A3
Newcastle-upon-Tyne, Lemington NE15 53 D7
Eldon Rd
Newcastle-upon-Tyne NE15 53 D7
Hexham NE46 45 D4
Eldon Square Sh Ctr NE1 99 A2
Eldon St Wallsend NE28 41 B2
South Shields NE33 42 B1
Gateshead NE8 56 A2
Sunderland SR4 102 A2
Eleanor St
Tynemouth NE30 32 C3
South Shields NE33 42 D3
Eleanor Terr
2 Whickham NE16 69 A7
Crawcrook NE40 52 A4
Electric Cres DH4 90 D4
Elemore Hall Sch DH6 97 A5
Elemore La
Easington Lane DH5 97 A7
High Pittington DH6 96 E6
Elemore St DH6 96 B5
Elemore View DH6 97 F7
Elenbel Ave NE22 11 C1
Eleventh Ave
Chester le Street DH2 88 B3
Gateshead NE11 70 E2
Blyth NE24 17 E6
Eleventh Ave *continued*
Morpeth NE61 9 B7
Eleventh Ave N NE11 70 E3
Eleventh Row NE63 6 B4
Elford Cl NE25 31 D5
Elfordleigh DH4 90 C4
Elgar Ave 3 NE5 36 C2
Elgin Ave NE28 40 F4
Elgin Cl Bedlington NE22 11 D2
Cramlington NE23 21 D6
Tynemouth NE29 41 C8
Elgin Ct NE10 57 B2
Elgin Gdns NE6 56 F6
Elgin Pl DH3 82 D2
Elgin Rd NE9 71 B8
Elgin St NE32 58 E4
Elgy Rd NE3 38 B3
Elisabeth Ave DH3 82 B6
Elizabeth Cres NE23 29 A8
Elizabeth Ct NE12 30 A1
Elizabeth Diamond Gdns NE33 59 B8
Elizabeth Dr NE12 40 A8
Elizabeth Rd NE28 41 A2
Elizabeth St
Houghton-le-Spring DH5 90 E1
Chopwell NE17 66 B1
East Cramlington NE23 22 F5
7 South Shields NE33 42 D2
Newcastle-upon-Tyne NE6 56 A6
Sunderland, Castletown SR5 74 B1
Sunderland, Monkwearmouth SR5 75 C3
Elizabeth Woodcock Maritime Inst The SR2 103 A1
Ell-Dene Cres NE10 71 E7
Ellen Ct 3 NE32 58 B7
Ellen Terr NE37 83 F8
Ellerbeck Cl 3 NE10 71 C8
Ellerby Ho NE6 56 E4
Ellersmere Gdns NE30 32 B2
Ellerton Way
Gateshead NE10 71 C8
Cramlington NE23 16 C2
Ellesmere DH4 89 D3
Ellesmere Ave
Newcastle-upon-Tyne, South Gosforth NE3 38 E4
Newcastle-upon-Tyne, Westerhope NE5 37 A2
Newcastle-upon-Tyne, Walkergate NE6 56 E8
Ellesmere Ct SR2 86 E1
Ellesmere Gdns NE62 11 C8
Ellesmere Rd NE4 54 E5
Ellesmere Terr SR6 75 E3
Ellington Cl Urpeth DH2 81 E2
Newcastle-upon-Tyne NE15 53 B7
Ryhope SR2 92 F5
Ellington Fst Sch NE61 1 E5
Ellington Terr NE63 5 F4
Elliot Cl DH4 90 B7
Elliot Ct NE61 9 B7
Elliot Gdns NE34 59 D2
Elliot Rd NE10 56 B1
Elliott Dr NE10 71 D8
Elliott St NE24 17 C4
Elliott Terr
3 Washington NE37 83 E8
Newcastle-upon-Tyne NE4 98 A1
Ellis Rd SR5 75 A3
Ellis Sq Pegswood NE61 4 F3
Sunderland SR5 75 B3
Ellison (C of E) Prim Sch NE32 58 B6
Ellison Pl
Newcastle-upon-Tyne NE1 99 B2
Jarrow NE32 58 B8
3 Gateshead NE9 70 F4
Ellison Rd NE11,NE8 69 F8
Ellison St Hebburn NE31 57 C7
Hebburn NE31 57 D6
10 Jarrow NE32 58 B7
Gateshead NE8 101 C3
Ellison Terr NE40 51 F1
Ellwood Gdns 3 NE9 70 F8
Elm Ave Dunston NE11 69 F7
Dinnington NE13 27 B7
Whickham NE16 69 C8
South Shields NE34 59 F4
Elm Bank Rd NE41 51 B5
Elm Cl Cramlington NE23 16 C2
Hexham NE46 44 E3
Elm Croft Rd NE12 39 E7
Elm Ct NE16 69 B5
Elm Dr Bedlington NE22 15 F8
Whitburn SR6 61 A2
Elm Gr Killingworth NE12 29 D1
Burnopfield NE16 78 F6
Newcastle-upon-Tyne NE3 37 F7
South Shields NE34 59 F4
Elm Pl DH4 90 D3
Elm Rd Ponteland NE20 26 A5
Blaydon NE21 53 D2
Shiremoor NE29 41 B8
Elm St
Chester le Street DH3 88 C3
Seaton Burn NE13 28 C8
Sunniside NE16 69 B2
Jarrow NE32 58 A7
Mickley Square NE43 64 E8
Elm St W NE16 69 B2
Elm Terr Birtley DH3 82 B5
Tantobie DH9 79 B2
Elm Trees NE24 17 D6
Elmfield Cl SR3 91 C6
Elmfield Gdns
Whitley Bay NE25 31 D3
Elmfield Gdns *continued*
Wallsend NE28 39 F4
Newcastle-upon-Tyne NE3 38 B4
Elmfield Gr NE3 38 B4
Elmfield Pk NE3 38 B3
Elmfield Rd
Walbottle NE15 35 E2
Newcastle-upon-Tyne NE3 38 C3
Hebburn NE31 57 F3
Elmfield Terr
Gateshead NE10 57 B2
Hebburn NE31 57 F4
Elms The
Easington Lane DH5 97 D8
Ellington NE61 1 D4
Sunderland SR2 103 A1
Elms W SR2 103 A1
Elmsford Gr NE12 39 B6
Elmsleigh Gdns SR6 60 A2
Elmtree Gdns NE25 31 E3
Elmtree Gr NE3 38 B3
Elmtrees NE3 38 B3
Elmway DH2 88 A5
Elmwood NE15 53 C8
Elmwood Ave
Wide Open NE13 28 C5
Wallsend NE28 40 F2
Sunderland SR5 74 F3
Elmwood Cres NE6 39 F1
Elmwood Dr NE20 25 E7
Elmwood Gdns NE11 70 B6
Elmwood Gr NE26 32 A6
Elmwood Rd NE25 31 E4
Elmwood Sq 5 SR5 74 F2
Elmwood St
Great Lumley DH4 89 E1
Sunderland SR2 102 B1
Elrick Cl NE5 36 C2
Elrington Gdns NE5 54 B8
Elsdon Ave NE25 23 D3
Elsdon Cl NE24 17 C7
Elsdon Ct NE16 69 A5
Elsdon Dr
Longbenton NE12 39 F8
Ashington NE63 6 C3
Elsdon Gdns NE11 70 A8
Elsdon Pl 7 NE29 42 A4
Elsdon Rd Whickham NE16 69 A6
Newcastle-upon-Tyne NE3 38 C5
Elsdon St NE29 42 A4
Elsdon Terr
4 Wallsend NE28 40 B1
North Shields NE29 41 D4
Elsdonburn Rd SR3 91 E5
Elsham Gn NE3 37 E6
Elsing Cl NE5 37 B4
Elstob Pl
Newcastle-upon-Tyne NE6 56 E4
Sunderland SR3 86 A2
Elston Cl NE5 36 C2
Elstree Ct NE3 37 B7
Elstree Gdns NE24 17 D3
Elstree Sq SR5 75 A3
Elswick East Terr NE4 100 B4
Elswick Rd
Washington NE37 83 A7
Newcastle-upon-Tyne NE4 100 A4
Elswick Row NE4 98 B1
Elswick St NE4 98 B1
Elswick Way NE34 59 A6
Elswick Way Ind Est NE34 59 A6
Elsworth Gn NE5 37 C3
Elterwater Rd DH2 88 B1
Elton St E NE28 40 B1
Elton St W NE28 40 B1
Eltringham Cl NE28 40 A2
Eltringham Cotts NE43 49 F1
Eltringham Rd NE42 50 A2
Elvaston Dr NE46 45 B3
Elvaston Gr NE46 45 B3
Elvaston Park Rd NE46 45 A3
Elvaston Rd Ryton NE40 52 C6
Hexham NE46 45 B4
Elvet Cl
Brunswick Village NE13 28 B6
6 Newcastle-upon-Tyne NE6 56 C7
Elvet Ct NE6 56 C7
Elvet Gn
Chester le Street DH2 88 C2
Hetton le Hole DH5 95 A1
Elvet Way 5 NE6 56 C7
Elvington St SR6 75 E3
Elwin Cl NE26 24 D5
Elwin Pl NE26 24 D5
Elwin Terr SR2 102 C2
Ely Cl NE12 39 D4
Ely St NE8 101 B1
Ely Way NE32 58 B1
Elysium La NE8 101 A1
Embankment Rd SR7 93 B1
Embassy Gdns NE15 54 B6
Emblehope NE37 83 A6
Emblehope Dr NE3 38 A4
Emblehope Ho SR3 91 E8
Embleton Ave
Wallsend NE28 40 E5
Newcastle-upon-Tyne NE3 38 A6
South Shields NE34 60 B8
Embleton Cres NE29 41 C8
Embleton Dr
Chester le Street DH2 88 A1
Blyth NE24 17 C5
Embleton Gdns
Gateshead NE10 56 D1
5 Newcastle-upon-Tyne NE5 37 D1

Embleton Rd
Gateshead NE10 57 B2
Tynemouth NE29 41 C8
Emden Rd NE3 37 F6
Emerson Pl NE27 30 E3
Emily Davison Ave NE61 8 E8
Emily St Newbottle DH4 90 D4
Newcastle-upon-Tyne NE6 56 E6
Gateshead NE8 56 B1
Emlyn Rd NE34 59 C6
Emma Ct SR2 103 B1
Emma View 6 NE40 51 F3
Emmanuel Cty Tech Coll NE11 70 A5
Emmaville NE40 52 A4
Emmaville Prim Sch NE40 51 F4
Emmbrook Cl DH5 94 D4
Emmerson Rd NE64 7 D5
Emmerson Terr NE38 83 E5
Emmerson Terr W 1 SR3 92 B7
Emperor Way SR3 91 C5
Empress Rd NE6 57 B4
Empress St 3 SR5 75 C1
Emsworth 4 SR5 75 A3
Emsworth Rd SR5 75 A3
Enderby Dr NE46 44 E3
Enderby Rd SR4 102 B3
Enfield Ave NE16 54 B1
Enfield Gdns NE16 69 B5
Enfield Rd NE9 70 F8
Enfield St SR4 85 F7
Engel St NE39 67 B2
Engine Inn Rd NE28 40 F4
Engine La NE9 70 F4
Engine Rd
Hedley on the Hill NE17 65 E4
Prudhoe NE42 65 F5
Englefeld NE10 71 F4
Englefield Cl NE3 37 D7
Englemann Way SR3 91 E5
English Martyrs Prim Sch SR5 74 E2
English Martyrs' RC Prim Sch NE5 54 C8
Enid Ave SR6 75 D3
Enid St NE13 28 A4
Ennerdale Birtley DH3 82 D2
Washington NE37 83 C7
Sunderland SR2 86 C4
Ennerdale Cres
Penshaw DH4 90 A8
Blaydon NE21 68 B8
Ennerdale Gdns
Wallsend NE28 41 A4
Gateshead NE9 71 A5
Ennerdale Pl DH2 88 C1
Ennerdale Rd Blyth NE24 16 F8
Tynemouth NE30 32 A2
Newcastle-upon-Tyne NE6 56 F6
Ennerdale St DH5 94 F2
Ennerdale Terr NE17 77 A5
Ennerdale Wlk NE16 68 F5
Ennis Cl NE62 11 D8
Ennismore Ct NE12 39 D6
Enslin St NE6 56 F3
Enterprise Ct
Cramlington NE23 15 F1
Seaham SR7 92 F2
Enterprise Ho NE11 70 D4
Epinay Specl Sch NE32 58 C6
Epinay Wlk NE32 58 C6
Epping Ct NE23 21 D6
Epping Sq 5 SR5 75 A3
Eppleton Prim Sch DH5 95 A6
Eppleton Row DH5 95 B4
Eppleton Terr E DH5 95 B4
Eppleton Terr W DH5 95 B4
Epsom Cl NE29 41 F4
Epsom Ct NE3 37 C7
Epsom Dr NE63 6 C2
Epsom Sq 6 SR5 75 A3
Epsom Way NE24 17 D3
Epwell Gr NE23 16 C2
Equitable St NE28 40 B1
Erick St NE1 99 B1
Erin Sq SR5 75 B3
Erith Terr SR4 85 F6
Ermine Cres NE9 71 B6
Ermyn Way NE34 59 B5
Ernest St
West Boldon NE35 74 A8
7 Sunderland SR2 86 E4
Ernest Terr
Chester le Street DH3 88 C2
5 Ryhope SR2 93 A6
Ernwill Ave SR5 74 B1
Errington Cl NE20 25 C2
Errington Pl NE42 50 C2
Errington Rd NE20 25 B2
Errington Terr NE12 29 E1
Errol Pl DH3 82 D2
Erskine Ct NE2 38 F2
Erskine Rd NE33 42 D2
Erskine Way NE33 42 D2
Esdale SR2 92 E6
Esher Ct NE3 37 C7
Esher Gdns NE24 17 D3
Esher Pl NE23 21 D6
Eshmere Cres NE5 36 C3
Eshott Cl
Newcastle-upon-Tyne, Fawdon NE3 38 A6
Newcastle-upon-Tyne, East Denton NE5 37 A1
Eshott Ct NE5 37 A1
Esk Ct 12 SR3 91 F6
Esk St N10,NE9 71 B7
Eskdale Birtley DH3 82 E1
Penshaw DH4 90 A8
Eskdale Ave Blyth NE24 17 A8
Wallsend NE28 40 C5
Eskdale Cres NE37 72 B1
Eskdale Ct NE34 59 C6
Eskdale Dr NE32 58 D3
Eskdale Gdns NE9 71 A3
Eskdale Mans NE2 99 B4
Eskdale Rd SR6 75 F6
Eskdale St
Hetton le Hole DH5 94 F2
South Shields NE34 59 C5
Eskdale Terr
Newcastle-upon-Tyne NE2 99 B4
Tynemouth NE26 32 C4
Eslington Ct NE8 70 B8
Eslington Ho NE2 99 B4
Eslington Mews NE63 6 F4
Eslington Rd NE2 99 B3
Eslington Terr NE2 99 B4
Esmaralda Gdns NE23 22 F1
Esplanade NE26 32 B5
Esplanade Ave NE26 32 B5
Esplanade Mews SR2 103 A1
Esplanade Pl NE26 32 B5
Esplanade The SR2 103 A1
Esplanade W SR2 103 A1
Espley Cl NE12 40 A8
Espley Ct NE3 37 E7
Essen Way SR3 86 B3
Essex Cl
Newcastle-upon-Tyne NE4 100 B3
Ashington NE63 6 A4
Essex Dr NE37 72 D1
Essex Gdns Wallsend NE28 40 E3
South Shields NE34 60 C7
Gateshead NE9 70 F7
Essex Gr SR3 92 A8
Essex St DH5 94 F4
Estate Houses DH4 89 E4
Esther Cambell Ct NE2 98 C3
Esther Sq NE38 83 E4
Esthwaite Ave DH2 88 B1
Eston Ct Blyth NE24 17 B8
Wallsend NE28 39 F5
Eston Gr SR5 75 C3
Estuary Way SR4 85 B7
Etal Ave Whitley Bay NE25 32 B4
North Shields NE29 41 D4
Etal Castle* TD12 107 B7
Etal Cl NE27 30 F3
Etal Cres Shiremoor NE27 30 F3
Jarrow NE32 58 E4
Etal Ct 2 NE29 42 A6
Etal Ho NE63 6 F4
Etal La NE5 37 B3
Etal Pl NE3 38 A7
Etal Rd NE24 17 B3
Etal Way NE5 37 B4
Ethel Ave Blaydon NE21 53 C2
Ryhope SR2 93 A6
Ethel St Dudley NE23 29 A6
Newcastle-upon-Tyne NE4 54 D4
Ethel Terr
South Shields NE34 59 B5
High Spen NE39 66 F3
7 Hexham NE46 45 A4
Sunderland SR5 74 B1
Etherley Rd NE6 56 D7
Etherstone Ave NE7 39 C3
Eton Cl NE23 16 C2
Eton Sq NE31 57 F6
Ettrick Cl NE12 29 C4
Ettrick Gdns
Gateshead NE8 71 B8
Sunderland SR4 85 F4
Ettrick Gr SR3 85 F4
Ettrick Lodge NE3 38 D4
Ettrick Rd NE32 58 A5
European Way SR4 85 E8
Euryalus Ct NE33 42 F1
Eustace Ave NE29 41 E5
Euston Ct SR5 75 A4
Eva St NE15 53 C6
Evanlade NE10 72 B6
Evelyn St SR2 102 B1
Evelyn Terr NE21 53 C3
Evenwood Gdns NE9 71 B5
Ever Ready Ind Est DH9 79 D2
Everard St NE23 16 B3
Everest Gr NE36 74 B7
Everest Sq SR5 75 A4
Eversleigh Pl NE15 35 E2
Eversley Cres SR5 75 B3
Eversley Pl Wallsend NE28 40 F3
7 Newcastle-upon-Tyne NE6 56 B7
Everton La SR5 75 A3
Evesham SR4 85 A6
Evesham Ave NE26 31 F6
Evesham Cl NE35 58 F1
Evesham Garth NE3 37 E3
Evesham Pl NE23 21 D7
Evistones Gdns NE6 56 E3
Evistones Rd NE9 71 A7
Ewart Cres NE34 58 E4
Ewart Ct NE3 38 A7
Ewbank Ave NE4 54 E7
Ewe Hill Cotts DH4 89 F1
Ewe Hill Terr DH4 89 F1
Ewe Hill Terr W DH4 89 F1
Ewehurst Cres DH9 78 E1
Ewehurst Gdns DH9 78 E1
Ewehurst Par DH9 78 E2
Ewehurst Rd DH9 78 E2
Ewehurst Terr DH9 78 E2
Ewen Ct NE29 41 B8
Ewesley NE38 89 A8
Ewesley Cl NE5 37 A1
Ewesley Gdns NE13 28 B6
Ewesley Rd SR4 85 F5
Ewing Rd SR4 102 A1
Exchange Bldgs NE26 32 B5
Exebly Cl NE3 38 D8
Exeter Cl
Cramlington NE23 21 E7
Ashington NE63 7 A2
Exeter Ct NE31 57 D5
Exeter Rd Wallsend NE28 40 A5
Tynemouth NE29 31 C1
Exeter St
Newcastle-upon-Tyne NE6 57 A4
Gateshead NE8 101 C1
Sunderland SR4 85 F7
Exeter Way NE32 58 B2
Exmouth Rd NE29 41 C5
Exmouth Sq SR5 75 A3
Exmouth St 2 SR5 75 A3
Extension Rd SR1 103 C2
Eyemouth Ct NE34 59 A5
Eyemouth La SR5 75 A4
Eyemouth Rd NE29 41 C5

F

Faber Rd SR5 75 A3
Factory Rd NE21 53 D4
Fair Gn NE25 31 C4
Fair View
West Rainton DH4 94 A2
Burnopfield NE16 78 E6
Prudhoe NE42 50 C2
Fairburn Ave
Houghton-le-Spring DH5 94 E6
Newcastle-upon-Tyne NE7 39 C4
Fairdale Ave NE7 39 C4
Fairfield Longbenton NE12 38 F6
Hexham NE46 44 F4
Fairfield Ave
3 Longbenton NE12 39 D8
Whickham NE16 69 A5
Blyth NE24 17 D4
Fairfield Cl NE11 54 E1
Fairfield Cres NE46 45 E8
Fairfield Dr
Whitley Bay NE25 31 D4
Tynemouth NE30 32 B2
Ashington NE63 7 A2
Whitburn SR6 60 F2
Fairfield Gn NE25 31 C4
Fairfield Ind Est NE10 57 A2
Fairfield Rd NE2 38 D1
Fairfield Terr NE10 57 B2
Fairfields NE40 52 B5
Fairgreen Cl SR3 91 F5
Fairhaven NE9 71 F2
Fairhaven Ave NE6 57 A6
Fairhill Cl NE7 39 C4
Fairholm Rd NE4 54 E5
Fairholme Ave NE34 59 F6
Fairholme Rd SR3 86 C3
Fairisle DH2 82 A1
Fairlands E SR6 75 D2
Fairlands W SR6 75 D2
Fairlawn Gdns SR4 85 E4
Fairles St NE33 42 D4
Fairmead Way SR4 85 A6
Fairmile Dr SR3 92 A4
Fairmont Way NE7 39 C4
Fairney Cl NE20 25 F6
Fairney Edge NE20 25 F6
Fairnley Wlk NE5 37 A2
Fairspring NE5 37 A2
Fairview Ave NE34 59 F7
Fairview Gn NE7 39 C4
Fairville Cl NE23 16 B2
Fairville Cres NE7 39 C4
Fairway Morpeth NE61 8 F5
Stakeford NE62 11 A8
Fairway Cl NE3 38 B8
Fairway The Ryton NE21 53 A4
Newcastle-upon-Tyne NE3 38 B8
Washington NE37 72 D3
Fairways Whitley Bay NE25 31 D5
1 New Silksworth SR3 92 B7
Fairways Ave NE7 39 C4
Fairways The NE36 74 A7
Fairwood Rd NE46 45 D4
Fairy St DH5 95 A4
Falcon Ct NE63 6 B1
Falcon Hill NE61 8 D7
Falcon Pl NE12 39 A7
Falcon Terr NE41 51 B6
Falcon Way NE34 59 B4
Falconar St NE2 99 B2
Falconar's Ct NE1 99 A1
Faldonside NE6 39 D2
Falkirk NE12 29 D4
Falkland Ave
Newcastle-upon-Tyne NE3 37 F3
Hebburn NE31 57 E6
Falkland Rd SR4 85 E6
Falla Park Com Prim Sch NE10 71 C8
Falla Park Cres NE10 71 C8
Falla Park Rd NE10 71 C8
Falloden Ave NE3 37 F8
Fallodon Gdns NE5 37 D2
Fallodon Rd NE29 41 D5
Fallow Park Ave NE24 17 C6
Fallow Rd NE34 60 D6
Fallowfeld NE10 72 A7
Fallowfield Ave NE3 37 F6
Fallowfield Way
Washington NE38 83 E2
Ashington NE63 6 B2
Falmouth Dr NE32 58 D5
Falmouth Rd
North Shields NE29 41 C5
Tynemouth NE29 41 D8
Newcastle-upon-Tyne NE6 56 B7
Sunderland SR4 85 E7
Falmouth Sq SR4 85 E6
Falmouth Wlk NE23 22 A8
Falsgrave Pl NE16 68 F5
Falstaff Rd NE29 41 D6
Falston Rd NE24 17 C5
Falstone Gateshead NE10 72 A5
Washington NE38 83 F2
Falstone Ave
Newcastle-upon-Tyne NE15 53 E8
South Shields NE34 60 A6
Falstone Cl NE12 40 A8
Falstone Cres NE63 6 E1
Falstone Sq NE3 38 A6
Falstone Way NE46 44 F3
Faraday Cl NE38 84 B5
Faraday Gr Gateshead NE8 70 E7
Sunderland SR4 85 F6
Faraday Terr DH6 97 E3
Farbridge Cres DH8 76 F3
Farding Lake Ct NE34 60 C6
Farding Sq NE34 60 C6
Fareham Gr NE35 73 D8
Fareham Way NE23 22 B7
Farlam Ave NE30 32 A1
Farlam Rd NE5 54 B8
Farleigh Ct NE29 41 B8
Farm Cl Sunniside NE16 69 B2
Washington NE37 72 B1
Farm Hill Rd SR6 60 A2
Farm St SR5 75 B1
Farn Ct NE3 37 D8
Farnborough Cl NE23 22 B8
Farnborough Dr SR3 92 B8
Farndale NE28 39 F5
Farndale Ave
Stakeford NE62 11 A8
Sunderland SR6 75 F6
Farndale Cl
Dinnington NE13 27 B7
Blaydon NE21 67 F8
Farndale Ct NE24 17 D4
Farndale Rd NE4 54 E5
Farne Ave
Newcastle-upon-Tyne NE3 38 A7
South Shields NE34 60 B8
Ashington NE63 6 D2
Farne Fst Sch NE5 37 A3
Farne Rd NE27 30 F3
Farne Sq SR4 85 D7
Farne Terr NE6 56 E6
Farnham Cl NE15 53 D6
Farnham Gr NE24 17 D4
Farnham Rd NE34 59 C6
Farnham St NE15 53 D6
Farnham Terr SR4 85 F4
Farnley Rd NE6 39 C1
Farnon Rd NE3 38 A5
Farnsworth Ct NE2 38 F2
Farquhar St 4 NE2 38 F1
Farrfeld NE10 71 F4
Farrier Cl NE38 83 E2
Farriers Ct NE22 11 C5
Farringdon Comm Sch SR3 91 D7
Farringdon Inf Sch SR3 91 D8
Farringdon Jun Sch SR3 91 D8
Farringdon Rd NE30 32 A2
Farringdon Row SR4 102 C3
Farrington Ave SR3 91 C8
Farrow Dr SR6 60 E1
Farthings The NE37 72 B2
Fatfield Pk NE38 83 D1
Fatfield Prim Sch NE38 83 D1
Fatfield Rd NE38 83 E4
Fatherly Terr DH4 94 B8
Faversham Ct NE3 37 D7
Faversham Pl NE23 22 B8
Fawcett St SR1 103 A2
Fawcett Terr 7 SR2 93 A6
Fawcett Way NE33 42 C3
Fawdon Cl NE3 37 F8
Fawdon Gr NE61 4 D3
Fawdon La NE3 37 F7
Fawdon Park Ctr NE3 37 F6
Fawdon Park Rd NE3 37 F6
Fawdon Pl NE29 41 C6
Fawdon Sta NE3 37 F6
Fawdon Wlk NE3 37 D7
Fawlee Gn NE5 37 C4
Fawn Rd SR4 85 C6
Feather Bed La SR2 93 A6
Featherstone NE38 82 F5
Featherstone Gr
Bedlington NE22 10 E2
Jarrow NE32 58 A3
Featherstone St SR6 75 F2
Federation Terr DH9 79 B2
Federation Way NE11 54 E1
Fee Terr SR2 92 E6
Feetham Ave NE12 40 A8
Feetham Ct NE12 30 A1
Felixstowe Dr NE7 39 D3
Fell Bank DH3 82 D4
Fell Cl Birtley DH3 82 E3
Sunniside NE16 69 B2
Washington NE37 83 B7
Fell Ct NE9 71 B5
Fell Dyke Com Prim Sch NE9 71 D3
Fell Rd Springwell NE9 71 F1
Sunderland SR4 85 D7
Fell Sq SR4 85 D7
Fell Terr NE16 79 B6
Fell View High Spen NE39 67 A3
15 Crawcrook NE40 51 F3
Fell View W 14 NE40 51 F3
Fell Way The NE5 36 D1
Fellcross DH3 82 C5
Felldyke NE10 71 F5
Fellgate Ave NE32 58 C1
Fellgate Cty Inf Sch NE32 58 B1
Fellgate Cty Jun Mix Sch NE32 58 B1
Fellgate Gdns NE10 72 C8
Fellgate Sta NE32 58 C2
Felling Bsns Ctr NE10 56 D2
Felling Dene Gdns NE10 56 E1
Felling House Gdns NE10 56 D2
Felling Shore Ind Est NE10 56 D3
Felling Sta NE10 56 D1
Felling View NE6 56 F3
Fellmere Ave NE10 72 A8
Fells Rd NE11 70 D7
Fellsdyke Ct NE9 71 C6
Fellside Birtley DH3 82 D3
Ponteland NE20 25 B1
South Shields NE34 60 B5
Fellside Ave NE16 69 B3
Fellside Cl NE20 25 B1
Fellside Com Prim Sch NE16 69 A6
Fellside Ct
Whickham NE16 69 A7
Washington NE37 83 B6
Fellside Rd
Byermoor NE16 79 C8
Sunniside NE16 68 F3
Fellside The NE3 37 F4
Felsham Sq SR4 85 E7
Felstead Cres SR4 85 D7
Felstead Pl NE24 17 D4
Felstead Sch SR4 85 D6
Felstead Sq SR4 85 D6
Felthorpe Ct NE5 37 B4
Felton Ave
Whitley Bay NE25 32 B4
Newcastle-upon-Tyne NE3 38 A6
South Shields NE34 60 A7
Felton Cl Shiremoor NE27 30 F3
Morpeth NE61 9 B6
Felton Cres NE8 70 E7
Felton Dr NE12 29 F1
Felton Gn 12 NE6 56 C6
Felton Ho 13 NE6 56 C6
Felton Terr NE63 6 D2
Felton Wlk 15 NE6 56 C6
Fence Houses Woodlea Prim Sch DH4 89 E1
Fence Rd DH3 89 E5
Fencer Ct NE3 38 C8
Fencer Hill Park NE3 38 C8
Fenham Chase NE4 54 E8
Fenham Ct NE4 54 E8
Fenham Hall Dr NE4 54 E8
Fenham Rd
Newcastle-upon-Tyne NE4 98 A2
Lynmouth NE61 1 F3
Fenkle St NE1 99 A1
Fennel NE9 71 C4
Fennel Gr NE34 59 E3
Fenning Pl 6 NE6 56 C4
Fenside Rd SR2 92 F8
Fenton Cl DH2 88 A2
Fenton Sq SR4 85 D6
Fenton Terr DH4 90 D6
Fenton Wlk NE5 37 A2
Fenwick Ave Blyth NE24 17 D5
South Shields NE34 59 A5
Fenwick Cl Penshaw DH4 90 B8
3 Newcastle-upon-Tyne NE2 38 F1
Fenwick Gr Hexham NE46 45 A5
Morpeth NE61 4 A1
Fenwick St DH4 90 B8
Fenwick Terr
2 Newcastle-upon-Tyne NE2 38 F1
North Shields NE29 42 A6
Fenwicks St NE35 58 E1
Ferdown Ct NE40 52 D4
Ferguson Cres NE13 28 A4
Ferguson St SR2 103 C2
Ferguson's La NE15 54 B6
Fern Ave
Newcastle-upon-Tyne, Jesmond NE2 38 F1
Cramlington NE23 16 B2
North Shields NE29 41 F6
Newcastle-upon-Tyne, Fawdon NE3 38 A7
Sunderland SR5 75 A2
Whitburn SR6 60 F2
Fern Ct NE62 10 E7
Fern Dene Rd NE8 70 E8
Fern Dr Annitsford NE23 29 B8
Cleadon SR6 59 F1
Fern Gdns NE9 70 F6
Fern St SR4 102 B3
Fern Terr DH9 78 F1
Fernbank NE26 24 C6
Fernclough NE9 71 C5

Ferndale Ave
Wallsend NE28 .40 C2
Newcastle-upon-Tyne NE3 .28 D1
4 East Boldon NE36 .74 D7
Ferndale Cl NE24 .17 A8
Ferndale Gr NE36 .74 D7
Ferndale La NE36 .74 D7
Ferndale Rd DH4 .90 A8
Ferndale Terr
Springwell NE9 .71 F1
Sunderland SR4 .85 E8
Ferndene NE28 .40 E4
Ferndene Cres SR4 .85 F6
Ferndene Ct NE3 .38 D4
Ferndene Gr Ryton NE40 .52 D6
Newcastle-upon-Tyne NE7 .39 C3
Ferndown Ct NE10 .72 B7
Ferngrove NE32 .73 C8
Fernhill Ave NE16 .69 A7
Fernlea NE23 .29 B8
Fernlea Cl NE38 .83 E2
Fernlea Gdns NE40 .52 A4
Fernlea Gn NE3 .37 F5
Fernley Villas NE23 .22 D6
Fernsway SR3 .86 B3
Fernville Ave NE16 .69 B2
Fernville Rd NE3 .38 B3
Fernville St SR4 .102 B1
Fernway NE61 .9 B8
Fernwood NE2 .99 B4
Fernwood Ave NE3 .38 D6
Fernwood Cl SR3 .92 A5
Fernwood Rd
Newcastle-upon-Tyne, Lemington NE15 .53 D6
Newcastle-upon-Tyne, Jesmond NE2 .99 B4
Ferrand Dr DH4 .94 D8
Ferriby Cl NE3 .38 D8
Ferrisdale Way NE3 .37 F7
Ferry Landing NE42 .49 F3
Ferry St Jarrow NE32 .58 B8
South Shields NE33 .42 B3
Ferryboat La
Sunderland, Castletown SR5 .85 A7
Sunderland, Hylton Castle SR5 .73 F2
Ferrydene Ave NE3 .37 F4
Festival Cotts NE12 .29 B5
Festival Park Dr NE11 .70 B7
Festival Way NE11,NE8 .100 A1
Fetcham Ct NE3 .37 C7
Fewster Sq NE10 .72 A6
Field Cl NE2 .99 C2
Field Fare Ct NE16 .79 C5
Field House Rd NE8 .70 E7
Field House Terr DH6 .97 F3
Field La NE10 .72 A8
Field Sq SR4 .85 D6
Field St
8 Gateshead NE10 .56 D1
Newcastle-upon-Tyne NE3 .38 E5
Field Terr
4 Throckley NE15 .35 D2
Jarrow NE32 .58 B5
Fieldfare Cl 2 NE38 .82 F3
Fieldfare Ho 9 NE24 .17 F8
Fieldhouse Cl NE61 .9 F5
Fieldhouse La NE61 .9 E5
Fielding Ct NE34 .59 A3
Fielding Pl NE9 .71 B8
Fieldside East Rainton DH5 94 C3
Whitburn SR6 .60 E1
Fife Ave
Chester le Street DH2 .88 C3
Brockley Whins NE32 .58 E3
Fife St NE8 .56 A1
Fife Terr NE17 .77 B6
Fifteenth Ave NE24 .17 D6
Fifth Ave
Chester le Street DH2 .88 B3
Gateshead DH98,NE11 .70 D5
Blyth NE24 .17 D6
Newcastle-upon-Tyne NE6 .56 C7
Morpeth NE61 .9 B7
Ashington NE63 .6 E3
Fifth Row NE61 .1 A3
Filey Cl NE23 .22 B8
Filton Cl NE23 .22 B8
Finchale NE38 .83 C3
Finchale Cl
Houghton-le-Spring DH4 .94 D8
Dunston NE11 .69 F6
Sunderland SR2 .103 B1
Finchale Gdns
Throckley NE15 .35 D3
Gateshead NE9 .71 C2
Finchale Rd NE31 .57 E3
Finchale Terr
Great Lumley DH4 .89 E1
Jarrow NE32 .58 D4
2 Newcastle-upon-Tyne NE6 .56 C4
Finchdale Cl NE29 .41 F4
Finchdale Terr
2 Chester le Street DH3 .88 C3
Newcastle-upon-Tyne NE6 .56 C5
Finchley Cres NE6 .57 A8
Finchley Ct NE6 .57 A8
Findon Gr NE29 .41 E4
Fine La DH8 .76 B3
Fines Rd DH8 .77 B1
Finsbury Ave NE6 .56 E6
Finsbury St 2 SR5 .75 C1
Finsmere Pl 1 NE5 .37 B1
Finstock Ct NE7 .38 F4
Fir Gr South Shields NE34 .59 F5
Ellington NE61 .1 D4
Fir St NE32 .58 A7
Fir Terr NE16 .79 B6
Firbank Ave NE30 .32 B2
Firbanks NE32 .58 D1
Firfield Com Sch NE5 .37 D2
Firfield Rd NE5 .37 D2
Firs The NE3 .38 B4
First Ave
Chester le Street DH2 .88 B8
Gateshead NE11 .70 C6
Blyth NE24 .17 D6
North Shields NE29 .41 C4
Newcastle-upon-Tyne NE6 .56 C7
Morpeth NE61 .9 B7
Ashington NE63 .6 E4
First Row Ellington NE61 .1 E4
Linton NE61 .1 A3
Ashington NE63 .6 A4
First St NE8 .101 A1
Firth Sq SR4 .85 D7
Firtree Ave
Longbenton NE12 .29 D1
Washington NE38 .83 C1
Newcastle-upon-Tyne NE6 .40 A1
Firtree Cres NE12 .29 C1
Firtree Gdns NE25 .31 F3
Firtree Rd NE16 .69 A6
Firtrees
Chester le Street DH2 .88 B5
Gateshead NE10 .71 E5
Firtrees Ave NE28 .41 B3
Firwood Cres NE39 .67 A3
Firwood Gdns NE11 .70 B5
Fisher Ind Est NE6 .57 B7
Fisher La
Cramlington NE13 .21 B5
Cramlington NE13,NE23 .21 B5
Fisher Rd NE27 .30 B6
Fisher St NE6 .57 B7
Fisherwell Rd NE10 .57 A1
Fitzpatrick Pl NE33 .42 E2
Fitzroy Terr 7 SR5 .74 F2
Fitzsimmons Ave NE28 .40 B3
Flag Ho NE33 .42 E1
Flag Lo NE33 .42 E1
Flagg Ct NE33 .42 D3
Flaunden Cl NE34 .60 B5
Flax Sq SR4 .85 C7
Flaxby Cl NE3 .38 D8
Fleet St SR1 .103 C2
Fleming Bsns Ctr NE2 .99 B4
Fleming Ct NE8 .100 C2
Fleming Gdns NE10 .71 D7
Fletcher Cres DH4 .90 E6
Fletcher Terr DH4 .90 D4
Flexbury Gdns
Gateshead, Mount Pleasant NE10 .71 C8
Newcastle-upon-Tyne NE15 .53 E7
Gateshead, Lyndhurst NE9 .71 A2
Flint Hill Bank DH9 .78 E1
Flock Sq SR4 .85 D7
Flodden NE12 .29 D4
Flodden Rd SR4 .85 D6
Flodden St NE6 .56 D5
Flora St 12 NE6 .56 B6
Floral Dene SR4 .85 A6
Floralia Ave 1 SR2 .93 A6
Florence Ave NE9 .71 A6
Florence Cres 4 SR5 .74 F2
Florence St NE21 .53 B1
Florida St SR4 .85 F8
Flotterton Gdns NE5 .54 C7
Flour Mill Rd NE11 .54 F2
Fold The Burnopfield NE16 .79 A7
Whitley Bay NE25 .31 E5
Newcastle-upon-Tyne NE6 .57 A8
New Silksworth SR3 .92 B5
Folds The
Fence Houses DH4 .94 B8
East Rainton DH5 .94 D4
Folldon Ave SR6 .75 D3
Follingsby Ave NE10 .72 D6
Follingsby Dr NE10 .72 C7
Follingsby La NE10 .72 E5
Follingsby Pk NE10 .72 D5
Follingsby Way NE10 .72 D6
Follonsby Terr NE10 .72 E7
Folly La NE40 .52 B2
Folly The NE36 .74 A7
Folly Yd NE40 .52 C2
Font Side NE61 .3 A1
Fontaine Rd SR1 .102 C3
Fontburn NE61 .1 E6
Fontburn Cres NE63 .6 F3
Fontburn Ct
North Shields NE29 .41 D4
Sunderland SR5 .74 F4
Fontburn Gdns NE61 .8 E7
Fontburn Pl NE7 .39 A5
Fontburn Rd
Bedlington NE22 .11 C1
Seaton Delaval NE25 .23 D3
Fontburn Terr NE30 .42 B6
Fonteyn Pl NE23 .16 B2
Fontwell Dr NE8 .70 D7
Forbeck Rd SR4 .85 D6
Forber Ave NE34 .60 B6
Forbes Terr SR2 .92 E6
Ford Ave
North Shields NE29 .41 D4
Ashington NE63 .6 D2
Sunderland SR4 .85 A6
Ford Cres Shiremoor NE27 .30 E3
Ford Cres *continued*
Jarrow NE32 .58 B3
Sunderland SR4 .85 A6
Ford Dr NE24 .17 C7
Ford Gr NE3 .38 B7
Ford Oval SR4 .85 B7
Ford Pk NE62 .11 C8
Ford St
Newcastle-upon-Tyne NE6 .56 A5
Gateshead NE8 .56 B1
Ford Terr Wallsend NE28 .40 F2
Riding Mill NE44 .63 A8
Guide Post NE62 .10 F7
5 Sunderland SR4 .85 F6
Ford The NE42 .50 D3
Ford View NE23 .22 A1
Fordenbridge Cres SR4 .85 E6
Fordenbridge Rd SR4 .85 D6
Fordenbridge Sq SR4 .85 E6
Fordfield Rd SR4 .85 D6
Fordhall Dr SR4 .85 E6
Fordham Rd SR4 .85 E6
Fordham Sq SR4 .85 E6
Fordland Pl SR4 .85 F6
Fordley Com Prim Sch NE23 .29 A8
Fordmoss Wlk NE5 .37 A2
Fore St
Newcastle-upon-Tyne NE2 .56 A8
Hexham NE46 .45 B5
Forest Ave NE12 .39 E8
Forest Dr NE38 .88 F8
Forest Hall Prim Sch NE12 .29 D1
Forest Hall Rd NE12 .29 E1
Forest Hall St Mary's RC Sch NE12 .29 D1
Forest Rd
Newcastle-upon-Tyne NE15 .54 C4
South Shields NE33 .42 C2
Sunderland SR4 .85 D6
Forest Rd Ind Est NE33 .42 C2
Forest Way NE23 .22 F1
Forestborn Ct 5 NE5 .36 F2
Forfar St SR6 .75 D2
Forge Cl NE17 .77 B6
Forge La Bournmoor DH3 .89 B2
Hamsterley Mill NE17 .77 E5
Forge Rd NE11,NE8 .70 A8
Forge Wlk NE15 .35 F1
Forres Pl NE23 .22 B8
Forrest Rd NE28 .40 A1
Forster Ave Sherburn DH6 96 A2
Bedlington NE22 .10 E1
South Shields NE34 .59 E6
Forster Ct 6 NE9 .70 F4
Forster St
Newcastle-upon-Tyne NE1 .99 C1
Blyth NE24 .17 F7
Sunderland SR6 .75 E1
Forsyth Rd NE2 .38 E1
Forsyth St NE29 .31 B1
Fort Sq 2 NE33 .42 C4
Fort St NE33 .42 D4
Forth Banks NE1 .101 A4
Forth Ct
South Shields NE34 .59 C5
7 Silksworth SR3 .91 F6
Forth La NE1 .101 A4
Forth Pl NE1 .100 C4
Forth St
Newcastle-upon-Tyne NE1 101 A4
Chopwell NE17 .66 C1
Fortrose Ave SR3 .86 A3
Forum Ct NE22 .10 F1
Forum The
Newcastle-upon-Tyne NE15 .53 F7
2 Wallsend NE28 .40 B1
Forum Way NE23 .22 A6
Foss Way Ebchester DH8 .76 E3
South Shields NE34 .59 B5
Fossdyke NE10 .71 F5
Fosse Law NE15 .35 E1
Fosse Terr NE9 .71 B6
Fossefeld NE10 .72 A7
Fossway NE6 .56 E7
Foster Ct NE11 .70 C3
Foster St
Newcastle-upon-Tyne, Low Walker NE6 .57 B6
Newcastle-upon-Tyne, Wincomblee NE6 .57 B5
Foundary Ct NE6 .56 C4
Foundry Ct NE6 .56 C4
Foundry La NE6 .56 A6
Fountain Cl NE22 .10 F1
Fountain Gr NE34 .59 F8
Fountain Head Bank NE26 .24 C6
Fountain La NE21 .53 C3
Fountain Row NE2 .98 B3
Fountains Cl
Dunston NE11 .69 F6
Washington NE38 .83 D4
Fountains Cres
Burnside DH4 .90 C2
Hebburn NE31 .57 E3
Four Lane Ends
Hetton le Hole DH5 .95 B2
Houghton-le-Spring DH5 .94 D6
Four Lane Ends Sta NE7 .39 C5
Fouracres Rd NE5 .37 E2
Fourstones NE5 .37 A2
Fourstones Cl NE3 .37 D5
Fourstones Rd SR4 .85 E6
Fourteenth Ave NE24 .17 D6
Fourth Ave
Chester le Street DH2 .88 B3
Fourth Ave *continued*
Gateshead NE11 .70 C5
Blyth NE24 .17 D6
1 Newcastle-upon-Tyne NE6 .56 C7
Morpeth NE61 .9 B7
Ashington NE63 .6 D3
Fourth Row NE61 .1 A4
Fourth St NE8 .101 A1
Fowberry Cres NE4 .54 E7
Fowberry Rd NE15 .53 F4
Fowler Cl DH4 .90 C4
Fowler Gdns 2 NE11 .54 F1
Fowler St NE33 .42 C3
Fox and Hounds La NE15 54 C6
Fox and Hounds Rd NE5 54 C7
Fox Ave NE34 .59 A4
Fox Covert La NE20 .25 D6
Fox Lea Wlk NE23 .22 E1
Fox St SR2 .102 B1
Foxcover NE63 .6 F1
Foxcover La SR3 .91 B7
Foxcover Rd
Sunderland SR3 .91 A8
Penshaw SR4 .84 F2
Foxglove Cl NE24 .17 C4
Foxglove Ct NE34 .59 B4
Foxhill Cl NE63 .6 B1
Foxhills Cl NE38 .83 E2
Foxhills Covert NE16 .68 E5
Foxhills The NE16 .68 E6
Foxholmes NE32 .73 D8
Foxhunters Light Ind Site NE25 .31 F3
Foxhunters Rd NE25 .31 F3
Foxlair Cl SR3 .92 A4
Foxley NE37 .83 E8
Foxley Cl NE12 .29 F4
Foxton Ave
Newcastle-upon-Tyne NE3 .37 F7
Tynemouth NE30 .32 B3
Foxton Cl NE29 .41 E3
Foxton Ct SR6 .60 A1
Foxton Gn NE3 .37 E5
Foxton Hall NE37 .72 D3
Foxton Way NE10 .57 B2
Foyle St SR1 .103 A2
Framlington Pl NE2 .98 C3
Frances St Blaydon NE21 .53 A2
9 New Silksworth SR3 .92 A7
Frances Ville NE62 .10 E4
Francis St SR6 .75 D2
Frank Pl NE29 .42 A6
Frank St Wallsend NE28 .40 B1
Greenside NE40 .51 F1
Sunderland SR5 .75 B2
Frankham St 1 NE5 .36 F2
Frankland Dr NE25 .31 E3
Franklin Ct 10 NE37 .83 D8
Franklin St
South Shields NE33 .42 C2
Sunderland SR4 .102 A3
Franklyn Ave NE26 .24 B7
Fraser Cl NE33 .59 B8
Frazer Terr NE10 .57 B2
Freda St SR5 .74 F1
Frederick Gdns DH4 .90 A7
Frederick Rd SR1 .103 A3
Frederick St
Chopwell NE17 .77 B8
South Shields NE33 .42 C1
Sunderland SR1 .103 A2
Sunderland, South Hylton SR4 .85 A6
Frederick Terr
Hetton le Hole DH5 .95 B1
South Hetton DH6 .97 F6
3 Whitburn SR6 .60 F1
Freehold Ave NE62 .10 F7
Freehold St 5 NE24 .17 F8
Freeman Hospl NE7 .39 A4
Freeman Rd NE3,NE7 .38 F4
Freeman Way
Whitley Bay NE26 .31 E7
Ashington NE63 .6 F1
Freesia Grange NE38 .83 E3
Freezemoor Rd DH4 .90 D6
Fremantle Rd NE34 .60 B5
French St NE24 .17 E8
Frenchman's Row NE15 .35 B2
Frenchman's Way NE34 .60 B8
Frensham NE38 .84 A4
Frenton Cl NE5 .36 C2
Friar Rd SR4 .85 D6
Friar Sq SR4 .85 D6
Friar Way NE32 .58 C7
Friar's Row NE16 .78 F5
Friarage Ave SR6 .75 D3
Friars NE1 .98 C1
Friars Dene Rd NE10 .56 C2
Friars Gate NE61 .8 D7
Friars St NE1 .98 C1
Friars Way NE5 .54 C8
Friarsfield Cl SR3 .91 E5
Friarside Cres NE39 .78 D8
Friarside Gdns
Burnopfield NE16 .78 F6
Whickham NE16 .69 A6
Friarside Rd NE4 .54 E8
Friary Gdns NE10 .56 C1
Frobisher Ct SR3 .91 F6
Frobisher St NE31 .58 A6
Frome Gdns NE9 .70 F2
Frome Pl NE23 .22 B8
Frome Sq SR4 .85 C6
Front Rd SR4 .85 D6
Front St
Chester le Street DH3 .88 C3
Front St *continued*
Fence Houses DH4 .94 A8
Newbottle DH4 .90 D4
Hetton le Hole DH5 .95 A3
Hetton le Hole, Low Moorsley DH5 .94 E1
Haswell DH6 .97 F3
High Pittington DH6 .96 B6
Sherburn DH6 .96 A1
Sherburn Hill DH6 .96 D1
South Hetton DH6 .97 F7
Tanfield DH9 .79 D3
Tantobie DH9 .79 B2
Killingworth NE12,NE23 .29 B5
Dinnington NE13 .27 B7
Burnopfield NE16 .79 B6
Burnopfield, Hobson NE16 .79 A4
Burnopfield, Lintz NE16 .78 E6
Whickham NE16 .69 B7
Whickham, Swalwell NE16 .54 A1
Blaydon NE21 .53 B1
Annitsford NE23 .22 B1
Cramlington NE23 .22 B6
Seghill NE23,NE13 .22 F2
Bebside NE24 .16 E7
Earsdon NE25 .31 A5
Whitley Bay NE25,NE26 .31 E4
North Shields NE29 .41 E5
Tynemouth, Preston NE29 .42 A8
Tynemouth NE30 .42 D7
Tynemouth, Cullercoats NE30 .32 C3
Boldon Colliery NE35 .58 E1
East Boldon NE36 .74 C7
Washington NE37 .83 D8
Prudhoe, Hagg Bank NE41 .50 F5
Prudhoe NE42 .50 D2
Corbridge NE45 .46 F5
Ellington NE61 .1 C5
Guide Post NE62 .10 E7
Newbiggin-by-the-Sea NE64 .7 E4
Longbenton NE7,NE12 .39 C5
Cleadon SR6 .60 A1
Whitburn SR6 .75 F8
Front St E Penshaw DH4 .90 B8
Bedlington NE22 .16 A8
Front St W Penshaw DH4 .90 B8
Bedlington NE22 .15 F8
Front Street Com Prim Sch NE16 .69 A7
Frosterley Cl DH5 .97 D8
Frosterley Gdns SR3 .86 B2
Frosterley Pl NE4 .98 A2
Frosterley Wlk NE16 .69 B3
Froude Ave NE34 .59 C3
Fuchsia Gdns NE31 .57 E3
Fuchsia Pl NE5 .37 D2
Fulbrook Cl NE23 .16 B2
Fulbrook Rd NE3 .37 F5
Fuller Rd SR2 .86 E4
Fullerton Pl NE9 .71 A8
Fulmar Dr Blyth NE24 .17 E3
Washington NE38 .82 F3
Fulmar Wlk SR6 .60 F2
Fulwell Ave NE34 .60 B7
Fulwell Gn NE5 .37 B1
Fulwell Inf Sch SR6 .75 D4
Fulwell Prim Jun Mix Sch SR6 .75 E4
Fulwell Rd SR6 .75 D2
Furnace Bank NE22 .11 D1
Furness Ct 1 SR3 .91 F6
Furrowfield NE10 .71 C6
Furrowfield Jun Sch DH3 .82 D3
Furrowfield Sch NE10 .71 C6
Furzefield Rd NE3 .38 B4
Fyling Ho 3 SR3 .91 F5
Fylingdale Dr SR3 .92 C7

G

Gables Ct SR4 .85 C3
Gables The
Newcastle-upon-Tyne NE13 .37 B6
3 Blyth NE24 .17 D8
4 Washington NE38 .83 E4
Gadwall Rd DH4 .94 B6
Gainers Terr NE28 .57 C8
Gainford
Chester le Street DH2 .88 A3
Gateshead NE9 .70 F2
Gainsborough Ave
Whiteleas NE34 .59 D2
Washington NE38 .83 E4
Gainsborough Cl NE25 .31 C7
Gainsborough Cres
Shiney Row DH4 .90 A5
Gateshead NE9 .71 B7
Gainsborough Pl NE23 .22 B3
Gainsborough Rd SR4 .85 C2
Gainsborough Sq SR4 .85 C2
Gainsbro Gr NE4 .54 F6
Gainsford Ave NE9 .70 E4
Gairloch Cl NE23 .16 B1
Gairloch Dr NE38 .83 A3
Gairloch Rd SR4 .85 C3
Gairsay Cl 5 SR2 .92 E8
Galashiels Gr DH4 .90 B5
Galashiels Rd SR4 .85 C3
Galashiels Sq SR4 .85 C3
Galen Ho NE1 .99 A1
Gallalaw Terr NE3,NE7 .38 F5
Gallant Terr NE28 .41 C1
Galleries The NE38 .83 C5
Galley's Gill Rd SR1 .102 C3

Galloping Green Cotts
NE9 .71 D2
Galloping Green Rd NE9 .71 D2
Gallowgate NE1 .98 C1
Gallowhill La NE15,NE42 .50 B7
Gallows Bank NE46 .45 B3
Galsworthy Rd
Biddick Hall NE34 .59 B3
Whiteleas NE34 .59 C3
Sunderland SR4 .85 C3
Galway Rd SR4 .85 B3
Galway Sq SR4 .85 B3
Gambia Rd [4] SR4 .85 B2
Gambia Sq [6] SR4 .85 B2
Ganton Ave NE23 .22 B4
Ganton Cl NE37 .72 C2
Ganton Ct NE34 .59 F3
Gaprigg Ct NE46 .45 B4
Gaprigg La NE46 .45 A4
Garasdale Cl NE24 .17 D4
Garcia Terr SR6 .75 E4
Garden City Villas NE63 .6 D3
Garden Cl NE13 .28 B8
Garden Cres DH8 .76 F4
Garden Croft NE12 .39 E8
Garden Dr NE31 .57 D4
Garden Est DH5 .95 B4
Garden House Est NE40 .51 E4
Garden La
South Shields NE33 .42 C2
Cleadon SR6 .74 F8
Garden Pk [9] NE28 .40 F4
Garden Pl Penshaw DH4 .90 B7
Sunderland SR1 .102 C3
Garden St Newbottle DH4 .90 D3
Blaydon NE21 .53 C3
Newcastle-upon-Tyne NE3 .38 C4
Garden Terr
Newbottle DH4 .90 D3
[9] Blaydon NE21 .53 B1
Earsdon NE25 .31 A5
Crawcrook NE40 .51 F4
Crawcrook, Ryton Woodside
NE40 .52 A3
Hexham NE46 .45 A5
Gardener St NE4 .100 A3
Gardens The
Chester le Street DH2 .88 B3
Whitley Bay NE25 .31 F4
Washington NE38 .83 E4
Gardiner Rd SR4 .85 B3
Gardiner Sq
Kibblesworth NE11 .81 C6
[4] Sunderland SR4 .85 B3
Gardner Pk NE29 .41 F5
Gardner Pl NE29 .42 B5
Garesfield Gdns
Burnopfield NE16 .78 F6
Rowlands Gill NE39 .67 E3
Garesfield Golf Course
NE17 .66 D4
Garesfield La NE21,NE39 .67 E6
Gareston Cl NE24 .17 B7
Garfield St [6] SR4 .85 F7
Garforth Cl NE23 .22 A4
Garland Terr [6] DH4 .94 A8
Garleigh Cl NE12 .29 F3
Garmondsway [15] NE6 .56 C5
Garner Cl NE5 .36 D3
Garnet St [3] SR4 .85 F7
Garrett Cl NE28 .40 F3
Garrick Cl NE29 .41 C7
Garrick St NE33 .59 C8
Garrigill NE38 .83 F1
Garsdale DH3 .82 E1
Garsdale Ave NE37 .83 C8
Garsdale Rd NE26 .24 E1
Garside Ave DH3 .82 C6
Garsin Cl NE7 .39 E3
Garth Cotts NE46 .45 A4
Garth Cres Blaydon NE21 .53 B1
South Shields NE34 .43 A1
Garth Farm Rd NE21 .53 B1
Garth Heads NE1 .99 C1
Garth Sixteen NE12 .29 D4
Garth The Medomsley DH8 77 C2
[7] Blaydon NE21 .53 B1
Newcastle-upon-Tyne, Kenton
NE3 .37 F4
Newcastle-upon-Tyne, West
Denton NE5 .36 E1
Garth Thirty Three NE12 .29 D3
Garth Thirty Two NE12 .29 E3
Garth Twenty NE12 .29 E3
Garth Twenty Five NE12 .29 F3
Garth Twenty Four NE12 .29 F3
Garth Twenty One NE12 .29 E4
Garth Twenty Seven
NE12 .29 F3
Garth Twenty Two NE12 .29 E3
Garthfield Cl NE5 .37 A3
Garthfield Cnr NE5 .37 A3
Garthfield Cres NE5 .37 A3
Gartland Rd SR4 .85 B3
Garvey Villas N10,NE9 .71 C6
Garwood St NE33 .59 B8
Gas House La NE61 .4 A1
Gas La NE21 .53 C4
Gaskell Ave NE34 .59 B3
Gatacre St NE24 .17 E8
Gateley Ave NE24 .17 D4
Gatesgarth NE9 .71 A5
Gatesgarth Gr SR6 .75 E5
Gateshead Highway
NE8 .101 C2
Gateshead International Stad
(Athletics Gd) NE10 .56 C3
Gateshead Jewish Boys Sch
NE8 .101 B1
Gateshead Jewish Prim Sch
NE8 .101 B1
Gateshead Jewish Teachers
Training Coll NE8 .101 B1
Gateshead Library★ NE8 .70 F8
Gateshead Metro Ctr Sta
NE11 .54 D2
Gateshead Rd NE16 .69 C3
Gateshead Sta NE8 .101 B3
Gateshead Stadium Sta
NE8 .56 A2
Gateshead Talmudical Coll
NE8 .101 B1
Gateshead Tech Coll NE9 70 F7
Gateshead Tech Coll
(Annexe) NE9 .71 A7
Gatwick Ct NE3 .37 C7
Gatwick Rd SR4 .85 B3
Gaughan Cl NE6 .56 F3
Gaweswell Terr DH4 .90 D4
Gayhurst Cres SR3 .92 B6
Gayton Rd NE37 .72 E1
Geddes Rd SR4 .85 B3
Gellesfield Chare NE16 .69 B4
Gelt Cres DH5 .95 B2
General Graham St SR4 102 A1
General Havelock Rd
SR4 .85 E6
General's Wood The
NE38 .89 B8
Geneva Rd [5] SR4 .85 B3
Genister Pl NE4 .54 D8
Geoffrey St
Whiteleas NE34 .59 C3
Whitburn SR6 .60 F1
George Pl NE1 .99 A2
George Rd
Bedlington NE22 .11 D2
Wallsend NE28 .57 B8
George Scott St NE33 .42 D4
George Smith Gdns
NE10 .56 C2
George Sq [6] NE30 .42 B6
George St Birtley DH3 .82 B4
Chester le Street DH3 .88 D2
Hetton le Hole DH5 .95 A5
Haswell DH6 .97 F3
Sherburn DH6 .96 A1
Newcastle-upon-Tyne NE1,
NE4 .100 C4
[5] Gateshead NE10 .56 F1
Brunswick Village NE13 .28 A6
Whickham NE16 .69 A7
Blaydon NE21 .53 D3
Blyth NE24 .17 E6
Wallsend NE28 .41 B1
Newcastle-upon-Tyne, Coxlodge
NE3 .38 A5
North Shields NE30 .42 B6
[4] Crawcrook NE40 .51 F3
Walbottle NE5 .35 F2
Ashington NE63 .6 E4
Ryhope SR2 .93 A6
New Silksworth SR3 .92 A8
George St N SR6 .103 A4
George St W [10] SR3 .92 A8
George Stephenson High Sch
NE12 .29 D3
George Stephenson Way
NE29 .42 A3
George Stephenson's
Cottage★ NE41 .51 D7
George's View NE23 .29 A7
Georges Rd
Newcastle-upon-Tyne NE4 .54 F4
Newcastle-upon-Tyne, Elswick
NE4 .54 F3
Georgian Ct
Longbenton NE12 .29 B1
Sunderland SR4 .86 A4
Gerald St Whiteleas NE34 .59 C3
Newcastle-upon-Tyne NE4 .54 D4
Gerrard Cl
Cramlington NE23 .22 B4
Whitley Bay NE26 .24 E1
Gerrard Rd
Whitley Bay NE26 .24 F1
[6] Sunderland SR4 .85 B3
Gertrude St DH4 .90 D2
Gibbon's Wlk NE34 .59 A2
Gibbs Ct [3] DH2 .88 C2
Gibside DH2 .88 A3
Gibside Chapel★ NE16 .68 A1
Gibside Cres NE16 .79 D8
Gibside Ct NE11 .69 F6
Gibside Gdns NE15 .54 B6
Gibside Terr NE16 .79 B6
Gibside View NE21 .68 B8
Gibside Way NE11 .54 B2
Gibson Ct NE35 .73 F8
Gibson Fields NE46 .45 B4
Gibson Ho [5] NE46 .45 A4
Gibson Pl NE46 .45 A5
Gibson St
Newcastle-upon-Tyne NE1 .99 C1
Wallsend NE28 .40 F5
Newbiggin-by-the-Sea NE64 .7 D4
Gibson Terr NE40 .52 A4
Gifford Sq SR4 .85 C4
Gilberdyke NE10 .72 A5
Gilbert Rd SR4 .85 B2
Gilbert Sq SR4 .85 B2
Gilbert St NE33 .59 C8
Gilderdale DH4 .89 E8
Gilderdale Way NE23 .22 A3
Giles Pl NE46 .45 A5
Gilesgate NE46 .45 A5
Gilesgate Rd DH5 .95 B1
Gilhurst Grange SR1 .102 B2
Gill Bridge Ave SR1 .102 C3
Gill Burn NE39 .67 E3
Gill Crescent N DH4 .89 E1
Gill Crescent S DH4 .89 E1
Gill Ct NE13 .28 A6
Gill Rd SR1 .102 C3
Gill Side Gr SR6 .75 E2
Gill St NE4 .54 E5
Gillas La DH5 .95 A7
Gillas La E DH5 .94 F7
Gillas La W DH5 .94 E6
Gillas Lane Inf Sch DH5 .94 F7
Gillhurst Ho SR1 .102 B3
Gillies St NE6 .56 D6
Gilliland Cres DH3 .82 C6
Gillingham Rd SR4 .85 C3
Gillside Ct NE34 .59 A5
Gillwood Ct DH4 .90 A6
Gilmore Cl NE5 .36 D3
Gilmore Ho NE8 .70 E8
Gilpin St DH4 .94 D8
Gilsland Ave NE28 .40 F3
Gilsland Gr NE23 .16 B1
Gilsland St SR4 .102 A2
Gilwell Way NE3 .28 B1
Gingler La NE40 .52 A2
Girtin Rd NE34 .59 D2
Girvan Terr DH5 .95 B1
Girvan Terr W DH5 .95 B1
Gisburn Ct NE23 .16 B1
Gishford Way NE5 .37 B2
Givens St SR6 .75 E2
Glade The Walbottle NE15 .36 A2
Hedworth NE32 .73 B8
Gladeley Way NE16 .69 B2
Gladewell Ct NE62 .10 E7
Gladstonbury Pl NE12 .39 C7
Gladstone Ave NE26 .31 F6
Gladstone Pl NE2 .99 B3
Gladstone St
Fence Houses DH4 .94 B8
Newcastle-upon-Tyne NE15 .53 C6
Blyth NE24 .17 D8
[3] Wallsend NE28 .41 B1
Hebburn NE31,NE32 .58 A6
Morpeth NE61 .9 B8
Sunderland SR6 .75 D1
Gladstone Terr
Birtley DH3 .82 B4
Penshaw DH4 .89 F8
Newcastle-upon-Tyne NE2 .99 B3
Bedlington NE22 .11 A1
[7] Whitley Bay NE26 .32 B4
[2] Boldon Colliery NE35 .58 E1
Washington NE37 .83 F8
Gateshead NE8 .101 C1
Gladstone Terr W NE8 .101 B1
Gladwyn Rd [2] SR4 .85 B2
Gladwyn Sq SR4 .85 B2
Glaholm Rd SR2 .103 C2
Glaisdale Ct NE34 .59 A4
Glaisdale Dr SR6 .75 E6
Glaisdale Rd NE7 .39 A5
Glamis Ave
Newcastle-upon-Tyne NE3 .28 C1
Sunderland SR4 .85 C4
Glamis Cres NE39 .68 B4
Glamis Ct NE34 .59 F3
Glamis Terr NE16 .69 A1
Glamis Villas DH3 .82 C6
Glanmore Rd [3] SR4 .85 B3
Glantlees NE5 .37 A2
Glanton Ave NE25 .23 C3
Glanton Cl
Chester le Street DH2 .88 A2
[3] Newcastle-upon-Tyne
NE6 .56 C4
Morpeth NE61 .9 B5
Glanton Ct NE11 .100 A1
Glanton Ho NE24 .17 B8
Glanton Rd
Tynemouth NE29 .41 D7
Hexham NE46 .45 D4
Glanton Sq SR4 .85 C3
Glanton Wynd NE3 .38 B7
Glanville Cl NE11 .70 B7
Glanville Rd SR3 .91 D5
Glasbury Ave SR4 .85 C4
Glasgow Rd NE32 .58 E3
Glassey Terr NE22 .11 D1
Glasshouse St NE6 .56 C4
Glastonbury NE38 .83 D4
Glastonbury Gr NE2 .38 F2
Glazebury Way NE23 .16 B1
Glebe Ave
Longbenton NE12 .39 D7
Whickham NE16 .69 B7
Glebe Cl Ponteland NE20 .25 E7
Newcastle-upon-Tyne NE5 .36 D3
Glebe Cres
Longbenton NE12 .29 D1
Washington NE38 .83 E6
Glebe Ct NE22 .10 F1
Glebe Dr SR7 .92 F2
Glebe Est SR7 .92 F2
Glebe Farm NE62 .10 F8
Glebe Mews NE22 .10 F1
Glebe Rd Longbenton NE12 29 D1
Bedlington NE22 .10 F1
Glebe Rise NE16 .69 B7
Glebe Sch The NE12 .29 D2
Glebe St NE4 .54 E6
Glebe Terr
[2] Houghton-le-Spring DH4 90 D1
[1] Dunston NE11 .69 F8
Glebe Terr *continued*
Longbenton NE12 .29 D1
Choppington NE62 .10 E4
Glebe The NE61 .14 C4
Glebe Village Prim Sch
NE38 .83 D5
Glebe Villas NE12 .29 C1
Glebe Wlk NE16 .69 B7
Glebelands NE45 .47 A6
Glen Ave NE43 .64 C7
Glen Barr DH2 .88 B4
Glen Cl NE39 .67 E3
Glen Ct NE31 .57 D5
Glen Luce Dr SR2 .86 F2
Glen Path SR2 .86 D3
Glen St NE31 .57 D5
Glen Terr
Chester le Street DH2 .88 A4
Washington NE38 .83 E4
Hexham NE46 .44 F5
Glen The SR2 .86 D3
Glen Thorpe Ave SR6 .75 E2
Glen's Flats DH6 .96 B5
Glenallen Gdns NE30 .32 C1
Glenavon Ave DH2 .88 B4
Glenbrooke Terr NE9 .70 F4
Glenburn Cl NE38 .82 F3
Glencarron Cl NE38 .83 A3
Glencoe NE12 .29 D4
Glencoe Ave
Chester le Street DH2 .88 B4
Cramlington NE23 .22 B3
Glencoe Rd SR4 .85 B2
Glencoe Rise NE39 .67 C1
Glencoe Sq SR4 .85 B3
Glencoe Terr NE39 .67 C1
Glencourse NE36 .74 E7
Glendale Ave
Whickham NE16 .69 A6
Blyth NE24 .16 E8
Whitley Bay NE26 .32 A7
Wallsend NE28 .40 B4
North Shields NE29 .41 F6
Newcastle-upon-Tyne NE3 .38 A4
Washington NE37 .83 C8
Stakeford NE62 .11 A8
Glendale Cl Blaydon NE21 .67 F8
Newcastle-upon-Tyne NE5 .36 D3
Sunderland SR3 .91 C6
Glendale Gdns
Stakeford NE62 .11 A8
Gateshead NE9 .71 B5
Glendale Gr NE29 .41 F6
Glendale Rd
Shiremoor NE27 .31 A3
Ashington NE63 .7 A2
Glendale Terr [5] NE6 .56 C6
Glendford Pl NE24 .17 D4
Glendower Ave NE29 .41 D6
Glendyn Cl NE7 .39 A1
Gleneagle Cl NE5 .36 D3
Gleneagles
Whitley Bay NE25 .31 D6
South Shields NE33 .42 F1
Gleneagles Cl NE7 .39 C5
Gleneagles Ct NE25 .31 D6
Gleneagles Dr NE37 .72 C2
Gleneagles Rd
Gateshead NE9 .70 E3
Sunderland SR4 .85 B2
Gleneagles Sq [1] SR4 .85 B2
Glenesk Gdns SR2 .86 C2
Glenesk Rd SR2 .86 C3
Glenfield Ave NE23 .16 B1
Glenfield Rd
Longbenton NE12 .39 B7
Longbenton NE12 .39 C7
Glengarvan Cl NE38 .83 A3
Glenholme Cl NE38 .82 F3
Glenhurst Dr
Whickham NE16 .68 F4
Newcastle-upon-Tyne NE5 .36 D3
Glenhurst Gr NE34 .59 F6
Glenkerry Cl NE38 .83 A3
Glenleigh Dr SR4 .85 C4
Glenluce Ct NE23 .22 B4
Glenluce Dr NE23 .22 B3
Glenmoor NE31 .57 D7
Glenmore Ave DH2 .88 C4
Glenmuir Ave NE23 .22 A3
Glenorrin Cl NE38 .83 A3
Glenridge Ave NE6 .39 B1
Glenroy Gdns DH2 .88 B4
Glenshiel Cl NE38 .83 A3
Glenside Hedworth NE32 .58 C2
Ellington NE61 .1 E5
Glenside Ct NE9 .70 E4
Glenthorn Rd NE2 .38 E2
Glenthorne Rd [1] SR6 .75 E2
Glenuce DH3 .82 E3
Glenwood NE63 .6 C2
Glenwood Wlk NE5 .36 D3
Gloria Ave NE25 .23 D6
Glossop St NE39 .66 F4
Gloucester Ave SR6 .75 E4
Gloucester Ct NE3 .37 C8
Gloucester Pl NE34 .60 A5
Gloucester Rd
Shiremoor NE29 .41 B7
Newcastle-upon-Tyne NE4 .98 A1
Gloucester St NE25 .23 D6
Gloucester Terr
Haswell DH6 .97 E1
Newcastle-upon-Tyne NE4 100 A4
Gloucester Way
Hedworth NE32 .58 B2
Newcastle-upon-Tyne NE4 100 B4
Glover Ind Est NE37 .83 E7
Glover Rd
Washington NE37 .83 F8
Sunderland SR4 .85 B2
Glover Sq SR4 .85 B2
Glynfellis NE10 .71 F4
Glynfellis Ct NE10 .71 F5
Glynn House NE4 .54 E4
Glynwood Cl NE23 .16 B1
Glynwood Com Prim Sch
NE9 .71 A5
Glynwood Gdns NE9 .71 A5
Goalmouth Cl [6] SR6 .75 E2
Goathland Ave
Longbenton NE12 .39 C6
Newcastle-upon-Tyne NE12 .39 C7
Goathland Cl SR3 .92 C7
Goathland Dr SR3 .92 B6
Goathland Prim Sch
NE12 .39 C6
Godfrey Rd SR4 .85 B3
Gofton Wlk NE5 .37 A2
Goldcrest Rd NE38 .82 F3
Goldfinch Cl NE4 .54 F4
Goldlynn Dr SR3 .91 E6
Goldsbrough Ct NE2 .98 C3
Goldsmith Rd SR4 .85 B2
Goldspink La NE2 .56 A7
Goldstone Ct NE12 .29 E4
Goldthorpe Cl NE23 .16 B1
Golf Course Rd DH4 .90 A4
Gompertz Gdns NE33 .59 B8
Gooch Ave NE22 .11 A4
Goodrich Cl DH4 .90 C5
Goodwood NE12 .29 E3
Goodwood Ave NE8 .70 C8
Goodwood Cl NE5 .36 D3
Goodwood Ct NE63 .6 D2
Goodwood Rd SR4 .85 A3
Goodwood Sq SR4 .85 A3
Goole Rd SR4 .85 C3
Goose Hill NE61 .9 A8
Gordon Ave
Newcastle-upon-Tyne NE3 .38 C4
Sunderland SR5 .85 A8
Gordon Ct [9] NE10 .56 D1
Gordon Dr NE36 .74 D7
Gordon Ho [2] NE6 .56 B5
Gordon Rd Blyth NE24 .17 F6
South Shields NE34 .59 C6
[3] Newcastle-upon-Tyne
NE6 .56 B5
Sunderland SR4 .85 B2
Gordon Sq
Whitley Bay NE26 .32 C4
Newcastle-upon-Tyne NE6 .56 B5
Gordon St NE33 .59 D8
Gordon Terr
Bedlington NE22 .16 A8
Whitley Bay NE26 .32 C5
Prudhoe NE42 .50 D2
Stakeford NE62 .11 C7
[3] Ryhope SR2 .93 A6
Sunderland SR5 .75 A2
Gordon Terrace W NE62 .11 C7
Gorleston Way SR3 .92 A4
Gorse Ave NE34 .60 A5
Gorse Hill Way NE5 .37 C3
Gorse Rd SR2 .103 A1
Gorsedene Ave NE26 .24 F1
Gorsedene Rd NE26 .24 F1
Gorsehill NE9 .71 C5
Gorseway NE61 .8 D7
Goschen St Blyth NE24 .17 D8
Gateshead NE8 .70 D8
Sunderland SR5 .75 A2
Gosforth Ave NE34 .59 C3
Gosforth Bsns Pk NE12 .38 F7
Gosforth Cen Mid Sch
NE3 .38 D6
Gosforth Ctr NE3 .38 C4
Gosforth East Mid Sch
NE3 .38 D7
Gosforth High Sch NE3 .38 C6
Gosforth Park Fst Sch
NE3 .38 D7
Gosforth Park Villas
NE13 .28 C4
Gosforth Park Way NE12 .38 F7
Gosforth St
[20] Gateshead NE10 .56 D1
Newcastle-upon-Tyne NE2 .99 C2
Sunderland SR6 .75 E1
Gosforth Terr
Gateshead NE10 .56 F1
Newcastle-upon-Tyne NE3 .38 E5
Gosforth West Mid Sch
NE3 .38 B5
Gosport Way NE24 .17 D4
Gossington NE38 .84 A5
Gossipgate Gallery★
CA9 .133 A1
Goswick Ave NE7 .39 B3
Goswick Dr NE3 .37 F8
Goundry Ave SR2 .93 A6
Gourock Sq SR4 .85 A3
Gowan Terr NE2 .38 F1
Gowanburn
Cramlington NE23 .22 A3
Washington NE38 .83 F2
Gower Rd SR5 .75 A2
Gower St NE6 .57 A4
Gower Wlk NE10 .71 C8
Gowland Ave NE4 .54 E6
Grace Darling Museum★
NE69 .109 B5

Grace Gdns NE28 ... 40 A4
Grace St Dunston NE11 ... 69 F8
Newcastle-upon-Tyne, Byker NE6 ... 56 C6
Newcastle-upon-Tyne, Walker NE6 ... 56 D6
Gracefield Cl NE5 ... 36 D3
Gradys Yd NE15 ... 35 D3
Grafton Cl 5 NE6 ... 56 B6
Grafton House 7 NE6 ... 56 B6
Grafton Rd NE26 ... 32 C4
Grafton St
11 Newcastle-upon-Tyne NE6 ... 56 B6
Sunderland SR4 ... 102 B3
Gragareth Way NE37 ... 83 A6
Graham Ave NE16 ... 69 B8
Graham Park Rd NE3 ... 38 C3
Graham Rd NE31 ... 57 D5
Graham St NE33 ... 42 D2
Graham Terr DH6 ... 96 B5
Grahamsley St NE8 ... 101 C2
Grainger Ct NE4 ... 54 F5
Grainger Mkt NE1 ... 99 A1
Grainger Park Rd NE4 ... 54 F5
Grainger St NE1 ... 99 A1
Graingerville N NE4 ... 98 A1
Graingerville S NE4 ... 98 A1
Grampian Ave DH2 ... 88 B2
Grampian Cl NE29 ... 31 F1
Grampian Gdns NE11 ... 70 B6
Grampian Gr NE36 ... 74 B7
Grampian Pl NE12 ... 29 B1
Granaries The
Fence Houses DH4 ... 94 B8
High Spen NE39 ... 66 F4
Penshaw SR4 ... 84 F3
Granby Cl Sunniside NE16 ... 69 B3
Sunderland SR3 ... 86 B3
Granby St NE16 ... 69 B2
Grand Par NE30 ... 32 D1
Grandstand Rd NE2 ... 38 B2
Grange Ave
Fence Houses DH4 ... 90 A1
Longbenton NE12 ... 39 E6
Bedlington NE22 ... 11 E3
Shiremoor NE27 ... 30 F4
Grange Cl Blyth NE24 ... 17 D4
Whitley Bay NE25 ... 31 D4
Wallsend NE28 ... 40 C2
Tynemouth NE30 ... 32 B2
Grange Cres
Gateshead NE10 ... 72 A7
Ryton NE40 ... 52 C4
Sunderland SR2 ... 103 A1
Grange Ct Gateshead NE10 72 A7
6 Jarrow NE32 ... 58 B7
Ryton NE40 ... 52 C4
Prudhoe NE42 ... 50 D2
Morpeth NE61 ... 9 A7
Grange Dr NE40 ... 52 C4
Grange Est NE11 ... 81 C6
Grange Farm Dr NE16 ... 69 A5
Grange Fst Sch NE3 ... 38 B6
Grange La NE16 ... 69 B5
Grange Lonnen NE40 ... 52 B5
Grange Nook NE16 ... 69 A5
Grange Park Ave
Bedlington NE22 ... 11 E3
Sunderland SR5 ... 75 C3
Grange Park Prim Sch SR5 ... 75 C2
Grange Pk NE25 ... 31 D4
Grange Pl NE32 ... 58 B7
Grange Rd
Gateshead NE10 ... 72 A7
Newburn NE15 ... 52 E8
Ponteland NE20 ... 25 F7
Newcastle-upon-Tyne, Gosforth NE3 ... 38 C7
Jarrow NE32 ... 58 B7
Newcastle-upon-Tyne, Fenham NE4 ... 54 D7
Ryton NE40 ... 52 C5
Morpeth NE61 ... 9 A6
Sunderland SR5 ... 85 A8
Grange Rd W NE32 ... 58 B7
Grange St S SR2 ... 86 F2
Grange Terr
Prudhoe NE42 ... 50 D2
Medomsley DH8 ... 77 B1
Kibblesworth NE11 ... 81 C6
1 East Boldon NE36 ... 74 D7
6 Gateshead NE9 ... 71 A8
Sunderland SR2 ... 103 A1
2 Sunderland, Southwick SR5 ... 75 B2
Grange The
Bedlington NE22 ... 10 A1
East Boldon NE36 ... 74 D7
Grange View
Newbottle DH4 ... 90 D3
East Rainton DH5 ... 94 D5
Ryton NE40 ... 52 C4
Sunderland SR5 ... 75 C3
Grange Villas NE28 ... 40 C2
Grange Wlk 3 NE16 ... 69 A5
Grangemere Cl SR2 ... 86 F1
Grangetown Prim Sch SR2 ... 86 F3
Grangeway NE29 ... 31 F1
Grangewood Cl DH4 ... 90 A5
Grangewood Ct 3 DH4 ... 90 A6
Grant St NE32 ... 58 A7
Grantham Dr NE9 ... 70 E4
Grantham Pl NE23 ... 22 A4
Grantham Rd
Newcastle-upon-Tyne NE2 ... 99 C3
Sunderland SR6 ... 75 E2
Grantham St NE24 ... 17 F6
Granville Ave
Longbenton NE12 ... 29 E1
Seaton Sluice NE26 ... 24 D5
Granville Cres NE12 ... 39 E7
Granville Ct NE2 ... 99 C4
Granville Dr
Shiney Row DH4 ... 90 C5
Longbenton NE12 ... 39 E7
Newcastle-upon-Tyne NE5 ... 36 D3
Granville Gdns
Newcastle-upon-Tyne NE2 ... 56 A8
Stakeford NE62 ... 11 A8
Granville Lodge NE12 ... 39 E8
Granville Rd
Newcastle-upon-Tyne, Jesmond NE2 ... 99 C4
Newcastle-upon-Tyne, Gosforth NE3 ... 38 D7
Granville St
Gateshead NE8 ... 101 C1
Sunderland SR4 ... 102 B3
Grasmere Birtley DH3 ... 82 E2
Cleadon SR6 ... 60 A1
Grasmere Ave
Easington Lane DH5 ... 97 C8
Gateshead NE10 ... 71 F8
Newburn NE15 ... 52 E7
Hedworth NE32 ... 58 D3
Newcastle-upon-Tyne NE6 ... 56 F5
Grasmere Cres
5 Penshaw DH4 ... 90 B6
Blaydon NE21 ... 68 B8
Whitley Bay NE26 ... 31 F7
Sunderland SR5 ... 75 C3
Sunderland, Monkwearmouth SR5 ... 75 C2
Grasmere Ct
Killingworth NE12 ... 29 C3
Newburn NE15 ... 52 E7
Grasmere Gdns
South Shields NE34 ... 59 E6
Washington NE38 ... 83 E4
Grasmere Ho NE6 ... 56 E5
Grasmere Pl NE3 ... 38 C7
Grasmere Rd
Chester le Street DH2 ... 88 B1
Whickham NE16 ... 69 C7
Wallsend NE28 ... 40 A1
Hebburn NE31 ... 57 F4
Grasmere St NE8 ... 101 B1
Grasmere St W NE8 ... 101 B1
Grasmere Terr
Washington NE38 ... 83 E5
Newbiggin-by-the-Sea NE64 ... 7 D4
Grasmere Way NE24 ... 17 A8
Grasmoor Pl NE15 ... 53 B7
Grassbanks NE10 ... 72 A6
Grassholm Pl NE12 ... 39 A7
Grassholme Mdws SR3 ... 86 B2
Grassington Dr NE23 ... 22 A4
Grasslees NE38 ... 88 F8
Grasswell Dr NE5 ... 37 D3
Gravel Wlks DH5 ... 90 F1
Gravesend Rd SR4 ... 85 B2
Gravesend Sq SR4 ... 85 C2
Gray Ave
Chester le Street DH2 ... 88 B2
Wide Open NE13 ... 28 C7
Gray Ct SR2 ... 86 D4
Gray Rd Sunderland SR2 ... 103 B1
Sunderland SR2 ... 103 C2
Gray St NE24 ... 12 E1
Gray's Wlk NE34 ... 59 A2
Graylands NE38 ... 88 E8
Grayling Ct SR3 ... 91 C5
Grayling Rd NE11 ... 70 B7
Grays Cross SR1 ... 103 B3
Grays Terr 7 NE35 ... 58 E1
Graystones NE10 ... 72 B6
Great Lime Rd
Killingworth NE12 ... 29 D1
Wide Open NE12,NE13, NE23 ... 29 A5
Killingworth NE12,NE3 ... 29 A3
Great North Rd
Newcastle-upon-Tyne, West Jesmond NE2 ... 38 D2
Newcastle-upon-Tyne, Gosforth NE3 ... 38 C7
Stannington NE61 ... 9 A2
Greathead St NE33 ... 59 B7
Grebe Cl Blyth NE24 ... 17 E5
Ashington NE63 ... 6 E1
Grebe Ct NE2 ... 38 F1
Greely Rd NE5 ... 36 F2
Green Acres
Ponteland NE20 ... 25 C1
Morpeth NE61 ... 8 E7
Green Ave DH4 ... 90 D4
Green Bank NE46 ... 45 C4
Green Cl Whitley Bay NE25 31 D4
Tynemouth NE30 ... 32 B1
Stannington NE61 ... 14 C4
Green Cres NE23 ... 28 F8
Green Gr NE40 ... 52 B3
Green Hill Wlk NE34 ... 60 C6
Green La Haswell DH6 ... 97 B3
Gateshead, Felling NE10 ... 56 D2
Gateshead, Pelaw NE10 ... 57 A1
Killingworth NE12 ... 29 E2
Woolsington NE13 ... 36 F8
Dudley NE23 ... 28 F8
South Shields NE34 ... 59 B4
Green La *continued*
East Boldon NE36 ... 74 E6
Morpeth NE61 ... 4 B1
Stannington NE61 ... 13 D2
Stannington, Duddo Hill NE61 ... 13 D5
Ashington NE63 ... 6 C3
Seaton SR7 ... 95 F6
Morpeth, Stobhillgate NE61 ... 9 B7
Green Lane Gdns NE10 ... 56 C2
Green Pk NE28 ... 39 E3
Green Sq NE25 ... 31 D4
Green St SR1 ... 103 A3
Green Terr SR1 ... 102 C2
Green The
Chester le Street DH2 ... 88 B3
Houghton-le-Spring DH5 ... 90 F1
Gateshead NE10 ... 71 E8
Walbottle NE15 ... 35 F1
Chopwell NE17 ... 77 B8
Ponteland NE20 ... 25 F7
Whitley Bay NE25 ... 31 E6
Newcastle-upon-Tyne NE3 ... 37 F3
Rowlands Gill NE39 ... 67 C2
Ovington NE42 ... 49 C4
Sunderland SR1 ... 102 C2
New Silksworth SR3 ... 92 C7
Sunderland, Southwick SR5 ... 75 A1
Green Way NE25 ... 31 D4
Green's Pl NE33 ... 42 C4
Green-Fields NE40 ... 52 B5
Greenacre Pk NE9 ... 70 E3
Greenacres Cl NE40 ... 52 A3
Greenbank Blaydon NE21 ... 53 C2
Jarrow NE32 ... 58 B7
Greenbank Dr SR4 ... 85 A5
Greenbank St 4 DH3 ... 88 D4
Greenbank Villas NE32 ... 58 B7
Greenbourne Gdns NE10 71 C7
Greencroft NE63 ... 6 C2
Greencroft Ave
Corbridge NE45 ... 47 A6
Newcastle-upon-Tyne NE6 ... 57 A8
Greendale Cl NE24 ... 17 A8
Greendale Gdns DH5 ... 94 F2
Greendyke Ct NE5 ... 37 A5
Greener Ct NE42 ... 50 B1
Greenesfield Bsns Ctr NE8 ... 101 B3
Greenfield Ave NE5 ... 37 A2
Greenfield Dr NE62 ... 10 E6
Greenfield Pl
Newcastle-upon-Tyne NE4 ... 98 C1
Ryton NE40 ... 52 D5
Greenfield Rd NE3 ... 28 B1
Greenfield Terr 2 NE10 ... 56 F1
Greenfields DH2 ... 82 A2
Greenfields Com Prim Sch NE13 ... 28 C6
Greenfields Specl Sch NE31 ... 58 A6
Greenfinch Cl NE38 ... 82 F3
Greenford NE11 ... 81 D6
Greenford La DH2,NE11 ... 81 F6
Greenford Rd NE6 ... 57 A4
Greenhaugh NE12 ... 29 B1
Greenhaugh Rd NE25 ... 31 B5
Greenhead NE38 ... 82 F4
Greenhead Rd NE17 ... 66 B3
Greenhead Terr NE17 ... 66 B2
Greenhill View NE5 ... 37 E2
Greenhills NE12 ... 29 D5
Greenholme Cl NE23 ... 16 B1
Greenhow Cl SR2 ... 92 F5
Greenlands NE32 ... 58 C2
Greenlands Ct NE25 ... 23 D4
Greenlaw NE5 ... 53 E8
Greenlaw Rd NE23 ... 22 A3
Greenlea NE29 ... 31 B1
Greenlea Cl
High Spen NE39 ... 67 A3
Sunderland SR4 ... 85 C3
Greenlee NE63 ... 6 E2
Greenlee Dr NE7 ... 39 D3
Greenock Rd SR4 ... 85 B2
Greenrigg Blaydon NE21 ... 53 D1
Seaton Sluice NE26 ... 24 C6
Greenrigg Gdns 2 SR3 ... 86 B3
Greenriggs Ave NE3 ... 28 D1
Greenrising NE42 ... 49 D4
Greenshields Rd SR4 ... 85 B2
Greenshields Sq 5 SR4 ... 85 B2
Greenside NE34 ... 60 B6
Greenside Ave
Brunswick Village NE13 ... 28 A6
Wallsend NE28 ... 40 F3
Greenside Cres NE15 ... 54 A7
Greenside Ho NE24 ... 17 B8
Greenside Prim Sch NE40 ... 51 F1
Greenside Rd
Crawcrook NE40 ... 51 F2
Crawcrook NE40 ... 51 F3
Greentree Sq NE5 ... 37 B2
Greenway
Newcastle-upon-Tyne, Fenham NE4 ... 54 D8
Newcastle-upon-Tyne, Westerhope NE5 ... 36 D4
Greenway The SR4 ... 85 C4
Greenwell Cl NE21 ... 53 A1
Greenwell Dr NE42 ... 50 D3
Greenwell Terr NE40 ... 51 E4
Greenwich Pl NE8 ... 56 A4
Greenwood NE12 ... 29 F3
Greenwood Ave
Bedlington NE22 ... 11 D3
Newcastle-upon-Tyne NE6 ... 40 A1
Greenwood Gdns
Gateshead NE10 ... 56 D2
Dunston NE11 ... 70 B5
Greenwood Rd SR4 ... 85 B3
Greenwood Sq 3 SR4 ... 85 B2
Greetlands Rd SR2 ... 86 C2
Gregory Rd 8 SR4 ... 85 B2
Gregory Terr DH4 ... 90 A1
Gregson Terr SR7 ... 92 F1
Grenada Cl NE26 ... 31 F8
Grenada Dr NE26 ... 31 F8
Grenada Pl NE26 ... 31 F8
Grenfell Sq 7 SR4 ... 85 B2
Grenville Ct
Ponteland NE20 ... 25 A4
Cramlington NE23 ... 22 A5
Grenville Dr NE3 ... 28 B1
Grenville Terr NE1 ... 99 C1
Grenville Way NE26 ... 31 E7
Grenwood Ave DH4 ... 94 C8
Gresford St NE33 ... 59 C6
Gresham Cl NE23 ... 22 B4
Greta Ave DH4 ... 90 A6
Greta Gdns NE33 ... 59 D8
Greta Terr SR4 ... 102 A1
Gretna Dr NE32 ... 58 F2
Gretna Rd NE15 ... 54 B6
Gretton Pl NE7 ... 39 A3
Grey Ave NE23 ... 22 A3
Grey Lady Wlk NE42 ... 50 D3
Grey Pl 10 NE61 ... 9 A8
Grey St
Houghton-le-Spring DH4 ... 90 D1
Newcastle-upon-Tyne NE1 ... 99 A1
Brunswick Village NE13 ... 28 A6
Wallsend NE28 ... 40 C2
North Shields NE30 ... 42 B6
Grey Terr 10 SR2 ... 92 F6
Grey's Ct NE1 ... 99 A1
Greybourne Gdns SR2 ... 86 C2
Greyfriars La NE12 ... 39 A6
Greystead Cl NE5 ... 36 D3
Greystead Rd NE25 ... 31 B5
Greystoke Ave
Whickham NE16 ... 69 B5
Newcastle-upon-Tyne NE2 ... 56 A7
Sunderland SR2 ... 86 C2
Greystoke Gdns
Whickham NE16 ... 69 B5
Newcastle-upon-Tyne NE2 ... 56 A8
10 Morpeth NE61 ... 3 F1
Gateshead NE9 ... 71 B2
Sunderland SR2 ... 86 C3
Greystoke Pk NE3 ... 38 C8
Greystoke Pl NE23 ... 22 A3
Greystoke Wlk 2 NE16 ... 69 A5
Greystone Pl SR5 ... 75 A2
Greywood Ave NE4 ... 54 E7
Grieve St NE24 ... 12 D1
Grieves' Row NE23 ... 22 A1
Griffith Terr 7 NE27 ... 30 E1
Grimsby St NE24 ... 17 E6
Grindleford Ct NE34 ... 59 E5
Grindon Ave SR4 ... 85 B5
Grindon Cl
Cramlington NE23 ... 22 A3
Whitley Bay NE25 ... 31 E2
Grindon Ct SR4 ... 85 C3
Grindon Gdns SR4 ... 85 C3
Grindon Hall Christian Sch SR4 ... 85 C4
Grindon Inf Sch SR4 ... 85 B2
Grindon La
Sunderland, Springwell SR3, SR4 ... 85 D3
Sunderland, South Hylton SR4 ... 85 B5
Grindon Mus★ SR4 ... 85 C3
Grindon Pk SR4 ... 85 C3
Grindon Terr SR4 ... 102 A1
Grinstead Cl NE34 ... 59 F7
Grisedale Gdns NE9 ... 71 A3
Grizedale NE37 ... 83 B6
Grizedale Ct SR6 ... 75 C5
Groat Mkt NE1 ... 99 A1
Grosvenor Ave
Whickham NE16 ... 69 B8
Newcastle-upon-Tyne NE2 ... 38 F1
Grosvenor Cl NE23 ... 22 A3
Grosvenor Cres NE31 ... 57 F4
Grosvenor Ct NE5 ... 36 D3
Grosvenor Dr
Whitley Bay NE26 ... 32 A4
South Shields NE34 ... 59 F8
Cleadon SR6 ... 74 E8
Grosvenor Gdns
Newcastle-upon-Tyne NE2 ... 56 A8
Wallsend NE28 ... 41 A3
South Shields NE34 ... 59 F6
Grosvenor Mews
1 North Shields NE29 ... 42 A6
4 South Shields NE33 ... 59 E8
Grosvenor Pl
Newcastle-upon-Tyne NE2 ... 38 F1
North Shields NE29 ... 42 A6
Grosvenor Rd
Newcastle-upon-Tyne NE2 ... 38 F1
South Shields NE33 ... 59 E8
Grosvenor St SR5 ... 75 A2
Grosvenor Villas NE2 ... 38 F1
Grosvenor Way NE5 ... 36 D3
Grotto Gdns NE34 ... 60 D6
Grotto Rd NE34 ... 60 D6
Grousemoor 2 NE37 ... 83 A7
Grousemoor Dr NE63 ... 6 C1
Grove Ave NE3 ... 38 D4
Grove Cotts 8 DH3 ... 82 C4
Grove Rd Walbottle NE15 ... 35 F2
Grove Rd *continued*
Gateshead NE9 ... 71 A6
Grove Terr
Burnopfield NE16 ... 79 B6
Sunniside NE16 ... 69 B1
Grove The
Houghton-le-Spring DH5 ... 94 D6
Longbenton NE12 ... 39 D6
Whickham NE16 ... 69 C6
Newcastle-upon-Tyne, Jesmond NE2 ... 38 F2
Ponteland NE20 ... 25 D5
Whitley Bay NE25 ... 31 F4
Newcastle-upon-Tyne, Gosforth NE3 ... 38 D4
Hedworth NE32 ... 73 B8
Rowlands Gill NE39 ... 67 F1
Stocksfield NE43 ... 64 C3
Newcastle-upon-Tyne, West Denton NE5 ... 36 D1
Ryhope SR2 ... 92 F6
Sunderland, Ashbrooke SR2 86 D4
6 Sunderland, Castletown SR5 ... 74 B1
Guardian Ct NE26 ... 32 C4
Guardians Ct NE20 ... 25 F7
Gubeon Wood NE61 ... 8 C2
Guelder Rd NE7 ... 39 C3
Guernsey Rd SR4 ... 85 B2
Guernsey Sq SR4 ... 85 B2
Guessburn NE43 ... 64 B6
Guide Post Mid Sch NE62 ... 10 F7
Guide Post Ringway Fst Sch NE62 ... 10 F8
Guildford Pl NE6 ... 56 B7
Guildford Sq NE61 ... 2 A3
Guildford St SR2 ... 86 E4
Guillemot Cl NE24 ... 17 E5
Guillemot Row NE12 ... 29 C4
Guisborough Dr NE29 ... 41 B8
Guisborough St SR4 ... 85 F5
Gullane NE37 ... 72 D3
Gullane Cl NE10 ... 57 C2
Gunn St NE11 ... 69 F8
Gunnerston Gr 1 NE3 ... 37 D5
Gunnerton Cl NE23 ... 22 B4
Gunnerton Pl NE29 ... 41 D6
Gut Rd NE28 ... 40 F1
Guyzance Ave NE3 ... 38 B6
Gypsies Green Sports Gd NE33 ... 42 F2

H

Hackwood Pk NE46 ... 45 B3
Hackworth Gdns NE41 ... 51 B6
Hackworth Way NE29 ... 41 F3
Haddington Rd NE25 ... 31 D7
Haddon Cl NE25 ... 31 B5
Haddon Gn NE25 ... 31 B5
Haddricksmill Ct NE3 ... 38 E4
Haddricksmill Rd NE2, NE3 ... 38 E4
Hadleigh Ct 9 DH4 ... 90 B6
Hadleigh Rd SR4 ... 85 D5
Hadrian Ave DH3 ... 88 D5
Hadrian Ct
Killingworth NE12 ... 29 E3
Ponteland NE20 ... 25 B1
Hadrian Gdns NE21 ... 53 D1
Hadrian Ho 2 NE15 ... 35 D2
Hadrian Hospl NE28 ... 40 C4
Hadrian Jun Mixed & Inf Sch NE33 ... 42 C4
Hadrian Lodge NE34 ... 58 F5
Hadrian Park Fst Sch NE28 ... 40 E7
Hadrian Park Mid Sch NE28 ... 40 E7
Hadrian Pl Walbottle NE15 35 E2
Gateshead NE9 ... 71 B7
Hadrian Rd Blyth NE24 ... 17 C3
Wallsend NE28 ... 40 D1
Jarrow NE32 ... 58 D4
Newcastle-upon-Tyne NE4 ... 54 E6
Hadrian Road Sta NE28 ... 40 E2
Hadrian St SR4 ... 102 A3
Hadrian's Wall (N.T.)★ NE47 ... 127 D4
Hadrian's Wall (N.T.)★ NE49 ... 126 D3
Hadrians Ct NE11 ... 70 D3
Hadrians Way DH8 ... 76 E3
Hadstone Pl 5 NE5 ... 37 C1
Hagg Bank Cotts NE41 ... 50 F5
Haggerston Cl NE5 ... 37 B4
Haggerston Cres NE5 ... 37 B4
Haggerston Ct NE5 ... 37 B4
Haggerston Terr NE32 ... 58 E4
Haggerstone Dr SR5 ... 85 A8
Haggie Ave NE28 ... 40 D3
Hahnemann Ct SR5 ... 75 B2
Haig Ave NE25 ... 31 F3
Haig Cres NE15 ... 54 B5
Haig Rd NE22 ... 16 B8
Haig St NE11 ... 69 F8
Haigh Terr NE9 ... 71 C1
Hailsham Ave NE12 ... 39 C7
Haininghead NE38 ... 83 E2
Hainingwood Terr NE10 ... 57 B2
Haldane Ct NE2 ... 99 B4
Haldane St NE63 ... 6 C4
Haldane Terr NE2 ... 99 B4
Halewood Ave NE3 ... 37 E4
Half Fields Rd NE21 ... 53 B1

Half Moon La
Tynemouth NE30 .42 D7
Gateshead NE8 .101 B2
Half Moon St NE62 .11 B8
Halidon Rd SR2 .86 D1
Halidon Sq SR2 .86 D1
Halifax Pl Dunston NE11 .54 E1
9 Sunderland SR2 .92 F6
Halifax Rd NE11 .54 E1
Halkirk Way NE23 .16 A1
Hall Ave NE4 .54 E6
Hall Cl West Rainton DH4 .94 A2
Seaton SR7 .92 D1
Hall Dene Way SR7 .92 F2
Hall Dr NE12 .29 C5
Hall Farm Cl NE43 .64 B8
Hall Farm Rd SR3 .92 A5
Hall Garth NE3 .38 C8
Hall Gdns Sherburn DH6 .96 A1
Gateshead NE10 .71 D7
Seaton Sluice NE26 .24 A6
West Boldon NE36 .74 A7
Hall Gn NE24 .17 B7
Hall La West Rainton DH4 .94 A2
Houghton-le-Spring DH5 .94 F7
Haswell DH6 .97 F3
Hall Pk NE21 .53 A4
Hall Rd Chopwell NE17 .66 C2
Hebburn NE31 .57 E5
Washington NE37 .83 E8
Hall Road Bglws NE17 .66 B2
Hall Terr Gateshead NE10 .57 B2
Blyth NE24 .17 E8
Hall View SR6 .75 F8
Halleypike C NE7 .39 D3
Hallfield Cl SR3 .92 A5
Hallgarth NE10 .72 A7
Hallgarth Ct SR6 .75 F1
Hallgarth La DH6 .96 B5
Hallgarth Rd NE21 .53 B2
Hallgarth View DH6 .96 C5
Hallgarth Villas DH6 .96 A1
Hallgate NE46 .45 B5
Halling Cl NE6 .57 A4
Hallington Dr NE25 .23 D3
Hallington Mews NE12 .29 C3
Halliwell St DH4 .90 D1
Hallorchard Rd NE46 .45 B5
Hallow Dr NE15 .35 D1
Hallside Rd NE24 .17 B6
Hallstile Bank NE46 .45 B5
Hallwood Cl NE22 .15 A8
Halstead Pl 2 NE33 .42 D1
Halstead Sq SR4 .85 D5
Halterburn Cl NE3 .38 A4
Halton Cl NE43 .64 D6
Halton Dr Wide Open NE13 28 C6
Backworth NE27 .30 D3
Hamar Cl NE29 .41 C4
Hambard Way NE38 .83 D4
Hambledon Ave DH2 .88 B2
Hambledon Ave NE30 .32 A3
Hambledon Cl NE35 .73 E8
Hambledon Gdns NE7 .39 A3
Hambledon St NE24 .17 D8
Hambleton Ct NE63 .6 F1
Hambleton Gn NE9 .71 B1
Hambleton Rd NE38 .83 B3
Hamilton Cres
Tynemouth NE29 .41 C8
Newcastle-upon-Tyne NE4 .98 B2
Hamilton Ct SR6 .75 F2
Hamilton Dr NE26 .31 F8
Hamilton Pl NE4 .98 B2
Hamilton Terr
West Boldon NE36 .74 A7
9 Morpeth NE61 .9 A8
Hamilton Way 2 NE26 .31 F8
Hammer Square Bank
DH9 .80 F1
Hampden Rd SR6 .75 E2
Hampden St NE33 .59 C8
Hampshire Ct NE4 .100 A2
Hampshire Gdns NE28 .40 E4
Hampshire Pl NE37 .72 D1
Hampshire Way NE34 .60 C7
Hampstead Cl NE24 .17 C3
Hampstead Gdns NE32 .58 D2
Hampstead Rd
Newcastle-upon-Tyne NE4 .54 E5
Sunderland SR4 .85 D4
Hampstead Sq SR4 .85 C4
Hampton Cl NE23 .22 D7
Hampton Ct
Chester le Street DH3 .88 D7
Whickham NE16 .54 B1
Hampton Dr
Gateshead NE10 .71 C8
Whitley Bay NE25 .31 C4
Hampton Rd NE30 .32 A2
Hamsterley Cres
Newcastle-upon-Tyne NE15 .53 B7
Gateshead NE9 .71 C3
Hamsterley Ct 6 SR3 .92 A6
Hamsterley Dr NE12 .29 C4
Hanby Gdns SR3 .86 A3
Hancock Mus★ NE2 .99 A3
Hancock St NE1,NE2 .99 A3
Handel St NE33 .42 D2
Handley Cres DH5 .94 C4
Handley Cross DH8 .77 C2
Handy Dr NE11 .54 E2
Hangmans La SR3,SR7 .91 E3
Hanlon Ct Hebburn NE32 .57 F7
Jarrow NE32 .58 A8
Hann Terr NE37 .83 F8
Hannington Pl 3 NE6 .56 A6
Hannington St 2 NE6 .56 A6
Hanover Cl 2 NE5 .36 C2
Hanover Ct
Annitsford NE23 .22 B1
5 Gateshead NE9 .71 A2
Hanover Dr NE21 .53 A1
Hanover Gdns 3 NE28 .41 A1
Hanover House NE32 .58 B4
Hanover Pl
Cramlington NE23 .16 A2
Sunderland SR4 .102 B4
Hanover Sq NE1 .101 A4
Hanover St NE1 .101 A4
Hanover Wlk
Blaydon NE21 .68 A8
1 Newcastle-upon-Tyne NE5 .36 C2
Harbord Terr NE26 .23 F5
Harbottle Ave
Shiremoor NE27 .31 A2
Newcastle-upon-Tyne NE3 .38 A6
Harbottle Cres NE32 .58 B2
Harbottle Ct NE6 .56 C4
Harbottle St 4 NE6 .56 C4
Harbour Dr NE33 .42 E4
Harbour The DH4 .90 B6
Harbour View
Cambois NE22 .12 B3
South Shields NE33 .42 D5
Sunderland SR6 .75 F2
Harcourt Pk 1 NE9 .71 A5
Harcourt Rd SR2 .86 D1
Harcourt St 2 NE9 .71 A5
Hardgate Rd SR2 .86 D1
Hardie Ave NE16 .69 A8
Hardie Dr NE36 .74 B7
Hardman Gdns NE40 .52 D5
Hardwick Ct NE8 .56 A1
Hardwick Pl NE3 .38 A3
Hardwick Rise SR6 .103 B4
Hardy Ave NE34 .59 B3
Hardy Ct 5 NE30 .42 B6
Hardy Gr NE28 .40 A5
Hardy Sq SR5 .75 A2
Hardyards Ct NE34 .59 C5
Harebell Rd NE9 .71 C4
Harehills Ave NE5 .37 D3
Harehills Tower NE3 .37 E3
Harelaw Dr NE63 .6 B1
Harelaw Gr NE5 .36 D1
Hareshaw Rd NE25 .31 B5
Hareside NE23 .22 A5
Hareside Cl NE15 .52 F8
Hareside Ct NE15 .52 F8
Hareside Wlk NE15 .52 F8
Harewood Cl
Whickham NE16 .69 A4
Whitley Bay NE25 .31 B4
Harewood Cres NE25 .31 B4
Harewood Ct NE25 .31 B4
Harewood Dr NE22 .11 C2
Harewood Gdns
Pegswood NE61 .4 E4
Sunderland SR3 .86 A3
Harewood Gn NE9 .71 B2
Harewood Rd NE3 .38 C6
Hareydene NE5 .36 F5
Hargill Dr NE38 .83 A1
Hargrave Ct NE24 .17 C6
Harland Way NE38 .83 D5
Harle Cl NE5 .36 E1
Harle Rd NE27 .30 D3
Harle St NE28 .40 B2
Harlebury NE27 .30 C1
Harlequin Lodge 9 NE10 .71 D8
Harleston Way NE10 .71 E6
Harley Terr NE3 .38 D5
Harlow Ave
Backworth NE27 .30 D3
Newcastle-upon-Tyne NE3 .37 F7
Harlow Cl NE23 .16 A1
Harlow Green Com Inf Sch NE9 .71 A2
Harlow Green Jun Sch NE9 .71 A2
Harlow Green La NE9 .71 A2
Harlow Pl NE7 .39 B3
Harlow St SR4 .102 B2
Harnham Ave NE29 .41 D5
Harnham Gdns NE5 .37 C1
Harnham Gr NE23 .22 A5
Harold Sq SR2 .103 B1
Harold St NE32 .58 C7
Harper St NE24 .17 D7
Harperley Dr SR3 .86 B2
Harperley La DH9 .79 B1
Harraby Gdns NE9 .71 B3
Harras Bank DH3 .82 C3
Harraton Prim Sch NE38 .83 B1
Harraton Terr
12 Birtley DH3 .82 C4
Bournmoor DH3 .89 C7
Harriet Pl 21 NE6 .56 C6
Harriet St Blaydon NE21 .53 C2
Newcastle-upon-Tyne NE6 .56 D6
Harrington Gdns NE62 .11 C8
Harrington St 6 NE28 .40 B2
Harriot Dr NE12 .29 B2
Harrison Ct Birtley DH3 .82 C3
Annitsford NE23 .29 B8
Harrison Gdns NE8 .70 D7
Harrison Pl NE2 .99 B3
Harrison Rd NE28 .41 A3
Harrogate St SR2 .103 B1
Harrow Cres DH4 .90 A6
Harrow Gdns NE13 .28 C5
Harrow Sq SR4 .85 D5
Harrow St NE27 .30 E4
Harrow's Scar Milecastle★ CA6 .126 A3
Hart Ct SR1 .103 A3
Hart Sq SR4 .85 E5
Hart Terr SR6 .75 F6
Hartburn NE10 .72 A6
Hartburn Dr NE5 .36 D3
Hartburn Pl NE4 .54 F7
Hartburn Rd NE30 .32 A1
Hartburn Terr NE25 .23 D3
Hartburn Wlk NE3 .37 D5
Hartford NE12 .29 D5
Hartford Bank NE23 .15 C4
Hartford Bridge Farm NE22 .15 C5
Hartford Cres
Bedlington NE22 .15 E8
Ashington NE63 .6 D2
Hartford Ct NE22 .15 E8
Hartford Dr NE22 .15 C5
Hartford House NE4 .98 B2
Hartford Rd
Bedlington NE22 .15 D6
Nedderton NE22 .15 D6
Newcastle-upon-Tyne NE3 .38 D7
South Shields NE34 .59 A5
Sunderland SR4 .85 D5
Hartford Rd E NE22 .15 F8
Hartford St 1 NE6 .56 C8
Hartforth Cres NE10 .57 C1
Harthope NE61 .1 E5
Harthope Ave SR5 .74 C3
Harthope Cl NE38 .88 F8
Harthope Dr NE29 .41 E3
Hartington Rd NE30 .32 B2
Hartington St
Newcastle-upon-Tyne NE4 .98 A1
Gateshead NE8 .101 C1
Sunderland SR6 .75 E1
Hartington Terr NE33 .59 D8
Hartland Dr DH3 .82 D3
Hartlands NE22 .15 E8
Hartleigh Pl NE24 .17 B7
Hartley Ave NE26 .31 E5
Hartley Ct
Brunswick Village NE13 .27 F5
New Hartley NE25 .23 D6
Hartley Gdns NE25 .23 C3
Hartley Ho NE26 .31 F5
Hartley La Holywell NE25 .31 B7
Whitley Bay NE25,NE26 .24 C2
Hartley Sq NE26 .24 D4
Hartley St
Seaton Delaval NE25 .23 C3
Sunderland SR1 .103 C3
Hartley St N NE25 .23 C3
Hartley Terr NE24 .17 C4
Hartleyburn Ave NE31 .57 D3
Hartoft Cl DH4 .90 D3
Harton Comp Sch NE34 .60 A6
Harton Cty Inf Sch NE34 .60 B6
Harton Gr NE34 .59 E7
Harton House Rd NE34 .59 F7
Harton House Rd E NE34 60 A7
Harton Jun Mix Sch NE34 .60 A6
Harton La NE34 .59 D6
Harton Quay NE33 .42 B2
Harton Rise NE34 .60 A7
Harton View NE36 .74 A7
Hartside Birtley DH3 .82 D1
Newcastle-upon-Tyne NE15 .53 C7
Hartside Cres
Blaydon NE21 .68 A8
Cramlington NE23 .16 A2
Backworth NE27 .30 D4
Hartside Gdns
Easington Lane DH5 .95 C1
Newcastle-upon-Tyne NE2 .38 F1
Hartside Pl NE3 .28 C1
Hartside Rd SR4 .85 D4
Hartside Sq SR4 .85 D4
Harvest Cl SR3 .91 F5
Harvey Cl
Washington NE38 .82 F5
Ashington NE63 .7 A3
Harvey Combe NE12 .29 B3
Harvey Cres NE10 .72 B8
Harwood Cl
Cramlington NE23 .22 A5
Washington NE38 .83 A1
Harwood Ct SR6 .75 E1
Harwood Dr NE12 .30 A3
Hascombe Cl NE25 .31 D6
Haslemere Dr SR3 .86 A3
Hassop Way NE22 .10 F2
Hasting Hill Prim Sch SR3 .85 C1
Hastings Ave
Longbenton NE12 .39 D7
Seaton Sluice NE26 .24 B7
Whitley Bay NE26 .24 F1
Newcastle-upon-Tyne NE3 .37 D7
Hastings Ct
Bedlington NE22 .11 C2
New Hartley NE25 .23 D6
Hastings Dr NE30 .42 C8
Hastings Gdns NE25 .23 D6
Hastings Par NE31 .58 A3
Hastings St
Cramlington NE23 .22 C5
Sunderland SR2 .86 E3
Hastings Terr
Cramlington NE23 .16 D1
New Hartley NE25 .23 D7
Sunderland SR2 .86 F3
Haswell Cl NE10 .72 D7
Haswell Gdns NE30 .42 A6
Haswell Prim Sch DH6 .97 E3
Hatfield Ave NE31 .57 F6
Hatfield Dr NE23 .23 A2
Hatfield Gdns
Whitley Bay NE25 .31 B5
Sunderland SR3 .86 A3
Hatfield Sq 11 NE33 .42 D3
Hathaway Gdns SR3 .86 A3
Hathersage Gdns NE34 .59 D5
Hatherton Ave NE30 .32 B3
Hathery La NE24 .16 D5
Haugh La
Ryton, Ryton Haugh NE21 .53 A5
Ryton NE21,NE40 .52 E6
Hexham NE46 .45 B5
Haughs The NE42 .50 D3
Haughton Cres
Hedworth NE32 .58 B2
Newcastle-upon-Tyne NE5 .36 E1
Haughton Ct NE4 .100 A3
Haughton Terr NE24 .17 E7
Hautmont Rd NE31 .57 F4
Hauxley NE12 .29 D5
Hauxley Dr
Cramlington NE23 .16 A1
Newcastle-upon-Tyne NE3 .37 F7
Hauxley Gdns NE5 .37 D2
Havanna NE12 .29 D5
Havannah Cres NE13 .27 B6
Havannah Rd NE37 .83 B7
Havant Gdns NE13 .28 B7
Havard Rd NE3 .37 E6
Havelock Cl NE8 .101 B2
Havelock Cres NE22 .11 F3
Havelock Ct SR4 .85 D6
Havelock Ho SR4 .85 D6
Havelock Mews NE22 .11 F3
Havelock Pl NE4 .98 B1
Havelock Prim Sch SR4 .85 D6
Havelock Rd NE27 .30 D3
Havelock St Blyth NE24 .17 E8
South Shields NE33 .42 B1
South Shields NE33 .42 C1
Sunderland SR1 .103 C3
Havelock Terr
Tantobie DH9 .79 B2
Chopwell NE17 .66 B1
Jarrow NE32 .58 B5
Gateshead NE8 .101 B2
Sunderland SR2 .102 B1
Haven Ct Blyth NE24 .17 C6
Sunderland SR6 .75 F1
Haven The Penshaw DH4 .90 B6
North Shields NE29 .42 A3
Prudhoe NE42 .50 D2
Haven View NE64 .7 E4
Havercroft NE10 .72 B7
Haverley Dr SR7 .92 E1
Haversham CL NE7 .39 A5
Haversham Pk SR5 .75 C5
Hawarden Cres SR4 .102 A1
Hawes Ave DH2 .88 C1
Hawes Ct SR6 .75 C5
Hawesdale Cres NE21 .68 B8
Haweswater Cl NE34 .59 D6
Haweswater Cres NE64 .7 C4
Hawick Cres NE6 .56 B4
Hawk Terr DH3 .82 E2
Hawkesley Rd SR4 .85 D5
Hawkey's La NE29 .41 F6
Hawkhills Terr DH3 .82 C5
Hawkhurst NE38 .83 E2
Hawkins Ct SR3 .91 F6
Hawks Rd NE8 .101 C4
Hawks St NE8 .56 A4
Hawksbury NE16 .69 A7
Hawksfeld NE10 .71 E4
Hawkshead Ct NE3 .37 D7
Hawkshead Pl NE9 .71 B4
Hawksley NE5 .36 F2
Hawksmoor Cl NE63 .6 C1
Hawkwell Rise NE15 .35 D1
Hawsker Cl SR3 .92 C7
Hawthorn Ave
Brunswick Village NE13 .28 A6
New Silksworth SR3 .92 B8
Hawthorn Cl NE16 .69 B5
Hawthorn Cres NE38 .83 C1
Hawthorn Dr
Dunston NE11 .69 F8
Hedworth NE32 .58 D2
Hawthorn Gdns
5 Gateshead NE10 .56 D1
Whitley Bay NE26 .31 F5
Tynemouth NE29 .41 F7
Newcastle-upon-Tyne NE3 .37 F4
Ryton NE40 .52 E4
Hawthorn Gr NE28 .40 B2
Hawthorn Mews NE3 .38 C4
Hawthorn Pl
Killingworth NE12 .29 C4
Newcastle-upon-Tyne NE4 100 B4
Hawthorn Prim Sch NE4 .100 A4
Hawthorn Rd
Blaydon NE21 .53 C1
Newcastle-upon-Tyne NE3 .38 C4
Ashington NE63 .6 E3
Hawthorn Rd W NE3 .38 C4
Hawthorn St
Burnside DH4 .90 C2
Jarrow NE32 .58 A7
Walbottle NE5 .35 F2
Sunderland SR4 .102 A2
Hawthorn Terr
Chester le Street DH3 .88 D2
Newcastle-upon-Tyne NE4 100 A4
Crawcrook NE40 .51 E3
Hawthorn Terr *continued*
Gateshead NE9 .71 D1
Sunderland SR6 .75 E6
Hawthorn Villas NE23 .22 D6
Hawthorn Way NE20 .25 D3
Hawthorn Wlk NE4 .100 B4
Hawthorne Ave
Hebburn NE31 .57 F6
South Shields NE34 .59 F4
Hawthorne Gdns NE9 .70 F6
Hawthorne Rd NE24 .17 F7
Hawthorne Terr DH9 .79 D3
Hawthorns The
East Boldon NE36 .74 D7
Newcastle-upon-Tyne NE4 100 A3
Gateshead NE9 .71 D1
Hay St SR5 .102 C4
Haydock Dr NE10 .72 C7
Haydon NE38 .83 E1
Haydon Cl NE3 .37 F8
Haydon Dr NE25 .31 F3
Haydon Gdns NE27 .30 D4
Haydon Rd NE63 .6 D2
Haydon Sq SR4 .85 D5
Hayes Wlk NE13 .28 B6
Hayfield La NE16 .69 B6
Hayhole Rd NE29 .41 E2
Haylands Sq NE34 .59 D5
Hayleazes Rd NE15 .53 F7
Haymarket NE1 .99 A2
Haymarket La NE1 .99 A2
Haymarket Sta NE1 .99 A2
Haynyng The NE10 .71 E7
Hayricks The DH9 .79 D4
Hayton Ave NE34 .60 A5
Hayton Cl NE23 .22 C7
Hayton Rd NE30 .32 A2
Hayward Ave NE25 .23 D3
Hazard La
Hetton le Hole DH5 .94 E3
West Rainton DH5 .94 E3
Hazel Ave
3 Houghton-le-Spring DH4 94 C8
Tynemouth NE29 .41 F7
New Silksworth SR3 .92 B8
Hazel Gr
Chester le Street DH2 .88 A5
Killingworth NE12 .29 B2
Burnopfield NE16 .79 C6
South Shields NE34 .59 F4
Ellington NE61 .1 E5
Hazel Rd Blaydon NE21 .53 D2
Gateshead NE8 .70 C8
Hazel St NE32 .58 A7
Hazel Terr DH4 .90 C2
Hazeldene
Whitley Bay NE25 .31 E5
Hedworth NE32 .73 C8
Hazeldene Ave NE3 .37 C5
Hazeldene Ct NE30 .42 C7
Hazeley Gr 4 NE3 .37 D5
Hazeley Way NE3 .37 D5
Hazelgrove NE10 .72 B7
Hazelmere Ave
Bedlington NE22 .10 E1
Newcastle-upon-Tyne NE3 .28 D1
Hazelmere Cres NE23 .22 C8
Hazelmere Dene NE23 .22 E1
Hazelmoor NE31 .57 D7
Hazelwood NE12 .29 F3
Hazelwood Ave
Newcastle-upon-Tyne NE2 .38 E2
Newbiggin-by-the-Sea NE64 .7 D5
Sunderland SR5 .74 F2
Hazelwood Cl NE9 .71 D2
Hazelwood Com Prim Sch NE13 .28 B5
Hazelwood Gdns NE38 .83 C1
Hazelwood Terr NE28 .41 A3
Hazledene Terr 2 SR4 .85 F6
Hazlitt Ave NE34 .59 B3
Hazlitt Pl NE23 .23 A1
Headlam Gn 2 NE6 .56 C5
Headlam Ho 11 NE6 .56 C6
Headlam St 3 NE6 .56 C6
Headlam View NE28 .41 A2
Healey Dr SR3 .86 B2
Heartsbourne Dr NE34 .59 F3
Heath Cl NE11 .70 B7
Heath Cres NE15 .54 A4
Heath Grange DH5 .90 E1
Heath Sq SR4 .85 E5
Heathcote Gn NE5 .37 B3
Heathdale Gdns NE7 .39 B3
Heather Cl SR6 .60 A2
Heather Dr DH5 .95 A5
Heather Gr NE10 .56 B2
Heather Lea DH9 .78 E2
Heather Lea La NE42 .50 D3
Heather Pl
Newcastle-upon-Tyne NE4 .54 E8
Crawcrook NE40 .52 A4
Heather Terr NE16 .79 B6
Heatherdale Terr NE9 .71 B3
Heatherlaw
Washington NE37 .82 F6
Gateshead NE9 .71 C5
Heatherlea Gdns 1 SR3 .86 B3
Heatherlee Gdns NE62 .11 A8
Heatherslaw Light Railway★ TD12 .107 B7
Heatherslaw Rd NE5 .54 C8
Heatherwell Gn NE10 .71 C7
Heathery La NE3 .38 E7
Heatheryhill NE46 .44 A4

Heathfield Morpeth NE61 9 B6
Sunderland SR2 86 C2
Heathfield Cres NE5 37 D3
Heathfield Farm NE40 52 A1
Heathfield Gdns NE40 52 A1
Heathfield Pl NE3 28 D1
Heathfield Rd NE9 70 F6
Heathway NE32 58 C2
Heathwell Gdns NE16 69 B8
Heathwell Rd NE15 53 F7
Heathwood Ave 1 NE16 69 A7
Heaton Cl NE6 56 B7
Heaton Gdns NE34 59 C2
Heaton Gr NE6 56 B7
Heaton Hall Rd NE6 56 B7
Heaton Manor Sch (Lower) NE7 39 A2
Heaton Manor Sch (Upper) NE7 39 C4
Heaton Park Ct 9 NE6 56 B7
Heaton Park Rd NE6 56 B7
Heaton Park View NE6 56 B7
Heaton Pl NE6 56 B6
Heaton Rd NE6 56 B7
Heaton Terr
North Shields NE29 41 E6
Newcastle-upon-Tyne NE6 56 A6
Heaton Wlk 4 NE6 56 B6
Hebburn Comp Sch NE31 57 E4
Hebburn Hospl NE31 57 D4
Hebburn St Aloysius RC Inf Sch NE31 57 E7
Hebburn Sta NE31 57 D6
Heber St NE1 98 C1
Hebron Ave NE61 4 E4
Hebron Pl NE63 6 F3
Hebron Way NE23 22 A5
Hector St NE27 30 F4
Heddon Ave NE13 28 A4
Heddon Banks NE15 34 E1
Heddon Cl
Newcastle-upon-Tyne NE3 38 A6
Ryton NE40 52 D5
Heddon View
Blaydon NE21 53 B2
Ryton NE40 52 D5
Heddon Way NE34 59 B6
Heddon-on-the-Wall St Andrew's CE Fst Sch NE15 34 E2
Hedge Cl NE11 70 B7
Hedgefield Ave NE21 52 F5
Hedgefield Cotts NE21 52 F5
Hedgefield Ct NE21 52 F5
Hedgefield Gr NE24 17 C3
Hedgefield View NE23 22 A1
Hedgehope 6 NE37 83 A6
Hedgehope Rd NE5 37 A4
Hedgelea NE40 52 B5
Hedgelea Rd DH5 94 C3
Hedgeley Rd
Tynemouth NE29 41 D7
Hebburn NE31 57 E6
Newcastle-upon-Tyne NE5 53 E8
Hedgeley Terr NE6 56 F6
Hedgerow Mews NE63 6 B2
Hedley Ave NE24 17 F6
Hedley Cl 7 NE33 42 C4
Hedley Ct NE24 17 F6
Hedley La NE11,NE16 80 C6
Hedley Pl NE28 40 B1
Hedley Rd
Seaton Delaval NE25 23 E2
North Shields NE29 41 F3
Wylam NE41 51 B6
Hedley St
Newcastle-upon-Tyne NE3 38 C5
5 South Shields NE33 42 C4
Gateshead NE8 70 D8
Hedley Terr
Newcastle-upon-Tyne NE3 38 C5
Ryhope SR2 93 A6
Hedworth Ave NE34 59 A4
Hedworth Ct SR1 103 B2
Hedworth La
Hedworth NE32 58 D2
Boldon Colliery NE35 58 E1
Hedworth Lane Prim Sch NE35 58 D1
Hedworth Pl NE9 71 C3
Hedworth St DH3 88 C3
Hedworth Terr DH4 90 B6
Hedworth View NE32 58 D3
Hedworthfield Comp Sch NE32 58 B1
Hedworthfield Prim Sch NE32 58 D1
Heighley St NE15 53 F5
Helen St Blaydon NE21 53 A2
Sunderland SR6 75 E4
Helena Ave NE26 32 B5
Hellpool La NE46 44 F5
Helmdon NE37 83 E8
Helmsdale Ave 13 NE10 56 D1
Helmsdale Rd SR4 85 D5
Helmsley Cl DH4 90 A6
Helmsley Ct SR5 74 E3
Helmsley Dr NE28 40 F2
Helmsley Gn NE9 71 B2
Helmsley Rd NE2 99 C3
Helston Ct NE15 53 B7
Helvellyn Ave NE38 83 A3
Helvellyn Rd SR2 86 D2
Hemel St 8 DH3 88 C2
Hemlington Cl 12 SR2 92 F6
Hemming St 9 SR2 86 F2
Hemsley Rd NE34 43 A1
Hencotes NE46 45 A4
Hencotes Ct 4 NE46 45 A4
Hencotes Mews 8 NE46 45 A4
Henderson Ave NE16 69 A8
Henderson Cl NE46 44 F3
Henderson Ct NE29 41 F3
Henderson Gdns NE10 72 B8
Henderson Rd
Wallsend NE28 40 B3
Wallsend, Battle Hill NE28 40 B4
South Shields NE34 58 F4
Sunderland SR4 85 F6
Henderson's Bldgs NE64 7 E5
Hendersyde Cl NE5 37 B3
Hendon Burn Ave SR2 103 B1
Hendon Burn Ave W 2 SR2 86 E4
Hendon Cl
North Shields NE29 42 A3
Sunderland SR1 103 B2
Hendon Gdns NE32 58 D2
Hendon Ho NE63 6 A4
Hendon Rd
Gateshead NE8,NE9 71 B8
Sunderland SR1 103 B3
Sunderland, Hendon SR1, SR2 103 C2
Hendon Rd E SR1 103 C2
Hendon St SR1 103 C2
Hendon Valley Ct 6 SR2 86 E4
Hendon Valley Rd SR2 103 B1
Henley Cl NE23 22 D7
Henley Gdns NE28 41 B4
Henley Rd
Tynemouth NE30 32 C1
Sunderland SR4 85 D5
Henley Sq NE61 2 A3
Henley Way NE35 73 E8
Henlow Rd NE15 53 C7
Henry Nelson St NE33 42 D4
Henry Robson Way NE33 42 C2
Henry Sq NE2 99 C2
Henry St Shiney Row DH4 90 B6
Hetton le Hole DH5 95 A5
Houghton-le-Spring DH5 90 E1
North Shields NE29 42 A4
Newcastle-upon-Tyne NE3 38 C5
South Shields NE33 42 D4
Henry St E SR2 103 C2
Henry Terr DH4 89 F2
Hensby Ct NE5 37 B4
Henshaw Ct NE63 6 B2
Henshaw Gr NE25 23 F2
Henshaw Pl NE5 54 B7
Henshelwood Terr 2 NE2 38 E1
Henson Cl NE38 83 D4
Hepburn Gdns NE10 56 C1
Hepburn Gr SR5 73 F1
Hepple Ct NE24 17 C6
Hepple Rd NE64 7 C3
Hepple Way NE3 38 A6
Hepscott Dr NE25 31 D6
Hepscott Terr NE33 59 D8
Hepscott Wlk NE61 4 E3
Herbert St NE8 56 A1
Herbert Terr SR5 75 B5
Herd Cl NE21 53 A1
Herd House La NE21 52 F2
Herdinghill NE37 82 F6
Herdlaw NE23 22 A6
Hereford Ct
Newcastle-upon-Tyne NE3 37 D8
Sunderland SR2 86 D1
Hereford Rd SR2 86 D1
Hereford Sq SR2 86 D1
Hereford Way NE32 58 B2
Hermiston NE25 31 E5
Hermitage Gdns DH2 88 B1
Hermitage Pk DH3 88 C1
Hermitage Sch The DH2 88 A2
Heron Cl Blyth NE24 17 E4
Washington NE38 83 A2
Ashington NE63 6 E1
Heron Dr NE33 42 C4
Heron Pl NE12 39 A7
Herrick St NE5 37 A3
Herring Gull Cl NE24 17 E3
Herrington Mews DH4 90 E6
Herrington Rd SR3,DH4 91 B6
Hersham Cl NE3 37 D7
Hertburn Gdns NE37 83 D7
Hertburn Ind Est NE37 83 E7
Hertford NE9 70 F2
Hertford Ave NE34 60 C7
Hertford Cl NE25 31 D6
Hertford Cres DH5 94 F4
Hertford Gr NE23 22 C7
Hesket Ct NE3 37 E7
Hesleyside 6 NE63 6 F2
Hesleyside Dr NE5 54 C8
Hesleyside Rd NE25 31 B5
Hessewelle Cres DH6 97 E1
Hester Ave NE25 23 D6
Hester Bglws NE25 23 D6
Hester Gdns NE25 23 E6
Heswall Rd NE23 16 A2
Hetton Lyons Country Park* DH5 95 C4
Hetton Lyons Ind Est DH5 95 B3
Hetton Lyons Prim Sch DH5 95 A2
Hetton Prim Sch DH5 94 F3
Hetton Rd DH5 94 E7
Hetton Sch DH5 94 F3
Heugh Hill NE9 72 A2
Hewitson Terr NE10 71 C8
Hewitt Ave SR2 92 E8
Hewley Cres NE15 35 D1
Heworth Burn Cres NE10 71 E8
Heworth Cres 1 NE37 83 D8
Heworth Ct NE34 59 A5
Heworth Dene Gdns NE10 56 E1
Heworth Gr NE37 83 C8
Heworth Grange Comp Sch NE10 71 F8
Heworth Rd NE37 72 D1
Heworth Sta (British Rail & Metro) NE10 71 F8
Heworth Way NE10 72 A8
Hewson Pl NE9 71 B6
Hexham NE38 82 F4
Hexham Abbey NE46 45 B5
Hexham Ave
Cramlington NE23 22 D7
Hebburn NE31 57 E3
Newcastle-upon-Tyne NE6 56 F5
Hexham Cl NE29 41 C7
Hexham Ct NE11 69 F6
Hexham East Fst Sch NE46 45 C4
Hexham General Hospl NE46 45 C4
Hexham Hackwood Park Sch NE46 45 B3
Hexham Mid Sch NE46 45 B4
Hexham Old Rd NE21, NE40 52 E5
Hexham Priory Sch NE46 45 C4
Hexham Race Course NE46 44 D1
Hexham Rd
Heddon-on-the-Wall NE15 34 E2
Throckley NE15 35 C2
Whickham NE16 54 A1
Sunderland SR4 85 D5
Hexham Sta NE46 45 C5
Hextol Cres NE46 45 A4
Hextol Gdns NE15 53 F7
Hextol Terr NE46 44 F4
Heybrook Ave NE29 41 F8
Heyburn Gdns NE15 54 D5
Hi-Tec Village NE35 73 D7
Hibernia Rd NE6 57 A4
Hibernian Rd NE32 58 B7
Hickling Ct NE5 37 C4
Hickstead Cl NE28 40 E7
Hickstead Gr NE23 22 D7
Hiddleston Ave NE7 39 B5
High Axwell NE21 53 D2
High Back Cl NE32 58 A4
High Barnes Terr SR4 102 A1
High Bridge NE1,NE99 99 A1
High Burswell NE46 44 F5
High Chare DH3 88 D3
High Cl NE42 50 F3
High Croft NE37 72 C1
High Croft Ct NE31 57 D4
High Dene NE7 39 B1
High Dewley Burn NE15 35 D3
High Downs Sq DH5 95 A5
High Farm Mid Sch NE28 40 B5
High Flatworth NE29 41 B4
High Friar La NE1 99 A1
High Gate The NE3 37 E4
High Gr NE40 52 D4
High Hamsterley Rd NE39 78 A5
High Hedgefield Terr NE21 52 E5
High Heworth La NE10 71 E7
High Horse Cl NE39 68 A4
High Horse Close Wood NE39 68 A4
High House Cl NE61 8 D2
High House Gdns NE10 56 E1
High La DH4 90 F4
High Lane Row NE31 57 F7
High Lanes NE10 71 F7
High Laws NE3,NE7 38 F4
High Level Rd NE8 101 B3
High Market NE63 6 A4
High Mdw NE34 59 F8
High Meadow NE34 59 F8
High Meadows NE3 37 E3
High Mill Rd NE39 78 A5
High Moor Ct NE5 37 E2
High Moor Pl NE34 59 C5
High Pasture NE38 83 E1
High Pk NE61 9 A7
High Primrose Hill DH4 89 D3
High Quay
Newcastle-upon-Tyne NE1 56 A5
Blyth NE24 17 F8
High Rd The NE34 60 A6
High Reach NE10 57 A2
High Ridge NE13 28 B4
High Row
Great Lumley DH4 89 E1
Newcastle-upon-Tyne NE15 53 C6
Washington NE37 72 D1
Ryton NE40 52 E4
High Sandgrove SR6 60 A1
High Shaw NE42 50 B1
High Spen Ct NE39 67 A4
High Spen Prim Sch NE39 66 F3
High St
Easington Lane DH5 95 C1
High Pittington DH6 96 B6
Gateshead, Felling NE10 71 D8
Newburn NE15 52 F7
High St *continued*
Blyth NE24 17 D7
Blyth NE24 17 E7
Newcastle-upon-Tyne NE3 38 C4
Jarrow NE32 58 C7
Jarrow NE32 58 D7
Choppington NE62 10 E6
Guide Post NE62 10 E7
Newbiggin-by-the-Sea NE64 7 F5
Gateshead NE8 101 C3
Gateshead, Wrekenton NE9 71 C3
Sunderland SR4 85 A6
High St Cuthbert's Ave 10 NE46 45 A4
High St E Wallsend NE28 40 C1
Sunderland SR1 103 B3
High St W
Newcastle-upon-Tyne NE28, NE6 40 A1
Wallsend NE28,NE6 40 A1
Sunderland SR1 103 A3
High Stobhill NE61 9 A6
High Swinburne Pl NE4 98 B1
High Usworth Cty Inf Sch NE37 72 C1
High Usworth Cty Jun Sch NE37 72 C1
High View Ponteland NE20 25 D2
Wallsend NE28 40 B3
Hedley on the Hill NE43 64 F3
High View N NE28 40 B4
High Well Gdns NE10 56 E1
High West St NE8 101 C2
Higham Pl NE1 99 B2
Highburn NE23 22 A5
Highbury Gateshead NE10 71 E8
Newcastle-upon-Tyne NE2 38 D2
Whitley Bay NE25 31 E5
Highbury Ave NE9 72 A2
Highbury Cl NE9 72 A2
Highbury Pl NE29 41 F6
Highcliffe Gdns NE8 71 A8
Highcroft Dr SR6 60 E1
Highcroft Pk SR6 60 F1
Highcross Rd NE30 32 A3
Highfield Birtley DH3 82 C6
Sunniside NE16 69 B3
Prudhoe NE42 50 D2
Highfield Ave NE12 39 D8
Highfield Cl NE5 36 F3
Highfield Cres DH3 88 C5
Highfield Ct NE10 71 E7
Highfield Cty Inf Sch NE34 43 A1
Highfield Day Hospl DH3 88 C5
Highfield Dr
Fence Houses DH4 94 B7
South Shields NE34 59 F8
Ashington NE63 7 A2
Highfield Gdns DH3 88 C5
Highfield Grange DH4 94 B7
Highfield Jun & Inf Schs NE39 67 C2
Highfield La NE42 50 C1
Highfield Pl
Brunswick Village NE13 28 A5
6 Sunderland SR4 85 F6
Highfield Rd
Shiney Row DH4 90 A6
South Shields NE33,NE34 59 F8
Rowlands Gill NE39 67 C1
Newcastle-upon-Tyne NE5 36 F3
Gateshead NE8 56 A1
Highfield Rise DH3 88 C5
Highfield Terr
Prudhoe NE42 50 B2
Newcastle-upon-Tyne NE6 57 A4
Highfields Mid Sch NE42 50 C2
Highford Gdns NE61 8 E7
Highford La NE46 44 E4
Highgate Gdns NE32 58 D2
Highgate Rd SR4 85 D5
Highgreen Chase NE16 69 A4
Highgrove NE5 36 D2
Highheath 1 NE37 83 A6
Highland Rd NE5 37 D3
Highlaws Gdns NE9 71 B2
Highmoor NE61 8 D7
Highridge DH3 82 C5
Highside Dr SR3 86 A3
Highstead Ave NE23 16 A1
Highsteads DH8 77 B1
Hightree Cl SR3 91 F5
Highwell La 4 NE5 36 E1
Highwood Rd NE15 53 F7
Highworth Dr
Newcastle-upon-Tyne NE7 39 D3
Springwell NE9 71 F1
Hilda Pk DH2 88 B5
Hilda St Gateshead NE8 101 A1
Sunderland SR6 75 D3
Hilda Terr
Chester le Street DH2 88 B4
7 Throckley NE15 35 D2
Hilden Bldgs NE7 39 C2
Hilden Gdns NE7 39 C2
Hill Ave NE23 23 A2
Hill Brow SR3 92 B6
Hill Crest Gateshead NE10 71 E6
Burnopfield NE16 79 B6
Hill Crest Gdns NE2 38 E4
Hill Croft NE15 33 C1
Hill Dyke NE9 71 C2
Hill Gate NE61 9 A8
Hill Head Dr NE5 36 D1
Hill Head Rd NE5 36 D2
Hill House Rd NE15 35 C2
Hill La DH4 84 C1
Hill Park Rd NE32 58 C5
Hill Pk NE20 25 D2
Hill Rise Washington NE38 83 E6
Crawcrook NE40 51 F3
Hill St Jarrow NE32 58 A7
South Shields NE33 42 B1
Corbridge NE45 46 F5
New Silksworth SR3 92 A7
Hill Terr DH4 90 E6
Hill The NE42 50 B4
Hill Top Birtley DH3 82 D4
Blaydon NE21 53 B1
Hill Top Ave NE9 71 B5
Hill Top Cl NE62 10 F8
Hill Top Gdns NE9 71 A5
Hill Top Sch NE10 71 E4
Hill View Gdns SR3 86 B3
Hill View Inf Sch SR2 86 D2
Hill View Jun Sch SR2 86 D2
Hill View Rd SR2 86 D2
Hill View Sq SR2 86 D2
Hillary Ave NE12 39 E8
Hillcrest Whitley Bay NE25 31 E5
Hedworth NE32 58 D2
South Shields NE34 60 B5
Prudhoe NE42 50 D2
Ashington NE63 7 A2
Sunderland SR3 91 B8
Hillcrest Ave NE62 10 F8
Hillcrest Ct NE42 50 D2
Hillcrest Dr Dunston NE11 69 E7
Hexham NE46 45 C4
Hillcrest Sch NE23 22 B6
Hillcroft 4 Birtley DH3 82 C5
Rowlands Gill NE39 67 C2
Gateshead NE9 71 A6
Hillfield NE25 31 D5
Hillfield Gdns SR3 86 B3
Hillfield St NE8 101 B2
Hillford Terr NE17 66 B1
Hillgate NE8 101 B4
Hillhead Gdns NE11 70 A6
Hillhead La NE16 68 D2
Hillhead Parkway NE5 36 C2
Hillhead Way NE5 36 E3
Hillheads Ct NE25 32 A4
Hillheads Rd NE25,NE26 32 A4
Hillingdon Gr SR4 85 A2
Hillrise Cres SR7 92 D1
Hills Ct NE21 53 E4
Hills St NE8 101 B3
Hillsden Rd NE25 31 D7
Hillside Birtley DH3 82 D4
Chester le Street DH3 88 C4
Dunston NE11 69 F7
Killingworth NE12 29 E2
Ponteland NE20 25 C1
Blaydon NE21 53 B2
South Shields NE34 60 B4
West Boldon NE36 74 A7
Morpeth NE61 8 F7
Ashington NE63 6 C4
Sunderland SR3 86 C3
Hillside Ave NE15 53 F8
Hillside Cl NE39 67 E3
Hillside Cres NE15 54 A4
Hillside Dr SR6 60 E1
Hillside Gdns SR3 86 C3
Hillside Grove DH6 96 B5
Hillside Pl NE9 71 A6
Hillside Rd NE46 45 D4
Hillside Way DH4 90 E1
Hillsleigh Rd NE5 37 D2
Hillsview Ave NE3 37 E5
Hillthorne Cl NE38 83 E4
Hilltop Gdns SR3 92 C7
Hilltop Ho NE5 37 A2
Hillview SR3 91 B7
Hillview Cres DH4 90 D3
Hillview Gr DH4 90 D3
Hillview Rd DH4 90 D3
Hilton Ave NE5 37 B2
Hilton Cl NE23 16 A2
Hilton Prim Sch NE5 37 B2
Hind St SR1 102 C2
Hindley Cl NE40 51 E3
Hindley Gdns NE4 54 D7
Hindmarch Dr NE35,NE36 74 B7
Hindson's Cres N DH4 90 A5
Hindson's Cres S DH4 90 A5
Hinkley Cl SR3 92 B6
Hippingstones La NE45 46 F6
Hipsburn Dr SR3 86 A3
Hiram Dr NE36 74 D7
Hirst Head NE22 11 A1
Hirst High Sch NE63 6 F2
Hirst Terr N NE22 11 A1
Hirst Villas NE22 11 B1
Histon Ct NE5 37 B3
Histon Way NE5 37 B3
Hither Gn NE32 58 D2
Hobart NE26 31 F7
Hobart Ave NE34 58 F3
Hodgkin Park Cres NE15 54 C5
Hodgkin Park Rd NE15 54 C5
Hodgson Terr 6 NE37 83 F8
Hodgson's Rd NE24 12 D1
Hodkin Gdns NE9 71 B6
Hogarth Cotts NE22 16 A8
Hogarth Dr NE38 83 E3
Hogarth Rd NE34 59 C2
Holbein Rd NE34 59 C3
Holborn Pl NE5 36 E1
Holborn Rd SR4 85 D5
Holborn Sq SR4 85 D4
Holburn Cl NE40 52 D5
Holburn Cres NE40 52 E5
Holburn Gdns NE40 52 E5

Holburn La NE40 .52 D6
Holburn Lane Ct NE40 .52 D6
Holburn Terr NE40 .52 E5
Holburn Way NE40 .52 D5
Holburn Wlk NE40 .52 E5
Holden Pl NE5 .37 D2
Holder House La NE34 .59 E3
Holder House Way NE34 .59 E2
Holderness Rd
Wallsend NE28 .41 B3
Newcastle-upon-Tyne NE6 .39 B1
Hole La Sunniside NE16 .69 B3
Whickham NE16 .68 F4
Holeyn Hall Rd NE41 .51 A7
Holeyn Rd NE15 .35 C1
Holland Dr NE2 .98 B3
Holland Park Dr NE32 .58 D2
Holland Pk NE28 .39 E3
Holley Park Prim Sch
NE38 .83 A3
Hollinghill Rd NE25 .23 E2
Hollings Cres NE28 .40 B4
Hollings Terr NE17 .66 A1
Hollingside Way NE34 .59 D5
Hollington Ave NE12 .39 B6
Hollington Cl NE12 .39 B6
Hollinhill NE39 .68 A5
Hollinhill La NE39 .67 F4
Hollinhill Rd NE37 .83 E7
Hollinhill Terr NE44 .62 F8
Hollinside Cl NE16 .69 A5
Hollinside Gdns NE15 .54 B6
Hollinside Rd
Whickham NE11 .54 B2
Sunderland SR4 .85 D4
Hollinside Sq SR4 .85 C5
Hollinside Terr NE39 .67 D2
Hollon St NE61 .3 E1
Hollow The NE32 .58 B2
Hollowdene DH5 .95 A3
Hollows The NE63 .7 B2
Holly Ave
Houghton-le-Spring DH5 .94 F8
Dunston NE11 .69 F7
Longbenton NE12 .29 D1
Newcastle-upon-Tyne, Jesmond
NE2 .38 F1
Winlaton Mill NE21 .68 C6
Earsdon NE25 .31 B5
Whitley Bay NE26 .32 A5
Wallsend NE28 .40 C1
Newcastle-upon-Tyne, Fawdon
NE3 .37 F6
South Shields NE34 .60 A5
Ryton NE40 .52 C6
Morpeth NE61 .8 E7
Newbiggin-by-the-Sea NE64 .7 C5
New Silksworth SR3 .92 B8
Whitburn SR6 .75 F8
Holly Ave W NE2 .38 E1
Holly Bush Gdns NE40 .52 E4
Holly Cl NE12 .29 C4
Holly Cres NE38 .83 C1
Holly Ct
Newcastle-upon-Tyne NE5 .37 B2
Sunderland SR4 .102 A2
Holly Gdns NE9 .70 F6
Holly Gr NE42 .50 B3
Holly Haven DH5 .94 D4
Holly Hill NE10 .71 D8
Holly Ho SR1 .103 C3
Holly Mews NE26 .32 A5
Holly Park View NE10 .71 D8
Holly Rd NE29 .41 F7
Holly St Jarrow NE32 .58 A7
Ashington NE63 .6 D3
Holly Terr NE16 .79 C5
Holly View NE10 .71 C8
Hollybush Rd 4 NE10 .71 C8
Hollycarrside Rd SR2 .92 E8
Hollycrest DH2 .88 B5
Hollydene
Kibblesworth NE11 .81 D6
Rowlands Gill NE39 .67 F2
Hollyhock Hebburn NE31 .57 E3
Washington NE38 .83 E2
Hollymount Sq NE22 .16 A8
Hollymount Terr NE22 .16 A8
Hollys The DH3 .82 B7
Hollywell Gr NE13 .36 F8
Hollywell Rd NE29 .41 D6
Hollywood Ave
Newcastle-upon-Tyne, Gosforth
NE3 .38 D6
Newcastle-upon-Tyne, Walkerville
NE6 .40 A1
Sunderland SR5 .74 F2
Hollywood Cres NE3 .38 D6
Hollywood Gdns NE11 .70 B5
Holm Gn NE25 .31 D4
Holman Ct NE33 .42 C2
Holmcroft NE64 .7 E5
Holmdale NE63 .6 C2
Holme Ave
Whickham NE16 .69 B7
Newcastle-upon-Tyne NE6 .39 F1
Holme Gdns
Wallsend NE28 .41 A2
Sunderland SR3 .86 B3
Holme Rise NE16 .69 B7
Holmesdale Rd NE5 .37 D1
Holmeside SR1 .103 A2
Holmewood Dr NE39 .78 D8
Holmfield Ave NE34 .59 E7
Holmland NE15 .54 C4
Holmlands NE25 .31 E5
Holmlands Cl NE25 .31 E5
Holmlands Pk DH3 .88 D2
Holmlands Pk N SR2 .86 C4
Holmlands Pk S SR3 .86 C4
Holmside Ave NE11 .70 A8
Holmwood Ave
Whitley Bay NE25 .31 D4
Newbiggin-by-the-Sea NE64 .7 D5
Holmwood Gr NE2 .38 D2
Holwick Cl NE38 .83 A2
Holy Cross RC Prim Sch
NE28 .40 F4
Holy Island NE46 .45 A5
Holy Jesus Bglws NE2 .98 B4
Holyfields NE27 .30 E2
Holylake Sq SR4 .85 D5
Holyoake Gdns
Birtley DH3 .82 C4
Gateshead NE9 .70 F8
Holyoake St NE42 .50 D3
Holyoake Terr 8 NE37 .83 D8
Holyrood Rd 2 SR2 .86 F2
Holystone Ave Blyth NE24 17 C5
Whitley Bay NE25 .32 B4
Newcastle-upon-Tyne NE3 .38 B6
Holystone Cl
Burnside DH4 .90 B2
Blyth NE24 .17 B5
Holystone Cres NE7 .39 B2
Holystone Ct NE8 .101 A1
Holystone Dr NE27 .30 C2
Holystone Gdns NE29 .41 D8
Holystone Grange NE27 .30 C1
Holystone Prim Sch
NE27 .30 C2
Holystone St NE31 .57 D6
Holystone Way NE12,
NE27 .40 C8
Holywell Ave
Holywell NE25 .23 F2
Whitley Bay NE26 .31 F6
Newcastle-upon-Tyne NE6 .56 E3
Holywell Cl Blaydon NE21 .53 D1
Holywell NE25 .23 F2
Newcastle-upon-Tyne NE4 .98 B2
Holywell Dene Rd NE25 .23 F2
Holywell La NE16 .69 B3
Holywell Mews NE26 .31 F6
Holywell Terr NE27 .30 D1
Holywell Village Fst Sch
NE25 .23 F2
Home Ave 2 NE9 .70 F4
Home Farm Cl NE63 .5 F4
Home Pk NE28 .39 E3
Homedale Prudhoe NE42 .50 E2
Hexham NE46 .45 C4
Homedale Pl NE42 .50 E1
Homedowne House NE3 .38 C5
Homeforth House NE3 .38 C5
Homeside Pl 6 NE6 .56 B7
Homestall Cl NE34 .59 D5
Honeycomb Cl 7 SR3 .91 F5
Honeycrook Dr NE7 .39 E3
Honeysuckle Ave NE34 .59 B5
Honeysuckle Cl SR3 .92 A5
Honister Ave NE2 .38 E3
Honister Cl NE15 .53 D7
Honister Dr SR5 .75 C3
Honister Pl NE15 .53 D7
Honister Rd NE30 .32 B2
Honister Way NE24 .17 C3
Honiton Cl DH4 .90 C4
Honiton Ct NE3 .37 B6
Honiton Way NE29 .41 B8
Hood Cl SR5 .75 C1
Hood St
Newcastle-upon-Tyne NE1 .99 A1
4 Whickham NE16 .54 A1
Morpeth NE61 .3 F1
Hookergate Comp Sch
NE39 .67 B3
Hookergate La NE39 .67 A2
Hope Shield NE38 .82 F1
Hope St Jarrow NE32 .58 C7
South Shields NE34 .59 B5
Sunderland SR1 .102 C2
Hope View SR2 .92 F7
Hopedene NE10 .72 A5
Hopgarth Ct DH3 .88 D4
Hopgarth Gdns DH3 .88 D4
Hopkins Ct SR4 .85 F7
Hopkins Wlk NE34 .59 A2
Hopper Pl NE8 .101 C3
Hopper Rd NE10 .71 C7
Hopper St
8 Wallsend NE28 .40 B2
5 North Shields NE29 .41 F5
Gateshead NE8 .101 C3
Horatio St
Newcastle-upon-Tyne NE1 .56 A5
Sunderland SR6 .75 E1
Hornbeam Pl NE4 .100 B3
Horncliffe Gdns NE16 .69 C8
Horncliffe Pl NE15 .35 B2
Horncliffe Wlk NE15 .53 A7
Horning Ct NE5 .37 B4
Hornsea Cl NE13 .28 B5
Hornsey Cres DH5 .95 B1
Hornsey Terr DH5 .95 B1
Horse Crofts NE21 .53 C3
Horsegate Bank NE17,
NE40 .66 D5
Horsham Gdns SR3 .86 A3
Horsham Gr NE29 .41 E4
Horsley Ave
Shiremoor NE27 .30 F2
Crawcrook NE40 .51 E3
Horsley Cl NE62 .10 F8
Horsley Ct NE3 .37 E6
Horsley Gdns
Dunston NE11 .70 A8
Seaton Delaval NE25 .23 F2
Horsley Gr SR3 .86 A3
Horsley Hill Rd NE33 .42 E1
Horsley Hill Sq NE34 .60 B7
Horsley Rd
Washington NE38 .84 A5
Ovingham NE42 .50 A5
Newcastle-upon-Tyne NE7 .39 B2
Horsley Terr
12 Tynemouth NE30 .42 D7
Newcastle-upon-Tyne NE6 .56 F5
Horsley Vale NE34 .60 A8
Horsley View NE42 .50 F3
Horsley Wood Cotts
NE15 .50 D7
Horton Ave
Bedlington NE22 .15 F8
Shiremoor NE27 .30 F2
Whiteleas NE34 .59 D3
Horton Cres NE13 .27 B7
Horton Dr NE23 .16 B2
Horton Pl NE24 .17 B4
Horton Rd NE22,NE24 .16 C5
Horton St NE24 .17 F7
Hortondale Gr NE24 .17 B7
Horwood Ave NE5 .36 E2
Hospital Dr NE31 .57 D4
Hospital La NE15 .53 B8
Hospital Of King James The
NE8 .56 B1
Hospl of St Mary the Virgin
The NE4 .100 B4
Hotch Pudding Pl NE5 .36 F1
Hotspur Ave
Bedlington NE22 .15 F8
Whitley Bay NE25 .32 A4
South Shields NE34 .59 F7
Hotspur Prim Sch NE2 .56 A6
Hotspur Rd NE28 .40 A5
Hotspur St
Tynemouth NE30 .42 D8
Newcastle-upon-Tyne NE6 .56 A7
Houghton Ave
Tynemouth NE30 .32 B3
Newcastle-upon-Tyne NE5 .37 E3
Houghton Cut DH5 .90 E1
Houghton Ent Ctr DH5 .94 E8
Houghton Enterprise Ctr
DH5 .94 E8
Houghton Gate DH3 .89 B3
Houghton Kepier Sch
DH4 .94 D8
Houghton Rd
Newbottle DH4 .90 D3
Hetton le Hole DH5 .95 A4
Houghton Rd W DH5 .95 A4
Houghton St SR4 .102 A2
Houghtonside DH4 .90 E1
Houlet Garth 11 NE6 .56 C5
Houlsyke Cl SR3 .92 C7
Houndelee Pl NE5 .37 C1
Houndslow Dr NE63 .6 B2
Hounslow Gdns NE32 .58 D2
House of Hardy Museum*
NE66 .113 B2
House Terr NE37 .83 D8
Housing La DH8,DH9 .77 D1
Housteads (Vercovium)
Roman Fort (N.T.)*
NE47 .127 D4
Housteads 6 NE28 .40 F4
Houston Ct NE4 .100 B4
Houston St NE4 .100 B4
Houxty Rd NE25 .31 B5
Hovingham Gdns SR3 .86 A3
Howard Cl NE27 .30 C1
Howard Ct NE30 .42 B5
Howard Gr NE61 .4 E3
Howard Pl NE3 .38 C5
Howard Rd NE61 .4 A1
Howard St
Newcastle-upon-Tyne NE1 .99 C1
Gateshead, Windy Nook
NE10 .71 C6
North Shields NE30 .42 B5
Jarrow NE32 .58 C6
Gateshead, Mount Pleasant
NE8 .56 B1
3 Sunderland SR5 .75 D1
Howard Terr
High Spen NE39 .66 F4
1 Morpeth NE61 .3 F1
Howardian Cl NE38 .83 B3
Howarth St SR4 .102 A2
Howarth Terr DH6 .97 F3
Howat Ave NE5 .37 E1
Howburn Cres NE61 .4 E3
Howdene Rd NE15 .53 F6
Howdon Green Ind Est
NE28 .41 B2
Howdon La NE28 .41 A2
Howdon Rd NE28,NE29 .41 E3
Howdon Sta NE28 .41 A2
Howe Sq SR4 .85 C5
Howe St Hebburn NE31 .58 A6
Gateshead NE8 .56 A1
Howick Ave NE3 .38 A7
Howick Hall Gardens*
NE66 .113 E4
Howick Pk SR6 .103 A4
Howlett Hall Rd NE15 .53 F6
Howley Ave SR5 .74 C2
Hownam Cl NE3 .38 A4
Hoy Cres SR7 .92 F1
Hoylake Ave NE7 .39 C5
Hoyle Ave NE4 .54 E6
Hoyle Fold SR3 .92 A4
Hubert St NE35 .73 F8
Hucklow Gdns NE34 .59 D5
Huddart Terr 2 DH3 .82 C5
Huddleston Rd NE6 .56 D7
Huddlestone Rise SR6 .103 B4
Hudleston NE26 .32 C4
Hudshaw Gdns NE46 .45 D4
Hudson Ave
Bedlington NE22 .11 B1
Annitsford NE23 .29 B8
Hudson Rd SR1 .103 B2
Hudson Road Prim Sch
SR1 .103 B2
Hudson St
North Shields NE30 .42 C6
South Shields NE33 .59 B6
Gateshead NE8 .101 B3
Hugar Rd NE39 .67 A3
Hugh Ave NE27 .30 F4
Hugh Gdns NE4 .54 E4
Hugh St Wallsend NE28 .40 B1
Washington NE38 .83 F4
Sunderland SR6 .75 E4
Hull St NE4 .54 F5
Hulne Abbey* NE66 .113 A3
Hulne Ave NE30 .42 D7
Hulne Park & Brizlee Tower*
NE66 .112 F3
Hulne Terr NE15 .53 C6
Humber Ct 11 SR3 .91 F6
Humber Gdns NE8 .56 B1
Humber St NE17 .66 C1
Humbert St NE32 .58 B6
Humbledon Pk SR3 .86 A3
Humbledon View 5 SR2 .86 C4
Hume St
Newcastle-upon-Tyne NE6 .56 A5
Sunderland SR4 .102 A2
Humford Gn NE24 .16 F7
Humford Way NE22 .16 A7
Humsford Gr NE23 .22 C8
Humshaugh Cl NE12 .40 A8
Humshaugh Rd NE29 .41 C6
Hunn's Buildings NE62 .10 E5
Hunstanton Ct NE9 .70 E3
Hunt Lea NE16 .68 E5
Huntcliffe Ave SR6 .75 E6
Huntcliffe Gdns NE6 .39 D1
Hunter Ave NE24 .17 F6
Hunter Cl NE36 .74 D6
Hunter House NE6 .57 A4
Hunter St Shiney Row DH4 90 A5
South Shields NE33 .42 D1
Hunter Terr SR2 .86 E3
Hunter's Moor Cl NE2 .98 B4
Hunter's Moor Hospl
NE2 .98 B4
Hunter's Pl NE2 .98 B4
Hunter's Rd
Newcastle-upon-Tyne,
Spital Tongues NE2 .98 B3
Newcastle-upon-Tyne,
South Gosforth NE3 .38 F5
Hunters Cl
Medomsley DH8 .77 C1
North Shields NE29 .41 D3
Hunters Ct Wallsend NE28 40 C2
Newcastle-upon-Tyne NE3 .38 E5
Hunters Hall Rd SR4 .102 B1
Hunters Lodge NE28 .40 C2
Huntingdon Cl NE3 .37 D8
Huntingdon Gdns SR3 .86 A3
Huntingdon Pl NE30 .42 D7
Huntington Dr NE23 .22 D7
Huntley Cres NE21 .68 A8
Huntley Sq SR4 .85 D5
Huntley Terr 4 SR2 .92 F6
Huntly Rd NE25 .31 D7
Hurst Terr NE6 .56 E6
Hurstwood Rd SR4 .86 A4
Hurworth Ave NE34 .60 B7
Hurworth Pl NE32 .58 B6
Hutton Cl
Chester le Street DH3 .88 E1
Houghton-le-Spring DH4 .94 C8
Washington NE38 .82 F5
Hutton St
Newcastle-upon-Tyne NE3 .38 A5
Boldon Colliery NE35 .58 F1
Sunderland SR4 .102 B1
Hutton Terr
Newcastle-upon-Tyne NE2 .99 C3
Gateshead NE9 .70 F4
Huxley Cl NE34 .59 B2
Huxley Cres NE8 .70 D7
Hyacinth Ct SR4 .102 B3
Hyde Pk NE28 .39 F3
Hyde St
South Shields NE33 .42 D2
Sunderland SR2 .86 F4
Hyde Terr NE3 .38 D5
Hydepark St NE8 .70 D8
Hylton Ave NE34 .60 B7
Hylton Bank SR4 .85 B6
Hylton Castle* SR5 .74 B2
Hylton Castle Jun Sch
SR5 .74 A2
Hylton Castle Rd SR5 .74 B1
Hylton Cl NE22 .10 D1
Hylton Ct NE38 .83 B5
Hylton Grange SR5 .84 F8
Hylton La NE36,SR5 .74 A5
Hylton Park SR5 .74 E1
Hylton Park Rd SR5 .74 E1
Hylton Rd Jarrow NE32 .58 B4
Sunderland SR4 .85 D5
Hylton Red House Prim Sch
SR5 .74 D2
Hylton Red House Sch
SR5 .74 E4
Hylton St Newbottle DH4 .90 D2
17 North Shields NE29 .42 A5
Gateshead NE8 .56 B1
Sunderland SR4 .102 A2
Hylton Terr
6 North Shields NE29 .42 A5
Ryhope SR2 .92 E6
Hylton Wlk SR4 .85 A5
Hymers Ave NE34 .58 F4
Hyperion Ave NE34 .59 A5

I

Ilderton Pl NE5 .53 E8
Ilex St NE11 .70 C6
Ilford Ave NE23 .16 A1
Ilford Pl NE8,NE9 .71 A8
Ilford Rd
Newcastle-upon-Tyne NE2 .38 D3
Wallsend NE28 .40 F3
Ilford Road Sta NE2 .38 D3
Ilfracombe Ave NE4 .54 E5
Ilfracombe Gdns
Whitley Bay NE26 .31 F6
Gateshead NE9 .70 F3
Ilminster Ct NE3 .37 C6
Imeary Gr 9 NE33 .42 D1
Imeary St NE33 .42 D1
Imperial Bldgs 9 DH4 .94 E8
Inchberry Cl NE4 .54 E4
Inchcliffe Cres NE5 .37 C2
Indigo St NE11 .70 C6
Industrial Rd NE37 .83 E7
Industry Rd NE6 .39 D2
Ingham Gr NE23 .16 A1
Ingham Grange NE33 .42 E1
Ingham Pl NE2 .99 C2
Ingham Terr NE41 .51 B6
Ingleborough Cl 3 NE37 83 A6
Ingleborough Dr NE40 .52 D4
Ingleby Terr Lynmouth NE61 2 A3
Sunderland SR4 .102 A1
Ingleby Way NE24 .17 D3
Inglemere Pl NE15 .54 A6
Ingleside Whickham NE16 .68 F6
South Shields NE34 .60 B6
Ingleton Ct SR4 .102 B1
Ingleton Dr NE15 .35 B2
Ingleton Gdns NE24 .17 C3
Inglewood Cl NE24 .16 F7
Inglewood Pl NE3 .28 C1
Ingoe Ave NE3 .37 F7
Ingoe Cl NE24 .17 C7
Ingoe St
Newcastle-upon-Tyne NE15 .53 C6
North Shields NE28 .41 C2
Ingoldsby Ct SR4 .85 E4
Ingram Ave NE3 .37 F8
Ingram Cl
Chester le Street DH2 .88 A1
Wallsend NE28 .40 F5
Ingram Dr Blyth NE24 .17 B7
Newcastle-upon-Tyne NE5 .36 D4
Ingram Terr NE6 .57 A6
Inkerman Rd NE37 .72 D1
Inkerman St SR5 .75 A1
Innesmoor NE31 .57 D7
Inskip Terr NE8 .70 F8
Institute Rd NE63 .6 B4
International Ctr for Life The
NE1 .100 C4
Inverness Rd NE32 .58 E2
Inverness St SR6 .75 D2
Invertay NE3 .38 E5
Invincible Dr NE4 .100 A3
Iolanthe Cres NE6 .56 E7
Iolanthe Terr NE33 .42 E1
Iona Pl NE6 .57 A6
Iona Rd
Gateshead N10,NE9 .71 B7
Brockley Whins NE32 .58 E3
Irene Ave SR2 .86 F1
Iris Cl NE21 .53 A2
Iris Cres DH2 .81 F2
Iris Pl NE4 .54 D7
Iris St NE11 .70 C6
Iris Steedman House
NE4 .98 A2
Iris Terr Bournmoor DH4 .89 E3
Crawcrook NE40 .51 F3
Iroko St NE11 .70 C6
Ironside St DH5 .90 E1
Irthing NE61 .1 E5
Irthing Ave NE6 .56 D4
Irton St NE3 .38 C5
Irvine Ho 7 NE12 .39 D8
Irwin Ave NE28 .40 C3
Isabella Cl NE4 .54 E3
Isabella Rd NE24 .17 C6
Isabella Wlk NE15 .35 D1
Islay Ho 9 SR3 .92 A6
Ivanhoe NE25 .31 E5
Ivanhoe Cres SR2 .86 B4
Ivanhoe Terr
11 Chester le Street DH3 .88 C2
Dipton DH9 .78 E1
Ivanhoe View NE9 .71 B2
Iveagh Cl NE4 .54 D4
Iveson Rd NE46 .44 E3
Ivor St SR2 .87 A2

Ivy Ave Ryton NE40 ....52 C6
Newbiggin-by-the-Sea NE64 .7 C5
Ivy Cl
Newcastle-upon-Tyne NE4 100 B3
Ryton NE40 ....52 C6
Ivy La NE9 ....71 A3
Ivy Pl DH9 ....79 C3
Ivy Rd Longbenton NE12 ...39 E8
Newcastle-upon-Tyne, Gosforth
NE3 ....38 C4
Newcastle-upon-Tyne, Walkergate
NE6 ....56 F8
Ivy Road Prim Sch NE12 .39 E8
Ivy St Gateshead NE11 ....70 C6
Seaton Burn NE13 ....28 C8
Ivy Terr DH4 ....90 B6
Ivymount Rd NE6 ....39 B1
Ixia St NE11 ....70 C6

J

Jack Common Ho 8 NE6 56 B7
Jack's Terr NE34 ....59 C5
Jackson Ave NE20 ....25 F7
Jackson Rd NE41 ....51 B6
Jackson St
Newcastle-upon-Tyne NE6 ..56 F6
Gateshead NE8 ....101 C3
Sunderland SR4 ....102 A1
Jackson St W NE30 ......42 B6
Jackson Terr 8 NE61 .....9 A8
Jacobins Chare NE4 .....98 C1
Jacques St SR4 ....85 F8
Jacques Terr DH2 ....88 B4
Jade Cl NE15 ....53 C8
James Armitage St SR5 .75 B2
James Ave NE27 ....30 F4
James Mather St NE33 ..42 D3
James St Tanfield Lea DH9 .79 F1
10 Whickham NE16 ....69 A7
Newcastle-upon-Tyne, Elswick
NE4 ....54 F4
Newcastle-upon-Tyne,
Westerhope NE5 ....36 F2
Sunderland SR5 ....75 A2
James Steel Pk* NE38 ...84 A2
James Terr
Fence Houses DH4 ....94 A8
Easington Lane DH5 ......97 B8
Wallsend NE28 ....40 B1
James Williams St SR1 .103 B3
Jameson Dr NE45 ....47 B7
Jane Eyre Terr NE8 ......56 B1
Jane St Hetton le Hole DH5 95 A6
22 Newcastle-upon-Tyne
NE6 ....56 C6
Jane Terr NE6 ....57 A4
Janet Sq NE6 ....56 C5
Janet St
17 Newcastle-upon-Tyne,
St Lawrence NE6 ....56 C5
Newcastle-upon-Tyne, St Peters
NE6 ....56 C4
Janus Cl NE5 ....36 C4
Jarrow Rd NE32,NE34 ....58 F6
Jarrow St Peter's C of E Prim
Sch NE32 ....58 C7
Jarrow Sta NE32 ....58 B7
Jasmin Ave NE5 ....36 C4
Jasmine Cl NE6 ....39 E1
Jasmine Ct Ashington NE63 .6 C1
Sunderland SR4 ....102 B3
Jasmine Terr DH3 ....82 D4
Jasmine Villas 7 NE16 ...69 A7
Jasper Ave NE40 ....52 B1
Jedburgh Cl
Tynemouth NE29 ....41 E8
Newcastle-upon-Tyne NE5 ..36 C4
Gateshead NE8 ....101 C1
Jedburgh Ct NE11 ....70 E2
Jedburgh Gdns NE15 ....54 B7
Jedburgh Rd DH4 ....90 B6
Jedmoor NE31 ....57 D7
Jefferson Cl SR5 ....75 C4
Jefferson Pl NE4 ....98 B2
Jellicoe Rd NE6 ....56 E3
Jenifer Gr NE7 ....39 A4
Jenison Ave NE15 ....54 C5
Jennifer Ave 9 SR5 ......74 B1
Jersey Sq NE61 ....2 A3
Jervis St NE31 ....57 F6
Jesmond Dene Rd
Newcastle-upon-Tyne, Jesmond
NE2 ....38 F2
Newcastle-upon-Tyne,
West Jesmond NE2 ......38 D3
Jesmond Gdns
Newcastle-upon-Tyne NE2 ..38 F1
Biddick Hall NE34 ....59 C3
Jesmond Park Ct NE7 ...39 B1
Jesmond Pk E NE7 ......39 B1
Jesmond Pk W NE7 ......39 A2
Jesmond Pl 1 NE2 ......38 E1
Jesmond Rd NE2 ....99 C4
Jesmond Rd W NE2 ......99 B3
Jesmond Sta NE2 ....99 C3
Jesmond Terr NE26 ......32 B4
Jesmond Vale NE2 ......56 A7
Jesmond Vale La NE6 ...56 B8
Jesmond Vale Terr NE6 ..56 B8
Jessel St NE9 ....70 F4
Jetty The NE10 ....57 A2
Jeycroft Ct NE30 ....42 B5
Joan Ave SR2 ....86 F1
Joan St NE4 ....54 D4
Joannah St SR5 ....75 C3
Jobling Ave NE21 ....53 B2
Jobling Cres NE61 ....9 B6
Joel Terr NE10 ....57 B2
John & Margaret Common
Homes for Aged Miners 5
NE24 ....16 F8
John Ave NE40 ....52 B1
John Brown Ct NE22 .....10 F1
John Candlish Rd SR4 .102 A3
John Clay St
3 South Shields NE33 ....42 D1
5 South Shields, Dean
NE33 ....59 D8
John Dobson St NE1,
NE99 ....99 B2
John F Kennedy Est
NE38 ....83 E5
John F Kennedy Prim Sch
NE38 ....83 E5
John Reid Rd NE34 .....59 C4
John Spence Community
High Sch NE29 ....42 A8
John St Prudhoe NE42 ....50 E3
Fence Houses DH4 ....94 A8
Hetton le Hole DH5 ......95 A3
Houghton-le-Spring DH5 ...94 F8
1 Gateshead, Pelaw NE10 .56 F1
Blyth NE24 ....17 B8
Earsdon NE25 ....31 A5
Wallsend NE28 ....40 B2
Newcastle-upon-Tyne NE3 ..38 A5
Tynemouth NE30 ....32 C3
West Boldon NE35 ....73 F8
Pegswood NE61 ....4 F3
Ashington NE63 ....6 C4
Gateshead, Old Fold NE8 ..56 B1
Sunderland SR1 ....103 A3
14 Ryhope SR2 ....93 A6
Sunderland, South Hylton
SR4 ....85 A7
John Taylor Ct SR5 ......75 A3
John Wesley Ct NE42 ....50 D2
John Williamson St
NE33 ....59 C7
Johnson St
6 Dunston NE11 ....54 F1
Newcastle-upon-Tyne NE15 .53 C6
South Shields NE33 ......59 C7
Gateshead NE8 ....100 B1
Sunderland SR1 ....102 C3
Johnson Terr
5 Washington NE37 ......83 F8
High Spen NE39 ....66 F4
Johnsons Villas NE62 ....10 B7
Johnston Ave NE31 ......57 D3
Joicey Aged Miners Homes
7 DH4 ....90 B6
Joicey Rd NE9 ....70 F6
Joicey Road Open Air Sch
NE9 ....70 F6
Joicey St NE10 ....57 A1
Jolliffe St DH3 ....88 D1
Jonadab Rd NE10 ....57 A2
Jonadab St NE10 ....57 A1
Jones St 3 DH3 ....82 C4
Jonquil Cl NE5 ....36 C4
Joseph Cl NE4 ....54 E4
Joseph Hopper Aged Miners'
Homes DH3 ....82 C7
Joseph Hopper Meml Homes
NE9 ....71 C6
Joseph Swan Comp Sch
NE9 ....70 E3
Joseph Terr NE17 ....66 B1
Jowett Sq SR5 ....75 A2
Joyce Cl NE10 ....72 D8
Joyce Terr 5 SR5 ....74 B1
Jubilee Ave NE9 ....71 C1
Jubilee Bldgs 2 NE46 ....45 B4
Jubilee Cotts
Houghton-le-Spring DH4 ...94 D8
Greenside NE40 ....66 D7
Lynmouth NE61 ....2 A3
Jubilee Cres
Sherburn Hill DH6 ....96 D1
Newcastle-upon-Tyne NE3 ..38 A5
Jubilee Ct Annitsford NE23 22 B1
Blyth NE24 ....17 D6
Hebburn NE31 ....58 A6
Jubilee Est NE63 ....6 D1
Jubilee Ho DH5 ....95 C1
Jubilee Ind Est NE63 .....6 D1
Jubilee Rd
Newcastle-upon-Tyne NE1 ..99 C1
Blyth NE24 ....17 E6
Newcastle-upon-Tyne, Coxlodge
NE3 ....38 B5
Ovington NE42 ....49 C4
Jubilee Sq
Easington Lane DH5 ......95 C1
South Hetton DH6 ....97 F7
Jubilee St 3 NE28 ....40 B2
Jubilee Terr Tantobie DH9 .79 A2
Seaton Burn NE13 ....28 B8
7 Whickham NE16 ....54 A1
Bedlington NE22 ....11 D2
Washington NE38 ....84 A2
Crawcrook NE40 ....51 E3
Newbiggin-by-the-Sea NE64 .7 E4
Jubilee Terrs NE6 ....56 D6
Julian Ave
South Shields NE33 ......42 D4
Newcastle-upon-Tyne NE6 ..56 E7
Julian Rd NE10 ....72 D8
Julian St NE33 ....42 D4
Juliet Ave NE29 ....41 D6
Juliet St NE63 ....6 E4
Julius Caesar St 5 SR5 .75 A2
Julius Ct NE33 ....42 C4
June Ave NE21 ....68 C6
Juniper Cl Blyth NE24 ....17 C4
Newcastle-upon-Tyne NE3 .28 D1
4 Sunderland SR2 ....86 E4
Juniper Ct NE21 ....53 C3
Juniper Wlk NE5 ....36 D4
Jutland Ave NE31 ....57 E6

K

Kalmia St NE11 ....70 C5
Kane Gdns NE10 ....71 C6
Kateregina DH3 ....82 D4
Katherine St NE63 ....6 E4
Katrine Ct DH2 ....88 B1
Katrine Ct SR3 ....92 A5
Kay's Cotts NE10 ....71 C7
Kayll Rd SR4 ....85 F6
Kearsley Cl NE25 ....23 D3
Kearton Ave NE5 ....36 C3
Keats Ave Blyth NE24 .....17 C5
West Boldon NE35 ....74 B8
Sunderland SR5 ....75 A2
Keats Gr NE63 ....6 F3
Keats Rd NE15 ....53 A6
Keats Wlk
Biddick Hall NE34 ....59 A3
Gateshead NE8 ....56 A2
Keeble Ct NE63 ....7 B3
Keebledale Ave NE6 .....56 F7
Keele Dr NE23 ....21 D6
Keelman's La SR4 ....85 C7
Keelman's Rd SR4 ....85 B7
Keelmans Terr NE24 .....17 E8
Keelmen's Hospl NE1 ....99 C1
Keighley Ave SR5 ....74 B4
Keighley Sq SR5 ....74 A4
Keir Hardie Ave NE10 ...72 A8
Keir Hardie Ct NE64 ......7 E5
Keir Hardie St
Fence Houses DH4 ....94 B8
Rowlands Gill NE39 ......67 B2
Keir Hardie Terr DH3 ....82 B6
Keir Hardie Way SR5 ....75 C1
Keith Cl NE4 ....54 E4
Keith Sq SR5 ....74 B4
Keldane Gdns NE4 ......54 E6
Kelfield Gr NE23 ....16 B2
Kelham Sq SR5 ....74 A4
Kell Cres DH6 ....96 C1
Kell's Way NE39 ....67 E1
Kellfield Ave NE9 ....71 A6
Kellfield Rd NE9 ....71 A5
Kells Gdns NE9 ....71 A5
Kells La NE9 ....70 F5
Kellsway NE10 ....71 F5
Kellsway Ct NE10 ....71 F5
Kelly Rd NE31 ....57 E3
Kelsey Way NE23 ....16 B2
Kelso Cl NE5 ....36 C4
Kelso Dr NE29 ....41 E8
Kelso Gdns
Newcastle-upon-Tyne NE15 .54 B6
Bedlington NE22 ....11 C1
Wallsend NE28 ....41 A4
Kelso Gr DH4 ....90 A6
Kelso Pl NE8 ....100 B1
Kelson Way NE5 ....36 C4
Kelston Way NE5 ....37 C2
Kelvin Gdns 3 NE11 .....54 F1
Kelvin Gr
Newcastle-upon-Tyne NE2 ..99 C3
Tynemouth NE29 ....42 A8
South Shields NE33 ......42 F1
Gateshead NE8 ....70 D8
Cleadon SR6 ....59 E1
Sunderland SR6 ....75 E2
Kelvin Grove Com Prim Sch
NE8 ....70 E8
Kelvin Pl NE12 ....30 A1
Kemble Cl NE23 ....16 B2
Kemble Sq SR5 ....74 B4
Kempton Gdns NE8 .....70 C7
Kendal DH3 ....82 E2
Kendal Ave Blyth NE24 ...17 D6
Tynemouth NE30 ....32 B2
Kendal Cres NE9 ....71 B5
Kendal Dr
Cramlington NE23 ....22 C8
East Boldon NE36 ....74 C8
Kendal Gdns NE28 ......41 A4
Kendal Gn 24 NE6 ....56 B6
Kendal House 27 NE6 ....56 B6
Kendal Pl 26 NE6 ....56 B6
Kendal St 1 NE6 ....56 B5
Kendale Wlk NE5 ....36 E3
Kendor Gr NE61 ....8 F6
Kenilworth NE12 ....29 D4
Kenilworth Ct
4 Washington NE37 ......83 F8
Newcastle-upon-Tyne NE4 100 A4
Kenilworth Rd
Whitley Bay NE25 ....31 F4
Newcastle-upon-Tyne NE4 100 A4
Ashington NE63 ....6 C3
Kenilworth Sq SR5 ......74 C4
Kenilworth View 7 NE9 ..71 A2
Kenley Rd
Newcastle-upon-Tyne NE5 ..54 A8
Sunderland SR5 ....74 C4
Kenmoor Way NE5 ....36 C3
Kenmore Cres NE40 .....52 B2
Kennersdene NE30 ......42 C8
Kennet Ave NE32 ....58 C3
Kennet Sq SR5 ....74 B4
Kennford NE9 ....71 A2
Kennington Gr NE6 .....56 E5
Kensington Ave NE3 .....38 C7
Kensington Cl NE25 .....31 F5
Kensington Cotts NE61 ...9 B8
Kensington Ct
5 Gateshead NE10 ......71 C8
South Shields NE33 ......59 E8
Kensington Gdns
Whitley Bay NE25 ....31 F5
Wallsend NE28 ....39 E3
1 North Shields NE30 ....42 B6
Kensington Gr NE30 .....42 B7
Kensington Terr
2 Dunston NE11 ....69 F8
Newcastle-upon-Tyne NE2 ..99 A3
Kensington Villas 5 NE5 .36 E3
Kent Ave 3 Dunston NE11 70 A8
Wallsend NE28 ....40 F2
Hebburn NE31 ....57 D5
Kent Cl NE63 ....6 A4
Kent Ct NE3 ....37 D8
Kent Gdns DH5 ....94 F4
Kent Pl NE34 ....60 A6
Kent St NE32 ....58 A6
Kent Terr DH6 ....97 E1
Kentchester Rd SR5 .....74 C4
Kentmere DH3 ....82 E1
Kentmere Ave
Newcastle-upon-Tyne NE6 ..56 F7
Sunderland SR6 ....75 C5
Kentmere Cl NE23 ......23 A2
Kenton Ave NE3 ....38 A3
Kenton Bank NE5 ....37 C5
Kenton Bar Prim Sch
NE5 ....37 D4
Kenton Cres NE3 ....37 F4
Kenton Ct NE33 ....42 D1
Kenton Gr SR6 ....75 D1
Kenton La NE3 ....37 E4
Kenton Lodge (Residential
Special Sch) NE3 ......38 B2
Kenton Park Sh Ctr NE3 .38 A4
Kenton Rd
Tynemouth NE29 ....41 C7
Newcastle-upon-Tyne NE3 ..38 A3
Kenton Sch NE5 ....37 E4
Kentucky Rd SR5 ....74 A4
Kenwood Gdns NE9 .....71 A2
Kenya Rd SR5 ....74 C4
Kepier Chare Prim Sch
NE40 ....51 F3
Kepier Gdns 6 SR4 .....85 A6
Keppel St Dunston NE11 ...54 F1
3 South Shields NE33 ....42 C3
Kepwell Bank Top NE42 .50 C3
Kepwell Bk NE42 ....50 D3
Kepwell Ct NE42 ....50 D3
Kepwell Rd NE42 ....50 C2
Kerby Cl NE34 ....58 F4
Kerry Cl NE24 ....17 E8
Kerry Sq SR5 ....74 B4
Kesteven Sq SR5 ....74 B4
Keston Dr NE23 ....16 B2
Kestrel Cl NE38 ....83 A2
Kestrel Ct 13 DH3 ......82 C4
Kestrel Dr NE63 ....6 B1
Kestrel Lodge Flats 6
NE33 ....42 D3
Kestrel Mews NE16 .....69 A7
Kestrel Pl NE12 ....39 A7
Kestrel Sq SR5 ....74 B4
Kestrel St NE11 ....70 C6
Kestrel Way
North Shields NE29 ......42 A3
South Shields NE34 ......59 B4
Keswick Ave SR6 ....75 D4
Keswick Dr NE30 ....32 B2
Keswick Gdns NE28 .....41 A3
Keswick Gr NE5 ....54 A8
Keswick St NE8 ....101 B1
Keswick Terr DH6 ......97 E8
Kettering Pl NE23 ......22 C8
Kettering Sq SR5 ....74 B4
Kettlewell Terr 7 NE30 ..42 B6
Ketton Cl NE12 ....39 B6
Kew Gdns NE26 ....31 F6
Keyes Gdns NE2 ....38 E3
Kibblesworth Bank NE11 .81 B6
Kibblesworth Prim Sch
NE11 ....81 D6
Kidd Sq SR5 ....74 B4
Kidderminster Dr NE5 ...36 C3
Kidderminster Rd SR5 ...74 B3
Kidderminster Sq SR5 ...74 B3
Kidland Cl NE63 ....6 F4
Kidlandlee Gn NE5 ......37 A4
Kidlandlee Pl NE5 ......37 A4
Kidsgrove Sq SR5 ....74 B3
Kielder NE38 ....82 F4
Kielder Ave NE23 ....21 D6
Kielder Castle Visitor
Centre* NE48 ....120 D8
Kielder Cl
Killingworth NE12 ....29 C4
Blyth NE24 ....17 B5
Newcastle-upon-Tyne NE5 ..37 A4
Kielder Dr NE63 ....6 C3
Kielder Gdns Jarrow NE32 58 B3
Stakeford NE62 ....6 A1
Kielder Pl NE25 ....31 B5
Kielder Rd
Newcastle-upon-Tyne NE15 .53 C7
Earsdon NE25 ....31 B5
Kielder Terr NE30 ....42 B6
Kielder Way NE3 ....38 B7
Kilburn Cl 4 SR2 ....93 A6
Kilburn Gdns NE29 ......41 D3
Kilburn Gn NE9 ....71 B1
Kilburne Cl NE7 ....39 E3
Kildale DH4 ....89 E8
Kildare Sq SR5 ....74 B4
Killarney Ave SR5 ....74 B4
Killarney Sq SR5 ....74 B4
Killiebrigs NE15 ....34 E2
Killin Cl NE5 ....36 C4
Killingworth Ave NE27 ...30 B4
Killingworth Ctr The
NE12 ....29 D3
Killingworth Dr
Killingworth NE12 ....29 B2
Sunderland SR3,SR4 .....85 E4
Killingworth La NE27 ....30 A5
Killingworth Mid Sch
NE12 ....29 D2
Killingworth Pl NE1 .....99 A2
Killingworth Rd
Killingworth NE12 ....29 E2
Newcastle-upon-Tyne NE3,
NE7 ....38 F5
Killingworth Way NE12,
NE27 ....29 D4
Killowen St NE9 ....70 E4
Kiln Rise NE16 ....69 A4
Kilnshaw Pl NE3 ....28 D1
Kilsyth Ave NE29 ....31 E2
Kilsyth Sq SR5 ....74 B4
Kimberley NE38 ....84 A5
Kimberley Ave NE29 .....41 E6
Kimberley Gdns
Newcastle-upon-Tyne NE2 ..56 A8
Stocksfield NE43 ....64 C7
Kimberley St Blyth NE24 ..17 D8
Sunderland SR4 ....85 F6
Kimberley Terr NE24 ....17 E8
Kinfauns Terr 5 NE9 ....71 A5
King Charles Ct 4 SR5 ..74 A4
King Charles Twr NE2 ...99 C2
King Edward Inf Sch
NE30 ....42 B7
King Edward Jun Sch
NE30 ....42 B7
King Edward Pl NE8 .....56 B1
King Edward Rd
Tynemouth NE30 ....42 C7
Ryton NE40 ....52 E4
Newcastle-upon-Tyne NE6 ..39 B1
Sunderland SR4 ....85 B7
King Edward St
Tanfield Lea DH9 ....79 C1
Gateshead NE8 ....56 B1
King Edward VI Sch The
NE61 ....3 F2
King George Ave NE11 ...69 F8
King George Rd
Newcastle-upon-Tyne NE3 ..37 E6
South Shields NE34 ......59 E5
King George V Comp Sch
NE34 ....59 E3
King George's Rd NE64 ...7 D5
King Henry Ct 5 SR5 ....74 A4
King James Ct SR5 ......74 A4
King James St NE8 .....101 C1
King John St NE6 ....56 B8
King John Terr NE6 .....56 B8
King John's Ct NE20 ....25 A4
King St Birtley DH3 ......82 B4
Newcastle-upon-Tyne NE1 101 B4
Gateshead, Pelaw NE10 ..57 A1
Blyth NE24 ....17 E8
North Shields NE30 ......42 B6
South Shields NE33 ......42 C3
Newbiggin-by-the-Sea NE64 .7 E5
Gateshead, Bensham NE8 ..70 C8
Sunderland SR1 ....103 A3
Sunderland, Fulwell SR6 ...75 D4
King's Ave NE61 ....3 F1
King's Dr Whitley Bay NE26 32 A4
Greenside NE40 ....52 B1
King's Gdns NE24 ....17 C8
King's Pl SR4 ....102 A3
King's Rd
Newcastle-upon-Tyne NE1,
NE2 ....99 A2
Bedlington NE22 ....11 D2
Whitley Bay NE26 ....31 F6
King's School Tynemouth
NE30 ....42 D7
King's Terr SR4 ....102 A3
King's Wlk NE1 ....99 A3
Kingarth Ave SR6 ....75 E5
Kingdom Pl NE29 ....42 A3
Kingfisher Cl NE63 ......11 E8
Kingfisher Lodge NE32 ..58 A6
Kingfisher Rd NE12 .....39 A7
Kingfisher Way
Blyth NE24 ....17 F4
Shiremoor NE28 ....41 A6
Kingham Ct NE7 ....38 F4
Kinghorn Sq SR5 ....74 B4
Kings Ave Hebburn NE31 ..57 F5
Sunderland SR6 ....75 E5
Kings Cl NE8 ....56 B1
Kings Meadow NE32 .....58 C1
Kings Meadows NE4 ...100 A3
Kings Pk NE62 ....10 F5
Kings Rd NE12 ....29 C1
Kings Rd N NE28 ....40 B4
Kings Rd S NE28 ....40 B3
Kings Rd The SR5 ....75 A2
Kings Terr NE9 ....71 F1
Kings Wlk NE5 ....36 C4
Kingsbridge NE12 ....38 F7
Kingsbridge Cl NE28 ....41 E4
Kingsclere Ave SR5 .....74 B3

Kingsclere Sq SR5 74 B4
Kingsdale Ave Blyth NE24 17 A7
Washington NE37 83 C8
Kingsdale Rd NE12 38 F7
Kingsgate NE46 45 A5
Kingsgate Terr NE46 45 A5
Kingsland NE2 99 B4
Kingsland Sq SR5 74 B3
Kingsley Ave
Whitley Bay NE25 32 A4
Newcastle-upon-Tyne NE3 28 D1
Biddick Hall NE34 59 A3
Kingsley Cl 4 SR5 75 A1
Kingsley Pl
8 Dunston NE11 54 F1
Whickham NE16 69 B8
Wallsend NE28 40 F3
8 Newcastle-upon-Tyne NE6 56 B7
Kingsley Rd NE61 2 A2
Kingsley Terr
Newcastle-upon-Tyne NE4 98 A1
Crawcrook NE40 51 E4
Kingsmeadow Com Comp Sch NE11 69 E8
Kingsmere DH3 88 C7
Kingsmere Gdns NE6 57 A4
Kingston Ave NE6 56 D4
Kingston Cl NE26 31 F8
Kingston Cres DH6 97 E3
Kingston Ct
6 Whitley Bay NE26 31 F8
Hebburn NE31 57 D5
Kingston Dr NE26 31 F8
Kingston Gn NE6 56 D5
Kingston Mews DH4 90 C5
Kingston Park Ave NE3 37 C6
Kingston Park Ctr NE3 37 C6
Kingston Park Prim Sch NE3 37 C6
Kingston Park Rd NE3, NE13 37 F7
Kingston Park Sta NE3 37 C6
Kingston Rd NE8 71 B8
Kingston Terr SR6 75 D2
Kingston Way 3 NE26 31 F8
Kingsway
Houghton-le-Spring DH5 94 F8
Sunniside NE16 69 A2
Ponteland NE20 25 E6
Blyth NE24 17 E6
Tynemouth NE30 42 C8
South Shields NE33 42 F2
Newcastle-upon-Tyne NE4 54 E8
Kingsway Ave NE3 38 C7
Kingsway Fst Sch NE24 17 E6
Kingsway Ho NE11 70 D4
Kingsway Interchange NE11 70 E3
Kingsway N NE11 70 C5
Kingsway Rd SR5 74 B4
Kingsway S NE11 70 D3
Kingsway Sq SR5 74 B4
Kingswood Ave NE2 38 D3
Kingswood Cl NE35 58 E1
Kingswood Dr NE20 25 C4
Kingswood Gr SR4 85 A2
Kingswood Rd NE23 22 C8
Kingswood Sq SR5 74 B3
Kinlett NE38 84 A5
Kinloch Ct DH2 88 B1
Kinloss Sq NE23 22 C8
Kinnaird Ave NE15 54 A6
Kinnock Cl DH6 96 A1
Kinross Cl DH3 82 D2
Kinross Ct NE10 57 B2
Kinross Dr NE3 37 F5
Kinsale Sq SR5 74 B4
Kinver Dr NE5 36 C3
Kipling Ave
Whickham NE16 69 B8
Hebburn NE31 57 F6
West Boldon NE35 74 B8
Kipling Ct NE16 69 B8
Kipling St SR5 75 A1
Kipling Wlk NE8 56 A2
Kirk St NE6 56 C5
Kirk View DH4 90 D3
Kirkbride Pl NE23 22 C8
Kirkdale Ct 2 NE34 59 A4
Kirkdale Gn NE4 100 B4
Kirkdale Sq SR5 74 B3
Kirkdale St DH5 94 F2
Kirkham NE38 83 D4
Kirkham Ave NE3 37 C7
Kirkharle Dr NE61 4 E4
Kirkheaton Pl NE5 54 C8
Kirkland Wlk NE27 30 E3
Kirklands NE23 29 C5
Kirklea Rd DH5 94 F8
Kirkleatham Gdns NE6 39 D2
Kirkley Ave NE34 60 A6
Kirkley Cl NE3 38 B6
Kirkley Dr Ponteland NE20 25 E7
Ashington NE63 6 E2
Kirkley Hall* NE20 130 D8
Kirkley Lodge NE3 38 B6
Kirkley Rd NE27 30 F2
Kirklinton Rd NE30 32 A2
Kirknewton Cl 7 DH5 94 F8
Kirkside DH4 90 E6
Kirkston Ave NE15 53 D7
Kirkstone DH3 82 D2
Kirkstone Ave
Tynemouth NE30 32 A2
Hedworth NE32 58 D3
Sunderland SR5 75 C3
Kirkstone Cl 8 DH5 94 F8
Kirkstone Gdns NE7 39 A3
Kirkstone Rd NE10 71 F8
Kirkwell Cl SR5 74 A1
Kirkwood NE23 29 C5
Kirkwood Ave SR4 85 A2
Kirkwood Dr NE3 37 F5
Kirkwood Gdns NE10 72 B8
Kirkwood Pl NE3 28 B1
Kirton Ave NE4 54 E6
Kirton Park Terr NE29, NE30 42 A7
Kirton Way NE23 22 C8
Kismet St SR5 75 A2
Kitchener Rd SR6 60 F4
Kitchener St
Gateshead NE9 71 A8
Sunderland SR4 85 F4
Kitchener Terr
New Herrington DH4 90 D6
North Shields NE30 42 C7
Jarrow NE32 58 B5
Sunderland SR2 86 F2
Kittiwake Cl Blyth NE24 17 E3
Shiremoor NE28 41 A7
Kittiwake Dr NE38 82 F3
Kittiwake House NE26 32 B5
Kitty Brewster Ind Est NE24 12 B1
Kitty Brewster Rd NE24 16 F8
Kiwi St NE11 70 C5
Knaresborough Cl NE22 10 D2
Knaresborough Sq SR5 74 C4
Knaresdale DH3 82 D1
Knarsdale Ave NE29 41 D6
Knarsdale Pl 3 NE5 36 E1
Knightsbridge
Newcastle-upon-Tyne NE3 38 C6
Sunderland SR3 91 E8
Knightside Gdns NE11 70 A7
Knightside Wlk NE5 36 C3
Knivestone Ct NE12 29 E4
Knobbyends La NE21 67 F8
Knoll Rise NE11 69 F7
Knoll The Ellington NE61 1 C5
Sunderland SR2 102 B1
Knollside Cl SR3 91 F5
Knop Law Fst Sch NE5 36 C3
Knott Flats 13 NE30 42 D7
Knott Pl NE15 54 B5
Knoulberry NE37 83 A6
Knoulberry Rd NE37 83 A6
Knowle Pl NE12 39 B5
Knowledge Hill NE21 53 B1
Knowsley Ct NE3 37 B5
Knox Cl NE22 11 D2
Knox Rd NE22 16 B8
Knox Sq SR5 75 A2
Knutsford Wlk NE23 22 C8
Kramel Fst Sch NE23 22 C5
Kristin Ave NE32 58 C4
Kyffin View NE34 60 B5
Kyle Cl NE4 100 B4
Kyle Rd NE8 70 C8
Kylins The NE61 9 A6
Kyloe Ave NE25 23 D2
Kyloe Cl NE3 37 E7
Kyloe Pl NE5 37 A3
Kyloe Villas NE5 37 A3
Kyo Bog La NE41,NE42 51 B1
Kyo Cl NE41 51 B1
Kyo La NE40 66 D7

L

L'Arbre Cres NE16 68 F7
La Sagesse High Sch NE2 38 E3
Laburnum Ave
Gateshead NE10 72 A7
Blyth NE24 17 D8
Whitley Bay NE26 32 A5
Wallsend NE28 40 B2
Washington NE38 83 B1
Newcastle-upon-Tyne NE6 56 F8
Laburnum Cl SR4 85 A6
Laburnum Cres NE11 81 C6
Laburnum Ct NE12 29 C4
Laburnum Gdns
6 Gateshead, Felling NE10 56 D1
Jarrow NE32 58 A4
Gateshead, Low Fell NE9 70 F6
Laburnum Gr
Sunniside NE16 69 B2
Whickham NE16 69 A7
Hebburn NE31 57 E3
South Shields NE34 59 F5
Sunderland SR5 85 A8
Cleadon SR6 60 A1
Laburnum Rd
Blaydon NE21 53 C2
Sunderland SR6 75 D3
Laburnum Terr NE63 6 D3
Laburnun Ct NE62 10 E7
Lacebark Shiney Row DH4 89 F6
Silksworth SR3 91 E4
Ladock Cl SR2 93 A8
Lady Beatrice Terr DH4 90 E7
Lady St DH5 95 A5
Lady Waterford Hall* TD15 107 C6
Lady's Piece La DH6 96 A5
Lady's Well (N.T.)* NE65 117 A5
Lady's Wlk
South Shields NE33 42 C4
Morpeth NE61 3 E1
Ladybank NE5 36 B4
Ladycutters La NE45 46 F3
Ladyhaugh Dr NE16 69 A4
Ladykirk Rd NE4 54 E5
Ladykirk Way NE23 21 E6
Ladyrigg NE20 25 D4
Ladysmith St NE33 42 D2
Ladywell NE43 64 D6
Ladywell Rd NE21 53 C2
Ladywell Way NE20 25 D7
Ladywood Pk DH4 89 F8
Laet St NE29 42 B5
Laindon Ave SR6 75 D4
Laing Art Gallery & Mus* NE1 99 B2
Laing Gr NE28 41 B3
Laith Rd NE3 37 E5
Lake App NE21 53 F1
Lake Ave NE34 60 C6
Lake Ct SR3 92 A6
Lake Rd DH5 94 E8
Lake View NE31 57 E4
Lakeside Blaydon NE21 53 F1
South Shields NE34 60 D6
Laleham Ct NE3 37 D7
Lamb St
East Cramlington NE23 22 F5
Newcastle-upon-Tyne NE6 57 A5
Lamb Terr 6 NE27 30 E1
Lambden Cl NE29 41 E3
Lambert Rd NE37 82 F7
Lambert Sq NE3 38 A5
Lambeth Pl NE8 71 A8
Lambley Ave NE30 32 B2
Lambley Cl NE16 69 A2
Lambley Cres NE31 57 D3
Lambourn Ave
Longbenton NE12 39 C7
North Shields NE29 41 E4
Lambourne Cl DH4 89 E3
Lambourne Rd SR2 86 C3
Lambton Ave NE16 69 C8
Lambton Cl NE40 51 F4
Lambton Ct
Washington NE38 88 E8
Sunderland SR3 91 C7
Lambton Dr DH5 95 A1
Lambton Gdns NE16 78 E5
Lambton Prim Sch NE38 83 B3
Lambton Rd
Newcastle-upon-Tyne NE2 99 B4
Hebburn NE31 57 F7
Lambton St
Chester le Street DH3 88 D2
Gateshead NE8 101 B3
Sunderland SR1 103 A3
Lambton Terr
Penshaw DH4 89 F8
Jarrow NE32 58 B4
Lambton Tower SR1 103 B3
Lampeter Cl NE5 37 B4
Lamport St NE31 57 C7
Lampton Ct NE22 11 C2
Lampton Lea DH4 90 A4
Lanark Cl NE29 41 C8
Lanark Dr NE32 58 E2
Lancaster Ct NE3 37 D7
Lancaster Dr NE28 40 D7
Lancaster House NE23 22 D5
Lancaster Pl NE11 54 E1
Lancaster Rd NE11 54 E1
Lancaster St NE4 98 B1
Lancaster Terr
Chester le Street DH3 88 D2
Morpeth NE61 4 A1
Lancaster Way NE32 58 A1
Lancastrian Rd NE23 22 A5
Lancefield Ave NE6 56 F4
Lancet Ct NE8 101 C2
Lanchester Ave NE9 71 E3
Lanchester Cl NE10 72 C6
Lanchester Gn NE22 10 F2
Lanchester Pk NE38 83 E2
Lanchester St NE34 59 B5
Lancing Ct NE3 37 C7
Landscape Terr NE40 52 B1
Landsdowne Gdns NE62 11 A8
Landseer Gdns
Whiteleas NE34 59 D2
Gateshead NE9 71 B7
Landswood Terr NE21 68 D7
Lane Cnr NE34 59 C5
Lane Head NE40 52 C5
Lanercost NE38 83 D5
Lanercost Ave NE21 53 B2
Lanercost Dr NE5 54 C8
Lanercost Gdns
Gateshead NE10 71 C6
Throckley NE15 35 D2
Lanercost Pk NE23 22 D5
Lanercost Rd NE29 41 E5
Lanesborough Ct NE3 38 A5
Langdale Birtley DH3 82 E1
Whitley Bay NE25 31 E5
Washington NE37 83 C7
Langdale Cl NE12 39 A6
Langdale Cres NE21 68 B8
Langdale Dr NE23 21 E6
Langdale Gdns
Wallsend NE28 41 A5
Newcastle-upon-Tyne NE6 57 A6
Langdale Rd
Penshaw DH4 90 A8
Gateshead NE9 71 A5
Langdale St DH5 95 A2
Langdale Terr NE17 77 A5
Langdale Way NE36 74 C7
Langdon Cl NE29 31 F1
Langdon Rd NE5 36 E2
Langford Dr NE35 58 F2
Langham Ave NE29 41 C8
Langham Rd NE15 54 A5
Langholm Rd
Newcastle-upon-Tyne NE3 38 C7
East Boldon NE36 74 D8
Langhorn Cl NE6 56 B7
Langhurst SR2 92 E8
Langleeford Rd NE5 37 A4
Langley Ave
Gateshead NE10 72 B6
Blyth NE24 17 B8
Whitley Bay NE25 31 D3
Shiremoor NE27 31 A3
Hexham NE46 45 D4
Langley Cl NE38 83 B4
Langley Fst Sch NE25 31 D3
Langley Mere 8 NE12 39 D8
Langley Rd
North Shields NE29 41 D6
Newcastle-upon-Tyne, West Denton NE5 53 F8
Newcastle-upon-Tyne, Walker NE6 56 F6
Ashington NE63 6 C3
Sunderland SR3 86 B2
Langley St DH4 90 D6
Langley Tarn 1 NE29 42 A4
Langley Terr NE32 58 B3
Langport Rd SR2 86 D3
Langton Cl SR4 102 B2
Langton Ct NE20 25 B4
Langton Dr NE23 16 C2
Langton St NE8 101 C1
Langton Terr
Bournmoor DH4 89 E2
Newcastle-upon-Tyne NE7 39 B2
Langwell Cres NE63 6 C4
Langwell Terr NE61 4 F4
Lanivet Cl 4 SR2 92 F8
Lannerwood 5 NE29 42 A4
Lansbury Cl DH3 82 B6
Lansbury Dr DH3 82 B5
Lansbury Gdns NE10 72 A8
Lansbury Rd NE16 69 C6
Lansbury Way SR5 74 B1
Lansdown SR2 92 E7
Lansdowne Cres NE3 38 C5
Lansdowne Ct NE46 44 F3
Lansdowne Gdns NE2 56 A8
Lansdowne Pl NE3 38 C5
Lansdowne Rd NE12 39 D8
Lansdowne St SR4 102 B3
Lansdowne Terr
North Shields NE29 41 F6
Newcastle-upon-Tyne NE3 38 C5
Lansdowne Terr E NE3 38 C5
Lansdowne Terr W NE29 41 F6
Lanthwaite Rd NE9 71 A4
Lanton St DH4 90 D6
Lapford Dr NE23 16 C1
Lapwing Cl Blyth NE24 17 E4
Washington NE38 82 F3
Lapwing Ct
Burnopfield NE16 79 C5
South Shields NE34 59 E5
Larch Ave
Houghton-le-Spring DH4 90 D1
South Shields NE34 60 A5
Whitburn SR6 61 A2
Larch Cl NE9 71 D2
Larch Rd NE21 53 D3
Larch St NE16 69 B2
Larch Terr DH9 79 A1
Larches The
Burnopfield NE16 79 B7
Newcastle-upon-Tyne NE4 100 A3
Larchlea NE20 25 C2
Larchlea S NE20 25 C2
Larchwood NE38 83 B1
Larchwood Ave
Wide Open NE13 28 C5
Newcastle-upon-Tyne, Fawdon NE3 37 F7
Newcastle-upon-Tyne, Walkergate NE6 56 E8
Larchwood Dr NE63 6 C1
Larchwood Gdns NE11 70 B5
Larchwood Gr SR2 86 C2
Lark Rise Cl NE7 39 D3
Larkfield Cres DH4 90 A5
Larkfield Rd SR2 86 C3
Larkspur NE9 71 C4
Larkspur Com Prim Sch NE9 71 C4
Larkspur Rd NE16 69 B6
Larkspur Terr NE2 38 E1
Larkswood NE34 60 B7
Larne Cres NE9 71 A5
Larriston Pl NE23 21 F6
Lartington Gdns NE3 38 F5
Larwood Cl DH3 88 E1
Lascelles Ave NE34 59 E5
Laski Gdns NE10 72 B8
Lassells Rise NE42 50 D4
Latimer St NE30 42 D8
Latrigg Ct 25 SR3 91 F6
Lauderdale Ave NE28 40 C4
Launceston Cl NE3 37 D8
Launceston Dr SR3 91 C7
Laura St SR1 103 B2
Laurel Ave
Killingworth NE12 30 A1
Newcastle-upon-Tyne NE3 38 A7
Laurel Cres Burnside DH4 90 C3
Newcastle-upon-Tyne NE6 39 F1
Laurel Ct
Chester le Street DH2 88 B5
Laurel Ct *continued*
North Shields NE30 42 B5
Laurel Dr NE63 6 C1
Laurel End NE12 30 A1
Laurel Gr SR2 86 D2
Laurel Rd NE21 53 D2
Laurel St Throckley NE15 35 D3
Wallsend NE28 40 C1
Laurel Terr
Burnopfield NE16 78 F6
Seaton Delaval NE25 23 E2
Laurel Way NE40 52 A3
Laurel Wlk NE3 38 C5
Laurelwood Gdns NE11 70 B5
Laurens Ct NE37 83 D8
Lavender Ct NE63 6 C1
Lavender Gdns
Newcastle-upon-Tyne NE2 38 D1
Gateshead NE9 70 F6
Lavender Gr SR5 74 A1
Lavender La NE34 59 B5
Lavender Rd NE16 69 A6
Lavender Row NE9 71 B5
Lavender St 4 SR4 85 A6
Lavender Wlk NE31 57 E3
Laverick NE10 71 F6
Laverock Ct 12 NE6 56 C5
Laverock Hall Rd NE24 17 B3
Laverock Pl Blyth NE24 17 B3
3 Newcastle-upon-Tyne NE3 37 D5
Lavers Rd DH3 82 C5
Lavington Rd NE34 59 E8
Lawe Rd NE33 42 D4
Lawn Cotts SR3 91 F6
Lawn Dr NE36 73 F6
Lawn The NE40 52 C6
Lawnhead Sq SR3 92 B6
Lawns The
Easington Lane DH5 95 C1
Whitburn SR6 75 F8
Lawnsway NE32 58 C1
Lawnswood DH5 94 F7
Lawrence Ave
Blaydon NE21 53 C3
Whiteleas NE34 59 D3
Lawrence Ct
Gateshead NE10 72 C8
Blaydon NE21 53 C3
Lawrence Hill Ct NE10 72 B8
Lawrence St SR1 103 C2
Laws St SR6 75 D4
Lawson Ave NE32 58 D3
Lawson Cres SR6 75 D4
Lawson Ct 6 DH2 88 C2
Lawson House NE4 54 E4
Lawson St Wallsend NE28 40 C1
North Shields NE29 42 A4
Lawson St W 8 NE29 42 A4
Lawson Terr
Hetton le Hole DH5 95 B1
Newcastle-upon-Tyne NE4 54 E4
Laxford DH3 82 D2
Laxford Ct SR3 92 A5
Laybourn Gdns 5 NE34 59 A4
Layburn Gdns NE15 53 E8
Laycock Gdns NE23 22 F1
Layfield Rd NE3 28 C1
Laygate NE33 42 C1
Laygate Lane Prim Sch NE33 42 C1
Laygate Pl NE33 42 C1
Laygate St NE33 42 B1
Lea Ave NE32 58 C2
Lea Gn DH3 82 E1
Lea Riggs DH4 94 A2
Lea View NE34 60 B8
Leabank NE15 53 D8
Leaburn Terr NE42 50 B2
Lead Gate NE15 33 C1
Lead La DH8,NE43 76 C6
Lead Rd
High Spen NE17,NE40 66 D6
Greenside NE40 52 B1
Stocksfield NE43 64 B2
Leadgate Cotts NE17 66 A4
Leafield Cres NE34 60 A8
Leagreen Ct NE3 38 A6
Leaholme Cres NE24 17 C6
Lealholm Rd NE7 39 A5
Leam Gdns NE10 72 C8
Leam La Gateshead NE10 72 B6
Jarrow NE32 58 C3
Leamington St SR4 102 B1
Leamside Gateshead NE10 71 F6
Jarrow NE32 58 C4
Leander Ave
Chester le Street DH3 88 D7
Stakeford NE62 11 B8
Leander Ct NE62 11 B8
Leander Dr NE35 73 E8
Leaplish NE38 83 F2
Leas The DH4 90 D3
Leasyde Wlk NE16 68 F5
Leatham SR2 92 E8
Leaway NE42 50 B2
Leazes Arc NE1 99 A2
Leazes Cres
Newcastle-upon-Tyne NE1 98 C2
Hexham NE46 44 F5
Leazes Ct NE4 98 B2
Leazes Dwellings NE4 98 B3
Leazes La
Newcastle-upon-Tyne NE1 99 A2
Corbridge NE45 47 A8

Leazes La *continued*
Hexham NE46 44 E5
Leazes Par NE2 98 B2
Leazes Park Rd NE1 99 A2
Leazes Parkway NE15 35 D1
Leazes Pk NE46 44 E5
Leazes Terr
Newcastle-upon-Tyne NE1 98 C2
Corbridge NE45 46 F6
Hexham NE46 44 F5
Leazes The
Throckley NE15 35 C1
Burnopfield NE16 78 F6
South Shields NE34 59 F6
Sunderland SR1 102 B2
Leazes View
Rowlands Gill NE39 67 D2
Ovington NE42 49 D4
Leazes Villas NE16 79 A6
Lecondale NE10 71 F5
Lecondale Ct NE10 71 F5
Ledbury Rd SR2 86 D3
Lee Cl NE38 84 B6
Lee St
[6] Sunderland, Southwick SR5 75 B1
Sunderland, Fulwell SR6 75 D4
Lee Terr DH5 95 B2
Leechmere Cres SR7 92 F1
Leechmere Ind Est SR2 86 E1
Leechmere Rd SR2 86 D1
Leechmere View [5] SR2 92 F8
Leechmere Way SR2 92 F8
Leeds St SR6 75 E2
Leeholme DH5 94 F7
Leeming Gdns NE9 71 B6
Legg Ave NE22 11 E3
Legges Dr NE13 20 D6
Legion Gr NE15 53 F7
Legion Rd NE15 53 F7
Leicester Cl NE28 40 A5
Leicester St NE6 56 E5
Leicester Way NE32 58 A1
Leighton Rd SR2 86 D2
Leighton St
South Shields NE33 42 E2
[7] Newcastle-upon-Tyne NE6 56 A6
Leighton Terr DH3 82 B5
Leith Ct NE34 59 C5
Leith Gdns DH9 79 D1
Leland Pl NE61 8 D7
Lemington Fst Sch NE15 53 D6
Lemington Gdns NE5 54 C7
Lemington Mid Sch NE15 53 D8
Lemington Rd NE15 53 B6
Lemon St NE33 59 B6
Lena Ave NE25 31 E4
Lenin Terr NE17 77 C8
Lenore Terr NE40 52 B2
Leominster Rd SR2 86 D2
Leopold St NE32 58 B6
Lesbury Ave
Shiremoor NE27 30 E3
Wallsend NE28 40 F3
Stakeford NE62 6 A1
Ashington NE63 6 D2
Lesbury Chase NE3 38 B7
Lesbury Gdns NE13 28 C6
Lesbury Rd NE6 56 B8
Lesbury St
Newcastle-upon-Tyne NE15 53 C6
North Shields NE28 41 C1
Lesbury Terr NE17 77 B8
Lesley Ct NE3 38 C5
Leslie Ave NE31 57 E5
Leslie Cl NE40 52 E4
Leslie Cres NE3 38 C3
Leslies View NE61 3 E2
Letch Way NE15 53 C7
Letchwell Villas NE12 29 E1
Leuchars Ct DH3 82 C3
Leven Ave DH2 88 B1
Leven Ho [10] SR3 92 A6
Levens Wlk NE23 21 E7
Levisham Cl SR3 92 C7
Lewis Cres SR2 103 C1
Lewis Dr NE4 54 F6
Lewis Gdns NE34 59 C3
Leybourne Ave NE12 29 D1
Leybourne Dene NE12 29 D2
Leybourne Hold DH3 82 C6
Leyburn Cl Urpeth DH2 81 D1
Houghton-le-Spring DH4 90 D1
Leyburn Dr NE7 39 A3
Leyburn Gr DH4 90 D1
Leyburn Pl DH3 82 B6
Leyfield Cl SR3 92 B5
Leyton Pl NE8 71 B8
Liberty Terr DH9 79 B2
Library NE42 50 D3
Liburn Cl NE36 74 C8
Lichfield Ave NE6 56 E4
Lichfield Cl
Newcastle-upon-Tyne NE3 37 E7
Ashington NE63 6 F2
Lichfield Rd SR5 75 A3
Lichfield Way NE32 58 A1
Lidcombe Cl SR3 92 C7
Liddell Ct SR6 75 F2
Liddell St
North Shields NE29,NE30 42 B5
Sunderland SR6 103 A4
Liddell Terr
Kibblesworth NE11 81 C6
Gateshead NE8 70 D8
Liddle Ct NE4 98 A1
Liddle Rd NE4 98 A1
Liddles St NE22 11 D3
Lieven St NE13 28 A4
Liffey Rd NE31 57 F3
Lightbourne Rd NE6 57 A6
Lightfoot Sports Ctr The NE6 56 F4
Lightwood Ave NE15 54 A4
Lilac Ave
[11] Houghton-le-Spring DH5 94 E8
Longbenton NE12 39 F8
Blyth NE24 17 D8
South Shields NE34 60 A5
New Silksworth SR3 92 B8
Whitburn SR6 60 F3
Lilac Cl NE5 36 B4
Lilac Cres NE16 79 A6
Lilac Ct Ellington NE61 1 E6
Ashington NE63 6 C1
Lilac Gdns
Whickham NE16 69 A6
Washington NE38 83 C1
Gateshead NE9 70 F6
Cleadon SR6 60 A2
Lilac Gr
Chester le Street DH2 88 A5
Sunderland SR6 75 D3
Lilac Rd NE6 40 A1
Lilac Sq DH4 89 E3
Lilac St SR4 85 A6
Lilac Wlk NE31 57 E3
Lilburn Cl [5] NE6 56 C4
Lilburn Gdns NE3,NE7 38 F4
Lilburn Pl SR5 75 A1
Lilburn Rd NE27 30 E2
Lilburn St NE29 41 F5
Lilburne Cl SR1 103 B3
Lilian Ave Wallsend NE28 40 A1
Sunderland SR2 92 E8
Lilley Gr SR5 74 B1
Lilley Terr NE39 67 F3
Lilleycroft NE39 67 F2
Lily Ave
Newcastle-upon-Tyne NE2 38 E1
Bedlington NE22 16 B8
Lily Bank NE28 40 C2
Lily Cl NE21 53 A2
Lily Cres
Newcastle-upon-Tyne NE2 38 E1
Whitburn SR6 60 F3
Lily Est NE15 35 D3
Lily Gdns DH9 78 E1
Lily St SR4 102 B3
Lily Terr Newbottle DH4 90 D4
Newcastle-upon-Tyne NE5 37 A3
Lilywhite Terr DH5 95 B1
Lime Ave DH4 90 C1
Lime Gr Ryton NE40 52 C5
Prudhoe NE42 50 B3
Lime St
Newcastle-upon-Tyne NE1, NE6 56 A5
Throckley NE15 35 D3
Blaydon NE21 53 D1
Sunderland SR4 102 B3
Limecroft NE32 58 C1
Limekiln Ct NE28 40 D2
Limekiln Rd NE28 40 D2
Limes Ave NE24 12 D1
Limes The Penshaw DH4 90 B8
Stannington NE61 14 C3
Sunderland SR2 86 D4
Limestone La NE20 25 B7
Limetree NE38 83 E2
Limetrees Gdns NE9 70 F7
Limewood Ct NE2 98 B4
Limewood Gr NE13 28 B5
Linacre Cl NE3 37 B6
Linbridge Dr NE5 36 E1
Linburn NE38 89 B8
Lincoln Ave
Wallsend NE28 40 A3
New Silksworth SR3 92 A8
Lincoln Cres DH5 94 F4
Lincoln Ct NE31 57 D5
Lincoln Gn NE3 28 C1
Lincoln Rd
Cramlington NE23 16 C1
South Shields NE34 60 B7
Lincoln St
Gateshead NE8 101 B1
Sunderland SR4 85 F7
Lincoln Way NE32 58 B1
Lindale Ave NE16 69 A5
Lindale Rd NE4 54 E8
Lindean Pl NE23 21 F6
Linden NE9 71 D4
Linden Ave
Newcastle-upon-Tyne, Gosforth NE3 38 C4
Newcastle-upon-Tyne, Fenham NE4 54 D7
Linden Cl NE62 11 A8
Linden Gdns SR2 86 C3
Linden Gr
Houghton-le-Spring DH4 94 D8
[1] Dunston NE11 70 A8
Linden Rd
Longbenton NE12 39 D7
Blaydon NE21 53 D2
Seaton Delaval NE25 23 B3
Newcastle-upon-Tyne NE3 38 C4
Sunderland SR2 86 C3
Linden Sch NE12 39 D8
Linden Terr
Longbenton NE12 39 D6
Whitley Bay NE26 32 A5
Springwell NE9 71 F1
Linden Way
Ponteland NE20 25 C3
Ellington NE61 1 D5
Gateshead NE9 71 D2
Lindfield Ave NE5 37 C1
Lindisfarne
Washington NE38 83 C4
Ryhope SR2 92 E6
Lindisfarne Ave DH3 88 D3
Lindisfarne Castle (N.T.)* TD15 105 ??
Lindisfarne Cl
Chester le Street DH2 88 A1
Burnside DH4 90 C2
Newcastle-upon-Tyne, Jesmond NE2 38 F2
Newcastle-upon-Tyne, West Denton NE5 36 F1
Morpeth NE61 9 A6
Pegswood NE61 5 A4
Lindisfarne Com Prim Sch NE8 56 A2
Lindisfarne Ct NE32 58 F6
Lindisfarne Dr NE8 101 C2
Lindisfarne Ho [2] NE63 6 F2
Lindisfarne La NE61 9 A6
Lindisfarne Pl NE28 40 D3
Lindisfarne Priory* TD15 105 ??
Lindisfarne Rd
Newcastle-upon-Tyne NE2 38 F2
Hebburn NE31 57 E3
Jarrow NE32 58 D4
Lindisfarne Recess NE32 58 D4
Lindisfarne Terr NE30 42 A7
Lindisfarne Wlk NE62 10 E7
Lindom Ave DH3 88 D3
Lindrick Ct NE10 72 C7
Lindsay Ave NE24 17 C8
Lindsay Cl SR2 103 B1
Lindsay Ct SR6 60 F2
Lindsay Rd SR2 103 B1
Lindsay St DH5 95 B5
Lindsey Cl NE23 21 E6
Lindum Rd NE9 70 F8
Linfield SR2 92 E6
Lingcrest NE9 71 C5
Lingdale Ave SR6 75 E6
Lingey Gdns NE10 72 C8
Lingey House Prim Schs NE10 72 B7
Lingey La NE10 72 B7
Lingfield DH5 94 F7
Lingholme DH2 88 A4
Lingmell NE37 83 B6
Lingshaw NE10 72 B7
Lingside NE32 58 C1
Linhope Ave NE3 37 F7
Linhope Fst Sch NE5 36 F2
Linhope Rd NE5 36 F2
Link Ave NE22 10 D1
Link Rd Hazlerigg NE13 28 A4
Newcastle-upon-Tyne NE5 37 E2
Link The NE46 44 F5
Links Ave
Whitley Bay NE26 31 F7
Tynemouth NE30 32 C2
Links Ct NE26 32 A7
Links Gn NE3 38 D6
Links Rd Blyth NE24 17 F4
Seaton Sluice NE24 18 A2
Tynemouth NE30 32 C2
Links The NE26 32 A7
Links View Blyth NE24 17 C4
Ashington NE63 12 A8
Links Wlk NE5 36 F2
Linkway NE32 58 D1
Linley Hill NE16 68 E4
Linnel Dr NE15 53 E7
Linnet Cl NE38 83 A3
Linnet Ct NE63 6 B2
Linnet Gr SR5 74 C1
Linnetsfield NE6 56 F8
Linney Gdns NE34 59 A4
Linnheads NE42 50 B1
Linshiels Gdns [1] NE63 6 F2
Linskell SR2 92 E8
Linskill Terr NE30 42 B7
Linskill Pl
Newcastle-upon-Tyne NE3 37 F3
North Shields NE30 42 B7
Linskill PRU NE30 42 B7
Linskill St NE30 42 B5
Linskill Terr NE30 42 B7
Linslade Wlk NE23 21 F6
Lintfort NE38 88 E7
Linthorpe Ct NE34 59 A5
Linthorpe Rd
Newcastle-upon-Tyne NE3 38 C7
Tynemouth NE30 32 B1
Linton NE12 29 D5
Linton Fst Sch NE61 1 A3
Linton Rd
Whitley Bay NE26 24 E1
Gateshead NE9 70 F3
Lintonville Rd NE63 6 C4
Lintonville Terr NE63 6 C5
Lintz Green La NE16,NE39 78 C6
Lintz La NE16 78 E4
Lintz Terr NE16 78 F6
Lintzford Gdns
Newcastle-upon-Tyne NE15 53 E7
Rowlands Gill NE39 78 D8
Lintzford La NE39 67 B1
Lintzford Rd
Hamsterley Mill NE39 78 C7
Rowlands Gill NE39 78 C7
Linum Pl NE4 54 E8
Linwood Pl NE3 28 C1
Lion Wlk NE29 42 A3
Lisa Ave SR4 85 A5
Lisburn Terr SR4 102 A3
Lish Ave NE26 32 C4
Lishman Terr NE40 52 A4
Lisle Gr NE28 41 A3
Lisle Rd NE34 60 A6
Lisle St
Newcastle-upon-Tyne NE1 99 A2
Wallsend NE28 40 B2
Lismor Terr NE9 71 F1
Lismore Ave NE33 59 D7
Lismore Pl NE15 54 D6
Lister Ave Dunston NE11 54 F1
Greenside NE40 66 F8
Lister Cl DH5 94 D6
Lister St NE15 53 F5
Listers La NE9 71 A8
Litchfield Cres [2] NE21 53 B1
Litchfield La NE21 53 B1
Litchfield St [1] NE21 53 B1
Litchfield Terr [3] NE21 53 B1
Little Bedford St NE29, NE30 42 B5
Little Dene NE2 38 D3
Little Villiers St SR1 103 B3
Little Way NE15 54 B4
Littleburn Cl DH4 90 C2
Littledene NE9 70 F7
Littletown La DH6 96 D3
Litton Ct [14] SR3 91 F6
Littondale NE28 39 F4
Liverpool St NE1 99 A2
Livingstone Pl [8] NE33 42 C4
Livingstone Rd SR1 102 C3
Livingstone St [2] NE33 42 D4
Livingstone View NE30 42 C7
Lizard La NE34,SR6 60 E4
Lloyd Ave DH5 94 C4
Lloyd Ct NE11 54 E2
Lloyd St [5] NE40 51 F3
Lobban Ave NE31 57 D3
Lobelia Ave NE10 56 B2
Lobelia Cl NE5 36 B3
Lobley Gdns NE11 70 A6
Lobley Hill Prim Sch NE11 70 A6
Lobley Hill Rd NE11,NE8 70 C7
Lobleyhill Rd
Byermoor NE16 79 D8
Sunniside NE16 79 D8
Local Ave DH6 96 C1
Locarno Pl NE64 7 E4
Lochcraig Pl NE23 21 F6
Lochfield Gdns NE11 81 C6
Lochmaben Terr SR5 75 D2
Lockerbie Gdns NE15 53 E7
Lockerbie Rd NE23 21 E7
Lockhaugh Rd NE39 68 A4
Locksley Cl NE29 31 B1
Locomotion Way
Killingworth NE12 29 B5
North Shields NE29 42 A4
Locomotive Ct NE42 50 C2
Lodge Cl NE39 78 A5
Lodges Rd The NE9 70 F3
Lodgeside Mdw SR3 92 B5
Lodore Ct [5] SR3 91 F6
Lodore Gr NE32 58 D3
Lodore Rd NE2 38 D3
Lofthill [6] SR3 91 E5
Logan Rd NE6 39 F1
Logan St DH5 95 A3
Logan Terr DH6 97 E8
Lola St NE13 27 F4
Lombard Dr DH3 88 D7
Lombard St
Newcastle-upon-Tyne NE1 101 B4
Sunderland SR1 103 B3
Lomond Cl NE38 83 B3
Lomond Ct [11] SR3 92 A6
Lomond Pl DH2 88 B1
London Ave NE37 72 B1
Londonderry St SR3 92 A7
Londonderry Terr SR3 92 B7
Londonderry Tower SR1 103 B3
Londonderry Way DH4 90 A7
Long Bank Birtley DH3 82 C7
Gateshead NE9 71 C1
Long Close Rd NE39 77 F5
Long Crag NE37 83 A5
Long Dr NE61 8 F5
Long Gair NE21 68 A8
Long Headlam [10] NE6 56 C6
Long Meadow Cl NE40 52 A3
Long Pk NE64 7 D4
Long Ridge Rd
Blaydon NE21,NE40 52 D2
Greenside NE21,NE40 52 D2
Long Rigg NE16 54 A2
Long Row NE33 42 B4
Long Row Cl NE40 66 F8
Longacre
Houghton-le-Spring DH4 94 C8
Washington NE38 83 E1
Longbenton Com Coll NE12 39 C7
Longbenton Sta NE12 39 A5
Longborough Ct NE7 39 A4
Longclose Bank DH8,DH9, NE17,NE39 77 E3
Longdean Cl NE31 57 C5
Longdean Pk DH3 88 D6
Longfellow St DH5 94 E7
Longfield Cl NE34 59 D4
Longfield Rd SR6 75 D3
Longfield Terr NE6 57 A4
Longframlington Gardens* NE65 118 E4
Longhirst Gateshead NE10 72 A7
Killingworth NE12 29 D5
Newcastle-upon-Tyne NE5 36 F2
Longhirst Dr NE13 28 B5
Longhirst Rd NE61 4 F4
Longhirst Village NE61 4 F7
Longlands Dr DH5 94 E7
Longleat Gdns
[10] South Shields NE33 42 D3
Pegswood NE61 4 E4
Longley St NE4 98 A2
Longmeadows
Ponteland NE20 25 B3
Sunderland SR3 91 C6
Longniddry NE37 72 C3
Longniddry Ct NE9 70 E3
Longridge NE21 53 A2
Longridge Ave
Washington NE38 83 B3
Newcastle-upon-Tyne NE7 39 D2
Longridge Dr NE26 31 E7
Longridge Sq SR2 86 D2
Longridge Way
Bedlington NE22 11 A4
Cramlington NE23 21 F6
Longrigg NE10 72 A7
Longrigg Rd NE11 54 B2
Longriggs The NE44 62 E7
Longshank La DH3 82 A6
Longstaff Gdns NE34 58 F4
Longston Ave NE30 32 B3
Longstone Ct NE12 29 E4
Longstone Lighthouse* 109 F7
Longstone Sq NE5 36 D1
Longwood Cl NE16 69 B3
Lonnen Ave NE4 54 D7
Lonnen Dr NE16 69 A8
Lonnen The
South Shields NE34 60 B4
Ryton NE40 52 E5
Lonsdale DH3 82 E1
Lonsdale Ave Blyth NE24 16 E8
Sunderland SR6 75 E7
Lonsdale Ct NE34 59 A4
Lonsdale Gdns NE28 41 A4
Lonsdale Rd SR6 75 E2
Lonsdale Terr NE2 38 E2
Loraine Terr NE15 53 C6
Lord Blyton Prim Sch NE34 58 F5
Lord Byrons Wlk SR7 93 B1
Lord Gort Cl [1] SR5 75 A1
Lord Lawson of Beamish Comp Sch DH3 82 D3
Lord Nelson St NE33, NE34 59 B6
Lord St
Newcastle-upon-Tyne NE1 100 C4
South Shields NE33 42 E1
New Silksworth SR3 92 B7
Lordenshaw NE5 36 F2
Lorne St DH5 97 B8
Lorne Terr SR2 103 A1
Lorrain Rd NE34 59 D2
Lort Ho NE2 99 C2
Lorton Ave NE30 32 A2
Lorton Rd NE9 71 A4
Losh Terr NE6 56 F5
Lossiemouth Rd NE29 41 C5
Lothian Cl DH3 82 D1
Lothian Ct NE5 37 C3
Lotus Cl NE5 36 B3
Lotus Pl NE4 54 D7
Loudon St NE34 59 C5
Lough Ct NE9 71 B5
Loughborough Ave
Tynemouth NE30 32 C1
Sunderland SR2 86 C3
Loughbrow Pk NE46 45 B2
Loughrigg Ave NE23 21 F6
Louie Terr NE9 71 A5
Louis Ave SR6 75 D3
Louise Terr DH3 88 C3
Loup St NE21 53 C3
Louvain Terr
Hetton le Hole DH5 95 A5
Guide Post NE62 10 F7
Louvain Terr W DH5 95 A5
Lovaine Ave
Whitley Bay NE25 32 A4
[8] North Shields NE29 42 A5
Lovaine Flats NE1 99 B2
Lovaine Pl NE29 42 A5
Lovaine Pl W [6] NE29 41 F5
Lovaine Row NE30 42 E8
Lovaine St NE15 52 E8
Lovaine Terr NE29 42 A6
Love Ave NE23 29 B7
Love Avenue Cotts NE23 29 B8
Love La NE1 99 C1
Loveless Gdns NE10 72 B8
Lovett Wlk NE8 100 C2
Low Burswell NE46 44 F5
Low Chare DH3 88 D3
Low Cl NE42 50 E3
Low Downs Rd DH5 95 A6
Low Farm NE61 1 D4
Low Fell Jun & Inf Sch NE9 70 F5
Low Flatts Rd DH3 88 C6
Low Fold NE6 56 B5

Low Friar St NE1 99 A1
Low Gate Prim Sch NE46 44 A4
Low Gosforth Ct NE3 28 D1
Low Haugh NE20 25 F7
Low Heworth La NE10 56 F1
Low La NE34 59 C5
Low Leam Ct NE5 36 F1
Low Main Pl NE23 22 B6
Low Mdw SR6 60 A1
Low Quay NE24 17 F8
Low Reach NE10 57 A2
Low Row Blaydon NE40 52 E3
Sunderland SR1 102 C2
Low St SR1 103 B3
Low Stobhill NE61 9 A7
Low Well Gdns NE10 56 E1
Low West Ave NE39 67 D1
Lowbiggin NE5 36 E5
Lowdham Ave NE29 41 E4
Lowdon Ct NE2 98 C3
Lower Crone St NE27 30 F4
Lower Dundas St SR6 103 A4
Lower Rudyerd St NE29 42 B5
Lowerson Ave DH4 90 A5
Loweswater Ave
Chester le Street DH2 88 B1
Easington Lane DH5 97 C8
Loweswater Cl NE24 11 F1
Loweswater Rd
Newcastle-upon-Tyne NE5 54 B8
Gateshead NE9 71 A4
Loweswood Cl NE7 39 A1
Lowfield Terr NE6 56 F4
Lowfield Wlk NE16 69 A6
Lowgate NE15 35 D1
Lowick Cl DH3 82 D1
Lowick Ct NE3 38 E4
Lowland Cl SR3 92 A5
Lownds Terr NE6 56 E6
Lowrey's La NE9 70 F5
Lowry Gdns NE34 59 D2
Lowry Rd SR6 75 E5
Lowther Ave DH2 88 B2
Lowther Cl NE63 6 F1
Lowther Sq NE23 21 E6
Lowthian Cres NE6 56 E5
Lowthian Terr NE38 83 F4
Lucknow St SR1 103 C3
Lucock St NE34 59 B5
Lucy St
[4] Chester le Street DH3 88 C4
Blaydon NE21 53 D3
Ludlow Ave NE29 41 E8
Ludlow Ct NE3 37 E7
Ludlow Dr NE25 31 B5
Ludlow Rd SR2 86 D3
Luffness Dr NE34 59 F3
Luke's La NE10,NE31 57 F1
Lukes Lane Prim Sch
NE31 58 A3
Lulsgate SR5 74 A1
Lulworth Ave NE32 58 E5
Lulworth Ct SR3 91 C7
Lulworth Gdns SR2 86 C3
Lumden's La NE61 8 F8
Lumley Ave
Whickham NE16 54 B1
South Shields NE34 60 B6
Lumley Cl
Chester le Street DH2 88 B3
Washington NE38 83 B5
Lumley Cres DH4 90 C4
Lumley Ct Bedlington NE22 11 C2
Hebburn NE31 57 F8
Sunderland SR3 91 C7
Lumley Gdns
Burnopfield NE16 78 E5
Gateshead NE8 56 B1
Lumley New Rd DH3,DH4 89 C1
Lumley St Newbottle DH4 90 C2
Sunderland SR4 102 B2
Lumley Terr
Chester le Street DH3 88 D2
Jarrow NE32 58 C4
[1] Ryhope SR2 92 F6
Lumley Tower SR1 103 B3
Lumley Wlk NE11 100 A1
Lumley's La NE43 65 B6
Lumsden's La NE61 3 F1
Lune Gn NE32 58 C2
Lunedale Ave SR6 75 C5
Lunesdale St DH5 95 A2
Lupin Cl NE5 36 C4
Luss Ave NE32 58 E3
Lutterworth Cl NE12 39 B6
Lutterworth Dr NE12 39 A6
Lutterworth Rd
Longbenton NE12 39 B5
Sunderland SR2 86 C3
Luxembourg Rd SR4 85 D7
Lychgate Ct NE8 101 C3
Lydbury Cl NE23 16 C1
Lydcott NE38 84 B5
Lyden Gate NE9 71 A3
Lydford Ct Newbottle DH4 90 C3
Newcastle-upon-Tyne NE3 37 C6
Lydford Way DH3 82 D3
Lydney Cl NE15 35 C1
Lyn-Thorpe Gr SR6 75 E3
Lyncroft NE63 6 C2
Lyncroft Rd NE29 41 E6
Lyndale NE23 16 C1
Lynden Gdns NE5 37 A3
Lynden Rd SR2 92 F8
Lyndhurst Ave
Chester le Street DH3 88 C6
Newcastle-upon-Tyne NE2 38 E2
Gateshead NE9 71 A4
Lyndhurst Cl NE21 68 A8
Lyndhurst Cres NE9 71 A4
Lyndhurst Dr NE9 71 A3
Lyndhurst Gdns NE2 38 D2
Lyndhurst Gn NE9 70 F4
Lyndhurst Gr NE9 71 A4
Lyndhurst Rd
Longbenton NE12 39 D7
Whitley Bay NE25 31 E5
Ashington NE63 6 F1
Lyndhurst St [3] NE33 42 D2
Lyndhurst Terr
[1] Whickham NE16 54 A1
Sunderland SR4 85 E8
Lyndon Cl NE36 74 B7
Lyndon Dr NE36 74 B7
Lyndon Gr NE36 74 B7
Lyndon Wlk NE24 16 F8
Lyne Terr NE61 1 F3
Lynemouth Fst Sch NE61 2 B3
Lynemouth Rd NE61 1 D4
Lynfield NE26 31 E7
Lynfield Ct NE5 37 B3
Lynfield Pl NE5 37 B3
Lynford Gdns SR2 86 C3
Lyngrove SR2 92 F8
Lynholm Gr NE12 39 D8
Lynmouth Pl NE7 39 B3
Lynmouth Rd
North Shields NE29 41 C5
Gateshead NE9 70 F3
Lynn Rd Wallsend NE28 40 A1
Tynemouth NE29 41 D7
Lynn St
Chester le Street DH3 88 C2
Blyth NE24 17 D7
Lynndale Ave NE24 17 A7
Lynnholm Cl NE7 39 B2
Lynnholme Gdns
[4] Gateshead NE9 70 F8
Gateshead, Deckham NE9 71 A8
Lynnwood Ave NE4 54 F5
Lynnwood Terr NE4 54 F5
Lynthorpe SR2 92 F8
Lynton Ave NE32 58 E5
Lynton Ct Newbottle DH4 90 C3
Newcastle-upon-Tyne NE5 37 B3
Lynton Pl NE5 37 B3
Lynton Way NE5 37 B3
Lynwood Ave
Blaydon NE21 53 C3
Newbiggin-by-the-Sea NE64 7 D5
Sunderland SR4 85 A2
Lynwood Cl NE20 25 C2
Lyon St NE31 57 D7
Lyons Ave DH5 95 B2
Lyons Cotts DH5 95 B2
Lyons La DH5 95 C1
Lyons The DH5 95 B2
Lyric Cl NE29 41 C8
Lysdon Ave NE25 23 D6
Lyster Cl SR7 92 E1
Lytchfield NE10 72 B7
Lytham Cl
Cramlington NE23 21 E6
Wallsend NE28 40 E7
Washington NE37 72 C2
Lytham Dr NE25 31 D5
Lytham Gn NE10 57 B2
Lytham Grange DH4 90 A4
Lytham Pl NE6 56 E5
Lythe Way NE12 39 C6

M

Mabel St NE21 53 C3
Macadam St NE8 70 D7
Macdonald Rd NE4 54 D4
Maclynn Cl SR3 91 E6
Macmerry Cl SR5 84 F8
Macmillan Gdns NE10 72 A8
Maddison Ct SR1 103 C3
Maddison Gdns NE23 22 E1
Maddison St NE24 17 E8
Maddox Rd NE12 39 D6
Madeira Ave NE26 31 F7
Madeira Cl NE5 36 C4
Madeira Terr [8] NE33 42 D1
Madras St NE34 59 A4
Mafeking Pl NE29 31 B1
Mafeking St
Whitley Bay NE26 32 B5
Newcastle-upon-Tyne NE6 56 F3
[5] Gateshead NE9 71 A8
Sunderland SR4 85 F7
Magdalene Ct NE2 98 B4
Magdelene Pl SR4 85 F7
Magenta Cres NE5 36 C4
Magnolia Ct NE4 54 D7
Magnolia Dr NE63 6 C1
Magpie Ct NE63 6 B2
Mahogany Row DH9 80 D1
Maiden La NE40 52 A2
Maiden Law DH4 94 A7
Maiden St NE4 100 B3
Maiden's Wlk NE46 45 C4
Maidens Croft NE46 44 F4
Maidstone Cl SR3 91 D6
Maidstone Terr DH4 90 D4
Main Cres NE28 39 F4
Main Rd Dinnington NE13 27 C6
Newcastle-upon-Tyne NE3 37 B6
Ryton NE40 52 B5
Wylam NE41 51 B6
Main St Ponteland NE20 25 E6
Crawcrook NE40 51 F4
Corbridge NE45 47 A5
Main St N NE23 22 F1
Main St S NE23 22 F1
Mains Park Rd DH3 88 D3
Mains Pl NE61 3 F1
Mainsforth Terr SR2 103 C1
Mainsforth Terr W SR2 86 E4
Mainstone Cl NE23 22 A6
Maitland Terr NE64 7 D4
Makendon St NE31 57 E7
Makepeace Terr NE9 71 F1
Malaburn Way [2] SR5 75 A1
Malaga Cl NE5 36 B4
Malaya Dr NE6 57 B5
Malcolm Ct NE25 31 D4
Malcolm St NE6 56 A6
Malden Cl NE23 21 F6
Maling Pk SR4 85 B7
Maling St NE6 56 A5
Malings Cl SR1 103 C2
Mallard Cl
Washington NE38 82 F4
Ashington NE63 11 D8
Mallard Ct NE12 29 C4
Mallard Lodge [11] NE10 71 D8
Mallard Way
Fence Houses DH4 94 B7
Blyth NE24 17 F3
Shiremoor NE28 41 A6
Mallowburn Cres NE3 37 C4
Malmo Cl NE29 41 B5
Malone Gdns DH3 82 D6
Malory Pl NE8 101 C2
Maltby Cl
Washington NE38 83 D4
[2] Silksworth SR3 91 E5
Maltings The SR3 92 C7
Maltkiln NE46 45 A4
Malton Cl
Newcastle-upon-Tyne NE15 53 E6
Blyth NE24 17 B7
Malton Cres NE29 41 F4
Malton Ct NE32 58 A7
Malton Gdns NE28 40 B4
Malton Gn NE9 71 B1
Malvern Ave DH2 88 B2
Malvern Cl NE63 6 F1
Malvern Ct Dunston NE11 70 A6
Newcastle-upon-Tyne NE15 53 B7
Cleadon SR6 59 F1
Malvern Gdns
Dunston NE11 70 A7
Sunderland SR6 75 E3
Malvern Rd
Seaton Sluice NE26 24 D5
Wallsend NE28 41 A3
Tynemouth NE29 41 E8
Washington NE38 83 B3
Malvern St NE33 59 C7
Malvins Close Fst Sch
NE24 17 C7
Malvins Close Rd NE24 17 C7
Malvins Rd NE24 17 B8
Manchester St NE61 3 F1
Mandale Cres NE30 32 A3
Mandarin Cl NE5 36 C5
Mandarin Lodge [8] NE10 71 D8
Mandarin Way NE38 84 C6
Mandela Cl SR1 103 C3
Mandela Way NE11 54 D2
Mandeville NE37 83 F8
Manet Gdns NE34 59 D4
Mangrove Cl NE5 36 C4
Manila St SR2 86 E4
Manisty Ho NE4 54 E4
Manley View NE63 7 A3
Manners Gdns NE25 23 C4
Manningford Cl NE23 22 A5
Manningford Dr SR3 91 E5
Manor Ave Newburn NE15 52 F8
Longbenton NE7 39 C5
Manor Chare NE1 99 B1
Manor Cl
Newcastle-upon-Tyne NE3 38 D5
Riding Mill NE44 62 F7
Manor Ct NE33 42 E1
Manor Dr
Newbiggin-by-the-Sea NE64 7 E5
Longbenton NE7 39 C5
Manor Gdns
Gateshead NE10 72 C8
Longbenton NE7 39 C5
Manor Gr
New Herrington DH4 90 F7
Newburn NE15 52 F7
Longbenton NE7 39 C5
Manor House Cl [1] NE6 56 C5
Manor House Farm Cotts
NE5 37 D4
Manor House Rd NE2 38 F1
Manor Pk
Washington NE37 83 D8
Corbridge NE45 46 F6
Manor Pl NE7 39 C5
Manor Rd Medomsley DH8 77 C1
Tynemouth NE30 42 D7
Washington NE37 83 D8
Longbenton NE7 39 C5
Manor Terr Blaydon NE21 53 A1
Winlaton Mill NE21 68 C7
Manor View
High Pittington DH6 96 B4
Washington NE37 83 E8
Newbiggin-by-the-Sea NE64 7 E5
Manor View E [2] NE37 83 E8
Manor Wlk NE7 39 C5
Manorfields NE12 39 D6
Manors Sta NE1 99 B1
Manors Sta (Metro) NE1 99 B1
Manors The NE42 50 E3
Manorway
Tynemouth NE30 42 D8
Hedworth NE32 58 C2
Mansel Terr NE24 16 E7
Mansell Pl NE3 37 E3
Mansfield Cres SR6 75 E2
Mansfield Ct NE36 74 A7
Mansfield Pl NE4 98 B1
Mansfield St NE4 98 B1
Mansion Ho NE36 74 A7
Manston Cl SR3 91 D6
Manx Sq SR5 75 B3
Maple Ave Dunston NE11 70 A7
Whitley Bay NE25 31 F4
New Silksworth SR3 92 B8
Maple Cl
Newcastle-upon-Tyne NE15 53 E6
Bedlington NE22 10 F1
Maple Cres NE24 16 F8
Maple Ct Killingworth NE12 29 C4
New Hartley NE25 23 D6
Maple Gr
Gateshead, Felling NE10 71 E8
South Shields NE34 59 F5
Prudhoe NE42 50 B2
Gateshead, Saltwell NE8 70 E7
Whitburn SR6 60 F1
Maple Rd NE21 53 C2
Maple Row NE11 54 B2
Maple St Jarrow NE32 58 A7
Newcastle-upon-Tyne NE4 100 B4
Ashington NE63 6 D3
Maple Terr
Shiney Row DH4 90 A5
Burnopfield NE16 78 F6
Newcastle-upon-Tyne NE4 100 B4
Maplebeck Cl SR3 91 D5
Mapledene NE38 83 E2
Mapledene Rd NE3 37 F6
Maplewood
Chester le Street DH2 88 B4
Newcastle-upon-Tyne NE6 56 E8
Maplewood Ave SR5 74 F3
Maplewood Cres NE38 83 B1
Maplewood Dr DH6 97 F3
Maplewood Sch SR5 74 E3
Maplewood St DH4 89 E1
Mapperley Dr NE15 53 E7
Marblet Ct NE11 70 B7
Marbury Cl SR3 91 D6
March Rd NE23 29 B7
March Terr NE13 27 A7
Marchburn La NE44 62 E7
Marcia Ave SR6 75 D3
Marconi Way NE11 54 B2
Marcross Cl NE15 36 B2
Marcross Dr SR3 91 E5
Mardale NE37 83 B7
Mardale Gdns NE9 71 A3
Mardale Rd NE5 37 B1
Mardale St DH5 95 A2
Marden Ave NE30 32 C3
Marden Bridge Mid Sch
NE25 32 A4
Marden Cl NE61 8 D7
Marden Cres NE26 32 C4
Marden Ct NE26 24 B7
Marden Farm Dr NE30 32 B3
Marden High Sch NE30 32 B1
Marden Rd NE26 32 A4
Marden Rd S NE25 32 B4
Marden Terr NE30 32 C3
Mare Cl NE23 23 A3
Mareburn Cres NE10 71 E8
Maree Cl SR3 91 E5
Margaret Alice St SR4 85 E7
Margaret Collins House
NE6 56 D6
Margaret Cotts NE25 31 F2
Margaret Dr NE12 40 A8
Margaret Gr NE34 59 A5
Margaret Rd NE26 32 C4
Margaret St SR2 87 A2
Margaret Sutton Sch The
NE34 59 D6
Margaret Terr
Penshaw DH4 90 C6
Tanfield Lea DH9 79 C1
Rowlands Gill NE39 67 C1
Margate St SR3 92 A8
Marguerite Ct SR4 102 B3
Maria St
Newcastle-upon-Tyne NE4 54 E4
New Silksworth SR3 92 A7
Marian Ct NE8 101 A1
Marian Dr NE10 57 C3
Marian Way
Ponteland NE20 25 B2
South Shields NE34 59 F3
Marie Curie Dr NE4 54 F4
Marigold Ave NE10 56 B2
Marigold Cres DH4 89 E3
Marigold Ct SR4 102 B3
Marigold Wlk NE34 59 B5
Marina Ave SR6 75 D3
Marina Ct SR6 75 D3
Marina Dr
Whitley Bay NE25 31 C4
South Shields NE33 42 E3
Marina Gr SR6 75 D3
Marina Terr
[8] Ryhope SR2 92 F6
Whitburn SR6 60 F1
Marina View
Wallsend NE28 40 F2
Hebburn NE31 57 D6
Marine App NE33 42 E2
Marine Ave NE26 31 F5
Marine Dr Jarrow NE31 58 A3
Sunderland SR2 93 A8
Marine Gdns NE26 32 A6
Marine Park Fst Sch
NE26 32 A6
Marine Park Jun Mix & Inf
Sch NE33 42 D3
Marine St NE64 7 E5
Marine Terr NE24 17 E7
Marine View NE26 24 C7
Marine Wlk SR6 75 F2
Mariner Sq SR1 103 C4
Mariners Point [8] NE30 42 D7
Mariners Wharf NE1 56 A5
Mariners' Cotts NE33 42 E3
Mariners' La NE30 42 C7
Marion St SR2 86 E4
Maritime St SR1 103 A2
Maritime Terr SR1 102 C2
Maritme Pl [3] NE61 3 F1
Marius Ave NE15 34 F2
Mariville E SR2 93 A5
Mariville W SR2 93 A5
Marjorie St NE23 22 F5
Mark Rise DH5 95 A5
Mark's La DH4 94 A3
Markby Cl [3] SR3 91 E5
Market Cres DH4 90 C6
Market La
Newcastle-upon-Tyne NE1 99 B1
Dunston NE11,NE16 69 D8
Market Pl
Houghton-le-Spring DH5 94 F8
Bedlington NE22 15 F8
Blyth NE24 17 E8
Corbridge NE45 46 F5
Hexham NE46 45 B5
Market Place Ind Est
DH5 90 F1
Market Sq Jarrow NE32 58 B7
Lynmouth NE61 2 B2
Sunderland SR1 103 A2
Market St
Hetton le Hole DH5 95 B4
Newcastle-upon-Tyne NE1 99 B1
Dudley NE23 29 A8
Blyth NE24 17 E8
Hexham NE46 45 B5
Market Way NE11 70 D6
Markham Ave SR6 61 A1
Markham St SR2 86 F2
Markington Dr SR2 92 F5
Markle Gr DH5 94 D5
Marlboro Ave NE16 69 B8
Marlborough App NE3 38 C7
Marlborough Ave NE3 38 C7
Marlborough Cres
Newcastle-upon-Tyne NE1 100 C4
Gateshead NE9 71 C3
Marlborough Ct
Houghton-le-Spring DH5 94 E6
Newcastle-upon-Tyne NE3 37 D7
Marlborough House
NE26 31 F6
Marlborough Rd
Washington NE37 83 F8
Sunderland SR4 85 A3
Marlborough St N NE33 59 D8
Marlborough St S NE33 59 D8
Marlborough Terr NE62 10 F4
Marleen Ave NE6 56 C8
Marleen Ct [2] NE6 56 C8
Marlesford Cl SR3 91 D6
Marley Cres SR5 74 F3
Marley Ct [16] NE6 56 C7
Marley Hill Cty Prim Sch
NE16 80 A8
Marlfield Ct NE5 37 B3
Marlow Dr SR3 91 D5
Marlow Pl NE12 39 C6
Marlow St NE24 17 D7
Marlow Way NE16 68 F5
Marlowe Gdns NE8 101 C1
Marlowe Pl DH5 94 F7
Marlowe Wlk NE34 59 A3
Marmion Rd NE6 57 A8
Marmion Terr NE25 31 F4
Marne St DH4 90 C6
Marondale Ave NE6 56 F7
Marquis Ave NE5 36 C4
Marquis Cl NE12 39 D5
Marquis Ct Prudhoe NE42 50 E4
Gateshead NE11 70 D3
Marquisway NE11 70 D2
Marr Rd NE31 57 F5
Marsden Ave SR6 60 F3
Marsden Cl DH4 94 C8
Marsden Cliffs Nature
Reserve★ NE34 60 E6
Marsden Gr NE9 71 D3
Marsden La
South Shields NE34 60 C7
Newcastle-upon-Tyne NE5 37 A3
Marsden Prim Sch SR6 60 F3
Marsden Rd
South Shields NE34 60 A7
Cleadon SR6 74 F8
Marsden St [6] NE33 59 D8
Marsden View SR6 60 F3
Marsh Ct NE11 70 B7
Marshall St SR6 75 D4
Marshall Wallis Rd NE33 59 C8
Marshall's Ct NE1 99 A1

Marsham Cl
Newcastle-upon-Tyne NE15 .53 E7
Cleadon SR6 .60 A2
Marsham Rd 3 NE5 .36 E3
Marshes' Houses NE62 .11 D7
Marshmont Ave NE30 .32 C1
Marske Terr NE6 .56 E6
Marston NE12 .29 D4
Marston Wlk NE16 .68 F5
Martello Gdns NE7 .39 D2
Martha St DH9 .79 B2
Martin Ct NE38 .82 F2
Martin Rd NE28 .41 A2
Martin Terr 7 SR4 .85 F7
Martindale Ave SR6 .75 C5
Martindale Pk DH5 .94 E8
Martindale Pl NE25 .23 E3
Martindale Wlk NE12 .29 C3
Marwell Dr NE37 .72 E2
Marwood Ct NE25 .31 D6
Marx Terr NE17 .77 C8
Mary Agnes St NE3 .38 A5
Mary Ave DH3 .82 B6
Mary Magdalene Bglws
NE2 .98 B4
Mary St Blaydon NE21 .53 C3
Blaydon, Winlaton NE21 .53 A2
Sunderland SR1 .102 C2
New Silksworth SR3 .92 A8
Mary Terr NE5 .37 A3
Mary Trevelyan Prim Sch
NE4 .100 A3
Mary's Pl NE6 .57 B6
Maryhill Cl NE4 .54 E4
Maryside Pl NE40 .51 F7
Masefield Ave NE16 .54 B1
Masefield Dr NE34 .59 A2
Masefield Pl NE8 .101 C2
Mason Ave NE26 .32 B5
Mason Rd NE28 .40 A4
Mason St
Brunswick Village NE13 .28 A6
4 Newcastle-upon-Tyne
NE6 .56 C5
Mason View NE13 .28 B8
Massingham Way NE34 .59 B5
Mast La NE30 .32 B3
Master Mariners' Homes
NE30 .42 C7
Master's Cres NE42 .50 B2
Matamba Terr SR4 .102 B2
Matanzas St SR2 .86 E3
Matfen Ave
Hazlerigg NE13 .28 A4
Shiremoor NE27 .31 A2
Matfen Cl
Newcastle-upon-Tyne NE15 .53 E6
Blyth NE24 .17 C7
Matfen Ct DH2 .88 A3
Matfen Dr SR3 .91 D6
Matfen Gdns NE28 .40 F5
Matfen Pl
Newcastle-upon-Tyne, Fawdon
NE3 .38 A6
Newcastle-upon-Tyne, Fenham
NE4 .54 F7
Matfen Terr NE64 .7 D3
Mather Rd NE4 .100 B4
Mathesons Gdns NE61 .8 F8
Matlock Gdns NE5 .36 F3
Matlock Rd NE32 .58 C5
Matlock Sq NE61 .2 A2
Matlock St SR1 .103 A3
Matthew Bank NE2 .38 E3
Matthew Rd NE24 .17 F5
Matthew St 13 NE6 .56 B6
Maud St
Newcastle-upon-Tyne NE15 .53 C6
Sunderland SR6 .75 E4
Maud Terr Tanfield DH9 .79 D3
5 Shiremoor NE27 .30 E1
Maud's Terr NE64 .7 E5
Maude Gdns 7 NE28 .40 B1
Maudlin Pl 2 NE5 .37 D1
Maudlin St DH5 .95 B6
Mauds La SR1 .103 B3
Maughan St NE24 .17 F7
Maurice Rd NE28 .57 B8
Maurice Road Ind Est
NE28 .57 B8
Mautland Sq DH4 .90 E1
Mautland St DH4 .90 E1
Maxton Cl SR3 .91 D5
Maxwell NE33 .42 C2
Maxwell Ho NE24 .17 B7
Maxwell St
South Shields NE33 .42 C2
Gateshead NE8 .70 D7
2 Sunderland SR4 .85 F7
Maxwell St Ind Est NE33 .42 C2
May Ave
Winlaton Mill NE21 .68 C7
Ryton NE40 .52 C6
Newbiggin-by-the-Sea NE64 .7 C5
May Gr SR6 .60 F3
May St Birtley DH3 .82 C4
Blaydon NE21 .53 B1
South Shields NE33 .42 D1
Sunderland SR4 .102 B3
Maydown Cl SR5 .84 F8
Mayfair Ct NE31 .57 D5
Mayfair Gdns
Ponteland NE20 .25 F6
South Shields NE34 .59 E7
Gateshead NE8 .71 A8
Mayfair Rd NE2 .38 D2
Mayfield Whickham NE16 .69 B5
Morpeth NE61 .8 E7
Mayfield Ave
Throckley NE15 .35 E1
Cramlington NE23 .22 C6
Mayfield Ct SR6 .75 D3
Mayfield Dr SR6 .75 B8
Mayfield Gdns
Throckley NE15 .35 E1
Wallsend NE28 .40 A3
Jarrow NE32 .58 A6
Mayfield Gr SR4 .85 A2
Mayfield Pl NE13 .28 A5
Mayfield Rd
Newcastle-upon-Tyne NE3 .38 C4
Sunderland SR4 .85 A6
Mayfield Terr NE5 .37 E1
Mayo Dr 1 SR3 .91 E5
Mayoral Way NE11 .70 D3
Maypole Cl 8 SR5 .75 B2
Mayswood Rd SR6 .75 D3
Maytree House NE4 .100 A4
Maywood Cl NE3 .37 E4
Mazine Terr DH6 .97 E2
McAnany Ave NE34 .59 D5
McAteer Ct DH6 .97 E1
McClaren Way DH4 .90 F7
McCracken Cl NE3 .38 C8
McCracken Dr NE13 .28 C7
McCutcheon Ct NE6 .56 E3
McCutcheon St 7 SR7 .92 E1
McErlane Sq NE10 .57 B2
McEwan Gdns NE4 .54 F5
McGowen Ct 6 NE6 .56 C5
McIlvenna Gdns NE28 .40 B4
Mcintyre Hall NE31 .57 F7
Mcintyre Rd NE31 .57 F7
McKendrick Villas NE5 .37 D1
McLennan Ct NE38 .83 D6
McNamara Rd NE28 .40 F3
Mcnulty Ct NE23 .28 F8
Meacham Way NE16 .69 A5
Mead Ave NE12 .39 E8
Mead Cres NE12 .39 F8
Mead Way NE12 .39 F8
Mead Wlk NE6 .56 F6
Meadow Bank Dr NE62 .10 E6
Meadow Brook Dr NE17 .66 C2
Meadow Cl
Houghton-le-Spring DH5 .94 F7
Dunston NE11 .54 E1
Longbenton NE12 .39 B7
Blaydon NE21 .52 F1
Seghill NE23 .22 F2
Ryton NE40 .52 D5
Meadow Ct
Ponteland NE20 .25 E5
Bedlington NE22 .10 E1
Meadow Dr
Seaton Burn NE13 .28 C8
Sunderland, East Herrington
SR3 .91 B6
Sunderland, South Hylton
SR4 .85 A5
Meadow Gdns SR3 .86 B3
Meadow Gr SR4 .85 B5
Meadow Grange DH4 .89 E2
Meadow La Dunston NE11 .54 F1
Crawcrook NE40 .52 A4
Sunderland SR3 .91 B6
Meadow Laws NE34 .60 A4
Meadow Pk NE44 .62 F7
Meadow Rd
Newcastle-upon-Tyne NE15 .53 D8
Whitley Bay NE25 .31 D4
Seaton Sluice NE26 .24 B6
Wallsend NE28 .40 F1
Meadow Rise
Newcastle-upon-Tyne NE5 .37 B4
Gateshead NE9 .71 C5
Meadow St DH5 .94 C3
Meadow Terr DH4 .90 C6
Meadow Vale SR2 .86 C4
Meadow View Dipton DH9 .78 E1
New Hartley NE25 .23 D6
North Shields NE28 .41 E4
Hedworth NE32 .73 D8
Sunderland SR3 .91 B5
Meadow Well Prim Sch
NE29 .41 D4
Meadow Well Sta NE29 .41 E4
Meadow Wlk NE40 .52 D5
Meadowbank NE23 .29 A8
Meadowbrook Dr NE10 .72 C7
Meadowcroft Mews
NE8 .101 A1
Meadowdale Cres
Bedlington NE22 .10 D1
Newcastle-upon-Tyne NE5 .37 D3
Meadowdale Mid Sch
NE22 .10 E1
Meadowfield
Ponteland NE20 .25 E7
Whitley Bay NE25 .31 D5
Ashington NE63 .7 A2
Meadowfield Ave NE3 .38 A6
Meadowfield Cres NE40 .52 A4
Meadowfield Ct NE20 .25 E7
Meadowfield Dr SR6 .60 B1
Meadowfield Est NE9 .71 F1
Meadowfield Gdns NE6 .40 A1
Meadowfield Ind Est
NE20 .25 E6
Meadowfield Pk NE20 .25 E6
Meadowfield Pk S NE43 .64 C5
Meadowfield Rd
Newcastle-upon-Tyne NE3 .38 B4
Meadowfield Rd continued
Stocksfield NE43 .64 C5
Meadowfield Terr
Killingworth NE12 .29 F1
Stocksfield NE43 .64 D7
Meadows La DH4,DH5 .94 B3
Meadows The
Bournmoor DH4 .89 D3
West Rainton DH4 .94 A3
Burnopfield NE16 .79 A4
Newcastle-upon-Tyne NE3 .37 F6
Ryton NE40 .52 D5
Meadowside SR2 .86 B4
Meadowsweet Cl NE24 .17 C4
Meadowvale NE20 .25 A2
Meadway Dr NE12 .39 F8
Meal Market NE46 .45 B5
Means Dr NE23 .29 B5
Medburn Ave NE30 .32 C2
Medburn Rd
Newcastle-upon-Tyne NE15 .53 C7
Seaton Delaval NE25 .23 E2
Medham Cl NE10 .71 E6
Medina Cl SR3 .91 E5
Medlar NE9 .71 D4
Medlar Cl DH4 .89 F6
Medomsley Gdns NE9 .71 E4
Medomsly St SR4 .102 A3
Medway NE32 .58 C2
Medway Ave NE31 .57 E3
Medway Cres NE8 .71 B8
Medway Ct NE3 .37 E5
Medway Gdns
Tynemouth NE30 .42 A7
Sunderland SR4 .85 D4
Medway Pl NE23 .16 D1
Medwyn Cl
Bournmoor DH4 .89 E3
Blyth NE24 .17 D5
Megstone Ave NE23 .22 A5
Megstone Ct NE12 .29 E4
Melbeck Dr DH2 .81 E2
Melbourne Cres NE25 .31 E3
Melbourne Ct
Newcastle-upon-Tyne NE1 .99 C1
Gateshead NE8 .101 B3
Melbourne Gdns NE34 .58 F3
Melbourne Pl SR4 .85 E4
Melbourne St NE1 .99 B1
Melbury NE25 .31 D6
Melbury Ct SR6 .75 D3
Melbury Rd NE7 .39 A1
Meldon Ave Sherburn DH6 96 A1
Newcastle-upon-Tyne NE3 .37 F7
South Shields NE34 .59 E6
Meldon Cl NE28 .40 E3
Meldon Ct NE40 .51 E3
Meldon Gdns
Dunston NE11 .70 A5
Stakeford NE62 .10 F8
Meldon Ho NE24 .17 B8
Meldon Rd SR4 .85 F7
Meldon St NE28 .41 C1
Meldon Terr
Greenside NE40 .51 F1
Newcastle-upon-Tyne NE6 .56 B8
Newbiggin-by-the-Sea NE64 .7 D3
Meldon Way NE21 .67 F8
Melgarve Dr SR3 .91 E5
Melkington Ct NE5 .37 B3
Melkridge Gdns NE7 .39 D3
Melkridge Pl NE23 .22 A5
Mellendean Cl NE5 .37 B3
Melmerby Cl NE3 .38 D7
Melness Rd NE13 .28 A5
Melock Ct NE13 .28 A5
Melrose NE38 .83 D3
Melrose Ave
Bebside NE22 .11 D1
Seaton Delaval NE25 .23 D2
Whitley Bay NE25 .31 F4
Backworth NE27 .30 C5
Tynemouth NE30 .32 A2
Hebburn NE31 .57 E3
Gateshead NE9 .71 A5
Melrose Cl
Newcastle-upon-Tyne NE15 .53 E6
Hazlerigg NE3 .28 B2
Melrose Ct NE22 .11 D2
Melrose Gdns
Newbottle DH4 .90 C3
Wallsend NE28 .41 A4
Sunderland SR6 .75 E3
Melrose Gr NE32 .58 E4
Melrose Terr
Bedlington NE22 .11 D2
Newbiggin-by-the-Sea NE64 .7 D3
Melrose Villas NE22 .11 D2
Melsonby Cl SR3 .91 D6
Meltham Ct NE15 .36 B2
Meltham Dr SR3 .91 E5
Melton Ave NE6 .56 F5
Melton Cres NE26 .24 D5
Melton Dr NE25 .23 D6
Melvaig Cl SR3 .91 E5
Melville Ave NE24 .17 D5
Melville Gdns NE25 .31 C4
Melville Gr NE7 .39 A4
Melville St DH3 .88 C2
Melvin Pl NE5 .37 B2
Melvyn Gdns SR6 .75 E3
Membury Cl 4 SR3 .91 E5
Memorial Sq NE64 .7 D5
Menai Ct 9 SR3 .91 F6
Menceforth Cotts DH2 .88 B4
Mendip Ave DH2 .88 C2
Mendip Cl
Tynemouth NE29 .31 F1
Mendip Cl continued
Ashington NE63 .6 E1
Mendip Dr NE38 .83 B3
Mendip Gdns NE11 .70 B6
Mendip Way NE12 .38 F6
Mentieth Cl NE38 .83 B3
Menvill Pl SR1 .103 B2
Mercantile Rd DH4 .94 C7
Merchants Wharf 10 NE6 56 C4
Mercia Way NE15 .53 E5
Mere Knolls Rd SR6 .75 E4
Meredith Gdns NE8 .101 C1
Meresyde NE10 .72 A7
Meresyde Ct NE10 .72 A7
Merevale Cl NE37 .72 E2
Merganser Lodge 10
NE10 .71 D8
Meridan Way NE7 .39 D3
Meridien Ho 3 NE33 .59 E8
Merlay Dr NE13 .27 B6
Merlay Hall NE6 .57 A4
Merle Gdns
16 Newcastle-upon-Tyne
NE6 .56 C5
Morpeth NE61 .3 D2
Merle Terr SR4 .85 F7
Merley Gate NE61 .9 A6
Merlin Cres NE28 .40 F3
Merlin Ct 17 NE10 .56 D1
Merlin Dr DH3 .88 D7
Merlin Pl NE12 .39 A7
Merlin Way Earsdon NE27 .31 A1
Shiremoor NE27 .41 A8
Merrick Ho 21 SR3 .91 F6
Merrington Cl
New Hartley NE25 .23 D7
Silksworth SR3 .91 D6
Merrion Cl SR3 .91 D6
Merryfield Gdns SR6 .75 E3
Merryshields Terr NE43 .64 C8
Mersey Ct 17 SR3 .91 F6
Mersey Pl NE8 .71 B8
Mersey Rd Hebburn NE31 .57 F3
Gateshead NE8 .71 B8
Mersey St NE17 .66 C1
Merton Ct NE4 .54 D4
Merton Rd NE20 .25 E6
Merton Sq NE24 .17 E8
Merton Way NE20 .25 E6
Methuen St NE9 .71 A8
Methven Way NE23 .16 C2
Metro Ctr The NE11 .54 C2
Metro Ret Pk NE11 .54 B2
Metroland Indoor Theme
Pk★ NE11 .54 C2
Mews The
Fence Houses DH4 .94 A7
Newcastle-upon-Tyne NE1 .99 A2
Gateshead NE10 .72 B8
Blaydon NE21 .53 E2
North Shields NE30 .42 A6
Tynemouth NE30 .42 E8
Sunderland SR3 .91 B7
Michaelgate 23 NE6 .56 C6
Mickle Cl NE37 .83 A6
Mickleton Gdns SR3 .86 B2
Micklewood Cl NE61 .4 E6
Mickley Fst Sch NE43 .49 E1
Middle Chare DH3 .88 D3
Middle Cl NE38 .83 B1
Middle Dr
Woolsington NE13 .26 F1
Ponteland NE20 .25 C3
Middle Engine La
Shiremoor NE27,NE28,NE29 41 A7
Wallsend NE27,NE28,NE29 .40 F5
Middle Farm Ct NE23 .22 B7
Middle Garth 1 NE5 .37 D1
Middle Gate
Newcastle-upon-Tyne NE5 .36 D1
Morpeth NE61 .8 F6
Middle Gn NE25 .31 C4
Middle Row
Great Lumley DH4 .89 E1
Blaydon NE40 .52 E3
Middle St Blyth NE24 .17 B4
Tynemouth NE30 .42 E7
Corbridge NE45 .46 F5
Newcastle-upon-Tyne NE6 .56 F6
Sunderland SR1 .102 C3
Sunderland SR1 .103 A3
Middle St E NE6 .57 A6
Middlebrook NE20 .25 B3
Middlefields Ind Est
NE34 .59 B6
Middleham Cl DH2 .81 E1
Middleham Ct SR5 .74 E3
Middleton Ave
Rowlands Gill NE39 .67 F1
Newcastle-upon-Tyne NE4 .54 E6
Middleton Cl SR7 .92 E1
Middleton Ct NE2 .99 C3
Middleton St NE24 .17 E7
Middlewood Pk NE4 .54 E7
Midfield Dr SR6 .75 E2
Midgley Dr SR3 .91 E5
Midhurst Ave NE34 .60 A8
Midhurst Cl SR3 .91 D6
Midhurst Rd NE12 .39 D7
Midmoor Rd SR4 .85 E7
Midsomer Cl SR3 .91 D5
Midway NE6 .57 A6
Milbanke Cl DH2 .81 F1
Milbanke St DH2 .81 F1
Milbur Cl NE46 .44 F2
Milburn Cl DH3 .88 E2
Milburn Dr NE15 .54 B6
Milburn Rd NE63 .6 D2
Milburn Terr
Shiney Row DH4 .90 B6
Stakeford NE62 .11 C6
Milcombe Cl SR3 .91 D6
Mildmay Rd NE2 .38 D2
Mildred St DH5 .90 E1
Mile End Rd NE33 .42 C4
Milecastle Ct NE5 .36 D2
Milecastle Fst Sch NE5 .36 C2
Milfield Ave
Shiremoor NE27 .31 A3
Wallsend NE28 .40 C4
Milford Ct NE10 .72 B6
Milford Gdns NE3 .28 B1
Milford Rd NE15 .54 C5
Military Rd
Heddon-on-the-Wall NE15 .34 C3
North Shields NE30 .42 B6
Military Vehicle Mus★
NE2 .99 A4
Milk Mkt NE1 .99 C1
Milkwell NE45 .47 A6
Milkwell La NE45 .47 A7
Mill Bank SR5 .75 C4
Mill Cl North Shields NE29 .41 E5
Riding Mill NE44 .62 F7
Mill Cres Penshaw DH4 .90 B6
Hebburn NE31 .57 C2
Mill Ct Bournmoor DH4 .89 E2
Hamsterley NE17 .77 B6
Ellington NE61 .1 C4
Mill Dam NE33 .42 B2
Mill Dene View NE32 .58 C5
Mill Dyke Cl NE25 .31 C6
Mill Farm NE61 .1 C4
Mill Farm Cl NE4 .98 B1
Mill Farm Rd NE39 .78 A5
Mill Gr Tynemouth NE30 .42 C8
South Shields NE34 .60 B4
Mill Grange NE44 .63 A8
Mill Hill DH5 .94 D6
Mill Hill Prim Sch SR3 .92 A5
Mill Hill Rd
Newcastle-upon-Tyne NE5 .53 F8
Silksworth SR3 .92 A6
Mill House NE2 .98 B4
Mill La Urpeth DH2 .81 D1
Sherburn DH6 .96 A1
Ebchester DH8 .76 E4
Hebburn NE10,NE31 .57 E2
Jarrow NE10,NE31 .57 E2
Heddon-on-the-Wall NE15 .34 F3
Winlaton Mill NE21 .68 B7
Seghill NE23 .22 D1
North Shields NE29 .42 B4
Newcastle-upon-Tyne NE4 100 A4
Slaley NE44 .62 A1
Whitburn SR6 .60 F2
Mill Pit DH4 .90 B6
Mill Race Cl NE17 .77 B6
Mill Rd Blackhall Mill NE17 .77 B8
Chopwell NE17 .77 B8
Gateshead NE8 .101 C4
Mill Rise NE3 .38 E4
Mill St SR4 .102 B3
Mill Terr Shiney Row DH4 .90 B6
Houghton-le-Spring DH5 .94 D6
Mill View Gateshead NE10 .71 C7
West Boldon NE36 .74 A7
Mill View Ave SR6 .75 D3
Mill View Rise NE42 .50 D4
Mill Way NE15,NE42 .50 D7
Millais Gdns NE34 .59 C2
Millbank Cres NE22 .11 A1
Millbank Ind Est NE33 .42 C2
Millbank Pl NE22 .16 B8
Millbank Rd
Bedlington NE22 .11 B1
Newcastle-upon-Tyne NE6 .57 A4
Millbank Terr NE22 .11 A1
Millbeck Gr DH5 .94 D6
Millbrook Gateshead NE10 71 E7
North Shields NE29 .41 E5
Millbrook Rd NE23 .16 D1
Millburn St SR4 .102 B3
Milldale Ave NE24 .17 A7
Milldene Ave NE30 .42 C8
Millennium Bridge★
NE1,NE8 .102 C4
Millennium Way SR5 .102 C4
Miller St NE8 .70 D8
Miller Terr SR3 .92 A8
Miller's La NE16 .54 B1
Millers Hill DH4 .90 C6
Millers Rd NE6 .56 C7
Millfield Bedlington NE22 .16 A7
Seaton Sluice NE26 .24 D5
Millfield Ave NE3 .37 E3
Millfield Cl
Chester le Street DH2 .88 A1
Newburn NE15 .52 F7
Millfield Ct
Whickham NE16 .69 C7
Bedlington NE22 .16 A8
Seaton Sluice NE26 .24 D5
Hexham NE46 .44 F5
Millfield E NE22 .16 A7
Millfield Gdns
Gateshead NE10 .71 C8
Blyth NE24 .12 D1
Tynemouth NE30 .42 C8
Hexham NE46 .44 F5
Millfield Gr NE30 .42 C8
Millfield La NE15 .52 F8
Millfield N NE22 .16 A8
Millfield Rd
Whickham NE16 .69 B6
Riding Mill NE44 .62 F7

Millfield S NE22 . . . . .16 A7
Millfield Sta SR4 . . . . . . .102 B3
Millfield Terr
Hexham NE46 . . . . .44 F5
Whitburn SR6 . . . . .60 F2
Millfield W NE22 . . . . .16 A8
Millford NE10 . . . . .72 B6
Millgrove View NE3 . . . . . .37 F3
Milling Ct NE8 . . . . .100 C2
Millom Pl NE9 . . . . .71 B4
Mills Gdns NE28 . . . . .40 B3
Millside NE61 . . . . .8 F8
Millthorp Cl SR2 . . . . .87 A1
Millview Dr NE30 . . . . .42 C8
Millway
Seaton Sluice NE26 . . . . . . .24 D5
Gateshead NE9 . . . . .71 A7
Millway Gr NE26 . . . . .24 D5
Milne Ct NE22 . . . . .10 F1
Milne Way NE3 . . . . .37 F6
Milner Cres NE21 . . . . . . .53 A1
Milner St NE33 . . . . .42 E2
Milrig Cl SR3 . . . . .91 E5
Milsted Cl SR3 . . . . .91 D5
Milsted Ct NE15 . . . . .36 B2
Milton Ave
Houghton-le-Spring DH5 . . .94 F7
Hebburn NE31 . . . . .57 E6
Milton Cl NE2 . . . . .99 C3
Milton Gn NE2 . . . . .99 C3
Milton Gr
North Shields NE29 . . . . . . .41 F6
Prudhoe NE42 . . . . .50 B2
Ashington NE63 . . . . .6 F3
Milton Pl
Newcastle-upon-Tyne NE2 . .99 C3
North Shields NE29 . . . . . . .41 F6
Springwell NE9 . . . . .71 E1
Milton Rd NE16 . . . . .69 B8
Milton Sq NE8 . . . . .56 A2
Milton St Jarrow NE32 . . . .58 B8
1 South Shields NE33 . . . .59 D8
Greenside NE40 . . . . .51 E1
Sunderland SR4 . . . . .102 A3
Milton Terr NE29 . . . . .41 F6
Milvain Ave NE4 . . . . .54 E6
Milvain Cl NE8 . . . . .101 C1
Milvain St NE8 . . . . .101 C1
Milverton Ct NE3 . . . . .37 C6
Mimosa Dr NE31 . . . . .57 E3
Mimosa Pl NE4 . . . . .54 D8
Minden St NE1 . . . . .99 B1
Mindrum Terr
North Shields NE29 . . . . . . .41 D4
Newcastle-upon-Tyne NE6 . .56 F5
Mindrum Way NE25 . . . . . .23 D3
Minehead Gdns 9 SR3 . . . .92 A8
Miner's Cotts NE16 . . . . . .69 C6
Miners Cotts NE15 . . . . . . .54 A7
Minerva Cl NE5 . . . . .36 C4
Mingarry DH3 . . . . .82 E2
Mingary Cl DH5 . . . . .94 C4
Minorca Cl SR1 . . . . .103 C2
Minorca Pl NE3 . . . . .37 F3
Minskip Cl SR3 . . . . .91 E5
Minster Ct NE8 . . . . .101 C3
Minster Gr NE15 . . . . .36 B3
Minster Par NE32 . . . . . . .58 C7
Minton Ct NE29 . . . . .41 F4
Minton La NE29 . . . . .41 F4
Minton Sq 4 SR4 . . . . .85 E7
Mirk La NE8 . . . . .101 B4
Mirlaw Rd NE23 . . . . .21 F5
Mistletoe Rd NE2 . . . . .38 E1
Mitcham Cres NE7 . . . . . . .39 B4
Mitchell Ave
Newcastle-upon-Tyne NE2 . .38 E2
Whitley Bay NE25 . . . . .31 D4
Mitchell Dr NE63 . . . . .7 B3
Mitchell Gdns NE34 . . . . . .59 F7
Mitchell St Birtley DH3 . . .82 C4
Crawcrook NE40 . . . . .51 E3
Newcastle-upon-Tyne NE6 . .57 B5
Mitchell Terr DH9 . . . . . . .79 B2
Mitchell's Bldgs NE9 . . . . .72 A1
Mitford Ave Blyth NE24 . . .17 C6
Seaton Delaval NE25 . . . . . .23 C3
Pegswood NE61 . . . . .4 E4
Mitford Cl
Chester le Street DH3 . . . . .88 D8
Washington NE38 . . . . .83 B4
Mitford Dr Sherburn DH6 . .96 A2
Newcastle-upon-Tyne NE5 . .36 E3
Ashington NE63 . . . . .6 D2
Mitford Gdns
Dunston NE11 . . . . .70 A5
Wide Open NE13 . . . . .28 C6
Wallsend NE28 . . . . .40 F5
Stakeford NE62 . . . . .10 F8
Mitford Pl NE3 . . . . .38 A6
Mitford Rd
South Shields NE34 . . . . . . .59 E6
Morpeth NE61 . . . . .3 E1
Mitford St
North Shields NE28 . . . . . . .41 C2
Sunderland SR6 . . . . .75 E4
Mitford Terr NE32 . . . . . . .58 B2
Mitford Way NE13 . . . . . . .27 B7
Mithras Gdns NE15 . . . . . .34 E2
Mitre Ind Est NE33 . . . . . .59 B7
Mitre Pl NE33 . . . . .59 B7
Moat Gdns NE10 . . . . .72 C8
Modder St NE6 . . . . .56 F3
Model Dwellings 1
NE38 . . . . .83 E4
Model Terr DH4 . . . . .90 A8
Modigars La NE43 . . . . . . .64 F4
Moffat Ave NE32 . . . . .58 E4
Moffat Cl NE29 . . . . .41 C8
Moine Gdns SR6 . . . . .75 E3
Moir Terr 12 SR2 . . . . .93 A6
Molesdon Cl NE30 . . . . . . .32 A1
Molineux Cl 6 NE6 . . . . . .56 B6
Molineux Ct 8 NE6 . . . . . .56 B6
Molineux St NE6 . . . . .56 B6
Mollyfair Cl NE40 . . . . . . .52 A4
Monarch Rd NE4 . . . . . . .100 A2
Monarch Terr NE21 . . . . . .53 C2
Monarch Way SR3 . . . . . . .91 C5
Monday Cres NE4 . . . . . . .98 B2
Monday Pl NE4 . . . . .98 B2
Monk Ct NE8 . . . . .101 C2
Monk St
Newcastle-upon-Tyne NE1 . .98 C1
Sunderland SR6 . . . . .75 D1
Monk's Terr NE46 . . . . . . .45 D4
Monkchester Gn NE6 . . . . .56 E5
Monkchester Rd NE6 . . . . .56 E4
Monkdale Ave NE24 . . . . . .17 A6
Monkhouse Ave NE30 . . . . .32 A1
Monkhouse Prim Sch
NE30 . . . . .32 B1
Monkridge
Newcastle-upon-Tyne NE15 .36 B2
Whitley Bay NE26 . . . . .31 E7
Monkridge Ct NE3 . . . . . . .38 E4
Monkridge Gdns NE11 . . . .70 A7
Monks Ave NE25 . . . . .31 D3
Monks Meadows NE46 . . . .45 D4
Monks Park Way NE12 . . . .39 A6
Monks Rd NE25 . . . . .31 C3
Monks Ridge NE61 . . . . .8 D7
Monks Way NE30 . . . . .32 C1
Monks Wood NE30 . . . . . . .41 F8
Monkseaton Com High Sch
NE25 . . . . .31 E2
Monkseaton Dr NE25,
NE26 . . . . .31 E6
Monkseaton Mid Sch
NE25 . . . . .31 E4
Monkseaton Rd NE25 . . . . .31 B5
Monkseaton Sta NE25 . . . .31 F5
Monkseaton Terr NE63 . . . . .6 E1
Monksfield NE10 . . . . .71 E7
Monksfield Cl 6 SR3 . . . . .91 F5
Monkside
Cramlington NE23 . . . . . . .21 F5
Newcastle-upon-Tyne NE6 .56 D8
Monkside Cl NE38 . . . . . . .83 A2
Monkstone Ave NE30 . . . . .42 C8
Monkstone Cl NE30 . . . . . .42 C8
Monkstone Cres NE30 . . . .32 C1
Monkstone Grange NE30 .32 B1
Monksway NE32 . . . . .58 E6
Monkswood Sq SR3 . . . . . .92 B6
Monkton NE10 . . . . .71 F6
Monkton Ave NE34 . . . . . . .59 A4
Monkton Bsns Pk NE31 . . .57 F2
Monkton Cty Inf Sch
NE34 . . . . .59 A3
Monkton Cty Jun Sch
NE34 . . . . .58 F4
Monkton Hall NE32 . . . . . .57 F4
Monkton La
Jarrow NE31,NE32 . . . . . . .57 F2
Hebburn NE32 . . . . .57 F4
Monkton Rd NE32 . . . . . . .58 B7
Monkton Terr NE32 . . . . . .58 C6
Monkwearmouth Hospl
SR5 . . . . .75 C3
Monkwearmouth Sch
SR6 . . . . .75 D5
Monkwearmouth Station
Mus* SR5 . . . . .103 A4
Monmouth Gdns NE28 . . . .41 A4
Monroe Pl NE5 . . . . .37 D2
Mons Ave NE31 . . . . .57 E6
Montagu Ave NE3 . . . . . . .38 A2
Montagu Ct NE3 . . . . .38 A2
Montagu Prim Schs NE5 . .37 E2
Montague Ct NE9 . . . . . . .70 F8
Montague St
Newcastle-upon-Tyne NE15 .53 D6
Sunderland SR6 . . . . .75 D3
Monterey
Washington NE37 . . . . .72 D1
Silksworth SR3 . . . . .91 E5
Montford Cl SR3 . . . . .91 D5
Montpellier Pl NE3 . . . . . .37 F3
Montpellier Terr SR2 . . . . .86 E3
Montrose Cl NE25 . . . . . . .23 D6
Montrose Cres NE9 . . . . . .71 B7
Montrose Dr NE10 . . . . . . .72 C7
Montrose Gdns
Morpeth NE61 . . . . .8 F7
Sunderland SR3 . . . . .86 A3
Monument Mall Sh Ctr
NE1 . . . . .99 A1
Monument Sta NE1 . . . . . .99 A1
Monument Terr
10 Birtley DH3 . . . . .82 C4
Penshaw DH4 . . . . .90 A8
Monument View DH4 . . . . .90 B8
Moonfield NE46 . . . . .45 B4
Moor Cl Tynemouth NE29 . .41 C8
Sunderland SR1 . . . . .103 C3
Moor Cotts DH6 . . . . .96 D4
Moor Cres NE3 . . . . .38 C3
Moor Crest Terr 2 NE29 .41 F8
Moor Croft NE64 . . . . .7 E5
Moor Ct Bournmoor DH4 . . .89 E3
Newcastle-upon-Tyne NE3 . .38 B2
Whitburn SR6 . . . . .75 E8
Moor Edge Prim Sch
NE12 . . . . .29 C3
Moor Edge Rd NE27 . . . . .30 E4
Moor Gdns NE29 . . . . .41 C8
Moor Grange NE42 . . . . . .50 D1
Moor La Ponteland NE20 . .25 C4
South Shields NE34 . . . . . . .59 E6
Newcastle-upon-Tyne NE5 . .37 D4
Stannington NE61 . . . . .14 C6
Whitburn SR6 . . . . .75 D8
Moor La E NE34 . . . . .59 F7
Moor Park Ct NE29 . . . . . .41 C7
Moor Park Rd NE29 . . . . . .41 C7
Moor Pl NE3 . . . . .38 C3
Moor Rd NE42 . . . . .65 E7
Moor Rd N NE3 . . . . .38 D4
Moor Rd S NE2,NE3 . . . . .38 D3
Moor St SR1 . . . . .103 B3
Moor Terr SR1 . . . . .103 C3
Moor View
Killingworth NE12 . . . . . . .29 C4
Crawcrook NE40 . . . . .52 A4
Newbiggin-by-the-Sea NE64 . .7 E5
Whitburn SR6 . . . . .75 E8
Moor View Cl NE61 . . . . . . .4 E3
Moor View Wlk NE12 . . . . .29 C4
Moorcroft Cl NE15 . . . . . .53 D7
Moorcroft Rd NE15 . . . . . .53 E6
Moordale Ave NE24 . . . . . .17 A6
Moore Ave Dunston NE11 . .69 F8
South Shields NE34 . . . . . . .59 F6
Moore Cres DH3 . . . . .82 C6
Moore Cres N DH5 . . . . . . .94 E7
Moore Cres S DH5 . . . . . . .94 E7
Moore Ct NE15 . . . . .52 B7
Moore St NE8 . . . . .56 A1
Moorfield NE2 . . . . .38 D3
Moorfield Gdns SR6 . . . . . .75 A8
Moorfields NE61 . . . . .9 A6
Moorfoot Ave DH2 . . . . . . .88 C2
Moorfoot Gdns NE11 . . . . .70 A7
Moorhead NE5 . . . . .37 E1
Moorhead Mews NE5 . . . . .37 E1
Moorhouse Cl NE34 . . . . . .59 D5
Moorhouse Est NE63 . . . . . .6 F3
Moorhouse Gdns DH5 . . . .95 B2
Moorhouse La NE63 . . . . . .6 F3
Moorhouses Rd NE29 . . . .41 C7
Moorings The 8 NE6 . . . .56 C4
Moorland Ave NE22 . . . . . .11 E3
Moorland Cotts NE22 . . . . .11 D3
Moorland Cres
Bedlington NE22 . . . . .11 E3
Newcastle-upon-Tyne NE6 . .56 E7
Moorland Ct NE22 . . . . . . .11 E3
Moorland Dr NE22 . . . . . . .11 E3
Moorland View NE17 . . . . .77 B8
Moorland Villas NE22 . . . .11 E3
Moorland Way NE23 . . . . .15 E1
Moorlands Hedworth NE32 58 D1
Prudhoe NE42 . . . . .50 E1
Moorlands The DH9 . . . . . .78 E1
Moormill NE11 . . . . .81 D6
Moormill La NE11 . . . . . . .81 E6
Moors Cl DH4 . . . . .94 B8
Moorsburn Dr DH4 . . . . . . .90 C1
Moorsfield DH4 . . . . .94 B8
Moorside Longbenton NE12 29 B2
Washington NE37 . . . . .83 B7
Moorside Com Prim Sch
NE4 . . . . .98 A2
Moorside Community Prim
Sch NE4 . . . . .98 A2
Moorside Ct NE5 . . . . .37 E1
Moorside Fst Sch NE64 . . .7 D5
Moorside N NE4 . . . . .54 F8
Moorside Pl NE4 . . . . .54 F8
Moorside Rd SR3 . . . . .91 D5
Moorside S NE4 . . . . .54 F7
Moorsley Rd DH5 . . . . .94 F2
Moorvale La NE5 . . . . .37 E2
Moorview Cres NE5 . . . . . .37 E2
Moorway NE37 . . . . .83 B6
Moorway Dr NE15 . . . . . . .53 E7
Moraine Cres NE17 . . . . . .77 B6
Moralee Cl NE7 . . . . .39 D3
Moran St SR6 . . . . .75 D4
Moray Cl DH3 . . . . .82 D1
Moray St SR6 . . . . .75 D3
Morcott Gdns NE29 . . . . . .41 F4
Morden St NE1 . . . . .99 A2
Mordey Cl SR2 . . . . .103 B1
Morecambe Par NE31 . . . .58 A2
Moreland Rd NE34 . . . . . . .59 D3
Moreland St SR6 . . . . .75 D2
Moresby Rd NE23 . . . . . . .16 C2
Morgan Bsns Ctr NE12 . . .29 B5
Morgan St SR5 . . . . .75 B2
Morgans Way NE21 . . . . . .53 A2
Morgy Hill E 2 NE40 . . . . .51 F3
Morgy Hill W 1 NE40 . . . . .51 F3
Morland Ave NE38 . . . . . . .83 E4
Morland Gdns NE9 . . . . . . .71 B7
Morley Ave NE10 . . . . .57 B2
Morley Hill Rd NE5 . . . . . .53 F8
Morley Pl NE27 . . . . .30 F4
Morley Terr
Fence Houses DH4 . . . . . . .90 A1
6 Gateshead NE10 . . . . . . .71 D8
Morningside NE38 . . . . . . .88 E8
Morningside Ct 5 DH3 . . .88 C4
Mornington Ave NE3 . . . . .37 F3
Morpeth Ave
Wide Open NE13 . . . . .28 C7
Jarrow NE32 . . . . .58 B3
South Shields NE34 . . . . . . .59 E7
Pegswood NE61 . . . . .4 E3
Morpeth Chantry Mid Sch
NE61 . . . . .3 E1
Morpeth Cl
Washington NE38 . . . . .83 A4
Morpeth Cl *continued*
Guide Post NE62 . . . . .10 E7
Morpeth Collingwood Sch
NE61 . . . . .9 B7
Morpeth Cottage Hospl
NE61 . . . . .8 F6
Morpeth Dr SR3 . . . . .91 D6
Morpeth Fst Sch NE61 . . . .9 A8
Morpeth Newminster Mid
Sch NE61 . . . . .3 E1
Morpeth Rd
Guide Post NE62 . . . . .10 E7
Ashington NE63 . . . . .5 F4
Morpeth Rd Fst Sch
NE24 . . . . .17 D8
Morpeth St NE2 . . . . .98 B4
Morpeth Sta NE61 . . . . .9 A7
Morpeth Stobhillgate Fst Sch
NE61 . . . . .9 B7
Morpeth Terr NE29 . . . . . .41 D4
Morpeth Wansbeck St
Aidan's CE Fst Sch NE61 .3 D2
Morris Ave NE34 . . . . .59 B3
Morris Cres NE35 . . . . . . .74 A8
Morris Ct NE23 . . . . .29 B8
Morris Gdns NE10 . . . . . . .72 B8
Morris Ho NE2 . . . . .98 C3
Morris Rd NE16 . . . . .69 B8
Morris St Birtley DH3 . . . .82 C4
Washington NE37 . . . . .83 C8
Gateshead NE8 . . . . .70 C8
Morrison Rd NE61 . . . . .4 A1
Morrison St NE8 . . . . . . .100 C2
Morriss Terr DH5 . . . . . . .94 F7
Morrit Ct NE7 . . . . .39 C5
Morston Dr NE15 . . . . . . .53 E6
Mortimer Ave
North Shields NE29 . . . . . . .41 D6
Newcastle-upon-Tyne NE5 . .36 F3
Mortimer Chase NE23 . . . .16 C3
Mortimer Comp Sch
NE34 . . . . .59 D7
Mortimer Prim Sch NE34 59 D7
Mortimer Rd NE33,NE34 . .59 D7
Mortimer St SR4 . . . . .85 F7
Mortimer Terr
Seaton Delaval NE25 . . . . . .23 E2
Pegswood NE61 . . . . .4 F4
Morton Cl NE38 . . . . .83 D4
Morton Cres
Great Lumley DH4 . . . . .89 F1
Woolsington NE5 . . . . .36 B6
Morton Grange Terr DH4 89 E1
Morton St
1 South Shields NE33 . . . .42 D4
Newcastle-upon-Tyne NE6 .56 D6
Morton Wlk 6 NE33 . . . . .42 C4
Morval Cl SR3 . . . . .91 D5
Morven Dr NE10 . . . . .57 B1
Morven Lea NE21 . . . . . . .53 B2
Morven Pl NE63 . . . . .6 B4
Morven Terr NE63 . . . . .6 B4
Morwick Cl NE23 . . . . .22 A5
Morwick Pl 3 NE5 . . . . . .37 D1
Morwick Rd NE29 . . . . . . .41 D8
Mosley St NE1 . . . . .99 B1
Moss Bank NE9 . . . . .71 B3
Moss Cl NE15 . . . . .53 C8
Moss Cres NE40 . . . . .52 A4
Moss Side NE9 . . . . .71 C3
Mosspool NE21 . . . . .53 A2
Mostyn Gn NE3 . . . . .37 F5
Motcombe Way NE23 . . . .16 D2
Moulton Ct NE5 . . . . .37 C2
Moulton Pl NE5 . . . . .37 C2
Mount Cl
Killingworth NE12 . . . . . . .29 D4
Whitley Bay NE25 . . . . .31 D3
Sunderland SR4 . . . . .85 B6
Mount Ct DH3 . . . . .82 D5
Mount Gr Dunston NE11 . .69 F7
Sunderland SR4 . . . . .86 A4
Mount La NE9 . . . . .82 E8
Mount Lonnen NE9 . . . . . .82 E8
Mount Pleasant
Birtley DH3 . . . . .82 C5
Houghton-le-Spring DH5 . . .94 F8
Dipton DH9 . . . . .78 E1
5 Blaydon NE21 . . . . .53 B1
9 Newcastle-upon-Tyne
NE6 . . . . .56 C6
3 Sunderland SR5 . . . . . . .75 A1
Mount Pleasant Bglws 5
DH3 . . . . .82 C5
Mount Pleasant Ct NE15 .35 D2
Mount Pleasant Gdns
NE8 . . . . .56 A1
Mount Rd Birtley DH3 . . . .82 D5
Gateshead NE9 . . . . .82 E8
Sunderland SR4 . . . . .85 F4
Mount Terr NE33 . . . . .42 C2
Mount The Throckley NE15 35 C2
Ryton NE40 . . . . .52 C5
Mount View
Whickham NE16 . . . . .69 B8
16 Crawcrook NE40 . . . . . .51 F3
Mount View Terr NE43 . . . .64 A7
Mountbatten Ave NE31 . . .57 E4
Mountfield Gdns NE3 . . . .37 F5
Mountfield Prim Sch
NE3 . . . . .37 E5
Mountford Rd NE25 . . . . . .23 D7
Mountside Gdns NE11 . . . .69 F7
Mourne Gdns NE11 . . . . . .70 A6
Mowbray Cl SR2 . . . . . . .103 A1
Mowbray Cty Jun Mix Sch
NE33 . . . . .42 F1
Mowbray Mews NE33 . . . .42 E2
Mowbray Rd
Longbenton NE12 . . . . .39 E8
North Shields NE29 . . . . . . .41 D6
South Shields NE33 . . . . . . .42 E1
Sunderland SR2 . . . . .103 B1
Mowbray St NE6 . . . . .56 A7
Mowbray Terr NE62 . . . . . .10 F7
Mowden Hall (Prep Sch)
NE43 . . . . .48 E7
Moyle Terr NE16 . . . . .79 A4
Mozart St NE33 . . . . .42 D2
Muirfield
Whitley Bay NE25 . . . . .31 D5
South Shields NE33 . . . . . . .42 F1
Muirfield Dr
Gateshead NE10 . . . . .71 E6
Washington NE37 . . . . .72 C2
Muirfield Rd NE7 . . . . .39 C5
Mulben Cl NE4 . . . . .54 E4
Mulberry Cl NE24 . . . . . . .17 D4
Mulberry Gdns NE10 . . . . .56 C2
Mulberry Gr NE16 . . . . . . .79 A4
Mulberry Pl NE4 . . . . . . .100 B3
Mulberry St NE10 . . . . . . .56 C1
Mulcaster Gdns NE28 . . . .40 A3
Mulgrave Dr SR6 . . . . .75 E1
Mulgrave Terr NE8 . . . . .101 B3
Mulgrave Villas NE8 . . . .101 B2
Mull Gr NE32 . . . . .58 E3
Mullen Dr NE40 . . . . .52 D4
Mullen Gdns NE28 . . . . . . .40 A4
Mullen Rd NE28 . . . . .40 B4
Mundella Terr NE6 . . . . . .56 B7
Mundle Ave NE21 . . . . . . .68 C6
Mundles La NE36 . . . . .74 D6
Municipal Terr NE38 . . . . .83 D6
Munslow Rd SR3 . . . . .91 D8
Murphy Gr SR2 . . . . .92 E7
Murray Ave DH4 . . . . .90 A1
Murray Ct DH2 . . . . .88 B3
Murray Gdns 1 NE11 . . . .70 A7
Murray Pl DH2 . . . . .88 C3
Murray Rd
Chester le Street DH2,DH3 .88 C3
Wallsend NE28 . . . . .40 F3
Murray St NE21 . . . . .53 C3
Murrayfield NE23 . . . . . . .22 F2
Murrayfield Rd NE5 . . . . .37 D3
Murston Ave NE23 . . . . . . .16 C2
Murton La
Easington Lane DH5 . . . . . .95 D1
Tynemouth NE27,NE29 . . . .31 B2
Murton St SR1 . . . . .103 B2
Muscott Gr NE15 . . . . .54 A6
Musgrave Rd NE9 . . . . . . .70 F6
Musgrave Sch NE9 . . . . . .70 F6
Musgrave Terr
Gateshead NE10 . . . . .57 B2
Washington NE38 . . . . .83 D6
Newcastle-upon-Tyne NE6 . .56 E6
Muswell Hill NE15 . . . . . .54 A5
Mutual St NE28 . . . . .40 B1
Mylord Cres NE12 . . . . . . .29 B5
Myre Hall 8 DH5 . . . . . . .94 E8
Myrella Cres SR2 . . . . . . .86 C2
Myreside Pl NE12 . . . . . . .39 B7
Myrtle Ave Dunston NE11 .69 F8
Whitburn SR6 . . . . .60 F1
Myrtle Cres NE12 . . . . . . .29 D1
Myrtle Gr Gateshead NE11 .70 F5
Burnopfield NE16 . . . . .78 F6
Newcastle-upon-Tyne NE2 . .38 E2
Wallsend NE28 . . . . .40 D1
South Shields NE34 . . . . . . .59 F4
Myrtle Rd NE21 . . . . .53 C1
Myrtle Terr NE63 . . . . .6 D4
Myrtles DH2 . . . . .88 B5

N

Nafferton Pl NE5 . . . . . . .54 C8
Nailsworth Cl NE35 . . . . .58 E2
Nairn Cl Birtley DH3 . . . .82 D2
Washington NE37 . . . . .72 C2
Nairn Rd NE23 . . . . .22 B7
Nairn St NE32 . . . . .58 E3
Nansen Cl NE5 . . . . .36 F2
Napier Cl DH3 . . . . .88 D8
Napier Ct NE16 . . . . .69 B4
Napier Rd NE16 . . . . .54 A1
Napier St
Newcastle-upon-Tyne NE2 . .99 C2
Jarrow NE32 . . . . .58 B7
South Shields NE33,NE34 . .59 B6
Napier Way NE21 . . . . . . .53 E2
Narvik Way NE29 . . . . . . .41 B4
Nash Ave NE34 . . . . .59 D3
Naters St NE26 . . . . .32 C4
National Glass Ctr (Mus)*
SR6 . . . . .103 B4
Natley Ave NE36 . . . . .74 E7
Navan Cl NE62 . . . . .11 D8
Navenby Cl
Newcastle-upon-Tyne NE3 .38 D8
Seaham SR7 . . . . .93 A1
Naworth Ave NE30 . . . . . .32 A1
Naworth Dr NE5 . . . . .36 E3
Naworth Terr NE32 . . . . . .58 D4
Nawton Ave SR5 . . . . .75 C2
Nayland Rd NE23 . . . . .22 A7
Naylor Ave NE21 . . . . .68 C6
Naylor Bldgs NE21 . . . . . .68 C6
Naylor Ct NE21 . . . . .53 E4
Naylor Pl NE26 . . . . .24 B7

Neale St Tantobie DH9 79 B2
Prudhoe NE42 50 D3
Sunderland SR6 75 E3
Nearlane Cl NE13 28 C8
Neasdon Cres NE30 32 B1
Neasham Rd SR7 93 A1
Nedderton Cl NE5 36 B4
Needham Pl NE23 22 B7
Neighbourhood Ctr The
NE5 37 A5
Neil St DH5 95 C1
Neill Dr NE16 69 B2
Neilson Rd NE10 56 B3
Nell Terr NE39 67 C1
Nellie Gormley House
NE12 29 B2
Nelson Ave
Cramlington NE23 21 F8
Newcastle-upon-Tyne NE3 38 A5
South Shields NE33 42 E3
Nelson Cl Ashington NE63 6 E2
Sunderland SR2 103 B1
Nelson Cres NE29 41 D2
Nelson Dr NE23 15 F1
Nelson House 14 NE30 42 D7
Nelson Ind Est NE23 15 E2
Nelson Park Ind Est
NE23 15 E1
Nelson Park West NE23 15 D1
Nelson Rd
Cramlington NE23 15 D1
Earsdon NE25 31 B5
Newcastle-upon-Tyne NE6 57 B4
Stakeford NE62 11 A7
Nelson St
Chester le Street DH3 88 C2
Hetton le Hole DH5 95 A3
Newcastle-upon-Tyne NE1 99 A1
Dunston NE11 54 F2
11 South Shields NE33 42 C3
Washington NE38 83 E4
Greenside NE40 51 F1
Gateshead NE8 101 C3
Ryhope SR2 92 F7
Nelson Terr Sherburn DH6 96 A1
Chopwell NE17 66 B1
North Shields NE29 41 D3
Nelson Way NE23 15 E2
Nene Ct 11 NE37 83 E8
Nent Gr NE46 45 C4
Neptune Rd
Newcastle-upon-Tyne,
Denton Burn NE15 53 E7
Newcastle-upon-Tyne, Lemington
NE15 53 D6
Wallsend NE28 57 B8
Nesburn Rd SR4 102 A1
Nesham Pl DH5 94 F8
Nesham Terr SR1 103 C3
Ness Ct NE21 53 A2
Nest Rd NE10 56 D2
Nether Farm Rd NE10 56 F1
Nether Riggs NE22 15 F8
Netherburn Rd SR5 75 C2
Netherby Dr NE5 54 C8
Netherdale NE22 10 D1
Netherton NE12 29 C4
Netherton Ave NE29 41 D7
Netherton Gdns NE13 28 B6
Netherton Gr NE29 41 D7
Netherton La NE22 10 C1
Netherton Park Assessment
Ctr NE61 14 D5
Nettleham Rd SR5 75 C2
Nettles La SR3 92 B6
Nevill Rd NE43 64 D7
Neville Cres DH3 82 C6
Neville Ct 3 NE37 83 F8
Neville Rd
Newcastle-upon-Tyne NE15 53 E7
Sunderland SR4 85 F7
Neville Sq NE61 2 A2
Neville St NE1 101 A4
Neville's Cross Rd NE31 57 F5
Nevinson Ave NE34 59 E3
Nevis Cl NE26 31 E8
Nevis Ct NE26 31 E8
Nevis Gr NE36 74 B7
Nevis Way NE26 31 E7
New Bridge St NE1 99 C1
New Bridge St W NE1,
NE99 99 B2
New Delaval Cty Sch
NE24 17 B4
New Dr SR7 93 B1
New Durham Rd SR2 102 C2
New Front St DH9 79 D1
New George St NE33 42 C1
New Green St NE33 42 C1
New Hartley Fst Sch
NE25 23 D6
New Herrington Ind Est
DH4 90 D6
New King St NE64 7 F5
New Mills NE4 98 B2
New Penshaw Prim Sch
DH4 90 B8
New Phoenix Yd 1 NE61 9 A8
New Quay NE29 42 B4
New Queen St NE64 7 E5
New Rd Gateshead NE10 72 C5
Dunston NE11 70 B6
Burnopfield NE16 79 B7
West Boldon NE35 74 B8
Washington NE38 89 C8
New Ridley Rd NE43 64 D5
New Seaham Prim Sch
SR7 92 F1
New Silksworth Inf Sch
SR3 92 B7
New Silksworth Jun Sch
SR3 92 B7
New South Terr DH3 82 D4
New St Sherburn DH6 96 A1
5 Sunderland SR4 85 A6
New York Prim Sch
NE29 41 C8
New York Rd
Shiremoor NE27 30 E2
Tynemouth NE29 31 B1
New York Way NE27 41 A8
Newark Cres SR7 93 A1
Newark Dr SR6 75 F8
Newark Sq NE29 41 F4
Newarth Cl NE15 53 E7
Newbank Wlk NE21 53 A1
Newbiggin La NE5 36 F4
Newbiggin Mid Sch NE64 7 C4
Newbiggin Rd NE63 6 E1
Newbold Ave SR5 75 C2
Newbold St NE6 56 D5
Newbolt Ct NE8 56 A2
Newbottle Prim Sch DH4 90 D3
Newbottle St DH4 90 E1
Newbridge Ave SR5 75 C2
Newbridge Bank DH3 88 F5
Newbrough Cres NE2 38 E2
Newburgh Ave NE25 23 D2
Newburn Ave SR5 75 C2
Newburn Bridge Rd
NE15,NE21 52 E6
Newburn Cres DH4 90 D1
Newburn Ct NE33 42 D1
Newburn Haugh Ind Est
NE15 53 C6
Newburn Ind Est NE15 53 A6
Newburn Lane End NE15 35 D2
Newburn Manor Fst Sch
NE15 52 F8
Newburn Motor Mus★
NE15 52 F8
Newburn Rd
Newburn NE15 52 F8
Throckley NE15 35 E1
Newbury NE12 29 D4
Newbury Ave NE8 70 D8
Newbury Cl NE15 53 D7
Newbury St
South Shields NE33 59 D7
Sunderland SR5 75 D3
Newby La DH6 96 C5
Newby Pl NE9 71 B4
Newcastle Arena NE4 100 C3
Newcastle Bank NE9 82 B7
Newcastle Bsns Pk NE4 100 A3
Newcastle Coll Trevelyan
Bldg NE4 100 B4
Newcastle Discovery Mus★
NE1 100 C4
Newcastle General Hospl
NE4 54 F6
Newcastle International
Airport NE13 26 D3
Newcastle Nuffield Hospl The
NE2 99 B4
Newcastle Rd Birtley DH3 82 C6
Chester le Street DH3 88 C5
Hedworth NE10,NE36 73 C7
Blyth NE24 17 C4
Jarrow NE34 58 F5
West Boldon NE36 73 E6
Sunderland SR5 75 C3
Newcastle St NE29 42 A5
Newcastle Terr 5 NE30 42 D7
Newcastle Upon Tyne Central
Sta NE1 101 A4
Newdene Wlk NE15 53 D7
Newfield Wlk NE16 69 A6
Newgate Sh Ctr NE1 99 A1
Newgate St
Newcastle-upon-Tyne NE1 99 A1
Morpeth NE61 3 F1
Newham Ave NE13 28 A4
Newhaven Ave SR5 75 C2
Newington Ct
Washington NE37 83 C8
Sunderland SR5 75 C1
Newington Rd NE6 56 A6
Newker Prim Sch DH2 88 B2
Newland Ct NE34 59 C5
Newlands NE30 32 A2
Newlands Ave Blyth NE24 17 D5
Whitley Bay NE25 31 D3
Newcastle-upon-Tyne NE3 28 D1
Sunderland SR3 86 B3
Newlands Pl NE24 17 D5
Newlands Prep Sch NE3 38 D4
Newlands Rd
Newcastle-upon-Tyne NE2 38 D3
Blyth NE24 17 D5
Newlands Rd W SR7 93 A1
Newlyn Cres NE29 41 E5
Newlyn Dr
Cramlington NE23 22 B8
Jarrow NE32 58 D6
Newlyn Rd NE3 37 E5
Newman Pl NE8 71 A8
Newman Terr NE8 71 A8
Newman's Way 1 NE46 45 B4
Newmarch St NE32 58 A7
Newmarket Wlk 1 NE33 42 D1
Newmin Way NE16 68 F5
Newminster Cl DH4 90 B2
Newminster Rd NE4 54 D7
Newport Gr 6 SR3 92 A8
Newquay Gdns 4 NE9 71 A2
Newriggs NE38 83 E2
Newsham Cl NE5 36 B4
Newsham Fst Sch NE24 17 C5
Newsham Rd NE24 17 C6
Newstead Ct NE38 83 C5
Newstead Rd DH4 90 C2
Newstead Sq SR3 92 A6
Newsteads Cl NE25 31 D5
Newsteads Dr NE25 31 D5
Newton Ave
Wallsend NE28 40 F3
Tynemouth NE30 32 B3
Newton Cl NE15 53 E7
Newton Gr NE34 59 A5
Newton House NE4 98 B2
Newton Pl NE7 39 B2
Newton Rd NE7 39 B2
Newton St Dunston NE11 54 F2
Gateshead NE8 70 D8
Newton Terr NE43 49 E1
Nichol Ct NE4 54 D5
Nichol St NE4 54 D5
Nicholas Ave SR6 75 F8
Nicholas St DH5 95 B5
Nicholson Cl SR1 103 B2
Nicholson Terr NE12 29 E1
Nidderdale Ave DH5 94 F2
Nidderdale Cl NE24 17 A8
Nidsdale Ave NE6 57 A7
Nightingale Cl SR4 85 B4
Nile Cl NE15 53 C8
Nile Ct NE8 56 A1
Nile St North Shields NE29 42 A5
South Shields NE33 42 B2
Sunderland SR1 103 B3
Nilverton Ave SR2 86 D3
Nimbus Ct 13 SR3 92 A6
Nine Lands DH4 94 C8
Ninth Ave
Chester le Street DH2 88 B3
Gateshead NE11 70 D3
Blyth NE24 17 D6
Newcastle-upon-Tyne NE6 56 C8
Morpeth NE61 9 B7
Ninth Ave E NE11 70 D3
Ninth Row NE63 6 B4
Nissan Way NE37,SR5 84 B7
Nithdale Cl NE6 57 B8
Nixon St NE8 56 A4
Nixon Terr NE24 17 F6
Noble Gdns NE34 58 F4
Noble St
2 Gateshead NE10 56 D1
Newcastle-upon-Tyne NE4 54 F3
Sunderland SR2 103 C1
Noble Terr
11 Morpeth NE61 9 A8
Sunderland SR2 103 C1
Noble's Bank Rd SR2 103 C1
Noel Ave NE21 68 C6
Noel Terr NE21 68 D7
Noirmont Way SR3 91 E6
Nook The
Whitley Bay NE25 31 F4
North Shields NE29 41 F5
Nookside SR4 85 C4
Nookside Ct SR4 85 C4
Nora St South Shields NE34 59 C5
Sunderland SR4 85 F4
Norbury Gr NE6 56 D5
Nordale Way NE24 17 A8
Norfolk Ave Birtley DH3 82 D1
New Silksworth SR3 91 F8
Norfolk Cl Ashington NE63 6 A4
Seaham SR7 93 A1
Norfolk Dr NE37 72 D2
Norfolk Gdns NE28 40 E4
Norfolk Mews 11 NE30 42 A6
Norfolk Pl DH3 82 D1
Norfolk Rd
South Shields NE34 60 C7
Gateshead NE8 56 A4
Norfolk Sq 19 NE6 56 B6
Norfolk St
Hetton le Hole DH5 94 F4
North Shields NE30 42 B5
Sunderland SR1 103 A3
Norfolk Way NE15 53 E7
Norham Ave N NE34 60 A8
Norham Ave S NE34 60 A8
Norham Castle★ TD15 104 C3
Norham Cl
Brunswick Village NE13 28 A5
Blyth NE24 17 C7
Norham Com Tech Coll
NE29 41 D5
Norham Ct
Bournmoor DH4 89 D1
Washington NE38 83 B4
Norham Dr
Newcastle-upon-Tyne NE5 36 E3
Morpeth NE61 9 B5
Norham Gdns NE62 6 A1
Norham Pl NE2 38 E1
Norham Rd
Whitley Bay NE25,NE26 31 F5
North Shields NE29 41 C5
Newcastle-upon-Tyne NE3 38 B6
Ashington NE63 6 D2
Norham Rd N NE29 41 B7
Norham Terr NE32 58 B3
Norhurst NE16 68 E5
Norland Rd NE15 53 F6
Norley Ave SR5 75 C2
Norma Cres NE26 32 C4
Norman Ave SR3 92 B7
Norman Rd NE39 67 F1
Norman Terr
High Pittington DH6 96 C5
Wallsend NE28 41 B2
Morpeth NE61 9 A8
Normanby Cl SR7 93 A1
Normanby Ct SR6 75 F1
Normandy Cres DH5 94 F8
Normanton Terr NE4 98 A1
Normount Ave 2 NE4 54 E5
Normount Gdns NE4 54 E6
Normount Rd NE4 54 E5
Norseland Gallery Studio
Two Ceramics★ NE70 108 F2
North App DH2 88 B4
North Ave
Longbenton NE12 39 D6
Newcastle-upon-Tyne, Gosforth
NE3 38 C4
South Shields NE34 59 F6
Washington NE37 72 C1
Newcastle-upon-Tyne,
Westerhope NE5 36 F2
Guide Post NE62 10 E7
North Balkwell Farm Ind Est
NE29 41 B7
North Bank Ct 7 SR5 75 B2
North Bridge St SR5 103 A4
North Burns DH3 88 C4
North Church St 2 NE30 42 B6
North Cl
South Shields NE34 59 F6
Ryton NE40 52 C5
4 Newcastle-upon-Tyne
NE6 56 C7
North Cres NE38 83 B1
North Croft NE12 39 E7
North Cross St NE3 38 C5
North Ct 5 NE32 58 B7
North Dr Hebburn NE31 57 C4
Chester le Street NE38 88 E7
Cleadon SR6 59 F1
North Durham St SR1 103 B3
North East Aircraft Mus★
SR5 73 E2
North Eastern Ct NE16 69 E8
North Farm NE22 15 A8
North Farm Ave SR4 85 B2
North Farm Rd NE31 57 D5
North Fawdon Prim Sch
NE3 37 F7
North Gr Ryton NE40 52 D5
Sunderland SR6 75 E3
North Grange NE20 25 E8
North Guards SR6 75 F8
North Hall Rd SR4 85 D4
North Hylton Rd SR5 74 E2
North Hylton Road Ind Est
SR5 74 D2
North Jesmond Ave NE2 38 E2
North King St NE30 42 B6
North La
Hetton le Hole DH5 95 E5
East Boldon NE36 74 C7
North Leech NE61 3 D2
North Leigh DH9 79 D1
North Lodge DH3 88 D7
North Lodge Apartments 10
NE21 53 B1
North Magdalene DH8 77 B1
North Mason Lodge
NE13 27 B8
North Mdws NE42 50 B5
North Milburn St SR4 102 B3
North Moor Ct SR3 85 E1
North Moor La SR3 91 E8
North Moor Rd SR3 85 E1
North Par
Whitley Bay NE26 32 B5
Choppington NE62 10 E6
North Pl NE61 3 E1
North Ravensworth St
SR4 102 B3
North Rd
Chester le Street DH3 88 C7
Hetton le Hole DH5 94 E4
Houghton-le-Spring DH5 94 E4
Dipton DH9 78 E1
Ponteland NE20 25 E8
Wallsend NE28 40 B2
Tynemouth NE29 42 A8
Boldon Colliery NE35 58 E1
West Boldon NE35,NE36 73 F7
East Boldon NE36 74 C7
Slaley NE47 62 A4
Seaham SR7 93 D1
North Ridge
Bedlington NE22 10 D1
Bedlington NE22 10 E1
Whitley Bay NE25 31 C6
North Row NE42 50 A2
North Sands Bsns Ctr
SR6 103 B4
North Seaton Ind Est NE63 6 F1
North Seaton Rd
Ashington NE63 6 D2
Newbiggin-by-the-Sea NE64 7 D3
North Shields Sta NE29 42 A5
North St Birtley DH3 82 E3
Newbottle DH4 90 D4
West Rainton DH4 94 A2
East Rainton DH5 94 D4
Newcastle-upon-Tyne NE1 99 A2
Blaydon NE21 53 A2
Jarrow NE32 58 B7
South Shields NE33 42 C3
New Silksworth SR3 92 A8
North St continued
5 Sunderland SR5 75 C1
Cleadon SR6 60 A1
North St E NE1 99 B2
North Terr Chopwell NE17 66 B2
Newcastle-upon-Tyne NE2 98 C3
1 Shiremoor NE27 30 E1
Wallsend NE28 40 E2
Hexham NE46 45 B4
11 New Silksworth SR3 92 A8
North Tyne Ind Est NE12 40 A8
North Tyneside Coll
NE28 40 E5
North Tyneside General
Hospl NE29 31 E1
North View Ouston DH2 81 F1
Bournmoor DH4 89 E2
Easington Lane DH5 95 C1
Haswell DH6 97 E1
Sherburn Hill DH6 96 D1
Medomsley DH8 77 B1
Whickham NE11 69 A7
4 Longbenton NE12 39 D8
Dinnington NE13 27 B7
Hazlerigg NE13 28 A4
Bedlington NE22 11 D3
Cambois NE24 12 C6
Wallsend NE28 40 C2
Tynemouth, Preston NE29 41 F8
Tynemouth, Cullercoats
NE30 32 C4
Jarrow NE32 58 A6
South Shields NE34 59 F8
Washington NE37 83 D8
High Spen NE39 66 F3
Rowlands Gill NE39 67 C2
Crawcrook NE40 51 E7
Ryton NE40 52 A5
Mickley Square NE43 49 E1
Newcastle-upon-Tyne NE6 56 B7
Newcastle-upon-Tyne NE6 56 C7
Stakeford NE62 11 C8
Ashington NE63 6 C4
Newbiggin-by-the-Sea NE64 7 D3
Gateshead NE9 71 B3
Sunderland, South Hylton
SR4 85 B5
Sunderland, Castletown
SR5 74 C1
Sunderland, Monkwearmouth
SR6 75 D3
North View Terr
Fence Houses DH4 94 B8
Prudhoe NE42 50 B2
Stocksfield NE43 64 C7
Gateshead NE8 56 C1
North View W NE39 67 C2
North Villas NE23 22 A1
North Walbottle Rd
Walbottle NE15 36 A2
Newcastle-upon-Tyne NE5 36 B4
Northbourne Ave NE61 3 F2
Northbourne Ho NE9 70 F5
Northbourne Rd NE31,
NE32 58 A6
Northbourne St
Newcastle-upon-Tyne NE4 54 F4
Gateshead NE8 70 F8
Northburn Fst Sch NE23 16 A1
Northcote NE16 69 A5
Northcote Ave
Whitley Bay NE25 31 D4
Newcastle-upon-Tyne NE5 36 C1
Sunderland SR1 103 B2
Northcote St
8 South Shields NE33 59 D8
Newcastle-upon-Tyne NE4 98 A1
Northcott Gdns NE23 22 E1
Northdene DH3 82 C7
Northern Counties Sch for
the Deaf NE2 38 D1
Northern Terr NE23 22 A1
Northern Way SR5 75 A2
Northfield NE22 12 B4
Northfield Cl NE16 68 F5
Northfield Dr
Killingworth NE12 29 B2
Sunderland SR4 85 B2
Northfield Gdns NE34 59 F8
Northfield Rd
Newcastle-upon-Tyne NE3 38 B4
South Shields NE33 42 F1
Northgate NE12 29 D4
Northgate & Prudhoe NHS
Trust Northgate Hospl
NE61 3 D4
Northland Cl SR4 85 B2
Northlands
Chester le Street DH3 88 C5
Blaydon NE21 53 B1
Tynemouth NE30 32 B1
Northlands Rd NE61 3 F2
Northlea NE15 53 E8
Northmoor Rd NE6 56 E8
Northolt Ave NE23 22 B7
Northside Pl NE25 23 E2
Northumberland Aged
Mineworkers Homes
NE23 22 D5
Northumberland Ave
Longbenton NE12 39 D7
Bedlington NE22 10 E1
Wallsend NE28 40 F2
Newcastle-upon-Tyne NE3 38 A3
Newbiggin-by-the-Sea NE64 7 D4
Northumberland Cl NE63 6 A4
Northumberland Coll
NE63 6 E2

Nor – Pal 167

Northumberland Ct NE31 57 D5
Northumberland Dock Rd NE28 41 C1
Northumberland Gdns
Newcastle-upon-Tyne, Jesmond Vale NE2 56 A8
Newcastle-upon-Tyne, North Walbottle NE5 36 B3
Northumberland National Park Visitor Centre* NE65 117 F4
Northumberland National Park Visitor Centre* NE66 111 E4
Northumberland Pl
Birtley DH3 82 D1
Newcastle-upon-Tyne NE1 99 A2
9 North Shields NE30 42 A6
Northumberland Rd
Newcastle-upon-Tyne NE1, NE99 99 B2
Newcastle-upon-Tyne, Lemington NE15 53 C6
Ryton NE40 52 C6
Northumberland Sq
Whitley Bay NE26 32 A5
4 North Shields NE30 42 B6
Northumberland St
Newcastle-upon-Tyne NE1 99 A2
Wallsend NE28 40 C2
North Shields NE30 42 C6
Gateshead NE8 100 C1
Northumberland Terr
Wallsend NE28 40 F2
Tynemouth NE30 42 D7
29 Newcastle-upon-Tyne NE6 56 B6
Northumberland Villas NE28 40 E2
Northumberland Way
Washington, Usworth NE10, NE37 72 D3
Washington, Columbia NE37, NE38 83 F4
Northumbria Lodge NE5 37 E1
Northumbria Police Headquarters NE20 25 D8
Northumbria Wlk
Newcastle-upon-Tyne, East Denton NE5 37 A2
Newcastle-upon-Tyne, West Denton NE5 36 F1
Northumbrian Rd NE23 22 B6
Northumbrian Way
Killingworth NE12 29 C2
North Shields NE29 42 A3
Northway Throckley NE15 35 D3
Guide Post NE62 10 F7
Gateshead NE9 71 B7
Northwood Ct SR5 75 C2
Norton Ave SR7 93 A1
Norton Cl DH2 88 A1
Norton Rd SR5 75 A3
Norton Way NE15 53 E6
Norway Ave SR4 85 E4
Norwich Ave NE13 28 B5
Norwich Cl NE63 7 A2
Norwich Way
Cramlington NE23 22 A7
Hedworth NE32 58 B1
Norwood Ave
Newcastle-upon-Tyne, Brunton Park NE3 28 C1
Newcastle-upon-Tyne, Heaton NE6 39 B1
Norwood Cres NE39 67 F2
Norwood Ct NE9 71 C2
Norwood Gdns 4 NE9 71 A8
Norwood Rd
Gateshead NE11 70 B7
Newcastle-upon-Tyne NE15 53 D8
Numbers Garth SR1 103 B3
Nun St NE1 99 A1
Nuneaton Way NE5 36 B4
Nunn St DH4 90 A5
Nunnykirk Cl NE42 50 A4
Nuns La
Newcastle-upon-Tyne NE1 99 A1
Gateshead NE8 101 C3
Nuns Moor Cres NE4 54 E7
Nuns Moor Rd NE4 54 E7
Nunthorpe Ave SR2 86 F1
Nunwick Gdns NE29 41 C6
Nunwick Way NE7 39 D4
Nursery Cl SR3 86 A2
Nursery Ct NE17 77 B6
Nursery La
Gateshead NE10 71 C7
Cleadon SR6 60 A1
Nursery Pk NE63 6 E1
Nursery Rd SR3 86 A2
Nutley Pl NE15 54 A5
Nye Baven Ho NE63 6 E2
Nye Dene SR5 74 B1

O

O'Hanlon Cres NE28 40 A4
Oak Ave
5 Houghton-le-Spring DH4 94 D8
Dunston NE11 69 F7
Dinnington NE13 27 C7
South Shields NE34 60 A5
Oak Cl NE46 44 E3
Oak Cres SR6 61 A2
Oak Gr Longbenton NE12 39 D8
Wallsend NE28 40 D1
Oak Rd NE29 41 B7
Oak Sq NE8 100 C1
Oak St Great Lumley DH4 89 E1
Seaton Burn NE13 28 C8
1 Throckley NE15 35 D2
Jarrow NE32 58 A7
Washington NE38 83 F4
Mickley Square NE43 64 E8
Sunderland SR1 103 C2
Oak Terr Tantobie DH9 79 B2
Burnopfield NE16 79 C6
Blaydon NE21 53 C1
Oakapple Cl NE22 10 F1
Oakdale NE22 15 B8
Oakdale Cl NE15 53 D6
Oakdale Terr DH3 88 C2
Oakenshaw NE15 53 E6
Oakeys Rd DH9 79 F1
Oakfield Ave NE16 69 B6
Oakfield Cl
Whickham NE16 69 B6
Sunderland SR3 91 C6
Oakfield Coll NE4 54 D6
Oakfield Ct SR3 91 C6
Oakfield Dr
Killingworth NE12 29 F3
Whickham NE16 69 B6
Oakfield Gdns
Newcastle-upon-Tyne NE15 54 D5
Wallsend NE28 39 F3
Oakfield Grange NE13 27 B7
Oakfield Inf & Jun Schs NE9 70 F3
Oakfield N NE40 52 B5
Oakfield Pk NE42 50 D2
Oakfield Rd Dunston NE11 70 A6
Whickham NE16 69 A5
Newcastle-upon-Tyne NE3 38 B3
Oakfield Terr
Gateshead NE10 57 B2
Killingworth NE12 29 E1
Newcastle-upon-Tyne NE3 38 B4
Oakfield Way NE23 22 F1
Oakfields NE16 79 B7
Oakham Ave NE16 68 F6
Oakham Gdns NE29 41 E5
Oakhampton Dr DH4 90 C4
Oakhurst Dr NE3 38 A3
Oakhurst Terr NE12 39 D7
Oakland Rd
Newcastle-upon-Tyne NE2 38 D2
Whitley Bay NE25 31 D4
Oakland Terr
Lynmouth NE61 2 A2
Ashington NE63 6 C3
Oaklands Whickham NE16 69 C8
Ponteland NE20 25 D4
Newcastle-upon-Tyne NE3 38 C3
Riding Mill NE44 62 F7
Stakeford NE62 11 A7
Oaklands Ave NE3 38 C3
Oaklands Ct NE20 25 D4
Oaklands Rise NE44 62 F7
Oaklands Terr SR4 102 A1
Oaklea DH2 88 A5
Oakleigh Gdns SR6 60 A2
Oakley Cl NE23 29 B8
Oakley Dr NE23 22 D7
Oakley Gardens Specl Sch SR6 60 B2
Oakmere Cl 2 DH4 90 B6
Oakridge NE16 68 F6
Oaks The Penshaw DH4 90 B8
High Spen NE39 67 A3
Greenside NE40 52 B1
Hexham NE46 44 F3
Sunderland SR2 103 B1
Oaks W The SR2 103 B1
Oaktree Ave NE6 40 A1
Oaktree Gdns NE25 31 E3
Oaktree Terr NE42 50 D2
Oakville NE63 7 A2
Oakwellgate NE8 101 C4
Oakwood Gateshead NE10 71 E5
Hebburn NE31 57 C7
Oakwood NE46 45 E8
Oakwood Ave
Wide Open NE13 28 C5
Newbiggin-by-the-Sea NE64 7 D5
Gateshead NE9 71 A3
Oakwood Bank NE46 45 C7
Oakwood Cl NE9 71 F1
Oakwood Gdns NE11 70 B5
Oakwood Pl 2 NE5 37 C1
Oakwood St SR2 102 B1
Oakwood Terr NE28 41 D2
Oatens Bank NE15 33 A2
Oates St SR4 102 A2
Oatfield Cl NE63 6 B2
Oatlands Rd SR4 85 E4
Oban Ave NE28 40 F4
Oban Ct NE6 56 C5
Oban Gdns 9 NE6 56 C5
Oban St Gateshead NE10 56 C1
Brockley Whins NE32 58 E3
Ocean Rd
South Shields NE33 42 D3
Sunderland SR2 86 F2
Ocean Rd N 6 SR2 86 F2
Ocean Rd S 7 SR2 86 F2
Ocean View
Whitley Bay NE26 32 B5
Newbiggin-by-the-Sea NE64 7 E4
Sunderland SR2 92 F8
Ochiltree Ct NE26 24 D6
Octavia Cl NE22 10 E2
Octavia Ct NE28 40 F4
Octavian Way NE11 70 C3
Odinel Ct NE42 50 D3
Offerton Cl 7 SR4 85 A6
Offerton La Penshaw SR4 84 F4
Sunderland SR4 85 A5
Offerton St SR4 102 B2
Office Pl DH5 95 A3
Office Row
New Herrington DH4 90 E7
Washington NE38 83 A1
Ogden St SR4 102 B2
Ogle Ave Hazlerigg NE13 28 A4
Morpeth NE61 8 E8
Ogle Dr NE24 17 C7
Ogle Gr NE32 58 A3
Oil Mill Rd NE6 57 B7
Okehampton Ct 2 NE9 71 A2
Okehampton Sq SR5 75 A3
Old Brewery Sq NE42 49 C4
Old Brewery The 10 DH4 94 E8
Old Coastguard Cotts NE30 42 E7
Old Coronation St NE33 42 C2
Old Course Rd SR6 75 A8
Old Durham Rd NE8,NE9 71 B6
Old Farm Ct NE16 69 B2
Old Fold Rd NE10,NE8 56 B2
Old Forge The NE43 48 C5
Old Main St NE40 51 E3
Old Mill Rd
Sunderland, Hendon SR2 103 C1
Sunderland, High Southwick SR5 75 A3
Old Orchard The NE44 63 A7
Old Rectory Cl DH9 79 D4
Old Sawmill NE61 8 A8
Old Station Ct NE20 25 C3
Old Vicarage Wlk 20 NE6 56 C6
Old Well La NE21 53 B1
Oldfield Rd NE6 56 F3
Oldgate NE61 8 F8
Oldgate Ct NE61 8 F8
Oldstead Gdns SR4 85 E4
Oldwell Ave 4 NE21 53 B1
Olga Terr NE39 67 C1
Olive Gdns NE9 71 A6
Olive Pl NE4 54 D7
Olive St South Shields NE33 59 B6
Sunderland SR1 102 C2
Oliver Ave NE4 54 E6
Oliver Cres DH3 82 C6
Oliver St 2 NE38 83 E4
Olivers Mill NE61 8 F8
Ollerton Dr NE15 35 B2
Ollerton Gdns NE10 71 C6
Olney Cl NE23 22 D7
Olympia Ave NE62 10 F7
Olympia Gdns NE61 4 A1
Olympia Hill NE61 3 F2
Ongar Way NE12 39 B7
Onslow Gdns NE9 70 F5
Onslow St SR4 85 E7
Open The NE1 99 A2
Oram Cl NE61 9 B8
Orange Gr Whickham NE16 69 C8
Annitsford NE23 22 B1
Orchard Ave NE39 67 D1
Orchard Cl
Killingworth NE12 29 F2
Sunniside NE16 69 B3
South Shields NE34 59 B5
Rowlands Gill NE39 78 D8
Prudhoe NE42 50 D1
Morpeth NE61 9 B8
Ashington NE63 6 C2
Orchard Cres NE45 47 A5
Orchard Ct
Tynemouth NE29 42 A8
Ryton NE40 52 C5
Greenside NE40,NE41 51 F1
Orchard Dene NE39 67 D1
Orchard Gdns
Chester le Street DH3 88 C1
Wallsend NE28 40 A4
Gateshead NE9 71 A4
Whitburn SR6 75 E8
Orchard Gn NE5 37 D4
Orchard Hill NE42 50 D3
Orchard Pk 7 DH3 82 C4
Orchard Pl NE2 38 F1
Orchard Rd
Whickham NE16 69 C7
Rowlands Gill NE39 67 D1
Orchard Rise NE15 53 B7
Orchard St Birtley DH3 82 C4
Newcastle-upon-Tyne NE1 101 A4
Sunderland SR4 85 F7
Orchard Terr
Chester le Street DH3 88 C1
Newcastle-upon-Tyne NE15 53 C6
8 Throckley NE15 35 D2
Rowlands Gill NE39 78 D8
Orchard The
Chester le Street DH3 88 D4
Newcastle-upon-Tyne NE15 53 D6
Whickham NE16 69 C7
4 North Shields NE29 42 A6
East Boldon NE36 74 C7
Wylam NE41 51 A6
Hepscott NE61 9 E5
Orchard-Leigh NE15 53 E6
Orchards The NE24 17 B8
Orchid Cl NE34 59 B5
Orchid Cres NE10 56 C2
Ord Ct NE4 54 D7
Ord St NE4 100 C3
Ord Terr NE62 11 B8
Orde Ave NE28 40 E3
Ordley Cl NE15 53 E6
Oriel Cl SR6 75 D1
Oriole House NE12 39 D7
Orkney Dr SR2 92 D8
Orlando Rd NE29 41 E6
Ormesby Rd SR6 75 D3
Ormiscraig NE15 53 E6
Ormiston NE15 53 E6
Ormonde Ave NE15 54 A6
Ormonde St Jarrow NE32 58 B7
Sunderland SR4 102 A1
Ormsby Gn NE5 54 A8
Ormskirk Cl NE15 53 D6
Ormskirk Gr NE23 22 C7
Ormston St NE23 16 B3
Orpen Ave NE34 59 C3
Orpine Ct NE63 6 C2
Orpington Ave NE6 56 E6
Orpington Rd NE23 22 C7
Orr Ave SR3 92 B6
Orton Cl NE4 54 E4
Orwell Cl NE34 59 B2
Osbaldeston Gdns NE3 38 B3
Osborne Ave
Newcastle-upon-Tyne NE2 99 C4
South Shields NE33 42 E1
Hexham NE46 44 F5
Osborne Cl NE22 11 C2
Osborne Ct NE2 99 C4
Osborne Gdns
Whitley Bay NE26 31 F5
Tynemouth NE29 42 A7
Osborne House NE28 40 E2
Osborne Rd
Chester le Street DH3 88 C3
Newcastle-upon-Tyne NE2 38 E2
Sunderland SR5 85 A7
Osborne St
South Shields NE33 42 E2
Sunderland SR6 75 D2
Osborne Terr
Newcastle-upon-Tyne NE2 99 B3
Cramlington NE23 22 A7
Gateshead NE8 101 A1
Osborne Villas NE2 99 B4
Osforth Park Way NE3 39 A8
Osier Ct NE62 11 C7
Oslo Cl NE29 41 B4
Osman Cl SR2 103 B1
Osprey Dr Blyth NE24 17 F5
Shiremoor NE28 41 A6
Osprey House 4 NE2 38 E1
Osprey Way NE34 59 B4
Oswald Rd
Hetton le Hole DH5 95 A5
Morpeth NE61 4 A2
Newbiggin-by-the-Sea NE64 7 D5
Oswald St Whiteleas NE34 59 C3
Sunderland SR4 102 A3
Oswald Terr
Gateshead NE8 101 A1
Sunderland, Grangetown SR2 86 F2
Sunderland, Castletown SR5 74 C1
Oswald Terr S SR5 74 C1
Oswald Wlk NE3 38 E5
Oswestry Pl NE23 22 C7
Oswin Ave NE12 39 D8
Oswin Ct NE12 29 E1
Oswin Rd NE12 29 E1
Oswin Terr NE29 41 D5
Otley Cl NE23 22 D7
Otter Burn Way NE42 50 B1
Otterburn Ave
Earsdon NE25 31 B4
Newcastle-upon-Tyne NE3 38 A4
Otterburn Cl NE12 39 F8
Otterburn Cres DH4 90 C1
Otterburn Ct
Whitley Bay NE25 31 B4
Gateshead NE8 101 A1
Otterburn Dr NE63 6 B1
Otterburn Gdns
Dunston NE11 70 A7
Whickham NE16 69 B7
South Shields NE34 59 E6
Gateshead NE9 70 E5
Otterburn Gr NE24 17 B5
Otterburn Rd NE29 41 F7
Otterburn Terr NE2 38 E1
Ottercap Cl NE15 53 D6
Ottercops NE42 50 B1
Otterington NE38 84 B4
Ottershaw NE15 53 E6
Otto Terr SR2 102 B1
Ottovale Cres NE21 53 A1
Ottringham Cl NE15 53 D6
Oulton Cl
Cramlington NE23 22 C7
Newcastle-upon-Tyne NE5 37 B4
Our Lady Queen of Peace RC Prim Sch DH4 90 A7
Ousby Ct NE3 37 D7
Ouse St NE1 56 A5
Ouseburn Cl SR2 92 F8
Ouseburn Rd
Newcastle-upon-Tyne, St Ann's NE1 56 A6
Newcastle-upon-Tyne, Jesmond Vale NE2,NE6 56 A8
Ouselaw NE11 81 D6
Ouslaw La NE11 81 B6
Ouston Cl NE10 72 C7
Ouston Inf Sch DH2 82 A1
Ouston Jun Sch DH2 81 F1
Ouston St NE15 53 F5
Outram St DH5 90 E1
Oval Park View NE10 71 D7
Oval The Ouston DH2 81 F2
Houghton-le-Spring DH4 94 D8
Longbenton NE12 39 E6
Woolsington NE13 36 F8
Bedlington NE22 11 C1
Blyth NE24 17 B3
Washington NE37 83 D8
Newcastle-upon-Tyne NE6 56 D4
4 Sunderland SR5 75 B2
Overdale Ct NE62 10 E6
Overdene NE15 53 F7
Overfield Rd NE3 37 F5
Overhill NE15 34 E2
Overhill Terr NE8 101 A1
Overton Cl NE15 53 D6
Overton Rd NE29 41 E8
Ovingham CE Fst Sch NE42 50 A3
Ovingham Cl NE38 83 F5
Ovingham Gdns NE13 28 B6
Ovingham Mid Sch NE42 50 A3
Ovingham Rd NE41 51 A6
Ovington Gr NE5 54 D8
Ovington View NE42 50 B1
Owen Brannigan Dr NE23 29 B7
Owen Ct NE2 98 C3
Owen Dr NE35,NE36 74 B8
Owen Terr Tantobie DH9 79 B2
Chopwell NE17 77 C8
Owlet Cl NE21 53 A1
Oxberry Gdns NE10 71 C7
Oxbridge St SR2 86 F2
Oxclose Rd NE38 83 E4
Oxclose Sch NE38 83 A4
Oxclose Village Prim Sch NE38 83 A5
Oxford Ave
Cramlington NE23 22 C7
Wallsend NE28 40 A3
10 South Shields NE33 59 D8
Washington NE37 83 B8
Oxford Cl SR3 91 F8
Oxford Cres
Hetton le Hole DH5 94 F4
Hebburn NE31 57 F6
Oxford Pl DH3 82 C1
Oxford Rd NE62 11 A7
Oxford Sq SR4 85 E7
Oxford St
Newcastle-upon-Tyne NE1 99 B2
Blyth NE24 17 F7
Whitley Bay NE26 32 B5
Tynemouth NE30 42 D7
South Shields NE33 59 D8
Sunderland SR4 85 E7
Oxford Terr
Shiney Row DH4 90 A6
Gateshead NE8 101 B1
Oxford Way NE32 58 B1
Oxnam Cres NE2 98 B3
Oxted Cl NE23 22 D7
Oxted Pl NE6 56 E3
Oystershell La NE4 98 C1
Oyston St NE33 42 C2
Ozanan Cl NE23 29 B7

P

Packham Rd SR4 85 C5
Paddock Cl
Shiney Row DH4 89 F5
Prudhoe NE42 50 E2
Cleadon SR6 59 E1
Paddock Hill NE20 25 F7
Paddock La SR3 92 C7
Paddock Rise NE63 6 B2
Paddock The
New Herrington DH4 90 F7
Gateshead NE10 71 F6
Woolsington NE13 36 F8
Walbottle NE15 35 F1
East Cramlington NE23 22 D5
Blyth NE24 17 C7
Seaton Delaval NE25 23 E3
Stocksfield NE43 64 C5
Ashington NE63 7 B2
Paddock Wood NE42 50 E2
Pader Cl NE13 28 B5
Padgate Rd SR4 85 C6
Padonhill 5 SR3 91 E5
Padstow Cl 2 SR2 92 F8
Padstow Ct NE9 70 F2
Padstow Rd NE29 41 E4
Page Ave NE34 59 E7
Page St NE31 57 F7
Page's Bldgs NE35 73 E8
Paignton Ave
Whitley Bay NE25 31 E4
Newcastle-upon-Tyne NE4 54 F5
Paignton Sq SR3 85 E2
Painshawfield Rd NE43 64 C6
Paisley Sq SR3 85 E2
Palace Rd NE22 11 D2
Palace St NE4 100 B4
Palatine View DH6 96 C1
Palermo St SR4 85 F8
Paley St SR1 102 C3
Palgrove Rd SR4 85 C5
Palgrove Sq SR4 85 C5
Pallinsburn Ct NE5 37 B3
Pallion Ind Est SR4 85 D7
Pallion New Rd SR4 85 F8
Pallion Pk SR4 85 F7

Pallion Prim Sch SR4 . . .85 E8
Pallion Rd SR4 . . . . .85 F6
Pallion Ret Pk SR4 . . . . . .85 E8
Pallion Sta SR4 . . . . .85 E8
Pallion Subway SR4 . . . . .85 F8
Pallion Way SR4 . . . . .85 E7
Pallion West Ind Est SR4 85 D7
Palm Ave
South Shields NE34 . . . . . . .60 A5
Newcastle-upon-Tyne NE4 .54 D7
Palm Ct NE12 . . . . .29 F1
Palm Terr DH9 . . . . .79 C3
Palmer Community Hospl
NE32 . . . . .58 B7
Palmer Cres NE31 . . . . . . .57 F6
Palmer Gdns NE10 . . . . . .72 C8
Palmer Rd DH9 . . . . .78 E1
Palmer St NE32 . . . . .58 A7
Palmer's Hill Rd SR6 . . .103 A4
Palmers Gn NE12 . . . . . . .29 F1
Palmerston Ave NE6 . . . . .56 E7
Palmerston Rd SR4 . . . . .85 B3
Palmerston Sq SR4 . . . . .85 C4
Palmerston St NE33 . . . . .59 C8
Palmerston Wlk NE8 . . .101 A2
Palmersville NE12 . . . . . . .29 F1
Palmersville Sta NE12 . . .30 A1
Palmstead Rd SR4 . . . . .85 C5
Palmstead Sq SR4 . . . . . .85 C5
Pancras Rd SR3 . . . . .85 E2
Pandon NE1 . . . . .99 B1
Pandon Bank NE1 . . . . . . .99 B1
Pandon Ct NE2 . . . . .99 C2
Pandon Quays NE1 . . . . . .99 C1
Panfield Terr DH4 . . . . . . .89 E2
Pangbourne Cl NE15 . . . .53 C8
Pankhurst Gdns NE10 . . .72 A8
Pann La SR1 . . . . .103 A3
Panns Bank SR1 . . . . . . .103 A3
Pantiles The NE37 . . . . . .72 D2
Parade Cl NE6 . . . . .57 A5
Parade The
Chester le Street DH3 . . . . .88 D1
Wallsend NE28 . . . . .40 D5
Washington NE38 . . . . .83 E4
Newcastle-upon-Tyne NE6 . .57 A5
Sunderland SR2 . . . . .103 C1
Paradise Row NE23 . . . . .22 B6
Park Ave Dunston NE11 . . .69 E7
Blaydon NE21 . . . . .53 C2
Bedlington NE22 . . . . .11 E3
Whitley Bay NE26 . . . . .32 A5
Shiremoor NE27 . . . . .31 A3
Wallsend NE28 . . . . .40 B2
Newcastle-upon-Tyne, Fawdon
NE3 . . . . .37 F7
Newcastle-upon-Tyne, Gosforth
NE3 . . . . .38 B6
North Shields NE30 . . . . . . .42 C7
South Shields NE34 . . . . . . .59 F4
Washington NE37 . . . . .83 D8
Prudhoe NE42 . . . . .50 E1
Hexham NE46 . . . . .44 F5
New Silksworth SR3 . . . . . .92 B7
Sunderland SR6 . . . . .75 E4
Park Chare NE38 . . . . . . .83 D5
Park Cl NE4 . . . . .100 A4
Park Cotts NE17 . . . . .77 B6
Park Cres Shiremoor NE27 .30 F3
North Shields NE30 . . . . . . .42 B7
Park Cres E NE30 . . . . . . .42 C7
Park Ct
Gateshead, Team Valley
NE11 . . . . .70 D3
Newcastle-upon-Tyne NE6 . .40 A1
Gateshead NE8 . . . . .101 C3
Park Dr Longbenton NE12 .39 E8
Whickham NE16 . . . . .69 C8
Blyth NE24 . . . . .17 B4
Newcastle-upon-Tyne NE3 . .28 C1
Morpeth NE61 . . . . .8 F7
Stannington NE61 . . . . .9 E1
Park Field NE40 . . . . .52 C5
Park Field Terr NE26 . . . .24 C6
Park Gate SR6 . . . . .75 E3
Park Gdns NE26 . . . . .32 A5
Park Gr Shiremoor NE27 . .30 F3
Washington NE37 . . . . .72 D1
Park Head Rd NE7 . . . . . .39 A1
Park House Gdns DH6 . . .96 A2
Park La Blaydon NE21 . . .68 B8
Shiremoor NE27 . . . . .30 F2
Prudhoe NE42 . . . . .50 D1
Gateshead NE8 . . . . .56 A3
Sunderland SR1 . . . . .103 A2
Park Lane Intc SR1 . . . .103 A2
Park Lane Sta SR1 . . . . .103 A2
Park Lea SR3 . . . . .91 B6
Park Lea Rd SR6 . . . . . . .75 E3
Park Par Whitley Bay NE26 32 A5
Sunderland SR6 . . . . .75 E2
Park Pl DH3 . . . . .88 D5
Park Pl E SR2 . . . . .103 A1
Park Pl W SR2 . . . . .103 A1
Park Rd
Gateshead NE10,NE8 . . . . .56 B2
Newburn NE15 . . . . .52 F8
Bedlington NE22 . . . . .16 A8
Blyth NE24 . . . . .17 F7
Seaton Delaval NE25 . . . . . .23 C3
Whitley Bay NE26 . . . . .32 A6
Shiremoor NE27 . . . . .30 F3
Wallsend NE28 . . . . .40 C1
Hebburn NE31 . . . . .57 E5
Jarrow NE32 . . . . .58 A6
Park Rd *continued*
Rowlands Gill NE39 . . . . . . .67 D2
Newcastle-upon-Tyne NE4 100 A3
Lynmouth NE61,NE63 . . . . . .2 A2
Ashington NE63 . . . . .6 B3
Sunderland SR2 . . . . .103 A1
Park Rd N DH3 . . . . .88 D4
Park Rd S DH3 . . . . .88 D1
Park Rise NE15 . . . . .53 C7
Park Road Central DH3 . .88 D3
Park Road East NE63 . . . . .6 C4
Park Row
3 Gateshead NE10 . . . . . . .71 D8
Sunderland SR5 . . . . .75 A1
Park Site NE61 . . . . .9 F5
Park St S SR5 . . . . .74 C1
Park Terr
Newcastle-upon-Tyne NE1,
NE2 . . . . .99 A3
Dunston NE11 . . . . .69 F8
Killingworth NE12 . . . . .29 B2
Burnopfield NE16 . . . . .79 A6
Whickham NE16 . . . . .54 A1
Blaydon NE21 . . . . .53 D2
Bedlington NE22 . . . . .11 D3
Whitley Bay NE26 . . . . .32 A6
Wallsend NE28 . . . . .40 B2
North Shields NE30 . . . . . . .42 C7
Washington NE37 . . . . .72 D1
Sunderland SR5 . . . . .75 A2
Park View
Chester le Street DH2 . . . . .88 B5
Bournmoor DH3 . . . . .89 D4
Shiney Row DH4 . . . . .90 B6
Hetton le Hole DH5 . . . . . . .95 A3
Longbenton, Forest Hall
NE12 . . . . .39 D8
Longbenton, West Moor
NE12 . . . . .29 B2
Wide Open NE13 . . . . .28 C6
Burnopfield NE16 . . . . .79 B6
Blaydon NE21 . . . . .68 C8
Blyth NE24 . . . . .17 F7
Seaton Delaval NE25 . . . . . .23 D3
Whitley Bay NE26 . . . . .32 A5
Wallsend NE28 . . . . .40 B2
Jarrow NE32 . . . . .58 B4
Newcastle-upon-Tyne NE6 . .57 A5
Ashington NE63 . . . . .6 B4
Park View Cl NE40 . . . . . .52 D5
Park View Com Sch DH3 .88 D3
Park View Com Sch (Lower)
DH3 . . . . .88 D7
Park View Ct NE26 . . . . . .32 A5
Park View Gdns NE40 . . .52 D5
Park Villas Wallsend NE28 .40 B2
Ashington NE63 . . . . .6 B4
Park Wall Cnr SR3 . . . . . .91 B6
Parkdale Rise NE16 . . . . .69 A7
Parker Ave NE3 . . . . .38 B3
Parker Ct NE11 . . . . .54 E2
Parkfield NE32 . . . . .58 C1
Parkgate La NE21 . . . . . . .68 B8
Parkham Cl NE23 . . . . . . .16 B1
Parkhead Com Prim Sch
NE21 . . . . .68 C8
Parkhead Gdns NE21 . . . .68 B8
Parkhead Sq NE21 . . . . . .53 C1
Parkhouse Ave SR5 . . . . .85 B8
Parkhurst Rd SR4 . . . . . . .85 B4
Parkin Gdns NE10 . . . . . .71 E7
Parkinson's Cotts NE40 . .52 E4
Parkland Longbenton NE12 39 D6
Ryton NE21 . . . . .53 A4
Parkland Ave NE21 . . . . . .68 B8
Parklands Gateshead NE10 72 C8
Ponteland NE20 . . . . .25 B2
Hamsterley Mill NE39 . . . . . .77 F5
Parklands Ct NE10 . . . . . .57 C1
Parklands Way NE10 . . . .72 C8
Parklea NE26 . . . . .24 C6
Parkmore Rd SR4 . . . . . . .85 A3
Parks The DH3 . . . . .88 E1
Parkshiel NE34 . . . . .60 A4
Parkside Tanfield Lea DH9 .79 C1
Dunston NE11 . . . . .69 F8
Throckley NE15 . . . . .35 E1
Bedlington NE22 . . . . .11 E3
Wallsend NE28 . . . . .40 D3
Tynemouth NE30 . . . . .32 D1
Hebburn NE31 . . . . .57 D4
Sunderland SR3 . . . . .91 B6
Parkside Ave
Blaydon NE21 . . . . .53 C1
Newcastle-upon-Tyne NE7 . .39 B5
Parkside Cotts DH9 . . . . .79 C1
Parkside Cres NE30 . . . . .42 D8
Parkside Ct NE26 . . . . . . .31 F5
Parkside Mid Sch NE23 . .22 B7
Parkside S SR3 . . . . .91 B6
Parkside Specl Sch
Wallsend NE28 . . . . .40 B2
Wallsend, Battle Hill NE28 .40 A5
Parkside Terr NE28 . . . . . .40 A4
Parkstone Cl SR4 . . . . . . .85 A2
Parkville NE6 . . . . .56 A7
Parkway Whickham NE16 . .68 E6
Washington, Biddick NE38 . .83 C4
Washington, Washington Village
NE38 . . . . .83 D5
Guide Post NE62 . . . . .10 F8
Parkway Sch NE5 . . . . . . .36 D2
Parkwood Ave NE42 . . . . .50 F3
Parliament St NE31 . . . . .57 C7
Parmontley St NE15 . . . . .53 F5
Parnell St DH4 . . . . .94 B8
Parry Dr SR6 . . . . .60 E1
Parson Rd NE41 . . . . .51 B6
Parson's Ave NE6 . . . . . . .56 F5
Parsons Ind Est NE37 . . . .83 B8
Parsons Rd NE37 . . . . . . .83 B7
Parsons' Gdns 5 NE11 . . .54 F1
Partick Rd SR4 . . . . .85 B4
Partick Sq SR4 . . . . .85 C4
Partnership Ct SR7 . . . . . .92 E2
Partridge Cl NE38 . . . . . . .82 F4
Pasteur Rd DH6 . . . . .97 F7
Paston Rd NE25 . . . . .23 D2
Pastures The Blyth NE24 . .17 D4
Stocksfield NE43 . . . . .64 B8
Morpeth NE61 . . . . .8 D7
Pathside NE32 . . . . .58 C2
Patience Ave NE13 . . . . . .28 C8
Patina Cl NE15 . . . . .53 C8
Paton Rd SR3 . . . . .85 F2
Paton Sq SR3 . . . . .85 F2
Patrick Cain Ho NE33 . . .59 B8
Patrick Cres DH6 . . . . . . .97 E8
Patrick Terr NE23 . . . . . . .29 B7
Patterdale Cl NE36 . . . . . .74 C7
Patterdale Gdns NE7 . . . .39 B4
Patterdale Gr SR5 . . . . . .75 C4
Patterdale Ho NE24 . . . . .17 A8
Patterdale Rd NE24 . . . . .17 A8
Patterdale St DH5 . . . . . . .95 A2
Patterdale Terr NE8 . . . . .70 F8
Patterson Cl NE46 . . . . . .44 E3
Patterson St NE21 . . . . . .53 E4
Pattinson Gdns
Gateshead, Old Fold NE10 . .56 C2
Gateshead, Carr Hill NE9 . . .71 B7
Pattinson Ind Est
Washington NE38 . . . . .84 B6
Washington, Swan NE38 . . .83 F3
Pattinson Rd NE38 . . . . . .84 B4
Patton Way NE61 . . . . .4 E3
Pauline Ave SR6 . . . . .75 D3
Pauline Gdns NE15 . . . . . .54 A7
Pauls Gn DH5 . . . . .95 A6
Pauls Rd SR1 . . . . .103 B2
Paulsway NE32 . . . . .58 E6
Pavilion Mews NE2 . . . . .99 C4
Pavilion The NE16 . . . . . .53 F1
Pavillion Ct SR1 . . . . . . .103 A2
Pawston Rd NE21,NE39 . .67 B5
Paxford Cl NE7 . . . . .39 A5
Paxton House★ TD15 . . .104 D5
Paxton Terr SR4 . . . . . . .102 A3
Peacehaven Ct NE37 . . . .72 C2
Peacock Ct NE11 . . . . . . .70 B7
Peacock St W SR4 . . . . . .85 F6
Pear Tree Terr
Great Lumley DH3 . . . . .89 B1
Chopwell NE17 . . . . .77 B8
Peareth Ct NE8 . . . . .101 C3
Peareth Gr SR6 . . . . .75 F3
Peareth Hall Rd NE37,
NE9 . . . . .72 A2
Peareth Rd SR6 . . . . .75 F4
Pearl Rd SR3 . . . . .85 F2
Pearson Pl
North Shields NE30 . . . . . . .42 B6
Jarrow NE32 . . . . .58 C8
Pearson St NE33 . . . . .42 D4
Pearson's Terr NE46 . . . . .45 A5
Peart Cl DH6 . . . . .96 A1
Peartree Bglws NE17 . . . .77 C6
Peartree Ct NE17 . . . . . . .77 C6
Peartree Gdns NE6 . . . . . .40 A1
Peary Cl NE5 . . . . .36 F2
Pease Ave NE15 . . . . .54 C6
Peasemoor Rd SR4 . . . . . .85 B5
Pebble Beach SR6 . . . . . .75 F7
Pecket Cl NE24 . . . . .17 A5
Peddars Way NE34 . . . . . .59 B5
Peebles Cl NE29 . . . . .41 C8
Peebles Rd SR3 . . . . .85 E2
Peel Ctr The NE37 . . . . . .83 F7
Peel Gdns NE34 . . . . .58 E4
Peel La NE1 . . . . .100 C4
Peel St
Newcastle-upon-Tyne NE1 100 C4
Sunderland SR2 . . . . .103 B1
Peepy Cotts NE43 . . . . . .48 D2
Pegswood Fst Sch NE61 . . .4 F4
Pegswood House NE4 . . .98 B2
Pegswood Ind Est NE61 . . .4 F4
Pegswood Sta NE61 . . . . . .4 F3
Pegwood Rd SR4 . . . . . . .85 C5
Pelaw Ave
Chester le Street DH2 . . . . .88 C5
Newbiggin-by-the-Sea NE64 .7 D5
Pelaw Bank DH3 . . . . .88 C4
Pelaw Cres DH2 . . . . .88 B5
Pelaw Grange Ct DH3 . . .88 C8
Pelaw Ind Est NE10 . . . . .72 A8
Pelaw Inf Sch DH2 . . . . . .88 B5
Pelaw Pl DH2 . . . . .88 C5
Pelaw Rd DH2 . . . . .88 C5
Pelaw Sq
Chester le Street DH2 . . . . .88 B5
Sunderland SR4 . . . . .85 C7
Pelaw Sta NE10 . . . . .57 A1
Pelaw Way NE10 . . . . .57 A1
Peldon Cl NE7 . . . . .38 F5
Pelham Ct NE3 . . . . .37 D7
Pelton Fell Rd DH2 . . . . .88 B4
Pelton La DH2 . . . . .88 B5
Pelton Rd SR4 . . . . .85 C4
Peltondale Ave NE24 . . . .17 A6
Pemberton Bank DH5 . . . .95 C1
Pemberton Cl 7 SR5 . . . .75 B1
Pemberton Gdns 3 SR3 . .86 B3
Pemberton St DH5 . . . . . .95 A4
Pembridge NE38 . . . . .83 A5
Pembroke Ave
Birtley DH3 . . . . .82 D1
Newcastle-upon-Tyne NE6 . .56 E7
New Silksworth SR3 . . . . . .92 A6
Pembroke Ct
Newcastle-upon-Tyne NE3 .37 D7
Newbiggin-by-the-Sea NE64 .7 E5
Pembroke Dr NE20 . . . . . .25 B4
Pembroke Gdns
Wallsend NE28 . . . . .41 A4
Ashington NE63 . . . . .7 A1
Pembroke Terr NE33 . . . .59 C7
Pendeford NE38 . . . . .84 A4
Pendle Cl NE38 . . . . .83 B3
Pendle Gn SR4 . . . . .102 A1
Pendleton Dr NE23 . . . . . .16 B1
Pendower Hall Sch NE15 54 C6
Pendower Way NE15 . . . .54 C5
Penfold Cl NE7 . . . . .39 C4
Penhale Dr SR2 . . . . .92 F7
Penhill Cl DH2 . . . . .81 F1
Penistone Rd SR4 . . . . . .85 A4
Penman Pl NE29 . . . . .42 A4
Penman Sq SR4 . . . . .85 C4
Penman St NE29 . . . . .42 A4
Penn Sq SR4 . . . . .85 C6
Penn St NE4 . . . . .100 B3
Pennant Sq SR4 . . . . .85 C6
Pennine Ave DH2 . . . . . . .88 B2
Pennine Ct 23 SR3 . . . . . .91 F6
Pennine Dr NE63 . . . . .6 E1
Pennine Gdns NE11 . . . . .70 A6
Pennine Gr NE36 . . . . . . .74 B7
Pennine View NE17 . . . . .77 B8
Pennine Way NE12 . . . . . .39 A6
Pennycross Rd SR4 . . . . .85 A4
Pennycross Sq SR4 . . . . .85 A5
Pennyfine Cl NE29 . . . . . .42 A8
Pennyfine Rd NE16 . . . . . .69 C2
Pennygate Sq SR4 . . . . . .85 A5
Pennygreen Sq SR4 . . . . .85 A5
Pennymore Sq SR4 . . . . .85 A4
Pennywell Bsns Ctr SR4 .85 C5
Pennywell Comp Sch
SR4 . . . . .85 B4
Pennywell Ind Est SR4 . .85 A3
Pennywell Rd SR4 . . . . . .85 C4
Pennywell Sh Prec SR4 .85 C4
Penrith Ave NE30 . . . . . . .32 A2
Penrith Gdns NE9 . . . . . . .71 B4
Penrith Gr NE9 . . . . .71 B4
Penrith Rd Hebburn NE31 .57 F4
Sunderland SR5 . . . . .75 C4
Penrose Gn NE3 . . . . .37 F5
Penrose Rd SR4 . . . . .85 B4
Pensford Ct NE3 . . . . .37 C6
Penshaw Gn NE5 . . . . . . .37 D3
Penshaw La DH4 . . . . .90 B8
Penshaw Monument★
SR4 . . . . .84 C1
Penshaw View
Birtley DH3 . . . . .82 E3
Gateshead NE10 . . . . .72 C8
Hebburn NE31 . . . . .57 E4
Jarrow NE32 . . . . .58 B4
Penshaw Way DH3 . . . . . .82 E4
Pensher St
Gateshead NE10 . . . . .56 C1
Sunderland SR4 . . . . .102 B2
Pensher St E NE10 . . . . . .56 C1
Pent Ct NE40 . . . . .52 A1
Pentland Cl
Cramlington NE23 . . . . .16 B1
Tynemouth NE29 . . . . .31 F1
Washington NE38 . . . . .83 B3
Ashington NE63 . . . . .6 E1
Pentland Ct 5 DH2 . . . . .88 C2
Pentland Gdns NE11 . . . .70 A7
Pentland Gr NE12 . . . . . . .29 B1
Pentridge Cl NE23 . . . . . .22 C7
Penwood Rd SR4 . . . . . . .85 C5
Penyghent Way NE37 . . .83 A6
Penzance Par NE31 . . . . .58 A2
Penzance Rd SR4 . . . . . .85 B4
Peplow Sq SR4 . . . . .85 C7
Peppercorn Ct NE1 . . . .101 B4
Peragrine CT NE28 . . . . .41 F6
Percival St SR4 . . . . .85 F7
Percy Ave
Whitley Bay NE26 . . . . .32 A5
Tynemouth NE30 . . . . .32 C3
Percy Cl NE46 . . . . .44 F3
Percy Cotts NE25 . . . . . . .23 E2
Percy Cres NE29 . . . . .41 D3
Percy Ct NE29 . . . . .41 D3
Percy Gardens Cotts
NE30 . . . . .42 D8
Percy Gdns Dunston NE11 .70 A7
Longbenton NE12 . . . . .39 D8
Whitley Bay NE25 . . . . .32 A4
Tynemouth NE30 . . . . .42 E8
Stakeford NE62 . . . . .11 A8
Percy Lonnen NE42 . . . . .50 D3
Percy Main Prim Sch
NE29 . . . . .41 D2
Percy Main Sta NE29 . . . .41 D3
Percy Park Rd NE30 . . . . .42 D8
Percy Pk NE30 . . . . .42 D8
Percy Rd NE26 . . . . .32 B5
Percy Scott St NE34 . . . . .59 C3
Percy St
Hetton le Hole DH5 . . . . . . .95 B4
Newcastle-upon-Tyne NE1 . .99 A2
Longbenton NE12 . . . . .29 F1
Newcastle-upon-Tyne, Lemington
NE15 . . . . .53 C6
Cramlington NE23 . . . . .22 C5
Blyth NE24 . . . . .17 F8
Percy St *continued*
Wallsend NE28 . . . . .40 C2
Tynemouth NE30 . . . . .42 E7
Jarrow NE32 . . . . .58 C7
5 South Shields NE33 . . . .42 D2
Ashington NE63 . . . . .6 E4
Percy St John's C of E Prim
Sch NE29 . . . . .41 E3
Percy St S NE24 . . . . .17 F7
Percy Terr Penshaw DH4 . .90 A8
Newburn NE15 . . . . .52 F7
Whitley Bay NE25 . . . . .31 E5
Newcastle-upon-Tyne NE3 . .38 E5
Sunderland SR2 . . . . .86 E4
4 Whitburn SR6 . . . . .60 F1
Percy Terr S SR2 . . . . . . .86 F3
Percy Way NE15 . . . . .36 A1
Peregrine Pl NE12 . . . . . .39 A7
Perivale Rd SR4 . . . . .85 B4
Perry St NE8,NE9 . . . . . . .70 F8
Perrycrofts SR3 . . . . .92 A4
Perth Ave NE32,NE34 . . . .58 E3
Perth Cl Wallsend NE28 . . .40 F4
Tynemouth NE29 . . . . .41 C8
Perth Ct Gateshead NE11 . .70 E3
Sunderland SR3 . . . . .85 E1
Perth Gdns NE28 . . . . . . .40 F4
Perth Rd SR3 . . . . .85 F2
Perth Sq SR3 . . . . .85 F2
Pescott Cl NE46 . . . . .45 B4
Pesspool Ave DH6 . . . . . .97 F3
Pesspool Bglws DH6 . . . .97 F3
Pesspool La DH6 . . . . . . .97 F3
Pesspool Terr DH6 . . . . . .97 F3
Peterborough Cl NE8 . .101 B2
Peterborough Way NE32 .58 B1
Petersfield Rd SR4 . . . . .85 B4
Petersham Rd SR4 . . . . . .85 C6
Peth Gn DH5 . . . . .95 B1
Peth Head NE46 . . . . .45 C5
Peth La NE40 . . . . .52 D6
Petherton Ct NE3 . . . . . . .37 C6
Pethgate Ct 5 NE61 . . . . . .9 A8
Petrel Cl 12 NE33 . . . . . . .42 C4
Petrel Way NE24 . . . . .17 F4
Petteril NE38 . . . . .83 A1
Petworth Cl NE33 . . . . . . .42 D3
Petworth Gdns NE61 . . . . .4 E4
Pevensey Cl NE29 . . . . . .31 F1
Pexton Way NE5 . . . . .54 A8
Pheasantmoor 3 NE37 . . .83 A7
Philadelphia Aged Miners
Homes 6 DH4 . . . . .90 B6
Philadelphia Complex
DH4 . . . . .90 D6
Philadelphia La DH4 . . . .90 C4
Philip Pl NE4 . . . . .98 A2
Philip Sq SR3 . . . . .85 E2
Philip St NE4 . . . . .98 A2
Philiphaugh NE28 . . . . . . .57 B8
Philipson St NE6 . . . . . . .56 F6
Phillips Ave NE16 . . . . . .69 A8
Phillips Cl DH6 . . . . .97 E3
Phobe Grange Cotts
NE42 . . . . .50 D2
Phoenix Chase NE29 . . . .41 C8
Phoenix Ct
Tynemouth NE29 . . . . .41 C8
Morpeth NE61 . . . . .8 F8
Phoenix Rd
Washington NE38 . . . . .82 E6
Sunderland SR4 . . . . .85 C6
Phoenix St NE24 . . . . .17 B4
Phoenix Way DH4 . . . . . . .94 C7
Piccadilly SR3 . . . . .91 E8
Picherwell NE10 . . . . .71 D7
Pickard St SR4 . . . . .102 A3
Pickering Ct NE32 . . . . . .58 A7
Pickering Gn NE9 . . . . . . .71 B2
Pickering Rd SR4 . . . . . . .85 B3
Pickering Sq SR4 . . . . . . .85 B4
Pickersgill Ho SR5 . . . . . .74 C3
Pickhurst Rd SR4 . . . . . .85 B3
Pickhurst Sq SR4 . . . . . .85 B3
Picktree Cotts 2 DH3 . . .88 D4
Picktree Cotts E 3 DH3 .88 D4
Picktree Farm Cotts
NE38 . . . . .88 E7
Picktree La
Chester le Street DH3 . . . . .88 D4
Chester le Street, Picktree
DH3,NE38 . . . . .88 E7
Picktree Lodge
Chester le Street DH3 . . . . .88 D8
Birtley NE38 . . . . .82 E1
Picktree Terr 1 DH3 . . . .88 D4
Pier Par NE33 . . . . .42 E4
Pier Rd NE30 . . . . .42 E7
Pier View SR6 . . . . .75 F2
Pikestone Cl NE38 . . . . . .83 A3
Pilgrim Cl SR5 . . . . .75 C1
Pilgrim St
Newcastle-upon-Tyne NE1 . .99 B1
Newcastle-upon-Tyne NE1 101 B4
Pilgrims Ct NE2 . . . . .99 B4
Pilgrims Way NE61 . . . . . . .8 D7
Pilgrimsway Jarrow NE32 .58 E6
Gateshead NE9 . . . . .71 B7
Pilton Rd NE5 . . . . .36 F3
Pilton Wlk NE5 . . . . .36 F3
Pimlico Ct NE9 . . . . .70 F4
Pimlico Rd
Hetton le Hole DH5 . . . . . . .95 B1
Sunderland SR4 . . . . .85 B4
Pinders Way DH6 . . . . . . .96 D1
Pine Ave
3 Houghton-le-Spring DH4 94 D8
Dinnington NE13 . . . . .27 C7

Pine Ave *continued*
Newcastle-upon-Tyne NE3 . .37 F7
South Shields NE34 . . . . . . .60 A5
Guide Post NE62 . . . . .10 D7
Pine Rd NE21 . . . . .53 C2
Pine St Birtley DH3 . . . . . .82 C5
4 Chester le Street DH3 . .88 C3
Seaton Burn NE13 . . . . . . .28 C8
Throckley NE15 . . . . .35 D3
Jarrow NE32 . . . . .58 A6
Greenside NE40 . . . . .52 B1
Sunderland SR4 . . . . .85 F7
Pinedale Dr DH6 . . . . .97 F7
Pinegarth NE20 . . . . .25 C2
Pines The
Newcastle-upon-Tyne NE4 100 A3
Greenside NE40 . . . . .52 B1
Pinesway 4 SR3 . . . . .86 B3
Pinetree Gdns NE25 . . . . . .31 E3
Pinetree Way NE11 . . . . . .54 B2
Pinewood NE31 . . . . .57 C7
Pinewood Ave
Wide Open NE13 . . . . .28 C5
Cramlington NE23 . . . . . . .16 B1
Washington NE38 . . . . .83 C1
Pinewood Cl
Newcastle-upon-Tyne,
Kingston Park NE3 . . . . . .37 B7
Newcastle-upon-Tyne, Walkerville
NE6 . . . . .39 F1
Pinewood Dr NE61 . . . . . . .3 D2
Pinewood Gdns NE11 . . . .70 A5
Pinewood Rd SR5 . . . . . . .74 F2
Pinewood Sq 8 SR5 . . . .74 F2
Pinewood St DH4 . . . . . . .89 E1
Pinewood Villas NE34 . . .60 A6
Pink La NE1 . . . . .100 C4
Pinner Pl NE6 . . . . .56 E4
Pinner Rd SR4 . . . . .85 C5
Pintail Ct 10 NE34 . . . . . .59 A4
Pioneer Terr NE22 . . . . . .11 C2
Pipe Ave NE16 . . . . .78 F6
Pipe Track La NE4 . . . . . .54 D4
Piper Rd NE42 . . . . .50 B5
Pipershaw NE37 . . . . .82 F6
Pipewellgate NE8 . . . . . .101 B3
Pit Row SR3 . . . . .91 F8
Pitcairn Rd SR4 . . . . .85 C5
Pitt St NE4 . . . . .98 C2
Pittington La DH6 . . . . . . .96 A6
Pittington Prim Sch DH6 96 B5
Pittington Rd DH4,DH5 . . .96 A7
Plains Farm Prim Sch
SR3 . . . . .85 F2
Plains Rd SR3 . . . . .85 F2
Plaistow Sq SR4 . . . . .85 C6
Plaistow Way NE23 . . . . . .16 B1
Plane Tree Ct SR3 . . . . . .91 E6
Planesway NE10 . . . . .71 E5
Planet Ho SR1 . . . . .103 A3
Planet Pl NE12 . . . . .29 C2
Planetree Ave NE4 . . . . . .54 D8
Planetrees Roman Wall*
NE46 . . . . .128 E4
Plantagenet Ave DH3 . . .88 D2
Plantation Ave
High Pittington DH6 . . . . . .96 E3
Whickham NE16 . . . . .69 A8
Plantation Gr NE10 . . . . .57 C2
Plantation Rd SR4 . . . . . .85 E7
Plantation Sq 2 SR4 . . . .85 E7
Plantation St NE28 . . . . .57 B8
Plantation The NE9 . . . . .71 A4
Plantation Wlk DH6 . . . . .97 F7
Plawsworth Gdns NE9 . . .71 C3
Pleasant Pl 6 DH3 . . . . . .82 C5
Plenmeller Pl NE16 . . . . .69 A3
Plessey Ave NE24 . . . . . .17 F6
Plessey Cres NE25 . . . . . .32 B4
Plessey Ct NE24 . . . . . . .17 B4
Plessey Gdns NE29 . . . . .41 D5
Plessey Rd NE24 . . . . . . .17 D5
Plessey Rd Fst Sch NE24 .17 F7
Plessey St NE23 . . . . .16 B3
Plessey Terr NE7 . . . . . . .39 B2
Plessey Woods Ctry Pk*
NE22 . . . . .15 B4
Plough Rd SR3 . . . . .91 F5
Plover Cl Blyth NE24 . . . . .17 E4
5 Washington NE38 . . . . .82 F3
Plover Dr NE16 . . . . .79 C5
Plover Lo DH3 . . . . .82 C6
Ploverfield Cl NE63 . . . . . .6 C2
Plummer St NE4 . . . . . . .100 C3
Plummer Tower Mus*
NE1 . . . . .99 B1
Plumtree Ave SR5 . . . . . .74 C2
Plunkett Rd DH9 . . . . . . .78 E1
Plymouth Sq SR3 . . . . . .85 E2
Point Pleasant Ind Est
NE28 . . . . .40 F1
Point Pleasant Terr NE28 40 E1
Polden Cres NE29 . . . . . .31 F1
Polebrook Rd SR4 . . . . . .85 C6
Pollard St NE33 . . . . .42 D3
Polmaise St NE21 . . . . . .53 C2
Polmuir Rd SR3 . . . . .85 F2
Polmuir Sq SR3 . . . . .85 E2
Polpero Cl DH3 . . . . .82 D3
Polperro Cl 6 SR2 . . . . .92 F8
Polton Sq SR4 . . . . .85 C6
Poltrossburn Milecastle*
CA6 . . . . .126 B3
Polwarth Cres NE3 . . . . .38 C8
Polwarth Dr NE3 . . . . . . .28 C1
Polwarth Rd NE3 . . . . . . .28 C1
Polworth Sq SR3 . . . . . . .85 F2
Pont Haugh NE20 . . . . . .25 F7
Pont St NE63 . . . . .6 D3
Pont View NE20 . . . . .25 F7
Pontdyke NE10 . . . . .71 F4
Pontefract Rd 2 SR4 . . . .85 B3
Ponteland Cl
Tynemouth NE29 . . . . .41 C7
Washington NE38 . . . . .82 F4
Ponteland Com High Sch
NE20 . . . . .25 F5
Ponteland Fst Sch NE20 .25 F7
Ponteland Mid Sch NE20 25 F5
Ponteland Rd
Woolsington NE13 . . . . . . .37 A7
Heddon-on-the-Wall NE15 . .35 D5
Newcastle-upon-Tyne,
Spital Tongues NE2 . . . . . .98 A3
Ponteland NE20 . . . . .26 A5
Newcastle-upon-Tyne,
Kenton Bankfoot NE3 . . . .37 B6
Newcastle-upon-Tyne, Blakelaw
NE5 . . . . .37 D3
Ponthaugh NE39 . . . . . . .67 F3
Pontop Sq SR4 . . . . .85 C7
Pontop St DH5 . . . . .94 C4
Pontop View NE39 . . . . . .67 D2
Poole Cl NE23 . . . . .22 C7
Poole Rd SR4 . . . . .85 C6
Pooley Cl NE5 . . . . .37 B1
Pooley Rd NE5 . . . . .37 B1
Poplar Ave
1 Houghton-le-Spring DH4 94 D8
Dinnington NE13 . . . . .27 C7
Burnopfield NE16 . . . . . . .78 F6
Blyth NE24 . . . . .12 D1
Newcastle-upon-Tyne NE6 . .39 F1
Poplar Cl NE31 . . . . .57 E3
Poplar Cres Birtley DH3 . .82 B5
Dunston NE11 . . . . .69 F7
Gateshead NE8 . . . . .101 B2
Poplar Dr SR6 . . . . .60 F1
Poplar Gr Bedlington NE22 11 C1
South Shields NE34 . . . . . .59 F5
7 Sunderland SR2 . . . . . .92 E8
Poplar Pl NE3 . . . . .38 C5
Poplar Rd NE21 . . . . .53 C1
Poplar St
3 Chester le Street DH3 . .88 C3
Throckley NE15 . . . . .35 D3
Ashington NE63 . . . . .6 D4
Poplar Terr DH3 . . . . .88 D4
Poplars The Penshaw DH4 90 B8
Easington Lane DH5 . . . . . .95 C1
Newcastle-upon-Tyne, Gosforth
NE3 . . . . .38 C3
Washington NE38 . . . . . . .83 D4
Newcastle-upon-Tyne, Elswick
NE4 . . . . .100 A3
1 Sunderland, South Hylton
SR4 . . . . .85 A6
1 Sunderland, Southwick
SR5 . . . . .74 F2
Popplewell Gdns NE9 . . .71 A4
Popplewell Terr NE29 . . .42 A8
Popular Ct 1 DH3 . . . . . .88 C3
Porchester Dr NE23 . . . . .22 C7
Porlock Ct NE23 . . . . . . .16 A1
Porlock Rd NE32 . . . . . . .58 D5
Portadown Rd 1 SR4 . . .85 B3
Portberry St NE33 . . . . . .42 B1
Portberry St Ind Est
NE33 . . . . .59 B8
Portberry Way NE33 . . . .42 B1
Portchester Gr NE35 . . . .73 E8
Portchester Rd SR4 . . . . .85 C5
Portchester Sq SR4 . . . . .85 C4
Porthcawl Dr NE37 . . . . . .72 C2
Portia St NE63 . . . . .6 E4
Portland Cl DH2 . . . . . . .88 A1
Portland Gdns
Cramlington NE23 . . . . . . .22 C7
Tynemouth NE30 . . . . .42 A7
1 Gateshead NE9 . . . . . . .70 F2
Portland Ind Est NE63 . . . .5 F5
Portland Mews NE2 . . . . .99 C3
Portland Rd
Walbottle NE15 . . . . .35 E2
Newcastle-upon-Tyne NE2 . .99 C2
Sunderland SR3 . . . . .85 F3
Portland Sch SR3 . . . . . .85 F3
Portland Sq SR3 . . . . . . .85 F3
Portland St
Gateshead NE10 . . . . .57 A1
1 Blyth NE24 . . . . .17 D8
Newcastle-upon-Tyne NE4 . .54 F4
Portland Terr
Newcastle-upon-Tyne NE2 . .99 C3
Hexham NE46 . . . . .44 F5
Ashington NE63 . . . . .5 F5
Portman Mews NE2 . . . . .99 C2
Portman Pl NE6 . . . . .56 E3
Portman Sq SR4 . . . . . . .85 C5
Portmarnock NE37 . . . . . .72 B2
Portmeads Rd DH3 . . . . .82 D4
Portmeads Rise DH3 . . . .82 D4
Portobello Ind Est DH3 . .82 E4
Portobello La SR5,SR6 . . .75 D1
Portobello Prim Sch
DH3 . . . . .82 D2
Portobello Terr DH3 . . . . .82 E2
Portobello Way DH3 . . . .82 D4
Portree Cl DH3 . . . . .82 D1
Portree Sq SR3 . . . . .85 E2
Portrush Cl NE37 . . . . . . .72 C2
Portrush Rd SR4 . . . . . . .85 C6
Portrush Way NE7 . . . . . .39 C5
Portslade Rd SR4 . . . . . .85 B4
Portsmouth Rd
North Shields NE29 . . . . . . .41 C5
Portsmouth Rd *continued*
Sunderland SR4 . . . . .85 B5
Portsmouth Sq SR4 . . . . .85 B5
Portugal Pl NE28 . . . . . . .40 B1
Post Office La NE29 . . . . .42 A8
Post Office St 4 NE24 . . .17 F8
Postern Cres NE61 . . . . . . .8 F7
Potland View NE61 . . . . . . .1 A3
Potter Sq SR3 . . . . .85 F2
Potter St Wallsend NE28 . .41 A1
Jarrow NE32 . . . . .58 A7
Potteries The NE33 . . . . .42 E1
Pottersway NE9 . . . . .71 B7
Pottery Bank
Newcastle-upon-Tyne NE6 . .56 F3
Morpeth NE61 . . . . .3 E2
Pottery Bank Ct NE61 . . . . .3 E2
Pottery La
Newcastle-upon-Tyne NE1 100 C3
Sunderland SR4 . . . . .85 A7
Pottery Rd SR5 . . . . .75 A1
Pottery Yd 3 DH4 . . . . . .94 E8
Potts St NE6 . . . . .56 C6
Pow Hill* DH8 . . . . .135 C4
Powburn Cl DH2 . . . . . . .88 A1
Powburn Gdns NE4 . . . . .54 E8
Powis Rd SR3 . . . . .85 F2
Powis Sq SR3 . . . . .85 F2
Powys Pl NE4 . . . . .98 B2
Poynings Cl NE5 . . . . . . .37 C5
Praetorian Dr NE28 . . . . .40 B1
Precinct The
Blaydon NE21 . . . . .53 D3
Sunderland SR2 . . . . .102 B2
Sunderland, Hillview SR2 . .86 C2
Prefect Pl NE9 . . . . .71 A7
Premier Rd SR3 . . . . .85 F2
Prendwick Ave NE31 . . . .57 D3
Prendwick Ct NE31 . . . . .57 D3
Prengarth Ave SR6 . . . . .75 D3
Prensgarth Way NE34 . . .58 F3
Prescot Rd SR4 . . . . .85 C6
Press La SR1 . . . . .103 A3
Prestbury Ave NE23 . . . . .16 A1
Prestbury Rd SR4 . . . . . .85 A3
Prestdale Ave NE24 . . . . .17 A7
Presthope Rd SR4 . . . . . .85 B4
Prestmede NE10 . . . . . . .71 E7
Preston Ave NE30 . . . . . .42 B7
Preston Ct NE29 . . . . . . .42 A8
Preston Gate NE29 . . . . . .31 F1
Preston Grange Prim Sch
NE29 . . . . .31 E1
Preston North Rd NE29 . .31 F1
Preston Pk NE29 . . . . . . .42 A7
Preston Rd
Tynemouth NE29,NE30 . . . .42 A7
Sunderland SR2 . . . . .86 F4
Preston Terr
12 Shiremoor NE27 . . . . . .30 E1
1 Tynemouth NE29 . . . . . .41 F8
Preston Tower* NE67 . . .113 B8
Preston Twrs NE29 . . . . .42 A7
Preston Wood NE30 . . . . .32 A1
Prestonhill 7 SR3 . . . . . .91 E5
Prestwick NE10 . . . . .71 E5
Prestwick Ave NE29 . . . . .41 C6
Prestwick Cl NE37 . . . . . .72 C2
Prestwick Dr NE10 . . . . . .72 C7
Prestwick Gdns NE3 . . . . .37 F4
Prestwick House NE4 . . . .98 B2
Prestwick Pit Hos NE20 .26 C3
Prestwick Rd SR4 . . . . . .85 C6
Prestwick Terr NE20 . . . .26 C3
Pretoria Ave NE61 . . . . . . .8 F8
Pretoria Sq SR3 . . . . .85 E2
Pretoria St NE15 . . . . . . .54 A5
Price St Hebburn NE31 . . .57 C7
Morpeth NE61 . . . . .3 E1
Priestclose Cotts NE42 . . .50 F2
Priestclose Rd NE42 . . . .50 D2
Priestfield Cl SR3 . . . . . .91 F5
Priestfield Gdns NE16 . . .78 F6
Priestlands Ave 1 NE46 .45 A4
Priestlands Cl NE46 . . . . .45 A3
Priestlands Cres NE46 . . .45 A4
Priestlands Dr NE46 . . . . .45 A4
Priestlands Gr NE46 . . . . .45 A3
Priestlands La NE46 . . . . .45 A4
Priestlands Rd NE46 . . . .45 A4
Priestley Ct NE34 . . . . . . .59 A3
Priestley Gdns NE10 . . . .72 B7
Priestly Cres SR4 . . . . . .102 B4
Priestman Ct SR4 . . . . . .85 D6
Priestpopple NE46 . . . . . .45 B4
Primary Gdns SR2 . . . . .103 C1
Primate Rd SR3 . . . . .85 E2
Primrose Ave NE34 . . . . .59 B5
Primrose Cl NE23 . . . . . . .29 A8
Primrose Cres
Bournmoor DH4 . . . . .89 E3
Sunderland SR6 . . . . .75 D3
Primrose Ct NE63 . . . . . . .6 B1
Primrose Gdns
Ouston DH2 . . . . .81 F2
Wallsend NE28 . . . . .40 A4
Primrose Hill NE9 . . . . . .71 A5
Primrose Hill Hospl
NE32 . . . . .58 C4
Primrose Hill Terr NE32 .58 C3
Primrose Prec SR6 . . . . .75 D3
Primrose St 3 SR4 . . . . .85 A6
Primrose Terr Birtley DH3 82 D4
Jarrow NE32 . . . . .58 C4
Prince Albert Terr NE2 . .99 C2
Prince Consort Ind Est
NE31 . . . . .57 C7
Prince Consort La NE31 .57 D6
Prince Consort Rd
Hebburn NE31 . . . . .57 C6
Jarrow NE32 . . . . .58 C6
Gateshead NE8 . . . . .101 C1
Prince Consort Way
NE29 . . . . .42 A3
Prince Edward Ct NE34 . .60 A5
Prince Edward Gr NE34 .60 C6
Prince Edward Rd NE34 .60 A5
Prince Edward Rd E
NE34 . . . . .60 C6
Prince George Ave SR6 . .75 D3
Prince Of Wales Cl NE34 .59 E5
Prince Philip Cl NE15 . . .54 C5
Prince Rd NE28 . . . . .40 B3
Prince St Chopwell NE17 . .66 B1
Sunderland SR1 . . . . . . .103 A3
Prince's Gdns NE24 . . . . .17 C8
Prince's Meadow NE3 . . .38 A5
Princes Ave
Newcastle-upon-Tyne NE3 . .38 B7
Sunderland SR6 . . . . .75 E5
Princes Cl NE3 . . . . .38 B8
Princes Gdns
Whitley Bay NE25 . . . . . . .31 E5
Sunderland SR6 . . . . .75 E5
Princes Pk Dunston NE11 .70 B6
Gateshead NE8 . . . . .70 C7
Princes Rd NE3 . . . . .28 B1
Princes St
Shiney Row DH4 . . . . .90 A5
Tynemouth NE30 . . . . .42 B7
Corbridge NE45 . . . . .47 A5
Princess Ct NE42 . . . . . .50 D4
Princess Dr NE8 . . . . . . .100 A1
Princess Gdns DH5 . . . . .95 A5
Princess Louise Fst Sch
NE24 . . . . .17 D7
Princess Louise Rd NE24 17 E7
Princess Mary Ct NE2 . . .99 A4
Princess St
Gateshead NE10 . . . . .57 A1
Sunniside NE16 . . . . .69 B2
Sunderland SR2 . . . . . . .102 C1
Princess Way NE42 . . . . .50 C4
Princesway
Gateshead NE11 . . . . .70 C3
Gateshead NE11 . . . . .70 C5
Princesway Central NE11 70 C4
Princetown Terr SR3 . . .85 E2
Princeway NE30 . . . . .42 D8
Prinn Pl NE16 . . . . .69 B2
Prior Terr Corbridge NE45 .46 F6
Hexham NE46 . . . . .45 A6
Prior's Ho NE30 . . . . . . .42 E7
Prior's Terr NE30 . . . . . .42 D7
Priors Grange DH6 . . . . .96 B5
Priors Way NE28 . . . . . . .40 E2
Priors Wlk NE61 . . . . .8 E7
Priory Ave NE25 . . . . .31 F4
Priory Ct Tynemouth NE30 .42 E8
South Shields NE33 . . . . . .42 D5
Gateshead NE8 . . . . .101 C3
Priory Gdns NE45 . . . . . .46 F7
Priory Gn 20 NE6 . . . . . . .56 B6
Priory Gr SR4 . . . . .85 F5
Priory Grange NE24 . . . . .17 C8
Priory Mews 7 NE30 . . . .42 D7
Priory Pl
Brunswick Village NE13 . . .28 A5
Stakeford NE62 . . . . .11 A8
Priory Prim Sch NE30 . . .42 D8
Priory Rd NE32 . . . . .58 C8
Priory Way NE5 . . . . .36 F4
Proctor Ct NE6 . . . . .57 A5
Proctor Sq SR3 . . . . .85 F2
Proctor St NE6 . . . . .57 A5
Promenade
Whitley Bay NE26 . . . . . . .32 B5
South Shields NE33 . . . . . .42 F3
Newbiggin-by-the-Sea NE64 .7 E4
Sunderland SR2 . . . . .87 A3
Seaham SR7 . . . . .93 D1
Promontory Terr NE26 . . .32 C4
Promotion Cl 9 SR6 . . . .75 E2
Prospect Ave
Seaton Delaval NE25 . . . . .23 C3
Wallsend NE28 . . . . .40 B3
Prospect Ave N NE28 . . . .40 B4
Prospect Cotts NE22 . . . .11 C5
Prospect Cres DH5 . . . . . .97 C8
Prospect Ct NE4 . . . . .98 A1
Prospect Gdns NE36 . . . .74 A7
Prospect Pl NE4 . . . . .98 A1
Prospect Row SR1 . . . . .103 C3
Prospect St
2 Chester le Street DH3 . .88 C4
Newbiggin-by-the-Sea NE64 .7 F5
Prospect Terr
1 Chester le Street DH3 . .88 C4
Ebchester DH8 . . . . .76 F4
Kibblesworth NE11 . . . . . .81 C6
Burnopfield NE16 . . . . . . .79 A4
North Shields NE30 . . . . . .42 C6
East Boldon NE36 . . . . . . .74 C7
Prudhoe NE42 . . . . .50 B2
Gateshead NE9 . . . . .71 D1
Providence Pl 18 NE10 . .56 D1
Provident Terr NE28 . . . .40 A2
Provost Gdns NE4 . . . . . .54 D4
Prudhoe Castle* NE42 . .50 C3
Prudhoe Castle Fst Sch
NE42 . . . . .50 B2
Prudhoe Chare NE1 . . . . .99 A2
Prudhoe Com High Sch
NE42 . . . . .50 D1
Prudhoe Ct NE3 . . . . .37 E7
Prudhoe Gr NE32 . . . . . . .58 B3
Prudhoe Pl NE1 . . . . .99 A2
Prudhoe St
Newcastle-upon-Tyne NE1 . .99 A2
North Shields NE29 . . . . . .42 A5
8 Sunderland SR4 . . . . . .85 F7
Prudhoe Sta NE42 . . . . . .50 B4
Prudhoe Street Bacl 19
NE29 . . . . .42 A5
Prudhoe Terr
18 North Shields NE29 . . . .42 A5
Tynemouth NE30 . . . . .42 D8
Prudhoe West Fst Sch
NE42 . . . . .50 C2
Pudding Chare NE1 . . . . .99 A1
Pudding Mews NE46 . . . .45 B5
Puffin Cl NE24 . . . . .17 F3
Pullman Ct NE9 . . . . .70 E5
Purbeck Cl NE29 . . . . . . .31 F2
Purbeck Gdns NE23 . . . . .22 C7
Purbeck Rd NE12 . . . . . . .39 B6
Purley NE38 . . . . .84 A4
Purley Cl NE28 . . . . .40 F4
Purley Gdns NE3 . . . . . . .37 F4
Purley Rd SR3 . . . . .85 E2
Purley Sq SR3 . . . . .85 E2
Putney Sq SR4 . . . . .85 B4
Pykerley Mews NE25 . . . .31 E4
Pykerley Rd NE25 . . . . . .31 E5

Q

Quadrant The
North Shields NE29 . . . . . .41 E5
Sunderland SR1 . . . . . . .103 C3
Quality Row NE6 . . . . . . .56 A5
Quality Row Rd NE16 . . . .54 A1
Quantock Ave DH2 . . . . . .88 A2
Quantock Cl
Longbenton NE12 . . . . .39 A6
Tynemouth NE29 . . . . .31 F2
Quarry Bank Ct NE4 . . . . .98 B1
Quarry Edge NE46 . . . . . .45 C3
Quarry House Gdns DH5 .94 C4
Quarry House La DH5 . . .94 D4
Quarry La
South Shields NE34 . . . . . .60 B5
South Shields, Marsden
NE34 . . . . .60 D6
Quarry Rd
Newcastle-upon-Tyne NE15 .53 C6
Hebburn NE31 . . . . .57 E5
New Silksworth SR3 . . . . . .92 B7
Quarry Row 19 NE10 . . . .56 D1
Quarry St SR3 . . . . .92 A7
Quarry View Inf & Jun Schs
SR4 . . . . .85 C6
Quarryfield Rd NE8 . . . .101 C4
Quatre Bras NE46 . . . . . .44 F5
Quay Rd NE24 . . . . .18 A7
Quay The DH5 . . . . .95 A3
Quay View NE28 . . . . . . .41 A2
Quayside
Newcastle-upon-Tyne NE1 101 B4
Newcastle-upon-Tyne, St
Lawrence NE1,NE6 . . . . . .56 A5
Blyth NE24 . . . . .17 F8
Quayside Ct 7 Blyth NE24 17 F8
North Shields NE30 . . . . . .42 B5
Quayside Ho SR1 . . . . . .103 B3
Queen Alexandra Rd
Tynemouth NE29 . . . . .42 A7
Sunderland SR2 . . . . .86 D3
Queen Alexandra Rd W
NE29 . . . . .41 E7
Queen Ann Ct 21 NE6 . . .56 C7
Queen Elizabeth Ave
NE9 . . . . .71 B6
Queen Elizabeth Dr DH5 .97 D8
Queen Elizabeth High Sch
NE46 . . . . .44 E4
Queen Elizabeth Hospl
NE9 . . . . .71 B6
Queen Elizabeth II Ctry Pk*
NE63 . . . . .6 F6
Queen St Birtley DH3 . . . .82 B4
Hetton le Hole DH5 . . . . . .95 A5
Newcastle-upon-Tyne NE1 101 B4
North Shields NE30 . . . . . .42 B6
South Shields NE33 . . . . . .42 C3
Lynmouth NE61 . . . . .2 A2
Morpeth NE61 . . . . .9 A8
Ashington NE63 . . . . .6 E4
Newbiggin-by-the-Sea NE64 .7 E5
Gateshead NE8 . . . . .70 C8
Sunderland SR1 . . . . . . .103 A3
Sunderland, Bishopwearmouth
SR1 . . . . .102 C3
Sunderland, Grangetown
SR2 . . . . .92 F8
Queen St E SR1 . . . . . . .103 B3
Queen Victoria Rd NE1,
NE2 . . . . .99 A3
Queen Victoria St NE10 . .57 A1
Queen's Cres
Wallsend NE28 . . . . .40 B3
Hebburn NE31 . . . . .57 D4
Sunderland SR4 . . . . .102 A1
Queen's Dr NE26 . . . . . . .32 A5
Queen's Gdns Blyth NE24 .17 C8
Morpeth NE61 . . . . .8 E7
Queen's Pk DH3 . . . . .88 D2
Queen's Rd
Newcastle-upon-Tyne NE2 . .38 F1
Bedlington NE22 . . . . .11 D2

Queen's Rd *continued*
Whitley Bay NE26 .31 F6
Sunderland SR5 .75 B1
Queen's Terr NE2 .38 F1
Queens Ave SR6 .75 E5
Queens Ct Walbottle NE15 36 A1
Newcastle-upon-Tyne, Brunton Park NE3 .28 C2
Newcastle-upon-Tyne NE4 .98 B2
Gateshead NE8 .100 C1
Queens Dr Sunniside NE16 69 B2
Whickham NE16 .69 C5
Queens Gdns
Longbenton NE12 .39 D6
Annitsford NE23 .22 B1
Queens La NE1 .101 A4
Queens Pl NE64 .7 E5
Queens Rd Walbottle NE15 36 A1
Annitsford NE23 .22 B1
Seaton Sluice NE26 .24 D6
Newcastle-upon-Tyne NE5 .37 A3
Queens Terr NE28 .40 C3
Queens Way NE46 .44 E5
Queensberry St SR4 .102 B3
Queensbridge NE12 .38 F7
Queensbury Dr NE15 .36 B2
Queensland Ave NE34 .58 F4
Queensmere DH3 .88 C7
Queensway
Houghton-le-Spring DH5 .94 F8
Ponteland NE20 .25 D2
Newcastle-upon-Tyne, Brunton Park NE3 .28 B1
Tynemouth NE30 .42 D8
3 Washington NE38 .83 E4
Newcastle-upon-Tyne, Fenham NE4 .54 D8
Morpeth NE61 .8 D7
Queensway N NE11 .70 C5
Queensway S NE11 .70 D4
Quentin Ave NE3 .37 D5
Quigley Terr DH3 .82 B6

R

Rabbit Banks Rd NE8 .101 A3
Raby Cl Fence Houses DH4 90 A1
Bedlington NE22 .10 D1
Raby Cres 7 NE6 .56 C6
Raby Cross 10 NE6 .56 C5
Raby Dr SR3 .91 C7
Raby Gdns
Burnopfield NE16 .78 E6
Jarrow NE32 .58 B4
Raby Rd NE38 .83 A5
Raby St
16 Newcastle-upon-Tyne, Byker NE6 .56 B6
Newcastle-upon-Tyne, St Lawrence NE6 .56 C5
Gateshead NE8 .70 F8
Sunderland SR4 .102 B2
Raby Way NE6 .56 C5
Rabygate 6 NE6 .56 C6
Rachel Cl SR2 .92 C7
Rackly Way SR6 .75 F8
Radcliffe Cotts 5 NE15 .35 D2
Radcliffe Pl 3 NE5 .37 D2
Radcliffe Rd
Hexham NE46 .45 C4
Sunderland SR5 .74 E2
Radcliffe St DH3 .82 C3
Radlett Rd SR5 .74 D2
Radnor Gdns NE28 .41 A3
Radnor St NE1 .99 B2
Radstock Pl NE12 .39 C7
Rae Ave NE28 .40 B4
Raeburn Ave NE38 .83 E4
Raeburn Gdns NE9 .71 B7
Raeburn Rd
Whiteleas NE34 .59 D2
Sunderland SR5 .74 C3
Raglan NE38 .83 A5
Raglan Ave SR2 .86 E3
Raglan Pl NE16 .79 B6
Raglan Row DH4 .90 C5
Raglan St NE32 .58 C7
Railton Gdns NE9 .71 B6
Railway Arches NE1 .99 B1
Railway Cotts Birtley DH3 .82 B4
Penshaw DH4 .90 A8
Bebside NE24 .16 E8
Cleadon NE36 .59 D1
Wylam NE41 .50 F5
Railway Mus NE41 .51 B6
Railway Row SR1 .102 B3
Railway St Newbottle DH4 90 D2
Hetton le Hole DH5 .95 A4
Dunston NE11 .54 F2
Dunston NE11 .100 A1
10 North Shields NE29 .42 A5
Hebburn NE31 .57 F7
Jarrow NE32 .58 A7
Newcastle-upon-Tyne NE4 100 B3
Sunderland SR1 .103 C2
Railway Terr
New Herrington DH4 .90 D6
Penshaw DH4 .90 A8
Blyth NE24 .17 D7
Blyth, South Newsham NE24 .17 C2
Wallsend NE28 .40 D1
North Shields NE29 .42 A5
Washington NE38 .83 F4
Railway Terr *continued*
Newcastle-upon-Tyne NE4 100 B3
2 Sunderland SR4 .85 A6
Railway Terr N DH4 .90 D7
Raine Gr SR1 .103 B2
Rainford Ave SR2 .86 E3
Rainhill Cl NE37 .72 F1
Rainhill Rd NE37 .72 F1
Rainton Bridge Ind Est DH4 .94 C7
Rainton Cl NE10 .72 C6
Rainton Gr DH5 .94 E6
Rainton Meadows (Nature Reserve)* DH4 .94 B6
Rainton St Penshaw DH4 .90 B8
Sunderland SR4 .102 A2
Rainton View DH4 .94 A2
Rake La NE29 .31 E1
Raleigh Cl NE33 .59 B8
Raleigh Rd SR5 .74 E2
Raleigh Sq SR5 .74 D2
Ralph Ave SR2 .92 E8
Ralph St NE31 .57 F7
Ramilies SR2 .92 D6
Ramillies Rd SR5 .74 C3
Ramillies Sq SR5 .74 C3
Ramparts The NE15 .53 F8
Ramsay Rd NE17 .66 B2
Ramsay Sq SR5 .74 E3
Ramsay St Blaydon NE21 .53 B1
High Spen NE39 .67 A5
Ramsey St DH3 .88 C2
Ramsgate Rd SR5 .74 E3
Ramshaw Cl NE7 .39 E3
Randolph St NE32 .58 C7
Rangoon Rd SR5 .74 C3
Ranmere Rd NE15 .54 A5
Ranmore Cl NE23 .22 B7
Rannoch Ave DH2 .88 B1
Rannoch Cl NE10 .72 C8
Rannoch Rd SR5 .74 C3
Ranson Cres NE34 .58 F5
Ranson St SR4,SR2 .86 B4
Raphael Ave NE34 .59 C2
Rathmore Gdns NE30 .42 A7
Ratho Ct NE10 .71 E6
Ravel Ct NE32 .58 C6
Ravenburn Gdns NE15 .53 F6
Ravenburn Wlk 6 NE15 .35 D2
Ravenna Rd SR5 .74 B3
Ravens Hill Dr NE63 .6 A2
Ravensbourne Ave NE36 .74 D8
Ravenscar Cl NE16 .68 F5
Ravenscourt Pl NE8 .101 A1
Ravenscourt Rd SR5 .74 C3
Ravensdale Cres NE9 .71 A6
Ravensdale Gr NE24 .17 A7
Ravenshill Rd NE5 .36 E1
Ravenside Rd NE4 .54 E8
Ravenside Terr NE17 .66 A1
Ravenstone NE37 .83 B7
Ravenswood Cl NE12 .39 E8
Ravenswood Gdns NE9 .70 F3
Ravenswood Prim Sch NE6 .39 C1
Ravenswood Rd
Newcastle-upon-Tyne NE6 .39 C1
Sunderland SR5 .74 B3
Ravenswood Sq SR5 .74 B3
Ravensworth Birtley DH3 .82 D5
Ryhope SR2 .92 D6
Ravensworth Ave
Fence Houses DH4 .90 A1
Gateshead NE9 .71 C2
Ravensworth Cl NE28 .40 F2
Ravensworth Cres NE16 .79 D8
Ravensworth Ct
South Hetton DH6 .97 F7
Dunston NE11 .100 A1
Bedlington NE22 .11 D3
Newcastle-upon-Tyne NE3 .37 D7
Ravensworth Gdns NE61 .1 D4
Ravensworth Rd
Birtley DH3 .82 B5
Fence Houses DH4 .89 F1
Dunston NE11 .100 A1
Ravensworth St
Bedlington NE22 .11 D3
Wallsend NE28 .40 F2
Sunderland SR4 .102 B3
Ravensworth Terr
Dunston NE11 .70 A8
Bedlington NE22 .11 D3
Jarrow NE32 .58 B3
South Shields NE33 .59 C8
Newcastle-upon-Tyne NE4 .98 B1
Ravensworth Terrace Prim Sch DH3 .82 C4
Ravine Terr SR6 .75 F3
Rawdon Ct NE28 .57 B8
Rawdon Rd SR5 .74 E3
Rawling Rd NE8 .70 D8
Rawlston Way NE5 .37 C3
Rawmarsh Rd SR5 .74 C3
Raydale SR5 .74 E3
Raydale Ave NE37 .83 B8
Raylees Gdns NE11 .70 A7
Rayleigh Dr NE13 .28 B7
Rayleigh Gr NE8 .70 D8
Raynes Cl NE61 .8 D7
Raynham Cl NE23 .21 F3
Raynham Ct NE33 .42 C2
Rea Pl NE3 .38 A5
Readhead Ave NE33 .42 E1
Readhead Bldgs 2 NE33 42 C2
Readhead Dr NE6 .56 F4
Readhead Rd NE34 .59 F8
Reading Rd
South Shields NE33 .59 D7
Sunderland SR5 .74 D3
Reading Sq SR5 .74 D3
Reasby Gdns NE40 .52 B5
Reasby Villas NE40 .52 B5
Reavley Ave NE22 .11 E3
Reay Cres NE35 .74 B8
Reay Ct 4 DH2 .88 C2
Reay Gdns NE5 .37 A3
Reay Pl NE34 .59 B5
Reay St NE10 .57 B2
Rectory Ave NE3 .38 E4
Rectory Bank NE36 .74 A7
Rectory Dene NE61 .8 F7
Rectory Dr NE3 .38 E4
Rectory Gn NE36 .73 F7
Rectory Gr NE3 .38 D5
Rectory La
Whickham NE16 .69 B7
Blaydon NE21 .68 B8
Rectory Pk NE61 .8 F7
Rectory Pl NE8 .101 A1
Rectory Rd
Hetton le Hole DH5 .95 A3
Gateshead, Carr Hill NE10 .71 C7
Newcastle-upon-Tyne NE3 .38 D4
Gateshead, Shipcote NE8, NE9 .70 E8
Rectory Rd E NE10 .71 D7
Rectory Terr NE3 .38 E4
Red Admiral Ct NE11 .70 B7
Red Barnes NE1 .99 C1
Red Berry Way NE34 .59 B4
Red Bglws NE9 .71 E1
Red Hall Dr NE7 .39 D3
Red House Dr NE25 .31 C6
Red House Farm NE22 .15 D8
Red House Rd NE31 .58 A6
Red Lion La NE37 .72 C2
Red Rose Prim Sch DH3 .88 D1
Red Rose Terr DH3 .88 D2
Red Row Dr NE22 .11 C3
Red Wlk NE7 .39 A1
Redburn Cl DH4 .94 C8
Redburn Rd NE5 .36 F4
Redby Cl 1 SR6 .75 D2
Redby Prim Sch SR6 .75 D2
Redcar Rd Wallsend NE28 .41 A3
Newcastle-upon-Tyne NE6 .39 D1
Sunderland SR5 .74 E2
Redcar Sq SR5 .74 E2
Redcliffe Way NE5 .37 B3
Redcroft Gn NE5 .37 B3
Redditch Sq SR5 .74 D3
Rede Ave Hebburn NE31 .57 E6
Hexham NE46 .45 C4
Rede Ct NE61 .1 E5
Rede St Gateshead NE11 .70 C5
Jarrow NE32 .58 A5
Redemarsh NE10 .71 F6
Redesdale Ave
Blaydon NE21 .67 F8
Newcastle-upon-Tyne NE3 .38 A6
Redesdale Cheese Farm* NE19 .123 A8
Redesdale Cl
Longbenton NE12 .39 C8
Newcastle-upon-Tyne NE15 .53 E7
Redesdale Fst Sch NE28 .39 F4
Redesdale Gdns NE11 .69 F7
Redesdale Gr NE29 .41 D6
Redesdale Pl NE24 .17 B7
Redesdale Rd
Chester le Street DH2 .88 A1
North Shields NE29 .41 D6
Sunderland SR5 .74 C3
Redewater Gdns NE16 .69 A6
Redewater Rd NE4 .54 E8
Redewood Cl NE5 .37 A1
Redford Pl NE23 .29 C5
Redheugh Bridge Rd NE1,NE4 .100 C3
Redheugh Ct NE8 .70 B8
Redheugh Rd NE25 .31 B5
Redhill SR6 .75 E8
Redhill Dr NE16 .68 E4
Redhill Rd SR5 .74 D3
Redhill Wlk NE23 .22 B7
Redhills Way DH5 .95 A2
Redland Ave NE3 .37 E6
Redlands DH4 .90 A7
Redmayne Ct 1 NE10 .71 D8
Redmires Cl DH2 .81 E1
Redmond Rd SR5 .74 E3
Redmond Sq SR5 .74 E3
Rednam Pl NE5 .37 B2
Redruth Gdns NE9 .70 F2
Redruth Sq SR5 .74 D3
Redshank Cl NE38 .82 F2
Redshank Dr NE24 .17 E4
Redstart Ct NE39 .67 D2
Redwell Ct
South Shields NE34 .60 C7
Prudhoe NE42 .50 D2
Redwell La NE34 .60 D7
Redwell Rd NE42 .50 E2
Redwing Cl NE38 .82 F3
Redwing Ct NE6 .56 E7
Redwood Cl
Hetton le Hole DH5 .94 F4
Killingworth NE12 .29 C4
Redwood Gdns NE11 .70 B5
Redwood Gr SR3 .92 B7
Reed Ave NE12 .29 C4
Reed St North Shields NE30 42 B6
South Shields NE33 .59 C8
Reedham Ct NE5 .37 B4
Reedling Ct SR5 .74 C4
Reedside NE40 .52 D5
Reedsmouth Pl NE5 .54 B8
Reedswood Cres NE23 .22 E5
Reestones Pl NE3 .37 D5
Reeth Rd SR5 .74 D2
Reeth Sq SR5 .74 D2
Reeth Way NE15 .35 C1
Regal Rd SR4 .102 A3
Regency Ct NE2 .99 C4
Regency Dr
Whickham NE16 .68 F6
New Silksworth SR3 .92 B8
Regency Gdns NE29 .41 E7
Regency Way NE20 .25 A5
Regent Ave NE3 .38 B5
Regent Centre Sta NE3 .38 C6
Regent Ct
Longbenton NE12 .29 B2
Blyth NE24 .17 D7
Hebburn NE31 .57 D5
South Shields NE33 .42 C1
Gateshead NE8 .101 C2
Regent Ctr The NE3 .38 C6
Regent Dr NE16 .68 F4
Regent Farm Ct NE3 .38 C5
Regent Farm Fst Sch NE3 .38 A6
Regent Farm Rd NE3 .38 B6
Regent Rd Wallsend NE28 .40 A3
Newcastle-upon-Tyne NE3 .38 C5
Jarrow NE32 .58 C6
Ryhope SR2 .93 A5
Regent Rd N NE3 .38 C5
Regent St
Hetton le Hole DH5 .95 A5
Blyth NE24 .17 E8
Regent Terr
North Shields NE29 .41 E6
Gateshead NE8 .101 B2
Sunderland SR2 .86 F2
Regents Ct NE28 .39 E4
Regents Dr Prudhoe NE42 .50 E4
Tynemouth NE30 .32 C1
Regents Pk NE28 .39 E3
Regina Sq SR5 .74 D3
Reginald St
West Boldon NE35 .73 F8
Gateshead NE8 .56 B1
4 Sunderland SR4 .85 F7
Reid Ave NE28 .40 B3
Reid Park Cl NE2 .38 F2
Reid Park Ct NE2 .38 F2
Reid Park Rd NE2 .38 F2
Reid St NE61 .9 A8
Reid's La NE23 .22 E1
Reigate Sq NE23 .22 B7
Reiverdale Rd NE63 .6 D4
Rekendyke Ind Est NE33 .42 B1
Rekendyke La NE33 .42 B1
Relton Ave NE6 .56 D4
Relton Cl DH4 .94 A7
Relton Ct NE25 .31 E5
Relton PL NE25 .31 E5
Relton Terr
Chester le Street DH3 .88 C2
Whitley Bay NE25 .31 E5
Rembrandt Ave NE34 .59 C2
Remington Ave NE30 .32 C1
Remscheid Way NE63 .6 C1
Remus Ave NE15 .34 D2
Remus Cl NE13 .28 B5
Rendel St NE11 .54 F1
Rendle Rd NE6 .57 B4
Renforth St NE11 .69 F8
Renfrew Cl NE29 .41 C8
Renfrew Gn NE5 .37 B3
Renfrew Pl DH3 .82 D2
Renfrew Rd SR5 .74 D3
Rennie Rd SR5 .74 B3
Rennie Sq SR5 .74 B3
Rennington NE10 .72 A5
Rennington Cl
Tynemouth NE30 .32 C1
Morpeth NE61 .9 B5
Rennington Pl NE5 .37 D2
Renoir Gdns NE34 .59 D2
Renwick Ave NE3 .37 E6
Renwick Ct NE8 .70 C8
Renwick Rd NE24 .17 D7
Renwick St NE6 .56 D6
Renwick Wlk NE61 .8 E8
Rescue Station Cotts DH5 .94 F6
Resida Cl NE15 .53 C8
Retford Rd SR5 .74 D3
Retford Sq SR5 .74 D3
Retreat The
Newburn NE15 .52 F7
Sunderland SR2 .102 B2
Revell Terr NE5 .37 E1
Revelstoke Rd SR5 .74 C3
Revesby St NE33 .59 C6
Reynolds Ave
Killingworth NE12 .29 B2
Whiteleas NE34 .59 D3
Washington NE38 .83 E4
Reyrolle Ct NE31 .57 D5
Rheims Ct SR4 .85 D7
Rheydt Ave NE28 .39 F2
Rhoda Terr SR2 .86 F1
Rhodes St NE6 .57 A5
Rhodesia Rd SR5 .74 D3
Rhondda Rd SR5 .74 B3
Rhuddlan Ct NE5 .37 B4
Rhyl Par NE31 .58 A2
Rhyl Sq SR5 .74 E3
Ribble Rd SR5 .74 C2
Ribble Wlk NE32 .58 C2
Ribbledale Gdns NE7 .39 B3
Ribblesdale Penshaw DH4 .90 B7
Wallsend NE28 .39 F4
Ribblesdale Ave NE24 .17 A8
Richard Ave SR4 .86 A4
Richard Avenue Prim Sch SR4 .86 A4
Richard Browell Rd NE15 35 E1
Richard St
Hetton le Hole DH5 .95 A3
Blyth NE24 .17 E7
Richardson Ave 2 NE34 .58 F4
Richardson Dees Fst Sch NE28 .40 D2
Richardson Rd NE1,NE2 .98 C3
Richardson St
Wallsend NE28 .40 C2
3 Newcastle-upon-Tyne NE6 .56 C8
Ashington NE63 .6 E1
Richardson Terr
Chopwell NE17 .66 B1
5 Washington NE37 .83 D8
6 Ryhope SR2 .93 A6
Richardson's Bldgs NE62 .10 E5
Richmond SR2 .92 D7
Richmond Ave
Gateshead NE10 .57 C2
Whickham NE16 .54 B1
Washington NE38 .83 D6
Richmond Cl NE22 .10 E2
Richmond Ct Jarrow NE32 58 A7
Gateshead NE8 .101 C1
1 Gateshead, Low Fell NE9 70 F4
Richmond Dr DH4 .89 D1
Richmond Gdns NE28 .40 E3
Richmond Gr NE29 .41 E5
Richmond Lodge NE3 .38 D4
Richmond Mews NE3 .38 B3
Richmond Pk NE28 .39 E3
Richmond Rd NE34 .59 C6
Richmond St SR5 .102 C4
Richmond Terr
Haswell DH6 .97 F3
13 Gateshead, Felling NE10 71 D8
Walbottle NE15 .35 F1
Whitley Bay NE26 .31 F7
Gateshead NE8 .101 B1
Richmond Way
Ponteland NE20 .25 A5
Cramlington NE23 .22 A3
Rickaby St SR1 .103 C4
Rickgarth NE10 .71 F5
Rickleton Ave DH3 .88 D5
Rickleton Prim Sch NE38 88 F8
Rickleton Way NE38 .83 A1
Riddell Ave NE15 .54 C5
Riddell Ct 7 DH2 .88 C2
Riddings Rd SR5 .74 D3
Riddings Sq SR5 .74 D3
Ridge Ct NE13 .28 B4
Ridge Terr NE22 .10 E1
Ridge The NE40 .52 C4
Ridge Villas NE22 .10 E1
Ridge Way NE25 .23 E1
Ridge Way The NE3 .37 F4
Ridgely Cl NE20 .26 A6
Ridgely Dr NE20 .26 A6
Ridgeway Birtley DH3 .82 C6
Gateshead NE10 .72 B6
Newcastle-upon-Tyne NE4 .54 E8
Stakeford NE62 .11 A8
Ashington NE63 .7 A2
Ryhope SR2 .92 C6
Ridgeway Cres SR3 .86 B3
Ridgeway Cty Jun Mix & Inf Sch NE34 .59 F4
Ridgeway The NE34 .59 F3
Ridgewood Cres NE3 .38 F5
Ridgewood Gdns NE3 .38 E5
Ridgewood Villas NE3 .38 E5
Riding Barns Way NE16 .69 A2
Riding Cl NE40 .51 E3
Riding Dene NE43 .49 F1
Riding Grange NE44 .62 E8
Riding La DH9,NE11 .81 B4
Riding Lea NE21 .53 A1
Riding Mill Sta NE44 .62 F8
Riding Terr NE43 .49 F1
Riding The NE3 .37 E3
Ridings Ct NE40 .51 E3
Ridings The NE25 .31 C6
Ridley Ave
Chester le Street DH2 .88 B2
Blyth NE24 .17 F7
Wallsend NE28 .41 B4
Sunderland SR2 .92 F7
Ridley Cl
Newcastle-upon-Tyne NE3 .37 F8
Hexham NE46 .44 F3
Morpeth NE61 .8 E8
Ridley Gdns NE16 .54 A1
Ridley Gr NE34 .60 A7
Ridley Mill Cotts NE43 .64 B6
Ridley Mill Rd NE43 .64 B5
Ridley Pl NE1,NE99 .99 A2
Ridley St Cramlington NE23 22 C5
Blyth NE24 .17 F8
Gateshead NE8 .70 E8
Sunderland SR5 .75 B2
Ridley Terr
Gateshead NE10 .71 E8
Cambois NE24 .12 D4
Sunderland SR2 .103 C1
Ridsdale NE42 .50 B1
Ridsdale Ave NE5 .36 E1

Ridsdale Cl
Seaton Delaval NE25 .. 23 C3
Wallsend NE28 .. 40 C4
Ridsdale Ct NE8 .. 101 A1
Ridsdale Sq NE63 .. 6 C3
Rievaulx NE38 .. 83 C4
Riga Sq SR5 .. 74 C3
Riggs The
Houghton-le-Spring DH5 .. 94 F8
Corbridge NE45 .. 46 F7
Rignall NE38 .. 84 A5
Riley St NE32 .. 58 A7
Riley Street Ind Est NE32 58 A7
Ringlet Cl NE11 .. 70 B7
Ringmore Ct SR2 .. 86 C2
Ringway Stakeford NE62 .. 6 A1
Sunderland SR5 .. 85 A8
Ringwood Dr NE23 .. 22 B7
Ringwood Gn NE12 .. 39 C7
Ringwood Rd SR5 .. 74 D3
Ringwood Sq SR5 .. 74 D3
Rink St NE24 .. 17 F8
Ripley Ave NE29 .. 41 E4
Ripley Cl NE22 .. 10 D2
Ripley Ct NE9 .. 71 B1
Ripley Dr NE23 .. 22 A3
Ripley Terr NE6 .. 56 E6
Ripon Cl NE23 .. 21 F3
Ripon Gdns
Newcastle-upon-Tyne NE2 .. 56 A8
Wallsend NE28 .. 40 E3
Ripon Sq NE32 .. 73 B8
Ripon St
Chester le Street DH3 .. 88 C1
Gateshead NE8 .. 101 B1
Sunderland SR6 .. 75 E1
Rise The Ponteland NE20 .. 25 B2
Ryton NE21 .. 53 A4
Seaton Sluice NE26 .. 24 E4
Newcastle-upon-Tyne NE3 .. 37 E4
Gateshead NE8 .. 56 B1
Rishton Sq SR5 .. 74 C3
Rising Sun Cotts NE28 .. 40 B5
Rising Sun Ctry Pk*
NE28 .. 40 B6
Ritson Cl NE29 .. 41 E7
Ritson St SR6 .. 75 E4
River Bank NE62 .. 11 C8
River Bank E NE62 .. 11 C8
River Dr NE33 .. 42 C4
River La NE40 .. 52 C6
River Terr 5 DH3 .. 88 D4
River View
Blackhall Mill NE17 .. 77 B6
Blaydon NE21 .. 53 B2
Bebside NE22 .. 11 D1
North Shields NE30 .. 42 C6
Ryton NE40 .. 52 E5
Ovingham NE42 .. 50 A4
Prudhoe NE42 .. 50 C2
Lynmouth NE61 .. 2 A3
River View Cl NE22 .. 11 D1
Riverbank Rd SR5 .. 74 D2
Riverdale SR5 .. 85 B8
Rivermead NE38 .. 83 E1
Rivermede NE20 .. 25 F7
Riversdale NE17 .. 77 B6
Riversdale Ave NE62 .. 11 A8
Riversdale Ct
Newcastle-upon-Tyne NE15 .. 53 C6
Stakeford NE62 .. 11 A7
Riversdale Ho NE62 .. 11 A7
Riversdale Terr SR2 .. 102 B1
Riversdale Way NE15 .. 53 C6
Riverside NE20 .. 25 E6
Riverside Ave NE62 .. 10 D7
Riverside Bsns Pk NE28 .. 41 A1
Riverside Ct
Dunston NE11 .. 100 A1
South Shields NE33 .. 42 B2
Riverside Lo NE15 .. 52 E7
Riverside Pk SR4 .. 85 B7
Riverside Rd SR5 .. 74 E2
Riverside The NE31 .. 57 C7
Riverside Way NE11,NE16 54 C3
Riverview Lodge NE4 .. 54 D4
Roachburn Rd NE5 .. 36 E2
Robert Owen Gdns NE10 71 C7
Robert St Blyth NE24 .. 17 E7
South Shields NE33 .. 42 D1
New Silksworth SR3 .. 92 B7
Sunderland SR4 .. 102 A3
Robert Terr NE39 .. 66 F4
Robert Terr Cotts NE39 .. 66 F4
Robert Westall Way
NE29 .. 42 A3
Robert Wheatman Ct
SR2 .. 86 E2
Roberts St NE15 .. 54 A5
Roberts Terr NE32 .. 58 B5
Robertson Rd SR5 .. 74 B2
Robertson Sq SR5 .. 74 B3
Robin Ct DH5 .. 94 C3
Robin Gr SR5 .. 74 C1
Robin La
East Rainton DH4,DH5 .. 94 C2
West Rainton DH4,DH5 .. 94 C2
Robinson Gdns
Wallsend NE28 .. 41 A3
2 Whitburn SR6 .. 60 F1
Robinson Sq NE64 .. 7 E5
Robinson St
8 South Shields NE33 .. 42 D2
4 Newcastle-upon-Tyne
NE6 .. 56 C6
Robinson Terr
Burnopfield NE16 .. 79 A4
Washington NE38 .. 83 F4
Robinson Terr *continued*
Sunderland SR2 .. 103 C1
Robinswood 8 NE9 .. 70 F5
Robsheugh Pl NE5 .. 54 C8
Robson Dr NE46 .. 44 F3
Robson Pl 10 SR2 .. 93 A6
Robson St
Newcastle-upon-Tyne NE6 .. 56 B6
7 Gateshead NE9 .. 70 F5
Robson Terr Tantobie DH9 .. 78 F1
High Spen NE39 .. 67 B3
Rochdale Rd SR5 .. 74 D3
Rochdale St
Hetton le Hole DH5 .. 95 A2
Wallsend NE28 .. 40 B1
Rochdale Way SR5 .. 74 D3
Roche Ct NE38 .. 83 C4
Rochester Cl NE63 .. 7 A2
Rochester Gdns NE11 .. 70 A8
Rochester Sq NE32 .. 58 B1
Rochester St NE6 .. 57 A4
Rochester Terr NE10 .. 71 E8
Rochford Gr NE23 .. 22 A3
Rochford Rd SR5 .. 74 C3
Rock Gr 4 NE9 .. 70 F5
Rock Lodge Gdns SR6 .. 75 F3
Rock Lodge Rd SR6 .. 75 F3
Rock Terr
Newcastle-upon-Tyne NE2 .. 99 C2
9 Washington NE37 .. 83 E8
Rockcliffe
Whitley Bay NE26 .. 32 C5
South Shields NE33 .. 42 F1
Rockcliffe Ave NE26 .. 32 C4
Rockcliffe Fst Sch NE26 .. 32 C4
Rockcliffe Gdns
Newcastle-upon-Tyne NE15 .. 53 F7
Whitley Bay NE26 .. 32 C4
Rockcliffe St NE26 .. 32 C4
Rockcliffe Way NE9 .. 71 D1
Rocket Way NE12 .. 39 F8
Rockhope NE38 .. 88 F8
Rockingham Rd SR5 .. 74 C3
Rockingham Sq SR5 .. 74 C3
Rockmore Rd NE21 .. 53 C1
Rockville SR6 .. 75 E4
Rockwood Gdns NE40 .. 51 E1
Rockwood Hill Est NE40 .. 66 E8
Rockwood Hill Rd NE40 .. 51 F1
Rockwood Terr NE40 .. 51 F1
Rodin Ave NE34 .. 59 D2
Rodney Cl
Tynemouth NE30 .. 42 D7
Ryhope SR2 .. 92 C6
Rodney Ct NE26 .. 31 D7
Rodney St NE6 .. 56 B5
Rodney Way NE26 .. 31 D7
Rodsley Ave NE8,NE9 .. 70 F8
Roeburn Way NE3 .. 37 F3
Roedean Rd SR5 .. 74 E3
Roehedge NE10 .. 72 B6
Rogan Ave 8 NE37 .. 83 A6
Roger St NE6 .. 56 B6
Rogerson Terr NE5 .. 36 E3
Rogues La NE39 .. 67 A5
Rokeby Ave NE15 .. 53 D6
Rokeby Dr NE3 .. 37 F4
Rokeby St
Newcastle-upon-Tyne NE15 .. 53 D6
Sunderland SR4 .. 102 B2
Rokeby Terr NE6 .. 39 C1
Rokeby View NE9 .. 71 A1
Roker Ave
Whitley Bay NE25 .. 31 F3
Sunderland SR6 .. 75 E1
Roker Baths Rd SR6 .. 75 E2
Roker Park Cl 10 SR6 .. 75 E2
Roker Park Rd SR6 .. 75 E3
Roker Park Terr SR6 .. 75 F2
Roker Terr SR6 .. 75 F3
Rokerby Ave NE16 .. 69 C6
Roland Burn Way NE39 .. 67 E2
Roland Rd NE28 .. 40 E2
Roland St NE38 .. 83 E4
Rollesby Ct NE5 .. 37 B4
Rolling Mill Rd NE32 .. 58 A8
Romaldskirk Cl SR4 .. 85 B5
Roman Ave
Chester le Street DH3 .. 88 D3
Newcastle-upon-Tyne NE6 .. 56 E6
Roman Rd Hedworth NE10 72 E8
South Shields NE33 .. 42 D4
Roman Rd N NE33 .. 42 C4
Roman Road Prim Sch
NE10 .. 72 A5
Roman Way NE45 .. 46 F6
Roman Way The NE5 .. 53 D8
Romford Cl NE23 .. 22 A3
Romford Pl NE9 .. 71 A8
Romford St 4 SR4 .. 85 F6
Romilly St NE33 .. 42 D2
Romley Gr NE10 .. 72 D7
Romney Ave
Whiteleas NE34 .. 59 D3
Washington NE38 .. 83 E4
Sunderland SR2 .. 86 E3
Romney Cl
Shiney Row DH4 .. 90 C5
Whitley Bay NE26 .. 32 C4
Romney Gdns NE9 .. 71 B7
Romsey Cl NE23 .. 22 B7
Romsey Dr NE35 .. 73 E8
Romsey Gr NE15 .. 53 C8
Ronald Dr NE15 .. 54 A6
Ronald Gdns NE31 .. 57 D4
Ronald Sq SR6 .. 75 D3
Ronaldsay Cl 4 SR2 .. 92 E8
Ronan Mews DH4 .. 94 A2
Ronsdorf Ct NE32 .. 58 B6
Rookery Cl NE24 .. 17 B7
Rookery La NE16 .. 68 E4
Rookery The NE16 .. 78 F6
Rooksleigh 6 NE21 .. 53 B1
Rookswood NE61 .. 9 A6
Rookswood Gdns NE39 .. 67 E3
Rookwood Dr NE13 .. 28 C8
Rookwood Rd NE5 .. 54 A8
Ropery La Bournmoor DH3 88 F3
Chester le Street DH3 .. 88 D2
Wallsend NE28 .. 40 F2
Hebburn NE31 .. 57 D6
Ropery Rd Gateshead NE8 .. 70 B8
Sunderland SR4 .. 102 B4
Ropery The NE6 .. 56 D4
Rosa St NE33 .. 42 D2
Rosalind Ave NE22 .. 11 B1
Rosalind St Ashington NE63 .. 6 E4
Ashington, Hirst NE63 .. 6 E3
Rosamond Pl NE24 .. 17 F7
Rose Ave
Fence Houses DH4 .. 89 F1
Whickham NE16 .. 69 B7
Cramlington NE23 .. 21 F8
Rose Cotts NE16 .. 78 E5
Rose Cres Bournmoor DH4 89 D3
Whitburn SR6 .. 60 F2
Rose Ct NE31 .. 57 D5
Rose Gdns
Kibblesworth NE11 .. 81 C6
Wallsend NE28 .. 40 B4
Rose St
7 Houghton-le-Spring DH4 94 D8
Hebburn NE31 .. 57 D5
Gateshead NE8 .. 100 C2
Sunderland SR4 .. 102 B3
Rose St E DH4 .. 90 B8
Rose St W DH4 .. 90 B8
Rose Terr Greenside NE40 .. 52 C2
Newcastle-upon-Tyne NE5 .. 37 E1
Rose Villa La NE16 .. 69 B7
Rosebank Cl SR2 .. 92 E8
Rosebank Hall NE28 .. 40 F2
Roseberry Grange NE12 .. 30 A1
Roseberry Pl NE2 .. 99 C4
Roseberry Terr 1 NE35 .. 58 E1
Rosebery Ave Blyth NE24 .. 17 D7
Tynemouth NE29 .. 42 A8
South Shields NE33 .. 42 E1
Gateshead NE8 .. 71 A8
Rosebery Cres NE2 .. 56 A8
Rosebery Pl NE2 .. 56 A8
Rosebery St 4 SR5 .. 75 D1
Rosedale Bedlington NE22 .. 10 E1
Wallsend NE28 .. 39 F4
Rosedale Ave SR6 .. 75 E6
Rosedale Cres DH4 .. 90 C2
Rosedale Ct NE5 .. 36 D2
Rosedale Rd NE40 .. 51 F3
Rosedale St
Hetton le Hole DH5 .. 94 E1
Sunderland SR1 .. 102 B2
Rosedale Terr
Newcastle-upon-Tyne NE2 .. 99 C3
North Shields NE30 .. 42 B7
Sunderland SR6 .. 75 E4
Roseden Ct NE12 .. 39 C7
Rosedene Villas NE23 .. 22 D6
Rosefinch Lodge NE9 .. 70 F5
Rosegill NE37 .. 83 B6
Rosehill NE28 .. 40 E2
Rosehill Rd NE28 .. 40 F2
Rosehill Way NE5 .. 37 C1
Roselea NE32 .. 58 C1
Roselea Ave SR2 .. 92 F7
Rosemary Gdns NE9 .. 71 D2
Rosemary Rd SR5 .. 74 D3
Rosemary Terr NE24 .. 17 F6
Rosemount
Newcastle-upon-Tyne NE5 .. 36 F2
Morpeth NE61 .. 9 A7
Sunderland SR4 .. 85 A5
Rosemount Ave NE10 .. 72 B7
Rosemount Cl NE37 .. 72 C2
Rosemount Ct NE36 .. 74 B7
Rosemount Way
Whitley Bay NE25 .. 31 C5
Newcastle-upon-Tyne NE7 .. 39 C5
Roseneath Ct NE63 .. 6 D3
Roseville St SR4 .. 102 B1
Rosewell Pl NE16 .. 69 A4
Rosewood NE12 .. 29 F3
Rosewood Ave NE3 .. 38 E6
Rosewood Cres
Seaton Sluice NE26 .. 24 D4
Newcastle-upon-Tyne NE6 .. 39 F1
Rosewood Gdns
Chester le Street DH2 .. 88 B5
Newcastle-upon-Tyne NE3 .. 37 F4
Gateshead NE9 .. 71 B5
Rosewood Sq SR4 .. 85 A2
Rosewood Terr
Birtley DH3 .. 82 B5
Wallsend NE28 .. 41 A2
Roseworth Ave NE3 .. 38 D3
Roseworth Cl NE3 .. 38 D4
Roseworth Cres NE3 .. 38 D3
Roseworth Terr
Whickham NE16 .. 69 B7
Newcastle-upon-Tyne NE3 .. 38 C4
Roslin Pk NE22 .. 11 C1
Roslin Way NE23 .. 22 A3
Ross DH2 .. 82 A1
Ross Ave NE11 .. 54 F1
Ross Castle (N.T.)*
NE66 .. 112 B8
Ross Gr NE23 .. 21 F7
Ross Lea DH4 .. 90 A5
Ross St SR5 .. 75 C1
Ross Way
Whitley Bay NE26 .. 31 E7
Newcastle-upon-Tyne NE3 .. 37 F8
Rosse Cl NE37 .. 83 B8
Rossendale Pl NE12 .. 38 F6
Rosslyn Ave
Newcastle-upon-Tyne NE3 .. 37 E5
Gateshead NE9 .. 71 A6
Ryhope SR2 .. 92 F7
Rosslyn Mews SR4 .. 102 A2
Rosslyn Pl DH3 .. 82 D2
Rosslyn St SR4 .. 102 A2
Rosslyn Terr SR4 .. 102 A2
Rosyth Rd SR5 .. 74 E3
Rosyth Sq SR5 .. 74 E3
Rotary Parkway NE63 .. 6 B4
Rotary Way Blyth NE24 .. 17 F5
North Shields NE29 .. 41 E3
Rothay Pl NE5 .. 37 C2
Rothbury SR2 .. 92 D6
Rothbury Ave
Gateshead NE10 .. 57 A1
Blyth NE24 .. 17 B6
Newcastle-upon-Tyne NE3 .. 38 B6
Hebburn NE32 .. 58 A4
Rothbury Cl
Chester le Street DH2 .. 88 A1
Killingworth NE12 .. 29 C4
Rothbury Gdns
Dunston NE11 .. 70 A5
Wide Open NE13 .. 28 C6
Wallsend NE28 .. 40 F3
Rothbury Rd SR5 .. 74 D3
Rothbury Terr
North Shields NE29 .. 41 D4
Newcastle-upon-Tyne NE6 .. 56 C8
Rotherfield Cl NE23 .. 22 B7
Rotherfield Gdns NE9 .. 71 A2
Rotherfield Rd SR5 .. 74 C3
Rotherfield Sq SR5 .. 74 C3
Rotherham Cl DH5 .. 94 D6
Rotherham Rd SR5 .. 74 C3
Rothesay DH2 .. 81 F1
Rothesay Terr NE22 .. 11 C2
Rothlea Gdns NE62 .. 11 A8
Rothley NE38 .. 83 F2
Rothley Ave
Newcastle-upon-Tyne NE5 .. 54 C7
Ashington NE63 .. 6 D2
Rothley Cl Ponteland NE20 25 D7
Newcastle-upon-Tyne NE3 .. 38 D5
Rothley Ct
Killingworth NE12 .. 29 D3
Sunderland SR5 .. 74 F4
Rothley Gdns NE30 .. 32 B1
Rothley Gr NE25 .. 23 C3
Rothley Terr DH8 .. 77 B1
Rothley Way NE26 .. 31 E7
Rothsay Terr NE64 .. 7 D3
Rothwell Rd
Newcastle-upon-Tyne NE3 .. 38 C5
Sunderland SR5 .. 74 C2
Roundhill NE32 .. 58 D1
Roundhill Ave NE5 .. 37 C2
Roundstone Cl NE7 .. 39 D4
Roundway The NE12 .. 39 B7
Row's Terr NE3 .. 38 E5
Rowan Ave NE38 .. 83 C1
Rowan Cl Bedlington NE22 .. 10 F2
Sunderland SR4 .. 85 B5
Rowan Ct
Longbenton NE12 .. 39 F8
Blyth NE24 .. 17 D6
4 South Shields NE34 .. 59 A4
Rowan Dr
Hetton le Hole DH5 .. 94 F4
Ponteland NE20 .. 25 E7
Newcastle-upon-Tyne NE3 .. 37 F6
Rowan Gr
Cramlington NE23 .. 22 D5
Prudhoe NE42 .. 50 B2
Rowanberry Rd NE12 .. 39 B6
Rowans The NE9 .. 71 D2
Rowantree Rd NE28,NE6 .. 40 A1
Rowanwood Gdns NE11 .. 70 B5
Rowedge Wlk NE5 .. 37 A2
Rowell Cl SR2 .. 92 C6
Rowes Mews NE6 .. 56 C4
Rowlands Gill Inf Sch
NE39 .. 67 F3
Rowlands Gill Jun Sch
NE39 .. 67 F3
Rowlandson Cres NE10 .. 71 D8
Rowlandson Terr
12 Gateshead NE10 .. 71 D8
8 Sunderland SR2 .. 86 E4
Rowley St NE24 .. 17 E7
Rowlington Terr NE63 .. 6 D2
Rowntree Way NE29 .. 42 A3
Rowsley Rd NE32 .. 58 C5
Roxburgh Cl NE21 .. 68 A8
Roxburgh House NE26 .. 32 A5
Roxburgh Pl 2 NE6 .. 56 B7
Roxburgh St SR6 .. 75 D2
Roxburgh Terr NE26 .. 32 A5
Roxby Gdns NE29 .. 41 E5
Royal Arc NE1 .. 99 B1
Royal Cres NE4 .. 54 E8
Royal Gram Sch NE2 .. 99 B3
Royal Ind Est NE32 .. 57 F8
Royal Quays Outlet Shopping
NE28 .. 41 E2
Royal Victoria Infmy NE2 98 C3
Royalty The SR2 .. 102 B2
Roydon Ave SR2 .. 86 E3
Royle St SR2 .. 86 F2
Royston Terr NE6 .. 57 A4
Ruabon Cl NE23 .. 22 A3
Rubens Ave NE34 .. 59 D3
Ruby St DH4 .. 90 D2
Rudby Cl NE3 .. 38 D8
Rudchester Pl NE5 .. 54 C8
Ruddock Sq 1 NE6 .. 56 C4
Rudyard Ave SR2 .. 86 E3
Rudyerd Ct NE29 .. 42 B5
Rudyerd St 13 NE29 .. 42 A5
Rugby Gdns
Wallsend NE28 .. 40 E3
Gateshead NE9 .. 71 C3
Ruislip Pl NE23 .. 21 F3
Ruislip Rd SR4 .. 85 A5
Runcorn SR2 .. 92 C7
Runcorn Rd SR5 .. 74 C3
Runhead Est NE40 .. 52 D4
Runhead Gdns NE40 .. 52 D5
Runhead Terr NE40 .. 52 E5
Runnymede SR2 .. 92 D7
Runnymede Gdns NE17 .. 77 B7
Runnymede Rd
Whickham NE16 .. 69 A6
Ponteland NE20 .. 25 C5
Sunderland SR5 .. 74 D3
Runnymede Way
Newcastle-upon-Tyne NE3 .. 37 E4
Sunderland SR5 .. 74 D3
Runswick Ave NE12 .. 38 F6
Runswick Cl SR3 .. 92 C7
Rupert Sq SR5 .. 74 E3
Rupert St SR6 .. 60 F1
Rupert Terr NE15 .. 52 F8
Rushall Pl NE12 .. 39 B6
Rushbury Ct NE27 .. 30 C5
Rushford SR2 .. 92 D6
Rushie Ave NE15 .. 54 C5
Rushley Cres NE21 .. 53 C3
Rushsyde Cl NE16 .. 68 E5
Rushton Ave SR2 .. 86 E3
Rushyrig NE37 .. 83 A6
Ruskin Ave
Easington Lane DH5 .. 97 D8
7 Dunston NE11 .. 54 F1
Longbenton NE12 .. 29 D1
Ashington NE63 .. 6 F2
Ruskin Cres NE34 .. 59 B3
Ruskin Ct NE42 .. 50 B1
Ruskin Dr
West Boldon NE35 .. 74 A8
Newcastle-upon-Tyne NE7 .. 39 E3
Ruskin Rd Birtley DH3 .. 82 C4
Gateshead N10,NE9 .. 71 B7
Whickham NE16 .. 69 A8
Russel Ct NE2 .. 38 F2
Russell Ave NE34 .. 60 A6
Russell Ct NE8 .. 100 C1
Russell Sq NE13 .. 28 B8
Russell St
8 North Shields NE29 .. 42 A5
Jarrow NE32 .. 58 C7
7 South Shields NE33 .. 42 C3
Washington NE37 .. 83 C8
Sunderland SR1 .. 103 B3
Russell Terr Birtley DH3 .. 82 B6
Newcastle-upon-Tyne NE1,
NE2 .. 99 C2
Bedlington NE22 .. 15 F8
Rustic Terr NE64 .. 7 E5
Ruswarp Dr SR3 .. 92 B6
Ruth Ave NE21 .. 53 C2
Rutherford Ave SR7 .. 92 F1
Rutherford Cl NE62 .. 10 E7
Rutherford Pl NE61 .. 8 E7
Rutherford Rd
Washington NE37 .. 72 E2
Sunderland SR5 .. 74 B3
Rutherford Sq SR5 .. 74 B3
Rutherford St
Newcastle-upon-Tyne NE1 .. 98 C1
Blyth NE24 .. 17 D7
Wallsend NE28 .. 41 B3
Rutherglen Rd SR5 .. 74 E3
Rutherglen Sq SR5 .. 74 E3
Rutland Ave
Newcastle-upon-Tyne NE6 .. 57 A7
New Silksworth SR3 .. 91 F7
Rutland Pl
North Shields NE29 .. 41 F6
Washington NE37 .. 72 D2
Rutland Rd Wallsend NE28 40 A1
Hebburn NE31 .. 57 F3
Rutland Sq DH3 .. 82 B5
Rutland St
Hetton le Hole DH5 .. 94 F4
Ashington NE63 .. 6 C3
Sunderland SR4 .. 85 F7
Rutland Terr DH6 .. 97 E1
Ryal Cl Blyth NE24 .. 17 C7
Seaton Delaval NE25 .. 23 E3
Ryal Terr NE6 .. 56 F5
Ryal Wlk NE3 .. 37 D4
Ryall Ave NE13 .. 28 A4
Rydal NE10 .. 72 A8
Rydal Ave
Easington Lane DH5 .. 97 C8
Tynemouth NE30 .. 32 A2
Rydal Cl Killingworth NE12 .. 29 F3
East Boldon NE36 .. 74 C8
Rydal Cres NE21 .. 68 B8
Rydal Gdns NE34 .. 59 E6
Rydal Mount
Newbiggin-by-the-Sea NE64 .. 7 C4

Rydal Mount *continued*
Sunderland, Castletown SR5 85 A8
Sunderland, Monkwearmouth SR5 75 C3
Rydal Rd
Chester le Street DH2 88 C1
Newcastle-upon-Tyne, Lemington NE15 53 D8
Newcastle-upon-Tyne, Gosforth NE3 38 D5
Rydal St NE8 101 B1
Rydal Terr NE13 28 B4
Ryde Pl NE23 22 B7
Ryde Terr NE11 100 A1
Rye Cl NE15 35 E1
Rye Hill
Newcastle-upon-Tyne NE4 100 B4
Newcastle-upon-Tyne NE4 100 C4
Rye Terr NE46 44 F5
Rye View SR2 92 F7
Ryedale Wallsend NE28 39 F5
Sunderland SR6 75 F7
Ryedale Cl NE63 6 B2
Ryedale Ct 7 NE34 59 A4
Ryehaugh NE20 25 F6
Ryehill View DH5 94 C5
Ryemount Rd SR2 92 D7
Ryhope Engine Mus* SR2 92 E5
Ryhope Gdns NE9 71 D4
Ryhope General Hospl SR2 92 F5
Ryhope Grange Ct SR2 86 F1
Ryhope Inf Sch SR2 92 F7
Ryhope Jun Sch SR2 92 F7
Ryhope Rd Ryhope SR2 93 A8
Sunderland SR2 86 E3
Ryhope St
Houghton-le-Spring DH5 94 F8
Ryhope SR2 92 E7
5 Sunderland SR2 86 F2
Ryhope St S SR2 92 F7
Ryhope Village C of E Prim Sch SR2 92 F6
Ryton Com Inf Sch NE40 52 A5
Ryton Com Jun Sch NE40 52 A5
Ryton Comp Sch NE40 52 B5
Ryton Ct NE33 42 D1
Ryton Hall Dr NE40 52 C6
Ryton Ind Est NE21 52 F5
Ryton Sq SR2 86 E3
Ryton Terr
Shiremoor NE27 30 D1
Newcastle-upon-Tyne NE6 56 F4

S

Sackville Rd
Newcastle-upon-Tyne NE6 39 C1
Sunderland SR3 85 E3
Sacred Heart High Sch NE4 54 D7
Sacred Heart Lower Sch NE4 54 F6
Sacred Heart RC Mid Sch Sch NE4 54 E7
Sacred Heart RC Prim Sch NE4 54 D7
Sacriston Ave SR3 85 F3
Sacriston Gdns NE9 71 C2
Saddleback NE37 83 B7
Saffron Pl NE6 57 A5
Saga Ct NE6 39 F1
Sage Cl NE15 53 C8
St Acca's Ct NE46 44 F5
St Agnes RC Prim Sch NE40 51 E4
St Agnes' Gdns NE40 51 E4
St Agnes' Gdns N NE40 51 E4
St Agnes' Gdns W NE40 51 E4
St Agnes' Terr NE40 51 E4
St Aidan's Ave
Wallsend NE12 30 C1
Sunderland SR2 86 F2
St Aidan's Cl NE29 41 D8
St Aidan's Cres NE61 9 A6
St Aidan's Ct NE30 42 C7
St Aidan's RC Comp Sch SR2 86 C4
St Aidan's RC Fst Sch NE63 6 D1
St Aidan's Rd
Wallsend NE28 40 A1
South Shields NE33 42 D4
St Aidan's Sq NE12 30 C1
St Aidan's St NE8 101 A1
St Aidan's Terr DH4 90 E6
St Alban's Cl NE25 31 A5
St Alban's Cres
Gateshead NE10 71 C7
Newcastle-upon-Tyne NE6 39 D2
St Alban's Pl NE10 71 C7
St Alban's RC Prim Sch NE10 57 A1
St Alban's RC Sch NE6 56 F6
St Alban's St SR2 86 F3
St Alban's Terr NE8 101 C1
St Albans Cl NE63 7 A2
St Albans View NE27 30 F2
St Aldate's Ct SR4 85 A2
St Aloysius RC Jun Mix Sch NE31 57 E7
St Aloysius View NE31 57 D6
St Andrew's Ct NE7 39 C5
St Andrew's Dr NE9 70 E3
St Andrew's La NE42 49 D4
St Andrew's RC Fst Sch NE24 17 C7
St Andrew's Rd
Tanfield Lea DH9 79 F1
Hexham NE46 45 A4
St Andrew's St
Newcastle-upon-Tyne NE1 98 C1
Hebburn NE31 57 C7
St Andrew's Terr
Ashington NE63 6 E3
3 Sunderland SR6 75 E2
St Andrews DH4 94 B8
St Andrews Ave NE37 83 B8
St Andrews Cl NE25 31 D5
St Andrews Ct 4 NE29 41 F8
St Ann's Cl NE1 56 A5
St Ann's St NE1 99 C1
St Anne's Ct NE25 31 E3
St Anne's RC Prim Sch
Newcastle-upon-Tyne NE4 100 C4
Gateshead NE9 71 B2
Sunderland SR4 85 B5
St Anselm Cres NE29 41 C7
St Anselm Rd NE29 41 C7
St Anthony's CE Prim Sch NE6 56 F3
St Anthony's Ct NE6 56 F6
St Anthony's Ho NE6 56 F3
St Anthony's RC Girls Sch SR2 102 C1
St Anthony's Rd NE6 56 E4
St Anthony's Wlk NE6 56 F3
St Asaph Cl NE12 39 D4
St Augustine's RC Prim Sch NE10 72 A6
St Austell Cl NE5 37 C4
St Austell Gdns NE9 70 F2
St Barnabas DH4 89 D3
St Barnabas Way SR2 103 C1
St Bartholomew's CE Prim Sch NE12 39 D6
St Bartholomews Cl
Cresswell NE61 2 A7
Ashington NE63 6 F5
St Bede's NE36 74 D7
St Bede's Cl DH5 95 A4
St Bede's Dr NE8 101 C2
St Bede's Ho NE9 71 A7
St Bede's Inf Sch NE32 58 C7
St Bede's Pk SR2 103 A1
St Bede's Prim Sch NE37 72 D1
St Bede's RC Fst Sch NE22 15 E8
St Bede's RC Prim Sch
Newcastle-upon-Tyne NE15 54 A6
Jarrow NE32 58 C7
South Shields NE33 42 D2
St Bede's Terr SR2 103 A1
St Bedes Pl NE24 17 B4
St Bedes Rd NE24 17 B4
St Bedes Wlk NE27 30 C1
St Benedict's RC Mid Sch NE63 6 F3
St Benet Biscop RC High Sch NE22 15 E8
St Benet's RC Prim Sch DH2 81 F1
St Benets RC Prim Sch SR6 75 D2
St Bernadette's RC Prim Sch NE28 40 B5
St Buryan Cres NE5 37 C4
St Catherine's Ct SR5 74 D1
St Catherine's RC Prim Sch NE2 56 A8
St Catherines Gr NE2 56 A7
St Cecilia's Cl SR2 86 F4
St Chad's Cres SR3 91 B7
St Chad's Rd SR3 91 B7
St Chad's Villas 6 NE36 74 D7
St Charles' RC Prim Sch NE3 38 B6
St Christopher Way NE29 41 C2
St Christopher's Ho NE61 8 E8
St Christopher's Rd SR3 86 A2
St Christophers Cl NE63 6 F5
St Clements Ct
Newcastle-upon-Tyne NE3 37 F8
Ashington NE63 7 A2
St Columba's Ct SR5 75 C2
St Columba's RC Prim Sch NE28 40 A2
Saint Ct SR3 92 A5
St Cuthbert Ave DH3 88 D3
St Cuthbert's Ave NE34 60 A8
St Cuthbert's Cave (N.T.)* NE70 108 C5
St Cuthbert's Cl DH5 95 A4
St Cuthbert's Ct
Newcastle-upon-Tyne NE3 38 A5
Gateshead NE8 101 A2
St Cuthbert's Dr NE10 71 F7
St Cuthbert's Gn NE5 54 C7
St Cuthbert's High Sch NE15 54 B6
St Cuthbert's La NE46 45 A4
St Cuthbert's Pl NE8 101 A1
St Cuthbert's RC Prim Sch
North Shields NE29 42 A5
Newcastle-upon-Tyne NE5 37 D4
Sunderland SR4 85 D3
St Cuthbert's Rd
New Herrington DH4 90 F7
Newbottle DH4 90 D3
St Cuthbert's Rd *continued*
Sunniside NE16 80 B7
Wallsend, Holystone NE27 30 C1
Wallsend, Holy Cross NE28 40 E3
Newcastle-upon-Tyne, Benwell NE5 54 B7
Newcastle-upon-Tyne, Fenham NE5 54 C8
Gateshead NE8 101 A2
Gateshead, Windmill Hills NE8 101 B3
St Cuthbert's Terr
Hexham NE46 45 A4
Sunderland SR4 102 B3
St Cuthbert's Wlk DH3 88 C3
St Cuthberts CE Jun Sch NE8 100 C1
St Cuthberts Cl
Wallsend NE27 30 C1
Prudhoe NE42 50 C2
Hexham NE46 45 A4
St Cuthberts Ct NE24 17 F7
St Cuthberts Lower Sch NE15 54 C6
St Cuthberts Pk NE16 80 A8
St Cuthberts RC Prim Sch DH3 88 D2
St Cuthberts Way
Blaydon NE21 53 D3
Wallsend NE27 30 C1
St David's Cl NE26 31 F8
St David's Way
Whitley Bay NE26 31 F8
Hedworth NE32 58 C1
St Davids Cl NE63 6 F5
St Ebba's Way DH8 76 E3
St Edmund Campion RC Sch NE9 71 D4
St Edmund's Ct NE8 56 A1
St Edmund's Dr NE10 71 F7
St Edmund's Rd NE8 101 C1
St Etienne Ct 12 NE10 56 D1
St Gabriel's Ave
Newcastle-upon-Tyne NE6 39 B1
Sunderland SR4 85 F5
St George's Ave NE33, NE34 59 E8
St George's Cl NE2 38 E2
St George's Cres NE29 41 F5
St George's Est NE38 83 C1
St George's Hospl NE61 4 A2
St George's Pl NE15 53 E5
St George's RC Sch NE15 53 D5
St George's Rd
Newcastle-upon-Tyne NE15 53 E5
Tynemouth NE30 32 C3
Hexham NE46 45 A4
St George's Terr
Newcastle-upon-Tyne, Lemington NE15 53 E5
Newcastle-upon-Tyne, West Jesmond NE2 38 E2
East Boldon NE36 74 D7
Sunderland SR6 75 F2
St George's Way SR2 103 A1
St Georges Cres NE25 31 F4
St Georges Ct NE10 72 B7
St Godric's Dr DH4 94 A2
St Gregory's Ct NE34 59 F5
St Gregory's RC Jun Mix & Inf Sch NE34 60 A7
St Helen's Cres NE9 70 E5
St Helen's St NE45 46 F6
St Hilda Ind Est NE33 42 C2
St Hilda St NE33 42 C2
St Hilda's Ave NE28 40 E3
St Hilda's RC Prim Sch SR5 75 A2
St Hilda's Rd NE46 45 A4
St Ignatius Cl SR2 103 B1
St Ives Way NE5 37 C4
St James Bvld NE1,NE4 100 C4
St James Cl NE44 62 F7
St James Ct NE8 56 B1
St James Lodge 4 NE4 54 D5
St James RC Prim Sch NE31 57 F4
St James Rd NE8 56 A2
St James Sq NE8 56 A2
St James St NE3 38 E5
St James Sta NE1 98 C1
St James Terr
Riding Mill NE44 63 A7
4 Morpeth NE61 3 F1
St James' Cres NE15 54 D4
St James' Gdns 6 NE15 54 D5
St James' Mall NE31 57 D5
St James' Pk (Newcastle Utd F.C.) NE1 98 C2
St James' Rd NE15 54 D5
St James' St NE1 98 C2
St James' Terr NE29 41 D3
St John & St Patrick's Church Sch SR1 103 C3
St John Bosco RC Prim Sch SR5 74 A4
St John Boste RC Prim Sch NE38 83 A5
St John St NE1 99 A1
St John the Baptist's RC Prim Sch NE10 71 D8
St John Vianney RC Prim Sch NE5 36 D1
St John's Ave NE31 57 D5
St John's Cl NE26 31 F8
St John's Cres NE22 11 D3
St John's Ct
Backworth NE27 30 C5
St John's Ct *continued*
Newcastle-upon-Tyne NE4 54 E4
St John's Gn NE29 41 D3
St John's Mall NE31 57 D5
St John's Pl Birtley DH3 82 C4
Bedlington NE22 11 D3
Whitley Bay NE26 31 F8
St John's Rd
High Pittington DH6 96 B5
Bedlington NE22 11 D2
Newcastle-upon-Tyne NE4 54 E4
St John's St NE29 41 D3
St John's Terr
North Shields NE29 41 D3
Jarrow NE32 58 B7
East Boldon NE36 74 E7
3 Seaham SR7 92 E1
St John's W NE22 11 D3
St John's Wlk
North Shields NE29 41 D3
Hebburn NE31 57 E5
Newcastle-upon-Tyne NE4 54 E4
St Johns SR1 103 C4
St Johns Pl NE10 71 D8
St Johns Rd NE46 45 A3
St Johns Vale SR4 85 A4
St Joseph's Ct
7 Birtley DH3 82 C5
Hebburn NE31 57 D3
St Joseph's RC Comp Sch NE31 57 D2
St Joseph's RC Mid Sch NE46 44 F4
St Joseph's RC Prim Sch
Newcastle-upon-Tyne NE15 54 D4
Blaydon NE21 53 B3
Hedworth NE32 58 B1
Washington NE38 83 D6
Gateshead NE8 101 C2
Sunderland SR4 102 A3
St Joseph's RC Sch NE39 67 B2
St Joseph's Way NE32 58 C1
St Jude's Terr NE33 59 C8
St Julien Gdns
Wallsend NE28 41 B3
Newcastle-upon-Tyne NE7 39 D2
St Just Pl NE5 37 C4
St Keverne Sq NE5 37 C4
St Kitt's Cl NE26 31 F8
St Lawerence's RC Prim Sch NE6 56 C6
St Lawrence Cl DH6 96 C5
St Lawrence Rd
High Pittington DH6 96 B5
Newcastle-upon-Tyne NE6 56 C4
St Lawrence Sq NE6 56 B5
St Leonard St SR2 86 F4
St Leonard's La NE61 3 B2
St Leonard's RC Prim Sch SR3 92 B7
St Leonard's Wlk NE61 3 C2
St Lucia Cl
Whitley Bay NE26 31 E8
Sunderland SR2 103 B1
St Luke's Rd
North Shields NE29 41 D3
Sunderland SR4 85 D7
St Luke's Terr SR4 85 F7
St Lukes Cl NE63 7 A5
St Lukes Ct NE31 57 D4
St Lukes Rd NE46 45 A4
St Margaret's Ave SR5 74 A1
St Margaret's Dr DH9 79 D4
St Margaret's Rd NE15 54 A4
St Margargets Ave NE12 39 D6
St Mark's Cl 11 NE6 56 C7
St Mark's Cres SR4 102 B2
St Mark's Ct NE29 41 D2
St Mark's RC Prim Sch NE5 36 F4
St Mark's Rd SR4 102 B2
St Mark's Rd N SR4 102 A2
St Mark's St
13 Newcastle-upon-Tyne NE6 56 C7
Morpeth NE61 3 E1
Sunderland SR4 102 B2
St Mark's Terr SR4 102 B2
St Mark's Way NE33 42 C1
St Marks Ct NE27 30 E3
St Marks Rd NE46 45 A3
St Martin's Cl NE26 31 E7
St Martin's Ct NE26 31 E7
St Mary & St Thomas Aquinas RC Prim Sch NE21 53 A4
St Mary Magdalene Hospl NE2 98 B4
St Mary RC Prim Sch NE32 58 D3
St Mary's Ave
Whitley Bay NE26 31 F7
South Shields NE34 59 F6
St Mary's Chare NE46 45 B4
St Mary's Church (Mus)* NE63 7 C6
St Mary's Coll NE4 54 E7
St Mary's College Flats NE4 54 E7
St Mary's Ct
South Shields NE33 59 B7
Gateshead NE8 101 C2
St Mary's Dr
West Rainton DH4 94 A2
Blyth NE24 17 B6
St Mary's Field NE61 8 F7
St Mary's Gn 4 NE16 69 B7
St Mary's Infs Sch NE8 101 B3
St Mary's Lodge NE26 31 F5
St Mary's or Bait Island* NE26 24 G2
St Mary's Pl
Newcastle-upon-Tyne NE1 99 A2
Walbottle NE15 35 E2
St Mary's Pl E NE1 99 A2
St Mary's RC Cath NE1 100 C4
St Mary's RC Comp Sch NE7 39 A5
St Mary's RC Fst Sch NE46 45 A4
St Mary's RC Prim Sch
Tynemouth NE30 32 A2
Sunderland SR2 86 B4
St Mary's St NE1 99 C1
St Mary's Terr
South Shields NE33 59 B7
East Boldon NE36 74 E7
Ryton NE40 52 B5
St Mary's Training & Enterprise Ctr NE4 98 B1
St Mary's Way SR1 103 A3
St Mary's Wynd
Seaton Sluice NE26 24 E4
Hexham NE46 45 B4
St Marys CE Jun Mix & Inf Sch NE33 59 B7
St Marys Cl DH2 88 B1
St Marys Dr NE63 6 F5
St Marys RC Prim Sch NE16 69 C7
St Mathews La NE42 50 D2
St Matthew's RC Fst Sch NE42 50 C2
St Matthew's RC Prim Sch NE32 58 B2
St Matthew's Terr DH4 90 D4
St Matthews Rd NE46 44 F3
St Matthews View SR3 92 A7
St Michael's Ave
New Hartley NE25 23 D6
South Shields NE33 42 E1
St Michael's Ave N NE33 42 D1
St Michael's Mount 3 NE6 56 C5
St Michael's RC Jun Sch NE4 54 F4
St Michael's RC Prim Sch DH5 94 E7
St Michael's Rd NE6 56 B5
St Michael's Way NE11 54 C1
St Michaels DH4 94 B8
St Michaels RC Inf Sch NE4 100 A3
St Michaels Way SR1 102 C2
St Michaels Workshops 10 NE6 56 B5
St Nicholas Cath NE1 99 B1
St Nicholas Ave
Newcastle-upon-Tyne, Gosforth NE3 38 C4
Newcastle-upon-Tyne, South Gosforth NE3 38 D4
Sunderland SR3 86 B3
St Nicholas Cl NE63 6 F5
St Nicholas Hospl NE3 38 A5
St Nicholas Rd
West Boldon NE36 74 A7
Hexham NE46 45 A4
St Nicholas View NE36 74 A7
St Nicholas' Church Yd NE1 99 A1
St Nicholas' Sq NE1 99 A1
St Nicholas' St NE1 101 A4
St Omers Rd NE11 54 F2
St Oswald Ave's NE6 56 E6
St Oswald's Gn NE6 56 E7
St Oswald's RC Prim Sch
Newcastle-upon-Tyne NE3 38 D7
Whiteleas NE34 59 D3
Gateshead NE9 71 C3
St Oswald's Rd
Wallsend NE28 40 E4
Hebburn NE31 57 F7
3 Hexham NE46 45 A4
St Oswald's Terr 8 DH4 90 B6
St Oswalds C of E Prim Sch NE31 57 F7
St Oswin's Ave NE30 32 C3
St Oswin's Pl NE30 42 D7
St Oswin's St NE33 59 D7
St Patrick's Cl NE10 71 D8
St Patrick's RC Prim Sch SR2 92 F6
St Patrick's Wlk NE10 71 D8
St Paul's CE Prim Sch NE4 100 B4
St Paul's Gdns NE25 32 A4
St Paul's Pl NE4 98 A1
St Paul's RC Fst Sch NE23 22 B5
St Paul's Rd NE32 58 C7
St Paul's Terr 5 SR2 92 F6
St Pauls Cl NE63 6 F5
St Pauls Ct NE8 100 C1
St Pauls Dr DH4 89 E8
St Pauls Rd NE46 44 F4
St Peter's Ave NE34 59 E7
St Peter's Ct NE6 56 C5
St Peter's Quayside E NE6 56 D4
St Peter's Quayside W 9 NE6 56 C4
St Peter's RC Mid Sch NE23 22 B4
St Peter's RC Prim Sch NE9 71 A6

St Peter's Rd
Wallsend NE28 40 D3
Newcastle-upon-Tyne NE6 56 C5
St Peter's View SR6 103 A4
St Peter's Wharf NE6 56 C4
St Peters Spec Sch NE3 38 F4
St Peters Sta SR5 103 A4
St Peters' Way SR6 103 B4
St Philip Neri RC Prim Sch NE11 70 A8
St Philips Cl NE4 98 B1
St Philips Way NE4 98 B1
St Robert of Newminster RC Sch NE38 83 D2
St Robert's of Newminster RC Fst Sch NE61 8 E8
St Rollox St NE31 57 D5
St Ronan's Dr NE26 24 B7
St Ronan's Rd NE25 31 F4
St Ronans View NE9 71 A2
St Simon St NE34 59 A4
St Stephen's Cl NE25 23 B3
St Stephen's RC Prim Sch NE12 39 B7
St Stephen's Way NE29 41 D3
St Stevens Cl DH4 89 E8
St Teresa's RC Sch NE6 56 B8
St Thomas Cl NE42 50 D2
St Thomas Mews NE42 50 D2
St Thomas More RC High Sch NE29 41 D7
St Thomas More RC Sch NE21 53 B3
St Thomas St 6 NE9 71 A5
St Thomas' Cres NE1 99 A2
St Thomas' Sq NE1 99 A2
St Thomas' St
Newcastle-upon-Tyne NE1 99 A2
Sunderland SR1 103 A3
St Thomas' Street Bsns Ctr NE1 99 A2
St Thomas' Terr NE1 99 A2
St Vincent Ct NE8 56 A1
St Vincent St
South Shields NE33 42 E1
Gateshead NE8 56 A1
Sunderland SR2 103 B1
St Vincent's Pl NE26 31 F8
St Vincent's RC Sch NE6 56 E4
St Vincent's Way 1 NE26 31 F8
St Vincents Cl NE15 53 E8
St Vincents Ho NE30 42 D7
St Wilfred's RC Mid Sch NE24 17 D7
St Wilfred's Rd NE45 47 A6
St Wilfrid's Ct 6 NE46 45 A4
St Wilfrid's Rd NE46 45 A4
St Wilfrid's RC Prim Sch NE10 56 B2
Saint Wilfrid's RC Comp Sch NE34 59 D6
Saints Peter & Paul RC Prim Sch NE33 59 B6
Saker Pl 1 NE28 40 B1
Salcombe Ave NE32 58 D6
Salcombe Gdns NE9 70 F2
Salem Hill SR2 103 B1
Salem Rd SR2 103 B1
Salem St Jarrow NE32 58 C7
South Shields NE33 42 C3
Sunderland SR2 103 B1
Salem St S SR2 103 B1
Salem Terr SR2 103 B1
Salisbury Ave
10 Chester le Street DH3 88 C2
Tynemouth NE29 42 A7
Salisbury Cl
Cramlington NE23 21 E6
9 Ashington NE63 6 F2
Salisbury Gdns NE2 56 A8
Salisbury Ho NE6 56 A6
Salisbury Pl NE33 42 E3
Salisbury St
Gateshead NE10 57 A1
Blyth NE24 17 D8
South Shields NE33 42 D2
Morpeth NE61 9 B8
Sunderland SR1 103 B2
Sunderland, South Hylton SR4 85 A7
Salisbury Way NE32 58 B1
Salkeld Gdns NE9 71 A8
Salkeld Rd NE9 71 A6
Sally Davison Ct 4 NE63 6 F2
Sallyport Cres NE1 99 B1
Sallyport Ho NE1 99 B1
Salmon St NE33 42 D4
Saltburn Cl DH4 90 C1
Saltburn Gdns NE28 41 B3
Saltburn Rd SR3 85 E3
Saltburn Sq SR3 85 E3
Salter La SR3 91 B8
Salter's La
Houghton-le-Spring DH5 91 E1
Seaton DH5,SR7 95 F6
Haswell DH6 97 E6
Hetton le Hole SR7 95 F6
Salterfen La SR2 93 A8
Salterfen Rd SR2 93 A8
Salters Cl NE3 38 E6
Salters Ct NE3 38 E6
Salters' La NE3,NE12 38 F7
Salters' Rd NE3 38 B4
Saltford NE9 71 A2
Saltmeadows Rd NE10, NE8 56 B4
Saltwell Park Mansion Mus★ NE9 70 E6
Saltwell Pl NE8 70 D8
Saltwell Rd NE8 70 D7
Saltwell Rd S NE9 70 E4
Saltwell St NE8 70 D8
Saltwell View NE8 70 E7
Sam's Ct NE23 28 F8
Samson Cl NE12 29 C2
Sancroft Dr DH5 94 E7
Sand Point Rd SR6 75 F1
Sandalwood NE34 59 E3
Sandalwood Sq SR4 85 B2
Sanderling Cl NE40 52 D4
Sanderlings 3 NE28 40 B1
Sanders Gdns 3 DH3 82 C5
Sanders' Memorial Homes DH2 88 C3
Sanderson Rd
Newcastle-upon-Tyne NE2 38 E2
Whitley Bay NE26 31 F5
Sanderson St NE4 54 F3
Sandfield Rd
Cambois NE22 12 B4
Tynemouth NE30 32 B3
Sandford Ave NE23 16 B1
Sandford Mews NE13 28 A5
Sandgate NE1 99 C1
Sandgrove SR6 60 A1
Sandhill NE1 101 B4
Sandhill View Comp Sch SR3 85 D2
Sandholm Cl NE28 40 F5
Sandhurst Ave NE30 32 C2
Sandiacres NE32 58 C1
Sandison Ct NE13 27 F6
Sandmartin Cl NE63 11 E8
Sandmere Pl NE15 54 A5
Sandmere Rd SR2 86 D1
Sandoe Gdns NE15 54 B5
Sandon Cl NE27 30 C5
Sandown NE25 31 D5
Sandown Cl NE25 23 D2
Sandown Ct NE28 41 A4
Sandown Gdns
Wallsend NE28 40 F4
Gateshead NE8 70 D8
New Silksworth SR3 91 F8
Sandpiper Cl Blyth NE24 17 F4
Washington NE38 82 F2
Ryton NE40 52 D4
Sandpiper Ct NE30 42 D8
Sandpiper Pl NE12 39 A7
Sandpiper Way NE63 6 D1
Sandray Cl DH3 82 D1
Sandridge NE64 7 F5
Sandringham Ave NE12 39 D6
Sandringham Cl NE25 31 B4
Sandringham Cres SR3 91 C6
Sandringham Ct
3 Longbenton NE12 39 A6
6 Gateshead NE10 71 C8
Sandringham Dr
Whickham NE16 69 A7
Blyth NE24 17 D3
Whitley Bay NE25 31 C4
Sandringham Gdns NE29 42 A7
Sandringham Mews 8 NE28 40 F4
Sandringham Rd
Newcastle-upon-Tyne, South Gosforth NE3 38 E4
Newcastle-upon-Tyne, West Denton NE5 53 E8
Sunderland SR6 75 D2
Sandringham Terr SR6 75 E2
Sandringham Way NE20 25 C4
Sands Ind Est The NE16 54 A1
Sands Rd NE16 54 A1
Sandsay Cl SR2 92 D8
Sandstone Cl NE34 58 F3
Sandwell Dr DH4 89 F8
Sandwich Rd NE29 31 F1
Sandwich St NE6 56 F3
Sandy Bank NE44 62 F7
Sandy Chare SR6 75 E8
Sandy Cres NE6 56 E4
Sandy La
Brunswick Village NE13 27 E6
Wide Open NE3,NE12 28 F4
Riding Mill NE44 62 E8
Ashington NE63 7 B2
Gateshead NE9 71 D1
Sandy Lane Ind Area NE3 28 E4
Sandyford Ave NE42 50 F3
Sandyford Pk NE2 99 C4
Sandyford Rd NE2 99 B3
Sandygate Mews NE16 69 B1
Sandypath La NE16 79 A7
Sandysykes NE42 50 B2
Sans St SR1 103 B3
Sans St S SR1 103 B2
Sarabel Ave NE62 10 E7
Sargent Ave NE34 59 D2
Satley Gdns
Gateshead NE9 71 C2
Sunderland SR3 86 B2
Saunton Ct DH4 90 C3
Saville Lodge 5 NE33 42 D3
Saville Pl SR1 103 B2
Saville Row NE1 99 A2
Saville St
North Shields NE30 42 B5
4 South Shields NE33 42 D3
Saville St W NE29 42 A5
Savory Rd NE28 40 F3
Sawmill Cotts DH9 78 E1
Saxilby Dr NE3 38 D8
Saxon Cl SR6 59 E1
Saxon Cres SR3 85 F3
Saxon Dr NE30 32 C1
Saxon Way NE32 58 C7
Saxondale Rd NE3 37 E5
Saxton Gr NE7 39 A4
Scafell DH3 82 D1
Scafell Ct 22 SR3 91 F6
Scafell Dr NE5 37 D3
Scafell Gdns NE11 70 A6
Scalby Cl NE3 38 D8
Scales Cres NE42 50 F2
Scarborough Ct
Cramlington NE23 22 B5
Newcastle-upon-Tyne NE6 56 D6
Scarborough Par NE31 58 A2
Scarborough Rd
Newcastle-upon-Tyne NE6 56 D6
New Silksworth SR3 91 F8
Sceptre Ct NE4 100 A4
Sceptre Pl NE4 98 A1
Sceptre St NE4 98 A1
Schalksmuhle Rd NE22 10 F1
Schimel St SR5 75 B2
School App NE34 60 A6
School Ave Dunston NE11 69 F8
Guide Post NE62 10 F7
School Cl NE9 71 D6
School Houses NE39 78 B8
School La Whickham NE16 69 C7
High Spen NE39 67 A3
School Loaning NE34 59 B5
School Rd
East Rainton DH5 94 C4
Bedlington NE22 11 D3
School Row NE43 64 F3
School St Whickham NE16 69 A7
Hebburn NE31 57 F7
School Terr DH4 89 E1
School View DH5 97 D8
Schoolhouse La NE16 79 E7
Scorer St NE29 41 F5
Scorer's La DH3 89 B1
Scot Terr NE17 66 B1
Scotby Gdns NE9 71 B3
Scotland Ct NE21 53 A1
Scotland Head NE21 68 A8
Scotland St SR2 93 A6
Scotswood Rd NE15,NE4 54 B4
Scotswood View NE11 54 C2
Scott Ave NE23 21 F8
Scott Cl NE46 44 F2
Scott St NE23 16 B3
Scott's Ave 12 NE40 51 F3
Scott's Ct NE10 72 B6
Scott's Terr DH5 95 A4
Scoular Dr NE63 7 A3
Scrogg Rd NE6 56 F6
Scruton Ave SR3 85 F3
Sea Banks NE30 42 E8
Sea Crest Rd NE64 7 E6
Sea La SR6 75 E4
Sea Rd South Shields NE33 42 E4
Sunderland SR6 75 E4
Sea View Lynmouth NE61 2 B3
Ashington NE63 12 A8
Ryhope SR2 93 A6
Sea View Gdns SR6 75 E3
Sea View La NE64 7 E5
Sea View Pk
Cramlington NE23 22 D6
Whitburn SR6 75 D8
Sea View Rd SR2 86 E3
Sea View Rd W SR2 86 D2
Sea View St SR2 86 F2
Sea View Villas NE23 22 D6
Sea Way NE33 42 E3
Seaburn Ave NE25 23 D6
Seaburn Cl SR6 75 E4
Seaburn Dene Prim Sch SR6 75 D5
Seaburn Dr 1 DH4 94 C8
Seaburn Gdns
Gateshead NE9 71 D3
Sunderland SR6 75 E4
Seaburn Gr NE26 24 C6
Seaburn Hill SR6 75 E4
Seaburn Sta SR5 75 C4
Seaburn Terr SR6 75 F4
Seaburn View NE25 23 D6
Seacombe Ave NE30 32 C3
Seacrest Appartments NE30 32 C1
Seacrest Ave NE30 32 C2
Seafield Rd NE24 17 E5
Seafield Terr NE33 42 E3
Seafield View NE30 42 D8
Seafields SR6 75 E5
Seaforth Rd SR3 86 A3
Seaforth St NE24 17 E8
Seaham Cl NE34 60 B6
Seaham Gdns NE9 71 C2
Seaham Grange Ind Est SR7 92 E2
Seaham Rd
Houghton-le-Spring DH5 95 A8
Ryhope SR2 93 A6
Seaham Sch SR7 93 A1
Seaham St SR3 92 A7
Seascale Pl NE9 71 B4
Seatoller Ct 3 SR3 91 F6
Seaton Ave
Houghton-le-Spring DH5 95 A7
Annitsford NE23 22 B1
Blyth NE24 17 C4
Newbiggin-by-the-Sea NE64 7 D4
Seaton Burn Com Coll NE13 28 C8
Seaton Cl NE10 72 B6
Seaton Cres Holywell NE25 23 F2
Seaton Cres *continued*
Whitley Bay NE25 31 E5
Seaham SR7 92 E1
Seaton Croft NE23 29 C8
Seaton Delaval Fst Sch NE25 23 B4
Seaton Delaval Hall★ NE26 24 A6
Seaton Gdns NE9 71 C3
Seaton La SR7 92 E1
Seaton Pl
Brunswick Village NE13 28 A6
Newcastle-upon-Tyne NE6 56 E3
Seaton Rd Shiremoor NE27 31 A4
Sunderland SR3 85 D3
Seaton Sluice Fst Sch NE26 24 D5
Seaton Sluice Mid Sch NE26 24 B7
Seaton Terr NE22 11 B1
Seatonville Cres NE25 31 E3
Seatonville Gr NE25 31 E3
Seatonville Rd NE25 31 E3
Second Ave
Chester le Street DH2 88 B2
Chester le Street DH2 88 B8
Dunston NE11 70 B6
Blyth NE24 17 D6
North Shields NE29 41 B4
Newcastle-upon-Tyne NE6 56 C7
Morpeth NE61 9 B7
Ashington NE63 6 D4
Second Row Ellington NE61 1 E4
Linton NE61 1 A3
Second St NE8 101 A1
Secretan Way NE33 42 C2
Sedbergh Rd NE30 32 B2
Sedgeletch Ind Est DH4 90 A2
Sedgeletch Rd DH4 90 A2
Sedgemoor NE12 29 D4
Sedgemoor Ave NE15 54 A4
Sedgewick Pl NE8 101 B1
Sedley Rd NE28 40 B1
Sedling Rd NE38 83 B2
Sefton Ave NE6 39 C1
Sefton Ct NE23 16 C1
Sefton Sq SR3 85 E3
Segedunum Way NE28 40 B1
Seghill Fst Sch NE23 22 F1
Seine Ct NE32 58 C6
Selborne Gdns NE2 56 A8
Selbourne Cl NE23 21 E6
Selbourne St
2 South Shields NE33 42 D2
Sunderland SR6 75 E1
Selbourne Terr NE24 12 D3
Selby Cl NE23 16 B1
Selby Ct 2 NE32 58 B7
Selby Gdns Wallsend NE28 40 B3
Newcastle-upon-Tyne NE6 56 F8
Selby Sq SR3 85 E3
Selby's Grave NE21 67 F8
Sele Ct 9 NE46 45 A4
Sele Fst Sch The NE46 45 A5
Selina Pl SR6 75 E1
Selkirk Cres DH3 82 C6
Selkirk Gr NE23 16 C1
Selkirk Sq SR3 85 D3
Selkirk St NE32 58 E3
Selkirk Way NE29 41 C8
Selsdon Ave SR4 85 A2
Selsey Ct NE10 71 E6
Selwood Ct NE34 59 F5
Selwyn Ave NE25 31 D3
Selwyn Cl NE5 37 D4
Senet Enterprise Workshop NE63 6 D2
Serin Ho NE5 37 A3
Serlby Cl NE37 72 C1
Seton Ave NE34 58 F4
Seton Wlk NE34 58 F4
Setting Stones NE38 89 A8
Settlingstone Cl NE7 39 E3
Sevenoaks Dr SR4 85 A2
Seventh Ave
Chester le Street DH2 88 B4
Gateshead NE11 70 D4
Blyth NE24 17 D6
Newcastle-upon-Tyne NE6 56 C7
Morpeth NE61 9 B7
Ashington NE63 6 E2
Seventh Row NE63 6 B4
Severn Ave NE31 57 E3
Severn Ct 8 SR3 91 F6
Severn Dr NE32 58 C2
Severn Gdns NE8 71 B8
Severn Hos NH37 84 A8
Severn St NE17 66 C1
Severs Terr NE5 36 B6
Severus Rd NE4 54 E7
Sewingshields Wall Turrets & Milecastle★ NE47 127 E5
Sextant Ho 6 NE24 17 F8
Seymour Ct
Dunston NE11 100 A1
Ashington NE63 7 B3
Seymour Sq SR3 85 E3
Seymour St
Dunston NE11 100 A1
North Shields NE29 42 A4
Seymour Terr
Hetton le Hole DH5 95 B1
Ryton NE40 52 A5
Shadfen Cres NE61 4 E3
Shadfen Park Rd NE30 32 A3
Shadon Way DH3 82 E3
Shaftesbury Ave
Whitley Bay NE26 31 F6
Shaftesbury Ave *continued*
Jarrow NE32 58 E5
Ryhope SR2 92 E7
Shaftesbury Cres
Tynemouth NE30 32 A3
Sunderland SR3 85 F3
Shaftesbury Gr NE6 56 B7
Shaftesbury Wlk NE8 101 A2
Shafto Ct NE15 54 B5
Shafto St
Newcastle-upon-Tyne NE15 54 A5
Wallsend NE28 40 E3
Shaftoe Cl NE40 51 F3
Shaftoe Cres NE46 45 A5
Shaftoe Ct
Killingworth NE12 29 D3
Newcastle-upon-Tyne NE3 38 A7
Shaftoe Leazes NE46 44 F4
Shaftoe Rd SR3 85 D2
Shaftoe Sq SR3 85 D2
Shaftoe Way NE13 27 B7
Shakespeare Ave NE31 57 E6
Shakespeare St
Houghton-le-Spring DH5 94 E7
Newcastle-upon-Tyne NE1 99 A1
Wallsend NE28 40 F3
Jarrow NE32 58 B8
18 South Shields NE33 42 D1
Sunderland SR5 75 B2
Shakespeare Terr SR2 102 C1
Shalcombe Cl SR3 92 A6
Shallcross SR2 86 B4
Shallon Ct NE63 6 C2
Shalstone NE37 72 F1
Shamrock Cl NE15 53 C8
Shandon Way NE3 37 E5
Shanklea Fst Sch NE23 22 B7
Shanklin Pl NE23 21 E6
Shannon Cl SR5 74 A1
Shannon Ct NE3 37 C7
Shap Cl NE38 83 D3
Shap Ct 2 SR3 91 F6
Shap La NE5 37 A1
Shap Rd NE30 32 A2
Sharnford Cl NE27 30 D5
Sharon Cl NE12 29 B2
Sharpendon St NE31 57 E7
Sharpley Dr SR7 92 E1
Shaw Ave NE34 59 B4
Shaw Gdns NE10 72 B8
Shaw La DH8,NE17 76 F4
Shawbrow Cl NE7 39 E3
Shawdon Cl NE5 37 B4
Shaws La Hexham NE46 44 D4
Hexham NE46 44 D5
Shaws Pk NE46 44 E6
Shearlegs Rd NE8 56 A3
Shearwater SR6 60 F3
Shearwater Ave NE12 39 A7
Shearwater Cl NE5 37 B4
Shearwater Way NE24 17 F4
Sheelin Ave DH2 88 C1
Sheen Cl DH4 94 A2
Sheen Ct NE3 37 B5
Sheep Hill NE16 79 B6
Sheepfolds N SR5 103 A4
Sheepfolds Rd SR5 103 A4
Sheepfolds S SR5 103 A4
Sheepwash Ave NE62 10 E7
Sheepwash Bank NE62 10 E7
Sheepwash Rd NE61 5 E3
Sheldon Ct NE12 29 C1
Sheldon Gr
Cramlington NE23 16 B1
Newcastle-upon-Tyne NE3 38 A3
Sheldon Rd NE34 42 F1
Sheldon St NE32 58 B7
Shelford Gdns NE15 53 E7
Shellbark DH4 89 F6
Shelley Ave
Easington Lane DH5 97 D8
South Shields NE34 60 B5
West Boldon NE35 74 A8
Springwell NE9 71 F1
Shelley Cres NE24 17 C5
Shelley Dr NE8 56 A2
Shelley Rd NE15 53 A7
Shepherd St SR4 102 A3
Shepherd Way NE38 83 F2
Shepherd's Quay NE29 42 B4
Shepherds Way NE36 74 A7
Sheppard Terr 1 SR5 74 B1
Sheppey Ct SR3 92 A6
Shepton Cotts NE16 69 C3
Sheraton NE10 72 A5
Sheraton St NE2 98 B4
Sherborne Ave NE29 41 D8
Sherburn Gn NE39 67 F3
Sherburn Gr DH4 90 C1
Sherburn Grange N NE32 58 A5
Sherburn Grange S NE32 58 A5
Sherburn Hill Prim Sch DH6 96 D1
Sherburn Park Dr NE39 67 F3
Sherburn Terr
Hamsterley NE17 76 F5
Gateshead NE9 71 C2
Sherburn Village Prim Sch DH6 96 A2
Sherburn Way NE10 72 C7
Sherfield Dr NE7 39 D2
Sheridan Gn NE38 83 A1
Sheridan Rd NE34 59 A3
Sheridan St 5 SR4 85 F7
Sheriff's Highway NE9 71 A6

Sheriff's Moor Ave DH5 97 C8
Sheriffs Cl NE10 71 B8
Sheringham Ave NE29 41 D7
Sheringham Cl SR3 92 A4
Sheringham Dr NE23 21 E6
Sheringham Gdns NE15 35 B2
Sherringham Ave NE3 37 E4
Sherwood NE27 31 B2
Sherwood Cl
Tynemouth NE27 31 B2
Washington NE38 83 D5
Sherwood Ct 5 SR3 92 A6
Sherwood Pl NE3 28 C2
Sherwood View NE28 40 A4
Shetland Ct 1 SR3 92 A6
Shibdon Bank NE21 53 D2
Shibdon Bsns Pk NE21 53 E3
Shibdon Cres NE21 53 D2
Shibdon Ct NE21 53 C3
Shibdon Park View NE21 53 D2
Shibdon Pond Nature Reserve★ NE21 53 E2
Shibdon Rd Blaydon NE21 53 D3
Blaydon NE21 53 E2
Shibdon Way NE21 53 F2
Shiel Gdns NE23 21 E6
Shield Ave NE16 54 B1
Shield Ct
Newcastle-upon-Tyne NE2 99 C3
Hexham NE46 45 B3
Shield Gr NE3 38 D6
Shield Rd SR6 75 C5
Shield St NE2 99 C2
Shieldclose 2 NE37 83 A6
Shieldfield Gn NE2 99 C2
Shieldfield Ho NE2 99 C2
Shieldfield La NE2 99 C2
Shields Rd
Chester le Street DH3 88 D5
Gateshead NE10 71 F8
Nedderton NE22 15 C5
Whitley Bay NE25 31 F3
Cleadon NE34 60 A3
Cleadon NE34,SR6 60 A2
Newcastle-upon-Tyne NE6 56 C7
Morpeth NE61 9 B7
Sunderland SR5,SR6 75 B5
Shields Rd W 5 NE6 56 A6
Shillaw Pl NE23 29 B5
Shilmore Rd NE3 37 F5
Shilton Cl NE34 60 B5
Shincliffe Ave SR5 74 C2
Shincliffe Gdns NE9 71 D3
Shiney Row Prim Sch DH4 90 B5
Shipcote La NE8 70 F8
Shipcote Terr NE8 70 F8
Shipley Art Gallery★ NE8 70 F8
Shipley Ave
Newcastle-upon-Tyne NE4 54 E6
Sunderland SR6 75 E4
Shipley Ct NE8 101 C1
Shipley Pl 18 NE6 56 B6
Shipley Rd NE30 42 C7
Shipley Rise 8 NE6 56 C6
Shipley St NE15 53 C6
Shipley Wlk 23 NE6 56 B6
Shipton Cl NE35 58 E1
Shire Farm Gr NE63 6 A2
Shiremoor Mid Sch NE27 30 F4
Shiremoor Prim Sch NE27 30 E3
Shiremoor Sta NE27 30 F4
Shirlaw Cl
Newcastle-upon-Tyne NE5 36 F4
Newcastle-upon-Tyne NE5 37 A4
Shirley Gdns SR3 86 B3
Shirwood Ave NE16 69 A5
Shop Row DH4 90 C5
Shop Spouts NE21 53 C3
Shopping Ctr The 4 NE5 36 C2
Shore St SR6 75 D1
Shoreham Ct NE3 37 C7
Shoreham Sq SR3 85 E3
Shorestone Ave NE30 32 B3
Short Row NE5 36 B6
Shortridge St 1 NE33 42 D3
Shortridge Terr NE2 38 F1
Shot Factory La NE4 100 C3
Shotley Ave SR5 75 B3
Shotley Ct NE63 6 B2
Shotley Gdns NE9 71 A7
Shotton Ave NE24 17 E6
Shotton La
Cramlington NE23 15 C2
Shotton NE61,NE13 20 F8
Shotton St NE23 16 B3
Shotton Way NE10 72 E6
Shrewsbury Cl NE12 39 D4
Shrewsbury Cres SR3 85 F3
Shrewsbury Dr NE27 30 C5
Shrewsbury St NE11 69 F8
Shrewsbury Terr NE33 59 C7
Shrigley Gdns NE3 37 F5
Shunner Cl NE37 83 A6
Sibthorpe St NE29 42 B5
Side NE1 101 B4
Side Cliff Rd SR6 75 E3
Sidlaw Ave
Chester le Street DH2 88 A2
Tynemouth NE29 31 F1
Sidlaw Ct NE63 6 E1
Sidmouth Cl DH4 90 C4
Sidmouth Rd
North Shields NE29 41 C5
Gateshead NE9 70 F3
Sidney Gr
Newcastle-upon-Tyne NE4 98 A2
Gateshead NE8 101 A1
Sidney St Blyth NE24 17 D7
North Shields NE29 42 A5
West Boldon NE35 73 F8
Siemens Way NE28 41 A7
Silkey's La NE29 41 F5
Silkstun Ct 8 SR3 92 A7
Silksworth Cl SR3 91 F8
Silksworth Gdns NE9 71 C2
Silksworth Hall Dr SR3 91 F6
Silksworth La
New Silksworth SR3 91 F7
Sunderland SR3 86 A2
Silksworth Rd
New Silksworth SR3 92 A7
Sunderland SR3 91 C6
Silksworth Row SR1 102 C3
Silksworth Terr SR3 92 A7
Silkwood Cl NE23 16 B1
Silkworth La 1 SR3 92 A8
Silkworth Way SR3 91 E6
Silloth Ave NE5 54 A8
Silloth Dr NE37 72 C2
Silloth Pl NE30 32 B2
Silloth Rd SR3 85 D2
Silvas Ct NE61 4 A1
Silver Ct 3 NE9 71 A8
Silver Fox Way
Earsdon NE27 31 A1
Wallsend NE27 40 F8
Silver Lonnen NE5 54 B8
Silver St Tynemouth NE30 42 D7
Sunderland SR1 103 C3
Silverbirch Ind Est NE12 29 B4
Silverdale SR3 92 A4
Silverdale Ave NE10 72 D8
Silverdale Dr NE21 68 A8
Silverdale Rd NE23 16 B1
Silverdale Terr NE8 70 F8
Silverdale Way
Whickham NE16 68 F4
Brockley Whins NE34 58 F3
Silverhill Dr NE5 54 B7
Silverhill Sch The NE5 54 C7
Silverlink N The
Shiremoor NE27 30 E1
Wallsend NE27 40 F8
Silverlink The NE28 41 A6
Silvermere Dr NE40 52 D4
Silverstone NE12 29 E3
Silverstone Rd NE37 83 E8
Silvertop Gdns NE40 52 A1
Silvertop Terr NE40 66 F8
Silverwood Gdns NE11 70 B5
Simon Pl NE13 28 A5
Simonburn NE38 82 F4
Simonburn Ave
North Shields NE29 41 C6
Newcastle-upon-Tyne NE4 54 E8
Simonburn La 3 NE63 6 F2
Simonside
Seaton Sluice NE26 24 D4
Prudhoe NE42 50 B1
Simonside Ave
Wallsend NE28 40 F4
Stakeford NE62 11 B8
Simonside Cl
Seaton Sluice NE26 24 D4
Morpeth NE61 8 D7
Simonside Fst Sch NE5 36 F5
Simonside Hall NE34 58 F5
Simonside Ind Est NE32 58 E5
Simonside Jun Mix & Inf Sch NE32 58 D4
Simonside Pl NE9 71 D3
Simonside Rd
Blaydon NE21 53 C1
Sunderland SR3 85 D3
Simonside Terr
Newcastle-upon-Tyne NE6 56 C8
Newbiggin-by-the-Sea NE64 7 E4
Simonside View
Ponteland NE20 25 D7
Jarrow NE32 58 C4
Simonside Way NE12 29 F4
Simpson Cl NE35 73 E8
Simpson Ct NE63 7 A3
Simpson St Blyth NE24 17 E8
North Shields NE29 41 E5
Tynemouth NE30 32 C4
Sunderland SR4 102 B4
Simpson Terr
Newcastle-upon-Tyne, Shieldfield NE1,NE2 99 B2
Newcastle-upon-Tyne, Lemington NE15 36 B1
Simpsons Memorial Homes NE40 52 A4
Sinclair Dr DH3 88 D8
Sinclair Gdns NE25 23 D3
Sinderby Cl NE3 38 D8
Sir Charles Parsons Sch NE6 56 F7
Sir GB Hunter Memorial Hospl NE28 40 C2
Sir Godfrey Thomson Ct NE10 71 C8
Sixth Ave
Chester le Street DH2 88 B3
Gateshead NE11 70 C4
Blyth NE24 17 D6
Newcastle-upon-Tyne NE6 56 C7
Morpeth NE61 9 B7
Sixth Ave *continued*
Ashington NE63 6 E2
Skaylock Dr NE38 83 A3
Skegness Par NE31 58 A2
Skelder Ave NE12 39 B6
Skelton Ct NE3 37 E8
Ski View SR3 91 F8
Skiddaw Dr SR6 75 C5
Skiddaw Pl NE9 71 B4
Skinnerburn Rd NE1, NE4 100 C3
Skipper Cl NE11 70 B7
Skipsea View SR2 92 D7
Skipton Cl
Bedlington NE22 10 D2
Cramlington NE23 16 C1
Skipton Gn NE9 71 B2
Skirlaw Cl NE38 83 D4
Skye Ct 2 SR3 92 A6
Skye Gr NE32 58 E2
Slake Rd NE32 58 D8
Slaley NE38 83 E1
Slaley Cl NE10 72 C7
Slaley Ct Bedlington NE22 11 A1
4 Silksworth SR3 92 A6
Slatyford La NE5 54 A8
Sled La NE40, NE41 51 D3
Sleekburn Ave NE22 11 E3
Slingley Cl 4 SR7 92 E1
Slingsby Gdns NE7 39 D3
Slipway The NE10 57 A2
Sloane Ct NE2 99 B3
Sloping Hall SR6 60 A1
Smailes La NE39 67 C2
Smallholdings NE64 7 C6
Smeaton Ct 5 NE28 41 A1
Smeaton St 2 NE28 41 A1
Smith Gr SR2 92 E6
Smith St
South Shields NE33 59 B8
Ryhope SR2 92 F6
Smith St S SR2 92 F6
Smith Terr NE8 100 B1
Smith's Terr DH5 95 B1
Smithburn Rd NE10 71 F7
Smithy★ TD12 107 B7
Smithy La NE11,NE9 70 F1
Smithy Sq NE23 22 B6
Smithy St 2 NE33 42 C3
Smithyford NE9 71 A1
Smyrna Pl SR1 103 B2
Snipes Dene NE39 67 E3
Snowdon Gdns NE11 70 A6
Snowdon Gr NE36 74 B7
Snowdon Terr NE39 66 F5
Snowdrop Cl NE21 53 A2
Soane Gdns NE34 59 D3
Softley Pl NE15 53 F7
Solar Ho SR1 102 C2
Solingen Est NE24 17 F5
Solway Ave NE30 32 B2
Solway Rd NE31 57 F4
Solway Sq SR3 85 E3
Solway St NE6 56 C4
Somerford NE9 71 F2
Somersby Dr NE3 37 E5
Somerset Cotts 4 SR3 92 A8
Somerset Gdns NE28 40 A3
Somerset Gr NE29 41 D8
Somerset Pl NE4 98 A1
Somerset Rd
Hebburn NE31 57 F3
Sunderland SR3 85 D3
Somerset Sq SR3 85 D3
Somerset St SR3 92 A8
Somerton Ct NE3 37 C6
Sophy St SR5 75 B2
Sorley St SR4 102 A2
Sorrel Cl NE63 6 C2
Sorrel Gdns NE34 59 E3
Sorrell Cl NE4 54 D7
Soulby Ct NE3 37 D8
Sourmilk Hill La NE9 71 A6
Souter Lighthouse★ SR6 60 F5
Souter Rd NE3 38 A5
Souter View SR6 60 F2
South App DH2 88 C2
South Ave Whickham NE16 69 B5
South Shields NE34 59 F5
Washington NE37 83 C8
Ryton NE40 52 C5
South Beach Fst Sch NE24 17 E4
South Bend NE3 28 B1
South Bents Ave SR6 75 F6
South Benwell Prim Sch NE4 54 E4
South Benwell Rd NE15 54 C4
South Burn Terr DH4 90 C6
South Burns DH3 88 C4
South Cl
Easington Lane DH5 97 D8
South Shields NE34 59 F5
Ryton NE40 52 C4
South Cliff SR6 75 F2
South Cres
Great Lumley DH4 89 F1
West Boldon NE35 73 F8
Washington NE38 89 B8
South Croft NE12 39 E7
South Cross St NE3 38 C5
South Dene NE34 59 B6
South Dr Shot NE13 20 E6
Woolsington NE13 37 A8
Hebburn NE31 57 D4
Cleadon SR6 59 F1
South Durham Ct SR1 103 B2
South Eldon St NE33 59 B8
South End SR6 74 E8
South Farm NE22 15 A8
South Frederick St NE33 59 B7
South Front NE2 99 B4
South Gosforth Fst Sch NE2 38 E4
South Gosforth Sta NE3 38 E4
South Gr NE40 52 D4
South Grange Pk SR7 92 F2
South Hetton Ind Est DH6 97 F7
South Hetton Prim Sch DH6 97 F7
South Hetton Rd DH5, DH6 97 D8
South Hill Cres SR2 102 B1
South Hill Rd NE8 101 A1
South Hylton Prim Sch SR4 85 A6
South Hylton Sta SR4 85 B6
South La NE36 74 C7
South Lea NE21 53 C1
South Leigh DH9 79 D1
South Magdalene DH8 77 B1
South Market St DH5 95 B4
South Nelson Ind Est NE23 21 E8
South Nelson Rd NE23 21 E8
South Newsham Rd NE24 17 D3
South Par Gateshead NE10 57 B2
Whitley Bay NE26 32 B5
Stocksfield NE43 64 A7
Choppington NE62 10 E6
South Preston Gr 1 NE29 42 A5
South Preston Terr 2 NE29 42 A5
South Rd Chopwell NE17 66 C1
Prudhoe NE42 50 D2
South Ridge
Newcastle-upon-Tyne NE3 38 B8
Ashington NE63 7 B2
South Riggs NE22 15 F8
South Row NE8 56 A4
South Sherburn NE39 67 E1
South Shields Sta NE33 42 C3
South Shore Rd
Gateshead, East Gateshead NE8 56 B3
Gateshead, Saltmeadows NE8 56 A4
South Side NE61 2 B7
South St
Chester le Street DH2 88 B4
9 Fence Houses DH4 94 A8
Newbottle DH4 90 D3
West Rainton DH4 94 A2
East Rainton DH5 94 C4
Sherburn DH6 96 A1
Newcastle-upon-Tyne NE1 101 A4
Shiremoor NE27 30 F4
Newcastle-upon-Tyne, Coxlodge NE3 38 A5
Hebburn NE31 57 F7
High Spen NE39 66 F4
Gateshead NE8 101 C1
Sunderland SR1 103 A3
South Street Prim Sch NE8 101 C1
South Terr Chopwell NE17 77 B8
Wallsend NE28 40 E2
Morpeth NE61 3 F1
Sunderland SR5 75 B1
South Tynedale Railway★ CA9 132 F1
South Tyneside Coll
Hebburn NE31 57 C2
South Shields NE33 59 E8
South Tyneside Coll Seamanship & Survival Ctr NE33 42 C4
South Tyneside General Hospl NE34 59 D5
South View Birtley DH3 82 D4
Shiney Row DH4 90 B6
Easington Lane DH5 97 D8
Sherburn Hill DH6 96 D1
Tantobie DH9 79 B2
Hazlerigg NE13 28 A4
Chopwell NE17 77 A8
East Sleekburn NE22 11 F3
Annitsford NE23 22 B1
Blyth NE24 17 C4
Cambois NE24 12 C6
Jarrow NE32 58 A6
Washington NE38 83 E1
High Spen NE39 66 F3
Crawcrook NE40 51 F4
Crawcrook NE40 51 F7
Prudhoe NE42 50 B2
Mickley Square NE43 49 E1
Newcastle-upon-Tyne NE5 53 E8
Pegswood NE61 4 F3
Guide Post NE62 10 E7
Ashington NE63 6 C4
Longbenton NE7 39 C5
Sunderland, South Hylton SR4 85 B5
Sunderland, Monkwearmouth SR6 75 D3
South View E NE39 67 C2
South View Gdns NE46 44 F4
South View Pl NE23 22 B6
South View Rd SR4 85 B5
South View Terr
Fence Houses DH4 94 B8
Whickham NE16 69 B6
South View Terr *continued*
Whickham, Swalwell NE16 69 B8
South View W
Rowlands Gill NE39 67 C2
Newcastle-upon-Tyne NE6 56 A6
South Wellfield Fst Sch NE25 31 B4
South Woodbine St 1 NE33 42 D2
Southburn Cl DH4 94 C8
Southcliff NE26 32 C4
Southcote NE16 69 A5
Southcroft NE38 83 D1
Southdowns DH2 88 C2
Southend Ave NE24 17 C6
Southend Par NE31 58 A2
Southend Rd
Gateshead NE9 71 B5
Sunderland SR3 85 E2
Southend Terr NE9 71 B6
Southern Cl NE63 7 B3
Southern Rd NE6 56 F4
Southern Way NE40 52 C4
Southey St NE33 59 D8
Southfield Gdns NE16 69 C6
Southfield Gn NE16 69 C6
Southfield La DH9,NE17 77 F3
Southfield Rd
Longbenton NE12 39 D6
Whickham NE16 69 C6
2 South Shields NE34 60 A8
Southfield Terr
Whickham NE16 69 C6
Newcastle-upon-Tyne NE6 57 A4
Southfields NE23 29 A8
Southfields Ho 1 NE6 56 B6
Southfork NE15 53 C8
Southgarth East 2 NE33 59 E8
Southgate NE12 29 D3
Southgate Wood NE61 9 A5
Southhill Rd NE34 60 A6
Southlands
Tynemouth NE30 32 B1
Hedworth NE32 58 D1
Hexham NE46 44 D4
Newcastle-upon-Tyne NE7 39 A2
Gateshead NE9 71 C2
Southlands Cty Mid Sch NE23 22 B3
Southlands Sch (Specl) NE30 32 A1
Southmayne Rd SR4 85 D4
Southmead Ave NE5 37 C1
Southmoor Rd NE6 56 F7
Southmoor Sch SR2 86 E3
Southport Par NE31 58 A3
Southridge Fst Sch NE25 31 D6
Southward NE26 24 D5
Southward Cl NE26 24 D5
Southward Way NE25 23 E1
Southway
Newcastle-upon-Tyne NE15 53 E7
Gateshead NE9 71 B6
Southwick Ind Est SR5 74 F2
Southwick Prim Sch SR5 75 A2
Southwick Rd SR5 75 C1
Southwold Gdns SR3 91 F8
Southwold Pl NE23 21 E6
Southwood Cres NE39 67 F2
Southwood Gdns NE3 37 F4
Sovereign Ct
Newcastle-upon-Tyne, Jesmond NE2 99 C4
Newcastle-upon-Tyne NE4 100 A4
Sovereign House 16 NE30 42 D7
Sovereign Pl NE4 100 A4
Spa Well Cl NE21 68 B8
Spa Well Dr SR5 74 C2
Spa Well Turn NE21 68 E7
Spalding Cl NE7 39 C4
Sparkwell Cl DH4 90 C4
Spartylea NE38 83 F1
Speculation Pl NE37 83 D8
Speedwell NE9 71 C5
Speedwell Ct NE63 6 B1
Spelter Works Rd SR2 86 F3
Spelvit La NE61 8 F7
Spen Burn NE39 67 A4
Spen La High Spen NE39 67 B3
Greenside NE39,NE40 66 F7
Spen Rd NE39 66 F5
Spence Terr 1 NE29 41 F5
Spencer Ct NE24 12 B1
Spencer Dr NE61 4 E3
Spencer Gr NE16 69 A8
Spencer Rd NE24 12 B1
Spencer St
20 North Shields NE29 42 A5
Hebburn NE31 57 F7
Newcastle-upon-Tyne NE6 56 C8
Spencer Terr NE15 36 B1
Spencers Bank 3 NE16 54 A1
Spenfield Rd NE5 37 D3
Spenser St NE32 58 B8
Spenser Wlk NE34 59 A3
Spetchells NE42 50 D3
Spinney Terr NE6 56 F6
Spinney The
Killingworth NE12 29 E2
Annitsford NE23 22 C1
Washington NE38 83 D2
Morpeth NE61 9 A6
Newcastle-upon-Tyne NE7 39 B2
Spinneyside Gdns NE11 69 F7
Spire Rd NE37 83 F7
Spires La NE6 56 C6
Spital Cres NE64 7 D3

Spital La NE46 ....44 F7
Spital Rd NE64 ....7 C3
Spital Terr NE3 ....38 D5
Spital Villas NE15 ....33 A3
Spittal Terr NE46 ....45 A5
Split Crow Rd NE10,NE8 ..71 B8
Spohr Terr NE33 ....42 D2
Spoor St NE11 ....100 A1
Spoors Cotts NE16 ....69 A6
Spout La Washington NE37 83 D7
  Washington, Concord NE37 .83 D8
  Washington, Washington Village NE38 ....83 D6
Spoutwell La NE45 ....47 A5
Spring Garden Cl SR1 ..103 B3
Spring Garden La NE4 ..98 B2
Spring Gardens Prim Sch NE29 ....41 F6
Spring Gdns NE29 ....41 F5
Spring St NE4 ....98 B2
Spring Terr NE29 ....42 A6
Spring Ville NE22 ....11 F4
Springbank Rd
  Newcastle-upon-Tyne NE2 ..56 A7
  Sunderland SR3 ....85 D3
Springbank Sq SR3 ....85 D3
Springfeld NE10 ....71 F4
Springfell DH3 ....82 D3
Springfield
  5 North Shields NE29 ....42 A6
  Ovington NE42 ....49 D4
Springfield Ave NE9 ....71 C1
Springfield Cl NE42 ....49 D4
Springfield Comp Sch NE32 ....58 B5
Springfield Gdns
  Chester le Street DH3 ....88 C5
  Wallsend NE28 ....39 F3
Springfield Gr NE25 ....31 E3
Springfield Pl NE9 ....71 A6
Springfield Rd
  Newbottle DH4 ....90 D3
  Blaydon NE21 ....53 C1
  Hexham NE46 ....45 C4
  Newcastle-upon-Tyne NE5 ..37 D2
Springfield Terr 1 NE10 ..71 C7
Springhill Gdns NE15 ..54 D6
Springhill Wlk NE61 ....8 E7
Springhouse Cl DH8 ....76 E2
Springhouse La DH8 ....76 E2
Springs The DH3 ....82 E3
Springsyde Cl NE16 ....68 E5
Springwell Ave
  Jarrow NE32 ....58 C6
  Newcastle-upon-Tyne NE6 ..56 E4
  Gateshead NE9 ....71 C3
Springwell Cl NE21 ....53 D1
Springwell Dene Sch SR3 ....85 E3
Springwell Dr NE61 ....1 E4
Springwell Rd
  Jarrow NE32 ....58 B5
  Gateshead NE9 ....71 D3
  Springwell NE9 ....71 F1
  Sunderland SR3,SR4 ....85 D3
Springwell Terr
  Hetton le Hole DH5 ....95 A2
  Gateshead NE9 ....71 E3
  Springwell NE9 ....71 F1
Springwell Village Prim Sch NE9 ....71 F1
Springwood NE31 ....57 C7
Square Houses NE10 ....71 C7
Square The
  3 Whickham NE16 ....69 B7
  Ponteland NE20 ....26 C5
  Riding Mill NE44 ....63 A8
  Guide Post NE62 ....10 F7
Squires Gdns NE10 ....71 D7
Stadium Ind Pk NE10 ....56 B3
Stadium of Light (Sunderland FC) SR5 ....102 C4
Stadium Rd NE10 ....56 B3
Stadium Sta SR5,SR6 ....75 D1
Stadium Villas NE28 ....40 C2
Stadium Way SR5 ....102 C4
Stafford Gr Ryhope SR2 ..92 E6
  Sunderland SR5 ....75 B2
Stafford St
  Hetton le Hole DH5 ....94 F4
  Sunderland SR1 ....103 C4
Stafford Villas NE9 ....71 F1
Staffords La 3 SR6 ....75 F8
Stagshaw NE12 ....29 C5
Stagshaw Rd NE45 ....46 F6
Staindrop NE10 ....72 A5
Staines Rd NE6 ....56 D4
Stainton Dr NE10 ....71 D8
Stainton Gdns NE9 ....71 C2
Stainton Gr SR6 ....75 C5
Staith La NE21 ....53 A4
Staithes Ave NE12 ....39 C6
Staithes La NE61 ....4 A1
Staithes Rd NE38 ....84 A3
Staithes St NE6 ....57 B6
Staiths Rd NE11 ....100 A2
Stakeford Cres NE62 ....11 B8
Stakeford Fst Sch NE62 ..11 C8
Stakeford La NE62 ....11 A7
Stakeford Rd NE22 ....11 C3
Stakeford Terr NE62 ....11 A7
Stalks Rd NE13 ....28 B6
Stamford NE12 ....29 D4
Stamford Ave
  Seaton Delaval NE25 ....23 E1
  Sunderland SR3 ....85 F3
Stamfordham Ave NE29 .41 D5
Stamfordham Cl NE28 ..40 A2
Stamfordham Mews 7 NE5 ....37 D1
Stamfordham Rd
  Ponteland NE15,NE5 ....35 D7
  Newcastle-upon-Tyne NE5 ..36 C4
  Woolsington NE5 ....36 C4
Stampley Cl NE21 ....68 A8
Stamps La SR1 ....103 C3
Stancley Rd NE42 ....50 E2
Standfield Gdns NE10 ..72 C8
Stanelaw Way DH9 ....79 F1
Staneway NE10 ....71 E5
Stanfield Bsns Ctr SR2 .103 C1
Stanfield Ct NE7 ....39 E3
Stang Wlk NE12 ....39 C7
Stanhope NE38 ....83 A5
Stanhope Cl DH4 ....94 D7
Stanhope Cty Inf Sch NE33 ....59 C6
Stanhope Cty Jun Mix Sch NE33 ....59 C7
Stanhope Par 7 NE33 ..59 D8
Stanhope Rd Jarrow NE32 58 D5
  South Shields NE33,NE34 ..59 C7
  Sunderland SR6 ....75 E4
Stanhope St
  South Shields NE33 ....42 C3
  Newcastle-upon-Tyne NE4 ..98 B2
  Greenside NE40 ....51 F1
Stanhope Way NE4 ....98 B2
Stanley Cres
  8 Whitley Bay NE26 ....32 B4
  Prudhoe NE42 ....50 E3
Stanley Gdns Seghill NE23 22 F1
  Gateshead NE9 ....71 C2
Stanley Gr
  Bedlington NE22 ....11 B1
  Newcastle-upon-Tyne NE7 ..39 B3
Stanley St
  Houghton-le-Spring DH5 ..90 E1
  Blyth NE24 ....17 F7
  Wallsend NE28 ....40 F3
  North Shields NE29 ....42 A5
  Jarrow NE32 ....58 C7
  South Shields NE34 ....59 B5
  Newcastle-upon-Tyne NE4 ..54 F4
  2 Sunderland SR5 ....74 B1
Stanley St W NE29 ....42 A5
Stanley Terr
  Chester le Street DH3 ....88 D2
  4 Penshaw DH4 ....90 B6
Stanmore Rd NE6 ....39 C1
Stannerford Rd NE40 ....51 F6
Stannington Ave NE6 ....56 B7
Stannington Fst Sch NE61 ....14 B4
Stannington Gdns SR2 ..86 C2
Stannington Gr
  5 Newcastle-upon-Tyne NE6 ....56 B7
  Sunderland SR2 ....86 D2
Stannington Pl
  Ponteland NE20 ....25 E8
  1 Newcastle-upon-Tyne NE6 ....56 B7
Stannington Rd NE29 ..41 D5
Stannington St NE24 ....17 F7
Stannington Station Rd NE61 ....14 D8
Stansfield St SR6 ....75 E1
Stanstead Cl SR5 ....85 A8
Stanton Ave Blyth NE24 ..17 B5
  South Shields NE34 ....59 E7
Stanton Cl NE10 ....72 D7
Stanton Dr NE61 ....4 E3
Stanton Gr NE30 ....32 A1
Stanton Rd
  Shiremoor NE27 ....30 E3
  Tynemouth NE30 ....32 A1
Stanton St NE4 ....98 A2
Stanway Dr NE7 ....39 A3
Stanwick St NE30 ....42 D8
Stanwix 1 NE28 ....40 F4
Stapeley Ct 5 NE3 ....37 D5
Stapeley View NE3 ....37 D5
Staple Rd NE32 ....58 C6
Stapleford Cl NE5 ....37 B1
Stapylton Dr SR2 ....86 B4
Star of the Sea RC Prim Sch NE25 ....31 E2
Starbeck Ave NE2 ....99 C3
Starbeck Mews NE2 ....99 C3
Stardale Ave NE24 ....17 A6
Stargate Gdns NE9 ....71 C2
Stargate La NE40 ....52 E4
Starlight Cres NE25 ....23 C3
Starling Wlk NE16 ....69 C2
Station App
  Gateshead NE11,NE9 ....70 D3
  Longbenton NE12 ....39 D6
  1 South Shields NE33 ....42 C3
  Cleadon NE36 ....74 E8
Station Ave DH5 ....95 A3
Station Ave N DH4 ....90 A1
Station Ave S DH4 ....90 A1
Station Bank Ryton NE40 .52 C6
  Mickley Square NE43 ....49 E2
Station Cl NE44 ....62 F8
Station Cotts
  Ponteland NE20 ....25 E6
  Seghill NE23 ....23 A1
  Burnopfield NE39 ....78 C6
  Morpeth NE61 ....9 A7
Station Field Rd DH9 ..79 F1
Station First Sch The NE22 ....11 D3
Station Ind Est NE42 ....50 B3
Station La DH2,DH3 ....82 B4
Station Mews 10 NE30 ..42 D7
Station Rd
  Chester le Street DH3 ....88 C3
  Houghton-le-Spring DH4 ..90 D1
  Penshaw DH4 ....89 E8
  Shiney Row DH4 ....90 A6
  Washington, Fatfield DH4, NE38 ....83 E1
  Hetton le Hole DH5 ....95 A2
  High Pittington DH6 ....96 A6
  Gateshead, Bill Quay NE10 .57 B2
  Killingworth NE12 ....29 B3
  Longbenton NE12 ....39 D7
  Newcastle-upon-Tyne, Kenton Bankfoot NE13 ..37 B6
  Heddon-on-the-Wall NE15 .35 A1
  Newburn NE15 ....52 F7
  Bedlington NE22 ....11 C2
  Cramlington NE23 ....22 B7
  Dudley NE23 ....28 F8
  Seghill NE23 ....23 A1
  Whitley Bay NE26 ....32 B4
  Backworth NE27 ....30 D3
  Wallsend NE28 ....40 B2
  Wallsend, Willington Quay NE28 ....41 A1
  North Shields NE29 ....41 D3
  Newcastle-upon-Tyne, South Gosforth NE3 ....38 E5
  Tynemouth NE30 ....32 C3
  Hebburn NE31 ....57 D6
  South Shields NE33 ....42 C2
  Boldon Colliery NE35 ....58 E2
  East Boldon NE36 ....74 D7
  Washington, Columbia NE38 83 E4
  Washington, Swan NE38 ..84 A4
  Rowlands Gill NE39 ....67 F1
  Crawcrook NE41 ....51 C5
  Wylam NE41 ....51 B5
  Prudhoe NE42 ....50 C3
  Corbridge NE45 ....46 F4
  Hexham NE46 ....45 C5
  Newcastle-upon-Tyne, Wincomblee NE6 ....57 A5
  Ashington NE63 ....6 B4
  Gateshead, Low Fell NE9 ..70 E5
  Ryhope SR2 ....93 A6
  Sunderland SR5,SR6 ....75 D4
Station Rd N
  Hetton le Hole DH5 ....95 A3
  Longbenton NE12 ....39 D8
Station St Haswell DH6 ..97 F3
  Bedlington NE22 ....11 D3
  Blyth NE24 ....17 E8
  Jarrow NE32 ....58 B7
  Sunderland SR1 ....103 A3
Station Terr
  Fence Houses DH4 ....89 F1
  Tynemouth NE30 ....42 D7
  East Boldon NE36 ....74 E7
  10 Washington NE37 ....83 E8
Station View DH5 ....95 A3
Staveley Rd SR6 ....75 C5
Stavordale Terr NE9 ....71 A7
Staward Ave NE25 ....23 D2
Staward Terr NE6 ....56 F4
Staynebrigg NE10 ....72 A6
Stead La NE22 ....11 C1
Stead Lane Fst Sch NE22 11 C1
Stead St NE28 ....41 A3
Steadings The
  Seaton Sluice NE26 ....24 E4
  Ashington NE63 ....6 A2
Steadlands Sq NE22 ....11 C1
Steads The NE61 ....9 A6
Stedham Cl NE37 ....72 E2
Steenbergs 8 NE1 ....56 A6
Steep Hill SR3 ....91 C7
Stella Bank NE21 ....52 F5
Stella Hall Dr NE21 ....53 A4
Stella Rd Blaydon NE21 ..53 B4
  Ryton NE21 ....53 B4
Stephen Ct NE32 ....58 C6
Stephen St
  East Hartford NE23 ....16 B3
  Blyth NE24 ....17 E8
  Newcastle-upon-Tyne NE6 ..56 A6
Stephenson Bldg NE2 ..99 C2
Stephenson Cl DH5 ....95 B4
Stephenson Ct
  North Shields NE30 ....42 B5
  Wylam NE41 ....51 C6
Stephenson Ind Est
  Killingworth NE12 ....29 C2
  Washington NE37 ....72 E2
Stephenson Meml Prim Sch NE28 ....41 A2
Stephenson Railway Mus* NE29 ....41 A7
Stephenson Rd
  Washington NE37 ....72 E2
  Newcastle-upon-Tyne NE7 ..39 B1
Stephenson St
  Wallsend NE28 ....41 B1
  North Shields NE30 ....42 B5
  1 Tynemouth NE30 ....42 D7
  Gateshead NE8 ....70 D8
Stephenson Terr
  Gateshead NE10 ....71 D8
  Newcastle-upon-Tyne NE15 .36 B1
  Throckley NE15 ....35 D2
  Wylam NE41 ....51 B6
Stephenson Way
  Blaydon NE21 ....68 B8
  Bedlington NE22 ....11 A4
Stephenson's La NE1 ..101 A4
Stepney Bank NE1 ....56 A6
Stepney La NE1 ....99 C1
Stepney Rd 1 NE1,NE2 ..56 A6
Sterling Cotts NE10 ....71 C7
Sterling St SR4 ....102 A2
Stevenson St DH4 ....94 D8
Steward Cres NE34 ....60 B6
Stewart Ave SR2 ....92 E6
Stewart Dr NE36 ....74 B7
Stewart St
  New Silksworth SR3 ....92 A7
  Sunderland SR4 ....102 B1
Stewartsfield NE39 ....67 D1
Stileford NE10 ....72 A7
Stillington Cl SR2 ....92 F5
Stirling Ave Jarrow NE32 ..58 E4
  Rowlands Gill NE39 ....67 E1
Stirling Cl NE38 ....84 A4
Stirling Ct NE11 ....70 E2
Stirling Dr
  Bedlington NE22 ....11 C2
  Tynemouth NE29 ....41 C8
Stirling La NE39 ....67 F1
Stobart St SR5 ....102 C4
Stobhill Villas NE61 ....9 A7
Stockfold NE38 ....83 E2
Stockholm Cl NE29 ....41 B5
Stockley Ave SR5 ....74 C2
Stockley Rd NE38 ....83 F6
Stocksfield Ave NE5 ....54 C7
Stocksfield Avenue Prim Sch NE5 ....54 B7
Stocksfield Gdns NE9 ..71 B2
Stocksfield Hall NE43 ..64 A8
Stocksfield Sta NE43 ..64 A7
Stockton Rd
  North Shields NE29 ....41 F3
  Sunderland SR2 ....103 A1
  Ryhope SR2,SR7 ....92 F2
Stockton Terr 8 SR2 ....86 F2
Stockwell Gn NE6 ....56 F8
Stoddart Ho NE2 ....99 C2
Stoddart St
  Newcastle-upon-Tyne NE1, NE2 ....99 C2
  South Shields NE34 ....59 C6
Stoker Ave NE34 ....58 F4
Stoker Terr NE39 ....67 A3
Stokesley Gr NE7 ....39 A3
Stokoe Dr NE63 ....7 A3
Stone Cellar Rd NE37 ..72 C2
Stone St NE10 ....71 C6
Stonechat Cl 3 NE38 ....82 F3
Stonechat Mount NE21 ..53 A4
Stonechat Pl NE12 ....39 A7
Stonecroft NE15 ....33 D1
Stonecroft Gdns NE7 ....39 D3
Stonecrop NE9 ....71 C5
Stonecross NE63 ....6 C2
Stonefold Cl NE5 ....37 B3
Stonehaugh Way NE20 ..25 B2
Stonelaw Mid Sch NE23 .22 A4
Stoneleigh NE61 ....9 E4
Stoneleigh Ave NE12 ....39 A7
Stoneleigh Cl DH4 ....90 C2
Stoneleigh Pl 1 NE12 ....39 A6
Stonesdale DH4 ....89 E8
Stonethwaite NE29 ....41 E3
Stoney La Springwell NE9 .71 F1
  Sunderland SR5 ....75 A1
Stoneycroft NE37 ....83 C7
Stoneycroft East NE12 ..29 E2
Stoneycroft West NE12 ..29 E2
Stoneygate Gdns NE10 ..56 E1
Stoneygate La NE10 ....56 E1
Stoneyhurst Ave NE15 ..54 B5
Stoneyhurst Rd NE3 ....38 E4
Stoneyhurst Rd W NE3 ..38 D4
Stoneylea Cl NE40 ....51 E3
Stoneylea Rd NE5 ....53 F8
Stoneywaites NE40 ....66 E8
Stonybank Way NE43 ....64 E8
Stonyflat Bank NE42 ....50 E2
Store Bldgs NE35 ....73 E8
Store Farm Rd NE64 ....7 C5
Store St
  Newcastle-upon-Tyne NE15 .53 C6
  Blaydon NE21 ....53 B1
Store Terr DH5 ....95 B1
Storey Cres NE64 ....7 C5
Storey La NE21 ....53 A4
Storey St NE23 ....22 C5
Stormont Gn NE3 ....37 F3
Stormont St NE29 ....42 A5
Stothard St NE32 ....58 C7
Stotts Rd NE6 ....57 A8
Stow The NE12 ....39 A5
Stowe Gdns NE61 ....4 E4
Stowell Sq NE1 ....98 C1
Stowell St NE1 ....98 C1
Stowell Terr NE10 ....71 E8
Straker Dr NE46 ....44 E3
Straker St NE32 ....58 D6
Straker Terr NE34 ....59 C5
Strand The SR3 ....91 E8
Strangford Ave 2 DH2 ..88 B1
Stranton Terr SR6 ....75 D2
Stratfield St SR4 ....85 E7
Stratford Ave SR2 ....86 E3
Stratford Cl
  Killingworth NE12 ....29 E3
  Cramlington NE23 ....21 E7
Stratford Gdns NE9 ....70 F6
Stratford Gr NE6 ....56 A7
Stratford Gr W NE6 ....56 A7
Stratford Grove Terr NE6 ....56 A7
Stratford Rd NE6 ....56 A7
Stratford Villas NE6 ....56 A7
Strathearn Way NE3 ....37 F7
Strathmore Ave NE39 ....67 E1
Strathmore Cres
  Byermoor NE16 ....79 D8
  Newcastle-upon-Tyne NE4 ..54 E6
Strathmore Rd
  Gateshead N10,NE9 ....71 B7
  Newcastle-upon-Tyne NE3 ..38 C7
  Rowlands Gill NE39 ....67 E1
  Sunderland SR3 ....85 E2
Strathmore Sq SR3 ....85 E2
Stratton Cl SR2 ....93 A8
Stratus Ct 12 SR3 ....92 A6
Strawberry Ave NE23 ....29 C5
Strawberry Cotts NE62 ..11 B8
Strawberry Gdns NE28 ..40 A4
Strawberry La NE1 ....98 C1
Strawberry Pl NE1 ....98 C2
Strawberry Terr NE13 ....27 F4
Street Gate Pk NE16 ....69 D3
Stretford Ct NE9 ....71 A1
Stretton Cl DH4 ....94 A7
Stretton Way NE27 ....30 C5
Stridingedge NE37 ....83 B6
Stronsay Cl 2 SR2 ....92 E8
Strothers Rd NE39 ....66 F5
Strothers Terr NE39 ....66 E4
Struan Terr NE36 ....74 E7
Struddars Farm Ct NE21 .53 F2
Stuart Ct NE3 ....37 C6
Stuart Gdns NE15 ....35 D2
Stuart Terr NE10 ....56 D1
Stubbs Ave NE16 ....69 A8
Studdon Wlk NE3 ....37 D5
Studland Cl NE29 ....31 F1
Studley Gdns
  Whitley Bay NE25 ....32 A4
  2 Gateshead NE9 ....70 F5
Studley Terr NE4 ....98 A3
Studley Villas NE12 ....39 E7
Sturdee Gdns NE2 ....38 E3
Styan Ave NE26 ....32 B5
Styford Gdns NE15 ....53 E7
Success Rd DH4 ....90 B4
Sudbury Way NE23 ....21 E6
Suddick St 2 SR5 ....75 B1
Suez St NE30 ....42 B6
Suffolk Cl NE63 ....6 A4
Suffolk Gdns
  Wallsend NE28 ....40 E4
  South Shields NE34 ....60 C7
Suffolk Pl Birtley DH3 ..82 D1
  Gateshead NE8 ....56 A4
Suffolk Rd NE31 ....57 F3
Suffolk St
  Hetton le Hole DH5 ....94 F4
  Jarrow NE32 ....58 B6
  Sunderland SR2 ....103 B1
Sugley Dr NE15 ....53 D6
Sugley St NE15 ....53 D6
Sugley Villas NE15 ....53 D6
Sulgrave Ind Est NE37 ..72 E1
Sulgrave Rd NE37 ....72 F1
Sullivan Wlk NE31 ....57 E5
Summer St NE10 ....56 D1
Summerfield NE17 ....77 A5
Summerfield Rd NE9 ....70 F7
Summerhill Blaydon NE21 .53 B3
  Hedworth NE32 ....58 D1
  Newcastle-upon-Tyne NE4 100 A4
  Sunderland SR2 ....102 B2
  Sunderland, Middle Herrington SR3 ....91 B7
Summerhill Ave NE3 ....28 D1
Summerhill Gr NE4 ....98 B1
Summerhill Rd NE34 ....60 A7
Summerhill St NE4 ....98 B1
Summerhill Terr NE1 ..100 C4
Summerhouse Farm DH5 ....94 D5
Summerhouse La
  Ashington, North Seaton NE63 ....7 B3
  Ashington, Woodbridge NE63 .7 B4
Summerson St DH5 ....95 B4
Summerson Way NE22 ..11 D2
Sun St NE16 ....69 B2
Sun View Terr SR6 ....59 E1
Sunbury Ave NE2 ....38 E2
Sunderland Ent Pk SR5 ..85 B8
Sunderland Eye Infmy SR2 ....86 D3
Sunderland High Sch SR2 ....103 A1
Sunderland High Sch Jun Sch SR2 ....86 D4
Sunderland Highway NE37,NE38 ....83 C6
Sunderland Mus & Art Gall* SR1 ....103 A2
Sunderland Rd
  Newbottle DH4 ....90 E4
  Gateshead, Felling NE10 ..71 E8
  Gateshead, Heworth NE10 .71 F8
  Gateshead, Wardley NE10 .72 C7
  South Shields NE33 ....59 E8
  South Shields, Harton NE34 .59 F6
  East Boldon NE36,SR5 ....74 E6
  Sunderland SR5 ....75 A2
  Cleadon SR6 ....75 B7
Sunderland Ret Pk SR6 .75 D1
Sunderland Royal Hospl SR4 ....102 A2
Sunderland Ski Ctr* SR3 ....85 F1

Sunderland St
2 Houghton-le-Spring, New Town DH4 .94 E8
Houghton-le-Spring DH5 .90 E1
Newcastle-upon-Tyne NE1 100 C4
Sunderland SR1 .103 B3
Sunderland Sta SR1 .103 A2
Sunderland Tech Pk SR1 .102 C2
Sundew Rd NE9 .71 C4
Sundridge Dr NE10 .72 C7
Sunhill NE16 .69 B2
Sunholme Dr NE28 .40 A5
Sunlea Ave NE30 .32 C2
Sunnidale NE16 .68 E5
Sunnilaws NE34 .60 A3
Sunningdale
Whitley Bay NE25 .31 D5
South Shields NE33 .42 E1
Sunningdale Ave
Wallsend NE28 .40 C2
Newcastle-upon-Tyne NE6 .57 A6
Sunningdale Cl NE10 .71 D7
Sunningdale Dr NE37 .72 C2
Sunningdale Rd SR3 .85 E3
Sunningdale Sch SR3 .85 E2
Sunnirise NE34 .60 A4
Sunniside
North Shields NE29 .41 E5
Sunderland SR4 .85 A6
Sunniside Ct NE16 .69 B3
Sunniside Dr NE34 .60 A4
Sunniside Gdns
Newcastle-upon-Tyne NE15 .54 B6
Gateshead NE9 .71 C2
Sunniside La NE34,SR6 .60 B2
Sunniside Rd NE16 .69 B3
Sunniside Sta* NE16 .69 B1
Sunniside Terr SR6 .60 A2
Sunny Brae NE40 .66 F8
Sunnybank Ave NE15 .54 D5
Sunnybrow SR3 .91 F8
Sunnycrest Ave NE6 .56 F6
Sunnygill Terr NE40 .51 F2
Sunnyside NE23 .22 A6
Sunnyway NE5 .37 C2
Sunrise Ent Pk SR5 .85 A8
Sunrise La 1 DH4 .90 D1
Surrey Ave SR3 .92 A6
Surrey Cl NE63 .6 A4
Surrey Pl Penshaw DH4 .90 C6
Newcastle-upon-Tyne NE4 .98 A1
Surrey Rd
North Shields NE29 .41 D6
Hebburn NE31 .57 F3
Surrey St Penshaw DH4 .90 C6
Hetton le Hole DH5 .94 F4
Jarrow NE32 .58 A6
Surrey Terr DH3 .82 C1
Sussex Gdns NE28 .40 E3
Sussex Pl NE37 .72 D1
Sussex St 2 Blyth NE24 .17 F8
Jarrow NE32 .58 A6
3 New Silksworth SR3 .92 A8
Sutherland Ave
Newcastle-upon-Tyne NE4 .54 E7
Newbiggin-by-the-Sea NE64 .7 D4
Sutherland Ct NE34 .59 D2
Sutherland Grange DH4 .90 D6
Sutherland St
Gateshead NE8 .101 C1
Sunderland SR6 .75 D2
Seaham SR7 .93 B1
Sutton Cl DH4 .90 A6
Sutton Ct NE28 .39 F5
Sutton St NE6 .56 E7
Sutton Way NE34 .60 B5
Swainby Cl NE3 .38 D8
Swaledale Wallsend NE28 .39 F5
Sunderland SR6 .75 F7
Swaledale Ave NE24 .17 A7
Swaledale Cl DH5 .94 F1
Swaledale Cres DH4 .90 A8
Swaledale Ct NE24 .17 A7
Swaledale Gdns
Newcastle-upon-Tyne NE7 .39 B3
Sunderland SR4 .85 F5
Swallow Cl NE63 .11 E8
Swallow Ct NE12 .29 C4
Swallow Tail Ct NE34 .59 B5
Swallow Tail Dr NE11 .70 B7
Swallows The NE28 .40 E7
Swalwell Bank NE16 .69 A8
Swalwell Cl NE42 .50 C2
Swalwell Cty Prim Sch NE16 .69 B8
Swan Ave NE28 .40 D3
Swan Ct NE11 .100 A1
Swan Dr NE11 .100 A1
Swan Ind Est NE38 .83 F4
Swan Ind Est (South) NE38 .83 F3
Swan Rd Washington NE38 83 F4
Newcastle-upon-Tyne NE6 .57 B4
Swan St Gateshead NE8 .101 C3
Sunderland SR5 .75 C1
Swansfield NE61 .8 E7
Swanton Cl NE5 .37 B4
Swanway NE9 .71 B7
Swards Rd NE10 .71 E7
Swarland Ave NE7 .39 B5
Swarland Rd NE25 .23 D2
Swarth Cl NE37 .83 A6
Sweetbriar Cl NE61 .3 E2
Sweetbriar Way NE24 .17 C4
Sweethope Ave
Blyth NE24 .17 D8
Ashington NE63 .6 F2
Sweethope Dene NE61 .9 A6
Swiftdale Cl NE22 .10 F1
Swiftden Dr SR4 .85 A4
Swinbourne Gdns NE26 .31 F6
Swinbourne Terr NE32 .58 B3
Swinburn Rd NE25 .23 D2
Swinburne Pl Birtley DH3 .82 C3
Newcastle-upon-Tyne NE4 .98 C1
Gateshead NE8 .101 C3
Swinburne St
Jarrow NE32 .58 E6
Gateshead NE8 .101 B3
Swindale Cotts NE41 .51 B6
Swindale Dr NE12 .29 C3
Swindon Rd SR3 .85 D3
Swindon Sq SR3 .85 E3
Swindon St NE31 .57 D6
Swindon Terr NE6 .39 B1
Swinhoe Gdns NE13 .28 B6
Swinhope NE38 .89 A8
Swinley Gdns NE15 .53 F6
Swinton Cl NE61 .9 B6
Swire NE1 .99 C1
Swirral Edge NE37 .83 C7
Swyntoft NE10 .72 B7
Sycamore DH2 .88 A5
Sycamore Ave
Dinnington NE13 .27 C7
Ponteland NE20 .25 D4
Blyth NE24 .12 D1
Whitley Bay NE25 .31 F4
South Shields NE34 .59 F4
Washington NE38 .83 B1
Guide Post NE62 .10 E7
Sycamore Cl NE2 .38 F2
Sycamore Dr SR5 .75 B3
Sycamore Gr
Gateshead NE10 .71 E8
Prudhoe NE42 .50 A2
Springwell NE9 .71 F1
Sycamore Pl NE12 .29 C4
Sycamore Rd
Blaydon NE21 .53 C2
Whitburn SR6 .60 F1
Sycamore St
Throckley NE15 .35 D3
Wallsend NE28 .40 C1
Ashington NE63 .6 D3
Sycamore Terr DH6 .97 F3
Sycamores The
Burnopfield NE16 .79 C5
Newcastle-upon-Tyne NE4 100 A3
Guide Post NE62 .10 E7
Sunderland SR2 .86 E3
Sydenham Terr
14 South Shields NE33 .42 D3
Sunderland SR4 .102 A1
Sydney Ct NE8 .101 B3
Sydney Gdns NE34 .58 F3
Sydney Gr NE28 .40 A5
Sydney St DH4 .89 E2
Syke Rd NE16 .78 F5
Sylvan Cl NE61 .8 D7
Sylverton Gdns NE33 .42 F1
Symington Gdns SR3 .91 F8
Symon Terr NE17 .77 B8
Synclen Ave NE45 .47 A6
Synclen Rd NE45 .47 A6
Synclen Terr NE45 .47 A6
Syon St NE30 .42 D8
Syron NE16 .68 F7
Syston Cl DH4 .94 A7

T

Taberna Cl NE15 .34 E2
Tadcaster Rd SR3 .85 C1
Tadema Rd NE33 .42 F2
Talbot Cl NE38 .83 D4
Talbot Cotts DH3 .82 C4
Talbot Gn NE5 .53 F8
Talbot House Specl Sch NE15 .35 F2
Talbot Rd
South Shields NE34 .59 C6
Sunderland SR6 .75 E3
Talgarth NE38 .84 B5
Talisman View 6 NE9 .71 A2
Talley Ct NE38 .83 C5
Tamar Cl NE29 .41 D8
Tamar Ct 6 SR3 .91 F6
Tamar St DH5 .97 C8
Tamarisk Way NE9 .71 C5
Tamerton Dr DH3 .82 D2
Tamerton St SR4 .85 F6
Tamworth Rd NE4 .98 A2
Tamworth Sq SR3 .85 C1
Tanbark DH4 .89 F6
Tanfield Gdns NE34 .60 B6
Tanfield Lea Ind Est DH9 79 D2
Tanfield Lea Jun & Inf Sch DH9 .79 C1
Tanfield Lea South Ind Est DH9 .79 F1
Tanfield Pl NE9 .71 C2
Tanfield Rd
Newcastle-upon-Tyne NE15 .54 A6
Gateshead NE9 .71 C2
Sunderland SR3 .85 D1
Tanfield Rly* NE16 .80 B7
Tanfield St SR4 .85 E7
Tangmere Cl NE23 .22 C7
Tankerville Pl 3 NE2 .38 E1
Tankerville Terr NE2 .38 E1
Tanners Row NE46 .45 A5
Tanners' Bank NE30 .42 C6
Tantallon DH3 .82 D2
Tantallon Ct DH4 .89 D1
Tantobie Rd NE15 .54 A6
Tarlton Cres NE10 .71 C8
Tarn Dr SR2 .86 F1
Tarragon Way NE34 .59 E3
Tarrington Cl NE28 .40 F5
Tarset Dr NE42 .50 D2
Tarset Pl NE3 .38 A6
Tarset Rd NE25 .31 B5
Tarset St NE1 .56 A5
Tasman Rd SR3 .91 C8
Tasmania Rd NE34 .58 F3
Tate St 8 NE24 .17 F8
Tatham St SR1 .103 B2
Tatham Street Back SR1 .103 B2
Tattershall SR2 .86 B4
Taunton Ave
Tynemouth NE29 .31 D1
Jarrow NE32 .58 E5
Taunton Cl NE28 .40 F5
Taunton Pl NE23 .22 B8
Taunton Rd SR3 .85 D2
Taunton Sq SR3 .85 D2
Tavistock Cl DH4 .90 C3
Tavistock Pl Jarrow NE32 .58 D5
Sunderland SR1 .103 A2
Tavistock Rd NE2 .38 E2
Tavistock Sq SR3 .92 A8
Tavistock Wlk NE23 .22 B8
Tay Rd SR3,SR4 .85 C2
Tay St Easington Lane DH5 .97 D8
Chopwell NE17 .66 C1
Taylor Ave
Wide Open NE13 .28 C6
Rowlands Gill NE39 .67 F1
Ashington NE63 .7 B3
Taylor Gdns
Gateshead NE10 .57 B2
Seaton Sluice NE26 .24 D6
9 Sunderland SR2 .86 E4
Taylor St Blyth NE24 .17 A8
South Shields NE33 .59 B8
Taylor Terr 8 NE27 .30 E1
Taylor's Bldgs NE22 .11 D2
Taynton Gr NE23 .22 F2
Teal Ave NE24 .17 F4
Teal Cl
7 Washington NE38 .82 F3
Longbenton NE7 .39 C5
Team St NE8 .100 B1
Team Valley Bsns Ctr NE11 .70 D6
Team Valley Trad Est NE11 .70 D4
Teasdale St SR2 .103 C1
Tebay Dr NE5 .53 F8
Tedco Bsns Wks 1 NE33 42 C2
Teddington Cl NE3 .37 B7
Teddington Rd SR3 .85 C2
Teddington Sq SR3 .85 C2
Tedham Rd NE15 .53 C7
Tees Ct South Shields NE34 59 C6
18 Silksworth SR3 .91 F6
Tees Rd NE31 .57 E3
Tees St
Easington Lane DH5 .97 D8
Chopwell NE17 .66 C1
Tees Terr 9 NE37 .83 D8
Teesdale Ave DH4 .90 A8
Teesdale Gdns NE7 .39 B3
Teesdale Gr NE12 .39 D8
Teesdale Pl 3 NE24 .16 F8
Teindland Cl NE4 .54 E4
Tel-el-Kebir Rd SR2 .86 E4
Telford Cl NE27 .30 C5
Telford Ct
North Shields NE28 .41 C2
Morpeth, Loansdean NE61 .8 F5
Morpeth, Stobhill NE61 .8 F6
Telford Rd SR3 .85 D2
Telford St
North Shields NE28 .41 C2
Gateshead NE8 .70 D7
Tempest St Ryton NE21 .53 A4
10 New Silksworth SR3 .92 A7
Temple Ave NE24 .17 C8
Temple Gn
South Shields NE34 .59 E5
Gateshead NE8 .70 C8
Temple Park Cty Inf Sch NE34 .59 D3
Temple Park Jun Mix Sch NE34 .59 D4
Temple Park Rd NE34 .59 D6
Temple St
Newcastle-upon-Tyne NE1 100 C4
Gateshead NE10 .56 D1
South Shields NE33 .59 B7
Temple St W NE33 .59 B7
Temple Town NE33 .59 B8
Tenbury Cres
Longbenton NE12 .39 C7
Tynemouth NE29 .31 E1
Tenby Rd SR3 .91 C8
Tenby Sq NE23 .22 C8
Tennant St Hebburn NE31 .57 D5
3 South Shields NE34 .59 A4
Tennyson Ave
Hebburn NE31 .57 F6
West Boldon NE35 .74 B8
Tennyson Cres NE16 .69 A8
Tennyson Ct
Prudhoe NE42 .50 B1
Gateshead NE8 .56 A2
Tennyson Gn NE3 .37 F3
Tennyson St
11 South Shields NE33 .42 D2
6 Sunderland SR5 .75 A2
Tennyson Terr NE29 .42 B4
Tenter Garth NE15 .35 C2
Tenter Terr NE61 .9 A8
Tenth Ave
Chester le Street DH2 .88 B3
Gateshead NE11 .70 D2
Blyth NE24 .17 E6
Newcastle-upon-Tyne NE6 .56 C8
Morpeth NE61 .9 B6
Tenth Ave W NE11 .70 D2
Tern Cl NE24 .17 F4
Terrace Pl NE1 .98 C2
Terrace The
Longbenton NE12 .39 C6
6 Boldon Colliery NE35 .58 E1
5 East Boldon NE36 .74 D7
Ovingham NE42 .50 A4
Terraces The NE38 .83 E4
Terrier Cl NE22 .11 C1
Tesla St DH4 .90 D4
Tetford Pl NE12 .39 C7
Teviot NE38 .83 A1
Teviot St
Easington Lane DH5 .97 C8
Gateshead NE8 .71 A8
Teviot Way NE32 .58 A5
Teviotdale Gdns NE7 .39 B3
Tewkesbury NE12 .29 D4
Tewkesbury Rd NE15 .53 C7
Thackeray Rd SR3 .85 D2
Thackeray St DH4 .94 D8
Thames Ave NE32 .58 C2
Thames Cres DH4 .94 A8
Thames Gdns NE28 .40 B1
Thames Rd Hebburn NE31 .57 F3
Sunderland SR3 .91 C8
Thames St
Easington Lane DH5 .97 C8
Chopwell NE17 .66 C1
Gateshead NE8 .56 A1
Thanet Rd SR3 .85 D1
Tharsis Rd NE31 .57 D5
Thatcher Cl NE16 .69 A5
Theatre Pl 21 NE29 .42 A5
Thelma St SR4 .102 B1
Theme Rd SR3 .91 C8
Theresa Russell Ho NE6 .56 C6
Theresa St NE21 .53 C3
Thetford NE38 .83 D4
Thieves Bank NE61 .5 E1
Third Ave
Chester le Street DH2 .88 B3
Chester le Street DH2 .88 B7
Gateshead NE11 .70 C6
Blyth NE24 .17 D6
North Shields NE29 .41 B5
Newcastle-upon-Tyne NE6 .56 C7
Morpeth NE61 .9 B7
Ashington NE63 .6 E3
Third Row Ellington NE61 .1 E4
Linton NE61 .1 A3
Third St NE28 .40 D1
Thirkeld Pl DH4 .90 A7
Thirlington Cl NE5 .37 B3
Thirlmere Birtley DH3 .82 E2
Gateshead NE10 .72 A8
Cleadon SR6 .60 A1
Thirlmere Ave
Chester le Street DH2 .88 B1
Easington Lane DH5 .97 C8
Tynemouth NE30 .32 A2
Thirlmere Cl NE12 .29 F3
Thirlmere Cres
Penshaw DH4 .90 B6
Blaydon NE21 .68 B8
Thirlmere Ct NE31 .57 F4
Thirlmere Terr NE64 .7 E4
Thirlmere Way Blyth NE24 12 A1
Newcastle-upon-Tyne NE5 .37 B1
Thirlmoor NE37 .83 A6
Thirlmoor Pl NE62 .11 A8
Thirlwell Gr NE32 .58 B3
Thirlwell Rd NE8 .56 A3
Thirsk Rd SR3 .85 D2
Thirston Dr NE23 .22 C6
Thirston Pl NE29 .41 D7
Thirston Way NE3 .37 D5
Thistle Ave NE40 .52 A4
Thistle Ct NE31 .57 D5
Thistle Rd SR3 .85 C1
Thistlecroft DH5 .94 E7
Thistledon Ave NE16 .68 F6
Thistley Cl NE6 .56 E8
Thistley Gn NE10 .57 B1
Thomas Bell Ho 8 NE34 .59 A4
Thomas Dr NE31 .57 D6
Thomas Hawksley Pk SR3 .86 A3
Thomas Hepburn Com Sch NE10 .71 E7
Thomas Horsley Ho NE15 54 B5
Thomas St
9 Chester le Street DH3 .88 C2
Hetton le Hole DH5 .95 B5
Whickham NE16 .69 A7
South Shields NE33 .42 C3
8 Washington NE37 .83 E8
Newcastle-upon-Tyne NE5 .36 F2
Gateshead NE9 .71 D1
Ryhope SR2 .92 F6
Thomas St N SR6 .103 A4
Thomas St S Ryhope SR2 .92 F6
Sunderland SR5 .75 A1
Thomas Taylor Cotts NE27 .30 C5
Thomas Walling Prim Sch The NE5 .37 C2
Thompson Ave NE12 .29 C4
Thompson Cres 7 SR5 .74 B1
Thompson Gdns NE28 .40 B2
Thompson Pl NE10 .71 D8
Thompson Rd SR5 .75 B2
Thompson St
Bedlington NE22 .11 D3
Blyth NE24 .12 D1
Blyth NE24 .12 E1
Thompson Terr 8 SR2 .93 A6
Thompson's Bldgs DH4 .90 C5
Thorburn St SR6 .75 D4
Thoresby Ho NE6 .56 E4
Thorn Cl NE13 .28 A5
Thorn Tree Dr NE22 .10 F2
Thornbank Cl SR3 .92 A4
Thornbeck Coll SR2 .102 C1
Thornborough Ho 17 NE6 .56 C6
Thornbridge NE38 .84 A5
Thornbury Ave NE23 .23 A2
Thornbury Cl
Newcastle-upon-Tyne NE3 .37 B5
Boldon Colliery NE35 .58 E1
Thornbury Dr NE25 .31 C6
Thornbury St SR4 .102 A3
Thorncliffe Pl NE29 .41 E5
Thorndale Pl NE24 .17 A8
Thorndale Rd
Newcastle-upon-Tyne NE15 .53 F5
Sunderland SR3 .85 D1
Thorne Ave NE10 .72 B8
Thorne Brake NE10 .72 A7
Thorne Rd SR3 .85 C1
Thorne Sq SR3 .85 C1
Thorne Terr NE6 .56 E7
Thornehill Gdns NE62 .11 A8
Thorney Close Prim Sch SR3 .85 D1
Thorney Close Rd SR3 .85 D1
Thorneyburn Ave NE25 .31 B5
Thorneyburn Cl DH4 .90 C2
Thorneyburn Way NE24 .17 C7
Thorneyfield Dr NE12 .29 B2
Thorneyford Pl NE20 .25 E7
Thornfield Gr SR2 .86 E2
Thornfield Pl NE39 .67 E3
Thornfield Rd NE3 .38 B4
Thorngill NE37 .83 C6
Thornhaugh Ave NE16 .68 F6
Thornhill Cl
Gateshead NE11 .70 A8
Seaton Delaval NE25 .23 D2
Thornhill Comp Sch SR2 .102 C1
Thornhill Cres SR2 .102 C2
Thornhill Gdns
Burnopfield NE16 .78 F5
Sunderland SR2 .102 C1
Thornhill Park Sch (Thornhill Unit) SR2 .102 C1
Thornhill Pk SR2 .102 C1
Thornhill Rd
Longbenton NE12 .39 D6
Ponteland NE20 .25 E7
Thornhill St DH4 .94 D8
Thornhill Terr SR2 .102 C1
Thornholme Ave NE34 .60 B6
Thornholme Rd SR2 .102 C1
Thornhope Cl NE38 .83 F6
Thornlea NE61 .9 E4
Thornlea Gdns NE9 .70 F6
Thornleigh Gdns SR6 .60 A3
Thornleigh Rd NE2 .38 E1
Thornley Ave
Gateshead NE10 .72 B6
Cramlington NE23 .22 C6
Thornley Cl NE16 .69 A4
Thornley La NE21,NE39 .68 A6
Thornley Rd NE5 .53 F8
Thornley Terr NE62 .11 C6
Thornley View NE39 .67 F2
Thornley Wood* NE21 .68 B6
Thornton Cl Penshaw DH4 90 B7
Morpeth NE61 .9 B6
Thornton Cotts NE40 .52 C6
Thornton Cres NE21 .53 C3
Thornton Ct NE38 .83 C5
Thornton St NE1 .98 C1
Thornton Terr NE12 .30 A1
Thorntree Ave NE13 .21 B1
Thorntree Cl NE25 .31 B4
Thorntree Ct NE12 .39 F8
Thorntree Dr
Newcastle-upon-Tyne NE15 .54 A7
Whitley Bay NE25 .31 C4
Thorntree Gdns NE63 .7 A2
Thorntree Mews SR3 .85 C2
Thorntree Way NE24 .16 F7
Thorntree Wlk NE32 .58 D2
Thornwood Gdns NE11 .70 B6
Thornyford House NE4 .98 B2
Thornygarth NE10 .71 E7
Thoroton St NE24 .17 E8
Thorp Ave NE61 .4 A2
Thorp Cl NE24 .17 B5
Thorp Cotts NE40 .52 A5
Thorpe Cl NE4 .98 A2
Thorpe Dr NE40 .52 E5
Thorpe St NE4 .98 A2
Thorpeness Rd SR3 .85 C1
Threap Gdns NE28 .40 E4
Three Mile Ct NE3 .38 C8
Three Rivers Ct NE36 .74 A7

- Threlkeld Gr SR6 75 C5
- Thrift St NE29 42 A4
- Thristley Gdns SR2 86 C3
- Throckley Fst Sch NE15 35 C2
- Throckley Mid Sch NE15 35 C2
- Throckley Way NE34 59 B5
- Thropton Ave Blyth NE24 17 C5
  - Newcastle-upon-Tyne NE7 39 B5
- Thropton Cl
  - Chester le Street DH2 88 A1
  - Gateshead NE10 72 C6
- Thropton Cres NE3 38 B6
- Thropton Ct NE24 17 C7
- Thropton Pl NE29 41 D7
- Thropton Terr NE7 39 B2
- Thrunton Ct 5 DH5 94 F8
- Thrush Gr 2 SR5 74 C1
- Thurleston DH4 90 C4
- Thurlow Way DH5 94 D6
- Thursby DH3 82 E2
- Thursby Ave NE30 32 B2
- Thursby Gdns NE9 71 B3
- Thurso Cl SR3 85 B1
- Tiberius Cl 6 NE28 40 B1
- Tidings The NE10 57 B2
- Tilbeck Sq SR3 92 A5
- Tilbury Cl DH4 90 C5
- Tilbury Gdns SR3 91 C8
- Tilbury Gr NE30 32 A2
- Tilbury Rd SR3 91 C8
- Tileshed La NE36 59 D1
- Till Ave NE21 53 B2
- Till Gr NE61 1 E5
- Till St 7 NE6 56 C4
- Tilley Cres NE42 50 D3
- Tilley Rd NE38 82 F5
- Tillmouth Ave NE25 23 E2
- Tillmouth Gdns NE4 54 C6
- Tillmouth Park Rd NE15 35 D1
- Tilson Way NE3 37 F6
- Timber Beach Rd SR5 74 D1
- Times Sq NE1 100 C4
- Timlin Gdns NE28 41 B3
- Timothy Duff Ct NE30 42 E7
- Tindal Cl NE4 98 B1
- Tindal St NE4 98 B1
- Tindale Ave NE23 22 C6
- Tindale Dr NE16 69 A6
- Tinkler Terr DH3 89 B1
- Tinkler's Bank NE45 46 F3
- Tintagel Cl
  - Cramlington NE23 22 B8
  - Sunderland SR3 85 B1
- Tintern NE38 83 C3
- Tintern Cl DH4 90 C2
- Tintern Cres
  - Tynemouth NE29 41 D8
  - Newcastle-upon-Tyne NE6 56 B7
- Tintern St SR4 102 B2
- Tiree Ct SR3 92 A6
- Tirril Pl NE5 37 A1
- Titan Rd NE6 57 A5
- Titchfield Rd NE38 83 C4
- Titchfield Terr
  - Pegswood NE61 4 F4
  - Ashington NE63 6 D2
- Tithe Barn* TD15 104 D7
- Tithe Cotts NE20 25 E7
- Titian Ave NE34 59 C2
- Titlington Gr NE31 57 D3
- Tiverton Ave
  - Tynemouth NE29 31 C1
  - 1 Newcastle-upon-Tyne NE4 54 E5
- Tiverton Cl Newbottle DH4 90 C4
  - Wallsend NE28 41 A5
- Tiverton Gdns NE9 70 F3
- Tiverton Pl NE23 22 B8
- Tiverton Sq SR3 85 C1
- Tivoli Bldgs DH4 90 C6
- Toberty Gdns NE10 72 B8
- Todd's Nook NE4 98 B1
- Togstone Pl 4 NE5 37 C1
- Toll Bar Rd SR2 92 E8
- Toll Bridge Rd NE21 53 F3
- Toll Sq NE30 42 C6
- Tollerton Dr SR5 74 A1
- Tollgate Fields DH4 94 A1
- Tollgate Rd NE39 77 F5
- Tolls Cl NE25 31 C6
- Tomlea Ave NE22 11 D1
- Tonbridge Ave NE29 41 E4
- Toner Ave NE31 57 D4
- Toner Avenue Cty Inf Sch NE31 57 D3
- Toner Avenue Jun Sch NE31 57 D3
- Topcliff SR6 103 B4
- Topcliffe Gn NE9 71 B2
- Toppings St NE35 58 E1
- Tor Mere Cl NE37 83 A6
- Torcross Way NE23 22 B8
- Toronto Rd SR3 85 D2
- Toronto Sq SR3 85 D2
- Torquay Gdns NE9 70 F3
- Torquay Par NE31 58 A3
- Torquay Rd SR3 85 D2
- Torrens Rd SR3 85 D2
- Torrington Cl DH4 90 C4
- Torver Cl NE13 28 B5
- Torver Cres SR6 75 D5
- Torver Pl NE9 71 B4
- Torver Way NE30 31 F2
- Tosson Cl NE22 11 B1
- Tosson Pl
  - North Shields NE29 41 D5
  - Ashington NE63 6 E3
- Tosson Terr NE6 39 C1
- Totnes Cl SR3 85 B1
- Totnes Dr NE23 22 B8
- Toward Rd
  - Sunderland SR1, SR2 103 A2
  - Sunderland SR2 103 B1
- Toward St 10 NE6 56 B6
- Tower Ct
  - Easington Lane DH5 95 C1
  - Dunston NE11 100 A1
- Tower Gdns NE40 52 C5
- Tower Ho NE1 99 C1
- Tower Knowe Visitor Centre* NE48 121 A5
- Tower Pl 1 SR2 86 E4
- Tower Rd NE37 83 E7
- Tower St
  - Newcastle-upon-Tyne NE1 99 B1
  - Sunderland SR2 103 C1
- Tower St W SR2 103 B1
- Tower View NE15 54 C6
- Towers Ave NE2 38 E3
- Towers Cl NE22 16 A8
- Towers Pl NE34 58 E5
- Towers The SR4 85 B5
- Town End Prim Sch SR5 73 F4
- Town Farm Field NE45 46 F6
- Town Sq 9 NE28 40 B2
- Towne Gate The NE15 34 E2
- Towneley Cotts NE40 52 A4
- Towneley Terr NE39 66 E4
- Townend Ct NE34 59 C5
- Townfield Gdns NE15 52 F8
- Townley Fields NE39 67 F2
- Townley Rd NE39 67 D2
- Townsend Cres NE61 8 D6
- Townsend Rd SR3 85 D1
- Townsend Sq SR3 91 C8
- Townsville Ave NE25 31 D3
- Towton NE12 29 D4
- Toynbee NE38 84 A5
- Tracey Ave NE36 74 B8
- Trafalgar House 17 NE30 42 D7
- Trafalgar Rd NE37 72 F1
- Trafalgar Sq SR1 103 C3
- Trafalgar St NE1 99 B1
- Trafford NE9 71 A1
- Trafford Rd SR5 75 A1
- Trafford Wlk NE5 36 E3
- Trajan Ave NE33 42 D4
- Trajan St NE33 42 D4
- Trajan Wlk NE15 34 D2
- Transbritannia Ct NE21 53 E4
- Tranwell Cl
  - Newcastle-upon-Tyne NE3 37 F8
  - Pegswood NE61 4 E3
- Tranwell Dr NE25 23 E2
- Travers St DH4 90 C6
- Treby St SR4 102 A3
- Tredegar Cl NE5 37 B4
- Tree Ct 26 SR3 91 F6
- Treecone Cl SR3 92 A5
- Treherne Rd NE2 38 D3
- Trent Ave NE31 57 E3
- Trent Dr NE32 58 C2
- Trent Gdns NE8 71 B8
- Trent Rd SR3 85 C1
- Trent St
  - Easington Lane DH5 97 C8
  - Chopwell NE17 66 C1
- Trentham Ave NE7 39 B5
- Trentham Gdns NE61 4 F4
- Trenton Ave NE38 83 D6
- Trevarren Dr SR2 92 F7
- Trevelyan Ave
  - Bedlington NE22 11 B1
  - Blyth NE24 17 C6
- Trevelyan Cl SR3 85 B1
- Trevelyan Ct 2 NE12 39 A6
- Trevelyan Dr NE5 37 A4
- Trevethick St NE8 70 D8
- Trevone Pl NE23 23 A2
- Trevor Gr SR6 75 A8
- Trevor Terr NE30 42 B7
- Trewhitt Rd NE6 56 C8
- Trewit Rd NE26 32 B5
- Tribune Pl NE9 71 B6
- Trident Rd SR3 92 A7
- Trimdon Gr NE9 71 D3
- Trimdon St SR4 102 B3
- Trimdon St W SR4 102 B4
- Trinity Bldgs NE30 42 C5
- Trinity Cl 2 NE29 42 A4
- Trinity Ct NE8 101 C3
- Trinity Ctyd NE6 56 D4
- Trinity Gr NE23 23 A2
- Trinity Maritime Mus* NE1 101 B4
- Trinity Pk DH4 90 B5
- Trinity Pl NE29 42 A4
- Trinity Sq SR1 103 B3
- Trinity St
  - North Shields NE29 42 A4
  - Sunderland SR5 74 F2
- Trinity Terr 3 NE29 42 A4
- Trinity Wlk NE33 42 B1
- Trojan Ave NE6 56 E7
- Tromso Cl NE29 41 C5
- Trool Ct SR3 92 A5
- Troon Cl NE37 72 C2
- Trotter Gr NE22 11 C1
- Trotter Terr SR2 92 F6
- Troutbeck Ave NE6 56 F5
- Troutbeck Gdns NE9 71 A3
- Troutbeck Rd SR6 75 C5
- Troutbeck Way NE34 58 F3
- Troutdale Pl NE12 38 F6
- Troves Cl NE4 54 E4
- Trowbridge Way NE3 37 F5
- Truro Gr NE29 41 D8
- Truro Rd SR3 85 D1
- Truro Way NE32 58 C1
- Tuart St DH3 88 C3
- Tudor Ave NE29 41 E6
- Tudor Ct NE20 25 C4
- Tudor Dr DH9 79 D3
- Tudor Gr SR3 85 F3
- Tudor Rd
  - Chester le Street DH3 88 D5
  - South Shields NE33 42 C2
- Tudor Way NE3 37 B6
- Tudor Wlk NE3 37 C6
- Tudor Wynd NE6 39 D2
- Tulip Cl NE21 53 B2
- Tulip St Prudhoe NE42 50 B2
  - Gateshead NE8 56 C1
- Tummel Ct SR3 92 A6
- Tumulus Ave NE6 57 A8
- Tunbridge Rd SR3 85 D2
- Tundry Way NE21 53 F4
- Tuneside NE10 72 B7
- Tunis Rd SR3 85 E2
- Tunstall Ave
  - South Shields NE34 60 B6
  - Newcastle-upon-Tyne NE6 56 D6
- Tunstall Bank SR2,SR3 92 D7
- Tunstall Hill Cl SR2 86 C2
- Tunstall Hope Rd SR3 92 C8
- Tunstall Pk SR2 86 C4
- Tunstall Rd SR2 102 C1
- Tunstall Terr
  - New Silksworth SR2 92 B7
  - Ryhope SR2 92 D7
  - Sunderland SR2 102 C2
- Tunstall Terr W SR2 102 C2
- Tunstall Vale SR2 86 C4
- Tunstall View SR3 92 B8
- Tunstall Village Gn SR3 92 C7
- Tunstall Village Rd SR3 92 B7
- Tunstall Villas SR3 92 B7
- Turbinia Gdns NE7 39 D2
- Turfside NE10 72 A7
- Turn The NE61 8 F5
- Turnberry Ouston DH2 81 F2
  - Whitley Bay NE25 31 C5
  - South Shields NE33 42 E1
- Turnberry Cl NE37 72 C2
- Turnberry Ct NE10 72 B7
- Turnberry Way
  - Cramlington NE23 22 C6
  - Newcastle-upon-Tyne NE3 38 E6
- Turnbull Ho 5 SR5 75 B1
- Turnbull St SR1 103 C4
- Turner Ave NE34 59 D2
- Turner Cl NE40 52 D4
- Turner Cres NE3 38 A5
- Turner St NE27 30 E1
- Turners Way NE61 8 D7
- Turnham Rd SR3 85 C1
- Turnstile Mews 7 SR6 75 E2
- Turnstone Dr NE38 82 F3
- Turret Rd NE15 53 F7
- Tuscan Rd SR3 91 C8
- Tweed Ave NE61 1 E5
- Tweed Bridge* TD12 106 D8
- Tweed Dr NE61 9 E1
- Tweed Gr NE15 53 C7
- Tweed St
  - Easington Lane DH5 97 C8
  - Chopwell NE17 66 C1
  - Hebburn NE31 57 E5
  - Jarrow NE32 58 A5
  - Washington NE38 83 F4
  - Newcastle-upon-Tyne NE4 54 F5
  - Ashington NE63 6 E4
- Tweedmouth Ct NE3 38 E4
- Tweedy St NE24 17 A8
- Tweedy Terr NE6 56 F5
- Tweedy's Bldgs NE40 52 B5
- Twelfth Ave
  - Chester le Street DH2 88 B4
  - Blyth NE24 17 D6
- Twentieth Ave NE24 17 C5
- Twentyfifth Ave NE24 17 D5
- Twentysecond Ave NE24 17 C5
- Twentysixth Ave NE24 17 C5
- Twentythird Ave NE24 17 C5
- Twickenham Ct NE23 22 F2
- Twickenham Rd SR3 85 C2
- Twizell Ave NE21 53 B2
- Twizell Pl NE20 25 E7
- Twizell St NE24 17 F6
- Two Ball Lonnen NE4 54 D8
- Twyford Cl NE23 22 B8
- Tyldesley Sq SR3 85 C1
- Tyndal Gdns 4 NE11 54 F1
- Tyne App NE32 58 A8
- Tyne Ct NE46 45 A6
- Tyne Dock Sta NE33 59 B6
- Tyne Gdns
  - Washington NE37 72 D1
  - Ryton NE40 52 E4
  - Ovingham NE42 50 B4
- Tyne Green NE46 45 A6
- Tyne Green Country Park NE46 45 B6
- Tyne Green Rd
  - Hexham NE46 45 A6
  - Hexham NE46 45 B6
- Tyne Ho 20 SR3 91 F6
- Tyne Main Rd NE10 56 C3
- Tyne Mills Ind Est NE46 45 C5
- Tyne Point Ind Est NE32 58 E5
- Tyne Rd E NE8 100 C2
- Tyne Riverside Ctry Pk* NE15 52 D8
- Tyne Riverside Ctry Pk* NE42 50 B3
- Tyne St
  - Easington Lane DH5 97 C8
  - Newcastle-upon-Tyne NE1 56 A5
  - Gateshead, Bill Quay NE10 57 A2
  - Gateshead, Felling Shore NE10 56 E2
  - Gateshead, Pelaw NE10 56 F2
  - Chopwell NE17 66 B1
  - Blaydon NE21 53 B1
  - North Shields NE30 42 B5
  - Jarrow NE32 58 B8
  - Ashington NE63 6 E4
- Tyne Terr NE34 59 C5
- Tyne Tunnel (Tynemouth) Trad Est NE29 41 B5
- Tyne Valley Gdns NE40 52 A5
- Tyne View
  - Newcastle-upon-Tyne NE15 53 D6
  - Blaydon NE21 53 C1
  - Hebburn NE31 57 C7
  - Crawcrook NE40 51 F7
  - Wylam NE41 51 B6
- Tyne View Ave NE16 69 C8
- Tyne View Com Prim Schs NE8 100 C2
- Tyne View Gdns NE10 56 F1
- Tyne View Pl NE8 100 C1
- Tyne View Terr
  - North Shields NE28 41 C1
  - Wallsend NE28 41 C1
  - Prudhoe NE42 50 D3
  - Stocksfield NE43 64 D7
- Tyne Wlk NE15 35 D1
- Tynebank NE21 53 B2
- Tynedale Ave
  - Whitley Bay NE26 31 F6
  - Wallsend NE28 40 B4
- Tynedale Cl NE41 51 B6
- Tynedale Cres DH4 90 B7
- Tynedale Ct NE28 41 A4
- Tynedale Dr NE24 17 A7
- Tynedale Gdns NE43 64 D5
- Tynedale Ho NE15 54 B5
- Tynedale Mid Sch NE24 17 A7
- Tynedale Rd
  - South Shields NE34 59 F8
  - Sunderland SR3 85 C1
- Tynedale St DH5 94 E1
- Tynedale Terr
  - Longbenton NE12 39 D6
  - Hexham NE46 44 F4
- Tynegate Office Precinct NE8 101 C2
- Tynemouth Castle* NE30 42 E7
- Tynemouth Cl 3 NE6 56 B6
- Tynemouth Coll NE29 41 F6
- Tynemouth Ct 7 NE6 56 C7
- Tynemouth Gr 9 NE6 56 C7
- Tynemouth Pl 6 NE30 42 D7
- Tynemouth Priory* NE30 42 E7
- Tynemouth Rd
  - Wallsend NE28 41 A3
  - North Shields NE30 42 C6
  - Jarrow NE32 58 B2
  - Newcastle-upon-Tyne NE6 56 C7
- Tynemouth Sealife Ctr* NE30 32 D1
- Tynemouth Sq SR3 85 D1
- Tynemouth Sta NE30 42 D7
- Tynemouth Terr NE30 42 D7
- Tynemouth Watch House (Mus)* NE30 42 E7
- Tynemouth Way 8 NE6 56 C7
- Tyneside Rd NE4 100 B3
- Tyneside Ret Pk NE28 41 A6
- Tynevale Ave NE21 53 C1
- Tynevale Terr
  - Newcastle-upon-Tyne NE15 53 C6
  - Gateshead NE8 100 C1
- Tyneview Pk NE12 39 D5
- Tyneview Prim Sch NE6 57 A5
- Tyneview Terr NE46 45 C3
- Tyzack Cres SR6 75 D2

U

- Uldale Ct NE3 37 E7
- Ullswater Ave
  - Easington Lane DH5 97 C8
  - Hedworth NE32 58 D3
- Ullswater Cl NE24 16 E8
- Ullswater Cres NE21 68 B8
- Ullswater Dr NE12 29 F3
- Ullswater Gdns NE34 59 D6
- Ullswater Gr SR5 75 C4
- Ullswater Rd
  - Chester le Street DH2 88 B1
  - Newbiggin-by-the-Sea NE64 7 C3
- Ullswater Terr DH6 97 E8
- Ullswater Way NE5 54 B8
- Ulverston Gdns NE9 71 B4
- Ulverstone Terr NE6 56 E7
- Umfraville Dene NE42 50 D3
- Underhill Dr NE62 10 E6
- Underhill Rd SR6 59 F1
- Underhill Terr NE9 72 A1
- Underwood NE10 72 A6
- Underwood Gr NE23 16 A1
- Union Alley NE33 42 C3
- Union Hall Rd NE15 53 D7
- Union La SR1 103 B3
- Union Quay NE30 42 C5
- Union Rd
  - North Shields NE30 42 C6
  - Newcastle-upon-Tyne NE6 56 C6
- Union St
  - Hetton le Hole DH5 95 A4
  - Newcastle-upon-Tyne NE2 99 C2
  - Blyth NE24 17 F7
  - Wallsend NE28 57 B8
  - North Shields NE30 42 B5
  - Jarrow NE32 58 B8
  - South Shields NE33 59 B6
  - Sunderland SR1 103 A3
  - Sunderland, South Hylton SR4 85 A6
- Union Stairs NE30 42 B5
- Unity Terr Tantobie DH9 79 B2
  - Cambois NE24 12 D4
- Univ of Newcastle-upon-Tyne NE1 99 A3
- Univ of Northumbria at Newcastle
  - Newcastle-upon-Tyne NE1 99 B2
  - Newcastle-upon-Tyne NE7 39 C4
- Univ of Sunderland SR1 102 C2
- Univ of Sunderland Ashburne Ho (School of Arts, Design & Media) SR2 86 D4
- Univ of Sunderland Bede Tower SR2 103 A1
- Univ of Sunderland Benedict Bldg SR2 103 A1
- Univ of Sunderland Langham Tower SR2 103 A1
- Univ of Sunderland Liby
  - Sunderland SR1 102 C2
  - Sunderland SR2 103 A1
- Univ of Sunderland St Peter's Campus SR6 103 B4
- University Sta SR1 102 C2
- Uplands NE25 31 D5
- Uplands The Birtley DH3 82 D5
  - Newcastle-upon-Tyne NE3 37 F4
- Uplands Way NE9 71 F2
- Upper Camden St 10 NE30 42 A6
- Upper Crone St NE27 30 F4
- Upper Elsdon St 6 NE29 42 A4
- Upper Fenwick Gr NE61 4 A2
- Upper Norfolk St NE30 42 B6
- Upper Pearson St NE30 42 B6
- Upper Precinct The NE21 53 D3
- Upper Queen St NE30 42 B6
- Upton St NE8 100 C1
- Urban Gdns NE37 83 D7
- Urfa Terr 4 NE33 42 D4
- Urswick Ct NE3 37 B5
- Urwin St DH5 95 B3
- Ushaw Rd NE31 57 F6
- Usher St 3 SR5 75 B1
- Usk Ave NE32 58 C3
- Usworth Colliery Prim Sch NE37 72 E1
- Usworth Cotts SR5 73 D3
- Usworth Grange Prim Sch NE37 72 F1
- Usworth Sch NE37 72 D2
- Usworth Station Rd
  - 4 Washington, Concord NE37 83 E8
  - Washington, Sulgrave NE37 83 F8
- Uxbridge Terr 3 NE10 56 D1

V

- Vale Ho NE2 56 A8
- Vale St Easington Lane DH5 97 B8
  - Sunderland SR4 102 B1
- Vale St E SR4 102 B1
- Vale Wlk NE2 56 A8
- Valebrook NE46 44 F4
- Valebrooke SR2 102 C1
- Valebrooke Ave SR2 102 C1
- Valebrooke Gdns SR2 102 C1
- Valehead NE25 31 D5
- Valentia Ave NE6 56 E7
- Valeria Cl NE28 40 E6
- Valerian Ave NE15 34 F2
- Valerian Ct NE63 6 B1
- Valeshead Ho NE28 40 B2
- Valeside NE15 35 C2
- Valley Cres NE21 53 A2
- Valley Ct SR2 103 B1
- Valley Dene NE17 77 B7
- Valley Dr Dunston NE11 69 F7
  - Whickham NE16 69 A8
  - Gateshead NE9 70 F7
- Valley Forge NE38 83 D6
- Valley Gardens Mid Sch NE25 31 D6
- Valley Gdns
  - Whitley Bay NE25 31 D5
  - Wallsend NE28 40 D3
  - Gateshead NE9 71 A7
- Valley Gn NE40 51 F2
- Valley La NE34 60 C6
- Valley Rd NE25 23 F2
- Valley Road Inf Sch SR2 86 F4
- Valley Road Jun Sch SR2 86 F4
- Valley Shopping Village NE11 70 D4
- Valley View Birtley DH3 82 B6
  - Hetton le Hole DH5 94 D1

Valley View *continued*
Newcastle-upon-Tyne, Lemington NE15 53 C7
Burnopfield NE16 78 F7
Newcastle-upon-Tyne, Jesmond NE2 38 F1
Jarrow NE32 58 B4
Washington NE38 83 E1
Rowlands Gill NE39 67 D2
Prudhoe NE42 50 E1
Hexham NE46 45 C4
Valley View Prim Sch NE32 58 B4
Vallum Ct NE4 98 B1
Vallum Pl NE9 71 B6
Vallum Rd Throckley NE15 35 E2
Newcastle-upon-Tyne NE6 56 E6
Vallum Way NE4 98 B1
Vanborough Ct NE25 23 D2
Vanburgh Gdns NE61 8 D7
Vance Bsns Pk NE11 70 B7
Vance Ct NE21 53 E4
Vancouver Dr NE7 39 D2
Vane St SR3 92 A7
Vane Terr SR2 103 C1
Vanguard Ct SR3 91 F6
Vardy Terr DH4 90 E6
Vauxhall Rd NE6 57 A8
Vedra St 1 SR5 75 B1
Velville Ct NE3 37 B6
Ventnor Ave NE4 54 F5
Ventnor Cres NE9 70 E5
Ventnor Gdns
Whitley Bay NE26 32 A6
Gateshead NE9 70 E6
Vera St NE40 66 F8
Verdun Ave NE31 57 E6
Vermont NE37 83 D8
Verne Rd NE29 41 D6
Vernon Cl NE33 59 B8
Vernon Dr NE25 31 E4
Vernon Pl NE64 7 E5
Vernon St NE37 83 D8
Veryan Gdns SR3 86 B3
Vespasian Ave NE33 42 D4
Viador DH3 88 C4
Viaduct St NE28 40 E2
Vicarage Cl SR3 91 F7
Vicarage La SR4 85 A6
Vicarage Rd SR3 92 A7
Vicarage St NE29 42 A4
Vicarage Terr NE22 16 A8
Vicars Way NE12 38 F6
Vicars' La NE7 39 A5
Vicarsholme Cl SR3 91 E5
Victor Ct SR6 75 E1
Victor St
5 Chester le Street DH3 88 C3
Sunderland SR6 75 E1
Victoria Ave
Gateshead NE10 71 C7
Longbenton NE12 39 D7
Whitley Bay NE26 32 B5
Wallsend NE28 40 B2
Sunderland, Grangetown SR2 86 E2
Sunderland, South Hylton SR4 85 B6
Victoria Ave W SR2 86 E2
Victoria Bldgs SR1 102 C2
Victoria Cres
8 North Shields NE29 41 F5
Tynemouth NE30 32 C3
Victoria Ct
Killingworth NE12 29 C1
Tynemouth NE30 32 C3
Hebburn NE31 57 D5
Gateshead NE8 100 C1
Victoria House NE8 100 C1
Victoria Ind Est NE31 57 C3
Victoria Mews
Newcastle-upon-Tyne NE2 56 A8
Blyth NE24 17 D7
Whitley Bay NE26 32 B5
Victoria Pl
Whitley Bay NE25 31 E4
7 Washington NE37 83 D8
Sunderland SR1 103 B2
Victoria Rd
South Shields NE33 42 C1
Washington NE37 83 D8
Gateshead NE8 70 C8
Victoria Rd E NE31 57 F6
Victoria Rd W NE31 57 D4
Victoria Sq
4 Gateshead NE10 71 D8
Newcastle-upon-Tyne NE2 99 B3
Victoria St
Hetton le Hole DH5 95 A4
Dunston NE11 100 A1
North Shields NE29 42 A4
Hebburn NE31 57 C6
Newcastle-upon-Tyne NE4 100 B4
Crawcrook NE40 51 F4
Victoria Terr
Penshaw DH4 90 C8
5 Gateshead, Felling NE10 71 D8
3 Throckley NE15 35 D2
Hamsterley NE17 77 B6
Bedlington NE22 11 C1
Whitley Bay NE26 32 B5
Jarrow NE32 58 A6
East Boldon NE36 74 C7
Rowlands Gill NE39 67 C1
Prudhoe NE42 50 D2

Victoria Terr *continued*
Newbiggin-by-the-Sea NE64 7 E4
Gateshead, Wrekenton NE9 71 C3
Springwell NE9 71 F1
Victoris Villas NE22 11 B1
Victory Cotts NE23 22 A1
Victory House 15 NE30 42 D7
Victory St SR4 85 E7
Victory St E DH5 95 B4
Victory St W DH5 95 B4
Victory Way SR3 91 C5
Viewforth Dr SR5 75 C3
Viewforth Gn 1 NE5 37 C1
Viewforth Rd SR2 92 F5
Viewforth Terr SR5 75 C3
Viewlands NE63 6 D4
Vigo La Birtley DH3 88 D8
Washington NE38 83 A1
Washington NE38 83 B1
Vigodale DH3 82 E1
Viking Precinct 8 NE32 58 B7
Villa Cl SR4 85 F6
Villa Pl NE8 101 B1
Villa View NE9 71 A6
Village Ct NE26 31 F5
Village Ctr
Washington, Albany NE37 83 B7
Washington, Donwell NE37 72 B1
Washington, Biddick NE38 83 D4
Washington, Glebe NE38 83 D5
Washington, Harraton NE38 88 F8
Washington, Lambton NE38 83 B3
Village E NE40 52 C6
Village Farm NE15 36 A1
Village Hts NE8 101 B2
Village La NE38 83 D6
Village Pl NE6 56 D5
Village Rd NE23 22 C6
Village The SR2 93 A6
Villas The Wide Open NE13 28 C5
Stannington NE61 13 C7
7 Sunderland SR5 74 C1
Villette Brook St 5 SR2 86 E4
Villette Path SR2 86 E4
Villette Rd SR2 86 E4
Villiers Pl 3 DH3 88 C4
Villiers St SR1 103 B3
Villiers St S SR1 103 B2
Vimy Ave NE31 57 E6
Vindolanda 2 NE28 40 F4
Vindomora Road DH8, NE17 76 E4
Vindomora Roman Fort* DH8 76 E4
Vindomora Villas DH8 76 E4
Vine Cl NE8 100 C1
Vine Ct NE46 45 B3
Vine La NE1 99 A2
Vine Pl
6 Houghton-le-Spring DH4 94 E8
Sunderland SR1 102 C2
Vine St Wallsend NE28 40 C1
South Shields NE33 59 C6
Vine Terr NE46 45 B4
Viola Cres DH2 81 F2
Viola St NE37 83 D8
Viola Terr NE16 69 B7
Violet Cl NE4 54 D4
Violet St
Houghton-le-Spring DH4 94 D8
Sunderland SR4 102 B3
Sunderland, South Hylton SR4 85 A6
Violet Terr DH4 89 D3
Violet Wlk NE4 54 D4
Viscount Rd 4 SR3 92 A7
Vivian Cres 1 DH2 88 C2
Vivian Sq SR6 75 D3
Voltage Terr DH4 90 D4
Vulcan Pl Bedlington NE22 16 A8
Sunderland SR6 75 D1
Vulcan Terr NE12 29 E1

W

Wade Ave NE15 33 A7
Wadham Terr NE34 59 B5
Wadsley Sq SR2 86 E3
Waggonway The NE42 50 D3
Wagon Way NE28 40 D1
Wagonway Rd NE31 57 E7
Wagtail Cl NE21 68 C8
Wakefield Ave NE34 60 B5
Walbottle Campus Tech Coll NE15 35 F2
Walbottle Rd
Wallbottle NE15 35 F1
Newburn NE15 52 F8
Walbottle St Cuthbert's RC Prim Sch NE15 35 F2
Walbottle Village Fst Sch NE15 35 F1
Walden Cl DH2 81 D2
Waldo St NE29 42 B5
Waldridge Cl NE37 83 A6
Waldridge Gdns NE9 71 D4
Waldridge La DH2 88 A2
Waldridge Rd DH2,DH3 88 B2
Waldron Sq SR2 86 E3
Walker Gate NE6 56 E8
Walker Gate Hospl NE6 39 E1
Walker Gate Ind Est NE6 57 B6
Walker Gate Sta NE6 56 E8
Walker Gr NE6 56 F8
Walker Park Cl NE6 57 A4
Walker Pl NE30 42 C6
Walker Rd NE6 56 E3
Walker Riverside Ind Pk NE6 57 B4
Walker Riverside Pk* NE6 56 F3
Walker Sch NE6 56 F6
Walker Terr NE8 101 B2
Walker View NE10 71 D8
Walkerburn NE23 22 B3
Walkerdene House NE6 57 B8
Walkergate Inf Sch NE6 56 E8
Walkergate Jun Sch NE6 56 E8
Wall Cl NE3 38 A5
Wall St NE3 38 A5
Wall Terr NE6 56 E7
Wallace Ave NE16 69 C8
Wallace Gdns NE9 71 E3
Wallace St
Houghton-le-Spring DH4 94 D8
Dunston NE11 100 A1
Newcastle-upon-Tyne NE2 98 B4
Sunderland SR5 75 C1
Wallace Terr NE40 52 C6
Waller St DH5 94 E7
Wallinfen NE10 71 F5
Wallingford Ave SR2 86 E2
Wallington (N.T.)* NE61 123 F4
Wallington Ave
Brunswick Village NE13 28 A6
Tynemouth NE30 32 A1
Wallington Cl NE22 11 C2
Wallington Ct
Killingworth NE12 29 C3
Seaton Delaval NE25 23 D3
Newcastle-upon-Tyne NE3 37 D7
Wallington Dr NE15 53 E8
Wallington Gr 9 NE33 42 D3
Wallington Rd NE63 6 F2
Wallis St Penshaw DH4 90 B8
12 South Shields NE33 42 C3
Wallridge Dr NE25 23 E1
Wallsend C of E Prim Sch NE28 40 E2
Wallsend Central Mid Sch NE28 40 D2
Wallsend Jubilee Fst Sch NE28 40 A4
Wallsend Rd
North Shields NE28,NE29 41 C3
North Shields, Percy Main NE29 41 D4
Wallsend Sports Ctr NE28 39 F2
Wallsend Sta NE28 40 C1
Walmer Terr NE9 71 D1
Walnut Gdns NE8 70 C8
Walnut Pl NE3 37 F3
Walpole Ct 1 SR4 85 F6
Walpole St
South Shields NE33 42 C1
Newcastle-upon-Tyne NE6 56 E8
Walsh Ave NE31 57 E7
Walsham Cl NE24 17 B5
Walsingham NE38 83 C4
Walter St
Brunswick Village NE13 28 A6
Jarrow NE32 58 B7
Walter Terr
Hetton le Hole DH5 95 B1
Newcastle-upon-Tyne NE4 98 A2
Walter Thomas St 3 SR5 74 F2
Waltham NE38 83 D4
Waltham Cl NE28 39 F3
Waltham Pl 4 NE5 37 B2
Walton Ave Blyth NE24 17 C8
Tynemouth NE29 41 F7
Walton Dr NE62 10 F8
Walton La SR1 103 B3
Walton Pk NE29 41 F8
Walton Rd
Washington NE38 84 B5
Newcastle-upon-Tyne NE5 37 A1
Walwick Ave NE29 41 D6
Walwick Rd NE25 31 B5
Walworth Ave NE34 60 C6
Walworth Gr NE32 58 B3
Wandsworth Rd NE6 56 B7
Wanless La NE46 45 B4
Wanley St NE24 17 E8
Wanlock Cl NE23 22 C3
Wanny Rd NE22 11 B1
Wansbeck NE38 83 A1
Wansbeck Ave Blyth NE24 17 E5
Tynemouth NE30 32 C2
Stakeford NE62 11 A8
Wansbeck Bsns Pk NE63 6 B5
Wansbeck Cl
Sunniside NE16 69 A3
Ellington NE61 1 E5
Wansbeck Cres NE61 4 E3
Wansbeck Ct 13 SR3 91 F6
Wansbeck General Hospl NE63 6 F4
Wansbeck Gr NE25 23 D6
Wansbeck Mews NE63 6 B4
Wansbeck Rd
Dudley NE23 28 F8
Jarrow NE32 58 B5
Ashington NE63 6 B2
Wansbeck Rd N NE3 38 A6
Wansbeck Rd S NE3 38 A6
Wansbeck Riverside Pk* NE62,NE63 5 F1
Wansbeck Road Sta NE3 38 A6
Wansbeck Sq NE63 6 C4
Wansbeck St
Chopwell NE17 66 C1
Morpeth NE61 9 A8

Wansbeck St *continued*
Ashington NE63 12 A8
Wansbeck Terr NE62 11 D7
Wansbeck View NE62 11 B8
Wansdyke NE61 3 D1
Wansfell Ave NE5 37 D3
Wansford Ave NE5 37 B1
Wansford Way
Whickham NE16 68 F5
Whickham NE16 69 A4
Wantage Ave NE29 41 D4
Wantage St NE33 59 D7
Wapping 1 NE24 17 F8
Wapping St NE33 42 B4
War Memorial Hospl NE46 45 B4
Warbeck Cl NE3 37 B6
Warburton Cres NE9 71 A8
Warcop Ct NE3 37 E7
Ward Ct SR2 103 B1
Warden Gr DH5 94 F7
Warden Law La SR3 91 F6
Wardenlaw NE10 71 F5
Wardill Gdns NE9 71 B7
Wardle Ave NE33 42 E1
Wardle Dr NE23 29 B8
Wardle Gdns NE10 71 E7
Wardle St NE3 38 E5
Wardle Terr NE40 51 F4
Wardley Ct NE10 72 D8
Wardley Cty Prim Sch NE10 72 B8
Wardley Dr NE10 72 D7
Wardley La NE10,NE31 57 C1
Wardroper House NE6 57 A4
Warenford Cl NE23 22 C4
Warenford Pl NE5 54 C7
Warenmill Cl NE15 53 B7
Warennes St 3 SR4 85 E7
Warenton Pl NE29 31 B1
Waring Ave NE26 24 B7
Wark Ave Shiremoor NE27 30 F4
North Shields NE29 41 C6
Wark Cres NE32 58 B2
Wark Ct NE3 38 E4
Wark St DH3 88 C1
Warkdale Ave NE24 17 A6
Warkworth Ave
Blyth NE24 17 E5
Whitley Bay NE26 32 A5
Wallsend NE28 40 C4
South Shields NE34 60 B7
Warkworth Castle* NE65 119 D6
Warkworth Cl NE38 83 B4
Warkworth Cres
Newburn NE15 52 F7
Newcastle-upon-Tyne NE3 38 B6
Ashington NE63 6 C3
Warkworth Dr
Chester le Street DH2 88 A1
Wide Open NE13 28 C6
Ellington NE61 1 E5
Pegswood NE61 4 F3
Warkworth Gdns NE10 71 C8
Warkworth Hermitage* NE65 119 D7
Warkworth La NE61 1 C6
Warkworth St
Newcastle-upon-Tyne, Lemington NE15 53 C6
2 Newcastle-upon-Tyne, Byker NE6 56 C6
Warkworth Terr
Tynemouth NE30 42 D8
Jarrow NE32 58 B3
Warnham Ave SR2 86 E2
Warnhead Rd NE22 11 B1
Warren Ave NE6 57 A8
Warren Cl DH4 90 C4
Warren Ct NE63 6 C2
Warren Sq SR1 103 C4
Warrenmor NE10 72 A7
Warrens Wlk NE21 53 A1
Warrington Rd
Newcastle-upon-Tyne, Fawdon NE3 37 E6
Newcastle-upon-Tyne, Elswick NE4 100 A4
Warton Terr NE6 56 C8
Warwick Ave NE16 69 B5
Warwick Cl
Whickham NE16 69 A5
Seghill NE23 22 E1
Warwick Ct NE3 37 D7
Warwick Dr
Houghton-le-Spring DH5 94 E7
Whickham NE16 69 B5
Washington NE37 72 D2
Sunderland SR3 91 C7
Warwick Gr NE22 10 D1
Warwick Hall Wlk NE7 39 D3
Warwick Rd
Wallsend NE28 40 B1
Hebburn NE31 57 F3
South Shields NE34 59 D7
Newcastle-upon-Tyne NE5 53 E8
Warwick St Blyth NE24 17 C4
Newcastle-upon-Tyne NE6 56 A7
Gateshead NE8 101 C2
Sunderland SR5 75 D1
Warwick Terr SR3 92 A8
Warwick Terr W SR3 92 A8
Wasdale Cl NE23 22 C3
Wasdale Ct SR6 75 C5
Wasdale Rd NE5 54 B8
Washington Arts Ctr NE38 83 D2
Washington Birtley Service Area DH3,NE38 82 E3
Washington F Pit Mus* NE37 83 C7
Washington Gdns NE9 71 C3
Washington Highway
Penshaw DH4,NE38 89 E8
Washington NE37,NE38 83 B4
Washington Hospl The NE38 88 E8
Washington Old Hall* NE38 83 E6
Washington Rd SR5 74 B2
Washington Sch NE37 83 D7
Washington St SR4 85 F6
Washington Terr NE30 42 C7
Washington Village Prim Sch NE38 83 E6
Washington Wildfowl & Wetlands Ctr* NE38 84 C5
Washingwell Com Prim Sch NE16 69 C6
Washingwell La NE16 69 D6
Washingwell Pk NE16 69 C6
Waskdale Cres NE21 68 B8
Waskerley Cl NE16 69 B3
Waskerley Gdns NE9 71 D3
Waskerley Rd NE38 83 F5
Watch House Cl NE29 42 A3
Watcombe Cl NE37 72 F2
Water Row NE15 52 E7
Water St NE4 100 B3
Waterbeach Pl NE5 37 B2
Waterbeck Cl NE23 22 C3
Waterbury Cl SR5 74 F3
Waterbury Rd NE3 28 B1
Waterfield Rd NE22 12 B4
Waterford Cl
East Rainton DH5 94 D4
Seaton Sluice NE26 24 D6
Waterford Cres 5 NE26 32 B4
Waterford Gn NE63 11 D8
Waterford Pk NE13 27 F6
Watergate NE1 101 B4
Waterloo Ct 5 NE37 83 E8
Waterloo Pl
North Shields NE29 42 A6
Sunderland SR1 103 A2
Waterloo Rd Blyth NE24 17 E7
Earsdon NE25 31 A5
Washington NE37 72 F3
Washington, Sulgrave NE37 72 E1
Waterloo Sq 10 NE33 42 C3
Waterloo St
Newcastle-upon-Tyne NE1 100 C4
Blaydon NE21 53 A1
Waterloo Vale 8 NE33 42 C3
Waterloo Wlk NE37 83 E8
Waterlow Cl SR5 74 F4
Watermill NE40 52 C5
Watermill La NE10 71 E8
Waterside Dr NE11 54 E2
Waterside Pk NE31 57 C6
Waterville Pl 16 NE29 42 A5
Waterville Prim Sch NE29 41 F4
Waterville Rd NE29 41 E4
Waterville Terr 9 NE29 42 A5
Waterworks Rd SR1 102 C2
Watford Cl SR5 74 F4
Watling Pl NE9 71 B6
Watling St
South Shields NE34 59 B5
Corbridge NE45 46 F5
Watson Ave Dudley NE23 29 A8
South Shields NE34 60 B5
Watson Gdns NE28 41 A3
Watson Pl NE34 60 B5
Watson St
Burnopfield NE16 79 B6
Jarrow NE32 58 C8
High Spen NE39 67 A5
Gateshead NE8 100 C1
Watson Terr
West Boldon NE35 73 F7
12 Morpeth NE61 9 A8
Watt St NE8 70 D7
Watt's La NE64 7 E5
Watt's Rd NE26 32 A6
Watts Moses Ho SR1 103 C3
Wavendon Cres SR4 85 E4
Waverdale Ave NE6 57 A7
Waverdale Way NE33 59 B7
Waverley Ave
Bedlington NE22 11 C2
Whitley Bay NE25 31 F4
Waverley Bldgs NE64 7 E5
Waverley Cl NE21 67 F8
Waverley Cres NE15 53 D7
Waverley Ct NE22 11 C2
Waverley Dr NE22 11 C2
Waverley Fst Sch NE15 53 E6
Waverley Lodge NE2 99 C3
Waverley Rd
Newcastle-upon-Tyne NE4 100 B4
Gateshead NE9 71 B1
Waverley Terr Dipton DH9 78 E1
Sunderland SR4 85 E7
Waverly Dr NE22 11 D2
Waverton Cl NE23 22 B3
Wawn St NE33 59 D8
Wayfarer Rd SR5 75 A1
Wayland Sq SR2 86 E1
Wayman St SR5 75 C1
Wayside
Newcastle-upon-Tyne NE15 54 B5
South Shields NE34 60 B6
Sunderland SR2 86 B4

Wea – Wes 179

Wealcroft NE10 .71 F5
Wealcroft Ct NE10 .71 F5
Wealleans Cl NE63 .7 B3
Wear Ct NE34 .59 C5
Wear Lodge DH3 .88 C7
Wear Rd NE31 .57 E3
Wear St
Chester le Street DH3 .88 D2
Fence Houses DH4 .94 A7
Hetton le Hole DH5 .95 A3
Chopwell NE17 .66 B1
Jarrow NE32 .58 B7
Sunderland SR1 .103 C2
Sunderland, South Hylton SR4 .85 A7
Sunderland, Low Southwick SR5 .75 A1
Wear Terr NE38 .83 E4
Wear View SR4 .85 B7
Weardale Ave
Longbenton NE12 .39 D8
Blyth NE24 .17 A8
Wallsend NE28 .40 B4
Washington NE37 .83 C8
Newcastle-upon-Tyne NE6 .57 A6
Sunderland SR6 .75 E7
Weardale Cres DH4 .90 B7
Weardale St DH5 .94 E1
Weardale Terr DH3 .88 D2
Wearfield SR5 .74 F1
Wearmouth Ave SR5 .75 D2
Wearmouth Dr SR5 .75 D2
Wearmouth St SR6 .75 D1
Weathercock La NE9 .70 F5
Weatherside NE21 .53 B1
Webb Gdns NE10 .72 A8
Wedder Law NE23 .22 B3
Wedderburn Sq NE63 .6 C3
Wedgewood Cotts NE15 .53 D6
Wedmore Rd NE5 .36 D3
Weetman St NE33 .42 B1
Weetslade Cres NE23 .29 A7
Weetslade Rd NE23 .29 A7
Weetslade Terr NE23 .29 C5
Weetwood Rd NE23 .22 C4
Weidner Rd NE15,NE4 .54 D6
Welbeck Com Fst Sch NE63 .7 A2
Welbeck Gn NE6 .56 E5
Welbeck Prim Sch NE6 .56 D5
Welbeck Rd
Newcastle-upon-Tyne NE6 .56 E5
Guide Post NE62 .10 E7
Welbeck Terr NE61 .4 F4
Welbottle Hall Gdns NE15 .36 A1
Welburn Cl NE42 .50 C5
Welbury Way NE23 .22 B3
Weldon Ave SR2 .86 E2
Weldon Cres NE7 .39 B2
Weldon Pl NE29 .41 D8
Weldon Rd
Longbenton NE12 .39 B6
East Cramlington NE23 .22 E5
Weldon Terr DH3 .88 D2
Weldon Way NE3 .38 B6
Welfare Cres
Ashington NE63 .6 F3
Newbiggin-by-the-Sea NE64 .7 C4
Welfare Rd DH5 .95 A4
Welford Ave NE3 .38 A5
Well Bank NE45 .46 F5
Well Bank Rd NE37 .72 B1
Well Close Wlk NE16 .69 A6
Well Dean NE42 .50 D3
Well La Tynemouth NE27 .31 B2
Tynemouth NE27 .31 C2
Well Rd NE43 .64 B5
Well Ridge Cl NE25 .31 C6
Well Ridge Pk NE25 .31 C7
Well St SR4 .85 F7
Well Way NE61 .3 F1
Wellands Cl SR6 .60 E1
Wellands Ct SR6 .60 E1
Wellands Dr SR6 .60 E1
Wellands La SR6 .60 E1
Wellbank Sch NE37 .72 B1
Wellbeck Terr NE63 .6 D2
Wellburn Rd NE37 .72 B1
Wellesley St NE32 .58 B5
Wellesley Terr NE4 .98 A1
Wellfield Cl NE15 .35 C1
Wellfield Ct NE40 .51 E3
Wellfield La NE5 .37 B2
Wellfield Mews SR2 .92 E5
Wellfield Mid Sch NE25 .31 B4
Wellfield Rd
Rowlands Gill NE39 .67 C2
Newcastle-upon-Tyne NE4 .54 D5
Newcastle-upon-Tyne NE4 .54 E5
Wellfield Terr
3 Gateshead NE10 .71 C7
Ryhope SR2 .92 E5
Wellgarth Rd NE37 .72 B1
Wellhead Dean Rd NE62 .5 F2
Wellhead Terr NE63 .6 A4
Wellhope NE38 .88 F8
Wellington Ave NE25 .31 A5
Wellington Ct
2 Gateshead NE10 .71 C8
6 Washington NE37 .83 E8
Wellington Dr NE33 .42 C4
Wellington La SR4 .102 B4
Wellington Rd
Dunston NE11 .54 E1
Dunston NE11 .54 F1
Stakeford NE62 .11 A7
Wellington Row DH4 .90 C5
Wellington St
High Pittington DH6 .96 B5
Gateshead, Felling NE10 .71 C8
Newcastle-upon-Tyne, Lemington NE15 .53 D6
Blyth NE24 .17 F7
11 North Shields NE29 .42 A5
Hebburn NE31 .57 D5
Newcastle-upon-Tyne NE4 .98 C1
Gateshead NE8 .101 B3
Wellington St E 10 NE24 .17 F8
Wellington St W 12 NE29 .42 A5
Wellington Wlk 2 NE37 .83 F8
Wellmere Rd SR2 .86 F1
Wells Cl NE12 .39 D4
Wells Gdns NE9 .70 F2
Wells Gr NE34 .60 A7
Wells St NE35 .58 E1
Wellshede NE10 .72 B7
Wellway NE32 .58 B2
Wellway Ct 11 NE61 .3 F1
Wellwood Gdns NE61 .4 A1
Welton Cl NE43 .64 D6
Welworth Way SR1 .102 C3
Welwyn Ave NE22 .11 D3
Welwyn Cl Wallsend NE28 .39 F4
Sunderland SR5 .85 A8
Wembley Ave NE25 .31 E4
Wembley Cl SR5 .74 F3
Wembley Gdns NE24 .12 B6
Wembley Rd SR5 .74 F3
Wembley Terr NE24 .12 C6
Wendover Cl SR5 .74 E4
Wendover Way SR5 .74 E4
Wenham Sq SR2 .86 B4
Wenlock NE38 .83 C4
Wenlock Dr NE29 .41 F8
Wenlock Pl 6 NE34 .59 A4
Wenlock Rd NE34 .59 A5
Wensley Cl Urpeth DH2 .81 E1
Newcastle-upon-Tyne NE5 .37 C4
Wensley Ho 2 SR3 .91 F5
Wensleydale NE28 .39 F5
Wensleydale Ave
Penshaw DH4 .90 A7
Washington NE37 .83 C8
Wensleydale Dr NE12 .39 D8
Wensleydale Mid Sch NE24 .17 F6
Wensleydale Terr NE24 .17 F6
Wentworth NE33 .42 E1
Wentworth Cl NE10 .71 D7
Wentworth Ct NE20 .25 C4
Wentworth Dr NE37 .72 C2
Wentworth Gdns NE25 .31 C4
Wentworth Grange NE3 .38 D4
Wentworth L Ctr NE46 .45 B5
Wentworth Pl
Newcastle-upon-Tyne NE4 .100 B4
Hexham NE46 .45 B5
Wentworth Terr SR4 .102 B3
Werhale Gn NE10 .71 D8
Wesley Ct
1 Gateshead, Felling NE10 .71 C8
Blaydon NE21 .53 D3
Wesley Dr NE12 .30 B1
Wesley Gr NE40 .51 E3
Wesley Mount NE40 .51 E3
Wesley St
Newcastle-upon-Tyne NE2 .99 C2
Prudhoe NE42 .50 D2
Gateshead, Low Fell NE9 .70 F5
Wesley Terr
Chester le Street DH3 .88 C3
Sherburn Hill DH6 .96 C1
Dipton DH9 .78 D1
Prudhoe NE42 .50 D2
Wesley Way
Longbenton NE12 .30 B1
Throckley NE15 .35 D2
Wessex Cl SR5 .74 F4
Wessington Terr NE37 .83 D7
Wessington Way
Sunderland, Castletown SR5 .85 B8
Sunderland, Low Southwick SR5 .74 E1
West Acres
Dinnington NE13 .27 B8
Blaydon NE21 .53 D2
West Ave Longbenton NE12 .29 F1
Longbenton NE12 .39 D6
Whitley Bay NE25 .31 E5
North Shields NE29 .41 D5
Newcastle-upon-Tyne, Gosforth NE3 .38 C4
South Shields NE34 .59 E6
Washington NE38 .83 B1
Rowlands Gill NE39 .67 D1
Newcastle-upon-Tyne, Westerhope NE5 .36 F2
Guide Post NE62 .10 D7
Whitburn SR6 .60 E1
West Bailey NE12 .29 B3
West Boldon Jun Sch NE36 .74 A7
West Bridge St
Penshaw DH4 .89 E8
Cambois NE24 .12 D3
West Chirton (Middle) Ind Est NE29 .41 B7
West Chirton (south) Ind Est NE29 .41 C5
West Chirton North Ind Est NE29 .41 B7
West Clifton NE12 .29 C4
West Copperas NE15 .53 F7
West Cres
Gateshead NE10 .72 C8
West Cres *continued*
Chopwell NE17 .77 B7
West Ct Blyth NE24 .17 C6
Newcastle-upon-Tyne NE3 .38 A5
West Dene Dr NE30 .42 A7
West Denton Cl NE15 .53 D8
West Denton Fst Sch NE5 .36 D1
West Denton High Sch NE5 .36 E2
West Denton Rd NE15 .53 D8
West Denton Ret Pk NE5 .37 A2
West Denton Way NE5 .36 E1
West Dr Blyth NE24 .17 C4
Cleadon SR6 .74 E8
West End
Seaton Sluice NE26 .24 D4
Wallsend NE28 .40 A1
West Farm
Medomsley DH8 .77 C2
Ponteland NE20 .26 C6
Burdon SR3 .92 B3
West Farm Ave NE12 .39 A6
West Farm Ct NE23 .22 B7
West Farm La DH8 .77 C2
West Farm Rd
Wallsend NE28 .40 F3
Newcastle-upon-Tyne NE6 .56 E7
Cleadon SR6 .75 B8
West Farm Wynd NE12 .38 F6
West Ford Rd NE62 .11 B8
West Gate Com Coll NE4 .54 D6
West George Potts St 17 NE33 .42 D1
West Gr SR4 .85 B5
West Grange SR5 .75 C3
West Greens 6 NE61 .9 A8
West Hextol NE46 .44 F4
West Hextol Cl NE46 .44 F4
West High Horse Cl NE39 .68 A4
West Hill Morpeth NE61 .8 E7
Sunderland SR4 .85 E4
West Holborn NE33 .42 B1
West Jesmond Ave NE2 .38 E2
West Jesmond Prim Sch NE2 .38 E1
West Jesmond Sta NE2 .38 E2
West La
Chester le Street DH3 .88 C2
Killingworth NE12 .29 D2
Byermoor NE16 .68 C1
Medomsley NE17 .77 B4
Blaydon NE21 .68 A8
West Law Rd DH8 .76 D1
West Lawn SR2 .86 C4
West Lawrence St SR1 .103 B2
West Lea
New Herrington DH4 .90 D6
Blaydon NE21 .68 C8
West Market St NE61 .2 B3
West Mdws NE5 .36 D4
West Meadows Dr SR6 .75 A8
West Meadows Rd SR6 .75 B8
West Moffett St 6 NE33 .42 D1
West Monkseaton Sta NE25 .31 D4
West Moor Ct NE12 .29 B1
West Moor Dr SR6 .75 A7
West Moor Terr 1 SR4 .85 E7
West Mount
Killingworth NE12 .29 C3
Sunderland SR4 .85 E5
West Par Hebburn NE31 .57 D5
Newcastle-upon-Tyne NE4 .100 B4
West Park Gdns NE21 .53 C1
West Park Rd
South Shields NE33 .59 C7
Gateshead NE8,NE9 .70 E7
Cleadon SR6 .60 A1
West Park View NE23 .28 F8
West Pastures
Hedworth NE36 .73 C5
Ashington NE63 .6 B2
West Percy Rd NE29 .41 F5
West Percy St NE29 .42 A5
West Pk Morpeth NE61 .8 E7
Sunderland SR3 .91 B6
West Quay Rd SR5 .74 F1
West Rd Tantobie DH9 .79 A1
Newcastle-upon-Tyne NE15, NE5 .54 B7
Ponteland NE20 .25 E6
Bedlington NE22 .11 D2
Prudhoe NE42 .50 B2
West Rig The NE3 .37 E4
West Riggs NE22 .15 F8
West Row DH3 .82 E3
West Salisbury St 4 NE24 .17 D8
West Sleekburn Mid Sch NE62 .11 F6
West Spencer Terr NE15 .36 B1
West St 4 Birtley DH3 .82 C4
Whickham NE16 .69 A7
Shiremoor NE27 .30 D1
Wallsend NE28 .40 A2
Hebburn NE31 .57 F7
High Spen NE39 .66 F4
Gateshead NE8 .101 B3
Sunderland SR1 .102 C3
New Silksworth SR3 .92 A8
West Stainton St 5 NE33 .42 D1
West Stevenson St 7 NE33 .42 D1
West Sunniside SR1 .103 A3
West Terr
Seaton Sluice NE26 .24 D6
Stakeford NE62 .11 C7
West Thorn Wlk NE16 .69 A6
West Thorp NE5 .36 F5
West Vallum NE15 .53 F7
West View
Chester le Street DH3 .88 C4
Bournmoor DH4 .89 E3
Newbottle DH4 .90 D2
Penshaw DH4 .90 B8
Shiney Row DH4 .90 B4
Haswell DH6 .97 D1
Sherburn Hill DH6 .96 C1
Kibblesworth NE11 .81 D6
5 Longbenton NE12 .39 D8
Wide Open NE13 .28 B7
Newcastle-upon-Tyne, Lemington NE15 .53 C6
Burnopfield NE16 .79 A6
Blaydon NE21 .53 C3
Bedlington NE22 .11 C3
Annitsford NE23 .29 A8
Seghill NE23 .22 F1
Cambois NE24 .12 C6
Earsdon NE25 .31 A5
Newcastle-upon-Tyne, Elswick NE4 .54 F4
Crawcrook NE40 .51 E6
Wylam NE41 .51 B6
Morpeth NE61 .3 C5
Pegswood NE61 .4 E3
Ashington NE63 .6 D3
Gateshead NE9 .71 C4
Ryhope SR2 .92 E6
3 Sunderland, Castletown SR5 .74 B1
Sunderland, Roker SR6 .75 D3
West View Terr NE46 .45 C4
West Walker Prim Sch NE6 .57 A4
West Walls NE1 .98 C1
West Walpole St NE33 .42 B1
West Way Dunston NE11 .70 A7
South Shields NE33,NE34 .59 C7
West Wear St SR1 .103 A3
West Wylam Dr NE42 .50 E3
West Wynd NE12 .29 D3
Westacre Gdns NE5 .54 C7
Westacres Ave NE16 .69 B5
Westacres Cres NE15 .54 C6
Westbourne Ave
Newcastle-upon-Tyne, Gosforth NE3 .38 C7
Newcastle-upon-Tyne, Walker NE6 .56 F7
Stakeford NE62 .6 A1
Gateshead NE8 .70 E8
Westbourne Dr DH4 .90 B5
Westbourne Gdns NE6 .57 A6
Westbourne Gr NE46 .44 F5
Westbourne Rd SR1 .102 B2
Westbourne Terr
2 Shiney Row DH4 .90 A6
Seaton Delaval NE25 .23 E3
Westburn Gdns NE28 .39 F4
Westburn Mews NE40 .51 E3
Westburn Terr SR6 .75 E2
Westbury Ave NE6 .57 A8
Westbury Rd NE29 .41 F8
Westbury St SR4 .102 B3
Westcliffe Rd SR6 .75 F4
Westcliffe Way NE34 .58 F3
Westcott Ave NE33 .42 E1
Westcott Rd NE34 .59 C6
Westcott Terr DH4 .90 C8
Westcroft Whiteleas NE33 .59 E1
Whitburn SR6 .60 E1
Westcroft Rd NE12 .39 E8
Wester Ct 1 SR3 .91 F5
Westerdale Penshaw DH4 .89 E8
Wallsend NE28 .39 F4
Westerdale Pl NE6 .57 B6
Westerham Cl SR5 .74 F3
Westerhope Fst Sch NE5 .36 E3
Westerhope Gdns 11 NE5 .37 D1
Westerhope Ind Unit NE5 .36 F3
Westerhope Rd NE38 .83 F5
Westerkirk NE23 .22 C3
Western App
South Shields, High Shields NE33 .42 C1
South Shields, Tyne Dock NE34 .59 A6
Western App Ind Est NE33 .42 C2
Western Ave
Gateshead NE11 .70 C4
Seaton Delaval NE25 .23 C3
Newcastle-upon-Tyne, Elswick NE4 .54 E5
Prudhoe NE42 .50 B2
Newcastle-upon-Tyne, West Denton NE5 .36 D1
Western Ct 5 NE26 .31 F8
Western Dr NE4 .54 F5
Western Fst Sch NE28 .40 A2
Western Highway NE38 .83 B2
Western Hill Ryhope SR2 .92 E7
Sunderland SR2 .102 B2
Western Mid Sch NE28 .40 A2
Western Rd
Wallsend NE28 .40 F2
Jarrow NE32 .58 A7
Western Terr Dudley NE23 .28 F8
West Boldon NE36 .74 B7
Western Terr *continued*
Washington NE37 .83 D7
Western View NE9 .71 C1
Western Way
Ponteland NE20 .25 A2
Blaydon NE21 .53 E2
Whitley Bay NE26 .31 F8
Ryton NE40 .52 C4
Westernmoor NE37 .82 F6
Westfield Gateshead NE10 .71 E6
Dudley NE23 .28 F8
Newcastle-upon-Tyne NE3 .38 B2
Hedworth NE32 .58 C1
Morpeth NE61 .8 E7
Westfield Ave
Brunswick Village NE13 .28 A6
Whitley Bay NE25 .31 D4
Newcastle-upon-Tyne NE3 .38 C3
Crawcrook NE40 .51 F3
Westfield Cl NE46 .44 F5
Westfield Cres
Crawcrook NE40 .51 F3
Newbiggin-by-the-Sea NE64 .7 D4
Westfield Ct
Wallsend NE28 .57 B8
Sunderland SR4 .85 E4
Westfield Dr NE3 .38 C3
Westfield Gr
Newcastle-upon-Tyne NE3 .38 B3
Sunderland SR4 .85 E4
Westfield La NE40 .52 B6
Westfield Lodge NE9 .70 E4
Westfield Pk
Wallsend NE28 .40 A2
Newcastle-upon-Tyne NE3 .38 C3
Westfield Rd
Newcastle-upon-Tyne NE15 .54 C5
Gateshead NE8 .70 E8
Westfield Sch NE3 .38 B3
Westfield Terr
Hexham NE46 .44 F5
Gateshead NE8 .70 E8
Springwell NE9 .71 E1
Westgarth NE5 .36 F4
Westgarth Terr 7 NE37 .83 E8
Westgate NE61 .8 D7
Westgate Ave SR3 .92 A8
Westgate Cl NE25 .31 C6
Westgate Ct NE4 .98 B1
Westgate Gr SR3 .92 A8
Westgate Hill Sch NE4 .98 A1
Westgate Hill Terr NE4 .98 C1
Westgate Rd NE1,NE4 .98 B1
Westgreen NE62 .10 F5
Westheath Ave SR2 .86 E1
Westhills DH9 .79 A2
Westholme Gdns NE15 .54 D6
Westholme Terr 1 SR2 .86 F2
Westhope Cl NE34 .60 A7
Westhope Rd NE34 .60 A7
Westlands
Seaton Sluice NE26 .24 C6
Tynemouth NE30 .32 B1
Hedworth NE32 .58 D1
Newcastle-upon-Tyne, West Denton NE5 .36 C1
Newcastle-upon-Tyne, High Heaton NE7 .39 A2
Sunderland SR4 .85 F5
Westlea NE22 .15 D8
Westleigh Rd DH4 .90 C3
Westley Ave NE26 .24 F1
Westley Cl NE26 .24 F1
Westline Ind Est DH2 .82 B2
Westloch Rd NE23 .22 B3
Westmacott St NE15 .52 E8
Westminster Ave NE29 .41 B8
Westminster Cl NE26 .32 C4
Westminster Cres NE31 .57 E2
Westminster Dr NE11 .69 F6
Westminster St
Gateshead NE8 .70 D8
4 Sunderland SR2 .86 F2
Westminster Way NE12 .39 D4
Westmoor Dr NE12 .29 B1
Westmoor Fst Sch NE12 .29 C1
Westmoor Mid Sch NE12 .29 B1
Westmoor Rd SR4 .85 D7
Westmoreland St NE28 .40 C2
Westmorland Ave
Bedlington NE22 .10 E1
2 Wallsend NE28 .41 B1
Washington NE37 .72 D1
Newbiggin-by-the-Sea NE64 .7 D4
Westmorland Ct NE31 .57 D5
Westmorland Gdns NE9 .70 F5
Westmorland La NE1 .100 C4
Westmorland Rd
Newcastle-upon-Tyne, Elswick NE1,NE4 .100 A4
Shiremoor NE29 .41 B7
South Shields NE34 .60 C7
Newcastle-upon-Tyne NE4 .100 C4
Westmorland Way NE23 .22 A6
Westmorland Wlk NE4 .54 F3
Westoe Ave NE33 .42 E1
Westoe Colliery Dr NE33 .42 E2
Westoe Cty Inf Sch NE33 .42 D1
Westoe Dr NE33 .42 E1
Westoe Hall 1 NE33 .59 E8
Westoe Rd NE33 .42 D1
Weston Ave NE16 .68 F5
Westover Gdns NE9 .70 F7
Westport Cl SR5 .74 F4
Westray DH2 .88 B1

Westray Cl 3 SR2 92 E8
Westsyde NE20 25 B3
Westward Ct NE5 36 E3
Westward Gn NE25 31 C4
Westward Pl NE38 83 B1
Westway Throckley NE15 35 E3
Blaydon NE21 53 B2
Westway Ind Est NE15 35 D3
Westwell Ct NE7 38 F4
Westwood Ave NE6 39 B1
Westwood Cl NE16 79 B7
Westwood Gdns
Newcastle-upon-Tyne NE3 37 E4
Stakeford NE62 5 F1
Gateshead NE9 71 D3
Westwood La NE17 77 B5
Westwood Rd NE3 28 C1
Westwood St SR4 85 F6
Westwood View
Chester le Street DH3 88 C1
Crawcrook NE40 51 F3
Wetheral Gdns NE9 71 A3
Wetheral Terr NE6 56 F4
Wetherby Cl NE63 6 C2
Wetherby Gr NE8 70 D7
Wetherby Rd SR2 87 A1
Wettondale Ave NE24 17 A7
Weybourne Sq SR2 86 E2
Weyhill Ave NE29 41 D4
Weymouth Dr DH4 89 F5
Weymouth Gdns NE9 71 A2
Whaggs La NE16 69 B6
Whalebone La NE61 8 F8
Whalton Ave NE3 38 A6
Whalton Cl Sherburn DH6 96 A1
Gateshead NE10 72 C7
Morpeth NE61 9 B5
Whalton Ct
Newcastle-upon-Tyne NE3 38 A6
South Shields NE34 59 E6
Wharfdale Pl NE6 57 B7
Wharfedale Penshaw DH4 90 A8
Wallsend NE28 39 F5
Wharfedale Ave NE37 83 C8
Wharfedale Dr NE33 59 C7
Wharfedale Gdns NE24 17 A8
Wharfedale Gn NE9 71 B1
Wharmlands Gr NE15 53 F7
Wharmlands Rd NE15 53 F7
Wharncliffe St SR1 102 B2
Wharrier St NE6 56 F4
Wharrier Street Prim Sch
NE6 56 F4
Wharton Cl DH5 94 D4
Wharton St Blyth NE24 17 C5
South Shields NE33 42 D2
Wheatall Dr SR6 60 F2
Wheatear Cl 1 NE38 82 F3
Wheatfield Cl NE42 50 B5
Wheatfield Gr NE12 39 C7
Wheatfield Rd NE5 36 F3
Wheatfields NE25 23 B4
Wheatley Gdns NE36 74 A7
Wheatridge NE25 23 B4
Wheatsheaf Ct SR6 75 F1
Wheler St 3 DH4 90 D1
Whernside Cl 4 NE37 83 A6
Whernside Ct 24 SR3 91 F6
Whernside Pl NE23 22 B3
Whernside Wlk NE40 52 D4
Whetstone Bridge Rd
NE46 44 F4
Whetstone Gn NE46 44 F4
Whickham Ave 6 NE11 69 F8
Whickham Bank 6 NE16 69 A7
Whickham Cl DH4 94 C8
Whickham Gdns 14 NE6 56 C5
Whickham Highway
NE11,NE16 69 E7
Whickham Ind Est NE16 68 F8
Whickham Lodge NE16 69 C7
Whickham Lodge Rise
NE16 69 C7
Whickham Parochial CE Prim
Sch NE16 68 F5
Whickham Pk NE16 69 C7
Whickham Rd NE31 57 E6
Whickham Sch NE16 69 A6
Whickham St SR6 75 E1
Whickham St E SR6 75 E1
Whickham View
Newcastle-upon-Tyne NE15 54 A6
Gateshead NE9 71 A4
Whickhope NE38 83 E2
Whinbank NE20 25 D2
Whinbrooke NE10 72 A6
Whinbush Pl NE15 54 A5
Whinfell NE37 83 B7
Whinfell Cl NE23 22 C3
Whinfell Ct 4 SR3 91 F6
Whinfell Rd NE20 25 D3
Whinfield Terr NE39 67 D2
Whinfield Way NE39 67 C1
Whinham Way NE61 9 B5
Whinlatter Gdns NE9 71 A4
Whinlaw NE9 71 C4
Whinmoor Pl NE5 37 E1
Whinney Cl NE21 68 A8
Whinneyfield Rd NE6 56 F7
Whinny La Ebchester DH8 76 E1
Morpeth NE61 3 A8
Whinshaw NE10 71 F7
Whinstone Mews NE12 39 D6
Whinway NE37 83 B7
Whistler Gdns NE34 59 D3

Whitbay Cres NE12 39 C6
Whitbeck Ct NE5 37 A1
Whitbeck Rd NE5 54 A8
Whitbourne Cl NE37 72 E2
Whitburn Bents Rd SR6 75 F7
Whitburn Comp Sch SR6 75 F8
Whitburn Gdns NE9 71 D3
Whitburn Hall SR6 75 F8
Whitburn Jun Mix Sch
SR6 75 E8
Whitburn Pl NE23 22 B3
Whitburn Rd Cleadon SR6 74 F8
Sunderland SR6 75 F4
Whitburn Rd E SR6 60 B1
Whitburn St SR6 103 A4
Whitburn Terr
East Boldon NE36 74 D7
Sunderland SR6 75 D4
Whitby Ave Hexham NE46 44 F5
Sunderland SR6 75 F6
Whitby Cl NE8 101 C1
Whitby Dr NE38 83 D3
Whitby Gdns NE28 40 E4
Whitby St NE30 42 B6
Whitchester House NE4 98 B2
Whitchurch Cl
Boldon Colliery NE35 58 E1
Sunderland SR5 74 F4
Whitchurch Rd SR5 74 F4
White Cross NE46 45 C4
White Gates Dr DH5 95 B2
White Hill Rd DH5 97 C8
White Horse View NE34 60 C6
White House Pl SR2 103 C2
White House Rd SR2 103 B2
White House Way NE10 71 E5
White Mere Com Prim Sch
NE10 72 C7
White Mere Gdns NE10 72 C8
White Oaks NE10 71 E5
White Rocks Gr SR6 60 F3
White Rose Way NE10 72 E5
White St NE6 57 B6
White-le-Head Gdns
DH9 79 A1
Whiteacres NE61 9 A7
Whitebark SR3 91 E4
Whitebeam Pl NE4 100 B3
Whitebridge Cl NE3 38 D7
Whitebridge Ct NE3 38 C7
Whitebridge Parkway
NE3 38 D8
Whitebridge Pk NE3 38 D8
Whitebridge Wlk NE3 38 D8
Whiteburn NE42 50 B1
Whitecliff Cl NE29 41 F8
Whitecroft Rd NE12 29 B2
Whitedale Ave NE24 17 A6
Whitefield Cres
Penshaw DH4 90 A7
Pegswood NE61 4 E3
Whitefield Gdns NE40 66 F8
Whitefield Gr NE10 71 D8
Whitefield Terr NE6 39 D1
Whiteford Pl NE23 23 A2
Whitefriars Way NE12 39 A6
Whitegate Cl NE11 54 F2
Whitehall Rd
Walbottle NE15 35 F2
Gateshead NE8 101 B1
Gateshead, Shipcote NE8 70 D8
Whitehall St NE33 59 C6
Whitehall Terr 7 SR4 85 F6
Whitehead St
South Shields NE33 59 B7
South Shields, West Harton
NE33 59 B6
Whitehill NE10 71 F5
Whitehill Dr NE10 71 D5
Whitehill Hall Gdns DH2 88 A4
Whitehill Rd NE23 16 A1
Whitehorn Cres NE5 37 E2
Whitehouse Cres NE9 71 E4
Whitehouse La
Tynemouth NE29 41 D8
Gateshead NE9 71 E4
Whitehouse Prim Sch
NE29 41 E8
Whitehouse Rd
Newcastle-upon-Tyne, Delaval
NE15 54 C4
Newcastle-upon-Tyne, Old Benwell
NE15 54 B4
Whiteladies Cl NE38 83 D6
Whitelaw Pl NE23 22 C4
Whiteleas Cty Jun Sch
NE34 59 C2
Whiteleas Way
Whiteleas NE34 59 C3
Whiteleas NE34 59 D2
Whitelees Ct NE3 37 E7
Whiteley Cl NE40 52 A1
Whiteley Rd NE21 53 E4
Whitemere Cl SR2 86 E1
Whites Gdns NE31 57 D6
Whiteside NE44 62 F7
Whitethroat Cl 6 NE38 82 F3
Whitewell Cl NE40 52 C5
Whitewell La NE40 52 C5
Whitewell Rd NE21 53 C2
Whitfield Dr NE12 39 C6
Whitfield Rd
6 Longbenton NE12 39 D8
Newcastle-upon-Tyne NE15 53 F5
Seaton Delaval NE25 23 D3
Whitfield Villas NE33 59 B6
Whitgrave Rd NE5 37 D3
Whitgray Ho NE6 56 E4

Whithorn Ct NE24 17 C7
Whitley Bay High Sch
NE26 31 E6
Whitley Bay Sta NE25 32 B4
Whitley Ct NE9 71 D3
Whitley Lodge Fst Sch
NE26 31 E8
Whitley Memorial CE Fst Sch
NE22 16 A8
Whitley Pl NE25 23 E2
Whitley Rd
Longbenton NE12 40 A8
Earsdon NE25 31 A5
Whitley Bay NE26 32 B4
Whitley Terr
Bedlington NE22 11 D3
Seaton Delaval NE25 23 E2
Whitmore Rd NE21 53 C3
Whitrig Cty Mid Sch
NE25 23 C4
Whitsun Ave NE22 11 A1
Whitsun Gdns NE22 11 A1
Whitsun Gr NE22 11 A1
Whittingham Cl
Tynemouth NE30 32 C2
Ashington NE63 6 A2
Whittingham Ct NE8 101 A1
Whittingham Rd
Tynemouth NE30 32 C1
Newcastle-upon-Tyne NE5 37 A4
Whittington Gr NE5 54 C8
Whittleburn NE10 71 F5
Whitton Ave NE24 17 B5
Whitton Gdns NE29 41 D7
Whitton Pl
Seaton Delaval NE25 23 D3
Newcastle-upon-Tyne NE7 39 B4
Whitton Way NE3 38 B6
Whittonstall NE38 83 F1
Whittonstall Rd NE17 66 A1
Whittonstall Terr NE17 66 A1
Whittonstone House NE4 98 B2
Whitwell Terr NE40 52 C6
Whitworth Cl
Newcastle-upon-Tyne NE6 57 A5
Gateshead NE8 70 D7
Whitworth Pl NE6 57 A5
Whitworth Rd NE37 82 F7
Whorlton Grange Cotts
NE5 36 E4
Whorlton Pl 1 NE5 36 E3
Whorlton Terr NE5 36 B4
Whorral Bank NE61 4 B2
Whyndyke NE10 71 F5
Whytlaw Cty Fst Sch
NE23 22 A5
Whytrigg Cl NE25 23 B3
Wickham Ind Est NE16 54 A1
Wicklow Ct NE62 11 D8
Widdrington Ave NE34 60 B8
Widdrington Gdns NE13 28 C6
Widdrington Rd NE21 53 C2
Widdrington Terr
Ryton NE21 53 A4
4 North Shields NE29 42 A5
Widnes Pl NE12 39 C7
Wigeon Cl NE38 83 A2
Wigham Terr NE16 79 A4
Wigmore Ave NE6 56 E4
Wilber Ct 9 SR4 85 F7
Wilber St SR4 85 F6
Wilberforce St
Wallsend NE28 57 B8
Jarrow NE32 58 C7
Wilberforce Wlk NE8 100 C2
Wilbury Pl NE5 37 C2
Wild Cattle Park*
NE66 112 B8
Wildbriar NE38 83 E2
Wilden Ct SR3 86 B2
Wilden Rd NE38 84 A3
Wildshaw Cl NE23 22 C3
Wilfred St
Chester le Street DH3 88 C2
West Boldon NE35 73 F8
Newcastle-upon-Tyne NE6 56 A6
Sunderland SR4 85 E7
Wilfrid St DH3 82 C3
Wilkes Cl NE5 36 F2
Wilkinson Ave NE31 57 D3
Wilkinson Ct 4 NE32 58 B7
Wilkinson Terr SR2 92 E6
Wilkwood Cl NE23 22 C4
Willerby Dr NE3 38 D8
William Allan Homes
NE22 15 D8
William Armstrong Dr
NE4 54 F3
William Cl NE12 40 A8
William Doxford Ctr SR3 91 F6
William IV Yd NE8 101 B4
William Morris Ave NE39 67 B2
William Roberts Ct NE12 29 D1
William St
Chester le Street DH3 88 C3
Gateshead NE10 56 D1
9 Whickham NE16 69 A7
Chopwell NE17 66 B1
Blyth NE24 17 E6
North Shields NE29 42 A5
Newcastle-upon-Tyne NE3 38 E5
Hebburn NE31 57 D7
6 South Shields NE33 42 C3
Pegswood NE61 4 F3
Sunderland SR1 103 A3
8 Sunderland, South Hylton
SR4 85 A6

William St W
14 North Shields NE29 42 A5
Hebburn NE31 57 D6
William Terr NE31 57 D7
Williams Pk NE12 39 C6
Williams Terr SR2 92 E6
Williamson Terr SR6 103 A4
Willington Comm High Sch
NE28 40 F4
Willington Terr NE28 40 E3
Willis St DH5 95 A5
Willmore St SR4 102 A2
Willoughby Dr NE26 31 E7
Willoughby Rd NE29 41 E6
Willoughby Way NE26 31 E7
Willow Ave Dunston NE11 69 F8
Blyth NE24 12 D1
Newcastle-upon-Tyne NE4 54 D8
Willow Bank Rd SR2 86 C3
Willow Cl Whickham NE16 69 B6
Morpeth NE61 9 B8
Willow Cres
Easington Lane DH5 95 D1
Blyth NE24 17 C4
Willow Ct Ryton NE40 52 D6
Stakeford NE62 11 B7
Willow Dyke NE45 47 A6
Willow Gdns NE12 29 C4
Willow Gr Gateshead NE10 71 E8
Wallsend NE28 40 D1
South Shields NE34 59 F5
Willow Grange NE32 58 A7
Willow Pl NE20 25 E4
Willow Rd
Houghton-le-Spring DH4 94 C8
Blaydon NE21 53 D2
Willow View NE16 79 A6
Willow Way NE20 25 E3
Willow's Cl NE38 83 F4
Willowbank Gdns NE2 38 E4
Willowdene NE12 29 E1
Willowfield Ave NE3 37 F6
Willowford Bridge
Abutment* CA6 126 B3
Willows Cl NE13 28 A5
Willows The
Throckley NE15 35 D1
Hebburn NE31 57 E4
Hedworth NE32 58 C1
Washington NE38 84 A4
Newcastle-upon-Tyne NE4 100 A3
Morpeth NE61 9 A8
Willowvale DH2 88 A5
Wills Mews NE7 39 E2
Wills Oval NE7 39 E2
Wilmington Cl NE3 37 B6
Wilson Ave Birtley DH3 82 C5
Cambois NE22 12 B3
Wilson Dr NE36 74 B8
Wilson Gdns NE3 38 B3
Wilson St Dunston NE11 69 F8
Wallsend NE28 40 B2
South Shields NE33 42 C2
Sunderland SR4 85 F6
Wilson St N SR5 102 C4
Wilson Terr
1 Longbenton NE12 39 D8
New Silksworth SR3 92 A8
Wilson's La NE9 70 F5
Wilsway NE15 35 C2
Wilton Ave NE6 56 E4
Wilton Cl
Cramlington NE23 22 C3
Whitley Bay NE25 31 C5
Wilton Cotts 5 NE35 58 E1
Wilton Dr NE25 31 B5
Wilton Gdns N NE35 58 E1
Wilton Gdns S NE35 58 E1
Wilton Manse NE25 31 B4
Wilton Sq SR2 86 E1
Wilton Terr DH8 76 E4
Wiltshire Cl SR5 74 E4
Wiltshire Dr NE28 39 F4
Wiltshire Gdns NE28 40 A3
Wiltshire Pl NE37 72 D2
Wiltshire Rd SR5 74 E3
Wimbledon Cl SR5 74 F3
Wimborne Cl NE35 73 E8
Wimbourne Ave SR4 85 E4
Wimbourne Gn NE5 36 F3
Wimpole Cl NE37 72 E2
Wimslow Cl NE28 39 F3
Winalot Ave SR2 86 E2
Wincanton Pl NE29 41 E4
Winchcombe Pl NE7 39 A3
Winchester Ave NE24 17 E7
Winchester Cl 8 NE63 6 F2
Winchester Ct NE32 58 B1
Winchester St 7 NE33 42 D3
Winchester Terr NE4 98 B1
Winchester Way NE22 10 F2
Winchester Wlk NE13 28 B6
Wincombee Rd NE6 57 B4
Windburgh Dr NE23 22 B3
Windermere Birtley DH3 82 D2
Cleadon SR6 60 A1
Windermere Ave
Chester le Street DH2 88 C1
Easington Lane DH5 97 C8
Gateshead NE10 71 F8
Windermere Cl NE23 22 B3
Windermere Cres
Penshaw DH4 90 C6
Blaydon NE21 68 B8
Hebburn NE31 57 F4
Hedworth NE32 58 D3
South Shields NE34 59 E6
Windermere Dr NE12 29 C3

Windermere Gdns NE16 69 C7
Windermere Rd
Newcastle-upon-Tyne NE5 54 B8
Newbiggin-by-the-Sea NE64 7 C3
Windermere St
Gateshead NE8 101 B1
Sunderland SR2 86 F2
Windermere St W NE8 101 B1
Windermere Terr NE29 41 F6
Windhill Rd NE6 56 F3
Winding The NE13 27 B7
Windlass Ct NE34 59 C5
Windlass La NE37 83 C7
Windmill Ct NE2 98 C4
Windmill Gr NE24 17 A8
Windmill Hill
South Shields NE33 42 B1
Hexham NE46 45 A5
Ellington NE61 1 E5
Windmill Hill Cl NE61 1 E6
Windmill Hills Prim Sch
NE8 101 B2
Windmill Hts NE61 1 E6
Windmill Ind Est NE23 15 C2
Windmill Sq SR5 75 C4
Windmill Way
Hebburn NE31 57 E8
Morpeth NE61 9 B8
Windshields Wlk NE15 35 C1
Windsor Ave
Whitley Bay NE26 32 C4
Newcastle-upon-Tyne NE3 38 E4
Gateshead NE8 70 E8
Windsor Cl
Whickham NE16 69 A4
Wallsend NE28 41 A4
Windsor Cotts NE28 41 A4
Windsor Cres
Houghton-le-Spring DH5 94 F8
Whitley Bay NE26 32 C4
Hebburn NE31 57 F6
Ovingham NE42 50 B5
Newcastle-upon-Tyne NE5 37 A3
Windsor Ct
7 Gateshead NE10 71 C8
Bedlington NE22 15 F8
Cramlington NE23 16 A1
Newcastle-upon-Tyne,
Kingston Park NE3 37 E7
Newcastle-upon-Tyne,
South Gosforth NE3 38 E5
Corbridge NE45 47 A6
Windsor Dr
Houghton-le-Spring DH5 94 E6
South Hetton DH6 97 F8
Blyth NE24 17 D3
Wallsend NE28 41 A4
New Silksworth SR3 92 A7
Cleadon SR6 59 F1
Windsor Fst Sch NE64 7 D3
Windsor Gdns
Gateshead NE10 71 C8
Bedlington NE22 15 F8
Whitley Bay NE26 31 F6
Tynemouth NE29 42 A7
South Shields NE34 59 E7
Windsor Gdns W NE26 31 F6
Windsor Pk NE28 39 F3
Windsor Pl
Newcastle-upon-Tyne NE2 99 B3
Ponteland NE20 25 B4
Longbenton NE27 30 C1
Windsor Rd Birtley DH3 82 B6
Whitley Bay NE25 31 E5
Newbiggin-by-the-Sea NE64 7 D4
Springwell NE9 71 F1
Windsor St 2 NE28 40 B2
Windsor Terr Haswell DH6 97 F2
Newcastle-upon-Tyne NE2 99 B3
Whitley Bay NE26 32 C4
Newcastle-upon-Tyne,
South Gosforth NE3 38 E4
Crawcrook NE40 52 A4
Corbridge NE45 47 A6
Hexham NE46 44 F5
Choppington NE62 10 F4
Newbiggin-by-the-Sea NE64 7 D4
3 Sunderland, Grangetown
SR2 86 F2
Sunderland, East Herrington
SR3 91 C6
Windsor Villas NE62 11 A7
Windsor Way NE3 37 D7
Windsor Wlk
Newcastle-upon-Tyne NE3 37 D7
Ashington NE63 7 A2
Windt St NE13 28 A5
Windy Gyle NE63 6 E4
Windy Nook Prim Sch
NE10 71 D6
Windy Nook Rd N10,NE9 71 B6
Windy Ridge NE10 71 C7
Windy Ridge Villas NE10 71 C7
Wingate Cl
Houghton-le-Spring DH4 94 D8
Newcastle-upon-Tyne NE15 53 E6
Wingate Gdns NE9 71 D3
Wingrove NE39 67 D1
Wingrove Ave
Newcastle-upon-Tyne NE4 54 F6
Sunderland SR6 75 E3
Wingrove Gdns NE4 54 F7
Wingrove Ho NE33 59 C6
Wingrove Prim Sch NE4 54 F6
Wingrove Rd NE4 54 F7
Wingrove Terr NE9 71 F1
Winifred Gdns NE28 40 C1
Winifred St SR6 75 E3

Win – Zio 181

Winifred Terr SR1 ... 103 B2
Winlaton Care Village NE21 ... 67 F6
Winlaton West Lane Com Prim Sch NE21 ... 68 A8
Winsford Ave NE29 ... 31 F1
Winshields NE23 ... 22 C4
Winshields Milecastle* NE47 ... 127 C3
Winship Cl NE34 ... 59 C3
Winship St NE24 ... 17 C4
Winship Terr 14 NE6 ... 56 C6
Winskell Rd NE34 ... 59 A4
Winslade Cl SR3 ... 92 B8
Winslow Cl
Boldon Colliery NE35 ... 58 F2
Newcastle-upon-Tyne NE6 ... 57 A6
Sunderland SR5 ... 74 F4
Winslow Gdns NE9 ... 70 E5
Winslow Pl NE6 ... 57 A6
Winster NE38 ... 83 A1
Winster Pl NE23 ... 22 B3
Winston Cres SR4 ... 85 E4
Winston Ct NE9 ... 71 F1
Winston Gn DH4 ... 89 F8
Winston Way NE43 ... 64 C3
Winton Cl NE23 ... 23 A2
Winton Way NE3 ... 37 F5
Wirralshir NE10 ... 72 A6
Wiseton Ct NE7 ... 38 F5
Wishart Ho NE4 ... 54 E4
Wishart Terr NE39 ... 66 F4
Wishaw Cl NE23 ... 22 C4
Wishaw Rise NE15 ... 53 E7
Witham Gn NE32 ... 58 C2
Witham Rd NE31 ... 57 F3
Witherington Cl NE7 ... 39 E3
Withernsea Gr SR2 ... 92 D7
Witherwack Prim Sch SR5 ... 74 F4
Witney Cl SR5 ... 74 F4
Witney Way NE36 ... 73 E7
Witton Ave NE34 ... 60 A6
Witton Ct
Newcastle-upon-Tyne NE3 ... 37 E6
Washington NE38 ... 83 B4
Sunderland SR3 ... 86 B2
Witton Gdns Jarrow NE32 ... 58 B3
Gateshead NE9 ... 71 D2
Witton Gr DH4 ... 94 C7
Witton Rd Shiremoor NE27 ... 30 F3
Hebburn NE31 ... 57 F8
Witty Ave NE31 ... 57 F5
Woburn NE38 ... 83 D4
Woburn Cl
Cramlington NE23 ... 16 A1
Wallsend NE28 ... 39 F3
Woburn Dr
Bedlington NE22 ... 11 C2
Silksworth SR3 ... 92 A6
Woburn Way NE5 ... 37 A2
Wolmer Rd NE24 ... 17 F5
Wolseley Cl NE8 ... 100 C1
Wolseley Gdns NE2 ... 56 A8
Wolseley Terr SR4 ... 102 A1
Wolsey Ct NE34 ... 59 C6
Wolsingham Ct NE23 ... 21 F7
Wolsingham Gdns NE9 ... 71 D3
Wolsingham Rd NE3 ... 38 B4
Wolsingham St NE4 ... 100 A3
Wolsley Rd NE24 ... 17 E7
Wolveleigh Terr NE3 ... 38 D5
Wolviston Gdns NE9 ... 71 D3
Wood Fields NE20 ... 25 F6
Wood Gr NE15 ... 53 E7
Wood La NE22 ... 11 B1
Wood Lea DH5 ... 95 A7
Wood St Dunston NE11 ... 69 F8
Burnopfield NE16 ... 79 A6
Sunderland SR4 ... 102 A3
Wood Terr
Gateshead NE10 ... 57 B2
Jarrow NE32 ... 58 A4
South Shields NE33 ... 59 D8
4 Washington NE37 ... 83 D8
High Spen NE39 ... 67 A2
Woodbine Ave
Wallsend NE28 ... 40 B2
Newcastle-upon-Tyne NE3 ... 38 C4
Woodbine Cl NE4 ... 54 F4
Woodbine Cotts NE40 ... 52 B5
Woodbine Pl NE8 ... 101 B1
Woodbine Rd NE3 ... 38 C5
Woodbine St
2 South Shields NE33 ... 42 D3
Gateshead NE8 ... 101 B1
Sunderland SR1 ... 103 C2
Woodbine Terr
Birtley DH3 ... 82 D4
Gateshead, Bill Quay NE10 ... 57 B2
Gateshead, Felling NE10 ... 71 B8
Blyth NE24 ... 17 F6
Corbridge NE45 ... 47 A6
Hexham NE46 ... 44 F5
Gateshead, Bensham NE8 ... 101 B1
Sunderland SR4 ... 85 F8
Woodbine Villas NE8 ... 101 B1
Woodbrook Ave NE5 ... 54 A8
Woodburn NE10 ... 71 E5
Woodburn Ave NE4 ... 54 E8
Woodburn Cl NE21 ... 68 A8
Woodburn Dr
Burnside DH4 ... 90 C1
Whitley Bay NE26 ... 31 E7
Woodburn Gdns NE11 ... 70 A6
Woodburn Sq NE26 ... 31 D7
Woodburn St NE15 ... 53 C7
Woodburn Terr NE42 ... 50 B2
Woodburn Way NE26 ... 31 E7
Woodchurch Cl NE12 ... 39 D4
Woodcroft Cl NE23 ... 22 B1
Woodcroft Rd NE41 ... 51 A6
Woodend NE20 ... 25 D2
Woodend Way NE3 ... 37 D8
Woodford NE9 ... 70 F1
Woodford Cl SR5 ... 74 F4
Woodgate Gdns NE10 ... 57 B1
Woodgate La NE10 ... 57 B2
Woodhall Cl DH2 ... 81 E2
Woodhall Ct NE25 ... 23 C3
Woodhall Spa DH4 ... 90 A4
Woodhead Rd
Prudhoe NE42 ... 50 F3
Newcastle-upon-Tyne NE6 ... 56 F8
Woodhill Dr NE61 ... 8 E8
Woodhill Rd NE23 ... 22 C4
Woodhorn Colliery Mus* NE63 ... 6 F5
Woodhorn Cotts NE63 ... 6 F5
Woodhorn Cres NE64 ... 7 D5
Woodhorn Dr NE62 ... 10 F8
Woodhorn Gdns NE13 ... 28 B6
Woodhorn La NE64 ... 7 E5
Woodhorn Rd
Ashington NE63 ... 6 E4
Newbiggin-by-the-Sea NE64 ... 7 D5
Woodhorn Villas NE63 ... 6 F5
Woodhouses La
Whickham, Fellside NE16 ... 68 E6
Whickham, Swalwell NE16 ... 69 A8
Woodhurst Gr SR4 ... 85 A2
Woodkirk Cl NE23 ... 23 A2
Woodland Cres NE15 ... 54 C4
Woodland Dr SR4 ... 85 E4
Woodland Grange DH4 ... 89 F1
Woodland Mews NE2 ... 38 F2
Woodland Rise SR3 ... 91 E6
Woodland Terr
Penshaw DH4 ... 90 A8
5 South Shields NE33 ... 42 D4
Washington NE37 ... 83 E8
Woodland View DH4 ... 94 A1
Woodlands
Chester le Street DH3 ... 88 C4
Great Lumley DH4 ... 89 F1
Throckley NE15 ... 35 C2
Ponteland NE20 ... 25 D3
Tynemouth NE29 ... 42 A7
Newcastle-upon-Tyne NE3 ... 38 C3
Washington NE38 ... 88 E8
Hexham NE46 ... 45 D4
Seaham SR7 ... 93 A1
Woodlands Cl
Earsdon NE25 ... 31 A5
High Spen NE39 ... 67 A3
Woodlands Ct
Kibblesworth NE11 ... 81 D6
Throckley NE15 ... 35 C2
Woodlands Dr SR6 ... 75 A8
Woodlands Grange NE12 ... 29 E1
Woodlands Ho NE24 ... 17 B8
Woodlands Park Dr NE21 ... 53 D2
Woodlands Park Villas NE13 ... 28 C4
Woodlands Pk NE13 ... 28 C5
Woodlands Rd
Newcastle-upon-Tyne NE15 ... 53 D7
Rowlands Gill NE39 ... 67 D2
Ashington NE63 ... 7 A2
Cleadon SR6 ... 75 A8
Woodlands Terr
Gateshead NE10 ... 71 C8
Longbenton NE12 ... 29 E1
Woodlands The NE11 ... 81 D6
Woodlands View SR6 ... 75 A8
Woodlawn Sch NE25 ... 31 D3
Woodlea Killingworth NE12 ... 29 D1
Newbiggin-by-the-Sea NE64 ... 7 E5
Woodlea Cl DH5 ... 95 A4
Woodlea Cres NE46 ... 45 C4
Woodlea Ct NE29 ... 41 E3
Woodlea Gdns NE3 ... 38 E6
Woodlea Rd NE39 ... 67 B2
Woodlea Sq NE29 ... 41 E3
Woodleigh Rd NE25 ... 31 E4
Woodleigh View NE5 ... 37 E3
Woodman Cl NE61 ... 8 E7
Woodman St NE28 ... 41 B3
Woodmans Way NE16 ... 68 F4
Woodpack Ave NE16 ... 68 F6
Woods Gn NE10 ... 57 C1
Woods Terr NE8 ... 101 C1
Woodside Ponteland NE20 ... 25 C2
Bedlington NE22 ... 11 C1
Blyth NE24 ... 17 F6
Prudhoe NE42 ... 50 F2
Hexham NE46 ... 45 D4
Morpeth NE61 ... 8 D7
Sunderland SR2 ... 102 C1
Sunderland, East Herrington SR3 ... 91 C6
Woodside Ave
Walbottle NE15 ... 35 E2
Seaton Delaval NE25 ... 23 D2
Corbridge NE45 ... 47 B6
Newcastle-upon-Tyne NE6 ... 57 B7
Woodside Cl NE40 ... 52 C5
Woodside Cres NE12 ... 39 E8
Woodside Ct NE12 ... 39 D8
Woodside Gdns NE11 ... 69 F7
Woodside Gr
Tantobie DH9 ... 79 C3
Sunderland SR3 ... 91 C6
Woodside La
Greenside NE40 ... 52 B3
Ryton NE40 ... 52 B4
Woodside Rd NE40 ... 52 B5
Woodside Terr
Chopwell NE17 ... 77 B8
Sunderland SR3 ... 91 C6
Woodside Villas NE46 ... 45 D4
Woodside Way
South Shields NE33 ... 59 B7
Ryton NE40 ... 52 C5
Woodside Wlk NE39 ... 67 C1
Woodstock Ave SR2 ... 86 E2
Woodstock Rd
Newcastle-upon-Tyne NE15 ... 54 A5
Gateshead NE9 ... 71 B2
Woodstone Terr DH4 ... 89 D1
Woodthorne Rd NE2 ... 38 E3
Woodvale NE20 ... 25 C2
Woodvale Dr NE31 ... 57 C4
Woodvale Gdns
Newcastle-upon-Tyne NE15 ... 53 E7
Wylam NE41 ... 51 B6
Gateshead NE9 ... 71 C6
Woodvale Rd
Killingworth NE12 ... 29 C4
Blaydon NE21 ... 53 D2
Woodville Cres SR4 ... 85 E4
Woodville Ct SR4 ... 85 E4
Woodville Rd NE15 ... 53 D8
Woodwynd NE10 ... 71 F6
Wooler Ave NE29 ... 41 D4
Wooler Cres NE8 ... 70 C8
Wooler Gn NE15 ... 53 B7
Wooler Sq
Wide Open NE13 ... 28 C7
Sunderland SR2 ... 86 E3
Wooler Wlk NE32 ... 58 A4
Woolerton Dr
Gateshead N10,NE9 ... 71 C6
Newcastle-upon-Tyne NE15 ... 53 E7
Gateshead NE9 ... 71 B6
Wooley St NE28 ... 40 B1
Woolmer Ct NE7 ... 39 E3
Woolsington Ct NE22 ... 10 F1
Woolsington Gdns NE13 ... 36 F8
Woolsington Pk S NE13 ... 36 F8
Woolsington Rd NE29 ... 41 C7
Woolwich Cl SR5 ... 74 F4
Woolwich Rd SR5 ... 74 F4
Wooperton Gdns NE5 ... 54 C7
Worcester Gn NE8 ... 101 B2
Worcester St SR2 ... 102 C1
Worcester Terr SR2 ... 102 C2
Worcester Way NE13 ... 28 C5
Wordsworth Ave
Easington Lane DH5 ... 97 D8
Whickham NE16 ... 69 B8
Blyth NE24 ... 17 C6
Hebburn NE31 ... 57 E6
Wordsworth Ave E DH5 ... 94 E7
Wordsworth Ave W DH5 ... 94 E7
Wordsworth Cres NE9 ... 71 F1
Wordsworth St NE8 ... 56 A2
Worley Ave NE9 ... 70 F4
Worley Cl NE4 ... 98 B1
Worley Mews NE9 ... 70 F4
Worley St NE4 ... 98 B1
Worley Terr DH9 ... 79 A1
Worm Hill Terr NE38 ... 83 E1
Worsdell St NE24 ... 12 E1
Worsley Cl NE28 ... 39 F4
Worswick St NE1 ... 99 B1
Worthing Cl NE28 ... 39 F3
Worthington Ct NE2 ... 99 C4
Wouldhave Ct NE33 ... 42 E3
Wouldhave St NE33 ... 42 E3
Wraith Terr SR2 ... 92 E6
Wraysbury Ct NE3 ... 37 D7
Wreay Wlk NE23 ... 22 C3
Wreigh St NE31 ... 57 D6
Wreken Gdns NE10 ... 72 C8
Wrekenton Row NE9 ... 71 C2
Wren Cl NE38 ... 83 A3
Wren Gr 1 SR5 ... 74 C1
Wretham Pl NE2 ... 99 C2
Wright Dr NE23 ... 29 A7
Wright St NE24 ... 17 D8
Wright Terr DH4 ... 90 A5
Wrightson St NE23 ... 16 B3
Wroxham Ct
Newcastle-upon-Tyne NE5 ... 37 B4
Sunderland SR2 ... 86 E2
Wroxton NE38 ... 83 C3
Wuppertal Ct NE32 ... 58 B6
Wych Elm Cl NE61 ... 1 D4
Wych Elm Cres NE7 ... 39 C3
Wychcroft Way NE5 ... 37 C2
Wycliffe Ave NE3 ... 37 F3
Wycliffe Rd SR4 ... 85 F4
Wydon Pk NE46 ... 45 A3
Wye Ave NE32 ... 58 C3
Wye Rd NE31 ... 57 E3
Wylam Ave NE25 ... 23 F2
Wylam Cl NE34 ... 59 E5
Wylam Fst Sch NE41 ... 51 B6
Wylam Gdns NE28 ... 40 F4
Wylam Gr SR1 ... 103 B2
Wylam Rd NE29 ... 41 F3
Wylam St NE32 ... 58 B7
Wylam Sta NE41 ... 51 C5
Wylam View NE21 ... 53 B2
Wylam Wood Rd NE41 ... 51 B5
Wyles Hill NE41 ... 51 B6
Wynbury Rd NE9 ... 71 A5
Wyncote Ct NE7 ... 39 B2
Wynd The
Killingworth NE12 ... 29 F1
Throckley NE15 ... 35 D1
Newcastle-upon-Tyne NE3 ... 38 A4
Tynemouth NE30 ... 42 A8
Wynde The
Ponteland NE20 ... 25 D4
South Shields NE34 ... 59 D5
Wyndfall Way NE3 ... 38 A3
Wyndham Ave NE3 ... 37 F3
Wyndham Prim Sch NE3 ... 38 A3
Wyndham Way NE29 ... 41 B8
Wynding The
Bedlington NE22 ... 10 E1
Annitsford NE23 ... 22 B1
Wyndley Cl NE16 ... 68 F5
Wyndley House NE3 ... 37 F3
Wyndley Pl NE3 ... 37 F3
Wyndrow Pl NE3 ... 37 F3
Wyndsail Pl NE3 ... 38 A3
Wyndtop Pl NE3 ... 38 A3
Wyndways Dr DH9 ... 78 E1
Wynn Gdns NE10 ... 56 F1
Wynyard DH2 ... 88 A3
Wynyard Dr NE22 ... 11 C3
Wynyard Gdns NE9 ... 71 C2
Wynyard Sq SR2 ... 86 E2
Wynyard St
Fence Houses DH4 ... 94 A8
Dunston NE11 ... 69 F8
New Silksworth SR3 ... 92 A7
Wythburn Pl NE9 ... 71 B4
Wyvern Sq SR2 ... 86 E2

Y

Yardley Gr NE23 ... 22 A8
Yarmouth Dr NE23 ... 22 A8
Yatesbury Ave NE5 ... 37 B3
Yeadon Ct NE3 ... 37 C7
Yeavering Bell (Camp)* NE71 ... 107 B2
Yeavering Cl NE3 ... 38 B4
Yellow Leas Farm NE36 ... 74 C7
Yelverton Cres NE6 ... 56 F3
Yelverton Ct NE23 ... 22 A8
Yemeni Sch The NE33 ... 42 B1
Yeoman St NE29 ... 42 B5
Yeovil Cl NE23 ... 22 A8
Yetholm Ave DH2 ... 88 B2
Yetholm Pl NE5 ... 37 A4
Yetholm Rd NE8 ... 100 B1
Yetlington Dr NE3 ... 38 A4
Yew Tree Dr NE22 ... 10 F2
Yewburn Way NE12 ... 39 C6
Yewcroft Ave NE15 ... 54 A6
Yewdale Gdns NE9 ... 71 A4
Yewtree Ave SR5 ... 74 F2
Yewtree Gdns NE6 ... 40 A1
Yewtrees NE10 ... 71 E5
Yewvale Rd NE5 ... 37 D1
York Ave NE32 ... 58 B3
York Cl NE23 ... 22 A8
York Cres DH5 ... 94 F4
York Ct DH3 ... 88 D2
York Dr NE28 ... 40 B1
York Gr NE22 ... 10 D2
York Ho SR5 ... 74 A4
York Rd Birtley DH3 ... 82 C1
Whitley Bay NE26 ... 32 B5
York St Hetton le Hole DH5 ... 94 E1
Gateshead NE10 ... 57 A1
Jarrow NE32 ... 58 A6
Newcastle-upon-Tyne NE4 ... 98 B1
Sunderland SR1 ... 103 A3
New Silksworth SR3 ... 92 A8
York Terr
Chester le Street DH3 ... 88 D2
Gateshead NE10 ... 71 D8
7 North Shields NE29 ... 42 A5
York Way NE34 ... 60 A6
Yorkdale Pl NE6 ... 57 A6
Yorkwood NE31 ... 57 C7
Young Rd NE12 ... 29 F1

Z

Zetland Dr NE25 ... 31 F2
Zetland Sq SR6 ... 75 E1
Zetland St SR6 ... 75 E1
Zion St SR1 ... 103 B3
Zion Terr Blaydon NE21 ... 53 B2
Sunderland SR5 ... 75 C3